REDEFINING ANCIEI

This book examines the fragmentary and contradictory evidence for
Orpheus as the author of rites and poems to redefine Orphism as
a label applied polemically to extra-ordinary religious phenomena.
Replacing older models of an Orphic religion, this richer and more
complex model provides insight into the boundaries of normal and
abnormal Greek religion. The study traces the construction of the category of "Orphic" from its first appearances in the Classical period,
through the centuries of philosophical and religious polemics, especially in the formation of early Christianity and again in the debates
over the origins of Christianity in the nineteenth and twentieth centuries. A paradigm shift in the scholarship of Greek religion, this study
provides scholars of classics, early Christianity, ancient religion, and
philosophy with a new model for understanding the nature of ancient
Orphism, including ideas of afterlife, cosmogony, sacred scriptures,
rituals of purification and initiation, and exotic mythology.

RADCLIFFE G. EDMONDS III is the Paul Shorey Professor of Greek
and Chair of the Department of Greek, Latin and Classical Studies at
Bryn Mawr College. He is author of *Myths of the Underworld Journey:
Plato, Aristophanes, and the "Orphic" Gold Tablets* (2004) and editor
of *The "Orphic" Gold Tablets and Greek Religion: Further Along the
Path* (2011).

REDEFINING ANCIENT ORPHISM

A Study in Greek Religion

RADCLIFFE G. EDMONDS III

Bryn Mawr College

CAMBRIDGE
UNIVERSITY PRESS

CAMBRIDGE
UNIVERSITY PRESS

University Printing House, Cambridge CB2 8BS, United Kingdom

One Liberty Plaza, 20th Floor, New York, NY 10006, USA

477 Williamstown Road, Port Melbourne, VIC 3207, Australia

314-321, 3rd Floor, Plot 3, Splendor Forum, Jasola District Centre, New Delhi - 110025, India

79 Anson Road, #06-04/06, Singapore 079906

Cambridge University Press is part of the University of Cambridge.

It furthers the University's mission by disseminating knowledge in the pursuit of education, learning and research at the highest international levels of excellence.

www.cambridge.org
Information on this title: www.cambridge.org/9781108730075

© Radcliffe G. Edmonds III 2013

First published 2013
First paperback edition 2018

A catalogue record for this publication is available from the British Library

Library of Congress Cataloging in Publication data
Edmonds, Radcliffe G. (Radcliffe Guest), 1970–
Redefining ancient Orphism : a study in Greek religion / Radcliffe G. Edmonds III.
pages. cm
Includes bibliographical references and index.
ISBN 978-1-107-03821-9 (hardback)
1. Dionysia. 2. Dionysus (Greek deity) – Cult. 3. Cults – Greece. I. Title.
BL820.B2E36 2013
292.9 – dc23 2013012164

ISBN 978-1-107-03821-9 Hardback
ISBN 978-1-108-73007-5 Paperback

Contents

Illustrations

Acknowledgments

This project has been many years in the making, and the people to whom I owe debts of gratitude are too many to name. Bruce Lincoln, Jonathan Z. Smith, James Redfield, and Chris Faraone aided and encouraged me in graduate school when I first encountered the problem of Orphism, introducing me to the scholarship and teaching me how to analyze it critically. It has become a cliché in scholarship to speak of standing "on the shoulders of giants" (even appearing as a trite acronym, OTSOG), but there is a profound truth in it nonetheless. I started my researches into Greek religion with the works of Burkert, Bremmer, Graf, Parker, and Sourvinou-Inwood, beginning with the conclusions they had drawn as they were changing the very way Greek religion is understood. Likewise, my study of Orphism began with Burkert, Graf, Brisson, and Detienne, so my understanding of it was shaped from the outset by the innovations of these giants in the field and the vision of it I have come to depends upon the point from which I started.

This work would not have been possible without Alberto Bernabé, whose monumental studies of the Orphic fragments have provided scholars in the twenty-first century with an invaluable resource. Although I disagree fundamentally with many of his conclusions, I have been fortunate indeed to have a scholarly opponent so friendly and courteous as well as so erudite. Many of my ideas have been honed in conversation with him, whether in print, at conferences, or even across the dinner table, and, while he will assuredly not agree with many of the conclusions I draw in this study, I am grateful nonetheless for his stimulating opposition.

My thanks are due as well to Fritz Graf and Sarah Johnston, who for many years have discussed matters Orphic with me (along with a plethora of other fascinating things); their kindness and conversations have been important to me. Claude Calame and Jan Bremmer have likewise provided helpful critiques and discussions, sharing their advanced researches with me as I embarked upon my own. Luc Brisson has generously given of his time and encouragement; I am indeed grateful to him as one of the giants without whom I could never have begun my own labors. His vast erudition has been a valuable resource for me, and his scholarly clarifications of the complex Neoplatonic tradition have been essential for the development of the study of Orphica in the twenty-first century. My progress along the way has been much aided by discussions with Miguel Herrero and Fabienne Jourdan, whose researches into the early Christian tradition have taught me much and for whose collegial conversations I remain very grateful.

The shape of this project owes much to my reading of several studies in the history of religions that have profoundly shaped my approach here. First and foremost of these is J. Z. Smith's *Drudgery Divine*, which I encountered early in my scholarly career and which first taught me to examine the history of scholarship with the same attention as the texts themselves. Michael Williams' *Rethinking "Gnosticism": An Argument for Dismantling a Dubious Category* and Karen King's *What is Gnosticism?* likewise provided me with models for thinking about Orphism as a category within the history of scholarship rather than a "thing" that existed in antiquity. Bruce Lincoln's *Theorizing Myth* (and the graduate seminar from which it stemmed) remains profoundly influential in my thinking.

This book is the result of many years of working, and different pieces of it have been published in various venues along the way. I have learned much from the conversations sparked by the responses to those publications, and most of the material previously published appears here in somewhat altered form, some bits with only the most superficial of changes and others with profound revisions. An earlier version of Chapter 6 appeared as "Orphic Mythology" within the Blackwell *Companion to Greek Mythology*, while sections of Chapter 8 are appearing as "A Lively Afterlife and Beyond: The Soul in Plato, Homer, and the Orphica," in a forthcoming volume of *Les Etudes Platoniciennes* entitled *Platon et ses prédécesseurs – Psukhê*. A version of one section of Chapter 9 appeared as "A Curious Concoction: Tradition and Innovation in Olympiodorus' 'Orphic' Creation of Mankind" in the *American Journal of Philology* 130 (2009): 511–532, while large portions of Chapters 9 and 10 were published online through the Center for Hellenic Studies as "Recycling Laertes' Shroud: More on Orphism and Original Sin" (http://chs.harvard.edu/chs/redmonds).

This project was begun during my time as a Fellow at the Center for Hellenic Studies, and I am grateful to the director, Gregory Nagy, and to my fellow Fellows for making my time there so fruitful and enjoyable. Bryn Mawr College made the work possible by supporting my research leaves at the beginning and end of the process. I am grateful too to my students over the past few years, who (mostly) refrained from rolling their eyes when I once again dragged the Orphica into discussions in class. I particularly want to thank Edward Whitehouse and Abbe Walker, whose sharp eyes and keen awareness were invaluable in putting together the indices and keeping the citations straight. My thanks also go to Michael Sharp and the editorial team at Cambridge University Press, who have shepherded this project through the many stages of its development. Finally, my love and gratitude to my wife and children, for their patience and support as I wrestled with this project for so many years.

Note on abbreviations

Abbreviations of ancient authors and works follow those of *The Oxford Classical Dictionary*, 3rd edn. (Oxford 1999), making use of the abbreviations in the *Greek Lexicon* of Liddell, Scott, and Jones for works not in the *OCD*. *BNP* refers to the entries in the electronic edition of the *Brill's New Pauly*, which are cited by the author's name and nd (no date).

PART I

Introduction: Definitions old and new

CHAPTER ONE

The name of Orpheus

Orpheus' name: that is what it all comes down to. It is a name that
no amount of trivial application or cold-blooded scholarship robs of
its fascination. (West 1983: 263)

Name-famed Orpheus, ὀνομάκλυτον Ὀρφην (*PMGF* 306 Davies) (*OF* 864
B) – one of the earliest textual witnesses we have for the mysterious figure of
Orpheus paradoxically indicates how much of the tradition we are missing.
Orpheus' name is already famous in the Archaic age of Ibykos, but nothing
remains of what that name signified – the poems composed by that famous
poet or the tales that told of his adventures. Even in the Classical period, the
evidence remains scant and fragmentary; the name of Orpheus is invoked
in a passing allusion or attached to a brief quotation. Later eras expand
upon the sentimental story of his lost love or credit him with the invention
of all the most holy rituals of the Greek religious tradition, but the name of
Orpheus remains mysterious to us – just what did this poet's name mean
to the Greeks and Romans who invoked it?[1]

Orpheus himself is a mythical character, not a historical person, so any
deeds belong to the realm of story, invented to fit with the name.[2] Likewise,
any poems or rituals credited to him – Orphica, as the Greeks referred to
them – bear the name of Orpheus, but the one thing of which we can be
certain is that some long-ago Orpheus was not the author; rather some
other author from a historical period has borrowed the name of Orpheus

---

[1] Harrison 1903: 471 rhapsodizes on the mysteriousness of Orpheus. "Always about him there is this
aloof air, this remoteness, not only of the self-sufficing artist, who is and must be always alone,
but of the scrupulous moralist and reformer; yet withal and through all he is human, a man, who
Socrates-like draws men and repels them, not by persuading their reason, still less by enflaming their
passions, but by sheer magic of his personality. It is this mesmeric charm that makes it hard even
now-a-days to think soberly of Orpheus."

[2] As Bernabé 2004: viii astutely points out, the task of collecting and editing the testimonies to
and fragments of Orpheus need not be concerned with the issue so crucial for other collections of
fragments, the distinction between true and spurious pieces of evidence: *editori autem fragmentorum
Orphicorum nihil interest utrum fragmentum Orphicum genuinum an spurium sit, cum omnia spuria
haberi possint quandoquidem Orpheus numquam fuerit.*

for his work (or has had it attached by another). There is no Orpheus to whom we can look; only the name of Orpheus.

Why would anyone label a text or rite with the name of Orpheus? What criteria would validate that labeling? Modern scholars of religion, always seeking to define ancient religions in the abstract category of "ism"s, have fabricated an Orph-ism, a category for all the religious phenomena associated with the name of Orpheus. This modern Orphism, I argue, distorts in important ways the evidence of the way the ancient Greeks used the name of Orpheus. It is the purpose of this study to redefine the category of ancient Orphism by identifying the criteria for this "Orphic" label that were used by the ancient Greeks (and Romans).

Ancient Orpheus

The people of the ancient Greco-Roman world attributed to the mythical poet Orpheus a number of poems in the dactylic hexameter and poetic language most familiar from Homeric poetry, as well as crediting him with the foundation of a number of rituals. Orpheus was the child of a Thracian king and a Muse, or of some similar semi-divine background, and his skill at poetic song was unrivaled by any – even the beasts and the trees drew near and listened when he played.[3] As a member of the Argonauts, he took part in one of the earliest heroic ventures, several generations before the war at Troy, so his poetic authority preceded even that of Homer. As Redfield has pointed out, to connect the name of Orpheus to a story or ritual is "to bypass tradition and claim (as it were) a fresh revelation," to claim the authority, not of the familiar cultural tradition, but of a specially privileged individual.[4] Such authority provided the incentive for many poets to circulate their poetry under the name of Orpheus, just as

---

[3] Bernabé has compiled all the testimonies to the life of Orpheus in the ancient materials as fragments 864–1095 in his recent edition of the Orphic fragments, the second volume of his edition of *Poetae Epici Graeci* (Bernabé 2004, 2005, 2007a), surpassing the collection in the older edition of Kern 1922. References to Bernabé's collection will be, e.g., *OF* 867 B, with corresponding references to Kern's edition, either OT 5 K for the testamenta, or OF 317 K for the fragments. References to the *Orphic Argonautica* (*OA*) are from Vian 1987, to the *Orphic Hymns* (*OH*) from Morand 2001. Although the official *editio princeps* of the Derveni papyrus has come out in Kouremenos *et al.* 2006, I cite the text and translation in Betegh 2004.

[4] Redfield 1991: 106. Of course, the potential for putting forth a new claim to religious authority was assisted by the medium of writing, which allowed for the multiplication of poems under the name of Orpheus, each of which could present a new alternative to the current norms. The caricature in Plato (*Resp.* 364b2–365a3) (*OF* 573i B = OF 3 K) and Euripides (*Hipp.* 948–957) (*OF* 627 B = OT 213 K) of the hubbub of books connected with Orpheus attests to the impression that this use of texts made on the contemporary audience. Since written texts attributed to an authority such as Orpheus were a useful device for religious innovators (or deviants) to urge their claims, such texts

the work of many poets went under the name of Homer. Later scholiasts identify authors, starting around the sixth century BCE, who wrote works under the name of Orpheus (Orphicists, we might call them), and, over a millennium later in the fifth century CE, the *Orphic Argonautica* styles itself as a work of Orpheus. Certain features of the verses, such as an address to Mousaios, the pupil of Orpheus, or the familiar *sphragis* (the poetic seal of authenticity) line, "I speak to those of understanding; close the doors of your ears, ye profane," serve as evidence within the text that it comes from Orpheus.[5]

Age old new age

Not only can a pseudepigrapher thus apply the label of Orphic to his own text, but, even without such self-labeling, others might also attribute a text or ritual to Orpheus. Whereas modern scholars have tended to make such attributions on the basis of supposed Orphic doctrines (of the immortality of the soul, of its stain by an original sin of the Titanic murder of Dionysos, and of its purification through a cycle of reincarnations), the ancients made no such doctrinal classifications.[6] Rather, the ancient label Orphic was more like the contemporary term "new age," which is associated, not specifically with particular religious ideas or organizations, but more vaguely with a set of ideas loosely defined by their distance from mainstream religious activity, especially by claims to extra-ordinary purity, sanctity, or divine authority.[7] Like "new age," the association with Orpheus can be positive, indicating special inspiration that goes beyond the ordinary, but often is negative, implying a holier-than-thou attitude that is either ludicrous or hypocritical. Euripides' Theseus accuses his son, Hippolytos, of being a fraud, pretending to extreme purity while secretly making advances on his stepmother:

could be associated with deviants or innovators like Hippolytos even though he did not make use of such books. See further ch. 4 below.

[5] Bernabé has collected the uses of the seal line in *OF* 1 B. Addresses to Mousaios appear in *OA* 7, 308, 858, 1191, 1347; *OH* proem. 1; *The Testament of Orpheus* (Διαθῆκαι) – [Justin] *Coh. Gr.* 15.1 (*OF* 372, 377i B = OF 245 K); Clem. Al. *Protr.* 7.74.3 (*OF* 375, 377iii B = OF 246 K); Euseb. *Praep. evang.* 13.12.4 (*OF* 378 B = OF 247 K); *Ephemerides* – Tzetz. *Prol. ad Hes.* 21 (Gaisford) (*OF* 759 B = OF 271 K); *Orphic Seismologion* (*OF* 778 B = OF 285 K); cp. fragments of Mousaios in Bernabé 2007a.

[6] Bernabé 1998a: 172: "El creyente órfico busca la salvación individual, dentro de un marco de referencia en que son puntos centrales: el dualismo alma-cuerpo, la existencia de un pecado antecedente, y el ciclo de trasmigraciones, hasta que el alma consigue unirse con la divinidad." Cp. Bernabé 1997: 39, Bernabé 2002d: 208–209. Guthrie 1952: 73 puts the same ideas in less guarded terms: "The Orphic doctrines included a belief in original sin, based on a legend about the origin of mankind, in the emphatic separation of soul from body, and in a life hereafter."

[7] For a study of the "New Age" in the twentieth century, see Sutcliffe 2003.

Do you, then, walk with the gods, as an extraordinary man? Are you so chaste and undefiled by evil? I would not believe your boasting, vilely attributing to the gods such ignorance in thinking. All right then, vaunt and puff yourself up through your vegetarian diet of soulless foods, and taking Orpheus as your leader engage in Bacchic revels, honoring the smoke of many books. For you have been caught now. I sound the warning for all to flee such men as you. For they do their hunting with reverent words while they devise evils.[8]

Therefore, whenever something is labeled as Orphic, it is always important to determine who is applying the label and in what context, whether it is self-applied or applied by another. The label may signal something extra-ordinarily good and authoritative, since Orpheus is the most ancient and divinely inspired poet, famous for his purity and rites that bring men closer to the gods. However, as for Euripides' Theseus, the label may be for something extra-ordinarily bad, either revolting or ineffectual, but, whether positive or negative, it always indicates something out of the ordinary.[9]

The Greek mythic tradition works by *bricolage*, to use Lévi-Strauss' metaphor of the rag-bag man who takes old pieces of things and patches them together to make new creations,[10] and the pieces used by the authors of the Orphic poems come from the same stock that every other mythmaker uses. Of course, not every subject found in the whole mythic tradition appears in Orphic poems, but every subject found in Orphic poems also appears elsewhere in the mythic tradition. It is the way the pieces are combined and the way the construct is framed that marks them as Orphic.

Redefining ancient Orphism

In this study, I am attempting to redefine ancient Orphism, that is, to come up with a way of defining the category of things the ancient Greeks

---

[8] Eur. *Hipp.* 952–957 (*OF* 627 B = OT 213 K): σὺ δὴ θεοῖσιν ὡς περισσὸς ὢν ἀνὴρ ξύνει; σὺ σώφρων καὶ κακῶν ἀκήρατος; οὐκ ἂν πιθοίμην τοῖσι σοῖς κόμποις ἐγὼ θεοῖσι προσθεὶς ἀμαθίαν φρονεῖν κακῶς. ἤδη νυν αὔχει καὶ δι᾽ ἀψύχου βορᾶς σίτοις καπήλευ᾽ Ὀρφέα τ᾽ ἄνακτ᾽ ἔχων βάκχευε πολλῶν γραμμάτων τιμῶν καπνούς· ἐπεί γ᾽ ἐλήφθης. τοὺς δὲ τοιούτους ἐγὼ φεύγειν προφωνῶ πᾶσι· θηρεύουσι γὰρ σεμνοῖς λόγοισιν, αἰσχρὰ μηχανώμενοι. Redfield 1991: 106 notes the unusual collection of elements in Theseus' condemnation: "Probably the Greeks themselves were vague about the category; Theseus assumes that since Hippolytus claims to be chaste (a claim not characteristic of the Orphics) he must also be a vegetarian and read Orphic books. All three would be tokens of a rejection of the world, and therefore mutually convertible." The vague associations are particularly striking here, since Hippolytos the obsessive hunter most certainly never displays any hint of vegetarianism. Nevertheless, vegetarianism is one of the peculiarities often linked with Orphic things, and Euripides' audience would have understood the kind of categorizing that lumps all of Theseus' charges together.

[9] See further Edmonds 2008a.   [10] Lévi-Strauss 1966: 16–36.

would have labeled Orphic. As recent scholarly efforts in reconstructing the ancient category of "magic" have shown, the reconstruction of the ancient category of "Orphic" must begin with the recognition that the label "Orphic" is also, in some sense, an ancient cultural classification as well as a modern scholarly category.[11] The ancient Greeks recognized a category of things that could be labeled *orphika* (texts and rituals credited to Orpheus) and people who could be labeled *Orpheotelestai* (practitioners of rites) or even *Orphikoi* (authors of Orphica). However, to limit the ancient category of Orphic only to those things "sealed with the name of Orpheus," as Linforth did, would be to exclude people and things that the ancient Greeks would have classified together.[12] In my process of redefinition, I start with Linforth's single criterion of the name of Orpheus to delineate evidence labeled as Orphic by the ancient witnesses, but I derive from this class of explicitly labeled evidence a set of criteria that characterize the material in different ways as extra-ordinary religious phenomena.

Although I agree with Linforth's conclusion more than half a century ago that there is no consistent list of criteria which define all the evidence for the Orphica, nevertheless, rather than conclude that the absence of any consistent criteria over the range of data means we must abandon the label of "Orphic" or apply it indiscriminately to anything that relates to Greek mystery religion, I suggest that Wittgenstein's concept of "family resemblances" permits us to construct a polythetic definition in which evidence characterized by any of several criteria may be labeled Orphic.[13] In this polythetic definition, there is no single feature, be it the name of Orpheus or some particular doctrine of the soul, that makes something Orphic. Rather, if something – person, text, or ritual – boasted of extra-ordinary purity or sanctity, made a claim to special divine connection or extreme antiquity, or was marked by extra-ordinary strangeness, perversity, or alien nature, then that thing *might* be labeled Orphic, classified with

---

[11] This idea is developed at greater length in Edmonds 2008a.

[12] Linforth 1941: xiii. Linforth rightly warns of the slippery slope encountered once one goes beyond this single criterion; however, attention to ancient ("emic") acts of classification, rather than to ("etic" categories of) doctrines or mythic motifs, provides a more secure methodology. Certain myths include the name of Orpheus as a character (e.g., his journey on the Argo, or his journey to the Underworld in search of his wife), but such myths are only Orphic when they are explicitly framed as the tellings of Orpheus himself.

[13] Wittgenstein 1958: 66–67. Alderink 1981: 20 also suggests that such a polythetic definition is useful for approaching Orphism, but his components differ from mine in that they are doctrinal. He defines Orphism as "characterized by a monistic tendency, an inclination to view the world as a created reality, and a disposition towards soteriological ideas of post-mortem existence" (Alderink 1981: 23). Ideas of monism, the creation of the cosmos, and soteriology, while they do appear in some evidence labeled "Orphic" in the ancient evidence, appear in far too many other contexts to make them valid indicators of what the ancient Greek considered "Orphic".

other Orphic things, and perhaps even sealed with the name of Orpheus. This polythetic definition permits us to include even material that is not sealed with the name of Orpheus but is classified as extra-ordinary in the same ways as other evidence that does bear Orpheus' name.

Moreover, whether something is labeled as Orphic depends, in the ancient evidence, not on the presence of particular mythic motifs or religious doctrines, but upon the act of classification by a particular classifier in a specific context; it is, therefore, always a polemical definition, not a disinterested one. Therefore, in my definition, I argue that:

> a text, a myth, a ritual, may be considered Orphic because it is explicitly so labeled (by its author or by an ancient witness), but also because it is marked as *extra-ordinary* in the same ways as other things explicitly connected with the name of Orpheus and grouped together with them in the ancient evidence. The more marked something is by claims to extra-ordinary purity or sanctity, by claims to special divine connection or extreme antiquity, or by features of extra-ordinary strangeness, perversity, or alien nature, the more likely it is to be labeled Orphic in the ancient evidence.

Such a definition provides modern scholars with a better idea of how the ancient Greeks thought about their religion, both ordinary and extra-ordinary, and makes better sense of the varied evidence from antiquity.

My approach here differs from that of earlier scholars, not just Linforth, on whom I build my methodology, but more significantly those such as Kern and Guthrie, who imagined an Orph-ism with identifiable believers and doctrines. I differ as well from contemporary scholars, such as Bernabé or Parker, who define Orphism more loosely as a current of religious ideas characterized by certain doctrines – of the immortality of the soul, of its stain by an original sin of the Titanic murder of Dionysos, and of its purification through a cycle of reincarnations. Such an approach, I argue, ignores the ancient classifications and labeling in favor of modern paradigms of doctrinal religion centered on belief, models ultimately grounded more in Christian ideas of faith than in the evidence for ancient religious practice.

What does this new way of defining Orphism help explain? By aligning the boundaries of the definition as closely as we can with the ancient notions of what was Orphic, we can get a better sense, not only of what the ancient Greeks thought of as extra-ordinary religion, but also what they saw as ordinary and normative. My definition permits a re-examination of the ancient evidence that takes seriously the model, proposed by Burkert and others, of itinerant religious specialists competing for religious authority among a varying clientele, like Theophrastos' Orpheotelest and his superstitious client.[14] Rather than looking for a coherent set of sacred texts canonical to people who considered themselves Orphics, texts expressive of doctrines pertaining to sin, salvation, and afterlife, we can look for things pieced together from widely available traditional material to meet the demand of clients looking for extra-ordinary solutions to their problems, the products of *bricolage*. If the texts and rituals are products of *bricolage*, however, and their creators *bricoleurs* competing for authority, we cannot expect to find consistency of either texts or doctrines, merely a loose family resemblance between composites of the same traditional elements. A redefinition of ancient Orphism requires a polythetic definition that accommodates the complexities of the ancient contexts rather than the sort of monothetic definition that identifies Orphism by its scriptures and doctrines.

A redefinition of Orphism along the lines I have proposed may seem a step backwards, jettisoning the conclusions drawn by many scholars in the past century and, to use Bernabé's image, making their labors as fruitless as Penelope's weaving.[15] However, re-examining the evidence with attention to its ancient contexts and making use of the new models for reconstructing these religious contexts provides a more accurate understanding, not only of the evidence itself, but also of the relation of different pieces to one another. The picture may not be as neat and tidy, nor as familiar as an Orphism constructed in the image of a Protestant sect, but this messy and incomplete picture nevertheless offers a less distorted view of ancient Greek religion and the place of Orphism within it. Moreover, much of the work done by scholars using older models need not be abandoned, but merely adapted; their insights contribute to our understanding of the evidence from new perspectives.[16] The disjointed and fragmentary pieces of evidence we have are not the relics of secret canonical doctrines and scripture, but the productions of countless *bricoleurs* in competition with one another for religious authority. Rather than trying to define the doctrines and scriptures crucial to a secret sect, we can try to reconstruct

---

[14] Cp. Burkert 1982. This idea has been further explored by Calame 1995 (republished in English translation in Edmonds 2011a) and particularly in Calame 2002. Parker 2005 is among those scholars who have taken this model furthest, although he still makes an exception for the Orphics in some regards.

[15] Bernabé 2002a, in which he argues against my arguments in Edmonds 1999, is entitled "La toile de Pénélope". My response, published online in 2008 (Edmonds 2008b) and adapted for this study as chapter 9, is "Recycling Laertes' Shroud", that is, finding a new way to make use of the evidence that has been removed from Bernabé's constructed model.

[16] As Alderink 1993: xiv suggests in his introduction to the reprint of Guthrie 1952, "Scholars love to argue with each other, which is well and good, but if we can reappropriate our predecessors as well as argue with and against them, we honor them as well as benefit ourselves."

the dynamics of this competition, the specialists and clients who were involved, and the traditional elements they used in their texts and rituals. This new way of defining Orphism thus provides a better understanding of the nature of ancient Greek religion in all of the periods from which our evidence for the Orphica comes.

CHAPTER TWO

Orphism through the ages
A history of scholarship

> As for "Orphism", the only definite meaning that can be given to
> the term is "the fashion for claiming Orpheus as an authority". The
> history of Orphism is the history of that fashion.   (West 1983: 3)

It is worth taking a brief survey of the evidence we have for the history of the
fashion for claiming the authority of Orpheus. Histories of the scholarship
of Orphism most often begin with Lobeck's 1829 *Aglaophamus*, a work that
applied modern philological methodology to the collection of evidence for
Orphica that survived into the modern era. Lobeck sifted critically through
the material, rejecting the Romantic notions of ancient Orphic wisdom for
a more cautious, historical assessment of the sources. His study redefined
the category of Orphica and was, in Smith's terms, one of the crucial acts
of comparison and generalization that established the parameters of the
religious phenomenon of Orphism for future scholars.[1] However, such acts
of comparison and generalization, of classification and critical analysis, did
not begin with Lobeck. Indeed, most of the earliest evidence is the product
of such scholarly activity, for the critical question of how to define the
Orphica began in antiquity, and the category of "Orphic" seems always to
have been a contested one, as different authors wrangled over how and to
what the label of "Orphic" should be applied.

As Linforth notes, the name of Orpheus always signifies one of two
different things, either Orpheus the character, the enchanting singer who

---

[1] Smith 1982: xi: "Religion is solely the creation of the scholar's study. It is created for the scholar's
analytic purposes by his imaginative acts of comparison and generalization." As I have noted in a
previous study, "Smith's 'acts of comparison and generalization', however, are performed not only
by modern scholars, but also by ancient thinkers, whose motivations are often as prejudiced as those
of modern scholars. Their prejudices, however, are different from those of modern scholars, and, as
such, constitute in and of themselves important data for the understanding of Greek religious ideas.
If 'religion' is a construct that varies from the perspective of the one constructing the category and
the circumstances of the construction, we, as modern scholars, can re-construct the religious ideas
of the ancient Greeks by paying close attention to the generalizations and comparisons made by
ancient thinkers and the circumstances in which they made them" (Edmonds 2008a: 17).

was a hero among the Argonauts, or Orpheus the author, the composer of verses and rituals.[2] The two Orpheuses intertwine in surprisingly few places. There are a few moments in the Argonautic tales (such as those of Apollonios Rhodios and the Orphic one) where the character of Orpheus founds a ritual or recites a cosmogony. The power of Orpheus' song becomes a trope for poets to talk about the power of poetry, from Vergil to Rilke and beyond, but the power of Orpheus' song to establish positive relations with the gods remains oddly separated.[3] The power of Orpheus' song to charm the beasts and even Hades and Persephone occasionally is used to validate the power of Orphic ritual or hymns, but more often these episodes of Orpheus the character are separated from Orpheus the author. The features that pertain to Orpheus the author are those that serve as the criteria for contemporaries to identify poems and rituals as Orphic, so the label of "Orphic" is applied to the works of Orpheus the author, rather than the deeds of Orpheus the character.

In some ways, therefore, the history of Orphism in antiquity is the history of scholarship on Orphica in antiquity, since so much of the evidence derives from the scholarly tradition, later scholars citing the critical works of their earlier predecessors. The fifth-century CE Neoplatonist Damascius, in his treatise on first principles, provides information not just about the Orphic poetry current in his day (presumably the *Orphic Rhapsodies*), but also about the Orphic cosmogonies described in the scholarly analyses of Eudemos and Hieronymos. Eudemos, a pupil of Aristotle, brings the scholarship on Orphica in Damascius back another eight centuries.

However, as Betegh has pointed out, Eudemos himself is working in an established tradition of scholarly inquiry into the Orphica.[4] Eudemos is

---

[2] Linforth 1941: 38: "Actually Orpheus appears as two persons, the legendary figure whose career we have followed, and the author of poetry and institutions which will be examined in the following chapters." My focus in this study is, like Linforth's, upon Orpheus the author, rather than Orpheus the character. For some discussion of the rare moments in the ancient evidence where the two intersect, in Christian polemics by Clement of Alexandria and Gregory Nazianzus, see Jourdan 2011: 15, 109.

[3] Pausanias, in the second century CE, 9.30.12 (*OF* 531ii, 682 B = OF 304 K), remarks that, while Orpheus' hymns are undoubtedly the most divine, they are inferior to the hymns of Homer in their poetic and musical character.

[4] Betegh 2002: 349–351; see also Betegh 2007: 140: "In the wake of Bruno Snell's original paper, Joachim Classen, Andreas Patzer and Jaap Mansfeld have shown that Hippias in this work presented fairly extensive doxographical material, together with an interpretation that identified the different gods of the poets with different elements. On the basis of this exegesis, he then claimed that groups of authors professed the same doctrine. Hippias' doxographical material, together with the interpretation he offered of the poetical and prose texts, became the starting-point for the allegorizing theological and philosophical interpretation of these authors. Hippias' material pops up in Plato's *Cratylus* and *Theaetetus* and Aristotle's doxographical surveys." Cp. esp. Snell 1966 and Mansfeld 1983 [1990].

using a list, one that appears first systematized in the sophist Hippias, of theologians, that is, poets and prose writers who make their logoi about the gods. Hippias, as Clement tells us, boasts that he has compiled the important ideas from the greatest of poets:

> Of these things some perchance are said by Orpheus, some briefly by Musæus; some in one place, others in other places; some by Hesiod, some by Homer, some by the rest of the poets; and some in prose compositions, some by Greeks, some by Barbarians. And I from all these, placing together the things of most importance and of kindred character, will make the present discourse new and varied.[5]

The thinkers in the fifth century begin the work of systematizing their cultural tradition, comparing the different authors and analyzing their works for the most significant ideas. The canonical list of Orpheus, Mousaios, Homer, and Hesiod appears earliest here, but it is repeated in later sources in much the same order. Aristophanes uses it in the *Frogs*, when he discusses the great contributions the poets have made, starting with Orpheus.[6] Part of this systematization is the classification of Orpheus as a culture hero and the analysis of his works.

Herodotus attests to some of this systematizing when he declares that Homer and Hesiod were the first to set out the genealogies and descriptions of the gods and that other poets who are said to be older than Homer (by which he must certainly mean Orpheus) are not actually older.[7] The works attributed to Orpheus, that is, are not really older than Homer's poems; they are later compositions by authors other than the mythical poet. Herodotus makes a similar claim grounded in this kind of classification when he claims that the rites thought to be Orphic and Bacchic are really Egyptian and Pythagorean.[8] Again, the claim bespeaks a kind of critical analysis of the tradition; someone (whether Herodotus himself or a previous thinker) has argued that rituals attributed to Orpheus actually belong in the category of rites taken from Egypt. The claim may likewise be attributing the authorship to a Pythagorean, again making the point that

---

[5] Hippias *FrGH* 6 F 4 = 86 B 6 DK *ap.* Clem. Al. *Strom.* 6.15.2 (*OF* 1146 B = OT 252 K): τούτων ἴσως εἴρηται τὰ μὲν Ὀρφεῖ, τὰ δὲ Μουσαίωι κατὰ βραχὺ ἄλλωι ἀλλαχοῦ, τὰ δὲ Ἡσιόδωι, τὰ δὲ Ὁμήρωι, τὰ δὲ τοῖς ἄλλοις τῶν ποιητῶν, τὰ δὲ ἐν συγγραφαῖς, τὰ μὲν Ἕλλησι, τὰ δὲ βαρβάροις· ἐγὼ δὲ ἐκ πάντων τούτων τὰ μέγιστα καὶ ὁμόφυλα συνθεὶς τοῦτον καινὸν καὶ πολυειδῆ τὸν λόγον ποιήσομαι.

[6] Ar. *Ran.* 1030–1032 (*OF* 547i, 510, 626i B = OT 90 K); cp. Hor. *Ars P.* 391–392 (*OF* 626ii B = OT III K).

[7] Hdt. 2.53 (*OF* 880i B = OT 10 K).

[8] Hdt. 2.81.2 (*OF* 45, 650 B = OT 216 K). I follow Burkert 1972: 127–128 in preferring the long version of the passage. For extensive bibliography on the disputed reading, see Bernabé *ad OF* 650 B.

the works labeled with the name of Orpheus belong not to the mythical figure but to a historical author. Herodotus does not cite his source for these classifications, but he provides evidence that the scholarly analysis of Orphic materials had already begun in his day, and that the Greeks were thinking critically about how to apply the label of "Orphic" to the materials in their tradition.

The Classical category

The evidence for this early analysis of the category "Orphic" as part of the more widespread systematic consideration of the poetic tradition comes mostly from later sources, looking back to the Classical period, but a few names stand out as worthy of attention. Pherekydes of Athens is said to have collected the works of Orpheus (τὰ Ὀρφέως συναγαγεῖν) in the fifth century BCE, perhaps the first in a long line of collections of Orphica up to Bernabé's recent edition.[9] Clement of Alexandria tells us that a certain Epigenes, identified by Linforth with the follower of Socrates, wrote a treatise on the poetry of Orpheus, in which he attributed various Orphica to particular authors.[10] Epigenes' treatise provides the first evidence for specific titles of Orphic works – *Katabasis*, *Hieros Logos*, *Peplos*, and *Physika* – as well as, like Herodotus, attributing to Pythagoreans (Kerkops and Brontinos) works that circulated under the name of Orpheus. Epigenes also seems to have discussed various features of Orphic poetry, like the description of the moon as Gorgonian because of its face or the use of the phrase "tears of Zeus" for rain showers, and he may even have interpreted Orphica allegorically, explaining that the parts of a loom represent the process of ploughing and sowing seeds.[11] Ion of Chios, a fifth-century tragedian and sophist, seems also to have discussed Orphica in his *Triagmoi*, claiming that Pythagoras himself put the name of Orpheus on his own poems. Herodoros

---

[9] *Suda* s.v. Φερεκύδης (φ 216, IV.713.23–24 Adler) (*OF* 1127 B = OT 228 K).

[10] Linforth 1941: 114–119 identifies Epigenes as the follower of Socrates mentioned by Plato (*Ap.* 33e, *Phd.* 59b) and Xenophon (*Mem.* 3.12).

[11] Clem. Al. *Strom.* 5.8.49 (*OF* 407i, 1128ii B = OF 33, OT 229 K): "Does not Epigenes, in his book on the *Poetry of Orpheus*, in exhibiting the peculiarities found in Orpheus, say that by the curved rods (κεραῖσι) is meant ploughs; and by the warp (στήμοσι), the furrows; and the woof (μίτος) is a figurative expression for the seed; and that the tears of Zeus signify a shower; and that the parts (μοῖραι) are, again, the phases of the moon, the thirtieth day, and the fifteenth, and the new moon, and that Orpheus accordingly calls them white-robed, as being parts of the light? Again, that the Spring is called flowery, from its nature; and Night still, on account of rest; and the Moon Gorgonian, on account of the face in it; and that the time in which it is necessary to sow is called Aphrodite by the Theologian." One could speculate that the explication of the weaving comes from an interpretation of the abduction of Kore while weaving, perhaps in the *Peplos*, in terms of natural phenomena. Cp. Herrero 2010: 207–209.

also wrote a treatise on the poetry of Mousaios and Orpheus, in which he resorted to the hypothesis of two different men named Orpheus to reconcile the chronology of the Argonaut with the appearance of various Orphic poems.[12] Not only were these thinkers of the Classical period (whether they should be called scholars or sophists) systematically collecting and analyzing the poetry of Orpheus, but they were working Orpheus into their histories of Greek culture. Orpheus appears, as he does in Aristophanes, as the inventor of special rituals (*teletai*), but also as the inventor of hexameter verse or even of letters.[13]

While most of this evidence comes in testimonia from much later sources, contemporary evidence does survive in the works of Plato and Aristotle. Plato seems to draw on Hippias for the canonical list of poets, but he also quotes passages in his dialogues.[14] With the possible exception of the Derveni papyrus, Plato indeed is the earliest source for direct quotations of Orphic poetry, and he seems to be familiar with a variety of poems. It is impossible to be certain what sort of poem the phrase "the season of enjoyment" (ὥραν τῆς τέρψιος) might come from, but it is a reasonable guess that "many bear the narthex, but few are bacchoi" comes from some work pertaining to Dionysos.[15] Orpheus is famous for his hymns, and Plato makes a reference in the *Laws* to a description of Zeus as the first, middle, and last, a line that turns up not only in the hymn to Zeus in the Derveni papyrus, but in later Orphica in expanded form.[16] Plato also quotes theogonic material, a line that makes Okeanos and Tethys the parents of the gods, in his argument in the *Cratylus* that Homer and Hesiod, along with Orpheus, subscribed to the Heraclitean principle of

---

[12] Cp. *FGrH* 31 F 42 = ΣAp. Rhod. *Argon.* 1.23–25a (8.22 Wendel) (*OF* 1010ii, 1129ii B = OT 5 K); *FGrH* 31 F 12 = Olymp. *ap.* Phot. *Bibl.* 80.61a 32 (1.180 Henry = 86 Migne 103 272c) (*OF* 1129i B = OT 230 K). *Suda* s.v. Ὀρφεύς (o 658, III.565.20–21 Adler) (*OF* 708i, 870v, 1103i B = OT 176, 223 K) and Const. Lascaris Προλεγόμενα τοῦ σοφοῦ Ὀρφέως 103 (36 Martínez Manzano) (*OF* 1103i–ii B) attribute works to Orpheus of Camarina, i.e., a later figure with the same name, in a rationalizing attempt to make the chronology work.

[13] Kritias 88 B 3 DK (fr. 3 Battegazzore-Untersteiner) *ap.* Mallius Theodorus, *De metris* 4.1 (p. 589.20 Keil) (*OF* 1029i, 1125iv B = OT 106 K); Alcidamas, *Ulysses* 24 (30 Muir) (*OF* 1027, 1030ii, 1046i, 1073i B = OT 123 K). (Even if the *Ulysses* is not authentic, the date is about right.)

[14] For the catalogues, see Pl. *Ap.* 41a (*OF* 1076i B = OT 138 K); *Ion* 536ab (*OF* 973 B = OT 244 K) (no Hesiod). Cp. Pl. *Prt.* 316de (*OF* 549i, 669iii, 806, 1013 B = OT 92 K) for the idea of Orpheus as crypto-sophist.

[15] Pl. *Leg.* 669d (*OF* 845 B, OF 11 K); *Phd.* 69c (*OF* 434iii, 549ii, 576i, 669ii B).

[16] Pl. *Leg.* 715e (*OF* 31iii B = OF 21 K), with scholiast *ad loc.* (317 Greene) (*OF* 31iv B); cp. the shorter version in the Derveni papyrus col. 17 (*OF* 14 B). Bernabé collects other testimonies to this line in *OF* 31 B, including Arist. [*Mund.*] 401a25 (*OF* 31i B = OF 21a K); for hymns, cp. the reference in *Leg.* 829d (*OF* 681 B = OF 12 K) to the sweet Orpheian hymns. Another of the earliest testimonies appears in the quotation of [Dem.] 25.8 (*OF* 33 B = OF 23 K) referring to Justice seated by the throne of Zeus.

flux.[17] The line quoted in the *Philebus*, "Stop the order of your song at the sixth generation," may also be from a theogonic context, although other genealogical contexts are imaginable.[18]

While the form of the Platonic dialogue is not geared to the systematic analysis of the Orphica, Plato shows his awareness of the critical tradition of his day. In discussing the genealogy of the gods, he has Timaios say, rather sarcastically, that,

> We should accept on faith the assertions of those figures of the past who claimed to be the offspring of the gods. They must surely have been well informed about their own ancestors. So we cannot avoid believing the children of the gods, even though their accounts lack plausible or compelling proofs.[19]

Timaios then recounts a brief theogony, beginning with Earth and Heaven, followed by Okeanos and Tethys as the parents of Kronos and Rhea. Since Homer and Hesiod do not claim to be divinely descended, whereas Orpheus and Mousaios do, it is plausible that Plato is referring to poems by the latter, at the same time expressing his doubts about the authorship of the poems. He does not, as Epigenes and Ion do, suggest alternate authors, but he does, like Herodotus, suggest that they are pseudepigrapha, poems to which the name of Orpheus has been attached.

The idea that Orphica are not the products of the mythical poet but of later pseudepigraphers comes out in the circumlocutions used to describe the authors. In the *Cratylus*, Plato has Socrates refer to "those concerned with Orpheus" (οἱ ἀμφὶ Ὀρφέα), rather than to Orpheus himself, as the authors of a particular etymology. Aristotle likewise mentions ideas found in "the so-called Orphic poems," at the same time acknowledging their supposed origin and denying its validity.[20] Plato and Aristotle show the controversies over the classification of Orphica in the Classical period, the debates over what it means to label something as Orphic.

The Hellenistic category

The loss of the vast majority of Hellenistic texts of all kinds makes it more difficult to determine how Hellenistic thinkers classified things as Orphic,

---

[17] Pl. *Cra.* 402b (*OF* 22i B = OF 15 K); cp. *Tht.* 180cd.
[18] Pl. *Phlb.* 66c8–9 (*OF* 25i B = OF 14 K): ἕκτηι δ᾽ἐν γενεῆι καταπαύσατε κόσμον ἀοιδῆς. See below pp. 151–2 for the problems of interpretation of this line in the scholarship on the theogonies.
[19] Pl. *Ti.* 40de (*OF* 21, 24, 910iii B = OF 16 K).
[20] Arist. *Gen. an.* B1 734a16 (*OF* 404 B = OF 26 K): ἐν τοῖς καλουμένοις Ὀρφέως ἔπεσιν; *De an.* A5 410b27 (*OF* 421i B = OF 27 K): ὁ ἐν τοῖς Ὀρφικοῖς ἔπεσι καλουμένοις λόγος.

but enough traces survive to show a continuity with the systematizing of the fifth and fourth centuries. Later sources such as Athenaios or the even later *Suda* refer to treatises on Orpheus and his rites by the otherwise almost unknown Apollonios of Aphrodisias and Nikomedes.[21] The Attidographer Androtion, responding to the earlier identifications of Orpheus as the inventor of writing, claims that an ignorant and illiterate Thracian could never have discovered this vital art. This very counter-claim reflects the impact of expanding literacy in the Greek world, as the distinction between literate and illiterate shifts its social significance and becomes a mark distinguishing Greeks and barbarians.[22] Another Attidographer, Philochoros, in addition to devoting works to the systematization of Attic history, wrote a treatise in several books on divination, in which he seems to have classified Orpheus as a *mantis*.[23]

In the universal history of Diodorus Siculus, Orpheus takes the role of the founder of important Greek religious practices, and Diodorus recounts how Orpheus took the ideas for these practices from that greatest of sources of ancient wisdom, Egypt. Diodorus is of course following in a tradition that goes back to (and no doubt before) Herodotus, but his account places Orpheus into a larger narrative of how Greek culture developed. As Bernabé has argued, Diodorus seems not to be drawing from a single work of Orpheus, but rather he is clearly familiar with a number of poems and rituals attributed in his day to Orpheus.[24] Diodorus systematizes the varied traditions he has at his disposal, creating a story that puts Orpheus in a plausible time to play his role as an Argonaut, but he retrojects the religious wisdom Orpheus brings to Greece even further back by tying it to the antiquity of the Egyptian tradition.

Whereas Diodorus puts Orpheus into a chronological schema, the later historian Strabo makes use of Orpheus in his excursus on ecstatic rituals, creating a geographical point of origin in Orpheus' homeland of

[21] Nikomedes (4th?/3rd c.), *FGrH* 772 F 3 *ap.* Ath. 14.637a (*OF* 1130 B = OT 231 K) mentions a work on Orpheus; *Suda* s.v. Ἀπολλώνιος (α 3424, 1.309.13–14 Adler) (*OF* 1132 B = OT 232 K) mentions that Apollonios of Aphrodisias wrote a work on Orpheus and his *teletai* (*FGrH* 740 T 1), possibly in the third century BCE.

[22] Androtion, *FGrH* 324 F 54a *ap.* Ael. *VH* 8.6 (*OF* 1028 B = OT 32 K). Androtion was a student of Isokrates. For the use made of the barbarian status of Orpheus in later Christian polemics, see Jourdan 2011: 224.

[23] *FGrH* 328 F 76 = Clem. Al. 1.21.134.4 (*OF* 1015i B = OT 87, OF 332 K). Philochoros was also apparently a practicing *mantis* himself, as well as the author of treatises on various ritual practices.

[24] Bernabé 2002b: 70: "Hay razones para pensar que los pasajes citados o aludidos por las fuentes de Diodoro proceden de tradiciones órficas diversas." Cp. the texts collected under *OF* 48 B: Diod. Sic. 1.92.2 (*OF* 48i B = OF 293 K); 1.96.3 (*OF* 48ii B = OT 96 K); 1.23.2 (*OF* 48iii B = OT 95 K); 4.25.3 (*OF* 48iv B = OT 97 K); 1.69.4 (*OF* 48v B).

Thrace. Apologizing for digressing from his geographical survey into matters mythological and theological, Strabo traces the ecstatic rites of the Kouretes, Dionysos, and the Mother of the Gods back from Phrygia and Helicon and Crete to Thrace, noting that Orpheus is among the ancient poets linked to Thrace. He refers to the Orphica to describe one class of rituals in this type of ecstatic ritual of which he is speaking, drawing a distinction between the rites of Dionysos among the Greeks and the rites of the Mother of the Gods among the Phrygians, the arts of Dionysos on the one hand and those of Orpheus on the other. For Strabo, then, the Orphica are of the type of ecstatic ritual, linked with the worship of the Mother of the Gods and her attendants, and similar to, but different from, the Dionysiac rituals of the same ecstatic type.[25]

The Orphica were also a topic in philosophical circles, and the systematizing work of the earlier thinkers was continued by the Hellenistic philosophers. Aristotle's pupil, Eudemos, as we know from Damascius, compared the cosmogonic ideas of Orpheus to those of Homer, Hesiod, Akousilaos, Epimenides, Pherekydes of Syros, as well as the Babylonians, Persian Magoi, and Phoenicians, and Betegh has argued that Eudemos' discussion extended beyond the first few principles that are all Damascius treats.[26] Eudemos contrasted Orpheus' beginning of the cosmogony with Night to Homer, who he claims began with Okeanos.[27] Eudemos' contemporary, Theophrastos, who took over the school after Aristotle, seems to have dealt with the Orphica not as a source for cosmogonic thought, but rather in his discussions of purification and piety, since he caricatures the superstitious man as one who visits an Orpheotelest once a month.[28]

Hieronymos of Rhodes is another Peripatetic who may have worked at systematizing materials from the Orphica, although much dispute remains in the scholarship as to whether he is indeed the Hieronymos mentioned by Damascius in that crucial fifth-century CE survey of previous treatments

[25] Strab. 10.3.7–23 (*OF* 570, 528, 1024i, 577v, 670 B = OT 160, 31 K).
[26] Betegh 2002: 346. He also points out that Hippias probably also included Akousilaos and Pherekydes in his survey, on which he argues that Eudemos is drawing, although it is unclear whether Hippias included the Babylonians, Persians, and Phoenicians in his treatment of the barbarians.
[27] Damascius rejects Eudemos' interpretation, but the idea that Homer had the flowing water of Ocean as his first principle appears not only in Plato (*Cra.* 402ac [*OF* 22i B = OF 15 K] and *Tht.* 152de above), but also in Arist. *Metaph.* 1.3 983b20–984a5 (*OF* 22iii B = OF 25 K), and becomes, as Betegh 2002: 349 notes, a commonplace.
[28] Theophr. *Char.* 16. His Περὶ εὐσεβείας, of which traces remain in Porphyry's *De abstinentia*, undoubtedly examined the history of the vegetarian ideal, which is labeled the βίος Ὀρφικός in Plato. Cp. Matelli 2010: 422–424. Porphyry, however, never mentions Orpheus in this connection, although he cites him elsewhere.

of first principles. "The theology circulating under the names of Hieronymos and Hellanikos, if indeed this is not the same, goes like this."[29] The
identities of both Hieronymos and Hellanikos have been much discussed.
West dismisses Lobeck's identification of Hieronymos with the Peripatetic
Hieronymos of Rhodes on the grounds that such a discussion of cosmogonic schemata does not fit well with what we know of Hieronymos' works,
but Matelli has recently argued that Hieronymos of Rhodes makes a good
candidate for Damascius' source, identifying the Hellanikos mentioned
with the fifth-century BCE mythographer from Lesbos.[30] Hellanikos is precisely the kind of systematizing mythographer to have made an account
of an Orphic theogony, and Hieronymos could simply have drawn his
information from this source. Damascius seems to indicate his uncertainty
whether the account he has stems from one source or two, but such confusion could easily arise from Hieronymos' use of Hellanikos as a source.[31]
One argument in favor of a later dating for the theogony recorded by
Hieronymos is the presence of elements that seem to draw from Stoic ideas.
The presence of mud and water as the primal elements of the theogony
looks to some modern scholars like the result of an allegorical interpretation
of a type attributed to Zeno, the founder of Stoicism. "Zeno also says that
Hesiod's 'Chaos' is water, from the settlement of which mud comes into
being, and when that solidifies the earth is established."[32] West also points to
the identification of certain deities as characteristic of Stoic allegorization,

[29] *De princ.* 123 (III.160.17 Westerink) (*OF* 69, 75i, 1138 B = OF 54, OT 242 K): Ἡ δὲ κατὰ τὸν
Ἱερώνυμον φερομένη καὶ Ἑλλάνικον, εἴπερ μὴ καὶ ὁ αὐτός ἐστιν, οὕτως ἔχει· One point of dispute
is the reference of ὁ αὐτός, whether it refers to the person (Hieronymos and Hellanikos may be the
same person) or a λόγος (the account of Hieronymos and Hellanikos may be the same).
[30] Matelli 2010: 445: "La più approfondita conoscenza critica dei testi di Ieronimo in base alla nuova
edizione dei frammenti, il nuovo quadro della religiosità di Rodi nel III sec. a. C., la considerazione
che all'interno della scuola di Aristotele ci fu interesse per l'orfismo, possono a mio giudizio portare
a rivedere la questione. L'attribuzione della paternità della Teogonia a un doppio nome 'Ieronimo
o Ellanico (a meno che siano la stessa persona)' da parte di Damascio (Pr. 123) potrebbe far pensare
che Ieronimo avesse riportato una Teogonia citando l'autorità dello storico del V sec. a. C., Ellanico,
sua fonte." Jacoby too had identified Hellanikos with the mythographer. Cp. Lobeck 1829: 340;
contra West 1983: 177: "What we know of it [Hieronymos' work], however, indicates that it was
concerned with literary history and anecdotal biography, and it would be extremely surprising if it
contained such details of an Orphic poem as Damascius has."
[31] West 1983: 176–178 suggests Sandon, son of Hellanikos, mentioned by the *Suda* as having written on
Orpheus, whose Cilician name might be rendered as Hieronymos, but ultimately prefers to identify
Hieronymos with Hieronymos the Egyptian mentioned by Josephos, about whom "we know next
to nothing."
[32] ΣAp. Rhod. *Argon.* 1.496–498b (44.4 Wendel = *SVF* I.29.17): καὶ Ζήνων δὲ τὸ παρ' Ἡσιόδῳ χάος
ὕδωρ εἶναί φησιν, οὗ συνιζάνοντος ἰλὺν γίνεσθαι, ἧς πηγνυμένης ἡ γῆ στερεμνιοῦται· Brisson 1985a
[1995]: 41 uses this evidence to date the Hieronymean theogony even later than the *Rhapsodies*: "Le
premier stade de cette théogonie, où interviennent l'eau et la matière dont vient la terre, pourrait
bien n'être qu'une adaptation de l'exégèse allégorique de Zénon de Cition."

but it remains an open question, given the absence of so much data from the Hellenistic period, whether such interpretations were exclusive to the Stoics or whether they could have been made by other thinkers of the period.[33] The identification of Hesiod's primordial Chaos with water and mud could easily be borrowed by one thinker from another, even if the two did not agree on other aspects of cosmology, ethics, or other philosophical matters, just as the identifications of divinities with concepts such as Time or Necessity could be put to use in a variety of different theological systems.

The treatise *On the World*, attributed to Aristotle, is another Peripatetic text that has been thought to contain Stoic elements.[34] In the final section, which describes the supreme deity of the cosmos, the author approvingly quotes in support of his ideas an *Orphic Hymn to Zeus*, which is an expanded form of that which appeared in the Derveni papyrus and in Plato's *Laws*.[35] Having introduced the lines by remarking "it is not badly said in the Orphica," he continues by citing a number of etymologies that identify principles of necessity (Anagke, Adrasteia, the Moirae, etc.) with the supreme deity.[36] The Stoics, however, were not the only ones to practice such etymological allegorization, which had been around long enough before Plato for him to mock it extensively in the *Cratylus*, so the question remains whether the elements that resemble Stoic ideas are drawn from the Stoics or are drawn by the Stoics and others (including the author of *On the World* and the Orphic cosmogony mentioned by Hieronymos) from a shared interpretive tradition.[37]

---

[33] West 1983: 219: "We have earlier found evidence both of Stoicizing embellishment in the Hieronymean Theogony (Chronos identified as Heracles, Ananke as Adrastea; Protogonos entitled Zeus) and of Stoic transmission of the poem (Hieronymus' formulation of the first material principles)."

[34] Furley 1955: 335–336: "The theology and cosmology of the *De Mundo* is, in general, Peripatetic, but the author borrows his details from many schools. . . . No doubt the *De Mundo* is influenced by Stoic religious thought. But the author rejects an important part of the Stoic doctrine: his god is not immanent in the world, but remote, unmoved, and impassive." Reale and Bos 1995 argue for a Peripatetic origin, perhaps even Aristotle himself. Bos 1991a: 312 notes that, although few are willing to accept that the treatise is actually by Aristotle, more have accepted that it may come from a Peripatetic context and that Stoics may have drawn on the ideas in it rather than vice versa.

[35] Arist. [*Mund.*] 401a27–401b6 (*OF* 31i B = OF 21a K): Ζεὺς πρῶτος γένετο, Ζεὺς ὕστατος ἀρχικέραυνος·| Ζεὺς κεφαλή, Ζεὺς μέσσα, Διὸς δ᾽ ἐκ πάντα τέτυκται·| Ζεὺς πυθμὴν γαίης τε καὶ οὐρανοῦ ἀστερόεντος·| Ζεὺς ἄρσην γένετο, Ζεὺς ἄμβροτος ἔπλετο νύμφη·| Ζεὺς πνοιὴ πάντων, Ζεὺς ἀκαμάτου πυρὸς ὁρμή·| Ζεὺς πόντου ῥίζα, Ζεὺς ἥλιος ἠδὲ σελήνη·| Ζεὺς βασιλεύς, Ζεὺς ἀρχὸς ἀπάντων ἀρχικέραυνος·| πάντας γὰρ κρύψας αὖθις φάος ἐς πολυγηθὲς | ἐκ καθαρῆς κραδίης ἀνενέγκατο, μέρμερα ῥέζων.

[36] καὶ ἐν τοῖς Ὀρφικοῖς οὐ κακῶς λέγεται.

[37] Baxter 1992 makes a thorough study of the tradition of allegory that lies behind the *Cratylus*. Cp. Long 1992 on the problems with attributing allegorization simply to the Stoics. For earlier

The Stoics certainly did cite this hymn to Zeus, with its praises of Zeus as supreme and all-encompassing deity, since Plutarch also quotes a version of it in a discussion of Stoic ideas as something they say themselves (ὡς αὐτοὶ λέγουσι).[38] Chrysippos, in addition to a work on Orpheus, is said to have written himself on a number of the same themes, reconciling the traditional cosmogonic tales of the succession of Ouranos, Kronos, and Zeus with the ideas of a supreme deity ruling over a rationally ordered cosmos.[39] Later authors such as Philodemos and Cicero attest to the interest of the Stoics in the Orphica, and Cicero's treatise *On the Nature of the Gods* provides evidence for the kind of systematizing in which these thinkers engaged.[40]

The Stoics, however, were not the only ones in the Hellenistic period to engage with the Orphica in general and with the hymn to Zeus in particular. Another version of the hymn turns up in a papyrus fragment,[41] and a revised and expanded version circulates as the *Testament of Orpheus*, Orpheus' recantation of polytheism and affirmation of monotheism. This *Testament* seems to be an Orphic work composed by a Hellenistic Jewish pseudepigrapher in the second or third century BCE. The Jewish Orphicists developed the idea of Zeus as supreme deity into an apology for the Jewish monotheistic tradition in the period when thinkers in the Jewish tradition were attempting to find ways of reconciling their ideas with those of the Greek philosophical and religious tradition.[42] This well known *Orphic Hymn*, already taken seriously in the philosophical tradition, provided an excellent way to borrow authority for the Jewish tradition by recasting it as

precedents, see not only Plato's *Cratylus*, but also Tiresias' explanations in Euripides' *Bacchae* 275 ff., with Roth 1984.

[38] Plut. *Comm. not.* 31.1074de (*OF* 31vi B): 'Ζεὺς ἀρχή, Ζεὺς μέσσα, Διὸς δ' ἐκ πάντα τέτυκται', ὡς αὐτοὶ λέγουσι. Note the substitution of ἀρχή in Plutarch's version for the metrically equivalent κεφαλή in the *De mundo*. Plut. *De def. or.* 415–416 (*OF* 358ii B = OF 250 K) likewise claims that the Stoics "graze" upon the Orphica as nourishment (τὰ Ὀρφέως ἐπινεμομένην ἔπη) for their idea of the universal conflagration (*ecpyrosis*).

[39] Chrysippos wrote on Orpheus (*OF* 1133 B = OT 233 K). Cp. Casadesús 2010 for a comparison of Stoic ideas with ideas attributed to Orphic texts.

[40] E.g., Cic. *Nat. D.* 3.58 (*OF* 497i B = OT 94 K) lists a whole series of gods called Dionysos, the third of which is associated with the Orphic rites. See further ch. 7 n. 153.

[41] *PSI* XV 1476 (*OF* 688a B): [ἐξ Ὀρφέως·] | [Ζεὺς] πάντων ἀρχή, Ζεὺς [μέσσα, Ζεὺς δὲ τε]λευτή· | Ζεὺς ὕπατος, [Ζεὺς καὶ χθόνι]ος καὶ πόντιός ἐστιν, | [Ζεὺς ἄρσην,] Ζεὺς θῆλυς | πάλιν | Ζεὺς δὲ [τὰ πάντα,] | [πά]ντα κύκλωι φαίνων, [Ζεὺς ἀρχή, μέσσα,] τ[ε]λευτή· | καὶ δύναται [Ζεὺς πᾶν, Ζεὺς π]ᾶ[ν] ἔχ<ε>ι αὐτὸς ἐν αὐτῶι. Bastianini 2005 describes the papyrus as an anthology dating to the second century CE, collecting verses, primarily from Euripides and other dramatists, arranged perhaps by topical headings. The quotation from Orpheus may have come in a list of verses about the greatness of Zeus.

[42] Riedweg 1993: 95 suggests that the Orphicist may have been Aristoboulos or at least that Aristoboulos may have redacted one of the versions that circulated.

Orpheus' recognition of the existence of a single, supreme god. As Jourdan
points out,

> Les raisons du choix d'Orphée par les auteurs du pseudépigraphie sem-
> blent davantage résider dans une appropriation de la conception païenne
> du poète et de son enseignement. Elle devait permettre de toucher les Juifs
> d'Alexandrie attirés par la culture hellénique et de leur fournir des arguments
> en faveur de leur propre religion, elle aussi pour ainsi dire 'révélée' par le
> tout premier théologien des Grecs.[43]

This text is preserved in several different forms by later Christian apologists who likewise found in it excellent ammunition for their critiques
of the Greek polytheistic tradition.[44] As Holladay notes, however, "in the
Pseudo-Orpheus poem we are not dealing with a single, relatively static text
with many variants but a *fluid* text preserved in *different* forms in *several*
witnesses, each with *many* variants."[45] Just as Peripatetics and Stoics found
the hymn useful to illustrate their ideas, tweaking its form to suit their particular concepts, so too the Hellenistic Jews adapted it for their purposes.[46]
The multiple appearances of this hymn to Zeus in the Hellenistic evidence
provide an illustration of the way that the Orphica were handled in this
period – cited for their authority and rewritten to fit the various individual
purposes.

In addition to the *Orphic Hymn to Zeus*, the figure of Orpheus himself is
appropriated in Hellenistic Judaism, through a wordplay upon the name of
Orpheus' pupil (or son) Mousaios, who is reinterpreted as Moses, the great
revelatory figure of the Jewish tradition. A certain Artapanus, Eusebios tells
us, relates in his treatise *On the Jews* that Moses was called Mousaios by
the Greeks and was the teacher of Orpheus.[47] This tale inverts the usual
relationship of Orpheus and Mousaios, making Orpheus dependent on

---

[43] Jourdan 2010: 45.
[44] There have been several recent detailed studies of this text and its history of transmission: Riedweg
1993, Holladay 1996, and most recently Jourdan 2010.
[45] Holladay 1996: 48.
[46] As West 1983: 225 says of the Stoic poet he imagines to have reworked the Hieronymean theogony,
"The Stoicizing poet's method was one of free re-composition, using lines and phrases from the
original but not following it slavishly. Hellenistic style and diction are detectable even in verses
describing events that must have been described in the old poem." Two other fragments of Orphic
verses, *OF* 691B = OF 248 K and *OF* 620 B = OF 299 K, both preserved in early Christian
apologists, have been identified as showing "influence of Judaism," suggesting a Jewish Orphicist.
Cp. West 1983: 35.
[47] Artapanus, *FGrH* 726 F 3 *ap.* Euseb. *Praep. evang.* 9.27 (*OF* 942 B = OT 44 K): "She being
barren took a supposititious child from one of the Jews, and called him Mouses (Moses): but by
the Greeks he was called, when grown to manhood, Mousaios. And this Moses, they said, was the
teacher of Orpheus; and when grown up he taught mankind many useful things. For he was the
inventor of ships, and machines for laying stones, and Egyptian arms, and engines for drawing

Moses/Mousaios, thus privileging the Jewish tradition over the Greek. The tradition of Orpheus' journey to Egypt, recorded in Diodorus, provides the opportunity to bring the two figures together in some unspecified time in the distant past, coordinating the origins of both the Greek and Jewish traditions but putting the Greek religious tradition in debt to Moses and the Jewish tradition.[48] Orpheus appears as a figure of great antiquity, a founder of religious traditions, a culture hero and inventor, and his name validates the traditions and cultural patterns to which it is attached.

The thinkers of the Classical and Hellenistic periods – the philosophers, the theologians, the mythographers, and the historians – handled the Orphica and the problem of Orpheus' name in similar ways. Orpheus was placed in the ranks of important "first discoverers" and other culture heroes, credited with inventing special rituals, hymns, writing, or even hexameter poetry itself. Mythographers and historians tried to work out the anomalies in the dates for this mythical hero who sailed on the Argo and yet whose poetic works kept appearing. As the philosophical schools developed, crafting theories about the nature of the gods and the universe, Orpheus' verses were used to support various ideas. Scholars collected his works and debated about their authenticity, while pseudepigraphers kept on producing new ones and tweaking the older verses to better support their own ideas.[49]

It is worth noting, however, that Orpheus' name is not the only, or even the predominant, name invoked as an authority. As West has shown, Mousaios, Linos, Epimenides, and other surpassingly ancient poets were

---

water and for war, and invented philosophy." ταύτην δὲ στεῖραν ὑπάρχουσαν ὑποβαλέσθαι τινὸς τῶν Ἰουδαίων παιδίον, τοῦτο δὲ Μώϋσον ὀνομάσαι· ὑπὸ δὲ τῶν Ἑλλήνων αὐτὸν ἀνδρωθέντα Μουσαῖον προσαγορευθῆναι. γενέσθαι δὲ τὸν Μώϋσον τοῦτον Ὀρφέως διδάσκαλον. ἀνδρωθέντα δ' αὐτὸν πολλὰ τοῖς ἀνθρώποις εὔχρηστα παραδοῦναι· καὶ γὰρ πλοῖα καὶ μηχανὰς πρὸς τὰς λιθοθεσίας καὶ τὰ Αἰγύπτια ὅπλα καὶ τὰ ὄργανα τὰ ὑδρευτικὰ καὶ πολεμικὰ καὶ τὴν φιλοσοφίαν ἐξευρεῖν·

[48] Cp. Gruen 1998: 159. As Herrero 2010: 225 notes, "More than an apologetic weapon, however, this was for the Jews above all a tool for integrating their own culture into the Greek historiographic frameworks."

[49] The extent of this tweaking must remain uncertain, but I see no reason to agree with West 1983: 224 that it was merely superficial, with no impact on the religious message: "I speak of 'embellishment', because none of it seriously affected the essence of the poem. It was not transformed into an exposition of Stoic theology. Doctrines such as the ecpyrosis and cyclicalism may lie behind some of the embellishments, but they were not imported into the text. It remained an Orphic poem with something like its original religious message." Even if the reworked poems were not intended as official expositions of Stoic doctrine (an anachronistic concept in any case), the Orphicist composed the poem to express his own ideas (Stoic or Peripatetic or an eclectic mix), and the modifications must have transformed the "original religious message" of the poem – or at any rate, the message of the previous version with which the Orphicist was working – into something congruent with his own ideas.

put into the systems alongside Orpheus by these Classical and early Hellenistic systematizers, and pseudepigraphers were hard at work composing poems in their names as well.[50] While Orpheus already appears as the most important of these poets, it is only in later periods that Orpheus becomes the predominant figure, the epitome of ancient Greek wisdom and representative of a Hellenic religious tradition that faced serious challenges, including from an emerging Christian tradition.[51]

Roman period

Just as the evidence of later commentators and apologists bears witness to the activities of various Orphicists with Stoic and Peripatetic interests during the Hellenistic period, so too the Middle Platonists must have had their fair share of Orphic pseudepigraphers, given the sorts of ideas that turn up in the Orphic verses quoted by Platonists in the Roman empire. It is to the later Neoplatonists – Iamblichus, Proclus, and Damascius – that we owe the bulk of all the fragments of Orphica, and the systematic picture of Orphic doctrines and ideas that they present has shaped the reception of Orphica ever since. Just as important, however, are the testimonies of their Christian opponents, who likewise built up a systematic portrait of Orpheus and all that he is associated with in order to condemn (or co-opt) the tradition of Greek polytheism. Indeed, the conflict between developing Christianity and those trying to preserve the authority of the Greek philosophical and religious tradition profoundly shaped the way Orpheus and his works were understood in the subsequent centuries.

Although the poets of the Hellenistic and Augustan periods, from Phanocles to Vergil and Ovid, elaborated upon the character of Orpheus, taking him as an image of the poet and extracting every bit of sentimental pathos from his love story, Orpheus the author is still discussed as the originator of certain religious practices and poems.[52] Plutarch, like Strabo, seems to regard Orpheus primarily as the founder of certain kinds of religious rites, specifically ecstatic rites similar to those for Dionysos and

---

[50] West 1983: 39–61. Cp. the fragments of Mousaios, Linos, and Epimenides collected by Bernabé in the third volume of his edition of Orphic fragments (Bernabé 2007a).

[51] As West 1983: 44, 52–53 notes, "The use of Musaeus as a pseudonym does not seem to have continued, like the use of Orpheus, through the Roman period. ... Epimenides seems to have become merely a saleable name. There is no sign that the usurpation of his name continued after the Hellenistic period, indeed it may have ceased in the third century."

[52] Cp. Ov. *Met.* 11.92 (*OF* 499, 527ii B = OT 160 K) for Midas receiving rites from Orpheus; Hor. *Ars P.* 391–392 (*OF* 626ii B = OT 111 K), echoing Ar. *Ran.* 1030–1032 (*OF* 547i, 510, 626i B = OT 90 K).

associated with the semi-barbarous land of Thrace.[53] Indeed, in his reference to the outlandish behavior of Olympias, mother of Alexander the Great, he proposes that the word θρησκεύειν, the excessive and extravagant practice of religion, derives from the Thracian origin of Orpheus – this mode of religious activity is fundamentally Orphic.[54] He also comments that the Roman rites of Bona Dea, a women's festival perhaps related to the Greek Thesmophoria, were similar to the Orphica.[55]

Plutarch also associates Orpheus' name with excessive religious practices not directly connected with such rituals, since he jokes that his friends thought that he might be avoiding eggs because of some superstition derived from the Orphica.

> But when Sossius Senecio was hosting us, they suspected me of adhering to the Orphic or Pythagorean teachings and holding the egg taboo, as some hold the heart and brain, because I considered it the first principle of creation.[56]

Such condescension toward excessive religiosity can also be seen in the anecdote related about an impoverished Orpheotelest who promised happiness in the afterlife for those initiated with him. The wise Spartan to whom he is speaking tauntingly asks, "then why don't you just die now?".[57] He likewise joins Plato in mocking the idea of the symposium of the blessed as everlasting drunkenness.[58] Although he indicates in various places that he

---

[53] Linforth 1941: 227–228 astutely notes the fact that Plutarch refers to both Orphic and Dionysiac rites, questioning why Plutarch should use both descriptors if the Dionysiac rites are to be attributed to Orpheus. His suggestion of a kind of stream of consciousness addition on Plutarch's part ("The answer probably is that Plutarch had in mind from the start the Thracian character of the women's performances and was consequently reminded of the legend of Orpheus as the founder of Thracian rites.") is not convincing, and it is worth considering that Plutarch may have, like Strabo and Herodotus and others who refer to Orphic and Dionysiac rites, meant two different sets of rituals.

[54] Plut. *Vit. Alex.* 2 665d (*OF* 556i B = OT 206 K): τὸ θρησκεύειν ὄνομα ταῖς κατακόροις γενέσθαι καὶ περιέργοις ἱερουργίαις.

[55] Plut. *Vit. Caes.* 9.4 (*OF* 584 B). Linforth 1941: 244 comments: "One suspects that when a Greek writer had occasion to speak of *foreign* orgiastic ritual and was reminded of *Greek* orgiastic ritual, he was naturally led to refer to the Greek ritual as Orphic."

[56] Plut. *Quaest. conv.* 2.3.1 635e (*OF* 645, 647i B = OF 291 K): ὑπόνοιαν μέντοι παρέσχον, ἑστιῶντος ἡμᾶς Σοσσίου Σενεκίωνος, ἐνέχεσθαι δόγμασιν Ὀρφικοῖς ἢ Πυθαγορικοῖς καὶ τὸ ᾠόν, ὥσπερ ἔνιοι καρδίαν καὶ ἐγκέφαλον, ἀρχὴν ἡγούμενος γενέσεως ἀφοσιοῦσθαι.

[57] Plut. *Apopth. Lacon.* 224d (*OF* 653 B = OT 203 K): "To Philip the Orpheotelest, who was entirely broke, but was claiming that those who underwent the rites with him were happy after the end of this life, Leotychidas said, 'Why then, you fool, don't you die as soon as possible so that you may at the same time cease from bewailing your misfortune and poverty?'" Πρὸς δὲ Φίλιππον τὸν ὀρφεοτελεστὴν παντελῶς πτωχὸν ὄντα, λέγοντα δ᾽ ὅτι οἱ παρ᾽ αὐτῷ μυηθέντες μετὰ τὴν τοῦ βίου τελευτὴν εὐδαιμονοῦσι, 'τί οὖν, ὦ ἀνόητε᾽ εἶπεν, 'οὐ τὴν ταχίστην ἀποθνῄσκεις, ἵν᾽ ἅμα παύσῃ κακοδαιμονίαν καὶ πενίαν κλαίων;'

[58] Plut. *Comp. Cim. et Luc.* 1.2 (*OF* 431ii B = OF 4 K). As Bernabé 1996 shows, Plutarch, like Plato, tends not to quote Orpheus seriously or attribute serious ideas to him. Cp. Herrero 2010: 84 n.

knows of Orphic cosmogonic poetry, Plutarch's category of things labeled with the name of Orpheus corresponds generally to that of excessive religious practices, either ecstatic women's rites or somewhat absurd ideas of purity or afterlife reward.[59] Orpheus may be categorized with other ancient wisdom figures, such as Zoroaster, Homer, or Hesiod, but he is still one among several of the most ancient poets and theologians (οἱ σφόδρα παλαιοὶ θεολόγοι καὶ ποιηταί), not yet the primary representative of ancient wisdom.[60]

For Pausanias, in his quest to set out the ancient roots of Greek culture, Orpheus remains a problematic figure, and the problem of to what to affix the name of Orpheus, as always, lies at the base of the problem. The Periegete recounts various versions of the life story of Orpheus, his lineage from the Muse Kalliope, his charming of the beasts, his descent into Hades to retrieve his wife, and even miracles after his death, but Pausanias concludes that these stories of Orpheus the character are false, and that conclusions can only be drawn about Orpheus the author. "Orpheus, it seems to me, surpassed those before him in the beauty of his verse, and he came to a great height of power because he was believed to have discovered rites for the gods and purifications from unholy deeds, cures for diseases and ways of averting divine angers." Pausanias claims to have conducted careful researches into the chronology of the poets, although he refrains from setting out his results because of the contentious nature of the debates.[61] He nevertheless weighs in on the question of the authenticity of various Orphica:

> Whoever has busied himself concerning poetry knows that the hymns of Orpheus are each very short, and that all of them together do not make a great number. The Lycomidae know them and chant them for their rituals. In beauty they may be said to come in second only to the hymns of Homer, but they come out far ahead of them in honor from the divine.[62]

126, who suggests that Plutarch's local allegiance to the prestige of Delphi causes him to reject the strategy of attaching the prestige of Orpheus to Greek antiquities.

[59] Bernabé 1996 examines the references to Orpheus in Plutarch, noting his critiques of excessive religiosity, but he makes a division between Plutarch's condemnation of "popular religion" and legitimate deep theology that imports later scholarly categories onto the evidence.

[60] Plut. *De def. or.* 436d (*OF* 31v B), where the Hymn to Zeus is attributed to these ancients as a group. Cp., e.g., Plut. *De def. or.* 415a (*OF* 524 B = OT 17 K).

[61] Paus. 9.30.3–4. For the hymns attributed to Orpheus and their place in the ritual tradition, see below, ch. 5, *Sacred texts* and *The form of Orphic poems*. Pausanias himself merely cites poems by Onomakritos at 1.22.7 (*OF* 1119 B = OT 195 K); 8.31.3 (*OF* 351, 1114ii B = OT 193 K); 8.37.5 (*OF* 39, 1113 B = OT 194 K); 9.35.5 (*OF* 254ii, 1114iii B).

[62] Paus. 9.30.12 (*OF* 531ii, 682 B = OF 304 K): ὅστις δὲ περὶ ποιήσεως ἐπολυπραγμόνησεν ἤδη, τοὺς Ὀρφέως ὕμνους οἶδεν ὄντας ἕκαστόν τε αὐτῶν ἐπὶ βραχύτατον καὶ τὸ σύμπαν οὐκ ἐς ἀριθμὸν

He rejects the name of Orpheus for an account of the lineage of Triptolemos, and he ascribes to Onomakritos a number of other verses that seem to
have been labeled Orphic.[63] In Pausanias' day, Onomakritos, the collector
of oracles in the court of the Peisistratids who, Herodotus famously relates,
was exiled for interpolating his own verses into the oracles of Mousaios,
becomes one of the favored candidates for the identity of the pseudepigrapher passing his own work under the name of Orpheus.[64] Although
this identification does not appear before the second century CE, several
of Pausanias' contemporaries recount the identification of Onomakritos as
the true author of Orphica as a commonplace. Tatian, an early Christian
apologist, gives the attribution with a vague "they say" (φασιν), while the
Pyrrhonist philosopher, Sextus Empiricus, simply cites Onomakritos in
the Orphica.[65] The identification is picked up by later authors, including
Clement of Alexandria in his list of authors of the Orphica that mentions
the identifications made by Epigenes and Ion of Chios, and is repeated
endlessly in the reception tradition down to the twentieth century.[66]

The crystallization of the category among the Christians and Neoplatonists

Despite all this scholarly activity in antiquity, from the fifth century BCE
onwards, that attempts to analyze and classify the works of Orpheus and to
determine to what the name of Orpheus should be affixed, the boundaries
of this category remain relatively loose until the efforts of the early Christian
apologists and their Neoplatonic opponents. The systematizing work of
both camps in the "culture wars" that surrounded the rise of Christianity
in the Roman empire creates a category of Orphism that is more sharply
defined than ever before, as both the Christian and Neoplatonic apologists

---

πολὺν πεποιημένους· Λυκομίδαι δὲ ἴσασί τε καὶ ἐπᾴδουσι τοῖς δρωμένοις. κόσμῳ μὲν δὴ τῶν ἐπῶν
δευτερεῖα φέροιντο ἂν μετά γε Ὁμήρου τοὺς ὕμνους, τιμῆς δὲ ἐκ τοῦ θείου καὶ ἐς πλέον ἐκείνων
ἥκουσι. Elsewhere (9.27.2 [*OF* 531i B = OF 305 K]) he claims as authentic the hymns composed
by Orpheus for the rites of the Lycomidae at Phyla.

[63] Paus. 1.14.3 (*OF* 382 B = OF 51 K). As Linforth 1941: 353 notes, "No one else throughout antiquity
quotes from works of Onomacritus or makes any allusion to them. It is an extremely probable
inference from these considerations that when Pausanias says Onomacritus he means Ps. Orpheus,
that all his quotations from Onomacritus are really quotations from Orphic poems, and that there
were actually no poems by Onomacritus and never had been. His words cannot be taken as a
statement of fact, but only as an echo of speculations concerning the authorship of Orphic poetry."

[64] Hdt. 7.6.2 (*OF* 807, 1109 B = OT 182 K).

[65] Tatianus *Ad Gr.* 41.3 (*OF* 1110i B = OT 183 K); Sext. Emp. *Pyr.* 3.30 (*OF* 1114i B = OT 187 K).

[66] Clem. Al. *Strom.* 1.21.131 (*OF* 876v, 1110ii, 409, 707, 1018iii, 406, 800i +1100i, 1101ii, 1128i B =
OT 183, 222, 173 K). Bernabé collects the references to Onomakritos as author of Orphica in *OF*
1109–1119 B.

seek to manipulate the authority of Orpheus and the prestige of his name for their own agenda. Surprisingly, both camps crystallize around a shared set of characteristics; they all agree upon what should be called Orphic, even as they make polar opposite interpretations of its significance.[67]

One point of agreement between both camps is the priority of Orpheus – Orpheus is the oldest of all the Greek poets, older than Homer or Hesiod and more important than any of the other ancient poetic figures like Linos or Mousaios or Olen that had contested for authority in previous centuries. The position of Orpheus as the oldest makes him the representative of the entire tradition that followed – for good or for ill. The old question of the chronology of Orpheus' life and works thus comes back into prominence, as his adventures on the Argo or the interpolations of Onomakritos into the Orphica in the Peisistratid era gain new importance for their impact on the authority of Orphic works.[68] Orpheus' special connection to divinity, through his mother Kalliope or through his extraordinarily inspired and divine hymns, likewise becomes a topic of special focus. Either Orpheus' claims are debunked, euhemerizing him into a Thracian prince or unscrupulous charlatan, or they are magnified, granting him supernatural authority.

The stamp of strangeness that marks Orpheus' works even in the complaints of moralizers in the Classical period becomes another feature of great importance in this shared definition. While detractors could deplore the literal details of the horrific tales of incest and mutilation, defenders could explain the theological profundity of these apparently awful stories through the complex processes of allegorization, arguing that the more dreadful the surface meaning, the more different and profound the hidden meaning must be. Again, this conflict replicates the debates over the Orphica that had been going on since the Classical period, but the stakes are raised as the Greek religious tradition defends itself against attack, no longer just from within, but from without as well.

The extraordinary focus on purity, which appears more in the earlier evidence, is less prominent in these debates, although occasional references to abstention from beans or meat appear, especially in conjunction with

---

[67] Such a set of shared principles among opponents in "culture wars" appears again in the end of the nineteenth and beginning of the twentieth century, when the category of Orphic again becomes a significant tool in the conflict of religious ideas, although the set – and thus the definition – is different in the modern era, tailored more to the particular conflicts of that period than those of the first few centuries of the Christian era. See further below.

[68] Onomakritos becomes a way to discredit claims specifically of the antiquity of Orphica, since he provides a sixth-century BCE date in contrast with the claim that Orpheus' works are older even than Homer, reaching back to the most ancient of wisdom, to the time of the heroes of the Argo.

(Neo)Pythagorean ideas.[69] In contrast with the debates over the category in the nineteenth and twentieth centuries, there is no particular interest in the idea of the immortality of the soul, the origin of human sin, or even the resurrection or apotheosis of Dionysos as a parallel to Christ. Although there are certainly debates about the nature of the soul and its fate after death, Orpheus is not a player in these particular disputes, nor is his name cited as an important authority.[70] So too, although the ascent of Dionysos into heaven is mentioned as a possible parallel to Christ's resurrection, the similarity of Christ to Dionysos and other dying and rising gods is not an issue of such importance to the early Christian apologists and their Neoplatonic opponents as it is to the historians of religion in the age of Frazer's *Golden Bough*.[71]

The formation of this late antique category of Orphism takes place in the broader cultural struggles that rage between Christian apologists on the one hand and Neoplatonic philosophers on the other, since other defenders of the polytheistic tradition (Stoics, etc.) chose other means of defense, just as the Christian apologists had other targets beyond Orpheus. Nevertheless, Orpheus becomes an increasingly important figure in the debates – Orpheus the author, that is, since Orpheus the character was of interest only insofar as his Argonautic adventures could be used to establish his temporal priority. As Herrero comments:

> Orpheus interested the apologists only for the religious value of his figure. Eurydice's tale, for example, is not mentioned in their writings at all. The great literary possibilities of Orpheus' myth, which many earlier and later writers have not hesitated to exploit, meant nothing to them if they did not have a connection to the one objective that mattered to them, the defense of

[69] As Jourdan 2011: 232–233 points out, the references by Jer. *Adv. Iovinian.* 2.14 (= *PL* 23.304c) (*OF* 630 B) to Orphic vegetarianism and Greg. Naz. *Or.* 27.10 (94 Gallay-Jourjon = *PG* 36.24c) (*OF* 648xiii = OF 291 K) to an Orphic prohibition of beans are the exceptions that prove the rule that the idea of Orphic purity "est peu evoqué par les chrétiens."

[70] As Herrero 2010: 213 notes, "there are no doctrines on the soul explicitly attributed to Orpheus in Christian pages." Gregory of Nazianzus does seem to be drawing material from the Orphica as his target in his poem on the soul (*Carm. arcana* 7 Sykes = *Carm. dogmatica* 8 [*PG* 37.446–456]), but, as Herrero 2007c has argued, he also draws from, e.g., Empedokles, and does not make Orpheus the focus of his attack. Even in this poem, the other issues of such import to the modern debates are absent: "There is no reference in the poem to the cause proposed by the *Rhapsodies* for the soul's wanderings – namely the myth of Dionysus – nor does there appear in Clement's, Arnobius's, or Firmicus's mentions of this myth the least allusion to any of the ideas that might be derived from it: the original impurity of mankind's soul, the cycle of reincarnations, the final liberation and entrance into a happy beyond" (Herrero 2010: 214). Cp. Jourdan 2011: 101–116 for an examination of Gregory's approach to Orpheus.

[71] Justin *Apol.* 1.54 and *Dial.* 69, as well as Origen *C. Cels.* 3.23 and 4.17, refer to an ascension of Dionysos that they explain as a demonic counterfeit of the death and resurrection of Christ, but Orpheus is never mentioned as the prophet of this false gospel.

Christianity and the attack on that paganism of which they made Orpheus
a principal figure.[72]

The Christian apologists' construction of Orphism

It is in the works of some of the early Christian apologists that Orpheus
begins to take a special prominence as a representative of the whole Greek
religious tradition, since the apologists need to concentrate their attack by
focusing on a single representative rather than the diffuse entirety of the
tradition.[73] While Tatian and Athenagoras make use of Orpheus, the most
important apologist in this regard is Clement of Alexandria. Two recent
studies have focused on the role that Clement plays in the formation of
the category of Orphism in this period. Fabienne Jourdan provides a more
detailed and nuanced picture of Clement's aims and tactics, while Miguel
Herrero focuses on Clement within the larger context of the Christian apologists before and after.[74] Both studies point out the centrality of Clement's
work in the process of systematization of the Christian idea of Orphism.
Clement is significant because later apologists used Clement as a source
and also because of the ways, both negative and positive, that Clement set
out for dealing with Orpheus, ways that were developed by later apologists.

Clement sets up Orpheus as a foil, a *repoussoir* as Jourdan puts it, for
Christ: the singer of the old song who puts into sharp relief the new
singer of the new song of the Christian gospel. Although Clement surveys a breathtaking amount of the Greek literary and religious tradition,
he places Orpheus at the head of that tradition, even before Homer, so
his treatment of Orpheus figures his treatment of the entire tradition.
Clement's treatment is surprisingly complex, especially in comparison to
other apologists both before and after him, and the details are handled
well in Herrero's and especially Jourdan's recent studies. Here, however,
it suffices to note that Clement does not simply condemn Orpheus and
the Greek religious tradition, but produces a blend of condemnation and
co-optation, both attacking the horrific features of the myths and rituals
which Orpheus recounts and pointing to certain features of Orpheus' work
as intuitions or even prefigurations of Christian doctrine.

---

[72] Herrero 2010: 139–140.
[73] As Jourdan 2011: 15–16 notes, the early Christian apologists took three basic approaches to Orpheus.
Most often he was simply attacked as the representative of Hellenic theology, but some viewed
him as the source from which later Greeks stole and distorted good ideas or even, following the
appropriation of Orpheus in Hellenistic Judaism, as a model of monotheism and conversion.
[74] Jourdan 2010 and Herrero 2010 (a revised English translation of his 2007 Spanish version). Jourdan
2011 continues her contextualization of Clement with studies of other early Christian writers.

One of the most important aspects of Orpheus for Clement was his role as the poet of the mystery rites. In the second book of his *Protrepticus*, Clement gives a lurid and impressionistic picture of all the Greek mysteries, blending them all into one horrifying blur of murders and perversions.[75] He cites Orpheus repeatedly as the poet of the rite (ὁ τῆς τελετῆς ποιητής), and since he blends all the different rituals together, Orpheus becomes, by inference, the figure responsible for them all. Later apologists follow Clement in his lumping together of all the Greek mysteries, and their texts often follow his descriptions directly. This strategy of blurring the distinctions between the different mystery rituals and treating them all as a single phenomenon was obviously a powerful way for the apologists to attack the Greek tradition, however confusing it has been for later historians of religion trying to uncover the specific nature of each rite. By building up a single and unified image of the ritual tradition, the Christian apologists create a concrete target for themselves to attack, and the figure of Orpheus, as the originator of the rituals, stands in for the whole tradition.

While Clement's attack on Orpheus sets the pattern for the assaults of other Christian apologists, he also provides a model for the co-optation of Orpheus, of borrowing the authority of the mythic poet to demonstrate that even the Greek tradition (properly understood) supports the Christian revelation. In the seventh book of the *Protrepticus*, Clement quotes the *Testament of Orpheus*, the Hellenistic (Jewish) Orphic text that hymns the praises of an omnipotent primary god, as evidence that Orpheus himself converted to monotheism, a prefiguration of the conversion to Christian doctrine. "But the Thracian Orpheus, the son of Oiagros, hierophant and poet at once, after his exposition of the orgies, and his theology of idols, introduces a palinode of truth with true solemnity, though tardily singing the strain."[76] Orpheus is once again the chief theologian for the Greek tradition, and, as goes Orpheus, so goes the rest of the Greek tradition. Like Stesikhorus, of whom Plato recounts in *Phaedrus* 243a that he regained his sight after blaspheming the divine Helen by singing a palinode proclaiming that she never went to Troy, Orpheus recants his blasphemous songs and

---

[75] Herrero 2010: 147 argues that "Clement's source was an alphabetic treatise on the mysteries from the end of the Hellenistic period." Clement moves through the rites of Aphrodite, Deo, Dionysos, and Korybantes, to Pherephatta, so the alphabetical order indicates that his source was likewise arranged, although there is no reason to believe, as Herrero suggests, that this source was itself based on a single Orphic poem. As Herrero argues, Clement's dependence on this source contradicts the assertion of Euseb. *Praep. evang.* 2.2.64 that Clement had been initiated in all these mysteries himself before his conversion.

[76] Clem. Al. *Protr.* 7.74.3 (*OF* 375, 377iii = OF 246 K): Ὁ δὲ Θράκιος ἱεροφάντης καὶ ποιητὴς ἅμα, ὁ τοῦ Οἰάγρου Ὀρφεύς, μετὰ τὴν τῶν ὀργίων ἱεροφαντίαν καὶ τῶν εἰδώλων τὴν θεολογίαν, παλινῳδίαν ἀληθείας εἰσάγει, τὸν ἱερὸν ὄντως ὀψέ ποτε, ὅμως δ᾽ οὖν ᾄδων λόγον.

praises the one true god. Orpheus' tardy and limited recantation serves as a model for understanding the truth value of the whole Greek tradition. "For if, at the most, the Greeks, having received certain scintillations of the divine word, have given forth some utterances of truth, they bear indeed witness that the force of truth is not hidden, and at the same time expose their own weakness in not having arrived at the end."[77] The Greek tradition, like the Orphica, is not valueless, but fundamentally limited even in the good it contains. Clement indeed cites Orphic poems positively in a number of places, especially in the fifth book of the so-called *Stromata*, where he brings verses from a number of different Orphic poems to support the idea of the inaccessibility, the greatness, and the oneness of God, but these citations corroborate the ideas from the Scriptures.[78]

The earlier apologists do not single Orpheus out as the representative of the whole Greek religious tradition to the extent that Clement does. Tatian includes Orpheus among a list of other poets, such as Mousaios and Linos, who brought these ideas to the Greeks, as well as various bar-barian races – Karians, Phrygians, Babylonians, Persians, and the like – who all claimed to receive messages from the divine.[79] He associates Orpheus with the story of the abduction of Persephone, just one of a list of horrific Greek tales about the gods, and he insists that Orpheus, like Linos, Mousaios, Thamyris, Philammon, and others, were all older than Homer, although Moses, the source of the Biblical revelation, is more ancient than any of these.[80] The Christian apologists eagerly pick up on the Jewish manipulation of Moses/Mousaios as the teacher of Orpheus to privilege the Biblical tradition over the Greek.

Justin Martyr, an apologist a generation or so before Clement, does not name Orpheus as the one responsible for either good or bad within the Greek religious tradition, although he condemns some of the same

---

[77] Clem. Al. *Protr.* 7.74.7: Εἰ γὰρ καὶ τὰ μάλιστα ἐναύσματά τινα τοῦ λόγου τοῦ θείου λαβόντες Ἕλληνες ὀλίγα ἄττα τῆς ἀληθείας ἐφθέγξαντο, προσμαρτυροῦσι μὲν τὴν δύναμιν αὐτῆς οὐκ ἀποκεκρυμμένην, σφᾶς δὲ αὐτοὺς ἐλέγχουσιν ἀσθενεῖς, οὐκ ἐφικόμενοι τοῦ τέλους.

[78] Cp. Clem. Al. *Strom.* 5.12.78 (*OF* 377iv B = OF 246 K); 5.14.123 (*OF* 377v, 378ii B = OF 246 K); and 5.14.133 (*OF* 377viii B). Herrero 2010: 182–186 notes that Clement is here citing from two different versions of the Zeus hymn found in the *Testament*, and adapting his quotations to suit his point in the passage. Herrero points out that Clement is drawing Orphica from a variety of hymns and other sources that seem to be circulating independently, some of which may perhaps come from an anthology, something like the second-century CE papyrus that quotes bits of the *Hymn to Zeus* along with Euripides and other poets (*PSI* XV 1476 [*OF* 688a B]). The variety of his sources indicates that Clement is not drawing from a standardized collection of Orphica in the *Rhapsodies*: "the majority of the Orphic material that Clement is using is pre-Rhapsodic" (Herrero 2010: 190).

[79] Tatianus *Ad Gr.* 1.1.

[80] Tatianus *Ad Gr.* 41.1–2 (*OF* 875i B = OT 15 K); the story of Persephone: *Ad Gr.* 8.4.

Dionysiac rituals as Clement.[81] Later pseudepigraphers using the name of Justin, however, follow Clement's lead in emphasizing the priority of Orpheus to Homer and then arguing that the Greeks, through Orpheus, are dependent on the even earlier Biblical tradition.[82] The *Cohortatio* quotes the *Testament* to claim that even Orpheus, the most polytheistic of the Greeks (Ὀρφεύς, ὁ τῆς πολυθεότητος ὑμῶν), saw the truth of monotheism, while the Pseudo-Justinian treatise *On Monarchy* quotes the *Testament* for the same purposes, to show that even the great founder of Greek rites converted to the worship of a single divine king.[83]

Clement's near contemporary, Athenagoras, gives more importance to Orpheus than the earlier apologists. Quoting Herodotus on the importance of Homer and Hesiod for systematizing the gods of the Greeks, he then places Orpheus prior to Homer and Hesiod, even clipping the quote to avoid Herodotus' disparaging comments about the poets who are not really older than Homer and Hesiod.[84] In making Okeanos the first of the gods in the cosmos, Homer, he claims, follows Orpheus, who was the first to invent their names and recount their births, and Athenagoras recounts an Orphic theogony very similar in its details to the theogony Damascius attributes to Hieronymos.[85] Athenagoras focuses on the horrific details in this myth of the generation of the gods, focusing particularly on the monstrous forms (20.2 [*OF* 82ii B = OF 58 K]) and on the incest and mutilations in their relations (20.3 [*OF* 84, 87i, 89i B = OF 58 K]). These horrible crimes and perversions that Orpheus attributes to the gods, Athenagoras argues, are far worse than the promiscuity and cannibalism (in the Eucharist) of which the Christians are accused.[86] Athenagoras, then, picks up on and elaborates two of the common elements in the Christian apologists' definition of Orphism, the temporal priority of Orpheus that makes him a fit representative of the whole tradition and the grotesque and perverse imagery of his myths, which bring the entirety of the Greek mythic tradition into disrepute.

---

[81] Justin *Dial.* 69.

[82] [Justin] *Coh. Gr.* 17b (*OF* 386i B). Riedweg 1994 has argued that the author of the *Cohortatio ad Graecos* attributed to Justin is probably the fourth-century CE Marcellus of Ancyra.

[83] Cp. [Justin] *Coh. Gr.* 15c3, 34d; [Justin] *De Monarch.* 104e.

[84] Athenagoras *Leg.* 17.1–2, citing Hdt. 2.53 (*OF* 880i B = OT 10 K).

[85] Athenagoras *Leg.* 18.3 (*OF* 75ii, 879iii, 1020ii, 1141iii B = OF 57 K): Ὀρφέως δέ, ὃς καὶ τὰ ὀνόματα αὐτῶν πρῶτος ἐξηῦρεν καὶ τὰς γενέσεις διεξῆλθεν. The theogony is recounted in 18.4–20.5 (*OF* 76ii, 79ii, 80ii, 82i, 83, 76iii, 88, 82ii, 84, 87i, 89i, 81, 80iii, 85 B = OF 57, 58 K). Cp. Dam. *De princ.* 123 (III.160.17–161.13 Westerink = 1.317.14–318.6 Ruelle). For the parallels, see West 1983: 176–226. Again, the issue of the date of Athenagoras' source is much debated, but if Hieronymos is to be identified with Hieronymos of Rhodes, then Athenagoras might be drawing (either first hand or at some further remove) from Hieronymos' account of the Orphic tale.

[86] Athenagoras *Leg.* 32.1 (*OF* 87ii B = OF 59 K).

Later apologists follow the same pattern, using the name of Orpheus to attack the Greek tradition, focusing on the perversity of the things labeled with the name of Orpheus. Origen, responding to Kelsos' attack on Christianity, complains that Kelsos, in recounting the superior wisdom of the Greeks, has omitted all the impious deeds attributed to the gods by Orpheus, "And he has intentionally overlooked the myth about the gods being considered as affected by human passions, a myth especially elaborated by Orpheus."[87] Kelsos only praises Orpheus as divinely inspired through his malicious desire to attack Jesus; if he were consistent with his own Platonic principles, he would reject Orpheus as Plato does Homer.

> And marveling at what in Orpheus does he say that, by common consent, he had lived nobly, inspired by a holy spirit? I am amazed if Kelsos does not hymn Orpheus simply from competitive envy with us and so that he may put down Jesus; and that, when he encountered Orpheus' impious myths about the gods, he did not turn them aside as more worthy, even than the poems of Homer, to be expelled from the noble state. For, indeed, Orpheus says far worse things than Homer about those whom they consider gods.[88]

Once again, Orpheus' work is characterized by the tales of perversion, by myths of "engaging in accursed unions and waging wars against their own fathers and chopping off their genitalia . . . or 'the father of men and gods', who had intercourse with his own daughter."[89] Origen does not always name Orpheus, however, and he extends his attack on the Greek tradition defended by Kelsos, rejecting the allegorical interpretation of all the stories that seem so scandalous.[90] The sixth of the *Homilies* attributed to Clement of Rome, pseudepigrapha dating perhaps to the second or third centuries, likewise has its hero critique allegorical interpretations of a theogony attributed to Orpheus, rejecting them as inadequate explanations for scandalous deeds.[91]

---

[87] Origen *C. Cels.* 1.16 (*OF* 1018vii B = OT 225a K): Καὶ ἑκὼν μὲν ἐπελάθετο τοῦ περὶ τῶν νομιζομένων θεῶν μύθου ὡς ἀνθρωποπαθῶν, ἀναγεγραμμένου μάλιστα ὑπὸ Ὀρφέως.

[88] Origen *C. Cels.* 7.54 (*OF* 1062ii B): Τί δὲ καὶ θαυμάσας Ὀρφέως ὁμολογουμένως φησὶν αὐτὸν ὁσίῳ χρησάμενον πνεύματι καλῶς βεβιωκέναι; Θαυμάζω δὲ εἰ μὴ καὶ Κέλσος διὰ μὲν τὴν πρὸς ἡμᾶς φιλονεικίαν, καὶ ἵνα Ἰησοῦν ἐξευτελίσῃ νῦν ὑμνεῖ Ὀρφέα, ὅτε δ᾽ ἐνετύγχανεν αὐτοῦ τοῖς ὡς περὶ θεῶν ἀσεβέσι μύθοις, οὐκ ἀπεστρέφετο τὰ ποιήματα ὡς μᾶλλον καὶ τῶν Ὁμήρου ἄξια ἐκβάλλεσθαι τῆς καλῆς πολιτείας· καὶ γὰρ πολλῷ χείρονα περὶ τῶν νομιζομένων εἶπε θεῶν Ὀρφεὺς ἢ Ὅμηρος.

[89] Origen *C. Cels.* 1.18 (*OF* 93i, 1022 B): ἐναγέσι μίξεσι χρωμένους καὶ κατὰ τῶν πατέρων στρατευομένους καὶ τὰ αἰδοῖα αὐτῶν ἀποτέμνοντας . . . τῇ ἑαυτοῦ θυγατρὶ ὁ "πατὴρ ἀνδρῶν τε θεῶν τε" συνελήλυθεν.

[90] Origen *C. Cels.* 4.48 (*OF* 187iii, 200viii, 201i, 214iv B): myths from Homer and Hesiod, as well as Chrysippos' interpretation of a fresco of Zeus and Hera engaged in fellatio; 4.17 (*OF* 326iv B): dismemberment of Dionysos.

[91] [Clem. Al.] *Hom.* 6. The story has Clement break in upon the allegorical interpretation given by Appian of the Orphic cosmogony, showing that he has fully mastered this kind of interpretation

Arnobius in the third century and Firmicus Maternus in the fourth also attack the Greek tradition for the standard list of scandalous stories – the castration of Ouranos, the dismemberment of Dionysos, and the various rapes of Zeus. Their list seems drawn largely from Clement, although neither names Orpheus as the figure responsible for the spread of such myths and the mystery rites the apologists associate with them.[92] Hippolytos, who in the third century is already more concerned with heretical schisms within the Christian community, blames Orpheus for the doctrines he associates with the Sethians.[93] Eusebios, responding to the attacks of Porphyry, draws directly from Clement to launch his counterattack, but he can likewise both critique and co-opt Orpheus. As Herrero points out, by Eusebios' time, "the balance of power has been reversed, with Christianity thriving and paganism on the defensive."[94] He borrows chunks from Clement in the critique of the Greek tradition focused on Orpheus, but he also uses the figure of Orpheus as a metaphor for the power of Christ, since, just as Orpheus could charm brute beasts with his music, so too Christ could soothe the souls of the savage nations with the Word of God.[95]

Lactantius puts forth an even more positive figure of Orpheus. Although he names Orpheus as the one who introduced the impious rites of Dionysos (Liber) into Greece, he more often credits him with insights into the nature of the supreme god.

> Orpheus, who is the most ancient of the poets, and on a par with the gods themselves (since indeed it is said that he sailed among the Argonauts along with the sons of Tyndarus and Hercules), speaks of the true and great God

and yet rejects it entirely. Jourdan 2011: 285–336 has the best recent study of this text, along with the parallel in [Clem. Rom.] *Recognitiones* 10.17–18. She argues that it derives from a forerunner to the cosmogony in the *Rhapsodies*, while Bernabé 2008a argues that it derives from the *Rhapsodies* themselves (cp. Roessli 2008). Despite their arguments, I am not convinced that a stemma of the transmission of the mythic tale can be constructed, and I would prefer to see formation of the theogonies in these texts as the looser product of *bricolage*. The contradictions with which they grapple can better be explained by a variety of sources loosely followed, some of which may have been later compiled into the *Rhapsodies* (see below, ch. 5).

92 Cp. Herrero 2010: 153–159 for discussion of the recent scholarship on the sources of Arnobius and Firmicus and their dependence on Clement in particular.

93 Hippol. *Haer.* 5.20.4 (*OF* 532i B = OF 243 K): "The whole system of their doctrine is from the ancient theologians, Mousaios, Linos, and Orpheus, who especially founded the *teletai* rituals and the mysteries. For their doctrine about the womb and the serpent and the navel, which is harmony, is explicitly the same as that in the Bacchic rites of Orpheus." Ἔστι δὲ αὐτοῖς ἡ πᾶσα διδασκαλία τοῦ λόγου ἀπὸ τῶν παλαιῶν θεολόγων, Μουσαίου καὶ Λίνου καὶ τοῦ τὰς τελετὰς καὶ τὰ μυστήρια μάλιστα καταδείξαντος Ὀρφέως. ὁ γὰρ περὶ τῆς μήτρας αὐτῶν καὶ τοῦ ὄφεως λόγος καὶ τοῦ ὀμφαλοῦ – ὅσπερ ἐστὶν ἁρμονία – διαρρήδην αὐτός ἐστιν τῷ ἐν τοῖς Βακχικοῖς τοῦ Ὀρφέως.

94 Herrero 2010: 143.   95 Euseb. *LC* 14.5 (*OF* 1090 B = OT 153 K).

as Protogonos, the first-born, because before him nothing was born, but from him all things were generated.[96]

Lactantius, even more unusually, argues that Orpheus could sing such true things of the true god because of his natural reason.[97] Even the bizarre elements of the theogonic myths, the target of early apologists, can be treated tolerantly. Orpheus, for example, depicts the primal deity Phanes as hermaphroditic because of his intuition that the supreme god did not require any other being for creation.[98]

Gregory of Nazianzus, facing the attempts of the Emperor Julian to turn the Roman empire back from Christianity and to re-establish the Greek religious tradition, is far more harsh in his condemnations. These take the now well-established path for Christian apologetics, ridiculing the absurdity and impiety of the myths. Whereas Lactantius was willing to credit Orpheus with imperfect intuitions of the supreme god, Gregory targets Orpheus in particular for his theogonic myth in which Phanes swallows all the other gods to become supreme.[99] He also mocks the idea that Zeus is so omnipresent that he may be found in dung, and he scorns the obscenity in Orpheus' verses describing the goddess displaying her genitalia.[100] The renewed vigor of Gregory's attack reflects the stakes in the conflict in his time; Orpheus once again must be condemned as the representative of the whole Greek religious tradition that Julian tries to restore.

By the time of Augustine, however, the battle is essentially over. As Herrero notes, Augustine "presents Orpheus as the principal theologian of pagan belief," but he does not engage in the same kind of harsh

---

[96] Lactant. *Div. inst.* 1.5.4–5 (60 Monat) (*OF* 876iv, 126ii, 125 B = OF 73 K): *Orpheus, qui est uetustissimus poetarum et aequalis ipsorum deorum, siquidem traditur inter Argonautas cum Tyndaridis et Hercule nauigasse, deum uerum et magnum* πρωτόγονον *appellat, quod ante ipsum nihil sit genitum, sed ab ipso sint cuncta generata*; cp. *Epitome* 3 (2.678.14 Brandt) (*OF* 153ii B = OF 88 K).

[97] As Herrero 2010: 136 notes, "not only is Lactantius the only author to draw some explicit positive parallels between Orphism and Christianity with regard to their portrayal of God as the uncreated Creator; more importantly, he ascribes such insights to Orpheus' reflection and natural reason alone."

[98] Lactant. *Div. inst.* 4.8.4 (2.296.2 Brandt) (*OF* 134iv B = OF 81 K).

[99] Greg. Naz. *Or.* 31.16 (306 Gallay-Jourjon = *PG* 36.149c–152b) (*OF* 191ii, 200vi, 201iii, 215i = OF 171 K); cp. *Or.* 4.115 (276.26 Bernardi = *PG* 35.653b) (*OF* 134v, 200vii, 201ii B).

[100] Greg. Naz. *Or.* 4.115 (272–276 Bernardi = *PG* 35.653). The verse on Zeus in dung (4.115 [274.17 Bernardi = *PG* 35.653b] [*OF* 848ii B = OT 245 K]) is of unknown origin; as West 1983: 53 dryly comments, "There may be some theological profundity here, but if so it eludes the uninitiate." The description of the obscene gesture (4.115 [276.22–25 Bernardi = *PG* 35.653b] [*OF* 395iii B = OF 52 K]) resembles the verse quoted in Clem. Al. *Protr.* 2.20.3 (*OF* 394i, 395i B = OF 52 K) of Baubo's action, but the verses are slightly different, suggesting that Gregory is working from a different version. Cp. Arn. *Adv. nat.* 5.25 (281.1 Marchesi) (*OF* 395ii B = OF 52 K).

condemnations of the specific content as Gregory and some of the earliest apologists.[101] The virulence and vehemence of the Christian apologists' attack – and the extent to which they focus specifically on Orpheus – is directly proportional to the threat posed by the authority of the Greek religious and philosophical tradition for the particular apologist. It is worth noting, for example, that Irenaeus of Lyons, never known for a gentle and delicate approach toward his theological opponents, does not mention Orpheus at all; the category of things to which the name of Orpheus was affixed was not a sufficient concern to him, in contrast to the other threats to true Christian doctrine that he perceived.[102] The late text known as the *Tübingen Theosophy* (perhaps the beginning of the sixth century CE) can quote Orpheus as an authority who supports the ideas of Christian doctrine, one of the many pagan witnesses to the divine truth of Christian revelation.[103]

The Neoplatonic construction of Orphism

Just as the Christian apologists use the name of Orpheus to create a focal point for their attack on the Greek tradition, so too their Neoplatonic opponents use Orpheus in the same way, but for the opposite reasons. Whereas the Christians emphasize the antiquity of Orpheus, his special connection with the divine, and his bizarre tellings of the myths in order to undermine the authority of the whole tradition at whose origin they place the Thracian poet, the Neoplatonists emphasize Orpheus' antiquity, divine connections, and bizarre stories in order to prove the profundity and philosophical power of the Greek tradition. Using not just the same principles, but very often the same passages, they draw contrary conclusions from their Christian opponents, highlighting the consistency of the Greek religious tradition from its earliest theologian, Orpheus, up to their own current works. The earlier Neoplatonists, like the earliest apologists, tend to cite Orpheus as merely one among several important early theological poets, but, starting with Iamblichus, the Neoplatonic authors increasingly use Orpheus as the single most important figure, eclipsing Homer as the spokesman for the tradition. The importance of Orpheus is crystallized

---

[101] Herrero 2010: 138. Cp. August. *De civ. D.* 18.14 (*OF* 885i B = OT 20 K), 18.24 (*OF* 888iii B = OT 20 K), 18.37 (*OF* 885ii B = OT 20 K).

[102] Herrero 2010: 133 n. 12: "Irenaeus is conspicuously absent from this list because he makes no explicit Orphic references."

[103] On the *Tübingen Theosophy*, see Jourdan 2011: 201–212, as well as the edition and commentary of Beatrice 2001.

by Syrianus, who systematizes the correspondences between Orpheus and the other authoritative texts of the Neoplatonic tradition, the Chaldaean Oracles and the texts of Plato (as interpreted by the Neoplatonists).

Kelsos, whose text survives only in the quotations by Origen, seems to have listed Orpheus only as one among the many sources of wisdom for the ancient Greek tradition. Origen complains that he does not include Moses among the great wise men of old.

> See, therefore, if he has not cast out Moses from his catalogue of sages in open malevolence, saying that Linos, Mousaios, and Orpheus, and Pherekydes, and the Persian Zoroaster, and Pythagoras have tackled these things and have set down their doctrines in books, and that they have been preserved up until now.[104]

The sources of Greek wisdom listed by Kelsos include not only other Greek poets, but prose authors and even the Persian Zoroaster.

Porphyry engages more directly with Orpheus, recounting – and interpreting allegorically – certain elements of Orpheus' poems as part of his explanation of the nature of the cosmos in the *Cave of the Nymphs*.[105] He quotes Orpheus' *sphragis* line, "Close the doors of your ears", as well as the *Hymn to Zeus* that appears in so many other citations.[106] But Orpheus is not the most important poet for Porphyry; he quotes Orpheus in the *Cave of the Nymphs* to explain Homer, and he cites Orpheus' reference to the river Styx only in company with Hesiod, in a list of other poets who refer to the rivers of the Underworld.[107] The name of Orpheus is conspicuously absent from Porphyry's treatise on vegetarianism, although he relies on

---

[104] Origen *C. Cels.* 1.16: Ὅρα οὖν εἰ μὴ ἄντικρυς κακουργῶν ἐξέβαλε τοῦ καταλόγου τῶν σοφῶν καὶ Μωϋσέα, Λίνον δὲ καὶ Μουσαῖον καὶ Ὀρφέα καὶ τὸν Φερεκύδην καὶ τὸν Πέρσην Ζωροάστρην καὶ Πυθαγόραν φήσας περὶ τῶνδε διειληφέναι, καὶ ἐς βίβλους κατατεθεῖσθαι τὰ ἑαυτῶν δόγματα καὶ πεφυλάχθαι αὐτὰ μέχρι δεῦρο.

[105] Porph. *De antr. nymph.* 7 (46.17 Simonini) (*OF* 279iii B), 14 (56.10 Simonini) (*OF* 286i B = OF 192 K), 16 (58.15 Simonini) (*OF* 222 B = OF 154 K), 16 (58.18 Simonini) (*OF* 220 B = OF 154 K), 16 (58.23 Simonini) (*OF* 187ii, 225v B = OF 154 K). Porphyry describes Persephone weaving as the process of generation of the body as the garment of the soul, while Orpheus describes Zeus trapping Kronos with honey, he explains, because "the theologian relates in allegory that the divine is bound through pleasure and drawn down into generation, and that, dissolved into pleasure, the divine begets certain powers." τοῦ θεολόγου δι' ἡδονῆς δεσμεῖσθαι καὶ κατάγεσθαι τὰ θεῖα εἰς γένεσιν αἰνισσομένου ἀποσπερματίζειν τε δυνάμεις εἰς τὴν ἡδονὴν ἐκλυθέντα.

[106] The references are preserved only in Eusebios; Porph. fr. 351 F Smith = Euseb. *Praep. evang.* 3.7.1 (*OF* lxiii B) (*sphragis*), fr. 354, the hymn to Zeus quoted in Porphyry's work on divine images = Euseb. *Praep. evang.* 3.8.2 (*OF* 243i B = OF 168 K). The other fragment of Porphyry in Eusebios that Bernabé lists among the Orphic fragments, 359 F Smith = Euseb. *Praep. evang.* 3.11.32 (*OF* 830av B), was probably not attributed to Orpheus by the ancients, and certainly no ancient attestation exists among the numerous quotations of the text.

[107] Porph. *Gaur.* 2.2.9 (*OF* 344 B = OF 124 K).

Pythagoras for the authority of the ancient tradition.[108] In Porphyry's *Life of Pythagoras*, Orpheus makes no appearance either, although abstentions from beans and other purifications are mentioned.[109]

It is Iamblichus who takes the decisive step in making Orpheus the crucial figure in the Greek religious tradition. In his *Life of Pythagoras*, he tells the story of how Pythagoras' great wisdom descends from Orpheus, through the medium of the mysterious initiatory priest Aglaophamos, and he argues that anyone who wishes to see the source of Pythagoras' ideas should look to the writings of Orpheus.[110] This genealogy of wisdom becomes canonical in the later Neoplatonists, as the Platonists take over the prestige of the Neopythagorean tradition and co-opt its authority for their own.[111] As for the Christian apologists, Orpheus is the oldest of the poets, but even in Iamblichus Orpheus has not yet become the exclusive representative of ancient wisdom. Pythagoras, Iamblichus tells us, also drew upon the wisdom of the Egyptians, Chaldaeans, the Persian magi, the mysteries at Eleusis and Samothrace, and even from the Kelts and Iberians.[112] Iamblichus, like Porphyry, mentions various Orphic texts, but he does not seem to have one standard Orphic poem to which he refers.[113]

Julian, in his attempts to convert the Roman empire back from Christianity, places great value on Iamblichus as a theologian and follows his lead in asserting the ancient and divine roots of the ancient Greek religious tradition. He does not, however, make Orpheus the centerpiece of his resistance to Christianity, although he does celebrate the figure of Orpheus, alluding to the power of Orpheus' lyre to soothe the pain of parting from his friend

---

[108] Porph. *Abst.* 2.36 (*OF* 635 B) refers to ὁ θεολόγος, but, despite Bernabé's special pleading, it is clearly Pythagoras, not Orpheus.

[109] Porph. *VP* 43 (*OF* 648xii B); Greg. Naz. *Or.* 27.10 (94 Gallay-Jourjon = *PG* 36.24c) (*OF* 648xiii = OF 291 K) refers to "Orphic beans", but other evidence associates them more with Pythagoras and his followers. The other passages in Bernabé's collection from the *VP* (*VP* 17, 43 [*OF* 571, 605ii B]) pertain to Pythagoras' initiatory descent into the cave of Zeus, but make no reference to Orpheus.

[110] Iambl. *VP* 28.145–147 (*OF* 507i B = OT 249 K).

[111] Cp. the references in *OF* 507 B. Iamblichus seems to have used it himself in his commentary on Plato's *Timaeus* (Iambl. *In Ti.* fr. 74 Dillon = Procl. *In Ti.* 3.168.9) (*OF* 507ii, 1144iv B = OT 107, 250 K).

[112] Iambl. *VP* 34.243 (*OF* 1023 B); *VP* 28.151 (*OF* 508i B = OT 249a).

[113] Iambl. *De an. ap.* Stob. *Flor.* 1.49.32 (1.366.17 Wachsmuth) (*OF* 421vi B = OF 27 K) refers to Aristotle; 1.49.38 (1.376.2 Wachsmuth) (*OF* 421vii B = OF 27 K) alludes to the same idea. In *Myst.* 8.3 (*OF* 149vii B = OF 109 K), the cosmogony mentioned bears some resemblance to the Orphic verses quoted in Hermias and Proclus (see *OF* 149i–vi B), but hardly enough to show that Iamblichus is relying on the authority of Orpheus here. Damascius quotes two fragments of Iamblichus in his *Philebus* commentary (Iambl. *In Phlb.* fr. 3 Dillon = Dam. *In Phlb.* 57 [29 Westerink] [*OF* 352iv B]; Iambl. *In Phlb.* fr. 7 = Dam. *In Phlb.* 243 [115 Westerink] [*OF* 114vii B]) to show that Iamblichus is in agreement with the ideas in the Orphica, but these passages are evidence of Damascius' systematizing Neoplatonic doctrine with the Orphica, not of Iamblichus' use of Orphic texts.

Salloustios.[114] For Julian, Orpheus is the most ancient of all the divinely inspired philosophers (ὁ παλαιότατος ἐνθέως φιλοσοφήσας), who used poetic myth to convey the deepest truths, and he is also the founder of the most sacred mystery rituals (ὁ τὰς ἁγιωτάτας τελετὰς καταστησάμενος), which are likewise the vehicles of the hidden truth.[115] Julian's Orpheus is thus the positive face of the Christian apologist's Orpheus, the most ancient representative of the Greek religious tradition and the one with special claims to divine connection, who first created the special rituals to connect mortals with immortals.

The greatest step in the creation of a systematic Orphism, however, comes after the failure of Julian's efforts, in the attempts of the later Neoplatonists to create a systematic correspondence between their own philosophical and theological doctrines and the ancient Greek religious tradition, represented by the poems of Orpheus.[116] Proclus and Damascius alone are responsible for a sizeable majority of the verses preserved with Orpheus' name, and the influence of the Neoplatonic construction of Orphism on the later reception tradition cannot be overstated. Brisson, in a series of recent studies, has analyzed the references to the Orphica within the late Neoplatonist authors, sifting through this incredibly dense and complicated material to pull out the significant patterns.[117] His analyses of these materials represent one of the greatest steps forward in the study of Orphism in modern scholarship, and they make possible an understanding of the Neoplatonists' use of the Orphica that is far more nuanced and comprehensive than was previously available.

Unfortunately, little remains of the works of the figure who seems to have played the greatest role in this Neoplatonic systematization, Syrianus. This Alexandrian scholar, who took over the leadership of the Platonic Academy in Athens after Plutarch of Athens in 431/2, wrote a treatise on the *Harmony of Orpheus, Pythagoras and Plato with the Chaldaean Oracles*, which does not survive.[118] Syrianus thus develops the point, set forth by Iamblichus,

---

[114] Julian. *Or.* 8.1.10 (not in *PEG*).
[115] Julian. *Or.* 7.10.9 (*OF* 102iii B = OT 14 K); *Or.* 7.12.9 (*OF* 550 B). Some of the fragments, e.g., *Ep.* 89b 292 (320ix B), *c. Galil.* fr. 4 Massarachia (*OF* 59vii B), and *Or.* 8.5 168b (*OF* 279ii B), listed under Julian in Bernabé's *PEG* do not actually refer to Orpheus; they make reference to various rituals – Korybantic, Dionysiac, Metroac, etc. – with which Orpheus is often associated, but it is significant that they do not invoke Orpheus' authority.
[116] Herrero 2010: 85 notes the increasing reliance in the Neoplatonic tradition on the authority of Orpheus: "Porphyry, Iamblichus, and Julian spoke with much greater reverence than Celsus about Orpheus, his poems, and his *teletai*, and the later Neoplatonists took this process to an extreme."
[117] Cp. the studies collected in Brisson 1995, as well as Brisson 2002 and 2009.
[118] *Suda* s.v. Συριανός (σ 1662, IV.478.23–479.2 Adler) (*OF* 677iii B = OT 238 K) attributes two books of *Orphic Theology* as well as a treatise of this name to him, but it remains unclear whether Syrianus

that the Platonic doctrines of their school express the same ideas as those of Pythagoras and of Orpheus, from whom Pythagoras took his ideas, and the Chaldaean Oracles confirm this correspondence with the authority of direct divine revelation. Syrianus seems to have worked out these correspondences in his commentaries on the Platonic dialogues, but only the commentary on the *Phaedrus* put together by his pupil Hermeias survives.[119] He put the authority of Orpheus to use in defending the Platonic system against Peripatetic attacks in his commentaries on Aristotle, only one of which, the commentary on the *Metaphysics*, remains extant.[120] His systematization of the ideas contained in the Orphic poems, which he probably knew from a collection sometimes called the *Orphic Rhapsodies*, set the stage for the great work with the Orphica by his successors: Proclus, Damascius, and Olympiodorus.

Proclus (412–487 CE), who succeeded Syrianus as the head of the Academy, is the single greatest source for Orphic fragments remaining from antiquity. Brisson has found a staggering 248 references to the Orphica in his works, and any reconstruction of the nature of the Orphic texts in antiquity must rely heavily on the evidence he provides.[121] Proclus was a systematizer extraordinaire, as works like his *Elements of Theology* attest, and he carried on the work of Syrianus in making systematic the ideas drawn from the Orphica and aligning them with the doctrines the Neo-platonic Academy drew from the works of Plato. Proclus claims that the entirety of theology for the Greeks is the offspring of the Orphica, trans-mitted through Aglaophamos to Pythagoras and then to Plato, and this lineage, drawn from Iamblichus, serves as the starting premise for all his commentary.[122] Brisson has outlined the correspondences Proclus creates between the principles of Neoplatonic theology, the dialogues of Plato, and the theogonic myths from the Orphica, and Proclus manages, over the course of his commentaries on Platonic works, to transform the bizarre

actually composed works with these titles or whether his notes on the topics were collected by his students.

[119] As Brisson 2009: 494 notes, "Ce présupposé [that Orpheus, Pythagoras, and Plato are in accord] amène Syrianus, dans ses commentaires aux dialogues de Platon, à établir systématiquement des correspondances entre des figures divines orphiques et des éléments du système néoplatonicien."

[120] Brisson 2009: 494: "Dans ses commentaires à Aristote, il utilise les *Rhapsodies orphiques* pour montre que les théologiens, en accord avec Pythagore et Platon, ne sont susceptibles des critiques que leur addresse Aristote."

[121] Brisson's study of Proclus and the Orphica in Brisson 1987 [1995] was groundbreaking and remains vital for the study of Orphism.

[122] Procl. *Theol. Plat.* 1.5 (1.25.26 Saffrey-Westerink) (*OF* 507iv B = OT 250 K): ἅπασα γὰρ ἡ παρ᾽ Ἕλλησι θεολογία τῆς Ὀρφικῆς ἐστὶ μυσταγωγίας ἔκγονος, πρώτου μὲν Πυθαγόρου παρὰ Ἀγλαοφήμου τὰ περὶ θεῶν ὄργια διδαχθέντος, δευτέρου δὲ Πλάτωνος ὑποδεξαμένου τὴν παντελῆ περὶ τούτων ἐπιστήμην ἔκ τε τῶν Πυθαγορείων καὶ τῶν Ὀρφικῶν γραμμάτων.

elements of the Orphic theogonies into representations of the abstract system of hypostases emanating from the One that the Neoplatonists understood as the true nature of the cosmos.[123]

Damascius (458–c.538 CE) continued the work of Proclus in the systematization of Orphism, developing the interpretations of the Orphic texts
to match the theological ideas of the Neoplatonists. While he is the second
single greatest source for Orphic fragments after Proclus, his fifty-six references represent less than a quarter of the number made by his predecessor.
Damascius was the last head of the Platonic Academy when it was finally
shut down by the Christian emperor Justinian, so he was responsible for
conducting the defense of the ancient Greek religious tradition at a point
when Christianity had become fully entrenched as the dominant religious
system in his society. Like Proclus (and Syrianus), Damascius makes a
point of the systematic consistency of his Hellenic theology, grounded in
the ancient traditions of Orpheus' poetry, in response to the generations of
Christian attacks upon the polytheistic tradition as a confused mass of perverse and inconsistent myths. For Damascius, all of the Orphica ultimately
tell the same, consistent story, even if considerable ingenuity in allegorical
interpretation might be required to bring that meaning out.

Olympiodorus (495–570), Damascius' successor as the head of the now
officially closed Academy, follows his predecessors in aligning the Orphic
material with the ideas of Plato. He makes use of Orphic myths to explain
key points in the Platonic texts on which he comments, at times coming
up with new and more elaborate explanations than his predecessors, in
keeping with the theory of myth interpretation that he elaborates.[124]

The Neoplatonic systematization creates an interpretive framework in
which the myths in the Orphica all point to the same process of emanation
from and return to the One that articulates all things in the cosmos. This
underlying meaning applies to all the tales, not just the explicitly theogonic
ones. For example, in addition to the cosmogonic myths that Damascius
treats in his treatise on first principles, the myth of the dismemberment
of Dionysos by the Titans is a significant source for Damascius' interpretations, as it was indeed for Proclus before him and Olympiodorus after
him. They all understand this tale in terms of the movement from the
One to the Many, an interpretation with a long tradition in the Platonic

---

[123] Brisson 1987 [1995]: 102. In his more recent study surveying the whole Neoplatonic tradition,
Brisson has set forth a similar chart with the correspondences, including with the Chaldaean
Oracles (Brisson 2008: 1514–1516).

[124] E.g., Olymp. *In Grg.* 46; cp. Edmonds 2009 for an example of Olympiodorus' innovations in
interpretation.

Academy, appearing earliest in extant evidence in Plutarch but dating perhaps as far back as Xenokrates.[125] Their emphasis on the importance of this
tale, however, has been misunderstood by later scholars, particularly in the
nineteenth and twentieth centuries, who, unlike the Christian apologists
of the first several centuries CE, focused on the parallels between Dionysos
and Christ as dying and rising gods of the Frazerian type. Olympiodorus'
story, in particular, has been made the cornerstone of the modern construct
of Orphism, and inferences have been drawn from it of an idea of the dual
nature of mankind that are alien to Olympiodorus' own ideas.[126] A correct
understanding of Olympiodorus' reading of the myth, as of Damascius'
and Proclus', can only come from an analysis of its place within this ongoing systematization of the correspondences between the Orphica and the
Platonic tradition.

Orphism as a systematic religion

In the works of Damascius and Olympiodorus, the category of Orphism
becomes firmly defined, making "Orphism" more of an objective reality
than it had ever been before. As Herrero concludes,

> Finally, once Christianity definitively prevailed after Julian's death, the last
> Neoplatonic philosophers in the fifth and sixth centuries AD – mainly Pro-
> clus, Damascius, Syrianus, Olympiodorus – recovered Orphism as one of
> the most ancient and divine religious traditions of their idealized and lost
> Greek past: they quoted Orphic poems as inspired poetry that only need
> to be rightly interpreted through allegory, and they imagined Orphic rites
> and communities of Orphics. Only once Orphism was definitely dead did
> it become, in these Neoplatonic re-creations, the consistent and systematic
> religion it had never been.[127]

So clearly has that path been established that Olympiodorus can claim
that Plato borrows everywhere from Orpheus (παρῳδεῖ γὰρ πανταχοῦ
τὰ Ὀρφέως).[128] Indeed, by his time, the systematization of the correspondences set out by Syrianus has been so thoroughly worked through that
Plato's debt to the Orphica must have seemed patently obvious to those
schooled in the Neoplatonic interpretive system. The Orphic verses, taken
out of the context of their texts and deployed to articulate the Neoplatonic
cosmological hierarchy, must have seemed intended to express those ideas
from their very composition.

---

[125] See ch. 9, pp. 343–345, 374–391.   [126] See Edmonds 1999 and below for analysis.
[127] Herrero 2010: 85–86.   [128] Olymp. *In Phd.* 7.10.10.

And, of course, many of them may well have been composed to express the Platonic ideas, since the pseudepigraphic tradition seems to have continued into the Hellenistic age and beyond. *The Orphic Hymn to Number*, for example, seems clearly a product of the Neopythagorean revival in the first century, and various Orphicists must have composed verses to express various Middle Platonic ideas, along with the Stoic, Peripatetic, and even Jewish Orphica. As Brisson notes, one of the problems for the modern scholar attempting to understand the way that the Neoplatonists manipulate the Orphic texts to make them fit their intended meaning is "celui d'interpréter Platon à partir d'un orphisme déjà platonisé."[129] The extent to which the Orphica available to the Neoplatonists were already Platonized is difficult to determine, since the only context in which the texts are preserved, apart from the polemics of the Christian apologists, is the systematizing commentaries of the Neoplatonists.

It remains unclear precisely what Orphic texts these authors were working from, in any case, and in what form they had access to them. Papyri such as the second-century CE anthology that contains quotations from various tragedians, lyric poets, as well as a version of the famous *Hymn to Zeus* of Orpheus, make clear that such anthologies were one resource on which the scholars of the first few centuries of the Common Era drew.[130] Some of these collections may have provided the titles for Orphic works, although such lists of titles (with the lists of names of the Orphicists who composed them) go back to the Classical and Hellenistic systematizers as well. The *Hymns* attributed to Orpheus in the collection that was passed down into the Renaissance along with the *Hymns* of Proclus were probably composed around the second century as well, even if they undoubtedly draw some of their verses from older works.[131] This collection of *Hymns* may well have been a synthesis of earlier and contemporary works, organized by an Orphicist of the time into a (more or less) coherent whole and provided with directions for sacrifices in ritual use.

The *Orphic Rhapsodies* may be another product of the canonizing trend of the first few centuries. The references to the title are very few and late, but it seems that many of the authors from this period who cite the Orphica are referring to a particular collection. In the Platonic tradition, it is unclear

---

[129] Janko 2005: 2886.
[130] Cp. *PSI* XV 1476 (*OF* 688a B), along with the discussion of Bastianini 2005, which points to the selections from Orpheus, Euripides, and others. Cp. Herrero's study of the sources of Clement in Herrero 2007b, suggesting that Clement drew from an alphabetically arranged collection of excerpts regarding various mystery rites.
[131] Cp. Ricciardelli 2000: xxviii–xxxi.

whether Porphyry and Iamblichus are working from such a collection, but Syrianus probably is. It is tempting to speculate that the canonization of an Orphic collection occurred at around the same time and in the same milieu as the canonization of the collection of Chaldaean Oracles, which served as the other great textual authority for the Neoplatonic tradition. Athanassiadi has argued for the important role of Iamblichus in the introduction of the Chaldaean Oracles, and the collection and organization of the Orphica would certainly suit the purposes of the followers of Iamblichus, especially the Emperor Julian.[132] While West has argued for a much earlier date, around the second to first century BCE, because of the parallels with the canonization of the Homeric texts in Pergamon, I would suggest that the canonization of Orphica is likely to have lagged behind that of Homer.[133] The systematization of the Homeric works, into collections of twenty-four rhapsodies for each epic, surely provides the model for the later systematization of the Orphic works, but the motivation to undertake this work arises later, as Orpheus grows in importance as the representative of the Hellenic tradition.

Whether the *Rhapsodies* were compiled in the wake of Iamblichean responses to the challenges of the Christians or as part of the late Hellenistic systematizing of Greek literature, Syrianus' work would, in any case, be aided by such a collection. His successor Proclus is clearly working from Syrianus' schema, but he also seems to draw directly from the Orphic works he is quoting. His most likely source is again the collection of the *Orphic Rhapsodies*, but he refers to the titles of a number of Orphic texts, and it remains unclear whether he knew such texts directly, whether he knew them from anthologized excerpts, or whether these titles in fact appeared as parts of the Rhapsodic collection.[134] His biographer and successor, Marinos, refers to Proclus' work with the Orphica, noting that he was deterred from writing a complete commentary himself by certain dreams, but that he annotated Syrianus' commentaries, providing his pupils with his thoughts on the Orphic material. Marinos notes, however,

---

[132] Cp. Athanassiadi 2010, esp. 138–141.

[133] West 1983: 251: "The rhapsody theory must have been worked out at Pergamum when Athenodorus was there. Theognetus must necessarily have been his contemporary. The compilation of the Rhapsodic theogony can therefore be firmly dated to the first third of the first century B.C."

[134] Brisson 1987 [1995]: 97 collects the references in an appendix. Proclus cites an *Astrologika*, a *Metroac Enthronements*, a *Krater*, as well as the *Hymn to Number*, among others. The Orphic astrological *Ephemerides* Proclus refers to in his commentary on Hesiod's *Works and Days* seems unlikely to have been incorporated into a Rhapsodic collection, while the Neopythagorean-influenced *Hymn to Number* also seems to have been independently known. Arguments could be made for the incorporation of the *Krater* and the *Enthronements*, but Proclus may have been working with multiple sources.

that he did not consent to do this annotation on the whole Orphic divine myth (πᾶσαν τὴν θεομυθίαν) or all the rhapsodies (πάσας τὰς ῥαψῳδίας), which suggests that Proclus and Syrianus were indeed working from the Rhapsodic collection.[135]

Damascius mentions several different Orphic theogonies in his survey of first principles, but he refers to one as the "usual Orphic theology" (ἡ συνήθης ὀρφικὴ θεολογία), the account found "in the rhapsodies which pass under the name of Orphic" (ἐν μὲν τοίνυν ταῖς φερομέναις ταύταις ῥαψῳδίαις ὀρφικαῖς).[136] He also provides the witness for Eudemos' and Hieronymos' accounts of Orphic theogonies, but the nature of his description suggests that he himself does not have access to the texts from which these earlier philosophers drew their account. Damascius is the first explicitly to mention the title of the *Orphic Rhapsodies*, and we can be certain that, by the time of Damascius – and probably as early as Iamblichus – the works of Orpheus had been systematized into a collection of twenty-four books, the better to serve as a representative of the wisdom of the ancients, just as the Homeric works had served as the backbone of the Hellenic education for centuries.

Gregory of Nazianzus, one of the most broadly read and scholastically educated of the Christian apologists, certainly seems acquainted with the Orphic material. Indeed, Claudian, around 400, praises Stilicho's daughter Maria for diligently learning from her mother all the writings of Homer, Orpheus, and Sappho, so the *Rhapsodies* may have become part of the educational program even outside the philosophical academies.[137] The *Rhapsodies* take on an almost Scriptural significance in Damascius' tale of Sarapion, a hermit who lived a godly life, despising money and bodily pleasures, with the book of Orpheus as nearly his only possession.[138]

---

[135] Marin. *Procl.* 27.16 (32 Saffrey-Segonds = 27.668–670 Masullo) (*OF* 677xii B = OT 239 K): καὶ ἐγένετο εἰς Ὀρφέα αὐτοῦ σχόλια καὶ ὑπομνήματα στίχων οὐκ ὀλίγων, εἰ καὶ μὴ εἰς πᾶσαν τὴν θεομυθίαν ἢ πάσας τὰς ῥαψῳδίας ἐξεγένετο αὐτῷ τοῦτο ποιῆσαι.

[136] Dam. *De princ.* 123 (III.159.17 Westerink = 1.316–317 Ruelle) (*OF* 90, 96, 109viii, 114viii, 677i B = OT 223d, OF 60 K).

[137] Claud. *de Nupt. Hon.* 232–235: "But Maria, with no thoughts of wedlock nor knowing that the torches were being got ready, was listening with rapt attention to the discourse of her saintly mother, drinking in that mother's nature and learning to follow the example of old-world chastity; nor does she cease under that mother's guidance to unroll the writers of Rome and Greece, all that old Homer sang, or Thracian Orpheus, or that Sappho set to music with Lesbian quill; (even so Latona taught Diana; so gentle Mnemosyne in her cave gave instruction to meek Thalia)."
illa autem secura tori taedasque parari | nescia divinae fruitur sermone parentis | maternosque bibit mores exemplaque discit | prisca pudicitiae Latios nec volvere libros | desinit aut Graios, ipsa genetrice magistra, | Maeonius quaecumque senex aut Thracius Orpheus | aut Mytilenaeo modulatur pectine Sappho | (sic Triviam Latona monet; sic mitis in antro | Mnemosyne docili tradit praecepta Thaliae).
(Platnauer's 1922 Loeb translation)

[138] *Suda* s.v. Σαραπίων (σ 116, IV.324.20 Adler) = Dam. *Isid.* fr. 41 (p. 37 Zintzen) (*OF* 677v B = OT 240 K): μόνον σχεδὸν τὸν Ὀρφέα ἐκέκτητο καὶ ἀνεγίνωσκεν. It is interesting to note that

The *Rhapsodies* were not, perhaps, the last product of the long tradition of Orphic pseudepigraphy. The *Orphic Argonautica* has been dated to the fifth century CE, and its proem clearly surveys the themes of Orphic literature of ages past before announcing its new theme, Orpheus' famous voyage on the Argo. Orpheus the author here joins with Orpheus the character in a way unprecedented in any of the earlier Orphica, since Orpheus recounts his own story here. However, this first person narration is really the extent of the presence of Orpheus the author, since the story does not seem marked as "Orphic" in any of the ways that earlier Orphic material is marked – the name of Orpheus is the only cue. On the other hand, the *Orphic Argonautica* clearly owes much to earlier Argonautic stories, particularly that of Apollonios Rhodios, but also, no doubt, to the more recent productions of Valerius Flaccus and Varro Atacinus. The *Orphic Argonautica* probably borrows some themes, images, and even verses from earlier Orphica, but the extent of such borrowing is impossible to determine, as is the extent to which it might draw from lost Argonautic stories that preceded Apollonios.

As for the other work which had been passed down under the name of Orpheus, the collection of lore on precious stones, the *Lithika*, as West says, "it does not really deserve a place in a discussion of Orphic literature, since it says nothing about Orpheus and makes no pretence of being by him. His name had become attached to it by the time of Tzetzes, and must have seemed appropriate to the subject matter."[139] Unfortunately, the *Argonautica* and the *Lithika*, the two works with the greatest number of lines between them of all the remaining poetry under the name of Orpheus, tell us little of how the category of Orphica was defined in antiquity. By contrast, the fragmentary references and decontextualized quotations in the polemics of the early Christian apologists and their Neoplatonic opponents show clearly the boundaries of the category and the criteria used – the antiquity of the poet, the bizarre details of his myths and rituals, and the special claim to divine connection that underlies the authority of his works.

Orpheus in the middle ages

When the authority of Orpheus and the tradition of Greek philosophy and theology he represents is no longer an active threat, the name of Orpheus

---

Sarapion is said to live the life of Kronos (τὸν μυθευόμενον Κρόνιον βίον, IV.324.24 Adler), rather than the βίος Ὀρφικός mentioned by Plato in the *Laws* and often imagined to be a widespread phenomenon. As this evidence shows, however, even a holy hermit in the Christian era, with the Orphica as his scriptures, was not said to live an Orphic life.

[139] West 1983: 36.

surfaces again as a metaphor for the power of the poetic tradition. As
in the Hellenistic and Roman poets, the character of Orpheus takes pre-
eminence, above Orpheus the author and founder of mysteries. As Herrero
puts it,

> During the Middle Ages, by contrast, when apologetic is no longer necessary
> following the complete Christianization of the empire, the literary themes of
> Orpheus the lover and the singer will once again become writers' favorites,
> while the theologian and founder of mysteries will be forgotten until the
> Renaissance.[140]

Orpheus becomes once more the enchanting singer, the Argonaut, the
bereaved lover of Eurydice who ventured into the Underworld to sway
even the heartless deities of death with his songs of love. The power of
Orpheus' song is allegorized in a variety of ways in this Christian tradition,
starting perhaps with Boethius' reading of the tale as an allegory of the soul's
ascent to heaven. Boethius' Orpheus is the spirit which, while ascending
up to the light, looks back down into the darkness, drawn by doubt
and desire, and the lesson not to become distracted by the lures of the
dark, material realm was retold in many ways in the centuries following
Boethius.[141] Boethius' Christian reading, however significantly influenced
by Platonism, nevertheless creates an Orpheus very different from the
Orpheus of his contemporary Neoplatonists. This Christianizing impulse
is taken to its greatest extreme in the interpretation of the fourteenth-
century Benedictine Pierre Bersuire, who, in his mythographic treatise the
Metamorphosis Ovidiana, identifies Orpheus with Christ. Bersuire, drawing
on the strand of interpretations from Boethius through the anonymous
thirteenth-century *Ovid Moralisée* that read Orpheus' descent into the
Underworld as an allegory of the soul's descent, transforms Eurydice into
the soul lost to the serpent's wiles, whom Christ-Orpheus descends into
Hell to save.[142]

The other influential strand of interpretation was that following upon
Fulgentius' fifth-century reading of the sentimental tale of Orpheus and
Eurydice as an allegory of music, wherein Orpheus (etymologized as *orea-
fone, id est optima vox* – the best voice) stands for musical practice, while

---

[140] Herrero 2010: 247. Cp. Vicari 1982: 65: "after the fifth or sixth century Orpheus scarcely seems to
have been thought of without Eurydice, except by the minstrels, for whom he was professional
archetype."

[141] Boeth. *Cons. phil.* 3 m12): *quicumque in superum diem | mentem ducere quaeritis; | nam qui Tartareum
in specus | uictus lumina flexerit, | quicquid praecipuum trahit | perdit dum uidet inferos.*

[142] Pierre Bersuire, *Metamorphosis Ovidiana* fol. 73.5. The identification of Christ and Orpheus is only
one of several allegorical readings Bersuire offers; see the discussion in Friedman 1970: 126–132.

Eurydice represents the theoretical understanding of music. Eurydice's death shows the way such understanding disappears into the secret places of the lower world, and Orpheus' prohibition to look upon her signifies that the attempt to explain the effects of music (e.g., the various modes) by theory is doomed to failure.[143] This musical sense of the myth continues on through the medieval period, in parallel with the Boethean moralizing interpretation, and both are sometimes even offered as alternatives by the same author.[144] Orpheus comes to stand for poetic eloquence, ultimately ending up in Dante as the representative of the *bella menzogna*, the beautiful lie that expresses the truth in an allegorical sense.[145]

The other role that Orpheus the character played in the Middle Ages was that of the lover/singer, the model of the troubadour.[146] Various narratives were spun around the tale of Orpheus' journey to win back his Eurydice. Some of these narratives continue the lines of the allegorical traditions, such as the racy twelfth-century *Prendantur oculos*, in which Orpheus the philosophical astronomer forgets his star-gazing for desire of Eurydice, who opens up the portals of her nether regions to the advances of the lover inflamed with desire. Others are as wildly different as the thirteenth/fourteenth-century English tale of *Sir Orfeo*, in which King Orfeo of Winchester goes to the land of the fairies to (successfully) win back his wife, Heurodis, who has been abducted by the fairies. The medieval tradition appropriates Orpheus' tragic love story for its own time: Orpheus the lover of Eurydice becomes the paragon of the courtly lover; Orpheus the singer becomes the ultimate troubadour, whose musical power is unstoppable.

The Renaissance of Orpheus

While the reception of Orpheus in the Middle Ages centers around the interpretation of the character Orpheus, known mostly from Ovid and Vergil, Orpheus the author is reborn in the Renaissance as the most ancient poet of religious hymns and rites. With the access to a wider variety of texts from antiquity comes a richer and more varied category of things to which the name of Orpheus pertains. Boccaccio, in his

---

[143] Fulg. *Myth.* 3.10 (77.10 Helm) (*OF* 979iv B = OT 64 K).
[144] Cp. Remigius of Auxerre, whose 904 CE commentary on Boethius offers the Boethean reading, while his references to the story in his commentary on Capella's *de Nuptiis* follow the Fulgentian musical interpretation. See Friedman 1970: 98–102.
[145] Dante, *Convivio* 2.1.3. Cp. Huss 2010: 482–483 for an overview of some of the medieval allegories.
[146] See Friedman 1970: 146–210 for the variety of examples of this theme.

Genealogia deorum gentilium, written some time between 1363 and 1373, can bring back Orpheus the Argonaut, as well as the tales of the head of Orpheus floating off to Lesbos and providing oracles after his death. He still finds in Orpheus an allegory of *eloquentia*, which tries to lead Eurydice (again as natural desire) back up to higher things, but the range of materials he has to work with has expanded. In the Renaissance, the *Orphic Argonautica*, the *Orphic Hymns*, and even the *Lithika* are held up as works of Orpheus, expanding the category of Orphic beyond its medieval boundaries.

Marsilio Ficino is perhaps the most important figure in shaping the category of Orphic in the Renaissance, as he picks up the Neoplatonists' Orpheus and fuses him with that of the Christian apologists to create the foremost of the *prisci theologi*, the primeval theologians whose pure pre-Christian theology harmonizes with the Christian revelation.[147] Ficino goes beyond even Proclus in his valorization of Orpheus; Proclus ultimately preferred the Chaldaean Oracles to the Orphica as a vehicle of divine revelation, but for Ficino, the Orphica are the most sublime. Ficino himself is dubbed the new Orpheus by his colleagues, and he even performs for his friends the hymns of Orpheus, which he himself has brought to the attention of the western world. "He set forth the hymns of Orpheus and sang them to the lyre in the ancient manner with incredible sweetness, so people say."[148] The collection of the *Hymns of Orpheus* is indeed far more important to Ficino than to ancient authors, who do not seem to quote the particular collection of hymns that has come down to the present day – in no small part due to the efforts of Ficino. Ficino revives the importance of Orpheus the author and theologian, making him, as did the Neoplatonists and the early Christian apologists, the representative of the ancient Greek religious and philosophical tradition – Orpheus to Pythagoras to Plato to Proclus. For Ficino and his friends, as for some of the apologists, Orpheus is also the heir of Moses/Mousaios, becoming the point of fusion where Jewish revelation and Greek philosophy conjoin, authenticating both as true and valid theology of the most ancient kind.[149] As western Europe grappled with the influx of ideas from the newly rediscovered and newly translated texts of the Greek world, Orpheus once again plays the role

---

[147] Warden 1982 remains one of the best treatments of this topic, along with Walker 1953, but a new and detailed study of Ficino's reception of the Orphica is greatly needed.

[148] *Orphei hymnos exposuit, miraque ut ferunt dulcedine ad lyram antiquo more cecinit.* C. G. Corsi *Vita Marsilii Ficini 6 ap.* Appendix 1 of Marcel 1958. Quote and translation from Warden 1982, who surveys the various representations of Ficino as Orpheus on pp. 86–88.

[149] The iconographic identification of Orpheus the singer with David the biblical psalmist that was important in the early Christian period surfaces again here with the new efforts to reconcile biblical and Hellenic traditions. See Friedman 1970: 38–85.

of the most ancient founder of the religious and philosophical tradition coming from Classical antiquity.

While Orpheus the author receives new life in the Renaissance, Orpheus the character continues to be significant, especially with the birth of the new art form of opera, designed as a rebirth of the Classical tragic performances. The first performance of such an opera, Jacopo Peri's 1600 production, takes Orpheus' story as its theme, while Monteverdi's 1607 *Orfeo* remains one of the most significant pieces from the period. Opera develops other stories, of course, but there are a series of *Orfeos* in the subsequent years, culminating in Gluck's 1762 *Orfeo ed Euridice*.[150] In all these versions, the sentimental story of Orpheus and Eurydice forms the basis for reflections on love and the power of music; the medieval allegorization is largely absent.

From the Renaissance to the nineteenth century

Of course, the debate continues over the boundaries of the category of Orphic, since the Renaissance thinkers are also heirs to all the controversies over Orpheus and his works that shaped the category in antiquity. Some, such as Bruni and Pico, latch on to the skepticism of Aristotle that Orpheus ever existed or wrote any of the works attributed to him, while others, including Steuco and Estienne, use more refined philological analyses to prove that some of the works, such as the *Orphic Hymns*, must have been written later than others.[151] Nevertheless, for those in the Renaissance seeking to harmonize the Christian and Classical traditions, Orpheus and his works remain important. As Walker notes, "those syncretists who make great use of Orpheus assumed that the Orphica, even if not all literally by Orpheus, were the genuine sacred writings of a very ancient religious tradition."[152] Extreme antiquity is the feature of the Orphic label that attracts the most interest in this context, rather than a focus on purity or even perversity.

The same assumptions and controversies continue in the following centuries, as the Orphica are examined and re-examined by scholars in

---

[150] As Huss 2010: 489 notes, "Gluck's overwhelming success at first largely silenced O. as a subject for serious opera."

[151] Steuco and Estienne date the *Hymns* later, while Leonardo Bruni and Gian-Francesco Pico rehearse the claim of Aristotle: Leonardo Bruni Aretino, *Humanistisch-philosophische Schriften*, ed. Hans Baron, Leipzig, 1928, p. 133; Gian-Francesco Pico, *Opera Omnia*, Basle, 1573, p. 36; Steuco, *De Perenni Philosophia*, Lyons, 1540, I, p. xxviii (Steuco, *Opera Omnia*, Venice, 1591, III, f. 24 vO); H. Estienne, *Praefatio* to his Οἱ τῆς Ἡρωικῆς ποιήσεως προτεύοντες ποιηταί, 1566, p. 487. See Walker 1953: 104 for references and details.

[152] Walker 1953: 104.

succeeding generations, each trying to define the boundaries of the category. In 1764, Johann Matthias Gesner produces the first collection of the Orphic fragments, bringing together the texts of the *Hymns*, the *Lithika*, and the *Argonautica* with the references in the Neoplatonists, Christian apologists, and earlier Classical authors, and other collections make available the same set of evidence for the category.[153] Using these resources, scholars debate which works sealed with the name of Orpheus might be earliest, which might be attributable to Pythagoras, which to Onomakritos, but the basic Neoplatonic (and Christian apologetic) assumption that there is a coherent system of theology laid out in the works of Orpheus remains the starting point for most of those who deal with the Orphica. For example, the eighteenth-century scholar Dieterich Tiedemann drew upon the skepticism of the ancient sources about the authorship of many of the Orphica to conclude that Orpheus was a pseudonym used by various authors to compose poems under Orpheus' name. He favors Pausanias' choice of Onomakritos for the Orphicist of the earliest (sixth-century) works, which form the basis of the pure "Orphic School", but he uses philological critiques to argue that some of the extant *Orphic Hymns*, for example, must have been composed later by Stoics, Pythagoreans, or Neoplatonists.[154] Tiedemann, like other scholars starting from the Renaissance, makes use of the Orphic material surviving in the Neoplatonists and the Christian apologists to try to reconstruct the ideas of this Orphic School. Again, like many of his predecessors, he takes seriously Diodorus Siculus' claims of the Egyptian origin of Orpheus' ideas, thus giving greater antiquity to the ideas (and putting them within the orbit of the revelations of Moses).[155] Tiedemann sifts critically through the materials provided by the Neoplatonists and Christian apologists, but his category of Orphic is thus fundamentally tied to the definitions his predecessors provide.

Tiedemann's contemporary, Thomas Taylor, takes his Neoplatonic predecessors even more seriously, agreeing with them not only that there is a systematic Orphic theology but also that it is a true ancient wisdom that is best explained through the doctrines of the Neoplatonists. Taylor

---

[153] Gesner 1764, published posthumously. Hermann's 1805 collection represents a philological advance, but is based on the same principles, as is Ábel's 1885 edition (which, however, is largely seen as a failure to capitalize on the advances made in source criticism in the intervening years).

[154] E.g., Tiedemann 1780: 83 argues that the first hymn of the collection, which calls upon Great Pan, must have been composed by a later Pythagorean or Neoplatonist, because Pan in the Classical period was only a rustic shepherd's god, in contrast to the later allegorization of his name to signify the All, the entirety of the cosmos. I owe this reference to the unpublished dissertation of Torjussen 2008, whose discussion of Tiedemann and Taylor has been very helpful.

[155] Tiedemann 1780: 16.

enthusiastically recreates the Orphic theology systematized by Proclus and the other Neoplatonists, translating not only the *Orphic Hymns* but also large numbers of the Neoplatonists' works into English and providing in his commentary the connections that show the systematic nature of the Orphic theology.[156] Taylor too follows the well-worn path tracing Orpheus' wisdom back to Egypt, through Hermes Trismegistos back to Moses, and he celebrates Orpheus as the source of all that is great in the Greek tradition, from Homer to Plato. He notes the controversies over the figure, but claims that, however difficult it may be to agree on the details of Orpheus' life, all may agree on his role as founder of the Greek religious tradition.

> Scarcely a vestige of his life is to be found amongst the immense ruins of time. For who has ever been able to affirm any thing with certainty, concerning his origin, his age, his parents, his country, and condition? This alone may be depended on, from general assent, that there formerly lived a person named Orpheus, whose father was Œagrus, who lived in Thrace, and who was the son of a king, who was the founder of theology, among the Greeks; the institutor of their life and morals; the first of prophets, and the prince of poets; himself the offspring of a Muse; who taught the Greeks their sacred rites and mysteries, and from whose wisdom, as from a perpetual and abundant fountain, the divine muse of Homer, and the philosophy of Pythagoras, and Plato, flowed.[157]

This universal agreement, of course, is the assumption made in common by both the Christian apologists and their Neoplatonic opponents, but it is hardly the view of Orpheus that emerges directly from the earlier evidence, however much this assumption dominates the reception of Orpheus from the Neoplatonists onward. Taylor takes the Orphic theology to be the purest representative of the Greek religious tradition, and his motivation in explicating it is "to show that God has not left himself without a witness among the wise and learned of the heathens."[158] Taylor's Orphism is like that of his favorite predecessor, Proclus, a privileged revelation of the deepest religious truth, the primal and unspoiled revelation of Greek theology.

---

[156] Taylor's (rather free and poetic) translations were the only versions in English for some of these Neoplatonic texts for centuries, although some recent publications in the last decade have begun to change that situation. Nevertheless, Taylor's influence (and interpretations) was significant in subsequent generations' understanding of the materials.

[157] Taylor 1792: 2–3. Cp. Taylor 1824: xliv. As he proceeds from surveying the evidence for Orpheus' life to the evidence for his theological system, he trumpets: "Let us now proceed to his theology; exchanging the obscurity of conjecture for the light of clear evidence; and the intricate labyrinths of fable for the delightful though solitary paths of truth" (Taylor 1792: 12).

[158] Taylor 1792: 45.

Taylor's mysticism and understanding of the Orphica as the witnesses to a lost ancient truth strikes a chord with the Romantic spirit, as the search for pure primeval wisdom becomes fashionable and widespread. The figure of Orpheus was important to poets, especially German Romantics such as Hölderlin and Novalis, not just as the archetypical poet but as the representative of ancient wisdom, older even than Ossian, that other mythical poet who was all the rage in Europe. Orpheus represented the poet's special access to that primitive wisdom, the *Urworte*, as Goethe put it, that combines poetry, religion, and philosophy in an "Orphic" expression of the "eternal yet enigmatic laws of life."[159] The scholarly manifestation of this Romantic admiration for Orpheus may be seen in the work of Creuzer, who in his *Symbolik und Mythologie der alten Völker, besonders der Griechen* traced the wisdom of the Greeks back to the east, whence the ineffable truths were transmitted through the symbolic means of myths and poetry.[160] Creuzer differs from other Romantics, e.g., Herder, in avoiding the search for a national spirit and looking instead for universal wisdom, and Orpheus, always coming from the outside, suits the purpose perfectly, allowing him to link the Indian traditions with those of the Greeks.

Despite their enduring appeal to romantics seeking the source of ancient wisdom, Creuzer's theories drew strong criticism from numerous quarters. K. O. Müller mocks Creuzer's idea of archaic Indian sages encoding deep truths in myths to convey them to the ignorant westerners as if they were "missionaries to the Greenlanders," and Christian August Lobeck, a pupil of Hermann (who had put together the most recent collection of Orphic fragments in 1805), mounts a sustained philological attack upon Creuzer's work. Lobeck's 1829 *Aglaophamus* is generally seen as the turning point in the scholarship on Orphism in the modern period, since Lobeck rejects the assumption (going back to the Neoplatonists and beyond) that the Orphica did indeed contain esoteric and mystical wisdom that dated back to the most primeval times. Lobeck shows that the supposed content of the mysteries was neither esoteric nor foreign in origin, but rather consonant with the general ideas of Greek religion as a whole – a point which unfortunately has been much neglected in subsequent studies.[161] Picking up on the long history of critical scholarship on the dating of the

---

[159] Huss 2010: 490.

[160] Creuzer's *Symbolik* was published first in 1810–12 (2nd edn. 1819, 3rd edn. 1837).

[161] Lobeck tends to dismiss the supposedly profound and esoteric ideas as primitive superstitions and bunkum foisted upon the ignorant by manipulative priests. In this critique, he of course follows Plato and Theophrastos (among others), but he approaches it from the bias of the Protestant critique of Catholic ritualism, comparing the priests to Jesuits, peddling ritual to enhance their own status (e.g., Lobeck 1829: 632–633, 964). See Gagné 2008 for a discussion of Lobeck's bias.

various Orphica, Lobeck argues that many of the "Oriental" elements were later additions and that there is no reason to suppose that all of the ideas found in the Neoplatonists represent the oldest strands of Orphic ideas.

The battle between Creuzer and Lobeck and their adherents thus revolves around many of the same issues as the disputes of the Christian apologists and their Neoplatonic opponents – the antiquity of the Orphica, their claims to antique wisdom, their foreign origin. The prodigious philological works of the nineteenth-century scholars, moreover, meant that they were working with many of the same pieces of evidence as the ancient scholars; even if large numbers of texts known in antiquity were lost forever, the nineteenth-century scholars at least had far more evidence at their disposal than their medieval or Renaissance predecessors.

The impact of new evidence: The "Orphic" gold tablets

The greatest shift in the debates over the category of Orphism comes with the introduction of new evidence at the end of the nineteenth century. In 1879, excavations at Thurii in Southern Italy uncover tombs with tiny gold tablets bearing hexameter verses. In the excavation reports and in an 1882 article, Domenico Comparetti identifies the texts as Orphic (despite the absence of any identifying name or familiar text), and these lamellae become the catalyst for a redefinition of Orphism in the succeeding decades. Comparetti takes the line on two of the tablets from Thurii, "Recompense I have paid on account of deeds not just", along with a line from another tablet discovered earlier in the southern Italian region of Petelia, "I am the child of Earth and starry Heaven," and concludes that the tablets provide evidence for "the main principles of the Orphic doctrine on psychogony and metempsychosis."[162] Comparetti uses the tale of the dismemberment of Dionysos found in the sixth-century CE Neoplatonist Olympiodorus to claim, contrary to the argument in Olympiodorus himself, that human beings' descent from the Titanic murderers of Dionysos brings a dual heritage – a good, divine Dionysiac nature and an evil Titanic one. "This Titanic element is the original guilt for which the human soul is excluded from the community of the other gods and from her blessed abode, and is condemned to a succession of births and deaths."[163]

---

[162] Gold Tablet A3 (*OF* 490 B = OF 32e K) ln. 4; cp. A2 (*OF* 489 B = OF 32d K) ln. 4: ποινὰν <δ'> ἀνταπέτε<ισ'> ἔργω<ν ἕνεκ'> ο<ὔ>τι δικα<ί>ων. See Edmonds 2011b: 16–39 for the texts and translations of the tablets.

[163] Comparetti 1882: 116. Olymp. *In Phd.* 20 uses the myth to explain the prohibition on suicide, arguing that the body contains divine elements and must not be harmed; he mentions nothing of a

Comparetti's interpretation, creating a doctrine of original sin at the heart of the Orphic religious ideas, is immediately taken up by his contemporaries and remains perniciously persistent, even today.

The reason Comparetti's explanation is so rapidly accepted is that it plays into one of the dominant questions of the day – the origins of Christianity, particularly the ideas of the soul. The origins of Christianity and the differences between Christianity and other religions were questions of vital interest, since the authority and validity of Christianity were being brought into question by the "culture wars" of the period, as Graf calls them, over the role of institutional religion in the modern nation state. The historicization of Christianity by tracing its connections with pagan antiquity thus had significant repercussions for contemporary society.[164] Darwin's *On the Origin of Species* in 1859 had shaken the faith of many, contributing to the social upheaval. Nietzsche's 1872 *Birth of Tragedy* diagnoses Christian ideas as a sickness that killed the spirit of the Greeks, while Frazer's 1890 *Golden Bough* places the death and resurrection of Christ in the context of dying and rising god stories all over the world, from contemporary primitives to the ancient Greeks. Comparetti himself notes the significance of the tablets as evidence for the "origins and precedents" of Christian doctrines of the soul, and Dieterich, in his 1893 *Nekyia*, postulates an esoteric Orphic *katabasis* tradition that contributed to early Christian eschatological imagery.[165] Nietzsche and Frazer are significant influences upon the most important studies of Greek religion in the period, Rohde's *Psyche* and Harrison's *Prolegomena to the Study of Greek Religion*.[166] The new definition of Orphism becomes codified in the collections of texts that are the equipment for the scholarly debates. Diels includes the gold tablets

dual heritage or a burden of inherited guilt, much less original sin. For Olympiodorus' innovations in combining the dismemberment story with an anthropogony, see Edmonds 2009 and further below.

[164] Graf and Johnston 2007: 58–61. Smith 1990 discusses the long history of the study of Greek mysteries in relation to early Christianity, pointing out many of the uses to which they were put.

[165] Comparetti 1910: 51: "Quindi grande è pure la discrepanza di opinioni emesse su tal soggetto dal dotti moderni, dal Lobeck al Rohde ed alla pleiade di dotti che in questi ultimi tempi hanno scrutato le non numerose notizie pervenuteci sui misteri antichi, **oggi particolarmente e con grande interesse studiati in correlazione colle origini e i precedenti del misticismo cristiano**" (emphasis added).

[166] A great spate of scholarly activity takes place at this time, of which I can take only brief notice. Cp. Maass 1898, Kern 1888, and, of course, Ábel's 1885 collection of Orphica. As Herrero 2010: 6 notes, "Though the majority of their hypotheses have been disproved, or at least modified, by subsequent scholarship, the works of these path-breaking scholars are not devoid of interest to the modern reader. They created the classical image of Orphism. Projecting the Christian model onto it, they posited a network of Orphic communities who read the Orphic poems as sacred texts, who celebrated rituals commemorating the sacrifice of Dionysus, and who held uniform practices and religious beliefs."

in his 1903 collection of fragments of Presocratic Philosophers, and Kern's 1922 collection of the Orphic fragments puts them among the earliest and most important witnesses. Kern omits the *Orphic Hymns*, the *Argonautica*, and the *Lithika* from his edition, showing the shift in the focus away from texts so important to earlier conceptions of Orphism and toward the fragments that are used to reconstruct the pre-Christian doctrines of Orphism. The category of "Orphic" becomes once again a useful tool in the definition of Christianity, as it was in the first several centuries CE.

The category, however, is different in the nineteenth and early twentieth centuries from the Orphism of the first few centuries CE, just as the issues at stake are different. Whereas the debate in the first few centuries centered on the antiquity and authority of the whole Greek religious tradition, of which Orpheus was made the representative, the nineteenth-century debate is more about the similarities between Christianity and the Greek mysteries, a special branch of ancient Greek religion, differing from the Homeric, of which Orpheus is made the representative. The Protestant/Catholic debates over ritualism and the purity of the early Church, fought out in Europe over the preceding centuries, certainly infect the question, as does the Nietzschean condemnation of Christianity's emphasis on the afterlife over this life.[167] As in the first few centuries, however, all sides make use of a similar category of Orphism to argue their points, whether it is that the Orphic reforms of Greek religion turned it from a vital primitivism to a sick-souled decay or that the Orphic ideas of purity and soul paved the way for the reception of the Christian revelation through their influence on the most important philosophers of the Greek tradition.[168] The nineteenth-century category of Orphism focused above all on extraordinary purity, the moral cleansing of the soul, as well as on the eschatological and soteriological ideas found in the Orphic texts that played up the importance of the special connection to the divine. The antiquity and foreign origin so important to the earlier category of Orphism play a far smaller role.

This focus on eschatology and soteriology, of course, plays into the debates over the nature and origin of Christianity, since Orphism is being

---

[167] See above all Smith 1990 for the history of the mystery cults in the Protestant/Catholic debates in the history of religions.

[168] Cp. Rohde 1925: 242: "Nor were they very susceptible **during their best centuries** to the infectious malady of a 'sick conscience'. What had they to do with pictures of an underworld of purgatory and torment in expiation of all imaginary types and degrees of sin, as in Dante's ghastly Hell?" (emphasis added); contrast Jaeger 1945: 168–169: "The Orphic conception of the soul marks an important advance in the development of man's consciousness of selfhood. Without it Plato and Aristotle could never have developed the theory that the human spirit is divine, and that man's sensual nature can be dissociated from his real self, which it is his true function to bring to perfection."

used to trace the development of the most authentically religious aspects of early Christianity. As Smith has shown, the Protestant and anticlerical critiques of Catholicism and its ritualized and hierarchical system define the terms for the understanding of the religions of the ancient Mediterranean world in the scholarship of the early modern period, especially on the mystery cults of the Greeks.[169] The category of Orphism, as it appears in the debates of the nineteenth and early twentieth centuries, often resembles the familiar model of Protestant Christianity, with a founding prophet Orpheus who reveals the scriptures that provide the key to salvation, imagined as a blissful afterlife that contrasts with the sorrows of this vale of tears. The parallels between Orphism and Protestantism are drawn most explicitly in the 1934 study of Watmough, but similar structures underlie much of the debate.

> In the ancient world we have the religion of Homer, entirely concerned with sacrifice and ritual, entirely dominated by the note of "Confiteor" – the confession of vows duly performed: and over against it the religion of "Orpheus", which emphasised the relation of the individual soul with God, for authority turning not to priests but scriptures. In the more modern world we have the mediaeval Church, a picturesque and colourful religious system based on sacerdotalism and ecclesiolatry: over against it the Protestant reformers with their "justification by faith" and bibliolatrous attitude to the canonical writings.[170]

The key elements are the choice of Orpheus as the revealer of the new gospel, the emphasis on sacred texts, and the focus on salvation and afterlife. Dieterich indeed claims that it was the similarities between Orphism and Christianity, specifically the reliance on sacred texts and the imagery of the afterlife, both positive and negative, that prompted the polemics of apologists such as Clement.[171] Comparetti's idea of an Orphic original sin, a stain upon mankind from which the dying and rising god Dionysos can redeem those who believe the doctrines written in the sacred texts of Orpheus, thus becomes a key piece in the definition of Orphism as a special, reforming strand of Greek religion that paves the way for the ideas of Christianity.

The elaboration of Orphism as a precursor of Christianity continues in the scholarship of the early twentieth century, culminating in Macchioro's vision of an Orphic Church, with special doctrines and rituals and congregations of the faithful spread throughout the Greek world. For Macchioro, this Orphic church and its doctrines were a formative influence on Paul

---

[169] Smith 1990: 43.   [170] Watmough 1934: 56–57.   [171] Dieterich 1893: 228.

and shaped Pauline Christianity.[172] This extravagance prompted a skeptical reaction, including that of Wilamowitz, who famously complained that "Moderns babble endlessly of Orphics."[173] Reacting to the critiques of scholars such as Boulanger, Guthrie sets out a toned down version of Macchioro's PanOrphic vision in his 1936 *Orpheus and Greek Religion*, but he still imagines an Orphic sect, with sacred books and special doctrines about the immortality of the soul and its need for purity – and the gold tablets are central to his reconstruction.

Linforth, on the other hand, in his 1941 *Arts of Orpheus*, refuses to include the gold tablets or any other evidence not explicitly "sealed with the name of Orpheus." Linforth's skeptical approach to the evidence demolished the grandiose structures fabricated by Macchioro and others, showing that there was no coherent Orphic sect or doctrine to be found among the evidence of things sealed with Orpheus' name in antiquity. As Dodds puts it a decade later,

> I must confess that I know very little about early Orphism, and the more I read about it the more my knowledge diminishes. Twenty years ago, I could have said quite a lot about it (we all could at that time). Since then, I have lost a great deal of knowledge; for this loss I am indebted to Wilamowitz, Festugière, Thomas, and not least to a distinguished member of the University of California, Professor Linforth. . . . The edifice reared by an ingenious scholarship upon these foundations remains for me a house of dreams – I am tempted to call it the unconscious projection upon the screen of antiquity of certain unsatisfied religious longings of the late nineteenth and early twentieth centuries.[174]

More new discoveries: The Linear B tablets, gold tablets, and the Derveni papyrus

The uneasy tension between Linforth's skeptical critique and Guthrie's specious construct remains in the following decades; the "house of dreams" constructed by Macchioro and the like had collapsed, but it was unclear what was left. Once again, the discovery of new evidence – particularly the

---

[172] Cp. Reinach 1909, Loisy 1919. Macchioro 1922 provides the most detailed exposition, but Macchioro 1930, his English work entitled, *From Orpheus to Paul*, popularized his ideas to a wider audience. As Graf notes, "the Columbia faculty, whom Macchioro thanks in his preface and who must have been instrumental in his invitation, were less interested in Greek religion than in this historical reductionism of dogmatic and totalitarian Christianity" (Graf and Johnston 2007: 60).

[173] Wilamowitz-Moellendorff 1931–32: II, 197: "Die Moderne reden so entsetzlich viel über die Orphiker. Wer macht das in Altertum?"

[174] Dodds 1951: 148.

gold tablet from Hipponion and the papyrus from Derveni – revitalizes
the scholarship on the Orphica, leading to new debates over the category
of Orphic. Although the Derveni papyrus is discovered earlier, in 1961,
and some scholarship begins to engage with the document, the absence
of a complete publication limits its impact, while the Hipponion tablet is
published very soon after its discovery in 1974.[175]

The lengthy text of the Hipponion tablet, parallel to the tablet discovered in Petelia more than a century earlier, and the mention at the end
of the *mystai* and *bacchoi* prompt new investigations into the religious
context of the gold tablets and their relation with Dionysiac and Orphic
ritual.[176] Zuntz's 1971 study collects the texts of the gold tablets, including
several more discovered in Crete and Thessaly in the intervening years,
but he emphatically rejects any possibility of a connection with Dionysos
or Orphica, preferring to see the tablets as witnesses to the ancient and
pure Pythagorean tradition that he traces in *Persephone*, his peculiar study
of the tablets, Empedokles, and other evidence for Goddess worship in
the ancient Mediterranean. The single word, *bacchoi*, fatally undercuts
his protestations that the tablets had nothing to do with Dionysos, and
scholars begin once again to imagine an Orphic context for the gold lamellae. The 1989 publication of two tablets in Pelinna with the line, "Say to
Persephone that Bacchios himself freed you," stirs further interest in an
Orphic/Bacchic mystic context, especially as more gold tablets are found
in subsequent excavations, albeit mostly with shorter texts or just the name
of an initiate.[177] Debates continue to rage over the interrelation of Orphic,
Bacchic, and Pythagorean contexts for the tablets, and the boundaries of
each of those categories undergo intense scholarly scrutiny. While Bernabé's
edition of the tablets labels them Orphic, and Graf and Johnston collect
the Bacchic lamellae, the recent publication of a tablet from Pherai with
the names of Demeter and Mater Oreia has re-opened the question of their
religious context.[178]

The other major impetus for the reconsideration of the category of
Orphic at the end of the twentieth century is the Derveni papyrus. The

---

[175] Foti and Pugliese Carratelli 1974.

[176] Tablet B10 (*OF* 474 B) ll. 15–16: καὶ δή καὶ σὺ πιὼν ὁδὸν ἔρχεα‹ι› ἄν τε καὶ ἄλλοι | μύσται καὶ
βάχχοι ἱερὰν στείχουσι κλε‹ε›ινοί. "And you too, having drunk, will go along the sacred road
that the other famed initiates and bacchics travel."

[177] Tablet D1 (*OF* 485 B) ln. 2 ≈ D2 (*OF* 486 B) ln. 2: εἰπεῖν Φερσεφόναι σ᾿ ὅτι Β‹άκ›χιος αὐτός
ἔλυσε.

[178] Tablet D5 (*OF* 493a B): "Send me to the thiasos of the initiates. I have [seen] the festivals | of
Demeter Chthonia, and the rites of the Mountain Mother." πέμπε με πρὸς μυστῶ‹ν› θιάσους· ἔχω
ὄργια [ἰδοῦσα] | Δημητρος Χθονίας, τε ‹τέ›λη καὶ Μητρὸς Ὀρεί[ας]. The tablet was discovered
in 1904, but not published until 2004 (Parker and Stamatopoulou 2004).

papyrus, the oldest piece of papyrus surviving from Greece, was preserved when it fell from the funeral pyre on which it had been placed, apparently in the hand of the deceased. As the body went up in flames, the bottom edge of the papyrus burned through and the top section, charred to carbon in its outer layers, fell from the pyre and was swept into the tomb, which can be dated to the first half of the third century BCE.[179] The carbonization preserved the papyrus from decomposition, and its recovery and deciphering represents one of the great triumphs of archaeology and paleography in the twentieth century. The tale of its publication, however, is less triumphant. Although the discovery is announced in 1962 and informal transcriptions circulate privately among scholars for years, no complete text is published until an unauthorized version appears in *Zeitschrift für Papyrologie und Epigraphik* in 1982.[180] This bootleg text (which still appears in the *TLG*) is missing some of the material from the first columns of the papyrus, but it nevertheless provides scholars with a basis from which to work on the remarkable text in the papyrus.

The unknown author of the text on the papyrus quotes and explains a number of verses from a poem of Orpheus, providing one of the earliest witnesses to such a poem, as well as one of the earliest examples of this kind of sustained hermeneutic activity. In 1983, West makes the Derveni theogony the basis for his study of the entire Orphic theogonic tradition, since the theogony in the papyrus provides an early witness to material that only surfaces again much later in the tradition. West's study subsumes and surpasses the philological studies of the previous century of scholarship on the fragments of the Orphic poems, connecting the new evidence with the earlier collections. West's textual stemma model, however, immediately provokes controversy, and in the past decade excellent studies by Betegh and Janko, followed by the official publication of the papyrus in 2006 (nearly half a century after its discovery!), have transformed the discussions, but debates are still ongoing regarding the date, the author, the genre, and indeed practically every aspect of the papyrus text.

Another discovery should be mentioned that also transformed the way that modern scholars think about Orphism, although its impact has been much less direct than the sensational appearances of the Derveni papyrus and new gold tablets. The publication of the Mycenaean-era tablets from Pylos and Khania with the name of Dionysos on them has finally laid to rest one of the oldest and most pervasive misunderstandings of Greek

[179] The description of the tomb was published by Themelis and Touratsoglou 1997, but a good summary may be found in Betegh 2004: 56–62.
[180] Anonymous 1982.

religion, the nature of Dionysos as an outsider.[181] The various theories of the
development of Greek religion through the invasion of Dionysiac cult from
the north (Thrace) or east (Phrygia) that were based on a literal historicizing
reading of the myths of the resistance to the advent of Dionysos have been
shown to be fallacious; Dionysos and his cult are not "a drop of foreign
blood" within the Greek religious system, as Rohde famously put it, but
an integral part of the Greek religion from its earliest witnesses.[182] The
part of an invading outsider that Dionysos plays within the structure of
Greek religion helps to illumine the testimonies that make Orpheus too
an outsider, who brings foreign religious ideas and practices into Greek
religion. Orpheus' foreign connections have been used in various ways in
different constructions of the category of Orphic from the early Christian
apologists onward, so understanding that this apparently alien nature is
an inherent part of Orpheus' role within the system of Greek religion
helps us to deconstruct those earlier classifications and to see how and
why they were put together. However, despite the fact that the Linear B
tablets were published early on in the latter half of the twentieth century,
scholars have been slow to grasp the full impact of the discovery on the
understanding of Greek religion, and the "foreign" nature of Dionysos and
Orpheus is still often taken to be historical fact rather than the Greek way
of expressing the distance of one element of the religious system from the
norm.

Studies by scholars such as Burkert, Graf, and Alderink begin to move
the debate about the nature of Orphism forward in new ways, but the
older models still remain influential.[183] The state of the question for
the category of "Orphic" in the late twentieth century is probably best

[181] Palaima 2004: 448–449. Tablet KH Gq5 from Khania records the offering of honey to Dionysos,
while a tablet from Pylos (PY Ea 102) refers to a fire altar for Dionysos. See Bernabé 2013 for a
study of the most important pieces of evidence, as well as a history of the scholarship.

[182] Rohde 1895: 27: "ein fremder Blutstropfen im griechischen Blut." By contrast, more recent scholars
have focused on his role as a deity who comes in to the community from abroad. As Sourvinou-
Inwood 2005: 150 puts it, "Dionysos is the god who *par excellence* arrived, in the myths, and whose
arrival was *par excellence* celebrated in cult." Cp. Detienne 1986, who draws upon ideas from Otto
1965.

[183] Burkert 1982 is a ground-breaking essay on the Orphics and Pythagoreans, showing that, while
the Pythagoreans may be understood by older models of a religious sect, the Orphics are better
understood with reference to a model of independent religious craftsmen. Graf 1974 analyzes the
evidence for the interplay between the Eleusinian Mysteries and the Orphica, concluding that
Orphic texts were composed to reflect local Athenian ideas of the Mysteries, although no coherent
Orphic movement existed in Athens. Alderink 1981, working from the new evidence of the Derveni
papyrus, proposes a polythetic definition of Orphism based on ideas of monism, the creation of
the cosmos, and soteriology, thus, like Burkert and Graf, moving away from the idea of an Orphic
religious group.

represented by Robert Parker's 1995 survey of "Early Orphism", which provides a good overview of the evidence and the debates, settling for a definition of Orphism that denies any coherent Orphic social organization, but sees Orphism as fundamentally concerned with eschatological and soteriological issues, focused (unlike the rest of Greek religion) upon texts, and tightly bound up with its ritual cultic activity. For Parker, as for many scholars throughout the twentieth century, the emphasis on purification and salvation, along with the rejection of ordinary religious practices, prompts comparison with "puritans", reformers of normal Greek religion like the Protestant reformers of Christianity who likewise emphasized purification and salvation.[184] The category of Orphism is thus defined at the end of the twentieth century as a reform movement within Greek religion that seeks through ritual means to achieve purification and ultimately salvation, relying on the texts ascribed to the poet Orpheus.

Orphism in the twenty-first century

The start of the new century in Orphic studies has been marked by the publication of Bernabé's monumental new edition of the Orphic fragments, along with several studies of the gold tablets and of the Derveni papyrus.[185] Bernabé's edition self-consciously marks a return to the ideas of Guthrie, the moderated version of the nineteenth-century model of Orphism as a doctrinal religion, but some of the new studies open up the possibility of moving beyond this outdated model.

Bernabé's three fascicles of the second volume of the *Poetae Epici Graeci* provide a much more massive collection of Orphica than any previous edition, even though he, like Kern, omits the non-fragmentary works – the *Orphic Argonautica*, the *Orphic Hymns*, and the *Lithika*. The nearly 1,200 fragments in this edition provide far more material for twenty-first-century scholars of Orphism than has been available for previous studies. Some of these represent the new discoveries made in the century since

---

[184] Cp. Parker 1995: 502: "In this gloomy alienation from the world and the senses, they were, of course, turning traditional Greek assumptions upside down. Equally untraditional, as we have noted, was the ambition with which these puritans aspired to godhead." One must not place undue emphasis on Parker's use of the Protestant model implicit in the word "puritans." From Parker's "puritans" (among whom he includes Empedokles and the Pythagoreans) to Harrison's "Protestant, prig" Orpheus is an enormous leap, that passes through the moderating influences of Dodds, among others. Even Harrison, moreover, does not go to the explicit extremes of Watmough, who devotes his whole monograph to illustrating the parallels between Orphism and Protestantism against Homeric religion and Catholicism.

[185] See Santamaria 2012 for an overview of the burgeoning scholarship in the field over the past decade.

Kern's edition, but many others are texts never before classified as Orphic. While Kern too includes texts that are not explicitly labeled as Orphic in the ancient sources, Bernabé includes many more (even omitting some of the ones that Kern does include).[186]

Bernabé's criteria for inclusion are directly based upon his own definition of Orphism as a religious current that has a unifying kernel of doctrines at its essence: the duality of body and soul, the stain of the soul by an original sin, the search for salvation through purification over a cycle of transmigrations of the soul, and the ultimate union of the purified soul with the divine.[187] Anything that reminds him of these doctrines is fair game for inclusion, so not only does he include a great deal of material that has to do with the dismemberment of Dionysos (on the grounds that it provides evidence for the idea of the original sin that stains mankind), but he also includes many testimonies to the idea of a lively afterlife or the judgment of the soul, as well as to the cycle of reincarnations.[188] This extremely broad category of Orphica defined by the appearance of certain ideas runs more than the usual risk of subjective bias, since Bernabé must decide, for example, which references to Dionysos he should include or which versions of Demeter's search for Persephone. Among the former, he includes several references to Semele as the mother of Dionysos, but by no means all, as well as references to Persephone as the mother of Dionysos, a relation that appears in several of the later myths attributed to Orpheus.[189] He is less generous in his inclusion of Demeter material, preferring to see more of the variants attested of this myth as non-Orphic stories. The bias toward Dionysiac material follows from the assumption of the centrality of the story of the dismemberment to Orphic

---

[186] For example, Bernabé rejects as not Orphic Pl. *Soph.* 242c (OF 18 K) and the chorus (1301–1369) from Euripides' *Helen*, which Kern 1922: 116 saw as preserving the traces of an ancient Orphic Demeter poem.

[187] Bernabé 1998a: 172: "El creyente órfico busca la salvación individual, dentro de un marco de referencia en que son puntos centrales: el dualismo alma-cuerpo, la existencia de un pecado antecedente, y el ciclo de trasmigraciones, hasta que el alma consigue unirse con la divinidad." Cp. Bernabé 1997: 39, Bernabé 2002d: 208–209. Note the similarity to Guthrie 1952: 73: "The Orphic doctrines included a belief in original sin, based on a legend about the origin of mankind, in the emphatic separation of soul from body, and in a life hereafter."

[188] Bernabé divides the fragments into categories of actual quotations, indirect fragments (paraphrases of or allusions to Orphic poetry), testimonia (references to particular poems or Orphica in general), and vestigia, "cioè passi che non sono di poesia orfica ma che ne portano chiare tracce" (Bernabé 2000: 70). For further critique of this methodology, see my review of Bernabé 2004 in *BMCR* (Edmonds 2004b).

[189] See Bernabé 1998b for discussion of the various births of Dionysos and his argument that Semele was part of the Orphic texts, although Bernabé's assumption that all the tales can be systematized into a single myth remains problematic.

soteriology, while the rites of Demeter, although more often connected to Orpheus in the ancient testimonies, have little place within the doctrinal definition.[190]

Bernabé also takes the process of fragmentation of the Orphic fragments even further than any of the previous editions of the Orphica, reinforcing the impression that the evidence is divorced from its historical context, pointing clearly and simply to Bernabé's essential nucleus of Orphism. This further fragmentation occurs in two ways, the dislocation of the fragments from the context in which they appear and the breaking up of the fragments into even smaller pieces. Bernabé criticizes Kern for including too much context with each of his fragments; the motivations of the authors who quote the material seem irrelevant to his task of uncovering the Orphic doctrines in the texts they quote or to which they allude.[191] However, as recent studies of the fragments of Presocratic philosophers have shown, the agenda of the citing author, even the most scholastic doxographer, can have a profound impact on the way the fragment is read subsequently.[192] The danger is particularly great for polemical sources, as so many of the sources for Orphic fragments indeed are, from the Neoplatonists to the Christian apologists and beyond.

Bernabé also breaks many of the fragments up into smaller pieces; where Kern had a single fragment (OF 54 K) for Damascius' summary of the Orphic theogony recorded by Hieronymos, Bernabé divides it into nine pieces (*OF* 90, 96, 109x, 114viii, 121i, 677i, 111v, 139i, 120iii B). Different parts of a passage are spread over several fragments, each attesting to a particular idea or element that Bernabé considers important in the understanding of Orphism. Bernabé even omits sections that appear to him irrelevant, such as the allegorization of Dionysos as the vine from the story of his dismemberment. Such athetization ignores the likelihood that the authors chose to tell a tale of dismemberment and rebirth (rather than another tale of Dionysos), and that they chose, e.g., Demeter or Rhea from among the various mothers of Dionysos found in the tradition precisely because of

---

[190] For the testimonies to the connection of Orpheus and Demeter rites, see below, ch. 6, *Poems for the sacred rites*, 'The aggrieved goddess'.

[191] Bernabé 2000: 74: "Non mi interesso di quei frammenti contenuti nei commentari neoplatonici che non offrono nessuna informazione per la ricostruzione del poema orfico. Il Kern è stato troppo generoso, a mio avviso, nella inclusione di questi commenti."

[192] Osborne 1987: 10 points out the importance of context for understanding these biases: "Reading an embedded instead of a fragmented text we read it as a functioning and meaningful system, governed by the preoccupation of an interpreter whose interests we can assess, rather than a set of disjointed parts, detached from the context in which they might mean something. Each interpretation will start from a biased approach, but once this factor is recognised we are in a better position to proceed."

the allegorical significance of both the mother and the dismemberment.[193] Such an organization erases the ancient author's collocation of elements, the elements in the ancient category, in favor of Bernabé's own classification system, based on his idea of an essential nucleus of Orphic doctrines.

While Bernabé's new edition of the Orphic fragments provides scholars in the twenty-first century an unprecedented wealth of material to work with, along with a staggering amount of critical apparatus and bibliographic records for the history of the scholarship for each fragment, the category of Orphic defined by his doctrinal criteria distorts and obscures the classifications made by the ancient sources. The collection of essays Bernabé has compiled with Casadesús knits together Bernabé's vision of Orphism, reinforcing the plan behind the edition of Orphica with nearly 1,600 pages of scholarship in Spanish, cataloging the various types of evidence for Orphism.[194] The monumental work of Bernabé and his team provides a rich resource on which scholars of Greek religion can draw, but the decontextualization distorts the ancient classifications, and the underlying principles of definition represent a return to the models of Guthrie, who in turn was dependent on nineteenth-century ideas of religion.

Some of the recent work on the new pieces of evidence has the potential to move the study of Orphism beyond the old models and to provide a better sense of how the ancient Greeks thought of their own religion. The new discoveries of gold tablets have catalyzed a renewed study of the texts and their religious context, just as the discovery of the tablets from Thurii did in the nineteenth century, while the Derveni papyrus provokes a reconsideration of many long-standing notions about the history of philosophy, religion, and literary criticism in the Classical period. For the Derveni papyrus, the official edition of Kouremenos, Parassoglou, and Tsantsanoglou in 2006 was preceded by the studies of Janko and Betegh, both of which focus heavily upon the parallels with Presocratic philosophy, and the nature of this Presocratic context has been one of the major issues in the study of the Derveni papyrus in recent years.[195] For the gold tablets, Bernabé and Jimenez produced an edition as part of Bernabé's edition of

---

[193] The physical allegory of Dionysos as the vine is athetized from the fragments such as Diod. Sic. 3.62.2–6 (*OF* 59iii B = OF 301 K) and Corn. *ND* 30 (58.6 Lang) (*OF* 59iv B).

[194] Bernabé and Casadesús 2008, which includes essays by a number of scholars within Bernabé's Madrid-based team, as well as by other scholars such as Graf and Brisson, who contribute pieces on their special interests (Eleusis, Neoplatonism, etc.).

[195] Cp. Janko 2001, 2002, 2002–03, 2008, while Betegh 2004 remains the most thorough study. Laks 1997 makes important contributions, and the essays in Tsantsanoglou 1997 (along with Janko 1997)

the Orphica, and their commentary follows the same lines as Bernabé's project overall.[196] By contrast, my own 2004 analysis of the gold tablets, in my study of different myths of the Underworld journey, focuses on the structure of the narrative and the way that the tablet texts manipulated the traditional mythic elements (in contrast to the way those elements appear in texts like Aristophanes' *Frogs* or the myths of Plato). Graf and Johnston 2007 likewise stress the process of *bricolage* by which the tablet texts put together familiar mythic elements, but they also classify the tablets as essentially Bacchic, belonging to a Dionysiac religious context. These studies all provide a richer understanding of these important texts and their contexts, but scholarly consensus on the background has yet to be achieved.[197]

New important work on the context of the older evidence for the Orphica has also advanced the study of Orphism in the twenty-first century. Brisson's series of studies on the Neoplatonists' handling of the Orphica has greatly illuminated these abstruse and difficult texts, providing scholars with a greater understanding of the context in which the majority of the Orphic fragments are preserved. Brisson's work has come as part of a broader revival of interest in the Neoplatonists as philosophers in their own right, not merely witnesses to the bizarre misunderstandings of Plato and Aristotle in late antiquity. New editions and translations of Iamblichus, Proclus, Damascius, and others bear witness to this renewed attention to these fascinating figures, and the social and historical contexts from which they came have been the subject of increasing study. Two recent studies of Clement of Alexandria and the Christian apologetic tradition, by Herrero and Jourdan, have similarly shed light upon the historical (and polemical) context in which the Orphica were preserved in antiquity.[198] While not entirely free from assumptions about the nature

---

represent the best collection of different perspectives. Recently, Brisson and Casadesús have argued that a Stoic or proto-Stoic context is more meaningful for understanding the cosmology and hermeneutics of the Derveni author; cp. Casadesús 2010 and 2011, along with Brisson 2006, 2009, 2011 (cp. Jourdan 2003: xxv), *contra* Betegh 2007. I make my arguments against Stoic influence in Edmonds forthcoming.

[196] Bernabé and Jiménez 2001, revised and translated into English as Bernabé and Jiménez 2008. Pugliese Carratelli 2001 presents a revised version of his 1993 edition of the tablets, which collected all the tablets found to date. Tortorelli Ghidini 2006 further expands this work, although she arranges the tablets geographically (like Graf and Johnston), rather than in the typology of Pugliese Carratelli or that of Zuntz, which was adapted by Riedweg 1998, Bernabé and Jiménez 2008, and Edmonds 2011a.

[197] Edmonds 2011a collects a variety of essays on the gold tablets, including ones by Bernabé, Edmonds, Calame, and Graf, to represent the scope of scholarly discussion on these texts. Cp. also Calame 2006, which builds upon his earlier studies in Calame 1995 and 2002.

[198] Herrero 2010, Jourdan 2010, 2011.

of Orphism conditioned by previous scholarship, all these studies help to situate the evidence for Orphica within the various historical contexts in which it appears. These insights into the historical contexts make the Orphica seem less like an ahistorical collection of fragments, as they appear in Bernabé's edition, embodying a timeless and unchanging set of ideas and doctrines.

Redefining ancient Orphism: Rejecting the Orphic exception

Building upon these recent studies, the evidence Bernabé has compiled in his collection of Orphica must be examined from a new perspective, with attention to the context of each fragment, both the context of the individual author's text in which the fragment is preserved and the broader historical context in which the author is writing. Moreover, the very type of definition used for the category of Orphic must be refined; rather than using the implicit model of doctrinal Christianity to define an Orphism by the appearance of certain doctrines (particularly focused on eschatology and soteriology), the evidence must be analyzed to indicate which sorts of things were labeled with the name of Orpheus in antiquity (and in which periods of antiquity).

One problem with doctrinal Christianity as the model for ancient Orphism is that such a religious organization stands in contrast to the way historians of religion in recent years have come to understand the dynamics of Greek religion.[199] Normal Greek religion does not have prophets who reveal the will of God for the chosen people; normal Greek religion does not have systematic theology or even a general orthodoxy; normal Greek religion does not have a set of sacred scriptures on which the doctrines of the religion are founded. Orphism, however, is repeatedly held up as the exception to the general rule in Greek religion. Greek religion does not have a prophet, except for the Orphics, who have Orpheus; Greek religion does not have a systematic theology, except for the Orphic theology with its complex soteriology and eschatology; Greek religion does not have sacred scriptures, except for the Orphics, who treated the poems of Orpheus as their scriptural authority. This idea of the "Orphic

---

[199] Burkert 1985 remains fundamental, but his study of Orphic and Pythagorean material within the context of Greek religion in Burkert 1982 is the starting point for much of the later work. The studies in Parker 1996, 2005, and 2011 represent the most significant work in reformulating ideas of ancient Greek religion, although Bremmer 1994 continues the work of Burkert in articulating new ideas about Greek religion.

exception" was clearly very important in the nineteenth- and early twentieth-century debates over the origins of Christianity, since it provided a means of connecting Christianity (for good or ill) with the Classical tradition. Even later, it lends a familiar kind of internal coherence to Orphism as a category. The "Orphic exception" thus provides the explanation for the persistence of things labeled Orphic throughout the times and places from which our evidence comes; for, without a set of doctrines and scriptures to hold it together, how could the Orphic religious movement have survived?[200]

However, Greek religion, recognized as a tradition of practices and ideas by those who engaged in the practices and discussed the ideas, survived through the centuries without any such doctrines or scriptures, so these components are not necessary to explain the persistence of the Orphic label. Recent anthropological studies of religion by Whitehouse and others have shown that many cultures have a mode of religious transmission that works quite differently from the doctrinal mode to which modern scholars, raised within societies where the Judaeo-Christian tradition is the norm, are accustomed, an "imagistic" mode.[201] Whereas doctrinal religions have regular forms of ceremony that include recitation of texts that reinforce the memory of particular doctrines and ideas, in imagistic religious contexts:

> Virtually no attempt was made to communicate religious ideas as bodies of doctrine. Revelations were codified in iconic imagery, transmitted primarily through the choreography of collective ritual performances. Religious representations were structured as sets of revelatory images connected by loose (and somewhat fluid) thematic associations, rather than as cohering strings of logically connected dogma.[202]

Such loose thematic associations and collective ritual performances characterize the nature of Greek religion as a whole, and the intense rituals of the *teletai*, with which Orpheus is often associated, as well as the bizarre myths in Orphic poetry would do quite well to provide the iconic imagery

---

[200] As Bernabé 2003: 39 claims, "Une telle persistance s'explique seulement si tous les passages renvoient à un schéma commun, qui a gardé sa cohésion en tout temps. Il doit donc correspondre à un mouvement religieux lui aussi d'une longue durée, d'une longue présence. Quel autre candidat à une aussi longue durée pourrions nous trouver, sinon l'orphisme?"

[201] Burkert 1987: 89–114 discusses such a mode of religiosity in the context of the mystery cults, but this mode is applicable to Greek religion as a whole, even if the mystery cults provide a more focused and intense experience.

[202] Whitehouse 2000: 14. For some attempts to apply Whitehouse's model of imagistic religion to Greek and Roman religions, see the essays in Martin and Pachis 2009.

central to such an imagistic mode of religion. A doctrinal model is thus not needed to explain the existence of the category of Orphic, nor is Bernabé's set of doctrines derived from the debates over the origins of Christianity in the nineteenth century the best way to classify the elements of the ancient Greek religious tradition that should be labeled "Orphic."

CHAPTER THREE

The problem of definition

In this study, I propose a different kind of definition in order to redefine ancient Orphism in a way that more accurately reflects the understanding of the category that the ancient sources themselves had.

A text, a myth, a ritual, may be considered Orphic because it is explicitly so labeled (by its author or by an ancient witness), but also because it is marked as extra-ordinary in the same ways as other things explicitly connected with the name of Orpheus and grouped together with them in the ancient evidence. The more marked something is by claims to extra-ordinary purity or sanctity, by claims to special divine connection or extreme antiquity, or by features of extra-ordinary strangeness, perversity, or alien nature, the more likely it is to be labeled Orphic in the ancient evidence.

This definition is not only polythetic, relying on a loose collection of features, none of which are necessary or sufficient; it also takes into account the nature of "Orphic" as a label that a specific ancient author may or may not choose to apply to a given phenomenon in a particular context. This attention to the labeler as well as the labeled object permits more attention to the historical and polemical contexts in which the labeling occurs. The concept of "cue validity," developed in cognitive psychology to describe the way that people formulate categories, provides a useful way in which to understand the relative importance of the factors involved in any act of labeling, as well as to expand the category of "Orphic" beyond those things explicitly labeled in antiquity with the name of Orpheus.[1] By assessing the validity of cues such as purity, antiquity, and the like, we can indicate elements that would be more likely to have been classified together with other elements that are explicitly labeled. Such a definition also helps explain why certain pieces of evidence, for example, certain

---

[1] For an application of the concept to Roman religion, see King 2003. This method helps to provide an answer to the question posed in Calame 2002 of what is Orphic in the Orphica.

verses of Empedokles, are labeled as Orphic in some sources but not in others.

Cue validity

The definition of an abstract class – and any religious phenomenon must be so classified – can rarely be accomplished with a single defining criterion. A monothetic definition demands a single element that is both necessary and sufficient to classify the thing in question as a member of the class. For example, a pen is a writing implement that uses ink. Any particular pen may have many other features – color, shape, size, material, etc. – but the fact it uses ink is sufficient to define it as a pen. If it does not use ink, then it is not a pen, however much a particular object may be shaped like a pen or in other ways resemble a pen.

Even for the simplest objects, however, the process of definition can be more complicated. Cognitive psychologists have studied the ways in which people classify, noting that there tend to be multiple criteria even for simple classes like fruit or furniture.[2] A polythetic definition is a definition based not on a single necessary and sufficient criterion, but on a set of criteria, none of which is necessary, but of which any might be sufficient. Subjects in studies were more likely to identify an object as a fruit (or a piece of furniture) if it had more of these critical elements, but some elements were more significant than others in determining the classification. Each of these critical elements, called "cues", thus had what could be termed "cue validity", the measure of probability that the cue would trigger a classification.[3] Certain cues, e.g., "sweet" or "having seeds," were more valid than others, e.g., "round" or "bright colored." Note that not all members of the class "fruit" have all of these features, but all these features are among the elements that all members of the class "fruit" may have.

Wittgenstein discusses such classifications and definitions with the metaphor of family resemblances. Looking at a group photo of an extended family, one can tell that the members are related even if all of them do not share a single feature, e.g., a prominent nose, that marks them all. The family nose may be shared by several members of the family, but hair color,

---

[2] See Rosch and Mervis 1975 for details of such experiments.
[3] Rosch and Mervis 1975: 575: "The validity of a cue is defined in terms of its total frequency within a category and its proportional frequency relative to contrasting categories. Mathematically, cue validity has been defined as a conditional probability – specifically, the frequency of a cue being associated with the category in question divided by the total frequency of that cue over all relevant categories."

ear size, cleft chin, or other features may also mark members of the family. Every member of the family has several of these features, even if none of them have all and there is no feature that is shared by every member. The nose may be the most valid marker of the family, appearing in more family members than other features and being unlike the noses found in people outside the family, but hair color too may be a fairly good marker, since it appears in many family members. However, since it also appears in many people who are not family, it is not as valid as the distinctive nose.[4]

The definition of the family can thus be set up as the class of those possessing the valid features, and such a definition can be used to identify people not in the group photo as likely members of the family, based on their possession of such features. Or rather, to switch perspectives, such a definition can be used to collect all the examples that people would be likely to identify as belonging to that family, on the basis of exhibiting the most valid cues. A polythetic definition, then, defines something as a member of the class on the basis of its possession of sufficient (and sufficiently) valid cues.

Beyond Linforth: A new definition

The significance of this procedure becomes apparent when we turn back to the problem of defining what is Orphic. Linforth's study demonstrated clearly that no single defining feature of Orphism can be found among the varied evidence from antiquity, and the new evidence that has come to light since Linforth has not altered that situation. A monothetic definition will not work, therefore, still less a monothetic definition in which the criterion is a complex of related doctrines all of which are imagined to be characteristic of all Orphic things. A polythetic definition is required to make sense of the evidence, the variety of texts and practices labeled Orphic in the ancient sources. The set of criteria identified as valid cues in the body of evidence explicitly labeled with the name of Orpheus can then be used to identify other evidence that, on the basis of the presence of valid cues, would be likely to be classified in the same way. The process of redefining ancient Orphism thus must have two logical steps. First, the evidence already labeled as Orphic, both that considered by Linforth and material that has

---

[4] Wittgenstein 1958: 66–67. Cp. Rosch and Mervis 1975: 575–576: "The principle of family resemblance relationships can be restated in terms of cue validity since the attributes most distributed among members of a category and least distributed among members of contrasting categories are, by definition, the most valid cues to membership in the category in question."

come to light since his study, must be examined for characteristic features, for valid cues that indicate the family resemblances among the various elements, even if there are none that are either necessary or sufficient for all. Second, other evidence, especially materials already grouped together with the explicitly labeled evidence in ancient sources, must be analyzed for the presence of these cues, expanding the set of evidence beyond Linforth's restricted set "sealed with the name of Orpheus."

Evidence may be explicitly labeled as Orphic in several different ways that are dependent upon the nature of the text or practice. A source may name Orpheus as the author of a given text or the founder of a particular ritual, as the Derveni author does for the poem by Orpheus which he is explaining or as Pausanias does for the rites of Hekate on Aigina, which he says the Aiginetans claim were founded by Orpheus.[5] In addition to such other-labeling, a text may also label itself as by Orpheus. Although author's bylines are unknown in the ancient world, certain features within the text can signal the authorship. Orpheus was known as a poet who composed in the most familiar and authoritative meter of the Greek language, dactylic hexameter. Any poet who wished to attribute his poem to the legendary Orpheus, therefore, would have to compose in dactylic hexameter, for no one would accept the claim of a poem to be by Orpheus that was not in hexameters. However, dactylic hexameter (and, for that matter, Greek dactylic hexameter) is not a particularly valid cue for Orphic poetry, simply because too many other authors composed in that meter. The appropriate language and meter for Orpheus was also the appropriate language and meter for Homer – and Hesiod and Empedokles and countless other Greek poets. The absence of Greek hexameters might negate the identification with Orpheus, but hexameters could only be a necessary, not sufficient condition.[6]

Two other features, by contrast, are particularly valid cues within the ancient evidence – an address to Orpheus' pupil Mousaios and the opening seal line "Close the doors of your ears, ye profane." Both of these features are found in multiple texts, and both serve to mark those texts as authored by Orpheus, even if there is no outside witness attesting to their Orphic

---

[5] Paus. 2.30.2 (*OF* 535i B = OT 120 K).

[6] Cp. Rosch and Mervis 1975: 580: "The salient attribute structure of these categories tended to reside, not in criterial features common to all members of the category which distinguished those from all others, but in a large number of attributes true of some, but not all category members." Hexameter, then, is a criterial feature common to a large number of Greek poetic works, but it is not a good criterion (valid cue) for deciding if a particular poem is Orphic. Rather, the most useful criteria are such things as extra-ordinary purity, antiquity, etc., each of which appears in some, but not all of the members of the class.

character. The collection of hymns to various divinities from around the second century CE is known as the *Orphic Hymns* because it is preceded by an address from Orpheus to Mousaios, just as poems in the Theognidea are characterized as by Theognis because of an address to Kyrnos, something that Theognis characterizes as a *sphragis*, a seal that marks the verses as his.[7]

The "close your ears" opening is likewise a *sphragis* line that is adopted by pseudepigraphers of Orphic poetry from the author of the Derveni poem (perhaps as early as fifth century BCE) through the Jewish author of the *Testament of Orpheus* (perhaps second century BCE) to the late *Rhapsodies* (perhaps second century CE) to mark their poems as authentically Orphic.[8] Its function as a marker of "Orphic-ness" has caused confusion among scholars seeking to date various texts attributed to Orpheus, since it is often assumed that, if this one line can be found in earlier sources, the whole text (with perhaps a few interpolations) must go back to the earliest attestations.

But, like the name of Orpheus itself, the earliest attestation of the tag already indicates that it has a long history of indicating that something is connected with Orpheus, that it is already a familiar sign establishing authorship and authority. When Alkibiades starts to tell the truth about his relationship with Socrates, he adapts this line to parody an Orphic poem revealing the secrets of the universe. Already by the time of Plato, "close the doors of your ears" was a valid cue to the Orphic nature of the following discourse because it served as the opening to poems attributed to Orpheus that circulated in the Greek world. Plato's audience would recognize the tag, with its characteristic claim to special privilege that separates the ones having performed the special rites from the uninitiate.

Even if they had not personally heard a poem by Orpheus with such an opening line, the holier-than-thou attitude of the verse might be classifiable as the sort of thing that was characteristic of Orphic poems. So many of the things that they knew of as Orphic conveyed a similar idea of exclusive and superior sanctity that this attitude itself could serve as an indicator of the Orphic nature. Given the appearance of this feature in so much of the evidence, we can designate it as a valid cue to define the text as Orphic. Similarly, a list of other valid cues can be reconstructed from the evidence of the things that do happen to preserve some explicit label that marks

---

[7] Addresses to Mousaios appear in *OA* 7, 308, 858, 1191, 1347; *OH*, proem 1; the *Testament of Orpheus* (Διαθῆκαι) [Justin] *Coh. Gr.* 15.1 (*OF* 372, 377i B = OF 245 K); Clem. Al. *Protr.* 7.74.3 (*OF* 375, 377iii B = OF 246 K); Euseb. *Praep. evang.* 13.12.4 (*OF* 378 B = OF 247 K); *Ephemerides* (Tzetz. *Prol. ad Hes.* 21 Gaisford [*OF* 759i B = OF 271 K]); *Orphic Seismologion* (*OF* 778 B = OF 285 K); cp. fragments of Mousaios in Bernabé 2007a.

[8] Bernabé has collected the uses of the *sphragis* line in *OF* 1 B.

them as Orphic. Such a list derived from the ancient evidence, however, differs considerably from the doctrinal criteria used by modern scholars to define Orphism. The resulting definition of the category of Orphic likewise differs in both form and content.

Emic vs. etic definitions

How then shall we go about defining the category of "Orphic" within Greek religion? Defining any religious phenomenon is a tricky business, particularly susceptible to bias from the definer's own perspective. Indeed, as J. Z. Smith provocatively notes, "Religion is solely the creation of the scholar's study. It is created for the scholar's analytic purposes by his imaginative acts of comparison and generalization."[9] The various ways in which Orphism, as the category of things Orphic, has been imagined by scholars in different periods would certainly seem to illustrate this principle, since the purposes of scholars have been all too apparent in the way that the evidence has been reconstructed.

Here, however, I would like to approach Smith's point in a different way. Smith's "acts of comparison and generalization," I would note, are performed not only by modern scholars, but also by ancient thinkers, whose motivations are often as prejudiced as those of modern scholars. While scholars from the Renaissance onward have formed their definitions from an etic perspective, standing outside of the tradition, ancient thinkers made their own categories, working within the ancient Greek religious tradition to create emic classifications. Such classifications were not arbitrary, based on clearly articulated rules and criteria; they were rather based on the specific purposes of the thinkers at the particular instance of classification – Teiresias and all diviners are quacks and charlatans; the gods convey their messages through omens, so it seems best to the people of Athens to designate certain representatives to watch the horizon for lightning omens; the gods love those who, like Hektor, provide copious animal sacrifices, so we should, as a community, sacrifice this ox; the gods are too pure to appreciate the reek of blood, so those who sacrifice animals attract only evil demons, etc.

The prejudices of ancient thinkers, however, are different from those of modern scholars, and, as such, constitute in and of themselves important data for the understanding of Greek religious ideas. Although it is axiomatic

---

[9] Smith 1982: xi. I explore this issue further in Edmonds 2008a.

that an outsider can never fully grasp an insider perspective, the clearest picture of an emic category arises from the acts of classification made by thinkers within the culture. If "religion" is a construct that varies from the perspective of the one constructing the category and the circumstances of the construction, we, as modern scholars, can reconstruct the religious ideas of the ancient Greeks by paying close attention to the generalizations and comparisons made by ancient thinkers and the circumstances in which they made them, the ancient acts of classification.

Linforth rightly warns of the slippery slope encountered once one goes beyond his single criterion of the name of Orpheus, but attention to ancient (emic) acts of classification, rather than to (etic categories of) doctrines or mythic motifs, provides a more secure methodology. Attention to the particular act is crucial: Who is labeling something as "Orphic" or describing it in terms that categorize it with other things labeled "Orphic"? What is the context for this classification? Even if the state of the evidence from antiquity often makes these questions difficult to answer, we can nevertheless try to determine whether the label is self-applied or applied by another. Again, the label applied to someone else's text or practices may be positive or negative, even if we do not find instances of people labeling their own practices as "Orphic" in a negative sense. This context cannot be taken into account if the evidence is treated as a set of disjoint Orphic fragments, divorced from their context and grouped by theme. The act of classification is performed by a particular classifier in a specific context; it is, therefore, not a disinterested definition, but always in some sense a polemical one, even if the intensity of the polemic can vary wildly from vitriolic condemnations or hyperbolic praise to the mild intention to properly sort out the conflicting testimonies of earlier authors.

Valid cues: Extra-ordinary purity, sanctity, antiquity, and strangeness

One of the cues most likely to indicate the label of Orphic is a special emphasis on maintaining or obtaining purity. Orpheus is known as the originator of many practices of purification, and the people associated with Orpheus and his practices are often depicted as obsessed with purity, usually with a negative valuation rather than a positive. Theseus berates his son, Hippolytos, whose avoidance of sex has aroused the anger of Aphrodite, telling him to follow Orpheus as his lord and maintain a meatless diet, since he pretends to be so pure and holy.[10] Theophrastos' caricature of the superstitious man not only engages in a ridiculously long list of purificatory practices, but goes once a month to the Orpheotelest, the specialist in rituals of Orpheus.[11] However, Orpheus is also the culture hero who taught mortals how to refrain from killing one another and to honor the gods properly.[12] Plato refers to the so-called Ὀρφικοὶ βίοι, the lives of purity led by people in the primeval past, who refrained from human sacrifice and even the killing of animals, sustaining themselves with a pure diet of honey and plants, and such a vegetarian diet is linked in other sources with Orpheus.[13] The rituals founded by Orpheus often involve purification of the individual as an instrument to special and privileged relations with the divine, as Pausanias notes when he credits Orpheus with inventing *katharmoi*, purifications from unholy deeds, as well as *teletai*, rituals that perfect the relations with the gods.[14] However, while such a goal of purification might in some

---

[10] Eur. *Hipp.* 948–957 (*OF* 627 B = OT 213 K): "Do you, then, walk with the gods, as an extraordinary man? Are you so chaste and undefiled by evil? I would not believe your boasting, vilely attributing to the gods such ignorance in thinking. All right then, vaunt and puff yourself up through your vegetarian diet of soulless foods, and taking Orpheus as your leader engage in Bacchic revels, honoring the smoke of many books. For you have been caught now. I sound the warning for all to flee such men as you. For they do their hunting with reverent words while they devise evils." σὺ δὴ θεοῖσιν ὡς περισσὸς ὢν ἀνὴρ ξύνει; σὺ σώφρων καὶ κακῶν ἀκήρατος; οὐκ ἂν πιθοίμην τοῖσι σοῖς κόμποις ἐγὼ θεοῖσι προσθεὶς ἀμαθίαν φρονεῖν κακῶς. ἤδη νυν αὔχει καὶ δι' ἀψύχου βορᾶς σίτοις καπήλευ' Ὀρφέα τ' ἄνακτ' ἔχων βάκχευε πολλῶν γραμμάτων τιμῶν καπνούς· ἐπεί γ' ἐλήφθης. τοὺς δὲ τοιούτους ἐγὼ φεύγειν προφωνῶ πᾶσι· θηρεύουσι γὰρ σεμνοῖς λόγοισιν, αἰσχρὰ μηχανώμενοι.

[11] Theophr. *Char.* 16.11 (*OF* 654 B = OT 207 K) (text and translation from Diggle 2004): "He makes a monthly visit to the Orphic ritualists to take the sacrament, accompanied by his wife (or if she is busy, the nurse) and his children." καὶ τελεσθησόμενος πρὸς τοὺς Ὀρφεοτελεστὰς κατὰ μῆνα πορεύεσθαι μετὰ τῆς γυναικός – ἐὰν δὲ μὴ σχολάζῃ ἡ γυνή, μετὰ τῆς τίτθης – καὶ τῶν παιδίων.

[12] Sext. Emp. *Math.* 2.31–32 (90.10–22 Mau) (*OF* 641i, 642 B = OF 292 K). The cessation of allelophagy is linked to the advent of civilization, humans becoming more than the beasts. Civilization brings justice, and with laws (*thesmoi*) comes agriculture, the other gift of the Thesmophoric goddesses.

[13] Pl. *Leg.* 782c1 (*OF* 625i B = OT 212 K): "Athenian: Indeed, we may see that the practice of men sacrificing one another survives even now among many peoples; and we hear of the opposite practice among others, when they dared not even taste an ox, and the offerings to the gods were not living creatures, but rather meal cakes and grain steeped in honey, and other such pure sacrifices, and they abstained from meat as though it were unholy to eat it or to stain the altars of the gods with blood. Rather, those of us men who then existed lived so-called Orphic lives, partaking entirely of inanimate food and doing the opposite with things animate." ΑΘ. Τὸ δὲ μὴν θύειν ἀνθρώπους ἀλλήλους ἔτι καὶ νῦν παραμένον ὁρῶμεν πολλοῖς· καὶ τοὐναντίον ἀκούομεν ἐν ἄλλοις, ὅτε οὐδὲ βοὸς ἐτόλμων μὲν γεύεσθαι, θύματά τε οὐκ ἦν τοῖς θεοῖσι ζῷα, πέλανοι δὲ καὶ μέλιτι καρποὶ δεδευμένοι καὶ τοιαῦτα ἄλλα ἁγνὰ θύματα, σαρκῶν δ' ἀπείχοντο ὡς οὐχ ὅσιον ὂν ἐσθίειν οὐδὲ τοὺς τῶν θεῶν βωμοὺς αἵματι μιαίνειν, ἀλλὰ Ὀρφικοί τινες λεγόμενοι βίοι ἐγίγνοντο ἡμῶν τοῖς τότε, ἀψύχων μὲν ἐχόμενοι πάντων, ἐμψύχων δὲ τοὐναντίον.

[14] Paus. 9.30.4 (*OF* 546, 551, 1082i B): "Orpheus, it seems to me, surpassed those before him in the beauty of his verse, and he came to a great height of power because he was believed to have discovered rites for the gods and purifications from unholy deeds, cures for diseases and ways of averting divine angers." ὁ δὲ Ὀρφεὺς ἐμοὶ δοκεῖν ὑπερεβάλετο ἐπῶν κόσμῳ τοὺς πρὸ αὐτοῦ καὶ ἐπὶ μέγα ἦλθεν

circumstances seem the very definition of pious intent, the element of excess or the use of alien means tends to mark the Orphic – the Orphic life is unlivable by normal folk, only prigs like Hippolytos or the mythical people of long ago would try to maintain such purity. Hyperbolic purity is therefore one of the most valid cues for the classification of something as Orphic, especially in the earliest evidence from before the Hellenistic period.

In some sources, Orpheus is the inventor of all mystery rites, the culture hero who brings the benefits of closer relations with the gods to mortals. These special rituals, often called *teletai*, designed to perfect the individual's relation to a particular deity, are unusual by their very nature; they provide a positive relation to a degree beyond that obtainable from the normal ritual interactions of mortals and gods in sacrifice and prayer. Specially reverent service to the gods is called *threskeuein*, after the Thracian poet.[15] Certain rituals of which Orpheus is said to be the particular founder have an even greater cachet; they are holier, better able to bring the favor of the gods on those who participate in them. Orpheus is the supreme founder of *teletai*, just as he is the supreme poet. In some sources, his supremacy in these fields is because he is divinely connected himself. Orpheus brings mortals closer to the gods, whether through his rituals or through the stories he tells in his poems, because he himself is closer to the gods. Often, his mother is said to be a Muse, usually Kalliope, and, although he often has a mortal father, at times his paternity is attributed to Apollo himself.[16] Special connection with the gods thus characterizes things Orphic, and extra sanctity is a good cue for the Orphic label. This feature is particularly significant in the early Christian and Neoplatonic uses of Orpheus as the representative of the entire Greek religious tradition, and this emphasis shapes later ideas in the reception tradition.

Another feature of Orpheus adds authority to his rites and songs; he is more ancient than other poets. Orpheus sailed on the Argo, a generation before the Trojan War, so he must be earlier than Homer, who recorded those events after they occurred. Several mythographers even make Orpheus the ancestor of both Homer and Hesiod, and he is often

---

ἰσχύος οἷα πιστευόμενος εὑρηκέναι τελετὰς θεῶν καὶ ἔργων ἀνοσίων καθαρμοὺς νόσων τε ἰάματα καὶ τροπὰς μηνιμάτων θείων.

[15] *Suda* s.v. Θρησκεύει (θ 486, II.728.12–15 Adler) (*OF* 556vii B = OT 37 K). Cp. Ar. *Ran.* 1032 (*OF* 510, 626i B = OT 90 K); Pl. *Prt.* 316de (*OF* 549i, 669iii, 806, 1013 B = OT 92 K).

[16] Cp., e.g., Apollod. *Bibl.* 1.3.2 (*OF* 501, 901ii, 954ii, 987, 1035i = OT 63 K), who notes that his father is said to be Oiagros or Apollo and his mother the Muse Kalliope, while Pausanias 9.30.4 (*OF* 546, 551, 1082i B) claims that some say his mother was a daughter of Pierus rather than Kalliope.

portrayed as the father of Mousaios.[17] One of the earliest testimonies we
have, indeed, attests to the widespread currency of this idea by vigorously
denying it. Herodotus disputes that Homer and Hesiod were any more
ancient than three hundred years before his own time, and, as for the
works of those poets who are said to be even older, Herodotus is decidedly
of the opinion that they are inventions by more recent authors.[18] Once
again, our earliest testimonies about Orpheus appear already looking back
at a long tradition that is lost to the modern scholar. Antiquity is a good
marker of things Orphic, but the most valid cue is not simply antiquity
but more antiquity – Orpheus is not just ancient, but more ancient.

In addition to being purer, holier, or older, things that are labeled Orphic
in the evidence are often marked as somehow stranger than other things.
The ancient sources attest in many ways to the stamp of strangeness that
characterizes the Orphic poems and rites. Often, this characterization is
negative: the Orphic poems are full of horrible stories that offend the
sensibilities not just of later Christian authors but even of Classical authors
like Plato and Isokrates. Once again, this strangeness is comparatively great.
Isokrates indeed claims that while other poets such as Hesiod and Homer
may tell offensive stories about the gods, Orpheus is really extraordinary.[19]
However, such unusual tales may also be viewed in a positive sense, as the
vehicles of sublime truths inexpressible in other ways. The unknown author
of the Derveni papyrus argues that Orpheus' bizarre tales actually compel
the reader to seek for their hidden meaning. In his discussion of an Orphic
poem, preserved on the earliest papyrus surviving from Greece, probably
dating back to the fourth century BCE, the author claims that Orpheus
recounts "sound and lawful things," even though "his poetry is something

---

[17] Both Homer and Hesiod – Hellanikos, *FGrH* 4 F 5b (= fr. 5b Fowler) (*OF* 871i = OT 7 K), 5a
(= fr. 5a Fowler) (*OF* 871ii B); Homer – Pherec. *FGrH* 3 F 167 (= fr. 167 Fowler) (*OF* 871i B =
OT 7 K); Damastes, *FGrH* 5 F 11b (= fr. 11b Fowler) (*OF* 871i B = OT 7 K); Charax, *FGrH* 103 F
62 (*OF* 872, 1134 B = OT 9 K). Plato and other authors frequently cite Orpheus first among a list
of authoritative poets, a list which may derive from Hippias (see above). Cp. Pl. *Ap.* 41a (*OF* 1076
B = OT 138 K); *Ion* 536b (*OF* 973 B = OT 244 K); Alexis fr. 140 KA (*OF* 1018i B = OT 220 K);
Hecat. *FGrH* 264 F 25 (*OF* 48iii, 55, 56, 61, 399i B = OF 95, 96, OF 293, 302 K).
[18] Hdt. 2.53 (*OF* 880i B = OT 10 K).
[19] Isoc. 11 (*Bus.*).39 (*OF* 26ii B = OF 17 K). Pl. *Euthphr.* 5e (*OF* 26i B = OF 17 K) claims to know
stories even more astounding than the bindings and castrations generally attributed to Homer and
Hesiod. In his critique of pagan religion in the beginning of the third century CE, the Christian
writer Origen (*C. Cels.* 7.54 [*OF* 1062ii B]) claims that Orpheus said much worse things than
Homer about the gods, while his slightly later contemporary Diogenes Laertius, in his biographies
of philosophers (1.5 [*OF* 1046ii, 8iii B = OT 125 K]), disputes with those who attribute to Orpheus
the beginning of philosophy: "But I don't know if one ought to call a philosopher one who has
spoken forth such things about the gods, nor what one should term someone who has recklessly
attributed to the gods the entirety of human passions and even obscene acts with the organ of
speech rarely performed by humans."

strange and riddling for people. But Orpheus did not intend to tell them captious riddles but momentous things in riddles."[20] Orpheus reveals more profound truths in his myths than Homer and Hesiod, precisely because of the strangeness of the way he expresses them.

This strangeness often manifests in an attribution to a foreign source. Orpheus himself is often called a Thracian, not a Greek but a member of a half-civilized tribe in the northern border regions of Greece. The myths he tells, and the rituals to which some of these myths pertain, are at times also labeled as foreign, deriving from some non-Greek source. Some of these mythic elements may actually have been foreign, but the name of Orpheus is often used as a way to mark things within the Greek tradition as strange or extraordinary where there is no real indication that they derived from another cultural tradition. The rites of Dionysos, for example, are consistently portrayed in the ancient sources as coming from without, alien intrusions on the normal religion of the Greek city-state, but they were nevertheless part of Greek religion from the Mycenaean period (and perhaps before).[21] So too, myths tell of the introduction of the rites of the Mother of the Gods from various places in Asia Minor, and even the ritual of Demeter that seems most widespread across the city-states of Greece, the Thesmophoria, is usually given a foreign origin, brought from Egypt by some extraordinary religious figure like Melampous or Orpheus.[22] Even if some of these elements might, historically speaking, actually have first been introduced into the Greek tradition from other sources (e.g., Phrygian, Egyptian, Thracian), the choice to refer to that foreign origin or to associate these elements with Orpheus is in itself a sign that their alien and extraordinary nature is being emphasized.[23]

[20] col. 7.2 (*OF* 2i B), 4–7 (*OF* 669i B) (tr. Betegh). Later Plut. fr. 157 Sandbach = Euseb. *Praep. evang.* 3.1.1 (*OF* 671 B) credits Orpheus with the same profundity.

[21] Contrast Rohde 1925. Detienne (e.g., 1979 and 1986) has developed the idea of Dionysos as a structural outsider by nature, and Versnel 1990: 96–205 explores the idea in interesting ways; for a recent overview, see Isler-Kerényi 2007: 252–254. "Normal" religion is of course a controversial term, since what seems normal may vary from age to age, from speaker to speaker, and from situation to situation. See Edmonds 2008a for more discussion of the categories of "normal" and "abnormal" religion.

[22] On the Thesmophoria, see Versnel 1993: 229–288. As Parker 1995: 502 notes, "The mythological mind often treats what is abnormal as being literally 'alien', of foreign origin. So too does the scholarly mind, and exotic origins for these exotic phenomena have been sought and found: the tradition goes back to Herodotus, who in the long text of 2.81 says that the 'so-called Orphic and Bacchic mysteries' are in reality 'Pythagorean and Egyptian'."

[23] Parker 1995: 502 again puts it well: "The case for particular borrowings has to be considered, and is occasionally good, but 'influence' or 'borrowing' can never provide more than a partial explanation for cultural change. Foreign thought is not picked up irresistibly, like a foreign disease; and the decision to take up this or that idea always requires an explanation. In fact, all that can plausibly

These cues have differing validity at different periods, as the motivations for applying the label of "Orphic" shift. Extraordinary purity going beyond normal practice seems a more valid indicator in the early evidence, whereas the Christian apologists and Neoplatonists are more concerned about the antiquity (and foreign origins) of Orpheus and his works. All of these cues, of course – strangeness, antiquity, sanctity, purity – can be found as characteristics of other religious phenomena in the Greek religious tradition; none of them is sufficient to classify something as Orphic. The greater the measure of any of these, however, the greater the likelihood that it will be labeled Orphic in the ancient sources, especially if the elements are not simply descriptive but comparative – stranger, older, holier, purer. The label of Orphic is most often employed in the context of a comparison, implicit or explicit, with more normal religion. Although the idea of what "normal" religion might be shifts from period to period (and indeed from source to source), evidence from what Bremmer calls the "messy margins" helps us to understand what could be normal in a religious system that had no real orthopraxy, much less orthodoxy.[24]

Consequences of the new definition

One consequence of a polythetic, rather than monothetic, definition appears when we consider the reconstruction of fragmentary evidence – and all of the evidence for Orphica is indeed fragmentary. With a monothetic definition, if certain traits (α, β, γ) are the criteria for determining whether something is Orphic, then if a fragmentary piece of evidence includes α and β then one could probably reconstruct the fragment with γ as well. If, on the other hand, α, β, and γ are only elements in the polythetic definition, the presence of any of which may indicate that the thing was considered Orphic, then the presence of α or β or even both does not mean that γ should be present.

For example, although the fragmentary Derveni papyrus contains no reference to the supposedly crucial doctrines of original sin, salvation through purification, and the cycle of reincarnations, many scholars have assumed that, because it has other features of Orphism, such as the name of Orpheus and certain mythological motifs, these missing features can be presumed. The poem must be an abbreviation of a longer myth with all those features,

be claimed is that particular elements in Orphism may have been borrowed; the synthesis is Greek, and must be explained in terms of Greek society."
[24] Bremmer 2010.

for, as Parker asks, "Could a poem abandon metempsychosis and vegetarianism and Titanic guilt and still be 'Orphic'?"[25] The Derveni author discusses none of these ideas in what remains of his commentary, yet scholars have imagined that these essential features must therefore have been found in the missing pieces. This presumption of a complete text that provides a doctrinal basis for Orphism is linked also to the idea that the Orphics were somehow the exception in Greek religion in having sacred scriptures. Rather than positing such an Orphic exception and hypothetical texts that fill this need for doctrinal scriptures, a polythetic definition identifies the poem in the Derveni papyrus as Orphic, not simply because it is attributed to Orpheus, but because of the ways in which the text marks itself as a special revelation of divine knowledge and as an extra-ordinary telling of a traditional cosmogonic tale. Moreover, abandoning the idea of a complete and coherent scriptural text means that the inconsistencies West identifies in the evidence for the Orphic poems need not be accounted for by a complex and fantastic stemma, but can simply be explained as the product of different Orphic authors telling different stories at different times.

A polythetic definition also resolves many of the controversies that have arisen about the nature of the Derveni author who speaks about the Orphic poem on the papyrus. Scholars have been frustrated in trying to figure out how the Derveni author's physical ideas relate to presumed Orphic eschatological and soteriological doctrines or even to glean a coherent and systematic set of ideas from the treatise. Rather than concluding that the Derveni author is an anti-Orphic, a heretical Orphic, or even an incompetent fool, I argue in Chapter 4 that he is Orphic simply by virtue of the fact that he cites the authority of Orpheus, as well as by the way in which he claims extra-ordinary wisdom and understanding. His lack of systematic doctrine is easily understood when his treatise is seen, not as supplying religious doctrines to the faithful, but as an advertisement of his skills as a religious specialist of the sort whom Plato sneers at for their hubbub of books by Orpheus. The Derveni author is making an *epideixis* of his exegesis, showing off his skills as an interpreter and promising potential clients the benefits of his special wisdom in their ritual experiences.

Attending to the ancient acts of classification also provides a way to understand how and why the label Orphic was attached to material that is not sealed by its author with the name of Orpheus. A Late Antique alabaster bowl, inscribed with four verses, provides evidence for the way non-Orphic texts can come into the Orphic orbit. (See Figure 1.) Three

---

[25] Parker 1995: 503.

Figure 1 Alabaster bowl (3rd–6th century CE), with details of the inscriptions. Images from a plaster cast in the Akademisches Kunstmuseum, Universität Bonn, courtesy of Ms. Jutta Schubert.

of the verses come from a hymn to the Sun that Macrobius quotes as by
Orpheus, but the last verse comes from Euripides' *Melanippe*, a line that
describes "how the heaven and earth were once a single form."[26] The line
is cited in Diodorus Siculus, who attributes the idea to Anaxagoras, but
the Byzantine Tzetzes associates the idea not only with Anaxagoras, but
also with Empedokles, Hesiod and Orpheus.[27] Euripides' poetic version
of some strange and new cosmological ideas in his time becomes grouped
with the poetry of Orpheus – physically on the bowl, more abstractly in
Tzetzes and elsewhere. This ancient act of classification makes Orphic the
Euripidean verse and the idea of heaven and earth as one form, but this
"Orphic-ness" is not transferable to other contexts – the idea of heaven
and earth as one form was not marked as Orphic in Euripides and might
not be recognized as such were it to appear in some other text.[28]

Likewise, verses of Empedokles sometimes appear in later sources as
verses of Orpheus, not because Empedokles was somehow recognized as
a genuine promoter of authentic Orphic doctrine, but rather because the
strangeness of the ideas fit with the category that source had of Orphica.
Aelian tells us that Empedokles claims that the noblest of people are
reincarnated among beasts as lions or as laurels among trees, but a scholiast
to the rhetorician Aphthonios' exercise on Daphne the laurel claims that
the lines are from the verses of Orpheus, the son of Oiagros. The idea of
reincarnation is unusual enough among the testimonies from the ancient
world that it could be lumped in with the ideas of Orpheus, despite the fact
that Empedokles' name is firmly attached to the verses in other sources.[29]
The conflation of Empedokles and Orpheus appears also in Tertullian, who
paraphrases some "verses of Orpheus or Empedokles" regarding blood as

---

[26] Eur. *Melanippe* fr. 484 K (= fr. 5 J.-V.L.) (*OF* 66i B): ὡς οὐρανός τε γαῖα τ᾽ ἦν μορφὴ μία; Macrob.
Sat. 1.23.22. For a description of the bowl, see Delbrueck and Vollgraff 1934, who date it somewhere
between the third and sixth century CE. Bernabé collects all the inscriptions as *OF* 66iii B.

[27] Diod. Sic. 1.7.7; Tzetz. *Exeg. Il.* 41.21 Hermann (*OF* 66ii B). Dion. Hal. *Rhet.* 8.10.6, 9.11.15 also
links the verse with Anaxagoras: see Jouan and Van Looy 2000 *ad loc.*

[28] Delbrueck and Vollgraff 1934: 134–135 imagine that the one form must be the Orphic egg, which
splits to make heaven and earth, but there is little basis for such a conclusion. While Athenagoras
18.3 (*OF* 75ii, 879iii, 1020ii, 1141iii B = OF 57 K) has the egg produce earth and heaven, other
versions have the egg produce Phanes. Even Damascius' account of the Hieronyman theogony,
which corresponds largely with Athenagoras' version, does not have heaven and earth produced by
the split (Dam. *De princ.* 123–124 [III.159.17–164.9 Westerink = 1.316–319 Ruelle] [*OF* 69, 75i, 76i,
77, 78, 79i, 80i, 86, 109x, 111vi, 1138, etc. B = OF 54, 60 K]).

[29] Ael. *NA* 12.7.36 = Emp. 31 B 127 DK (fr. 131 Wright): ἐν θήρεσσι λέοντες ὀρειλεχέες χαμαιευναι
| γίγνονται, δάφναι δ᾽ ἐνὶ δένδρεσιν ἠυκόμοισιν. Hermann 1805: 511 #32 quotes a scholiast on
Aphthonios' *Progymnasmata*: Ὀρφεὺς ὁ παῖς Οιάγρου που φησὶν ἐν λόγοις· ἐν θήρεσσι λέοντες
ὀρειλεχέες χαμαιευναι | γίγνονται, δάφναι δ᾽ ἐνὶ δένδρεσιν ἠυκόμοισιν. Empedokles' interest in
laurels is attested in another fragment (31 B 140 DK [fr. 127 Wright]), which Plut. *Quaest. conv.*
3.1.2 646d cites in his discussion of laurels: δάφνης φύλλων ἄπο πάμπαν ἔχεσθαι.

the principle of mind.[30] The peculiarity of the idea, its distance from the mainstream (as the labeler perceives it), means that it can be classified as Orphic, coming from the poetry of Orpheus, identified by the name of Orpheus.

On the other hand, even the name of Orpheus is not a perfectly valid cue for the classification, since there are some things sealed with the name of Orpheus that cannot be considered either exceptional or characteristic of other Orphic things. For example, Clement of Alexandria quotes Orpheus as saying that nothing is more shameless than a woman, but this idea is far from unique in Greek thought. Indeed, Clement is using it as an example of the tendency to plagiarism among the Greek authors.[31] The idea can no more be considered characteristic of Orphism than it can of the Homeric poems.

The gold lamellae that have been labeled as Orphic by modern scholars since their discovery in the nineteenth century provide another test of the different ways of defining what is Orphic. These tablets, with their hexameter verses, mention Orpheus nowhere, causing Linforth to refuse to admit them in his survey of the evidence. Moreover, the fact that they are mentioned nowhere in the literary record means that we have no evidence of how these texts were classified by the ancients. Nevertheless, these texts exhibit, in the self-identifications of the deceased in the tablets, the kind of claims to extra-ordinary purity and divine connection that is characteristic of other evidence sealed with the name of Orpheus. "Pure I come from the pure," boasts the woman at Thurii; "For I claim that I come of your blessed race." "I am the child of Earth and starry Heaven," proclaims the woman from the necropolis at Hipponion, just like many others from Crete, Thessaly, and other parts of southern Italy. While we have no direct

---

[30] Tert. *De anim.* 15.5: *ut et ille uersus Orphei uel Empedoclis: namque homini sanguis circumcordialis est sensus.* Cp. Emp. 31 B 105.3 DK (fr. 94 Wright): αἷμα γὰρ ἀνθρώποις περικάρδιόν ἐστι νόημα, which appears within a set of hexameters in Stobaeus, quoting from Porphyry, who is citing Empedokles (*de Styge ap.* Stob. *Ecl.* 1.49.53 [424.14 Wachsmuth]). Curiously, Arist. *De an.* A2 405b5 attributes this idea to Kritias, and Philoponus, in his commentary on the passage, quotes this line as one of Kritias' (Kritias, 88 B 8 DK = Joannes Philoponus, *In Aristotelis libros de anima commentaria* 15.9.21).

[31] Clem. Al. *Strom.* 6.2.5.3 (*OF* 846 B = OF 234 K): "Making use of the testimonies of some of the most customary and well-reputed men among the Greeks, I have exposed their plagiarizing nature. Making use of examples from various periods, I shall turn to the following. Orpheus, then, having composed the line: 'For nothing else is more shameless and horrible than woman,' Homer plainly says: 'Since nothing else is more dreadful and shameless than a woman'." ὀλίγοις δὲ τῶν καθωμιλημένων καὶ παρὰ τοῖς Ἕλλησιν εὐδοκίμων ἀνδρῶν χρησάμενος μαρτυρίοις, τὸ κλεπτικὸν διελέγξας εἶδος αὐτῶν, ἀδιαφόρως τοῖς χρόνοις καταχρώμενος, ἐπὶ τὰ ἑξῆς τρέψομαι. Ὀρφέως τοίνυν ποιήσαντος· ὡς οὐ κύντερον ἦν καὶ ῥίγιον ἄλλο γυναικός, Ὅμηρος ἄντικρυς λέγει· ὡς οὐκ αἰνότερον καὶ κύντερον ἄλλο γυναικός.

evidence, such claims to purity and special relations with the gods suggest that they, like Euripides' Hippolytos who made similar claims to purity and special connections, would have been associated with Orpheus. As West notes, "We have no warrant for calling the gold leaves themselves Orphic, as has so often been done. But certainly their owners were the sort of people who would have been attracted to Orphic revelations and mystery cults."[32]

This kind of modern act of categorization, of generalization, is precisely parallel to the kind of classificatory move that ancient audiences might well have made regarding the gold tablets. We may be more specific, however, in analyzing exactly why we might classify the owners as "the sort of people," since the tablets are characterized by the appeal to special connection with the gods and strong emphasis on (ritual) purity that are two of the strongest cues for the Orphic label – in addition to being in the hexameters that are characteristic of all Orphic verses.[33]

For the last century, however, the tablets have been regarded as Orphic for doctrinal reasons. The presence of lightning and the penalty for unjust deeds on some tablets and the claim to be the child of Earth and starry Heaven on others caused Comparetti, in 1882, to define them as Orphic on the basis of an imagined doctrine of original sin, inherited by mankind from the Titans' murder of Dionysos Zagreus. As I have shown in earlier studies, such a doctrine (and indeed the whole connection of the dismemberment of Dionysos with anthropogony and human guilt) is a fabrication of the nineteenth century and scholars' continued reliance on this idea obscures other explanations, not just of the gold tablets, but of many other texts as well.[34]

Attention to ancient acts of classification produces some unexpected differences from modern classifications, since what the ancients found extra-ordinary does not always correspond with modern expectations. For example, many scholars have assumed that the idea of differentiated lots for the dead in the afterlife, as found for example in Pindar's *Second Olympian*, was Orphic, but a survey of the evidence shows that the idea is present throughout Greek literature and religion and that the idea is never attributed to Orpheus. Orpheus may be credited with rites that improve your chances for a better lot in the afterlife, but there were many other ways to influence one's afterlife – from heroic action to moral behavior – and, despite the influence of the Homeric epic ideal that only immortal glory

---

[32] West 1983: 26.
[33] See further my analysis of the self-identifications in the tablets in Edmonds 2004a.
[34] Cp. Edmonds 1999, 2008b.

in poetic form could provide a meaningful existence after death, the basic assumption of a differentiated afterlife appears in a wide range of sources. If the ancient Greeks did not, in fact, think that a differentiated afterlife was an abnormal, marginal idea, then the idea should not fall within our category of Orphic, especially if there is no evidence that the concept was ever linked to the name of Orpheus.

If, on the contrary, they did think that reincarnation was a peculiar idea, we can examine whether, when, and how it was linked with Orpheus or with the sort of people who were linked with Orpheus, such as the Pythagoreans who were said to have written Orphica. Only a limited set of sources refer to the idea of reincarnation, and the idea is always marked as extra-ordinary, even in the sources in which it is portrayed positively. Differentiated afterlife is ordinary; reincarnation is extra-ordinary and therefore, at times, can be labeled Orphic, just as certain other unusual ideas about the nature of the soul are sometimes associated with Orpheus. Attending to the ways ideas are classified in the ancient evidence, rather than simply trying to trace a stemma of a particular idea, doctrine, or mythic motif, provides a clearer picture of how the ancient Greeks thought about issues such as life after death and removes the need for clumsy, undocumentable hypotheses about, for example, the creeping influence of Orphic ideas of afterlife on mainstream Greek religion.

Conclusion: Redefining ancient Orphism

The name of Orpheus is famous; Orpheus is known as the poet of the mysteries and the author of texts. The rites founded by Orpheus are extra-ordinary, providing special connection and favor with the gods, while his poems are famous texts, important texts, enigmatic and disturbing texts. But what kind of texts are these? What sort of rituals? In the following chapters, I examine the texts attributed to Orpheus and the rites associated with his name, employing my definition of "Orphic" to gain a clearer understanding of the way the ancient Greeks used the label to create a category of things Orphic. This category of extra-ordinary religion in turn helps to throw into relief the shifting boundaries of the category of ordinary religion in the ancient Greek world. The rest of this study is divided into two main sections, the first relating to Orphic texts and the second to Orphic doctrines and practices.

To understand Orpheus the author, we must examine not only the content of the poems attributed to the mythical poet, but also the form in which these poems were collected and preserved, as well as the ways these texts were understood. Modern scholars have often read the evidence for Orphic texts through the lens of the sacred scriptures of the Judaeo-Christian religious traditions most familiar to us. Plato refers to the texts circulating under the name of Orpheus as a "hubbub of books," while his near contemporary Euripides mentions "the smoke of many books," so many modern scholars have assumed an essential link between Orphica and the written text of books. Because the content of the books involves the gods, some modern scholars have gone further and imagined these books to be holy books, the Bible of the Orphics, the scriptures of Orphic religion. "The Orphic," claims Guthrie, "did nothing unless there was a warrant for it in his books."[35] These religious books of Orpheus would thus be a guide to proper action, as well as a revelation of divine truth, the understanding of which was essential to salvation.

A careful re-examination of the evidence, however, suggests that the texts attributed to Orpheus are not as anomalous in Greek religion or Greek society as this scriptural model would suggest. In Chapter 4, I examine the evidence from the Classical period for Orphic texts, showing that the emphasis on the book form of the Orphic texts reflects the anxieties about the newly expanding use of the technology of writing in this period. Orphic texts are categorized with other scientific, religious, medical, and philosophical texts; they are all new age forms of technology, making unfamiliar claims to authority, in a society still suspicious of their use. Specialists like the Derveni author use this new technology of the written book to display their knowledge and expertise, just as the Hippocratic doctors, the sophists and philosophers, and even poets like Euripides all do. Orphic texts only become treated like scriptural authority when the Neoplatonists turn to them seeking an alternative to the Christian scriptural tradition, a textual authority even older than the books of Moses that nevertheless affirms the ideas of Plato (or at least Plato's ideas as understood by the Neoplatonists).

By contrast, the earlier evidence for Orphic texts suggests that Orpheus is best known for his hymns, poetry created for performance at a ritual occasion, rather than a liturgical text providing instructions for ritual or a theological text explaining the underlying doctrines. In Chapter 5, I analyze the evidence for the Rhapsodic collection, suggesting that it was more likely a loose collection of previous material from various periods than a comprehensive account of the creation of the world down to the present day. In its form, it was more like the *Sibylline Oracles* than Hesiod's *Theogony* – or

---

[35] Guthrie 1952: 202.

even the Bible. While the collection was undoubtedly modeled upon the twenty-four rhapsodies stitched together for each epic of Homer, the *Orphic Rhapsodies* are more likely a later product of *bricolage*, created in the Roman empire as the Hellenic tradition struggled to articulate its religious tradition in the face of emerging Christianity.

The content of the poems attributed to Orpheus thus covered a wider range than the pieces of a cosmogonic saga that is often imagined. In addition to a variety of hymns to individual gods, many of the poems bearing the name of Orpheus relate to rites of Demeter and Dionysos in various aspects, the aggrieved and mourning goddess or the threatened infant god. Although the Orphic tales of Dionysos have received much, perhaps even undue, attention, the myths of Demeter and Persephone linked with Orpheus' name have been neglected in the scholarship. In the ancient evidence, however, Orpheus' name is linked more often with the goddesses than with Dionysos, so this analysis of the evidence restores an important aspect of the ancient ideas of what should be called "Orphic."

Far from being the exceptional sacred scriptures of the Orphic Bible, then, the texts attributed to Orpheus have a much less anomalous status in Greek religion. To be sure, they often pertain to the special mystery rites of Demeter and Dionysos, and they claim the authority of the ancient poet who has special connections to the gods. Nevertheless, the hubbub of books attributed to Orpheus illuminates the contestive atmosphere of Greek religion, where the name of Orpheus is used to validate a variety of special claims to religious authority in a range of times and places in the Greek tradition.

In Part III, I turn to the ritual practices linked with the name of Orpheus, along with the ideas of purity and afterlife salvation that have been derived from them. In antiquity, Orpheus is also known as the founder of rituals and other practices that bring mortals closer to the gods. The association of Orpheus with practices of purification has, however, often been misunderstood by modern scholars, who have interpreted the evidence using models tainted with Christian ideas of sin and salvation. The rituals labeled with the name of Orpheus, whether purificatory practices or the special rites known as *teletai* (often misleadingly translated as "initiations"), provide a special connection with the divine, an extra-ordinary way of gaining the god's favor. Those engaging in such rites should likewise not be imagined as adherents of a religious sect, but rather as the clientele of the ritual experts who make use of the authority of Orpheus' name to advertise their expert services. No community of Orphics ever existed, nor is there any indication that those who made use of the services of a ritual expert for

Orphic rituals felt themselves united by a common set of beliefs, practices, or secret doctrines. In Chapter 7, I examine the evidence for rites that are labeled Orphic, placing them within the larger context of purificatory rites and *teletai* in the Greek religious tradition.

One of the things most often imagined by modern scholars to distinguish Orphism from normal Greek religion is a belief in a lively afterlife, featuring morally tinged rewards and punishments for the dead in contrast to the uniformly shadowy world of the dead in Homeric epic. Orphic rituals, it is thought, provide the means to salvation in the afterlife for the elect, while the uninitiated suffer torments because of their unexpiated guilt. A closer examination of the evidence in context, however, reveals that the idea of the lively afterlife is more the norm than the exception in the evidence for Greek views of life after death. Homeric epic provides a peculiarly epic view that only epic glory provides any kind of meaningful afterlife, but this idea, while remaining influential throughout all periods of Greek history, is in tension with the idea that appears in funerary practices and literary depictions of the dead who retain awareness of the world of the living and seek honor from and bestow favor or ill-will upon the living. The lot of the dead in the afterlife reflects their lot in life; if they had the favor of the gods, they remain so blessed, while if the gods hated them in life, their torments continue after death. Some ideas of life after death, such as reincarnation, are marked as extra-ordinary and often labeled with the name of Orpheus, but this idea of a lively afterlife is not itself marked as extra-ordinary, nor is it attributed to Orpheus in particular. To be sure, the *teletai* of Orpheus can win favor with the gods that will continue in the afterlife, and Orpheotelests who could not guarantee material manifestations of the gods' favor in this life seem to have promised compensatory delights in the next. However, belief in Orphic ideas or adherence to Orphic practices was not necessary for salvation; undergoing a ritual attributed to Orpheus was merely an extra-ordinary way to gain the favor of the gods, quicker and easier than a life of heroic virtue, cheaper and more effective than Homeric hecatombs or golden statues. Chapter 8 explores the contrast between the Homeric and the normal ideas of afterlife, as well as examining the smaller set of ideas marked as extra-ordinary or Orphic. This study provides a clearer understanding of what the Greeks normally thought about the nature of death and the existence thereafter, as well as the ideas that seemed bizarre to them.

The final chapter in Part III returns to the evidence that has been used in modern scholarship to fabricate the idea of the Zagreus myth at the heart of Orphism. According to this idea, all the Orphic practices and myths depend upon this central tale of the creation of mankind from the ashes of the Titans who dismembered Dionysos Zagreus. The life of man, according to this imagined Orphic doctrine, is a perpetual penance for this primordial crime, and Orphic religion is the belief in this sin-stained human nature and the practices of purification, carried out if need be through multiple reincarnations, that provide escape from the guilt. This definition of Orphism, however, is born from nineteenth-century debates over the origins of Christianity and relies upon distortions of the evidence from antiquity. Upon closer examination, the evidence shows the artificial nature of the Zagreus myth and, when properly interpreted and placed in its ancient contexts, illumines the nature of ideas of purification and inherited guilt within Greek religion, as well as casting light upon the Platonic philosophical tradition in which much of the evidence appears. In this chapter, I review the pieces of evidence used by scholars from Comparetti to Bernabé to fabricate the Zagreus myth and show where these threads fit within the larger tapestry of Greek religion.

This study of the category of Orphic within ancient Greek religion thus aims to illuminate not simply the marginal practices and ideas that were labeled Orphic in the ancient sources, but also ancient Greek religion in general, the varying currents of ideas and practices in different times and places that nevertheless were imagined by the Greeks as their tradition. This redefinition of Orphism according to the patterns of classification made by the ancient sources helps to clear away the distortions that have arisen as the name of Orpheus has been invoked and re-invoked over the centuries. The Neoplatonic crystallization of the texts and rites of Orpheus as the representative of the Greek religious tradition, just at the point when that tradition was being overwhelmed, created an Orphism that served as the basis for further reinterpretation from Late Antiquity to the modern era, while the disputes over the origins of Christianity that raged in the nineteenth and twentieth centuries created yet another new Orphism, even further from the category that was familiar to those ancient sources that considered the Greek religious tradition to be their own. Even if no modern, etic study can entirely recreate the emic definition, this study's redefinition of Orphism based on the ancient acts of classification should provide a clearer understanding of the ancient Greek category of things that could be labeled "Orphic."

PART II

Orphic scriptures or the vaporings of many books?

CHAPTER FOUR

Orphic textuality
A hubbub of books

Taking Orpheus as your leader, go engage in Bacchic revels, honoring the vaporings of many books.[1]

When Euripides' Theseus accuses his son Hippolytos of raping his step-mother, he depicts him as a hypocrite, someone who pretends to be extra-ordinarily holy in order to cover up his perversity and wickedness. Theseus' characterization of the kind of person who would acknowledge the author-ity of Orpheus includes not just an association with ecstatic and mystic ritual, but also a special connection with texts; such people hold books and their contents in high honor. Scholars of Orphism in the past century have often misunderstood this connection, however, ignoring the wider social and historical context in which Euripides frames Theseus' charge and postulating a special kind of Orphic attitude toward written works – Orphism as textual orientation. I argue that this supposed textual orienta-tion distorts the evidence for the multiple ways in which Orphic texts were regarded and their complex relations with ritual practice.

Orphic texts have often been held up as the exception to the general rule that there are no sacred scriptures in Greek religion, but a close examination of the ways in which Orphic texts are characterized in the evidence shows that Orphic texts were not regarded in an essentially different way than other texts that made claims to insights into the nature of the gods and the cosmos. Nor are the Orphic texts characterized by special Orphic myths, exclusive to the Orphica, that have special doctrinal significance to the ini-tiate. On the contrary, the Orphic texts make use of the same mythological material available to all the *bricoleurs* working in the Greek mythological tradition, and the meanings of those myths shift from version to version, just as in the rest of the mythological tradition, without preserving some core of Orphic doctrine that identifies the myths as Orphic.

---

[1] Eur. *Hipp.* 953–954 (*OF* 627B = OT 213 K): Ὀρφέα τ' ἄνακτ' ἔχων βάκχευε πολλῶν γραμμάτων τιμῶν καπνούς.

Lingering traces of the outdated idea of Orphic scriptures has led to a privileging of cosmogonic themes in the modern scholarship, along with the assumption that Orphic cosmologies provide a doctrinal underpinning for ritual practice. Although cosmogonic and cosmological themes are certainly present in some Orphic texts, the whole range of mythic themes in the Orphica cannot be subordinated to a cosmogonic frame. Cosmogony served as one medium for innovative thinkers to express cosmological and theological ideas under the name of Orpheus, but other themes, such as those relating to the experiences of Demeter and Dionysos, provided different ways of expressing religious ideas. The relation, if any, of these mythic texts to ritual differed from text to text and cannot be confined to a single model, whether a Christianocentric scriptural one or even a liturgical model better suited to the ancient world. A survey of the various mythic themes present in the Orphica reveals that the name of Orpheus was often attached to tales relating to goddesses such as Demeter and Persephone or to Rhea, Kybele, and the Mother of the Gods, along with their attendant divinities, variously called Kouretes, Korybantes, Kabeiroi, and the like. Myths of Dionysos, or similar Bacchic figures, and their experiences can also be found, but, given the prevalence of Demeter material, the evidence does not support the identification of Orphica with Bacchic myths and rites.

In this chapter, I examine the ideas of Orphic textual orientation and place the characterizations of the Orphic smoke of many books in their proper historical context, the contests for discursive authority in the period of transition from orality to literacy. In the following chapter, I explore the interrelations of the Orphic texts and the rituals attributed to Orpheus, and I look at the range of evidence for Orphic texts that actually remains. I propose that the *Orphic Rhapsodies*, the form of the Orphica best known in the Imperial Roman and later periods, were not a single, comprehensive theogony, but rather a collection of previous Orphic texts of diverse subject matter and form. In Chapter 6, I then explore the traces of some of these themes and forms, surveying the evidence for cosmological Orphica and poems related to Demeter and Dionysos, as well as other minor themes. The variety of Orphic texts, this vaporings of many books, cannot be constrained in the model of Orphic scriptures without stifling some of the fascinating voices raised in the hubbub of books that were the ancient Orphica.

Orphic textuality

Contrary to the assumption in prior scholarship, a focus on texts is not a particularly valid cue for the label of "Orphic" across the range of time from which the evidence comes. The evidence for Orphica is not marked by a special reliance on texts, except in the trivial sense that all of the works of Orpheus of which we have evidence are texts, the hexameter poems composed in various periods under the famous name of Orpheus. Yet even this point ignores the many references to rituals founded by Orpheus – the other type of Orphica – that have no mention whatsoever of texts. The evidence of Pausanias is often used to mark the essentially textual nature of Orphic materials. However, when Pausanias claims, referring to the idea that Demeter cannot be credited with the discovery of beans, that "whoever has seen the *telete* at Eleusis or has read what are called the Orphica knows what I am saying," he is not making a distinction between the ritual nature of Eleusis and the textual nature of Orphism.[2] On the contrary, he is claiming that the texts (falsely) circulating under the name of Orpheus happen to agree in this respect with an idea that is also present in the Eleusinian Mysteries. Orphic texts are not thereby marked as a special type of text that is functionally equivalent to ritual performance, text that provides a special kind of doctrinal instruction and authority that other mythic texts never provide.[3]

The idea of a peculiar Orphic textual orientation is actually founded on very few pieces of evidence and derives, for the most part, from outdated models of the role of texts in religion. Although it is commonly agreed that Greek religion in general does not have sacred texts, the references to texts by Orpheus have been taken as the exception, since they are often mentioned in conjunction with religious rituals. Such an "Orphic exception" distorts the relation between the texts and religious practices, simplifying it into a model grounded in modern paradigms rather than the ancient context.

In addition to the passage from Euripides cited above, the other piece of evidence is the famous passage in Plato that mentions a hubbub of books by Orpheus and Mousaios that characterizes the activities of certain religious practitioners in Socrates' Athens. It is no coincidence that both these passages reflect the social and historical conditions of Classical Athens, and they must be understood in that context, not ripped out and used to generalize about Orphism across the whole range of time and space that our evidence covers. In the *Republic*, Socrates' interlocutors Glaucon and

---

[2] Paus. 1.37.4 (*OF* 649i B = OT 219 K): ὅστις δὲ ἤδη τελετὴν Ἐλευσῖνι εἶδεν ἢ τὰ καλούμενα Ὀρφικὰ ἐπελέξατο, οἶδεν ὃ λέγω.

[3] *Contra*, e.g., Rangos 2007: 42: "Pausanias implies that the reasons for the prohibition were provided by the *ritual* of Eleusinian Mysteries and the *text* of Orphic poetry. It follows that at least some Orphic poetry was considered to be the *verbal equivalent to mystery initiation*."

Adeimantos are complaining that too many forces in their cultural tradition induce people to choose injustice over justice.

> But of all these arguments the most astounding are those they make about the gods and excellence, how indeed the gods also allot misfortune and a bad life to many good people, and the opposite fate to their opposites. Begging priests and diviners, going to the doors of the rich, persuade them that there is a power provided to them by the gods in sacrifices and incantations to make amends with pleasures and feasts if he or any of his ancestors has committed some injustice. And if he wants to harm some enemy, he will harm just and unjust alike with spells and curses for only a small expense, having persuaded, as they claim, the gods to obey them. And as witnesses for their claims, they bring in the poets. Some, on the topic of vice, granting ease, say that "vice may readily be seized in abundance; the way is easy and she dwells nearby. But the gods have placed sweat before excellence," and a long, steep, rough road. Then they call on Homer as a witness that the gods may be swayed by men; since that poet says: "Even the gods themselves may be moved by prayers; and men avert their wrath by praying to them and by sacrifices and soothing pleas, and by libations and the smell of burning fat, when someone has transgressed and done wrong." And they present a hubbub of books by Musaios and Orpheus, offspring of Selene and the Muses, as they say, according to which they perform their rituals. And they persuade not only individuals but whole cities that there are absolutions and purifications from unjust deeds through sacrifices and the pleasures of play, both for them while still living and after they have died. These *teletai*, as they call them, release us from evils in the hereafter, but terrible things await those who have not performed the rituals.[4]

This passage provides some of the most important evidence for the nature of Orphic texts and the people who used them. Most importantly here, the religious specialists who employ the books of Orpheus are characterized

---

[4] Pl. *Resp.* 364b2–365a3 (*OF* 573i B = OF 3 K): τούτων δὲ πάντων οἱ περὶ θεῶν τε λόγοι καὶ ἀρετῆς θαυμασιώτατοι λέγονται, ὡς ἄρα καὶ θεοὶ πολλοῖς μὲν ἀγαθοῖς δυστυχίας τε καὶ βίον κακὸν ἔνειμαν, τοῖς δ' ἐναντίοις ἐναντίαν μοῖραν. ἀγύρται δὲ καὶ μάντεις ἐπὶ πλουσίων θύρας ἰόντες πείθουσιν ὡς ἔστι παρὰ σφίσι δύναμις ἐκ θεῶν ποριζομένη θυσίαις τε καὶ ἐπῳδαῖς, εἴτε τι ἀδίκημά του γέγονεν αὐτοῦ ἢ προγόνων, ἀκεῖσθαι μεθ' ἡδονῶν τε καὶ ἑορτῶν, ἐάν τέ τινα ἐχθρὸν πημῆναι ἐθέλῃ, μετὰ σμικρῶν δαπανῶν ὁμοίως δίκαιον ἀδίκῳ βλάψει ἐπαγωγαῖς τισιν καὶ καταδέσμοις, τοὺς θεούς, ὥς φασιν, πείθοντές σφισιν ὑπηρετεῖν. τούτοις δὲ πᾶσιν τοῖς λόγοις μάρτυρας ποιητὰς ἐπάγονται οἱ μὲν κακίας πέρι, εὐπετείας διδόντες, ὡς "τὴν μὲν κακότητα καὶ ἰλαδὸν ἔστιν ἑλέσθαι | ῥηϊδίως· λείη μὲν ὁδός, μάλα δ' ἐγγύθι ναίει· | τῆς δ' ἀρετῆς ἱδρῶτα θεοὶ προπάροιθεν ἔθηκαν" καί τινα ὁδὸν μακράν τε καὶ τραχεῖαν καὶ ἀνάντη· οἱ δὲ τῆς τῶν θεῶν ὑπ' ἀνθρώπων παραγωγῆς τὸν Ὅμηρον μαρτύρονται, ὅτι καὶ ἐκεῖνος εἶπεν "λιστοὶ δέ τε καὶ θεοὶ αὐτοί, | καὶ τοὺς μὲν θυσίαισι καὶ εὐχωλαῖς ἀγανᾶισιν | λοιβῇ τε κνίσῃ τε παρατρωπῶσ' ἄνθρωποι | λισσόμενοι, ὅτε κέν τις ὑπερβήῃ καὶ ἁμάρτῃ." βίβλων δὲ ὅμαδον παρέχονται Μουσαίου καὶ Ὀρφέως, Σελήνης τε καὶ Μουσῶν ἐκγόνων, ὥς φασι, καθ' ἃς θυηπολοῦσιν, πείθοντες οὐ μόνον ἰδιώτας ἀλλὰ καὶ πόλεις, ὡς ἄρα λύσεις τε καὶ καθαρμοὶ ἀδικημάτων διὰ θυσιῶν καὶ παιδιᾶς ἡδονῶν εἰσι μὲν ἔτι ζῶσιν, εἰσὶ δὲ καὶ τελευτήσασιν, ἃς δὴ τελετὰς καλοῦσιν, αἳ τῶν ἐκεῖ κακῶν ἀπολύουσιν ἡμᾶς, μὴ θύσαντας δὲ δεινὰ περιμένει.

as ἀγύρται καὶ μάντεις, itinerant practitioners who wander about seeking a clientele for a range of religious services, mostly purifications from past offenses but also magical attacks upon one's enemies. The tools of their trade are described as a βίβλων ὅμαδον, a hubbub of books, that is a din or clamor of competing voices from the texts, and their primary activity is persuasion of their clients, whom they convince to employ their services. We must understand the evidence for Orphic texts and their use precisely in this competitive context, the clamor of rival practitioners seeking to advertise their expertise and to win over clients.

In this context, books are merely the tools of the trade characteristic of this kind of expert, but this kind of expert is not limited to the Orphic practitioner. On the contrary, a wide variety of experts making claims to special wisdom were characterized by their use of texts in fifth-century Athens. Moreover, even those who use Orphic books in particular present not a singular text of Orpheus, with doctrinal authority or ritual efficacy, but a hubbub of books with which they make a clamor of competing claims. Understanding the competitive context not only illuminates the evidence from Plato and Euripides, but it sheds light on another crucial piece of evidence for early Orphic texts, the Derveni papyrus. The treatise of the Derveni author and his relation to the text of Orpheus can be better understood in the context of the sort of competitive religious practitioners depicted in Plato, and many of the puzzles modern scholars have struggled with stem not from the Derveni author's text but from the model of Orphic textuality with which scholars have approached the material.

Textual orientation

In the scholarship of the past century, scholars have imagined Orphism as characterized by three different modes of textual orientation. Before the discovery of the Derveni papyrus, the bibliolatry model prevailed, in which Orphics venerated their sacred scriptures, but the Derveni author's comments upon the Orphic poem have led some scholars to imagine Orphism as a kind of post-modern textual orientation, seeking meaning through the act of interpretation, while others have focused on the ritual aspects, seeing Orphic writing as essentially linked to initiatory experiences. While this ritual interpretation is, in some important respects, less wrong than the others, all of these ideas distort the evidence for Orphic texts by constraining the way these texts were used into a single model deemed Orphic.

Bibliolatry

The older paradigm, elements of which still persist today, treated Orphic texts on the model of Judaeo-Christian sacred scriptures and imagined Orphics who revered their texts of Orpheus in the way devout Christians, especially Protestant Christians, might revere the Bible. In his monograph exploring the nature of Orphism, Watmough makes perhaps the most egregious formulation of the idea, making an analogy between the relation of Orphics to mainstream (Homeric) Greek religion and that of Protestants to Catholics.

> In the ancient world we have the religion of Homer, entirely concerned with sacrifice and ritual, entirely dominated by the note of "Confiteor" – the confession of vows duly performed: and over against it the religion of "Orpheus", which emphasised the relation of the individual soul with God, for authority turning not to priests but scriptures. In the more modern world we have the mediaeval Church, a picturesque and colourful religious system based on sacerdotalism and ecclesiolatry: over against it the Protestant reformers with their "justification by faith" and bibliolatrous attitude to the canonical writings.[5]

Watmough's analogy reveals the way this older paradigm is grounded in theological disputes within Christianity over the place of ritual, priests, and scriptures, disputes that, as J. Z. Smith has shown, were played out repeatedly in the scholarship of the history of religions.[6] Guthrie, as usual, provides a more nuanced and careful picture, but he nevertheless places Orphic sacred scriptures firmly at the heart of his idea of Orphism. Orphic texts, for Guthrie, provide the fundamental authority for Orphic believers, the scriptural basis for their way of life. "The Orphic did nothing unless there was a warrant for it in his books."[7]

While the societies of Orphic believers imagined by earlier scholars have largely vanished from current accounts, traces of this older model persist, not only in outdated surveys but even in some of the most advanced and thoughtful scholarship on the subject. While it is problematic that undergraduate textbooks like Morford and Lenardon's refer to the Zagreus myth that "provides the biblical authority for Orphism," the traces of a scriptural model within more sophisticated scholarship are even more

---

[5] Watmough 1934: 56–57. Note that, in the "modern world," the Catholic church is nevertheless "mediaeval."

[6] Smith 1990. Cp. Edmonds 1999 and Graf and Johnston 2007: 50–65, for further discussion of the role of Protestant/Catholic disputes in the scholarship on Orphism.

[7] Guthrie 1952: 202.

pernicious, since it is harder to see the ways in which these flaws affect the otherwise legitimate work.[8]

Some scholarship, especially coming from the standpoint of the history of philosophy or the history of medicine with a narrative of the evolution from irrational belief to rational science, tends to adopt, almost by default as it were, the categories of science and religion that figure in the contemporary debates. Texts pertaining to religion are thus automatically considered as scriptures. Janko, for example, draws such a modern analogy to the Derveni author's use of Leukippos, Herakleitos, and Anaxagoras in his exegesis of the Orphic poem. "This is as if someone were to argue, while citing Nietzsche, that the *Book of Mormon* is a coded account of Einstein's and Hawking's theories about the origins of the universe."[9] He sees the Derveni author's allegorical interpretation as inherently, and indeed deliberately, contrary to the faith of his fundamentalist contemporaries. "The ultimate outrage would have been the allegory itself – the interpretation of the holy poem as a coded version of the latest physics, and the equation of God with the most basic element, Air."[10] Here the Orphic poem appears as holy writ, and any tampering with its literal meaning is calculated to arouse the outrage of the faithful. Such a context for the understanding of the text infects his otherwise excellent interpretations, leading, for example, to a peculiar and anachronistic emphasis on questions of "faith" in the treatise.[11]

Another way in which the scriptural paradigm creeps back into the scholarship is through "the Orphic exception." While it is admitted that ancient Greek polytheism in general cannot be understood with models based on Christian ideas of doctrine or scripture, the Orphics are held up as the exception that proves the rule. No one in ancient Greece had sacred scriptures – except the Orphics. Even Parker, whose work on ancient Greek polytheism has done so much to break down the older paradigms and create a new and better understanding, nevertheless allows "the Orphic exception" to slide in. "Both in social and religious terms Orphism is profoundly unorthodox; and it displays several characteristics of a 'religion of the book',

---

[8] Morford and Lenardon 1999: 246.

[9] Janko 2002–03: 3. Janko's categories of rational science against irrational religion are clear, for example, when he dismisses Betegh's arguments against sarcastic condemnation of the Derveni author's hermeneutics, "as if one can study religious thought without remarking its frequent departures from rationality" (Janko 2005).

[10] Janko 2002–03: 13. Cp. Janko 2001: 2: "It is my contention that he sets out to criticize most of his contemporaries on the ground that they believed too literally in the rites and holy texts of traditional religion."

[11] Janko 2002–03: 5: "The link which holds together this chain of apparently disparate topics is the question of religious faith. If faith is to be maintained, interpretation is essential, both for rituals and holy texts." See also his readings of col. 5 in terms of belief in the afterlife.

being indeed transmitted through a 'hubbub of books'."[12] The category of the "religion of the book" of course comes from the criterion by which the monotheistic religions of Islam, Judaism, and Christianity distinguished themselves from the polytheistic pagans. Religions of the book treat their holy texts differently, rely on them for canonical formulations of doctrine, take their meaning more seriously as a guide for action than religions that have only myths. Such a paradigm is at work when Parker characterizes the Orphic accounts of the Underworld as exceptional. "Orphic poetry can almost be defined as eschatological poetry, and it was in such poems perhaps that 'persuasive' accounts of the afterlife – accounts designed, unlike that in *Odyssey* xi, to influence the hearer's behaviour in the here and now – were powerfully presented for the first time."[13] In this model, all Orphic poetry, regardless of its apparent topic, must have eschatological significance, must present the doctrines by which the faithful should live in hopes of salvation hereafter. On the contrary, rather than making an exception for Orphic material, we can gain a much better understanding by applying Parker's insights for Greek religion generally to this evidence as well.

The writing of Orpheus

The discovery of the Derveni papyrus has brought new ways of approaching the issue of Orphic texts, since the treatise, with its comments on the Orphic text, provides a perspective quite different from the Euripidean or Platonic mockery of the hubbub of books. The sophistication of the Derveni author's handling of language, as well as his apparent determination to make new meaning in the text of Orpheus, appeals to scholars of literary criticism, especially those for whom the reader plays a more active role in the creation of the meaning of a text. Perhaps the most eloquent of such scholars is Marcel Detienne, whose essays on the writing of Orpheus have been both thought-provoking and influential. Focusing specifically on the Derveni papyrus, Detienne celebrates the polyphonic and open-ended nature of Orphic writing.

> The discovery of the Derveni papyrus, an Orphic book of Plato's day, indicates clearly enough that the writing of Orpheus is an open-ended text. His speech continues through exegesis – that is, through the commentaries that

---

[12] Parker 1996: 55.
[13] Parker 1995: 500. Cp. the excellent studies by Parker of the nature of Greek religion in Parker 2011, Parker 2005, and Parker 1996.

it prompts educated initiates to write.... The song of Orpheus generates interpretations, gives rise to exegetic constructions that become or are an integral part of the Orphic discourse. This is polyphonic writing, a book with several voices.[14]

Ultimately, he depicts Orphic writing as an ongoing conversation between scholarly intellectuals, with the act of interpretation itself taking the place of religious ritual. Not only do such conversations sound suspiciously like the dialogues of post-modern deconstructionists, but even Detienne's vision of salvation seems peculiarly existential.

> Orphism thus involves a choice of writing, and an impulse to produce a plural book, an impulse that runs as deep as others' renunciations of the world and of the political and religious values of the city. For the kind of salvation that is cultivated amid circles of the purified and intellectuals can also be achieved through literature. It can be won through writing that tells of Orpheus' triumph over death and oblivion. The literate initiates of Orphism became the champions of books but at the same time rejected the world, setting up for themselves a secret library that revolved around Orpheus' unique voice.... In the space of Orpheus and the writing of his disciples, the sole purpose of the eschatological vocation that prompts them to write is knowledge, real knowledge of the genesis of the gods and of the world, knowledge that extends to the extreme isolation of the individual.[15]

While this image of salvation through literature may be even more appealing to twenty-first-century scholars than the image of a proto-Protestant Orphism was to those of the twentieth, it is grounded even less securely in ancient evidence. Indeed, Detienne's reconstructions of Orphism are often "unburdened," as he puts it, with footnotes or references to specific evidence, and the gaps between the evidence with which he is working and the vision he comes up with are often huge.

One example seems to me illustrative of Detienne's approach and its problems. In discussing the relation of Orpheus, writing, and the Orphic life, Detienne refers to a particular image.

> An Etruscan mirror, now in Boston, depicts a box of books lying at the feet of an Orpheus surrounded by animals drawn out of their world of silence. The box contains a piece of writing entitled the Initiation and also a Telete designed to be recited or chanted, which recounts how the child Dionysus is lured by the Titans and then put to death in the course of a most horrible sacrifice.[16]

---

[14] Detienne 2003: 135. [15] Detienne 2003: 136.
[16] Detienne 2003: 154. See my review in *BMCR* (Edmonds 2004c) for more on this subject.

Figure 2 Etruscan mirror, *Corpus Speculorum Etruscorum*, U.S.A. 2:14. Drawing by
Richard De Puma and reproduced with his kind permission.

The image, as Detienne describes it, conveniently pulls together a number
of separate themes in Detienne's study – the magical voice of Orpheus,
the association of Orpheus with writing, and the association of Orpheus
with ritual. However, very little of the description comes from the actual
object (Figure 2); most of it comes from the imagination of the commentator. Detienne does not bother to cite the image, nor does he provide
an illustration that would reveal the discrepancies between the object and
his description.[17] In the first place, although the lyre-playing figure is
unlabeled, it is generally identified as Apollo, who also often appears with
animals, rather than as Orpheus. Although a reasonable case could be made

---

[17] The image is published as *Corpus Speculorum Etruscorum*, U.S.A. 2:14. The image also may be found
in LIMC as Apollo/Aplu 88. Special thanks to Jean Turfa for the guidance in tracking down this
item.

to identify the figure as Orpheus instead of Apollo (or even as Orpheus connected to Apollo by the iconography), the significance of the image changes if it is not actually Orpheus associated with the writings. A box nearby does indeed seem to contain two scrolls, but there is no title on either of them. As for the contents of the writings, an initiatory ritual that involves reciting a myth of the Titans' murder of the infant Dionysos in a perverted sacrifice, they are entirely a fabrication, something that could never have been depicted on a mirror, even by the most gifted of Etruscan artists. Such a disregard for the ancient evidence vitiates Detienne's clever reconstructions, despite the fact that some of his insights and ideas are not only plausible, but illuminating.[18] However, his model of Orphic textual orientation remains largely a figment of his creative imagination, and scholars must be careful not to import his fabrications back into the ancient evidence.[19]

Ritual texts

While the Derveni author's interest in hermeneutics has sparked one type of modern theory about Orphism as a textual orientation, his concern with ritual practice has led to another way of imagining the relation between Orphism and its texts. The Derveni author's interest in the cosmogonic Orphic poem, coupled with his interest in the performance of ritual, led Burkert to adduce Near Eastern parallels for the use of cosmogonic myth in ritual.

> It has been concluded from Plato's words that these Orphic books must have contained ritual prescriptions and liturgies, whereas the surviving fragments of Orphic literature are nearly exclusively mythological in character. It is, however, the Mesopotamian model which illustrates the use of mythology precisely in the sphere of the magical practitioner: he has to overcome disease and other forms of crisis, to reinstall normal order, and the most basic means of doing so is to repeat cosmogony.[20]

---

[18] Detienne's structuralist studies of Dionysos (esp. Detienne 1979 and 1986) greatly illuminate the variety of ways in which this figure appears in the Greek religious tradition, and his idea (Detienne 1975) that Dionysiac rites are, along with Orphism and Pythagoreanism, one of the "chemins de déviance" available within the Greek tradition for non-normative religious activity has been formative for my own understanding of the category of Orphism, even if I find his definition of Orphic problematic in other ways.

[19] Even Bernabé, who does not generally tend to such excesses, succumbs to the lure of Detienne's model when he claims, on the basis of the reference in the *Meno* 81a to priests who provide an account, that "the exegesis of their own texts is characteristic of the Orphics" (Bernabé 2007b: 128). Such exegesis, as we will see below, is characteristic, not particularly of Orphics, but of all types of intellectuals making claims to special wisdom.

[20] Burkert 1982: 8.

On this theory, then, the cosmogonic themes in Orphic poetry – not just in the Derveni poem, but in other Orphica – are significant to the sort of people who take Orpheus as their authority, not because they provide a scriptural account of creation equivalent to the Biblical Genesis, but rather because they provide a myth of the original order, a description of the things *in illo tempore*, which can be used in the rituals practiced by the ἀγύρται καὶ μάντεις in Plato – or perhaps even the Derveni author himself.[21]

This theory represents a marked advance over the older scriptural model insofar as it is grounded, not on a Christianocentric model of religions of the book, but on a model of religions in the ancient Mediterranean world. Rather than imagining a set of the faithful who rely on their sacred text to provide them with doctrinally defined understanding of the cosmos, Burkert's model instead envisages religious specialists who, in the words of the Derveni author, "make a craft of the rites," providing ritual services to a variety of clientele in different circumstances. In a series of studies, Burkert has traced the evidence for such practitioners in the ancient Near East as well as in Greece, noting the important contacts between the cultures that promoted the spread of ritual technologies.[22] This model explains the evidence for Plato's ἀγύρται καὶ μάντεις far better than the older models, not to mention the various references to Orpheotelestai, and, indeed, Burkert's identification of those involved with Orphica as craft practitioners, rather than a sect, remains perhaps the most significant advance in the study of Orphism in the twentieth century.[23]

Some caution must be used, however, when inferring the function of Orphic texts in Greek society from the Mesopotamian parallels. While the dynamic cultural exchange between Greece and the Near East makes a transfer of such ritual techniques entirely plausible, the absence of any Greek evidence for the use of cosmogonic myth in a ritual of healing, purification, or the like, must give us pause. Even in Mesopotamian cultures, the recital of a cosmogony was only one technique that could be employed, and it is quite possible that this particular technique never really made the transfer from one culture to the other.[24] The creation story of the *Enûma elis* was recited at the official New Year's festival marking the recreation of the divine order each year along with the renewal of the power of the

---

[21] Cp. Eliade's model of mythic originary time that provides the basis of all sacred ritual in Eliade 1987 and 1965, but note the critiques of Smith 1978 of the limitations of this model and the abuses to which it has been put.

[22] Cp. Burkert 1982, 1987, 1992 , and 2004.   [23] Burkert 1982.

[24] Cp. Smith 1978 on the problems with Mesopotamian cosmogony rituals as a model for everything.

king.[25] While portions of the text could also be used in charms to facilitate childbirth or to prevent a toothache, part of the prestige of such texts may well have derived from their use in the central festival, and such prestige would be lacking when transferred to a cultural context without such a centralized festival. So too, the mechanics of the employment of such a mythic text in Greek rituals of purification or healing remain uncertain, since the admittedly meager evidence for such rituals contains nothing similar.[26]

Ultimately, of course, the absence of any Greek evidence cannot prove, especially given the Mesopotamian parallels, that Orphic cosmological poetry was not used in rituals of healing or purification. However, to assume that all Orphic poetry must have served such a function distorts the evidence that does exist, since cosmology was hardly the only theme found in the Orphica. Moreover, some scholars who have picked up on Burkert's idea have extrapolated from the idea of cosmogony being used in ritual to the idea of anthropogony, specifically the anthropogony imagined in the Zagreus myth, where mankind arises from the ashes of the Titanic murderers of Dionysos. According to this hypothesis, the narration of this primordial crime would serve the same function as the Mesopotamian creation story, to heal the problem (be it disease or impurity) by restoring normal order. However, such an argument mixes up two different kinds of procedures, the Mesopotamian cosmogony practice to which Burkert referred and the Greek mantic practice of determining a past event that has brought the anger of the gods, for which expiation is needed to cure the disease or remove the impurity.

---

[25] This detail comes from the problematic account of Cornford, who is drawing on the "myth and ritual" school of orientalist scholars such as Oesterly and Hooke. Cp. his imaginative reconstruction (Cornford 1950: 111–112) of the process by which primitive magical ritual decays into myth: "Suppose you start with a ritual drama, in which the powers of evil and disorder, represented by a priestly actor with a dragon's mask, are overcome by the divine king, as part of a magical regeneration of the natural and social order. Then you may compose a hymn, in which this act is magnified, with every circumstance of splendour and horror, as a terrific battle between the king of the gods and the dragon of the deep. And you will recite this hymn, every time the ritual drama is performed, to reinforce its efficacy with all the majesty of the superhuman precedent. Now so long as the myth remains part of a living ritual, its symbolic meaning is clear. But when the ritual has fallen into disuse, the myth may survive for many centuries." As he notes, "What excited me was the idea (which I got from Hooke's books) that early philosophic cosmogony is not only a transcription of mythic cosmogony, but finally has its root in *ritual*, something tangibly existing, not baseless 'fancies' and speculation" (116).

[26] There is a distinction, moreover, between the recitation of a mythic precedent for ritual purposes and the use of cosmogony in particular. The former is a common pattern, found not only in the Near East, but throughout what might be called the Indo-European tradition as well (see Burkert 1992: 124–125, and West 2007: 336–339 on *Legendezauber*). Recitation of cosmogony is a special case, and we cannot conclude from the general validity of the former that the recitation of cosmogony was used ritually in any given culture at any given time.

Obbink indeed refers to the opening of Sophocles' *Oedipus Rex*, where the Thebans call upon the diviner Teiresias to determine what might have caused the gods to send plague upon Thebes, but suggests that the Orphic solution was to posit a single offense that infected mankind universally, in place of having to find a different past event for each case.

> For it was the task of such healers to discover the "ancient guilt" (παλαιὸν μήνιμα) at the basis of present suffering. This would require singling out a specific past offence in every single case of affliction, from among a vast repertoire of paradigmatic mythic examples that were authoritative but susceptible of periodic reinvestment with new meanings. It is precisely for this reason that the surviving poetry of "Orpheus", just as the Orphic verses treated by the Derveni author, dwells upon cosmogony and theogony including anthropogony: for it contained the story of the most ancient and general kind of guilt for humankind: the "ancient grief of Persephone" as Pindar says (fr. 133 [Snell-Maehler][*OF* 443 B]).[27]

Not only is this Zagreus anthropogony, with the burden of Titanic original sin, a fabrication of the nineteenth and twentieth centuries, as I have demonstrated,[28] but, even if it were not, the conflation of the two models of the relation of myth and ritual does not work. The logical structure of the ritual that employs the cosmogony is not actually compatible with that of the purging of ancient guilt. In the former, the ordering principles of the cosmos are narrated, performatively setting all things into their proper order. The episode of the first creation of mankind could thus be excerpted from the longer cosmogony and related to facilitate the birth of a new child, performatively narrating the process of creation and new birth to ensure that the current process succeeds. Likewise, an excerpt recounting how the hero Atrahasis prayed to the gods to get rain during drought could be used as a spell to bring rain, invoking the successful petition in the myth to bring success to the current petition.[29] In the latter procedure, the purging of ancient guilt, the diviner must interpret the enigmatic messages

---

[27] Obbink 1997: 50. Cp. Burkert 1992: 125–126: "The necessary link between ritual and anthropogony can be seen from the function of the charismatic healers: The sick person desperately asks what the source of the affliction might be, 'whence it sprang, what the root of evil can be, which gods they should appease with sacrifice in order to find relief from their sufferings.' [Eur. fr. 912 K (= *Cret.* fr. 7 J.-V.L.) (*OF* 458B)] The answer must lie somewhere in the past: Thus Epimenides the seer 'prophesied not about the future, but about the past.' The most general answer which can be given, extending far beyond the individual case, is the interpretation of human existence as the consequence of an ancient crime, as a punishment going back to the oldest 'wrath' of the gods."

[28] Cp. Edmonds 1999, 2008b, and below, ch. 9.

[29] As, e.g., in the Old Babylonian version of the myth told in the *Atrahasis* that is used as an incantation for childbirth, ANET 99–100. Lambert and Millard 1969: 28, refer to the passage in which Atrahasis gets Adad to send rain during a drought being used as an incantation to bring rain.

of the gods to discover what offense occurred in the past and what must be done to expiate it.[30] The mere narration of the past offense does not bring expiation; the offended powers must be appeased, usually by sacrifices and other ritual honors. As a fragment from Euripides attests, the questions involved are always: "whence it sprang, what the root of evil can be, which gods they should appease with sacrifice in order to find relief from their sufferings."[31] Whereas the narration of cosmogony can be a performative utterance, setting the cosmos in its proper order, the narration of a past offense cannot serve the same function.[32] If the narration concerned the restoration of proper order after some disruption, one could perhaps make the case that such a narrative could serve the same performative function of restoring the normal order, but such a narrative of salvation is completely absent, even from the texts that some scholars have used for evidence of original sin stemming from the Zagreus myth.

One consequence of this conflation of the Mesopotamian cosmogony model with the anthropogony has been that scholars have tried to understand any text that contains any reference that might be construed as alluding to this supposed anthropogony as a ritual text. Obbink asserts that "the surviving poetry of 'Orpheus', just as the Orphic verses treated by the Derveni author, dwells upon cosmogony and theogony including anthropogony," but the Derveni verses have nothing to do with anthropogony, and cosmogony is only one of the many themes that appears in the evidence for the Orphica. We run the risk of constraining our perception of the variety of Orphic texts by adopting a single model for understanding the relation of the texts to ritual.

Parker provides a good warning when discussing the common nature of Orphic texts, noting that texts that had a ritual function could be of diverse natures and suggesting that all Orphic texts might not have had a ritual function.[33] Despite his cautions, however, Parker assumes that the

---

[30] See Borgeaud 1999 for a discussion of this type of divination and purification.

[31] Eur. fr. 912 K (= *Cret.* fr. 7 J.-V.L.) *ap.* Clem. Al. *Strom.* 5.11.70 (*OF* 458 B): πόθεν ἔβλαστον, τίς ῥίζα κακῶν, τίνα δεῖ μακάρων ἐκθυσαμένους εὑρεῖν μόχθων ἀνάπαυλαν. Macías Otero 2010 goes astray in her interpretation of this fragment by trying to read it in terms of a specific guilt for all humanity from the murder of Dionysos Zagreus, for which neither the text nor Clement's context provides any support. This is one of the many fragments improperly classified as Orphic in Bernabé's collection on the basis of a supposed resemblance to the hypothetical Zagreus myth.

[32] As Smith 1987: 99 notes, "Many of the first times described in myth – particularly those dealing with the origin of death, sickness, illness, sin, and evil – may well be existentially repeated in the human condition itself, but they are neither celebrated nor ritually repeated."

[33] Parker 1995: 486: "One obvious reason why Orphic poems might have shared common features is their shared ritual function. To be of use to a working Orpheotelest, busy with initiations and expiations, a text obviously had to be of a particular type. We must, however, at once weaken this

cosmogony in the Derveni poem had a ritual use and that most of the other early Orphica may be assumed to have had a ritual function as well. By assuming that the cosmogony must be linked with the anthropogony and thus the original sin from which mankind needs salvation, he concludes that the focus of most of this ritual would be "securing the initiate's welfare in the afterlife," redeeming the initiate from the stain of the primordial crime. Indeed, he dismisses as a Platonic misrepresentation the fact that the religious practitioners in the *Republic* passage speak not of Titanic guilt but of the unjust deeds of individuals.[34] Once again, the assumption that the Zagreus myth underlies all Orphic ideas results in disregard of the actual evidence, which in this case presents a very different picture. We would do better to heed Parker's caveats than to follow his reconstruction here, noting that the relation between the mythic text and a ritual might work in a variety of different ways (including, perhaps in evidence no longer extant, the Mesopotamian cosmological model) and that some Orphic texts might have no direct ritual function at all.

If there is no special Orphic textual orientation that determines the relation between an Orphic text and its readers, how then are we to make sense of the references to the hubbub of Orphic books or the smoke of many books of those who take Orpheus as their leader? These texts cannot be understood simplistically and anachronistically as the sacred scriptures of the Orphics, vessels of doctrine for the believers, nor as the sophisticated religious productions of an intellectual elite who find their salvation through exegetical writing, nor even as liturgical texts designed for use in initiations that bring salvation from original sin. While some Orphic texts undoubtedly had some sort of ritual function, the relation between text and ritual cannot be understood solely in terms of the model

powerful argument by two reservations. First, it is not strictly demonstrable that all early Orphic poems were written for ritual use. It is true that this is the context in which they are mentioned in the rare early allusions; and it looks, as we shall see, as if the *Theogony*, perhaps the most important among them, was specifically designed for ritual use. But anyone who maintains that *Net*, say, or *Robe* was a purely speculative composition cannot be proved wrong. Second, even text that has a ritual function could have been, up to a point, quite diverse. Different recipes for securing the initiate's welfare in the afterlife could have been followed, different eschatological conceptions appealed to; and there are some hints, in early references to 'charms' and 'cures' of Orpheus, that Orpheotelestes may also have offered help with the ills of this world."

[34] Parker 1995: 504: "In hinting here at the practices of the Orpheus-initiators, Plato does not speak of Titanic guilt as the stain to be effaced, but only of the 'unjust acts of an individual or his ancestors'; and as means of expiation he mentions 'playful ritual', not the asceticism of the Orphic life. Of course, between this text and the actual content of Orphic books, two filters obtrude: first that of Plato himself, who is very likely to have misrepresented the values of the Orpheus-initiators; and second that of the Orpheus-initiators themselves, who were free to select from the texts and interpret them in whatever way they thought would meet their clients' wishes."

of restoration of the normal order through the performative narration of the creation of cosmic order.

The hubbub of books in Classical Athens

Rather than relying on these models, grounded in modern paradigms of religion, we must examine the evidence for Orphic texts in the context of ancient Greek religion and culture, not assuming an "Orphic exception", but exploring the ways in which the Orphic materials fit into the classificatory systems of their time. Specifically, the association between those who look to Orpheus and texts, as it is highlighted in the passages from Plato and Euripides, must be seen in the context of fifth-century Athens and the technological innovations that made the book the new tool of all those who aspired to a special claim to wisdom. No peculiar Orphic textual orientation distinguished those who made use of Orphic texts from other types of claimants to wisdom; the contemporary evidence shows that others who made use of books at that time were regarded in similar ways.

When considering the evidence for Plato's hubbub of books, two elements must be kept in mind – the hubbub and the books. I first examine the book as a technological innovation in fifth-century Athens, demonstrating that other book users were treated with the same blend of suspicion, awe, and scorn that characterizes the evidence for the users of Orphic texts. I then turn to the hubbub, the competitive context in which these books were employed, showing that the book served as a tool in the fierce competitions for authority and influence among the different types of experts who claimed special wisdom. This agonistic context shaped the nature of certain early written texts, which served as display pieces demonstrating the claims to special wisdom and denouncing rival claims.

Illuminating this context provides a better understanding of the puzzling treatise of the Derveni author, since the Derveni author can be seen as a religious practitioner providing an *epideixis* of his exegetic skills and attempting to disparage his rivals for a similar clientele. The absence of systematic doctrine or even any focus on the doctrinal points often imagined as most important to Orphism becomes unsurprising when we abandon the anachronistic models by which the Derveni author's Orphism has been evaluated. Likewise, we can better understand the other Orphic writings and their relations to ritual if we examine the different types of Orphica without a single model of the relation of myth to ritual.

The Technology of the Book

The hubbub of books in fifth-century Athens was not confined to Orphic books only; all sorts of books were chattering in the busy marketplace of ideas that characterized the intellectual climate of that period. Even though the technology of writing had been available for centuries, the first significant challenges to the oral poetic tradition as the primary authoritative discourse came in this period.[35] Plato provides some of the most thoughtful testimony to the issues that might arise with the spread of this new technology, even as he proved himself a master of it in his innovative dialogues.[36] Books were the latest technology, and all those who wanted to promote their claims to advanced knowledge were making use of this technological innovation to bolster their credibility and authority. Like any technical innovation whose use is limited to a select few, the use of books inspired both awe and scorn. As Woodbury puts it, "Books did not yet fit easily into the general view of life. They were the latest thing, but somehow odd and out of place, and the object of some suspicion and derision."[37] This mixed reaction to books and bookishness characterizes all the evidence on the users of books from this period, not just the Orphic evidence.

All types of experts who wished to display their expertise could make use of this new technology, whether they were called by the general term "sophists" or by more technical labels of doctors, diviners, or even rhapsodes or philosophers.[38] Although the term "sophist" has acquired an irremediably bad connotation from the polemics of Plato, who wished to distinguish his brand of wisdom from his competitors', it is a useful term to designate all those who made a claim to special wisdom (*sophia*).[39] Although

---

[35] Morgan 2000: 15–45 discusses this rise of textualization and the conflict between the poetic "masters of truth" as described by Detienne and the new claimants to special wisdom. "The textualisation of mythological material led first to criticism and then to the opportunity to manipulate and play against this material considered as a fixed entity. The development of allegorical interpretation and of sophistic mythological epideixis are rooted in the same phenomenon" (24). Cp. the studies of Detienne 1996 and Havelock 1963.

[36] The *Phaedrus* provides the most striking example, but the issue is ubiquitous in Plato's work. As Brisson 1999: 38 comments, Plato's testimony is "balanced on a razor's edge" as he sits at the precise historical moment of transition between the dominance of orality and that of literacy.

[37] Woodbury 1986: 242.

[38] Thomas 2003: 170: "Again and again, when written texts are mentioned as problematic in any way, they are by a wider collection of writers than just sophists. Written texts were evidently available in increasing numbers by all kinds of intellectuals, poets, sophists and philosophers." The book trade in Athens, mentioned for example in Plato's *Ap.* 26de, caters to these types of intellectuals.

[39] Pl. *Prt.* 316de (*OF* 549i, 669iii, 806, 1013 B = OT 92 K) claims all the great poets, musical theorists, doctors, and religious specialists as sophists, even if they were afraid to use the word for themselves. On Plato and his polemics, see, e.g., Lincoln 1993; Nightingale 1995: 22–25; Morgan 2000: 89–94; and Gagarin 2002: 4.

polemics among such marginal figures might draw very firm differences, from the perspective of the mainstream, all such intellectuals could be lumped together in a single category, regardless of what expertise they professed, what fees they charged (or not), or what they said about one another.[40] One example of such ancient categorization appears in Aristophanes' *Clouds*, where the Cloud goddesses of the Socratic Thinkery are described as caring for a list of ridiculous types of sophists, a list which includes diviners and doctors as well as poets and physicists.[41] Although modern scholars tend to separate the expertise of religious practitioners such as diviners or purifiers from that of doctors or geometers, the ancient classifications often lumped them all together as sophists and did not distinguish in the same ways between the grounds of their expertise.

The ultimate figure of avant-garde intellectualism associated with books in fifth-century Athens is of course the tragedian Euripides, the master of the old poetic discourse who embraced the new ideas and technologies. Although Euripides is a favorite target in many places, Aristophanes mercilessly mocks Euripides' bookishness in the contest with Aeschylus in the *Frogs*. Not only does he have Euripides claim that he tried to get Athens back in shape with a medical regime that included "giving a dose of drivel strained from books" (χυλὸν διδοὺς στωμυλμάτων ἀπὸ βιβλίων ἀπηθῶν), he also has Aeschylus retort that he can defeat Euripides in the weighing of words even if he steps in the scales himself, taking all his books along with him (συλλαβὼν τὰ βιβλία).[42] An extra-ordinary tool that marks the exceptional claims of its users to wisdom, the new technology of the book is associated with avant-garde poets like Euripides, as well as with all the other sophists in fifth-century Athens – the doctors, the rhetoricians, the diviners, and the geometers.

Books are characteristic of all these types; they are the tools of the trade for professional wise men as well as the way in which they displayed their expertise. Some of the earliest prose treatises of which we have

---

[40] As Dover 1968: lii puts it, "In order to understand *Nu.* we must make an imaginative effort to adopt an entirely different position, the position of someone to whom all philosophical and scientific speculation, all disinterested intellectual curiosity, is boring and silly. To such a person distinctions which are of fundamental importance to the intellectual appear insignificant, incomprehensible, and often imperceptible."

[41] Ar. *Nub.* 331–334: "For don't you know, by Zeus, that they nourish very many sophists, Thurian diviners, medical practitioners, long-haired-onyx-seal-wearing idlers, song-twisters for the cyclic dances, and quacks with their heads in the clouds. They feed lazy people who accomplish nothing, because such men celebrate them in verse." οὐ γὰρ μὰ Δί᾽ οἶσθ᾽ ὅτιὴ πλείστους αὗται βόσκουσι σοφιστάς, | Θουριομάντεις ἰατροτέχνας σφραγιδονυχαργοκομήτας, | κυκλίων τε χορῶν ἀσματοκάμπτας ἄνδρας μετεωροφένακας, | οὐδὲν δρῶντας βόσκους᾽ ἀργούς, ὅτι ταύτας μουσοποιοῦσιν.

[42] Ar. *Ran.* 943, 1049.

testimony seem to have been exhibitions of their authors' particular crafts. The *Tetralogies* of Antiphon, like Gorgias' *Helen* and *Palamedes*, were surely meant to demonstrate the skill with words their composer had. Antiphon is also credited with a book on dream interpretation, in which he likewise displays his ability to provide interpretations that surpass those of other experts, and his *Truth* may have been, like Gorgias' *On Not-Being*, a demonstration that he could win an argument on any point, regardless of its truth.[43] Such displays of technical prowess naturally created concern as well as admiration. The story that Protagoras' books were burned in Athens because of his subversive and newfangled ideas is probably a later invention, but it nevertheless attests to the tradition that sophists and their books were viewed with suspicion.[44] In Plato's *Apology*, Socrates refers to the books of Anaxagoras, which anyone can get for a drachma, as proof that he is not the source of the ideas his accusers claim are corrupting the youth.[45] Likewise, a fragment of Aristophanes refers to someone who has been corrupted, either by Prodikos or by a book.[46] The book here marks the sophist and can even substitute for him, just as the Euripidean smoke of many books or the Platonic hubbub of books marks those connected with Orpheus.

But bookishness was not confined to the likes of Antiphon and Gorgias; as Aristophanes' mockery indicates, doctors were considered in much the same category. While the dating of the Hippocratic writings is notoriously problematic, the first treatises seem to be circulating in the fifth century, making use of the new technology to promote their new systems.[47] Once again, the wisdom of the medical sophists is as clearly linked with books as that of the other types. In a conversation that indeed centers on the problem

---

[43] The identity of "Antiphon the sophist" with "Antiphon the Athenian" and "Antiphon the logographer" has been well argued by Gagarin 2002: 37–62, *contra* Pendrick 2002: 1–26. For discussions on the nature of *Truth*, see Gagarin 2002: 62–93; Pendrick 2002: 32–38.

[44] Cic. *Nat. D.* 1.63, Diog. Laert. 9.52.

[45] Pl. *Ap.* 26de: "And do you so look down upon these men and consider them so unversed in letters that they do not know that the books of Anaxagoras the Clazomenian are full of these arguments? And indeed, do the young learn these things from me, which it is possible for them sometimes to buy (if it is very costly) for a drachma in the bazaar and to laugh at Socrates, if he claims they are his own, especially since they are so bizarre?" καὶ οὕτω καταφρονεῖς τῶνδε καὶ οἴει αὐτοὺς ἀπείρους γραμμάτων εἶναι ὥστε οὐκ εἰδέναι ὅτι τὰ Ἀναξαγόρου βιβλία τοῦ Κλαζομενίου γέμει τούτων τῶν λόγων; καὶ δὴ καὶ οἱ νέοι ταῦτα παρ' ἐμοῦ μανθάνουσιν, ἃ ἔξεστιν ἐνίοτε εἰ πάνυ πολλοῦ δραχμῆς ἐκ τῆς ὀρχήστρας πριαμένοις Σωκράτους καταγελᾶν, ἐὰν προσποιῆται ἑαυτοῦ εἶναι, ἄλλως τε καὶ οὕτως ἄτοπα ὄντα; Note that the audience for these books are those who are not "unversed in letters".

[46] Ar. *Tagenistae* fr. 490 KA: τοῦτον τὸν ἄνδρ' ἢ βυβλίον διέφθορεν | ἢ Πρόδικος ἢ τῶν ἀδολεσχῶν εἷς γέ τις.

[47] Cp. Jouanna 1999: 56–71.

of trying to acquire true wisdom through books, Xenophon's Socrates mocks the young Euthydemus by a comparison with the knowledge of doctors, noting that the writings of the doctors are many.[48] The doctors' books are only a selection among Euthydemus' collection; Socrates also mentions architects, geometers, and astronomers, other types of experts in knowledge whose wisdom Euthydemus might acquire from their books. These books are the medium through which these experts communicate their expertise to the limited set of those who wish likewise to claim expertise.

Aristophanes, in his *Birds*, mocks a similar series of experts who show up at the newly founded CloudCuckooland, all pushing their claims to authority with books in hand. Meton, parodied as an astrogeometer, waves his tools and treatises about, while the inspector and the decree-seller both have books (βιβλία) with decrees they claim give them power and authority in the city.[49] "What's this book?" Peisthetairos asks as the last of his visitors interrupts his sacrifice, "What is the problem now?"[50] The book and the troublesome claim of an interfering expert to authority are one and the same. The most extended controversy over the authority of a book comes earlier in the scene, when the oraclemonger repeatedly bolsters his claims to special treatment by reference to his book with a collection of oracles. "And giving a share of the sacrificial entrails to you, that's in there?" asks Peisthetairos. "Look at the book," replies the oraclemonger. After a whole series of these claims, each of which is backed up by the book, Peisthetairos loses patience and invents his own oracle, authorizing him to smack the charlatan between the ribs, and, whenever the oraclemonger protests, he retorts, "look at the book."[51] Once again, the book stands for the claim to special knowledge and authority that Aristophanes is mocking in the scene, and Peisthetairos' invention of an imaginary book of his own comically suggests the insubstantiality of such claims.

Such oracle collections seem to have been the tools of the trade for experts who claimed mantic authority, even if such claims are mocked in comedy. Isokrates relates the story of a *mantis*, Polemainetos, who, since he lacked a son to whom he could pass on the family profession, passed down his

---

[48] Xen. *Mem.* 4.2.10: πολλὰ γὰρ καὶ ἰατρῶν ἐστι συγγράμματα.

[49] While the books of the inspector (1024) and the decree-seller (1036) are mentioned explicitly, Meton's κανόνες are probably a pun, indicating not only his measuring tools but also his treatises on proper measurement, like the *Kanon* of Polykleitos, a treatise on measurement in sculpture that seems to have been well-known in Athens at this time. Cp. Stewart 1998 for the nature of Polykleitos' text. I owe this suggestion to Alex Herda.

[50] Ar. *Av.* 1036: τουτὶ τί ἐστιν αὖ κακόν, τὸ βυβλίον;

[51] Ar. *Av.* 975–976; 981–989.

books to a guestfriend, Thrasyllos, who thereupon took up the profession of an itinerant diviner himself.[52] The use of such collections, however, was not limited to full-time professionals like Thrasyllos; various political figures seem to have derived at least some of their political influence from their expertise at deploying the interpretation of oracles in the Assembly debates.[53] Aristophanes parodies such figures in the conflict in his *Knights* between the Kleon-figure, the Paphlagonian, and his rival, the Sausage-Seller, for the direction of Demos. Both rascals claim to have a huge store of oracles that will delight Demos, and they bring their texts out for their contest of oracles to win the favor of Demos. Even if, practically speaking, they could no more flip through these texts on stage to find the oracle for the moment than Peisthetairos or his oraclemonger in the *Birds*, the point is nonetheless that this kind of claim to special knowledge and authority was always imagined as being bolstered by a text, whether anyone actually read it or not.

The book, then, is not a sign of a particular religious orientation that takes sacred texts more seriously than other types of Greek religion. Particularly in fifth-century Athens, the context from which the evidence for the hubbub of Orphic books comes, the book signifies a claim to special expertise, to extra-ordinary wisdom. It marks the avant-garde intellectual of any type, not simply the religious deviant, although the books of Orpheus seem to have found their place, along with collections of oracles and treatises on divination, among the tools of religious specialists who claimed extra-ordinary wisdom and authority.

The contest context

The hubbub of books by Orpheus and Mousaios described by Plato is therefore just part of an even larger hubbub of books going on in Athens in the fifth century, and Plato himself, in his attacks on the sophists, provides the most vivid pictures of such clamor, the disputes back and forth between rival experts professing special knowledge. This hubbub is importantly and essentially agonistic; the books are deployed in struggles for

---

[52] Isoc. 19.5–6, 45. In addition to the books, Polemainetos also passed on some property, which is being claimed in the case by one of the (many) illegitimate sons Thrasyllos fathered in his wanderings. On this story, see Bowden 2003: 259; for the distinctions, often fuzzy, between *mantis* and *chresmologos*, see Dillery 2005.

[53] Hierokles, who appears as an expert consulted by the Assembly in *IG*³ 40.64–66, is referred to in Ar. *Pax* 1043–1047 as a charlatan and oraclemonger. He seems to have been honored by the Athenian Assembly with the right of *sitesis* at the Prytaneion, a privilege reserved for the greatest benefactors of the state, although Flower 2008b: 123 n. 43 expresses some reasonable doubts.

discursive authority, in contests where the prize is the reputation for wisdom and all the influence that comes with it. Aristophanes' contest between the weaker and stronger argument in the *Clouds* takes such contests to an absurd extreme, but it is worth noting that the function of the contest is to convince the onlookers that Socrates has wisdom worth acquiring. As Gagarin notes, these sophistic contests are the direct descendants of the wisdom contests that provided the performance contexts for most of the poetry and prose in the Greek tradition, a competitive tradition that continued in the poetic competitions (of tragedy, comedy, and other forms) of the religious festivals.[54]

An early Hippocratic treatise describes this milieu, in which various pretenders to medical knowledge dispute with one another over the superiority of their ideas. In his own polemical attempt to distinguish himself from his rivals, the author complains that they show no understanding or consistency in their terminology or principles. He draws a vivid picture of the public arena, in which such disputations, like wrestling matches, might be won by whoever knocked down his opponent three times in a row.

> One could understand this best, if he were present when they were debating. For when the same speakers dispute with one another in front of the same audience, the same man never wins in the discussion three times in a row, but sometimes this one wins, sometimes that one, and sometimes whoever happens to have the most fluent tongue in addressing the mob.[55]

The written rhetoric of the texts seems to mirror this oral performance contest context. Many of the Hippocratic treatises begin with polemical sections, rhetorically denouncing rival practitioners and explaining why the speaker's own method is the best.[56] Betegh has noted that the appeal to systematic knowledge and the ability to explain in a consistent and logical fashion is one strategy that such medical treatises share with the author of the Derveni papyrus.[57] Systematization and the claim to a reasoned

---

[54] Gagarin 2002: 18–22. For this contestive tradition, see Griffith 1990.

[55] Hippoc. *Nat. Hom.* 1.15–20: Γνοίη δ' ἄν τις τόδε μάλιστα παραγενόμενος αὐτέοισιν ἀντιλέγουσιν· πρὸς γὰρ ἀλλήλους ἀντιλέγοντες οἱ αὐτοὶ ἄνδρες τῶν αὐτέων ἐναντίον ἀκροατέων οὐδέποτε τρὶς ἐφεξῆς ὁ αὐτὸς περιγίνεται ἐν τῷ λόγῳ, ἀλλὰ ποτὲ μὲν οὗτος ἐπικρατέει, ποτὲ δὲ οὗτος, ποτὲ δὲ ᾧ ἂν τύχῃ μάλιστα ἡ γλῶσσα ἐπιρρυεῖσα πρὸς τὸν ὄχλον. Jouanna 1975: 55–60, attributes this text to Polybos, the son-in-law of Hippocrates, and conjectures that it was written sometime in the last decade of the fifth century.

[56] Hippoc. *Art.* 1, e.g., consists largely of such polemics. Cp. Jouanna 1999: 80–85.

[57] Betegh 2004: 354–359. Betegh is at pains to distinguish the empirical verifiability of medical technique from the lack thereof in ritual practice, but, setting aside the question of how empirically verifiable medical practice really was in fifth-century Athens, I would emphasize the shared rhetorical strategy of systematic exposition as a means of winning the clientele's trust in the expert's authority.

account become in themselves evidence for the expertise and authority of the speaker, regardless of the area of expertise claimed or the specifics of the system.

Such contests, however, reflect a hubbub of advertisements for clientele, rather than an organized competition for official positions. Although some scholars of ancient medicine have imagined a public audition for doctors seeking an official post of "public doctor," the references to such competitions reflect rather these unofficial debates that help to establish the reputation of an expert.[58] Of course, a reputation for wisdom and expertise was good not just for private clients, but also for public authority, since, as Oliver points out, "During the fifth century boards of experts were customarily set up to study special problems for which special knowledge was required and to make recommendations in the form of *xyngraphai*."[59] Oliver, however, is discussing not medical experts, but religious ones, and he refers to an Athenian decree regulating the offering of first fruits at Eleusis as a case in which a panel of experts, including the famous *mantis* Lampon, were selected to provide recommendations on how the city should act.[60] Lampon was notorious for his political involvement, but others must have been constantly vying for influence in the Assembly on the basis of their religious expertise. Hierokles, who appears as the prominent expert in another decree, was at some point, like Lampon, granted the great civic

As Betegh concedes, "The explanatory account provided for ritual action can have more persuasive power, which can certainly enhance also the psychological efficacy of the practice joined to it, when it satisfies certain criteria of validity applicable also in the domain of medical theories. And this is especially so in a culture where people have been made sensitive to such features as internal logical consistency, the economy of causal principles and so forth, through the critical discussions and professional rivalry that went on notably in medicine and philosophy. If so, certain representatives of the priestly *techne* could also feel that their explanatory accounts have to satisfy such criteria in order to retain their persuasive power" (Betegh 2004: 359).

[58] Jouanna 1999: 76–80 seriously misconstrues the evidence in imagining auditions for an official post of public doctor. The jokes about Pittalos in Ar. *Ach.* 1030–1032 do not imply that he had an official post, just that he was well-known as a healer; indeed Cohn-Haft 1956: 11 n. 24 suggests that the otherwise unidentifiable Pittalos was probably not even a doctor, since the jokes would be funnier if he were, for example, a well-known *hippiatros*. For the idea of public auditions, Jouanna relies on several passages of Plato's *Gorgias* taken out of context (455b, 456b, 514de). A closer examination of these passages in the context of the dialogue, however, shows that such doctors, like the shipbuilders and architects, are seeking to use their established reputations to be chosen for a particular project whose funding and execution are under debate in the Assembly. The passages from Xenophon likewise refer to someone seeking to undertake medical work for the city (παρὰ τῆς πόλεως ἰατρικὸν ἔργον) or for a military expedition (Xen. *Mem.* 4.2.5, cp. *Cyr.* 1.6.15).

[59] Oliver 1950: 8.

[60] *IG* i³ 78 = ML 73: περὶ δὲ τὸ ἔλαίο ἀπαρ χ ἐς χ συγγράφ | σας Λάμπον ἐπιδει χ σάτο τῆι βολῆι ἐπὶ τὲς ἐνάτες πρυτανείας· | θε δὲ βολὲ ἐς τὸν δῆμον ἐχσενενκέτο ἐπάναγκες. Lampon is undoubtedly the Thuriomantis to whom Aristophanes refers in *Nub.* 332, and he was a prominent figure in Athens at the time, an associate of Perikles (cp. Plut. *Vit. Per.* 6.2) who was one of the founders of the colony of Thurii (Diod. Sic. 12.10.3–4, cp. ΣAr. *Nub.* 332). Cp. Dillery 2005: 196–197.

privilege of dining in the Prytaneion for his services to Athens. The Platonic Euthyphro, however, complains that he is often mocked when he speaks in the Assembly, urging various causes on the basis of his expertise in religious matters. We need not imagine Euthyphro a farcical crank, however, who was just a joke in the Assembly; he was influential enough to become a target of Plato's critiques in two dialogues, even if his assertions of special wisdom were not always accepted in public debates.[61] Even the successful were not immune from mockery. Lampon and Hierokles, for example, despite the official recognition by the Assembly of their expertise, are portrayed as money-grubbing charlatans in Aristophanes.[62] Just as tendentiously, Plato lumps together the beggar-priests (ἀγύρται) and diviners who not only come to the doors of the rich, but convince whole cities of their special power and expertise. For every type of expertise, there was a whole spectrum of experts seeking authority and public recognition of their wisdom, and to collapse the distinctions between the widely respected and the lunatic fringe is in itself a polemical move, rejecting all rival claims to wisdom.

Indeed, victory in such a contest could be tantamount to proving oneself a legitimate wise man or divinely inspired interpreter, while the price of loss could be the reputation for fraud. The idea that Onomakritos was a charlatan given to forging oracles and other texts (including, as scholars as early as Pausanias have claimed, Orphic poems) may stem from his famous loss to Lasos of Hermione, who, as Herodotus tells us, caught him in the act of interpolating an oracle of Mousaios that the islands off Lemnos would slide into the sea.[63] Dillery has persuasively argued that this episode is best understood in the context of a traditional wisdom contest, in which Lasos and Onomakritos are competing in the Peisistratid court to show which is best at recounting and explaining the difficult oracle texts.[64] The precise details of how one could be caught in the act (ἐπ᾽ αὐτοφώρῳ ἁλούς) of adding in (ἐμποιέων) an oracle of Mousaios remain

---

[61] In addition to the *Euthyphro*, much of the *Cratylus* concerns Euthyphro's expertise. Cp. Kahn 1997 for the suggestion that the Derveni author was Euthyphro or someone much like him.

[62] E.g., *Nub.* 332, *Av.* 987–988, *Pax* 1043–1047. The fact that Hierokles, who seems to have been consulted as an *exegetes* and perhaps even acted as a *mantis*, could be called a *chresmologos* and *alazon*, shows that the terminology was not precise, but depended, as so often, on the speaker's point of view or axe to grind. *Exegetes* was a term implying public acceptance, whereas *mantis* and *chresmologos* could have less positive connotations. Cp. Dillery 2005: 194–197.

[63] Hdt. 7.6.3: "Onomakritos had been banished from Athens by Hipparchos, the son of Peisistratos, when he was caught by Lasos of Hermione in the act of interpolating into the works of Mousaios an oracle to the effect that the islands off Lemnos would disappear into the sea." ἐξηλάσθη γὰρ ὑπὸ Ἱππάρχου τοῦ Πεισιστράτου ὁ Ὀνομάκριτος ἐξ Ἀθηνέων, ἐπ᾽ αὐτοφώρῳ ἁλοὺς ὑπὸ Λάσου τοῦ Ἑρμιονέος ἐμποιέων ἐς τὰ Μουσαίου χρησμόν, ὡς αἱ ἐπὶ Λήμνῳ ἐπικείμεναι νῆσοι ἀφανιζοίατο κατὰ τῆς θαλάσσης.

[64] Dillery 2005, esp. 188–191. Cp. Privitera 1965: 48, for the poetic contest.

unclear, but a scenario in which Onomakritos is publicly humiliated by Lasos and made to seem a fool who tries to make things up rather than a wise man who explicates the existing texts seems more plausible than some scenario in which Lasos somehow comes upon Onomakritos in the act of forging (rather than recopying) an oracle of Mousaios. Lasos triumphs on that occasion, to the extent that Hipparchos drives Onomakritos out of Athens, but, in later times, Hipparchos' brother Hippias is happy to make use of Onomakritos' services when they both are at the Persian court and trying to solicit Persian assistance to return to Athens. The winner in the wisdom contest, Lasos, is better known for his innovative poetry, although none is preserved, while Onomakritos ends up with the reputation of a fraudulent diviner, a charlatan who invents or manipulates false oracles to curry favor with his clients.

Although the way in which Lasos triumphed over Onomakritos is not clear, another episode in Herodotus, the debate over the famous Delphic "wooden wall" oracle, provides more details about the actual process of the disputation. As Herodotus relates, when faced with an imminent Persian invasion, the Athenians asked the oracle at Delphi what they should do.[65] Dissatisfied with the first dire response, which mostly described the devastation of Attica, the officially appointed delegates to the oracle brought home a second response.

> Pallas, praying with many arguments and her clever cunning, is not able to propitiate Olympian Zeus. But to you again I will speak my verse, having made it firm as adamant. While other things, all those that the boundary of Kekrops holds within it and the vales of holy Kithairon, will be captured, far-seeing Zeus will give a wooden wall to Tritogeneia that alone will stand untaken. But, you, do not wait in quiet for the cavalry and great army of foot soldiers coming from the mainland, but depart from the land, turning your back. There still will come a time when you will be face to face. Divine Salamis, you will destroy the sons of women, whether perhaps when Demeter's grain is scattered or when it is gathered in.[66]

---

[65] This fascinating episode has been the subject of many studies that have focused on various aspects of the oracle and the Athenian response, e.g. Struck 2003 and Dillery 2005. While the absolute historicity of anything in Herodotus can never be taken for granted, I find it plausible that the Athenians would have consulted the oracle as early as Herodotus says they did and that the oracle could have made such a reply (in verse!), since the power of the Persian army, the significance of the proposed wall across the isthmus, and the strategic importance of Salamis would have been topics of discussion in the Assembly of Athens and probably elsewhere. Even if the episode is an invention after the battle of Salamis, however, it still provides insights into the ways Herodotus and his contemporaries thought about the interpretation of oracles as contests of wisdom with political implications.

[66] Hdt. 7.141: Οὐ δύναται Παλλὰς Δί' Ὀλύμπιον ἐξιλάσασθαι, | λισσομένη πολλοῖσι λόγοις καὶ μήτιδι πυκνῇ· | σοὶ δὲ τόδ' αὖτις ἔπος ἐρέω, ἀδάμαντι πελάσσας. | Τῶν ἄλλων γὰρ ἁλισκομένων ὅσα

What they did not bring home was a plan of action in response to this oracle; it was the task of the Assembly to debate what to do. Obviously, however, what to do depended on what the oracle meant, and Herodotus describes the conflict in the Assembly over the interpretation of the oracle. In this public disputation, the rising politician Themistokles proved himself the best interpreter of the oracle, pointing out an interpretation of the oracle that provided the Athenians with a constructive solution to their problem. Rejecting the interpretation of the "wooden wall" as the hedge around the acropolis, he sided with those who had understood it as the Athenian fleet. However, he also provided an explanation of the line that had baffled other interpreters, explaining that Salamis who would bring death to women's sons was called "divine" because those deaths would be Persian deaths rather than Athenian.[67] Such parsing of the meaning of a single word gave Themistokles his opportunity to show his interpretive skills and to demonstrate his religious and political wisdom, and his performance in this public contest proved the most convincing to the Athenian people, who agreed to his plan and granted him authority to execute it.[68] While Herodotus refers to *chresmologoi*, people giving accounts of oracles, who offered opinions on the oracle's meaning, these figures need not only have been professionals whose only livelihood came from interpreting oracles. Themistokles is competing here, not against some official board of oracular interpreters, but against a hubbub of different voices, each putting forth their own credentials and explanations for their own interpretations. The stakes in such contests might be very high, especially when conducted in public, and the grounds on which they were decided very small, just the interpretation of a single word.

Aristophanes' *Knights* provides a comic look at such disputes over religious expertise and their political implications. Aristophanes stages a competition in wisdom between a Paphlagonian slave, representing the

---

Κέκροπος οὖρος | ἐντὸς ἔχει κευθμῶν τε Κιθαιρῶνος ζαθέοιο, | τεῖχος Τριτογενεῖ ξύλινον διδοῖ εὐρύοπα Ζεύς | μοῦνον ἀπόρθητον τελέθειν, τὸ σὲ τέκνα τ' ὀνήσει. | Μηδὲ σύ γ' ἱπποσύνην τε μένειν καὶ πεζὸν ἰόντα | πολλὸν ἀπ' ἠπείρου στρατὸν ἥσυχος, ἀλλ' ὑποχωρεῖν | νῶτον ἐπιστρέψας· ἔτι τοί ποτε κἀντίος ἔσση. | Ὦ θείη Σαλαμίς, ἀπολεῖς δὲ σὺ τέκνα γυναικῶν | ἤ που σκιδναμένης Δήμητερος ἢ συνιούσης.

[67] As Dillery 2005: 212 comments about Themistokles, "in the story of Salamis he plays the role of the clairvoyant religious expert who can see what other experts and authorities cannot. The controversy surrounding the interpretation of 'divine Salamis' takes on the look of a competition, along the lines of what we see with Onomacritus and Lasus, Trygaeus and Hierocles, or perhaps even Calchas and Mopsus."

[68] Struck 2003: 185 describes the contest of oracular interpretations as a test of the best man, "a situation in which, in practice, a divine sign comes to mean precisely what the best of the men who read it say it means. The correct reading of it is, by definition, that which is delivered by the hero who is best equipped, with the tools of persuasive speech, to press his case on his peers."

prominent politician Kleon, and an even more knavish Sausage-Seller for the influence of Demos, the master of the house and representative of the Athenian *demos*. Not only does each have a huge collection of books with oracles, indicating their avant-garde intellectual pretensions, but the contest itself centers around the display of interpretations. This being Aristophanes, the interpretations are absurd, and scatological and sexual humor is never far away, but the form of the contest is in interpretation of the enigmatic words of the oracles, and each competitor tries to outdo the other in providing a comprehensible explanation of the oracle that takes into account as much of the verses as possible. So, for example, when the Paphlagonian quotes an oracle that he claims refers to himself as the lion of Athens who must be preserved (σῴζειν), the Sausage-Seller points out that he has not explicated the reference to the wall of wood and brass and proceeds to win the round by explaining the wall as a collar to bind (δῆσαι) this savage beast down (1036–1049). The superior interpreter shows his ability to explain the text, in itself and in its entirety, and to find meanings that relate most appropriately to the context – in this case, the relation of Kleon to the Athenians.[69] The stakes of the contest are influence and authority with Demos, the representative of the Athenian *demos*, who at the end of the contest vows, "I shall yield myself to you; guide me in my old age and educate me anew."[70]

Whatever the forum, the contest is always for such influence, whether for political authority in the Assembly, medical clientele in an Agora debate, or students in a sophistic display. Indeed, the competition described in Plato's *Protagoras* over the interpretation of a poem by Simonides provides the most detailed account of such a wisdom contest in fifth-century Athens, showing how the exegesis of an authoritative text could provide the opportunity for someone claiming extra-ordinary wisdom to demonstrate the validity of his claim and his superiority over his rivals. Plato's scene is set with an all-star cast of sophists, the better to display the prowess of his champion Socrates. Not only does Protagoras, the man famous for introducing the teaching of disputation for profit in Athens, take the role as Socrates' chief adversary, but many of the other leading intellectuals of the day (especially Hippias and Prodikos) just happen to be present to pitch in and be defeated in their turn.[71] Of course, in his typical fashion, Plato has Socrates eventually

---

[69] It is worth comparing the principles of interpretation that Most 1994: 132–133 outlines, especially the emphasis on contextualization and the principle of economy.

[70] Ar. *Eq.* 1098–1099: Καὶ νῦν ἐμαυτὸν ἐπιτρέπω σοι τουτονὶ γεροντ αγωγεῖν κἀναπαιδεύειν πάλιν.

[71] As Ford 2005: 4 puts it, "If Plato were writing the *Protagoras* for our time, he would set it around 1970: young Hippocrates would be thinking about graduate study in literature, and would drag

change the rules of the game and invent his own kind of contest, more suited to Platonic philosophical inquiry, but, before the Socratic shift, he makes it clear that Socrates can compete in the traditional kind of wisdom contest and win against the greatest possible opponents.[72]

Protagoras sets up the contest by claiming that "The most important part of education is being clever concerning poetry (περὶ ἐπῶν δεινὸν); that is, to understand what is said by the poets, both rightly and not, and to be able to tell the difference and to give an account when challenged" (339a). He quotes a poem of Simonides and proceeds to demonstrate his cleverness by claiming that the wise Simonides contradicts himself by first claiming that to be good is hard and then denying Pittakos' claim that it is hard to be good. Protagoras thus shows himself to be wiser not only than Simonides, a respectable old poet whom he himself had ranked with Homer as one of those who practiced his own art of sophistry in ancient times, but also than Socrates, who had just approved this poem of Simonides as finely and correctly composed (καλῶς τε καὶ ὀρθῶς). Socrates responds with his own elaborate interpretation, in which he resolves Protagoras' contradiction, proving himself better both at the analysis of the fine details of the words and at the explication of the text and context of the poem as a whole.[73] On the one hand, Socrates draws the distinction between γενέσθαι and ἔμμεναι as "becoming" and "being", allowing him to twist the sense of the verses to fit the meaning for which he is arguing. On the other, he contextualizes the poem within a wisdom competition between Simonides and Pittakos, providing explanations not only for more of the poem but for the motivations of the poet in writing the lines. Regardless of Plato's larger purposes for this contest within the dialogue, his depiction of the way the contestants use the exegesis of a traditional text as a way to exhibit their *sophia* helps to fill in the picture for all the other wisdom contests in our evidence for fifth-century Athens, setting out more fully the exchanges that Aristophanes merely brings up for a joke or that other authors mention only in passing.

Like the contests of oracle explanations, the Simonides contest involves the exegesis of an existing text, rather than the creation of a new one, as

---

Socrates out of bed to get into the School of Criticism & Theory at Irvine, where Derrida, de Man and Jameson all happened to be passing through. We readers would be allowed to eavesdrop on the discussion, in which the savants would explain why our young man should study with them and would illustrate their claims by analyzing a tough poem of – say – Mallarmé along the way."

[72] Cp. the analysis of Ledbetter 2003: 99–118, for some indications of the way Plato uses the debate over the ode to set up his more complex points later in the dialogue.

[73] Cp. Most 1994 for an account of Socrates' method here as a model of interpretation.

in the case of the sophistic long speeches or the medical treatises.[74] At stake in each contest is the reputation of the participants as wise men in the face of the audience that observes them, a reputation that not only determines who and how many will choose to employ their services (as healers, teachers, or advisors), but also how those who take their wisdom seriously will choose to live. Plato's Socrates may belittle the whole contest as the sort of thing that boorish folk do at the symposium when they have drunk too much, but the choice of a Protagorean or Socratic view of the world could have a substantial impact on an Athenian's way of life, just as the choice between following the medical regime of a Hippocratic doctor or some other, not to mention the choice between Themistokles' (or Kleon's) interpretation of an oracle or someone else's. Neither Socrates' nor the sophists' interpretations nor even the chresmologues' oracle readings should be taken as a meaningless joke, since each interpreter sees an important meaning in the text he is explaining, however bizarre the twists of reasoning may seem to other observers.

The epideixis of exegesis: The Derveni author and his text

It is precisely in such a context that we can best understand the aims and methods of the Derveni author. The Derveni author is a religious specialist who is putting his wisdom and expertise on display in the treatise on the Derveni papyrus, and one of the primary ways in which he demonstrates his abilities is through his exegesis of the Orphic poem. The Derveni author's attention to the minute details of the lines of the Orphic poem has led some modern scholars to think the Derveni author a literary critic, an innovator writing a commentary before commentaries were invented, while his bizarre interpretations and ruthless wrenching of the text to fit the cosmological principles he describes have misled others trying to understand his relation to the poem of Orpheus. Scholars who view the Orphic poem either as sacred scripture or as a ritual text for the Derveni author have great trouble in understanding what the Derveni author might be doing with his exegesis.[75] The comparison with the methods used in the Simonides contest in the *Protagoras*, as well as in the interpretation of

---

[74] Hippias' offer (347b) to perform a long speech on the same subject shows, however, that these two modes were seen as comparable games, even if Plato's Socrates repeatedly rejects the legitimacy of the long speech as a mode of philosophic activity.

[75] Cp. Parker 1995: 488–489: "It is hard to see a practicing Orpheotelest finding this particular commentary very helpful. A scandalous story about the gods becomes, in the author's hands, not an unscandalous story about the gods, but rather about physics; and he speaks with scorn of the way in which clients of 'those who make a profession out of rites' (i.e., Orpheotelests) are left

oracles, however, shows that the Derveni author is not so anomalous; his techniques are actually quite commonplace in such discourse.

Like the interpreters of oracles or like the sophists tackling the text of Simonides, the challenge is to determine the true meaning of the existing and authoritative text.[76] Just as the moral authority of the famous and canonical poet Simonides is taken for granted by all the interlocutors, so too the extra-ordinary authority of Orpheus is assumed by the Derveni author. The Derveni author explicitly claims that Orpheus is communicating important truths in his holy account of the accession of Zeus to supreme power in the cosmos. "But Orpheus did not intend to tell them captious riddles, but momentous things in riddles. Indeed, he is telling a holy discourse from the first."[77] Like Plato disparaging eristic sophists like Euthydemos and Dionysodoros in the *Euthydemus* or like the Hippocratic doctors denouncing, in their rhetorical treatises, other doctors who merely use words to bedazzle their audiences, the Derveni author dismisses mere eristic word-juggling for the understanding of Orpheus' text; his own interpretations reveal the important meaning. However much his own hermeneutic maneuvers may seem indistinguishable to us from sophistic eristic, the Derveni author stakes his claim to expertise through this standard move of differentiating himself from his rivals.

Indeed, the similarity of his interpretive strategies to those of the oraclemongers mocked by Aristophanes or of the sophists criticized by Plato have led some modern scholars to doubt either the intelligence or the sincerity of the Derveni author. "Our preposterous commentator", as West refers to him, seems to go out of his way to avoid the obvious meaning of the text, with the result that "his interpretations are uniformly false. Not once does he come near to giving a correct explanation of anything in his text."[78] However, giving an explanation finely and correctly (καλῶς τε καὶ ὀρθῶς) was, as we saw, the aim in the Simonides contest too, and we should assess the Derveni author's expertise in the context of this sort of contest, rather than by the standards of nineteenth- and twentieth-century philology. The Derveni author, like the contestants in the *Protagoras*, seeks

completely unenlightened about the meaning of those rites. If the commentator thought of himself as an Orphic, he was surely one of a very singular stamp. For our purposes, he is just the misty glass through which we seek to gaze at Orpheus."

[76] Betegh 2004: 365: "The task does not consist in proving *that* the pronouncement is true, but in understanding *how* it is true."

[77] col. 7.5–7 (*OF* 669i B): [ὁ δ]ὲ [Ὀρφεὺ]ς αὐτο[ῖς] [ἐ]ρίστ' αἰν[ίγμα]τα οὐκ ἤθελε λέγειν, [ἐν αἰν]ίγμασ[ι]ν δὲ [μεγ]άλα. ἱερ[ολογ]εῖ ται μὲν οὖγ καὶ α[πὸ το]ῦ πρώτου.

[78] West 1983: 82, 79. See his assessment: "the commentator, who is in general the least trustworthy of guides" (88). Rusten 1985: 125, likewise, speaks of "the unscrupulous commentator."

to make an explanation that demonstrates his own *sophia*, his acuity and cleverness in explicating the details as well as his understanding of the significance of the text as a whole.

The Derveni author insists, in one of the most controversial passages, that every word of Orpheus must be treated carefully. "Since in his whole work he speaks about matters enigmatically, one has to speak about each word in turn."[79] In this case, the Derveni author is speaking about the phallus (αἰδοῖον), presumably of Ouranos the first-born god, which he explains must be understood as the sun, since both the phallus and the sun are generative of new life.[80] The Derveni author shows how an event within the Orphic poem enigmatically signifies the role of the sun and its fire in the generation of life in the cosmos, and he calls attention to his own act of exegesis, displaying his own skill at revealing the obscure significance of a possibly scandalous line.

Some of his techniques are fairly sophisticated, displaying his ability to situate the Orphic poem within a wider poetic context. Following his policy of word by word exegesis, he tackles the potentially problematic line in which Zeus desires to sleep with his own mother (μητρὸς ἑᾶς). "Mother" he explains as Mind, but he makes a more complex argument about ἑᾶς. Just as Socrates makes a point about the Lesbian dialect of Simonides' address to Pittakos, so too the Derveni author points out that in epic language the word ἑᾶς can mean "good", rather than "his own."[81] He cites two other verses in which ἑάων is used in the sense of "good things" and argues that Orpheus could have used ἑοῖο had he wanted to convey the sense of ἑαυτοῦ.[82] Such an argument may seem ludicrous to a modern philologist, but, within the context of these wisdom contests, it should be taken seriously as a display of the Derveni author's facility with

---

[79] col. 13.6–7 (*OF* 2iii B): ὅτι μὲμ πᾶσαμ τὴμ πόησιν περὶ τῶν πραγμάτων αἰνίζεται κ[α]θ' ἔπος ἕκαστον ἀνάγκη λέγειν. (Betegh's trans. modified).

[80] col. 13.8–11. The interpretation of this line has caused much controversy, but I agree with Betegh 2004 and others in assuming that the Orphic poem had αἰδοῖον as phallus, rather than imagining that the Derveni author has introduced the idea of the phallus into the text, as West 1983 and others have argued. (See further below, ch. 6, *Cosmogony*, "Close the doors of your ears".)

[81] Pl. *Prt.* 346e1: "ἐπαίνημι – and there he has used a Mytilenaean word, since he is speaking to Pittakos." ἐπαίνημι – καὶ τῇ φωνῇ ἐνταῦθα κέχρηται τῇ τῶν Μυτιληναίων, ὡς πρὸς Πιττακὸν λέγων.

[82] col. 26.8–13. The lines he cites to bolster his argument are equivalent to *Od.* 8.335 and *Il.* 24.527–528, but it is not clear whether the Derveni author cites them as lines of Orpheus or of Homer. Kouremenos *et al.* 2006: 272 *ad loc.* take δηλοῖ as impersonal and reject the idea that the Derveni author might have considered the lines Orphic. Noting the suggestion of Obbink 1997: 41 n. 4, however, Betegh 2004: 100 points out that all the other uses of δηλοῖ in the text are personal and suggests that the question must be left open. The question makes little difference to the strategy of the Derveni author, however, especially if these lines are considered part of a common stock of hexameters utilized by epic poets, Orphic as well as Homeric, in their compositions.

his hermeneutic tools and of his ability to make satisfactory sense out of a troublesome text.

Even more strikingly, the Derveni author, like Socrates in the *Protagoras*, uses the concept of hyperbaton to provide an explanation of verses, the two earliest uses extant of this word as a technical term. Socrates claims that the adverb "truly" is transposed from modifying the whole concept of it being difficult to become good to the word "good."[83] The Derveni author argues that Orpheus uses hyperbaton in verses describing Zeus taking over the rulership of the cosmos.

> "And when Zeus took from his father the prophesied rule | And the strength in his hands and the glorious daimon." They ignore the fact that these words are transposed (ὑπερβατά). They are to be taken as follows: "Zeus when he took the strength from his father and the glorious daimon."[84]

In both cases, the interpreter is arguing that one must look beyond the obvious ordering of the words in the verse to see the true meaning of the poet's lines, and this true meaning discovered by the interpreter is substantially different from the obvious one. Not only is the new meaning preferable to the old one because of its correspondence with the ideas and values of the interpreter, but the very act of uncovering this meaning shows the interpreter's wisdom and hermeneutical expertise.

Many of the allegorical interpretations explicate things in the poem according to the cosmological vision of the Derveni author, such as the equation of Moira (Fate) with *pneuma* (breath) and *phronesis* (understanding) or the connection between Okeanos, air, and Zeus. Again, it is notable how the Derveni author calls attention to his own expertise. "This verse has been made misleading and it is unclear to the many, but to those who understand correctly it is clear that Okeanos is the air and air is Zeus."[85] Orpheus has composed enigmas that only someone as skilled as the Derveni author can explain, and the interpreter backs up his exegesis not only with reference to his general cosmological framework, but also with specific reference to details of the text, in this case the epithets "broad-flowing" applied to Okeanos.[86] At another point, he makes an even more subtle

---

[83] Pl. *Prt.* 343de.

[84] col. 8.4–8 (*OF* 5i B): Ζεὺς μὲν ἐπεὶ δὴ πα[τρὸς ἐο]ῦ πάρα θέ[σ]φατον ἀρχὴν | [ἀ]λκήν τ᾽ἐγ χείρεσσι ἔ[λ]αβ[εγ κ]αὶ δαίμον[α] κυδρόν | [τα]ῦτα τὰ ἔπη ὑπερβατὰ ἐό[ν]τα λανθά[νει], [ἔσ]τιν δὲ ὧδ᾽ ἔχοντα· Ζεὺς μὲν ἐπεὶ τ[ὴν ἀλ]κὴν [πα]ρὰ πατρὸς ἐοῦ ἔλαβεγ καὶ δαίμονα [κυδρ]όν.

[85] col. 23.1–3 (*OF* 16iii B): τοῦτο τὸ ἔπος πα[ρα]γωγὸμ πεπόηται καὶ το[ῖς μ]ὲν πολλοῖς ἄδηλόν ἐστι τοῖς δὲ ὀρθῶς γινώσκουσι εὔδηλον ὅτι Ὠκεανός ἐστιν ὁ ἀήρ.

[86] col. 23.5–10: "But those who do not understand think that Okeanos is a river because he [*sc.* Orpheus] added the epithet 'broadly flowing'. But he indicates his meaning in current and customary expressions. For they say that the very powerful among men 'flowed great'." οἱ δ᾽οὐ γινώσκοντες τὸν

argument with epithets, arguing that "Olympos" must mean "time", since Orpheus never uses the epithet "broad" of Olympos, whereas he does use that term of "heaven" (Ouranos).

> Olympos and time are the same. Those who think that Olympos and the heaven are the same are entirely mistaken, for they do not know that the heaven cannot be longer rather than wider; but if someone were to call time long, he would not be wrong at all. And whenever he (sc. Orpheus) wanted to speak about heaven, he added the epithet "wide," whereas whenever (he wanted to talk) about Olympos, on the contrary, he never (added the epithet) "wide", but "long."[87]

Here the Derveni author shows not only that he has an understanding of the lines superior to those who think that Olympos, the celestial home of the gods, is the same as the heaven, the celestial realm in which the gods make their home, but also that he has such a broad knowledge of the poetry of Orpheus that he can claim that Orpheus never used that epithet for that noun in any of his work. Again and again, the Derveni author's interpretations serve not so much to expound a systematic cosmological doctrine as to exhibit his own wisdom in understanding the hidden cosmological ideas and his own skill at uncovering them in the enigmatic poem of Orpheus.

Previous explanations of the Derveni author's methods have been problematic because they have seen as his principal aim the exposition of some doctrine, whether it be Orphic eschatology, Presocratic cosmology, or even the correspondence between the two. If the purpose of the text is rather to demonstrate the author's skill at his craft, the peculiar exegeses become more comprehensible. He is not incompetently expounding a system; he is selecting examples to display his expertise.[88] Like Antiphon's *Tetralogies* or Gorgias' *Defense of Helen*, the treatise in the Derveni papyrus illustrates

---

Ὠκεανὸν ποταμὸν δοκοῦσιν εἶναι ὅτι εὑρὺ ῥέοντα προσέθηκεν. ὁ δὲ σημαίνει τὴν αὑτοῦ γνώμην ἐν τοῖς λεγομέν[ο]ις καὶ νομιζομένοις ῥήμασι. καὶ γὰρ τῶν ἀν[θ]ρώπων τοὺς μέγα δῠνατ[οῦ]ντας μεγάλους φασὶ ῥυῆναι.

[87] col. 12.3–10: Ὀλυμπ[ος καὶ χ]ρόνος τὸ αὐτόν. οἱ δὲ δοκοῦντες Ὄλυμπ[ον καὶ] οὐρανὸν [τ]αὐτὸ εἶναι ἐξαμαρτάν[ουσ]ι[ν οὐ γ]ινώσκοντες ὅτι οὐρανὸν οὐχ οἷόν τε μακ[ρό]τερον ἢ εὑρύτε[ρο]ν εἶναι, χρόνον δὲ μακρὸν εἴ τις [ὀνομ]άζο[ι] οὐκ ἂ[ν ἐξα]μαρτάνοι· ὁ δὲ ὅπου μὲν οὐρανὸν θέ[λοι λέγειν, τὴμ] προσθήκεν εὐρὺν ἐποιεῖτο, ὅπου [δὲ Ὄλυμπον, το]ὐναντίον, εὐρὺμ μὲν οὐδέποτε, μα[κρὸν δέ.] Brisson 1997 provides the most detailed study of this passage.

[88] As Betegh 2004: 182 notes, the text is not organized to set out the underlying system: "Apart from the lacunose nature of the papyrus, what make the reconstruction so difficult is that the Derveni author does not explain his theory in a linear way, but distributes the elements of it in his exegetical remarks. In other words, the exposition is not governed by the internal logic of the theory." The cosmological ideas of the Derveni author have been deduced and reconstructed by a number of scholars, most importantly Betegh 2004, but also, e.g., Burkert 1968, Laks 1997, Bernabé 2002c, Janko 2002.

the cleverness of the author; it is a textual example of the kind of sophistic debate portrayed in the Hippocratic treatise and Plato's *Protagoras*.[89] The Derveni author's treatise takes the Orphic poem line by line, but he never seems to make a systematic exposition of either his cosmological theories or his religious ideas. The Derveni papyrus is thus part of Plato's hubbub of books, competing for clientele in the marketplace of the fifth century amid the swirling controversies of the sophists of all types. The Derveni author is advertising his skill at his craft, that of a religious specialist, the type parodied by Aristophanes, denounced as charlatans by the Hippocratics, and scorned by Plato. All the same, the evidence for public honors and successful careers for such figures should not be forgotten – Lampon, Hierokles, and Diopeithes in the fifth century, as well as later figures like Philochoros or Kleidemos, who seem to have served as *exegetai* as well as having written treatises on the ancient religious customs of Attica.

The Derveni author's boasts of superior knowledge, along with his demonstrations of exegetical cleverness, show that his treatise is aimed at winning clients in the public marketplace, not at showing a select group of sectarians the secret of salvation. The references to the secrets known only to a few are thus best understood as a rhetorical device that enhances the value of the speaker's expertise, not an atheist's public revelation of the sacred mysteries or even an indication of the limited circle of initiates who might understand his sermons.[90] The Derveni author's interpretations do not serve to expound a systematic cosmology to his audience, explaining his doctrine to his (potential) converts; rather, they put the emphasis on exhibiting his own wisdom in understanding the hidden cosmological ideas and his own skill at uncovering them in the enigmatic poem of Orpheus.

His expertise, moreover, is not merely in textual matters, but also in ritual. The Derveni author's concern with ritual practice has been evident ever since the first columns of the Derveni papyrus were published, revealing that the text was not merely a commentary on the poem. The Derveni author discusses making several kinds of offering to divine powers: libations in columns 2 and 6, sacrifices of birds in columns 2 and 6, and of many-knobbed cakes in column 6. The powers to whom these offerings are directed may be the Erinyes or Eumenides or the souls of the dead, but the Derveni author is providing not only instructions for what sort of offerings

---

[89] Cp. Thomas 2003 on the prose *epideixis* and its serious purposes for the sophists.

[90] *Contra* Brisson 2010: 24–25: "Le secret souhaité par Orphée est néanmoins préservé. Si le commentaire offre l'accès au texte à un public plus large, ses destinataires sont cependant les seuls lecteurs susceptibles de comprendre l'exégèse. La désignation constante de la foule ignorante est le repoussoir qui fait d'eux un cercle restreint et choisi."

are made, but also explanations for why such offerings are appropriate. "They sacrifice innumerable and many-knobbed cakes, because the souls, too, are innumerable."⁹¹ Again, the author is providing, not doctrinal or ritual instructions, but exegesis, demonstrating his understanding of the procedures rather than telling his readers what to do or to believe.

The Derveni author is not just expert in sacrificial procedures, he also refers to his mantic expertise. In column 5, he refers to clients who want to consult an oracle, wondering if a certain thing (unfortunately lost in a lacuna) is right (θέμις) or not, a standard oracular question. "For them we go into the oracular shrine to inquire for oracular answers."⁹² In addition to oracular shrines, the Derveni author also mentions oracular dreams, complaining that some people fail to understand the significance of dreams and, indeed, of other kinds of omens as well (τῶν ἄλλων πραγμάτων), all of which can serve as παραδείγματα, as warning signs of the will of the gods.⁹³ In the same way that Plato condemns those who fail to heed the correct path of philosophy, the Derveni author passes a moral judgment on those who disregard such omens; they are overcome by error and by pleasures, and so they fail to learn and to understand.⁹⁴ The Derveni author, then, is not only an expert at bringing back a meaningful response from an oracular shrine for a client with a question; perhaps like Antiphon, he could also provide interpretations of dreams and other omens.⁹⁵

The Derveni author was certainly not an anti-religious thinker, working to destroy traditional religion with his new-fangled cosmological ideas, as some have suggested. Aristophanes might regard him as such and classify

⁹¹ col. 6.7–8 (OF 471B): ἀνάριθμα [κα]ὶ πολυόμφαλα τὰ πόπανα θύουσιν, ὅτι καὶ αἱ ψυχα[ὶ ἀν]αριθμοί εἰσι. Cp. Henrichs 1984a, Johnston 1999: 137–138.
⁹² col. 5.4–5 (OF 473 B) χρησ[τ]ηριάζον[ται]. . . . αὐτοῖς πάριμεν [εἰς τὸ μα]ντεῖον ἐπερ[ω]τήσ[οντες], τῶν μαντευομένων [ἕν]εκεν, εἰ θέμι[. . .]. Janko attempts to make the whole consultation hinge on belief in the afterlife, casting the consultation as an inquiry of whether it is right to disbelieve in the terrors of Hades and comparing the later argument of Sext. Emp. Math. 9.56 (OF 641i, 642 B = OF 292 K) about the implausibility of the gods based on the implausibility of the terrors of Hades. Janko 1997: 68 imagines that Protagoras' treatise "on the things in Hades" must have had a similar argument and served as a source for the Derveni author.
⁹³ col. 5.6–8: οὐ γινώσ[κοντες ἐ]νύπνια οὐδὲ τῶν ἄλλων πραγμάτων ἕκαστ[ον], διὰ ποίων ἂν παραδειγμάτων π[ι]στεύοιεν. Rangos 2007: 37–38 rightly points out that οὐ γινώσκοντες ἐνύπνια must mean "not understanding what kind of things dreams are," rather than simply not understanding the (meaning of the) dream.
⁹⁴ col. 5.8–10: ὑπό τ[ῆς] ἄλλης ἡδον[ῆ]ς νενικημέν[οι, οὐ] μανθ[άνο]υσιν [οὐδὲ] πιστεύουσι. ἀπ[ι]στίη δὲ κἀμα[θίη] τὸ αὐτό.] In Pl. Prt. 357d, for example, Socrates reaches the conclusion that "being overcome by pleasure is ignorance in the highest degree," τὸ ἡδονῆς ἥττω εἶναι ἀμαθία ἡ μεγίστη.
⁹⁵ As Tsantsanoglou 1997: 98–99 rightly argues, although he mistakes the general purpose of the treatise as being "to divulge his professional secrets to the faithful." For Antiphon, cp. Cic. Div. 51.116: hic magna quaedam exoritur neque ea naturalis, sed artificiosa somniorum Antiphonis interpretatio eodemque modo et oraclorum et vaticinationum. sunt enim explanatores, ut grammatici poetarum.

him along with the other sophists who belong in Socrates' Thinkery, but the Derveni author should be seen, like the Aristophanic Socrates, as trying to recruit clientele rather than to destroy the whole edifice of traditional religion. Janko argues to the contrary that the Derveni author, whom he identifies as the Diagoras of Melos known in antiquity as an atheist, seeks to undermine the validity of mystery rites in general.

> By reinterpreting the Orphic cosmogony and mocking the Orphic initiates in col. xx of the papyrus, Diagoras might well have made his audience doubt whether it was worth the trouble and expense of getting initiated. This would certainly have offended the itinerant priests who peddled salvation from the terrors of Hades, which are the topic of col. v, by selling initiation rites to those feeling in need of indulgence for their sins.[96]

On the contrary, the Derveni author would no doubt be delighted to convince clients to come back regularly for the rituals, like the client of the Orpheotelestai in Theophrastos who performs the *teletai* every month for himself and his children.[97] The apparently "rationalizing" exegeses that explain Orpheus' cosmogonic hymn according to the motion of air, fire, and other elements, are not anti-religious but rather representative of the most avant-garde trends in theological discourse. Such ideas might seem extra-ordinarily strange and perverse to some, but they were intended to appeal to their audience as extra-ordinarily arcane and wise.

The exegeses provided by the Derveni author of the mythic events in the Orphic poem do indeed resemble the sorts of explanations that sophists are depicted as giving in the literature of the period, but it is important not to accept uncritically the polemical portrayals by Aristophanes, Plato, or others with their own axes to grind. Perhaps the closest parallel to the Derveni author's hermeneutics is the sort of explanation provided by Teiresias in Euripides' *Bacchae*, a character who is neither a simple parody nor the object of a rival's critique, but, as diviners always are in

---

[96] Janko 2002–03: 13.
[97] Theophr. *Char.* 16.11a (*OF* 654 B = OT 207 K): "Once a month he will go to see the Orpheotelests to undergo the rituals, taking his children along and his wife or, if she is busy, their nursemaid." καὶ τελεσθησόμενος πρὸς τοὺς Ὀρφεοτελεστὰς κατὰ μῆνα πορεύεσθαι μετὰ τῆς γυναικός – ἐὰν δὲ μὴ σχολάζῃ ἡ γυνή, μετὰ τῆς τίτθης – καὶ τῶν παιδίων. This passage provides the important reminder that undergoing a *teletê* was not a once in a lifetime event, like baptism, but rather more like a chiropractic treatment or psychotherapy session, done whenever the client felt the need. Such a client also would seek out a professional whenever he had a dream. Theophr. *Char.* 16.11a (*OF* 654 B = OT 207 K): "Whenever he has had a dream, he will consult the dream-interpreters, the seers, the augurs, to find out to which god, to which goddess, he ought to pray." καὶ ὅταν ἐνύπνιον ἴδηι πορεύεσθαι πρὸς τοὺς ὀνειροκρίτας, πρὸς τοὺς μάντεις, πρὸς τοὺς ὀρνιθοσκόπους ἐρωτήσων τίνι θεῶν ἢ θεᾶι εὔχεσθαι δεῖ.

tragedy, someone with special access to the truth. As Roth has pointed out, Teiresias' identification of the gods Dionysos and Demeter with the elements of wet and dry resembles Empedokles' penchant for connecting the traditional gods with his elemental theory, while his praise of them as benefactors of mankind through their gifts of wine and grain resembles Prodikos.[98] Teiresias calls Demeter the Earth, just as the Derveni author does, and his syncretistic praises of Dionysos with the functions of Ares, Apollo, and Aphrodite recall the ways in which the Derveni author seems to elide the differences between gods. Like the Derveni author, Teiresias uses etymologies and wordplays to draw out hidden meanings, such as the connection between μαντική and Dionysiac μανία (299), or the elaborate retelling of Dionysos' birth story with the plays on μῆρος, ὅμηρος, and μέρος (286–297).

Roth argues that Euripides' Teiresias is similar, not only to figures like Plato's Euthyphro, with his interest in etymology and extra-ordinary versions of traditional myths, but also to other diviners such as Lampon, Dion's seer Miltas, or even Antiphon in his work as a dream-interpreter. Most interestingly, he compares the way the atthidographer Philochoros, who acted as an *exegetes* and a *mantis*, makes use of similar hermeneutic tools, etymologies, and syncretistic identifications, to provide a superior account of the significance of the traditional stories about the gods. Such similarities are reinforced if indeed, as Obbink has argued, Philokhoros actually quotes the Derveni author in his identification of Ge, Demeter, and Hestia.[99] Lampon, Euthyphro, Philokhoros, and the Derveni author, then, may all be seen as the same type, religious thinkers who make use of sophisticated hermeneutic tools, not to destroy religion or respect for the gods, whatever a conservative satirist like Aristophanes might say, but to improve it. Although allegoresis, etymology, and other such devices have long had a bad reputation among historians of religion as markers of inauthenticity or insincerity, recent scholarship has shown the role that such interpretive traditions played in the continuing life of the Greek religious tradition. Allegoresis "saved myth," as Brisson has argued, and Henrichs has pointed out that many of the sophistic ideas of Prodikos and others that were condemned by Aristophanes and his contemporaries as

---

[98] Roth 1984: 61. Cp. Scodel 2011: 86–89.

[99] Obbink 1994 compares col. 20.12 with Philokhoros, *FGrH* 328 F 185 in Phld. *Piet.* (*P. Herc.* 248 I pp. 63, 23 Gomperz). Betegh 2004: 99 n. 20, however, suggests that it is more likely that Philokhoros and the Derveni author used a common source, or even (I might suggest) drew similar conclusions from the same Orphic poem. Any of these possibilities, however, still indicates the similarities between the Derveni author and a figure like Philokhoros.

irreligious nevertheless show up in Hellenistic religion as part of authentic religious worship, the sincerely expressed ideas of worshipers honoring their gods.[100] It is worth noting that the spread of such ideas coincided, not with the disappearance of mystery cults and the demand for religious specialists, but rather with their spread and expansion in the Hellenistic period. The Derveni author's hermeneutics, peculiar as they might seem to us, were actually appropriate to winning the confidence of his clientele in his religious expertise.

Like all of the other sophists, regardless of their field of expertise, the Derveni author disparages his rivals, pitying the clients of "those who make a craft for themselves out of the rites", since they fail to get their money's worth from these inferior practitioners.[101] The Hippocratic doctors pity the clients of other doctors, and the expert *manteis* are astonished at the inferior service people get from other interpreters of oracles, but neither would reject the entire practice of medicine or of divination. So too, the Derveni author is not an Enlightenment rationalist centuries before his time, trying to debunk the practices of consulting oracular shrines or undergoing *teletai*. Rather, he is arguing that he is better qualified to provide such services than his rival technicians, since he would provide the client not only with the performance of the ritual but also with an understanding of what they have done and seen and heard. Just so, Ion, the superstar rhapsode who boasts of his supreme competence in his branch of wisdom and his numerous victories in the competitions, is eager to show Socrates that he can give an explanation of the Homer passages he performs so beautifully.[102] Ion's superiority rests not just in his ability to perform but also to provide explanations, and he looks down on the amateurs who can only recite memorized bits. Likewise, the Derveni author scoffs at his rivals, who send their clients off without answering their questions about the rites, without providing them with any sense of the significance of what

---

[100] Brisson 2004, titled *How Philosophers Saved Myths: Allegorical Interpretation and Classical Mythology*, provides the best treatment of the importance of the allegorical tradition in the development of philosophy. Cp. Henrichs 1984b, who traces some of the ideas of Prodikos in the Isis aretalogies. Burkert 1987: 78–88 discusses the use of allegory in various mystery cults. Struck 2004 traces the development of allegory in the literary tradition, showing that it was far more important far earlier than previous scholarship had been inclined to credit.

[101] Col. 20.3–4: "But all those who (hope to acquire knowledge?) from someone who makes craft of the holy rites deserve to be wondered at and pitied. Wondered at because, thinking that they will know before they perform the rites, they go away after having performed them before they have attained knowledge." ὅσοι δὲ παρὰ τοῦ τέχνην ποιουμένου τὰ ἱερά, οὗτοι ἄξιοι θαυμάζεσθαι καὶ οἰκτε[ί]ρεσθαι· θαυμάζεσθαι μὲν ὅτι δοκοῦντες πρότερον ἢ ἐπιτελέσαι εἰδήσειν, ἀπέρχονται ἐπιτελέσαντες πρὶν εἰδέναι.

[102] Cp. Brisson 1997: 165.

they have experienced. Like the wise priests and priestesses whom Socrates mentions in the *Meno*, by contrast, the Derveni author is one of those "who have made it a practice to be able to give an account of the things they have in hand."[103] The Derveni treatise is not such an account in itself, but rather an exhibition of his ability to give such accounts, touching on both ritual matters in the first part of the surviving text and the hymn of Orpheus quoted so extensively in the second.

This distinction helps us to understand the intended audience for the text, not a congregation of the faithful but an audience of potential clients. The Derveni author is not the local theologian, explaining the fine points of doctrine for interested initiates or even preaching schismatic heresies to convert them away from their previous understanding of Orphic doctrine to his own peculiar brand.[104] Rather, he is an independent practitioner trying to convince potential clients to retain his services, even if they have already performed telestic rites before with rival practitioners, since that experience will have left them not only ignorant of the significance of the experience but also bereft of hope that they could ever achieve such under-standing. The Derveni author's display of his exegetical skills proffers hope to his clients that they could have a meaningful experience of the *teletai*; it does not offer that meaningful experience or even all the knowledge necessary for salvation through the reading of the text.[105] Scholars have sought to find in the Derveni treatise a set of doctrines unifying the first part, dealing with rituals involving dead souls, and the second part, which deals with cosmology, but such efforts are in vain, because the Derveni author is not, in fact, systematically setting out doctrines that provide salvation after death by explaining the nature of the soul and its place in the cosmos. Such systematic soteriological doctrines are alien to Greek religion of the Classical period, and the Derveni author and his treatise

---

[103] Pl. *Meno* 81a10–b2 (*OF* 424, 666 B): "The speakers were certain priests and priestesses who have made it a practice to be able to give an account of the things they have in hand." οἱ μὲν λέγοντές εἰσι τῶν ἱερέων τε καὶ τῶν ἱερειῶν ὅσοις μεμέληκε περὶ ὧν μεταχειρίζονται λόγον οἵοις τ' εἶναι διδόναι.

[104] West seems to envision such a tame theologian for his hypothesized Ionian Orphic-Bacchic cult, as Kouremenos notes: "such societies always reserved a place for the speculative theologian who, for a fee, was ready to explain to the members the esoteric meaning of their rites and holy texts and myths" (Kouremenos *et al.* 2006: 47). The schismatic hypothesis is elaborated in Most 1997a.

[105] Cp. Detienne's path to salvation through exegetical reading and writing, above. Rangos 2007: 43 offers a modified version: "Quite obviously, mere reading of an Orphic epic or hymn did not suffice to make one a *mystês*. But much of what will have taken place in an Orphic initiation would be cryptically contained in Orphic myths. In this sense, it is more than probable that the mythology contained in the Derveni poem was originally meant as the symbolic kernel of Orphic initiation. If the author thought of his cosmological exposition as the right method for imparting mystic knowledge, he may not have been very far from the poet's original purpose."

should not be seen as the exception, but rather understood in the context of other experts with claims to special wisdom that they promote in their books.

The name of Orpheus

The Derveni author, then, was one of those figures mocked in Plato, part of the crowd of religious specialists who compete for clientele on the basis of their books of Orpheus. Indeed, given the authority that the Derveni author attributes to Orpheus, we can see how the Euripidean Theseus might scorn him as someone who takes Orpheus for his lord and honors the vaporings of many books. His invocation of the name of Orpheus as his authority is above all what marks him as Orphic; it distinguishes his claim to wisdom from that of other sophists and distinguishes his claim to religious expertise from that of other religious practitioners. Betegh rightly emphasizes the difference between the Derveni author or others who invoke the name of Orpheus and an innovator like Empedokles, who lays claim to religious authority in his own name and through his own divine insight.[106] Both are competing in the marketplace for religious authority, but their strategies for impressing their clientele differ. Of course, Empedokles is sometimes labeled an Orphic in ancient sources, precisely because he lays claim to extra-ordinary insight into the matters having to do with the divine and because his ideas are strange enough, different enough from those of his competitors, that he might be grouped together with others who are labeled Orphic. The Derveni author, by contrast, has the label of Orphic first and foremost because of his own invocations of Orpheus' authority. His claims to extra-ordinary insight into divine things, another Orphic characteristic, stem directly from his superior understanding of Orpheus' enigmas, and he advertises his expertise in such things as *teletai* and oracular revelations, yet another marker of the Orphic, through his exegesis of the Orphic text.

Such characteristics, not any adherence to supposedly Orphic doctrines, define the Derveni author as Orphic. The doctrinal definition is deeply problematic for the Derveni author, since he seems unconcerned with all the pieces of doctrine that are supposed to be central to Orphics – Titanic guilt,

---

[106] Betegh 2004: 371: "The core of the difference between the Derveni author and the Orphic initiators on the one hand, and Empedocles on the other is this: while the former try to sell their ideas and services under Orpheus' authority, the latter tries to elevate himself to Orpheus' religious and cultural standing by claiming the poet's most important functions for himself."

purification and vegetarianism, metempsychosis, etc.[107] None of these ideas appear anywhere in the Derveni papyrus, either in the Orphic poem or in the treatise that contains it. While the references to the souls of the dead and the terrors in Hades have led some scholars to attribute an eschatological focus to the Derveni author, the mere idea of a differentiated afterlife is not particularly Orphic, nor does it appear as a central focus of the Derveni author's treatise.[108] Those who define Orphic by doctrinal criteria must regard the Derveni author as not-Orphic, despite his explicit citations of Orpheus' authority, whereas, under the polythetic definition I have formulated, the Derveni author meets multiple criteria for classification as Orphic.[109] Burkert likewise argues for a non-doctrinal definition. "It did not matter for an Orpheotelest whether he himself or his colleague was truly 'Orphic', but whether he was good at his profession."[110] The Derveni author repeatedly, through his *epideixis* of exegesis in his treatise, tries to convince his audience that he is good at his profession.

The focus of the Derveni author throughout his treatise is not on doctrinal consistency or even systematic exposition of his cosmological or theological ideas; rather, he focuses again and again upon his own superiority at exegesis and the importance of making use of his skills to arrive at a true understanding. His treatise is his exhibition of his technique, just as other sophists in the marketplace of ideas made use of the new technology of books to demonstrate and validate their expertise. The references in Plato and Euripides to Orphic books must be understood in this context, not as references to a peculiar Orphic textual orientation that distinguished Orphic believers from others. Avant-garde thinkers of all stripes were flaunting their books, from the doctors and oraclemongers to the geometers and rhetoricians, from Meton to Euripides. While this tactic seems, by its very ubiquity, to have been a successful strategy, it also exposed them to the ridicule of the comedians, the suspicions of the conservative, and the polemics of their rivals. But the users of Orphic texts are not

---

[107] Parker 1995: 503 asks: "Could a poem abandon metempsychosis and vegetarianism and Titanic guilt and still be 'Orphic'?"

[108] For further discussion of eschatological ideas, see below, ch. 8.

[109] Cp. Parker 1995: 488–489: "If the commentator thought of himself as an Orphic, he was surely one of a very singular stamp. For our purposes, he is just the misty glass though which we seek to gaze at Orpheus." Casadio 1987: 386: "Lo spirito dell' anonimo commentatore è decisamente estraneo alla temperie orfica." By contrast, Bernabé 2002c: 97 opts to suspend his usual doctrinal qualifications: "Il ya beaucoup de manières d'être 'orphique' et notre commentateur, du moment où il recherche le 'sens véritable' du text d'Orphée, peut être considéré comme orphique."

[110] Burkert 1982: 10.

essentially text-centered, except in the trivial sense that they can be identified as users of Orphic texts simply because they use the texts attributed to Orpheus. These Orphics had no sacred scriptures, nor were the poems attributed to Orpheus always used as the basis for initiatory ritual, bringing new life and salvation to the initiate through the recitation of the birth of the cosmos. While cosmogony is indeed one theme of Orphic poetry, other poems have other topics, and the relation of any of these texts – or the mythic themes within them – to ritual is a topic that must be explored in detail, with attention to the different themes and varied performance contexts and audiences.

The Derveni papyrus, then, includes two kinds of Orphic texts, the poem attributed to Orpheus and the treatise of the Derveni author that makes use of it to display his exegetic skills. The bookishness of the Derveni author does not mark him as Orphic, but rather as an avant-garde intellectual of the Classical period, the period in which the technology of the book comes to the fore among the tools of the intellectual elite. It is his claims to special knowledge about purification, sacrifice, divination and other ritual matters, as well as his attribution of religious authority to Orpheus, that mark the Derveni author as Orphic. The Orphic poem itself is marked as Orphic, not only by the attribution to Orpheus, but by some of its features that show through, even in its fragmentary form – the claims to special wisdom and the peculiar twists that characterize the mythic narrative.

No particular textual orientation distinguishes those who make use of Orphic texts. The texts of Orpheus, like the texts of Homer or Hippocrates, circulated widely and were used in different ways by various individuals. The peculiar references to Orphic texts in Plato and Euripides reflect the particular context of Classical Athens and the status of books as the markers of the intellectual avant-garde of the time. References to the texts of Orpheus outside of that particular context never have that same mark of peculiarity, while other references to books and book users from Classical Athens treat them in the same way. An examination of the context shows that the itinerant religious practitioners who used the books of Orpheus were just a few among the many intellectuals making use of this new technology in the competition for a share of influence and authority. The competitive context further helps us understand the rhetoric of the Derveni author, just as the parallels with other wisdom contexts demonstrate that his methods are not as anomalous as is sometimes supposed. The Derveni author is not trying to convey religious doctrine, eschatological or cosmological; he is showing off his abilities as an interpreter of enigmatic texts, as a thinker conversant with advanced philosophical cosmologies, and as ritual specialist who can provide a meaningful account of his religious activities. Without the strictures of outdated interpretive models, we can provide a better picture of such users of Orphic texts, the sort whom Euripides mocks as taking Orpheus for their lord – in short, the Orphics in ancient terms.

CHAPTER FIVE

Orphic hieroi logoi
Sacred texts for the rites

Orphism, then, cannot be defined as a special textual orientation. The ancient Greeks did not particularly associate books with those who were connected with Orpheus, nor were the Orphic texts treated with any kind of scriptural reverence. While the claims to special knowledge that often characterize the Orphic in ancient evidence produce an overlap in the feature of book use, especially in the Classical period, with others who claimed special wisdom, it is not the books, but the kinds of knowledge claimed that distinguish the Orphic. Orphic texts were indeed associated with ritual, but not as scriptures from which the participants in the ritual would derive sectarian doctrines, nor were the texts recited in the ritual as magical incantations to create some initiatory effect through the performative utterance. Rather, I would suggest that many of the poetic compositions attributed to Orpheus were associated with ritual simply because they were performed (or imagined to be performed) in the context of ritual. Poetic performance, be it choral or monodic, hymnic or some other form, was a standard part of nearly every Greek religious ritual, and a wide variety of different types of poetry could be associated with ritual performance.

Sacred texts: Myth and ritual again

The distinction here is between ritual texts, used like the Mesopotamian creation excerpt to create a magical effect through the performative narration of primal events, and texts used on the occasion of ritual performance. Although the Derveni author's Orphic text is not a ritual text, any more than it is a systematic exposition of doctrine, be it religious or physical, some of the texts associated with Orpheus clearly did have a place in ritual. Plato's religious specialists (*Resp.* 364b2–365a3 [*OF* 573i B = OF 3 K]) have books according to which they perform their rites and sacrifices (καθ᾽ ἃς θυηπολοῦσιν). The precise meaning of the preposition (κατά) is unclear here, and some scholars have assumed that these were books of ritual instructions. As Burkert points out, however, there is almost no evidence for such instruction manuals among the Orphica; the Orphic fragments that survive are overwhelmingly mythological in nature.[1] Once again, the Orphic texts differ little in this respect from non-Orphic texts in Greek religion; the Orphica are not the exception within Greek religion.

Greek religion as a whole is indeed notable, by contrast with other religions of the ancient Mediterranean world, for the minimal role that texts and a class of specialized text-users play. As Parker explains, "Writing was not, by contrast, used to build up a complicated specialized corpus of ritual knowledge." The absence of such a body of specialized ritual knowledge, he goes on to argue, has implications for the nature of the religious specialists. "Elaborate ritual texts are the hallmark of a more specialized priesthood and a more autonomous religious order than those of Greece."[2] The absence of a corpus of ritual instructions, such as those found in Mesopotamian or Hittite cultures, makes the reconstruction of ancient Greek ritual much more difficult, since basic patterns of ritual procedure seem to have been transmitted orally and the details of the ritual performance were left to the individual performer. Nevertheless, as Henrichs points out, textual evidence of various sorts abounds for Greek religion, although "the majority of these texts refers to ritual practices without being themselves ritual texts or blueprints for rituals."[3] Not only do we have many literary references to people performing rituals, but many references survive that attest to the place of poetic performance in ritual.

While sacrifice, of animals or of other things (incense, grains, objects, etc.) plays a central role in many Greek rituals, poetic song often has an equally vital role in the contact with the gods that is the central function of such rituals. A hymn or other song performed in the context of a ritual is a religious act, an offering to the god designed to please and win the favor of the deity. The mythic narrative contained in such poetic texts serves as the pleasing offering (*agalma*) in the network of reciprocal relations that constitutes worship in Greek religion.[4] Furley and Bremer describe the place of hymns in Greek religion: "By reminding a god through hymnic worship of his mighty and beneficent deeds in the past, the worshiper wishes both to define the deity addressed and his powers, and to secure a

---

[1] Burkert 1982: 8.

[2] Parker 1996: 54. He also points out, "A crucial aspect of this integration of religion in Greece is the ordinariness of the priests; they were ordinary in many ways, but above all lacking all pretension to distinctive learning."

[3] Henrichs 2003: 43.

[4] Cp. Pulleyn 1997: 39–55 for a discussion of how hymns of praise fit into the reciprocal networks of Greek religion.

measure of that power for himself through divine grace."[5] These reminders and definitions of the god's power and beneficence take the form of mythic narratives, and the poetic form serves to elaborate, to adorn, and to make pleasing this telling of the traditional tale. As Furley and Bremer note, "What is seldom adequately realized, however, is that myth is the substance of hymns, and that the stories told about the gods in myths were in fact the stories sung *to* the gods in worship in order to flatter, remind, praise, and cajole a recalcitrant stone image into beneficial action."[6]

The myths told in such poetic performances might be tales of the foundation of the cult or some particular ritual within it, but such narrowly aetiological myths were only one way to sing the praises of the god. Any tale that highlighted the divinity's powers or described its past beneficence to mankind in general or to the worshiping community in particular would be a good myth to recount to build up the relationship with the god and to bind more closely deity and worshipers. As Detienne argues, "There is no reason to imagine any deep cleavage between, on the one hand, 'real' myths that are bound to rituals deeply anchored in beliefs, and, on the other, stories that have become literary and seem no longer to have anything to do with the mythological tradition."[7] While the development of a tale in a literary format might differ from its deployment in a hymn performed in ritual, the basic traditional stock of mythic stories remained the same. Myths that do not seem to reflect any ritual pattern or sequence may very well have had their place in a ritual, even if modern scholars cannot use the shape of the mythic narrative to try to reconstruct the shape of the ritual.[8] Ancient Greeks, however, could easily associate a wide variety of poetic tellings of myths with ritual, since the performance of myths in hymns and other forms was a regular part of many rituals.

These poetic texts do not seem to be fixed, canonical texts that were performed on every occasion. Rather, certain types of performances were appropriate for certain occasions – paians for Apollo, tragedies at the Dionysia, choruses of maidens singing and dancing for Artemis, all of which might be grouped under the loose heading of "hymns" as poetic

---

[5] Furley and Bremer 2001: 7.   [6] Furley and Bremer 2001: 6.   [7] Detienne 2003: xiii–xiv.
[8] Various scholars have sought to define the relation between myth and ritual, often attempting to use the myths that are extant to reconstruct the shape and pattern of ritual performances that have left little trace in the evidence. While some myths may indeed reflect that pattern of rituals, the connection is usually not as helpful for reconstructive work as such scholars might wish. As Furley and Bremer 2001: 7 note, "Whilst the whole 'myth and ritual' school of interpretation has worked on the premiss that there is an intrinsic connection between the two modes – the ritual and the mythical – it has not been adequately grasped just how close the link in fact was: the myths formed the substance of hymns sung before or during the ritual."

songs addressed to a god.[9] Even when the performance was prescribed by
the community, it is the general form, rather than the text, that is specified.
A sacred law at Magnesia includes the direction: "The temple warder shall
further engage choirs of maidens to sing hymns to Artemis Leucophryene",
but who is to compose the hymns, what the subject matter of these hymns
is to be, all such details are left unspecified.[10] The texts of the hymns or
other poetic performances are created for the occasion, possibly but not
necessarily reperformed on subsequent occasions.

The fact that there was no prescribed or canonical form for the hymn
means that no single version of a mythic story ever became prescribed or
canonical for a ritual. While it might always be appropriate to tell of the
birth of Apollo at Delos during a Delian festival, the precise details of the
myth would vary from version to version, even in significant ways. Since
any myth about the nature and actions of a divinity embeds the theological
ideas of its author in the narrative, the variation of myth means that every
ritual occasion provides a new retelling, along with constant but imperceptible shifts of meaning.[11] These constant shifts make mythic hymns a
particularly poor vehicle for the transmission of religious doctrine in constant form across the generations, since not only is there no specialized
body of priests to maintain the interpretation of the text, but the text of
the myths themselves changes with each new performance. As Kowalzig
notes, "in a world where right, privilege or obligation to worship in a
particular cult were rarely uncontested, this yields interesting battles for
the truth, expressed in the almost infinite number of competing myths."[12]

---

[9] Cp. the classification of Men. Rhet. 331.21–332.2: "Thus hymns to Apollo are called *paeans* and
huporchemata, hymns to Dionysos dithyrambs and iobacchoi and the like, those to Aphrodite 'erotic
hymns', while those appropriate to other gods are either called by the generic title 'hymns' or, more
specifically, e.g., 'To Zeus'." τοὺς μὲν γὰρ εἰς Ἀπόλλωνα παιᾶνας καὶ ὑπορχήματα ὀνομάζομεν, τοὺς
δὲ εἰς Διόνυσον διθυράμβους καὶ ἰοβάκχους, καὶ ὅσα τοιαῦτα, τοὺς δὲ εἰς Ἀφροδίτην ἐρωτικούς,
τοὺς δὲ τῶν ἄλλων θεῶν ἢ τῷ γένει ὕμνους καλοῦμεν ἢ μερικώτερον οἷον πρὸς Δία. (trans. Russell
and Wilson)

[10] συντελείτω δὲ ὁ νεωκόρος καὶ χοροὺς παρθένων ἀϊδουσῶν ὕμνους εἰς Ἄρτεμιν Λευκοφρυηνήν
(*LSAM* 33a.21; *SIG* 3 695 at Magnesia PH260444; Magnesia 3, lines 28–29). Cp. Paus. 5.15.10, who
mentions performances to Nymphs and Mistresses at Elis, or Paus. 2.74, a reference to hymns for
Dionysos at Sicyon.

[11] Myth, as a form of discourse, provides a narrative in which a culture's models of the world and for
action within it may be manipulated according to the author's ideological aims. As I have defined it
elsewhere: "A myth, then, is a telling of a traditional tale, in which the teller shapes the traditional
material in response to his context and audience, and in which aspects of the culture's models of
the world are selected or rejected by the teller in his crafting of the story according to his view of
the significant tensions and issues involved with the narrative" (Edmonds 2004a: 7).

[12] Kowalzig 2007: 29. Kowalzig rightly points to the way in which this performance of myth in cultic
contexts "is central to an incessant process of forging and re-forging religious communities over
time, and to expressing relations between the different groups involved in a cult" (8).

Such battles for the truth, or at least for religious authority, are part of the contestive nature of mythic performance, a competitive element enhanced by the fact that the performance of song in many festivals was indeed part of a contest between performers.

While innovation has a certain place in such a competitive atmosphere, the key to success is of course to balance the original elements with a firm grounding in the tradition. A song, a ritual, even a whole festival could derive authority not only from its expressive power, but also from the antiquity of its tradition. While rituals too were being constantly reinvented and modified, they nevertheless had to seem ancient and traditional, the customs of the ancestors, the same thing that had always been done. As modern scholars, we should not be deceived by this rhetoric of antiquity into considering ritual an inherently static medium that actually preserves unchanged the forms of practice through the centuries. As Kowalzig argues:

> Being antique is a strategy of ritual. Ritual convinces, ritual persuades by its antiquity. Rituals have to be ancient in order to be accepted and to be effective. All rituals only work on the assumption that they continue old practices. Being old is an appearance of ritual, but more importantly it is a technique, something that ritual aspires to. All the characteristics of ritual are geared toward this goal – its formality, archaism, symbolism, repetition.[13]

The same features of traditionality are valuable in the mythic expressions that form part of rituals; an ancient hymn becomes a treasure passed down in the tradition that is offered to the god.

Such a premium on antiquity serves as an incentive for pseudepigraphy, for attributing more recent texts to famous names of the past, and no name has more prestige for poetry in ritual than that of ὀνομάκλυτος Orpheus. Orpheus' name was attached to a number of poems that were associated with rituals, particularly those of Demeter and Dionysos, but many of the Orphic poems not explicitly associated with rituals may have been hymns or other such forms written to be (or as if to be) performed in rituals. There is no way to know, for example, if the hymn to Zeus in the Derveni papyrus was ever performed in a ritual for Zeus, but the poem's narrative of Zeus' rise to power in the cosmos would be an appropriate subject for such a hymnic performance. The antiquity and prestige associated with the supposed author, Orpheus, would shed luster upon any rite in which it was performed. On the other hand, even if the hymn never was actually performed in ritual or never even intended to be performed, the form of a

---

[13] Kowalzig 2007: 34.

hymnic praise of a god nevertheless would have been an appropriate form in which to make a mythological expression of ideas about the gods and the cosmos. Orpheus was associated with poetic texts that were performed in religious rituals of various kinds, and the name of Orpheus would be a good label to attach to a text to ensure its reception and transmission.

The form of Orphic poems

It is worth examining the extant evidence to see what sort of works were attributed to Orpheus. Nearly all of the works that are connected to Orpheus in the ancient evidence are in the characteristic dactylic hexameter, but the form and genre vary – Orpheus' works include hymns to the gods, didactic poetry, and even epic narrative. The most complete list is in an entry for Orpheus in the Byzantine encyclopedia, the *Suda*, which attributes various works to particular pseudepigraphers. Some of these attributions may go back to Epigenes in the fourth century BCE, but few firm conclusions can be drawn about the dates of any particular works.

> Among them are the so-called Hierostolica [Sacred Missives]; Cosmic calls; Neoteuktika; Sacred speeches in 24 rhapsodies, but these are said to be by Theognetos of Thessaly, or by the Pythagorean Kerkops; Oracles, which are attributed to Onomakritos; Rites, though these too are attributed to Onomakritos; among these is the Concerning Cutting on Stones, entitled Eighty Stone; Deliverance, but these are said to be by Timokles the Syracusan or by Persinos the Milesian; Mixing Bowls, said to be by Zopyros; Thronismoi of the Mother and Bacchica, said to be by Nicias of Elea; Descent into Hades, said to be by Herodikos of Perinthos; Robe and Net, also said to be by Zopyros of Heracleia, though others say Brotinus; an Onomasticon in epic hexameter, a Theogony in epic hexameter; Astronomy, Amocopia, Thyepolikon, Oiothytika or Oeoscopy in epic hexameter, Katazostikon, Hymns, Korybanticon, and Physika, which they attribute to Brotinos.[14]

---

[14] *Suda* s.v. Ὀρφεύς (ο 654, III.564.27–565.11 Adler) (*OF* 91, 92, 411, 605i, 606, 608, 609, 611, 612, 685i, 692, 709, 725, 782, 800iii, 805, 809, 811, 835, 838, 839, 840, 1018iv, 1100ii, 1101iii, 1102, 1105, 1106iii, 1111, 1120, 1123, 1125iii B = OT 173, 174, 175, 178, 179, 184, 186, 196, 199, 223, 223d K): ἐν δὲ τούτοις τὰ Ἱεροστολικὰ καλούμενα· Κλήσεις κοσμικαί· Νεοτευκτικά· Ἱερούς λόγους ἐν ῥαψῳδίαις κδ'· λέγονται δὲ εἶναι Θεογνήτου τοῦ Θεσσαλοῦ, οἱ δὲ Κέρκωπος τοῦ Πυθαγορείου· Χρησμούς, οἳ ἀναφέρονται εἰς Ὀνομάκριτον· Τελετάς· ὁμοίως δέ φασι καὶ ταύτας Ὀνομακρίτου· ἐν τούτοις δ' ἐστὶ περὶ λίθων γλυφῆς, ἥτις Ὀγδοηκοντάλιθος ἐπιγράφεται· Σωτήρια· ταῦτα Τιμοκλέους τοῦ Συρακουσίου λέγεται ἢ Περσίνου τοῦ Μιλησίου· Κρατῆρας· ταῦτα Ζωπύρου φασί· Θρονισμοὺς Μητρῴους καὶ Βακχικά· ταῦτα Νικίου τοῦ Ἐλεάτου φασὶν εἶναι· Εἰς ᾅδου κατάβασιν· ταῦτα Ἡροδίκου τοῦ Περινθίου· Πέπλον καὶ Δίκτυον· καὶ ταῦτα Ζωπύρου τοῦ Ἡρακλεώτου, οἱ δὲ Βροτίνου· Ὀνομαστικὸν ἔπη, Θεογονίαν ἔπη, Ἀστρονομίαν, Ἀμοκοπία, Θυηπολικόν, Ὠοθυτικά ἢ Ὠοσκοπικά, ἐπικῶς· Καταζωστικόν, Ὕμνους· Κορυβαντικόν· καὶ Φυσικά, ἃ Βροτίνου φασίν. On the source of the list in Epigenes, see West 1983: 7–15.

Unfortunately, these titles are all we have of most of the works listed here, and even these titles shed little light on the form or content of these works. Only a few late works survive in any form more comprehensive than fragmentary quotations in other authors: the epic narrative of the *Orphic Argonautica*, the *Orphic Lithika* – a didactic poem on the properties of stones – and a collection of *Orphic Hymns*.[15] Fragments and allusions to earlier works, however, suggest a long and creative tradition of forging works in Orpheus' name.[16]

The earliest testimonies suggest hymns to the gods and didactic material, mostly cosmological in nature, starting possibly as early as the end of the sixth century. Many of the earliest references to the works of Orpheus mention hymns in particular as the form that Orpheus' poetry took. Euripides refers to the bewitching hymns of Orpheus that might sway the ruler of Hades, while Plato mentions the hymns of Orpheus as particularly sweet.[17] The Derveni author even quotes a line he says is found in the hymns of Orpheus, and much of his treatise is concerned with the Orphic poem that seems to be a hymn to Zeus.[18] Pausanias, who is much concerned with the authenticity of poetry attributed to Orpheus, claims that the only genuine works of Orpheus are a small set of short hymns used by the Lycomidae at Phlya, which he compares to the *Homeric Hymns*.[19]

The hymns accepted as most ancient and revered by Pausanias are assuredly not the extant *Orphic Hymns*, which date probably to Pausanias' time or later.[20] All these hymns, however, are indeed rather short, shorter

---

[15] All these works date from the Roman imperial era; the *Hymns* may be perhaps as early as the second century CE, while the *Lithika* and the *Argonautica* may be as late as the fifth century CE. For the *Orphic Argonautica*, see Vian 1987; for the *Lithika*, see Halleux and Schamp 1985; for the *Hymns*, see Morand 2001 and Ricciardelli 2000.

[16] West 1983: 7–15 summarizes the testimonies for early Orphica. The fragmentary nature of the evidence makes dating individual themes and elements very difficult, and it is often necessary to use a composite of evidence from different sources of different eras to reconstruct the patterns of a story. It is important to note, however, that the particular details and combinations in each piece of evidence are the products of mythic *bricolage* in particular circumstances and cannot be extrapolated for other times and sources.

[17] Eur. *Alc.* 357–359 (*OF* 680 B = OT 59 K); Pl. *Leg.* 829d (*OF* 681 B = OF 12 K).

[18] Col. 22.11–13 (*OF* 398i B). col. 7.2 (*OF* 2i B) mentions a hymn that is probably a reference to the Zeus poem. For the Derveni poem as a hymn to Zeus, see Bernabé 2002c.

[19] Paus. 9.30.12 (*OF* 531ii, 682 B = OF 304 K). Pausanias provides no reasons for accepting this group of Orphic texts, which he claims are second only to the *Homeric Hymns* in their composition (κόσμῳ) but have more honor from the divine. He refers to other texts as those attributed to Orpheus or simply as the writings of Onomakritos. Cp. Linforth 1941: 350–353.

[20] The whole collection survived in a single manuscript brought from Constantinople to Rome in 1423, a manuscript that included not only the *Orphic Hymns*, but the *Homeric Hymns* and the *Hymns* of Proclus. Linforth 1941: 179–189 remains the most useful brief introduction to this manuscript and its origins.

than many of the more substantive *Homeric Hymns*, and are characterized by their collections of divine epithets rather than extended mythical
narratives.[21] This collection of eighty-seven hymns does seem to have been
designed for use in rituals, since each hymn is preceded by instructions for
a sacrifice of incense.[22] Some scholars have located the cult association that
made use of the hymns in Pergamon, since Pergamon provides evidence
for the worship of a larger portion of the collection of deities addressed
in the *Hymns* than other places. However, although deities such as Hipta
do seem to come from that region of Asia Minor, there is no reason that
the collection could not have been used elsewhere to celebrate deities that
seemed slightly exotic with hymns designed by the prestigious Orpheus.[23]

While some of the hymns attributed to Orpheus thus were really
designed for ritual use, others must have just made use of the recognized form so often associated with Orpheus, reinforcing the plausibility
of their pseudepigraphy by the choice. Of course, the generic category
of the hymn could be fairly broad; any form of praise addressed to the
gods could be considered a hymn. The third-century CE Menander Rhetor
includes not only all types of metrical hymns but even prose hymns. He
classifies the hymns of Orpheus under his rubric of "scientific hymns"
(*hymnoi physikoi*), along with the poems of Empedokles and Parmenides,
since all these poems focus on the nature (*physis*) of the gods, rather than
on narrative action, as the mythic hymns do.[24] While modern scholars
might categorize Empedokles and Parmenides as didactic rather than hymnic, Menander Rhetor's ancient grouping of the hymns (in the broadest
sense) of Orpheus with these two Presocratics should help us understand
how some Orphic poems might have been understood by their ancient
audiences.

Indeed, the fragments of Empedokles, as scattered and problematic as
they are, probably provide the best insight into the nature of many Orphic
cosmological writings, of which little more than the titles are preserved.
Empedokles' didactic hexameters, describing the nature of blood, bone,
and flesh or the four elements that make up all perceptible matter, show
how an innovative thinker can use the traditional medium of dactylic hexameter verse and the traditional mythic figures like Zeus, Hephaistos, and

---

[21] The best study is Morand 2001, although much more remains to be done with these long-neglected
texts.
[22] Cp. Graf 2009 on the ritual nature of the texts.
[23] Linforth 1941: 179–189 summarizes the disputes over the origins, rightly concluding that the arguments for locating the cult in any particular place remain unconvincing.
[24] Menander Rhetor 333.

Aphrodite to put forth new ideas about the nature of the cosmos.[25] Empedokles claimed his own authority for his revelations, but others preferred to use the name of Orpheus, whether the Pythagoreans of the Archaic and Classical age, like Brontinos and Zopyros to whom the *Net*, the *Robe*, the *Krater*, and other *Physika* are attributed, or the Neopythagoreans of a later era who composed the *Lyre* and the *Hymn to Number*.[26] Aristotle refers to a poem of Orpheus, which may, like Empedokles' poem, have been called *Physika* by later writers, in which souls are said to be carried on the winds to incarnation, and Gagné has suggested that this poem may have used the mysterious Tritopatores, ancestral spirits who in later evidence are also associated with the winds, to make this point about the nature of the soul and its incarnation.[27] The Orphica of the late Archaic and Classical period thus seem to have treated similar themes and grappled with similar cosmological issues as the works of other thinkers of the periods.

In the Hellenistic period, Orpheus' didactic repertoire may have expanded to include *Lithika* and *Astrologika*, as well as other special knowledge, and new hymns and cosmogonies appeared reflecting the new theological and philosophical developments of the era. The extant *Orphic Lithika*, however, probably has little connection to these earlier works. It is very much akin to other didactic works of the Imperial period, and the attribution to Orpheus may indeed have come only from the Byzantine commentator Tzetzes, who identified the work with a lost treatise on stones attributed in earlier sources to Orpheus.[28] The work lacks any of the features that characterize other Orphica; there are no explicit references to Orpheus or addresses to Mousaios, nor is the text characterized by any strange or alien features. Even the claims to special knowledge about the properties of stones are not particularly marked, given the genre of the didactic. The name of Orpheus, however, is a good way to mark as remarkable otherwise ordinary material, and Orpheus' reputation for wisdom of all kinds ensured that didactic poems continued to be attributed to him.

The evidence from the lists of early titles suggests that until the Hellenistic period, a wide variety of Orphic works circulated. Sometime in the first few centuries CE, however, much of the extant Orphic poetry seems to have been compiled into a collection of twenty-four Rhapsodies, on the model of the Homeric poems. The *Iliad* and the *Odyssey* had each been arranged, probably by the first century BCE, into twenty-four

---

[25] Emp. fr. 31 B 6, 31 B 96, 31 B 98 DK (frr. 7, 48, 83 Wright).
[26] Cp. West 1983: 7–15, 29–33.   [27] Gagné 2007.   [28] See Halleux and Schamp 1985: 31.

Rhapsodies, which correspond to the modern book divisions.[29] The grammarian Dionysios Thrax defines a rhapsody as "a part of a poem encompassing a certain subject," and he explicitly takes Homer as the model.[30] The word is derived by the commentators from the action of stitching together the words and the verses, as Callimachus says, weaving together the myth with the rod (ῥάβδος).[31] Each rhapsody forms a coherent unit, as if performed by a rhapsode. The rhapsodies of each Homeric epic are more or less similar pieces that together comprise a whole, but, after the division of the Homeric epics into twenty-four rhapsodies, such a division became canonical, inspiring many imitations, from twenty-four rhapsodies on Alexander the Great to the Sacred Speeches of Orpheus.[32] This collection of Orphica, which survives primarily in quotations by the Neoplatonist philosophers Proclus and his successors, seems to have been the form in which most of the later Classical world (from whom the majority of our evidence stems) knew the Orphic tradition.

The nature of the Rhapsodic collection

The *Rhapsodies* have at times been imagined as a coherent poem on the model of Hesiod's *Theogony*, structured as a genealogical account of the creation of the world from first principles through the gods and culminating

[29] West 1983: 247–251 locates the collections of the *Rhapsodies* in Pergamon in the first third of the first century BCE (in connection with the Homeric scholarship), but Brisson 1995: 2886 prefers a date in the first century CE. Brisson's argument that Chronos could not have been added to the cosmogony before the spread of Mithraism in the first century CE is not persuasive, but West's date relies on his unconvincing interpretation of the reference in Cic. *Nat. D.* 1.107 (*OF* 889i, 110iiv B = OT 13 K) to provide a *terminus ante quem*. Cicero's testimony does not imply that he knew of only one canonical Orphic poem, but rather suggests that he had access to the same treatise of Epigenes cited by Clement that raised doubts about the authorship of Orphic poems.

[30] Dion. Thrax 1.1.8.4 (*OF* 889i, 110iiv B = OT 13 K): Ῥαψῳδία ἐστὶ μέρος ποιήματος ἐμπεριειληφός τινα ὑπόθεσιν. Later scholiasts differentiate the ποίησις, as the whole epic, from ποιήματα, as self-contained poetic units within the whole, equivalent to rhapsodies, but the idea remains that rhapsodies are defined as having their own subject matter (ὑπόθεσις).

[31] Cp. Eust. *Il.* I.9.27 van der Valk: "They are called rhapsodies on account of the stitching something together, such as a song, according to the conventional technical term." ῥαψῳδίαι καλοῦνται διὰ τὸ κατὰ συνθήκην τεχνικὴν ῥάπτεσθαι οἷον τὴν ᾠδήν. Cp. 1.10.4–7 van der Valk, which refers to the laurel wand held by the rhapsodes in performance: Ὅτι δὲ καὶ παρὰ τὴν ῥάβδον ἡ ῥαψῳδία εἴρηται, οἱονεὶ ῥαβδῳδία τις οὖσα, φασὶ καὶ τοῦτο οἱ παλαιοί, ἀκολουθοῦντες Καλλιμάχῳ εἰπόντι "τὸν ἐπὶ ῥάβδῳ μῦθον ὑφαινόμενον". δαφνίνη δὲ ἦν ἡ ῥάβδος, ἣν κατέχοντες ἐποιοῦντο τὰς τοιαύτας ᾠδάς.

[32] *Suda* s.v. Ἀρριανός (α 3867, 1.350.4–7 Adler) mentions a poet who composed an Alexandriad in 24 rhapsodies: Ἀλεξανδριάδα· ἔστι δὲ κατὰ τὸν Μακεδόνα ἐν ῥαψῳδίαις εἴκοσι καὶ τέσσαρσιν. *Suda* s.v. Ὀρφεύς (ο 654, III.564.29 Adler) (*OF* 91, 110iiii, 1120, 1123, 1125iii B = OT 173, 174, 222 K) also mentions the Sacred Speeches in 24 Rhapsodies, Ἱεροὺς λόγους ἐν ῥαψῳδίαις κδ', in a list of the works of Orpheus (see above, n. 14), but most of the references to this text simply mention ἐν ῥαψῳδίαις.

in mankind. West indeed provides an elaborate account, tracing all the pieces of evidence to their imagined place in this grand scheme, creating a stemma for the different variants to account for any discrepancies. His whole account, however, depends on the assumption that a variety of myths can be charted like varying readings in a manuscript tradition, rather than being the products of *bricolage* that combine and recombine the same pieces in many different ways and forms.[33] On the contrary, the *Rhapsodies* were more likely a loose collection of Orphic poetry, containing a variety of poems that had been composed and reworked over the centuries by a number of different *bricoleurs*. Like the *Sibylline Oracles*, another collection of hexameter verse poetry attributed to a mythical author but composed in different periods by different poets, the *Orphic Rhapsodies* probably contained material that overlapped with and contradicted other parts of the collection.[34] Like the Orphica, the *Sibylline Oracles* seem to have been collected in the first century as a repository of ancient wisdom, since the Sibyl, like Orpheus, was imagined to have predated the Trojan War and had direct access to the divine.

The *Sibylline Oracles*, in the form that they have survived to modernity, comprise a set of books of varying lengths and contents. The shape of this collection, however, seems not to differ too much from that available to early Christian witnesses like Lactantius, who quotes from several different books corresponding to the extant ones and often notes that he is bringing his quotations from different parts.[35] Whereas the Homeric rhapsodies are fairly even in length, ranging between 400 and 900 lines, the *Sibyllines* are much more varied. The longest book in the extant collection is over 800 lines long, while the shortest is a mere 28 lines.[36] By contrast, almost no evidence survives about the shape of the *Orphic Rhapsodies* collection; the *Suda* refers to the *Hieroi Logoi* in twenty-four books, so we may presume that the *Orphic Rhapsodies* were shaped into this form in imitation of the *Homeric Rhapsodies*. However, only a few citations to individual books exist, and they provide little information about the contents of the *Rhapsodies*. One refers to the race of Gigantes, born from Earth and the blood of

[33] West 1983, which remains, despite the criticisms, the standard account. Even before his effort, however, the idea of creating a stemma of Orphica was rejected. West himself cites Hans Schwabl, *RE* Suppl. IX 1962 s.v. Weltschöpfung, 1481.60–62, who had said "Es ist wohl überhaupt verkehrt, ein Stemma aller orphischen Theogonien aufstellen zu wollen."

[34] Buitenwerf 2003: 65–91 traces the development of the *Sibylline Oracles* collection.

[35] Buitenwerf 2003: 66–72 tries to reconstruct the formation of the extant collection from the manuscripts.

[36] The modern division between books 1 and 2 does not appear in the manuscripts, which put books 1 and 2 together, sometimes along with the first 92 lines of 3 (a total of 839 lines). Book 6, by contrast, seems a single hymn of only 28 lines.

Heaven, in the eighth book of the *Orphic Rhapsodies*, while there is a quote from the fourth *Rhapsody* to Mousaios in the *Tübingen Theosophy*, as well as a reference to the twelfth revelation in Malalas' quotations.[37] None of this evidence provides any clue about the length or composition of the *Rhapsodies*, but there is no reason to suppose that each *Orphic Rhapsody* was as long as a Homeric book, rather than that individual books varied in length and content like the *Sibyllines*.

Although the most familiar style of Sibylline oracle consists of an extended prophecy of doom that recounts the collapse of successive empires, describing the devastation that descends upon each one, the Sibylline verses tackle other topics too. All the verses are in dactylic hexameter, but the nature of the contents differs, from book to book and even within individual books. Hymns of praise are interwoven with the moral exhortations and other didactic verse; certain passages even provide instructions for ritual.[38] This mixture of genres in even the heavily edited and selected collection that survives suggests that in the *Orphic Rhapsodies* we may imagine a similar variety of texts attributed to Orpheus. Orpheus is known above all for his hymns, and older hymns with extended mythological sections may have been expanded and combined into sections of the *Rhapsodies*. Moral and didactic poetry may likewise have been incorporated, as digressions within the mythological narratives, as gnomic conclusions to the tales, or even as separate sections conveying the wisdom of Orpheus. Like the *Sibyllines*, the *Rhapsodies* probably did not contain a single, extended narrative (in the manner of a Homeric poem), but a variety of texts assembled under the rubric of their famous putative author.

The hypothesis of a varied selection of texts provides a better explanation of the variety of material quoted by the authors to whom we owe our extant fragments of the *Rhapsodies*. Many of the puzzling questions that have troubled the scholarship on the *Rhapsodies* can be resolved if we abandon the

---

[37] *Etym. Magn.* s.v. Γίγας (231.21)· (*OF* 188 B = OF 63 K): Παρὰ τὸ γῶ, τὸ χωρῶ, γίνεται γᾶς· καὶ κατὰ ἀναδιπλασιασμόν, γίγας· ἢ παρὰ τὸ ἐκ τῆς γῆς ἰέναι· οἶον, Οὓς καλέουσι γίγαντας ἐπώνυμον ἐν μακάρεσσιν, | οὔνεκα γῆς ἐγένοντο, καὶ αἵματος οὐρανίοιο. | Οὕτως Ὀρφεὺς ἐν τῷ ὀγδόῳ τοῦ ἱεροῦ Λόγου. Cp. *Tübingen Theosophy* 61 (*OF* 138i B = OF 61 K); Mal. *Chron.* 4.8 (73.12 Dindorf) (*OF* 102i B = OF 62 K).

[38] All of *SO* 6 is a hymn to Christ, while *SO* 8.429–455 is a hymn to God the Father built into the overall historical narrative. *SO* 5 contains a section of fairly generic wisdom literature, moral advice that in fact also appears in Ps.-Phokylides (*SO* 5.6–148 = [Phoc.] 5–79). *SO* 7.76–91 contains instructions for sacrifice, a feature often found in the remains of *Sibylline Oracles* attested from the Roman Republic and early Empire. Many of the oracles mentioned, for example, in Livy provide instructions for propitiatory sacrifices to avert the doom threatened by the omen that prompted the consultation of the Sibylline books. Orlin 1997 provides an appendix with a list of Sibylline consultations.

assumption that the text was a single, coherent narrative.[39] The elaborate hypotheses of West regarding the stemma of Orphic theogonies, building on and eclipsing the efforts of many other previous scholars in the early twentieth century, are intended to resolve the contradictions in the evidence regarding the number and composition of the first generations of the gods and mortals. If, however, the apparent contradictions are merely references to different tales contained within the corpus of the *Orphic Rhapsodies*, tales that are not (meant to be) consistent with one another, then the need for complex and hypothetical explanations disappears.

The parallels with the *Sibyllines* are instructive. Since an extensive text of the *Sibylline Oracles* is extant, we can test the sort of assumptions made about the *Orphic Rhapsodies* in the process of deducing the whole from the fragmentary quotations. For example, on the question of the sequence of generations in the *Rhapsodies*, scholars have assumed that the *Rhapsodies* contain a single, coherent sequence of divine generations, starting from the First Principle onwards. This theogonic narrative, usually presumed to be "the usual Orphic theogony" to which Damascius refers, is thought to have six generations, on the basis of Plato's quotation of an Orphic line that calls for the song to come to a close at the sixth generation.[40] For the *Sibyllines*, Servius, in his commentary on Vergil's *Fourth Eclogue*, claims that the Sibyl recounted ten generations, so scholars have sought a sequence of ten generations in the remaining *Sibylline Oracles*. However, a look at the extant books reveals several different sequences. Books 1 and 2, which seem originally to have been parts of a single book, have a sequence of generations that may once have had ten, but book 1 only goes through seven generations, while book 2 picks up in the final generation. The third book of *Sibylline Oracles*, by contrast, describes eight generations after the primordial family, while book 4 has just four. Anyone trying to reconstruct the contents of the books as a single sequence

---

[39] For example, West 1983: 214 complains: "The testimonia which represent Phanes as permanently settled in the cave with Night are hard to reconcile with others in which he is said to travel around the cosmos." So too, in the stories involving Persephone, he claims "the myth of the snake-mating cannot well coexist with the chariot snatch. Secondly there is the discrepancy between the prophesied and actual father of the Eumenides [Apollo vs. Hades]" (West 1983: 95). He also notes (95–96) the complications created by the Cretan elements and place names that appear in some sources and the Phrygian ones that show up in others. All of these complications, and many more, are easily resolved by abandoning the hypothesis of a single, consistent storyline.

[40] Pl. *Phlb.* 66c8–9 (*OF* 25i B = *OF* 14 K): ἕκτηι δ᾽ἐν γενεῆι καταπαύσατε κόσμον ἀοιδῆς. Cp. Dam. *De princ.* 123 (III.159.17 Westerink = 1.316–317 Ruelle) (*OF* 90, 96, 109viii, 114viii, 677i B = OT 223d, OF 60 K), who describes as the usual Orphic theology (ἡ συνήθης ὀρφικὴ θεολογία) the theogony in the purported *Orphic Rhapsodies* (Ἐν μὲν τοίνυν ταῖς φερομέναις ταύταις ῥαψῳδίαις ὀρφικαῖς ἡ θεολογία).

of ten by relying on Servius' information would seriously distort the text.

So too, the idea, based on the fragment of Orpheus from Plato's *Philebus*, that the standard Orphic theogony had six generations is fundamentally misguided. First of all, there is no reason to suppose that Plato is referring to a theogonic poem that covered six generations, since Plato, along with all the other Platonic sources that cite this line, merely uses it to enumerate a set of six (or five) arguments.[41] It is, of course, not impossible that Plato is borrowing the line from a text in which it actually did describe six divine generations, but, even if so, other Orphic poems may have detailed fewer (or more) generations, and more than one such poem may have been included in the Rhapsodic collection. While Proclus does describe six divine generations, Olympiodorus, for example, cites an Orphic theogony of only four generations, and much needless scholarly effort has been expended in the attempt to get all the evidence for Orphic theogonies to conform to the six-generation mode.[42]

Likewise, the *Sibylline Oracles* provide, in different books, different accounts of the origin of mankind. The first book starts off with a paraphrase of the creation story in Genesis, describing God's creation of the world, the creation of Adam and Eve, and their fall.[43] However, the third book starts its historical narrative with the generation of the Titans, children of Earth and Heaven. This narrative, adapted from Hesiod via the Euhemeristic tradition, tells of the birth of Zeus to Rhea, his escape from the danger of being torn apart as an infant, and his return to power through the battle against the Titans, which the Sibyllist portrays as the first coming of war to mankind.[44] The Sibylline anthropogony, then, could be either of these tales, depending on which part of the collection was cited, and the

---

[41] Bernabé collects all nine quotations of this line in *OF* 25 B, but, when one examines the context of each fragment, it is clear that none of them refer directly to a sequence of divine generations. Plato is referring to elements of the good, describing pure and harmless pleasures as the fifth element; Plut. *De E ap. Delph.* 15.391d (*OF* 25ii B) refers to the same in a treatise on the number five. Damascius quotes the line several times but never in reference to generations of gods. At *In Phlb.* 251 (119 Westerink) (*OF* 25iv B), he is just citing the *Philebus* passage. The other references, *De princ.* 53 (II.34.22 Westerink) (*OF* 25v B); *In Prm.* 199 (*OF* 25vi B), *In Prm.* 253 (*OF* 25vii B), *In Prm.* 278 (*OF* 25viii B), *In Prm.* 381 (*OF* 25ix B), are all just making a list of six arguments. Procl. *In R.* 2.100.23 Kroll (*OF* 25iii B) lists the hierarchy of entities in the myth of Er: Ananke and Fates, Sirens, celestial gods, guardian *daimones*, judges, and punishing *daimones*, but even this list of divine beings is not a theogonic sequence of generations.

[42] Procl. *In Ti.* 3.168.15 Diehl (*OF* 98iii B = OF 107 K); Olymp. *In Phd.* 1.3 (*OF* 174 viii, 190ii, 227iv, 299vii, 304i, 313ii, 318iii, 320i B = OF 220 K); in his notes to *OF* 25 B, Bernabé collects the various attempts scholars have made to force the evidence into the preconceived pattern.

[43] *SO* 1.1–64.

[44] *SO* 3.110–155. Buitenwerf 2003: 172–177 compares this story to the euhemerizing versions in Ennius and Diodorus Siculus. It is interesting to note that this version has the group of Titans threatening

fact that the Titans are mentioned as a later generation in other historical narratives in the *Sibyllines* leaves much room for confusion.[45] What then of the first generations of men in the *Rhapsodies*? Two conflicting versions appear. Following the Hesiodic pattern of an artifice anthropogony, Proclus relates that Phanes created a golden race, Kronos a silver one, while Zeus produced a Titanic one from the limbs of the Titans.[46] However, Lactantius quotes Orphic verses that tell how Kronos was the first to rule over men on earth, which rules out the race that Phanes created.[47] The conflict ceases to be a problem, however, if two (or more) stories of anthropogony coexisted in the *Rhapsodies*, each fitting into a different narrative. Only if one presumes a single narrative covering the entire span from first principles to the life of humans are the contradictions problematic.

The comparison with the *Sibylline Oracles* is again useful in trying to assess how the biases of the sources who quote the Orphica may skew modern scholars' reconstruction of the *Rhapsodies*. Lactantius often cites the *Sibylline Oracles* in support of his arguments, in much the same way that Proclus or other Neoplatonists cite the Orphica in support of theirs. When we examine Lactantius' quotations in their original context, however, we can see the way his preoccupations shape the reading of the quoted texts. For example, when Lactantius discusses the second coming of Christ, he cites the *Sibylline Oracles* three times to argue that this fundamentally important Christian idea was present even in pagan wisdom.[48] When one examines the passages in their original context within the *Sibylline Oracles*, however, it is clear that only the third quotation actually refers to the second coming of Christ; the others refer to the arrival of other kings in other situations in the historical narratives. The first passage comes from a brief reference to a figure who will oppose the destruction being wrought by a "Persian king," who, in the peculiar system of the *Sibyllines*, is probably Nero. The second passage describes a king, probably Cyrus, who will restore the

---

to tear apart (διέσπων) the infant Zeus (*SO* 3.132–138), a role they more often have with the infant Dionysos, whereas in Hesiod, Kronos himself devours the children Rhea bears.

45 Cp. Titans as the seventh race in *SO* 1.375 and as one of the races at the last judgment in *SO* 2.285.

46 Procl. *In R.* 2.74.26 Kroll (*OF* 159, 216i, 320ii B = OF 140 K); Procl. *In Hes. Op.* 127–129 (5.15 Pertusi) (*OF* 216ii B = OF 141 K); cp. Dam. *In Phd.* 1.8 (33 Westerink) (*OF* 320iv B). For the artifice model of anthropogony, see Loraux 2000: 2, who distinguishes between the model of artifice and the model of fertility for the generation of mankind (and woman). See also Brisson 2002: 444–454.

47 Lactant. *Div. inst.* 1.13.11 (146 Monat) (*OF* 363 B = OF 139 K); cp. Serv. *In Bucol.* 4.10 (3.46.3 Thilo-Hagen) (*OF* 364 B = OF 29a K). Bernabé, to avoid the contradiction, places these two fragments with the alternate anthropogony in the section "Alia fragmenta theogonica origo incerta", although there is no reason to suppose that Lactantius or Servius used a different source for this Orphic citation than for all the rest that they drew from the *Rhapsodies*.

48 Lactant. *Div. inst.* 7.18, in which 7.18.6 = *SO* 5.107–109, 7.18.7 = *SO* 3.652–653, and 7.18.8 = *SO* 8.326–328. See the notes of Collins 1983–85 on each of these passages.

Temple in Jerusalem, but some of the language describing this king seems to derive from earlier oracles that prophesied the coming of a native Egyptian king who would free Egypt from foreign domination. The third passage does indeed come from a section that recounts the life of Christ, describing Christ's return after his resurrection to save Zion. If the *Sibyllines* Lactantius is quoting were not extant, it would be extremely difficult to tell from the quotations that Lactantius was drawing on descriptions of different kings from different books, even though in this chapter he does helpfully mark each quote as coming from another Sibylline. Indeed, it would be easy to imagine a single narrative of the second coming of Christ that incorporated all the passages, just as West imagines the *Orphic Rhapsodies* incorporating all the references into a single narrative.

Likewise, Lactantius cites the *Sibylline Oracles*, along with Vergil's *Fourth Eclogue*, to describe the paradise that will follow upon the last judgment.[49] However, although the paradise, in which there is peace and plenty, does come after a fiery destruction and judgment in the *Oracle* from the third Sibylline book, which Lactantius quotes from several times, there is no fiery day of wrath in the fifth Sibylline, which Lactantius also quotes, nor does Vergil mention any such thing in his *Eclogue*. Again, if the *Sibyllines* or Vergil's *Eclogue* were not extant, it would be easy to imagine that their visions of the return of the Golden Age all included a description of a preceding fiery day of judgment rather than postulating several different narratives, some of which bring about a paradise without it.

Even our modern impression of the weight and focus of the text is skewed by the way it is quoted. If we had only Lactantius, we might imagine that the *Sibylline Oracles* focused much more on the stories of last judgment and the return of a king to redeem the world, rather than the rise and fall of successive empires. The downfall of the Macedonian or Egyptian empires, for example, receives little attention in Lactantius, in comparison to the number of verses spent on these topics in the extant Oracles. In a similar manner, we may suspect that the Neoplatonists' attention to the creation of the world from the first principles or the generation of many from one in the story of Dionysos' dismemberment produces a biased view of the content of the *Orphic Rhapsodies*, which may have contained much more about the wanderings of Demeter and the grief of Persephone at her abduction – or even the ecstasies of the Kouretes and Korybantes – than is

---

[49] Lactant. *Div. inst.* 7.24, in which 7.24.11 = Verg. *Ecl.* 4.21–45, 7.24.12 = *SO* 3.787–791, 7.24.13 = *SO* 3.619–623, and 7.24.14 = *SO* 5.281–283. Lactantius cites the Sibyl in the previous book to describe the fiery destruction that precedes the paradise (7.23.4 = *SO* 4.40–45).

apparent from the quotations in Proclus and the other Neoplatonists that make up the majority of the surviving fragments of the *Rhapsodies.*[50] The Christian Lactantius and the Neoplatonist Proclus, moreover, both tend to quote from the portions of their collections that were produced by pseudepigraphers who built Christian or Neoplatonic ideas into their verses. Just as Jewish and Christian Sibyllists composed many of the verses in the collection known to Lactantius, adapting and transposing older versions of the verses attributed to the Sibyl, so, too, many of the verses in the *Orphic Rhapsodies* must have been composed by Stoic and Platonic Orphicists, whose theological ideas shaped the Orphic mythic narratives as much as the Sibyllists' did theirs. West, by contrast, claims that the *Rhapsodies* were largely unaffected by such compositions, since the Orphic religious context somehow dominated the form and content of the narrative.[51] But, just as the Sibyllists can transform the pagan mythic theme of the return of the Golden Age, familiar from Hesiod to Vergil, into a fiery last judgment, where the world is destroyed and sinners are judged and cast into the fire, so too the Orphicists must have transformed the meaning of the poems that were collected into the *Rhapsodies.* Indeed, such transformations are always part of the process of *bricolage* by which the Greek mythological tradition operates; each telling of the myth has differences that shape its meaning to its audience.

West's reconstruction of the *Rhapsodies,* followed by Bernabé in his arrangement of the Orphic fragments, assumes that the whole collection had a "theogonic frame" on which all of the material was arranged.[52] The ancient evidence, however, contradicts the idea that the *Rhapsodies* were theogonic in overall form, since ancient authors make a distinction between the theogonic material and the *Rhapsodies* as a whole.[53] Despite citing

[50] As Linforth 1941: 178 notes, "the fact that certain portions of Orphic mythology have been repeatedly cited by later writers because they suited their own particular purposes has led to the unjustifiable conclusion that they held a prominent place in the Orphic poems."

[51] West 1983: 224: "I speak of 'embellishment', because none of it seriously affected the essence of the poem. It was not transformed into an exposition of Stoic theology. Doctrines such as the ecpyrosis and cyclicalism may lie behind some of the embellishments, but they were not imported into the text. It remained an Orphic poem with something like its original religious message."

[52] West 1983: 245: "The hymn to Zeus as embodiment of the world indicates that he did not limit himself to theogonies for his raw materials, but also made use of other Orphic poems if they fitted easily into the theogonic frame."

[53] Clem. Al. *Strom.* 6.2.26 (*OF* 330, 223 B = OF 206, 149 K) cites the theogony of Orpheus, in contrast to his other material, while Procl. *In Ti.* 3.186.7–25 Diehl (*ad* 40e) (*OF* 191i, 195iii B = OF 117 K) refers to Orpheus' poem and contrasts it with Hesiod's *Theogony.* Cp. ΣLycoph. *Alex.* 399 (*OF* 214i B = OF 147 K). Procl. *Theol. Plat.* 4.5 (4.21.15 Saffrey-Westerink) (*OF* 179vi, 206v B = OF 128 K) makes references to the Orphic theogonies, while Mal. *Chron.* 4.8 (73.12 Dindorf) (*OF* 102i B = OF 62 K) lists the theogony as one of the themes of Orpheus. Fulg. *Myth.* 3.9 (74.8 Helm) (*OF* 353i

this evidence, West nevertheless proceeds to reconstruct the *Rhapsodies* and the sources for the *Rhapsodies* on the assumption that they are all theogonies, subordinating all other material to this theogonic framework.[54] The *Suda* mentions *Theogony* as the title of a work attributed to Orpheus, but theogonic material can appear in forms other than a whole poem devoted to the topic. While Hesiod's *Theogony* is indeed a full poem of over a thousand hexameters devoted to the generations of the gods, most theogonic myth appears in briefer forms, either short narratives that provide the background for some other account or allusions that merely outline a mythic genealogy.

The praise of Zeus at the beginning of Hesiod shows that one venue for cosmological myth would be a hymn to the ruler of the cosmos, and Pindar provides an account of the cosmogony in his *Theban Hymn to Zeus*, a poem of perhaps two hundred lines of which nearly fifty survive.[55] However, Homer provides another model of cosmogonic myth, the brief mythic allusion.[56] In the *Iliad*, Hera asks for the magic *kestos* of Aphrodite, so that she can soothe the quarrel between Okeanos and Tethys, who are described as the father and mother of all the gods.[57] This line is sufficient for later Greeks, starting at least as early as Plato, to attribute a cosmogony to Homer in which Okeanos and Tethys replace Ouranos and Gaia as the first gods.[58] Damascius, in the fifth century CE, discusses the cosmogonies of various authors, and his summaries form the basis of modern scholars' reconstructions of the theogonies of the *Rhapsodies*, as well as of earlier Orphica. Damascius mentions the "usual Orphic theology" (ἡ συνήθης ὀρφικὴ θεολογία) of the *Rhapsodies*, as well as a different version preserved in the works of Hieronymos or Hellanikos (Damascius is not sure if the

---

B = OF 173 K) (cp. *Myth. Vat.* 3.10.7 [*OF* 353ii B = OF 173 K]) claims that Orpheus mentioned three types of musical activity in his Theogony, but the context for this categorization is unclear.

[54] West 1983: 68: "Having said that, I shall continue to call these poems theogonies, without I hope committing myself to too rigid a view of their form or function. By a theogony I mean a poem of which the major part consists in an account of the gods from the beginning of the world to the present."

[55] For a recent analysis, see Hardie 2000.

[56] Such allusory mythic narratives merely evoke the tale, rather than narrating it in detail. Such an allusion does not necessitate the existence of a lost but complete version full of detail, since the mythic *bricoleur* may simply be using a traditional story pattern (like cosmogony, maiden's maturation, or hero quest) with a new set of characters or contexts. Other allusory cosmogonies can be found, for example, in Eur. *Antiope* fr. 182a K (= fr. 4 J.-V.L.); *Hypsipyle* fr. 758a K = 1103–1108 (*OF* 65 B = OF 2 K) and even in the *Homeric Hymn to Hermes* 423–433.

[57] *Il.* 14.201 = 302; Okeanos as father of all: *Il.* 14.245–246.

[58] Pl. *Cra.* 402b (*OF* 22i B = OF 15 K) quotes *Il.* 14.201 = 302 as evidence that Homer followed the Heraclitean doctrine of flux at the root of all being, following this quote immediately with two lines from Orpheus on Okeanos and Tethys to argue that Orpheus too was a Heraclitean.

two names refer to a single person) and another recounted in the work of the fourth-century BCE Peripatetic Eudemos.[59]

West postulates a complete and comprehensive theogonic poem, like that of Hesiod, for each of the versions Damascius mentions, even though the only piece of information Damascius reveals about the Eudemian theogony is that it began with Night.[60] However, the dangers of such speculative reconstruction are aptly illustrated by comparing what Damascius says about the cosmogonies of Homer and Hesiod with those he attributes to Orpheus. His summary of Homer's cosmogony, based on the line about Okeanos and Tethys, would lead us to expect as full and detailed a narrative as that of Hesiod, if the full content of those poems did not survive.[61] There is no reason to suppose, however, that the cosmological material in the *Orphic Rhapsodies* or any other poem followed as comprehensive a narrative as Hesiod's, rather than comprising a set of allusions to cosmogonic figures in the manner of Homer. West's whole elaborate reconstruction of the Orphic theogonies depends on the assumption of a comprehensive narrative from first principles to the affairs of men of a scope surpassing even Hesiod's *Theogony*, but the contradictions and inconsistencies are more easily explained by taking Homer's cosmological references as the model.

If the *Rhapsodies* were not a coherent, single narrative that fit everything into a cosmogonic frame, but rather a miscellany of poems attributed to Orpheus, the relation of these texts to the rituals founded by Orpheus must be more complex than has been previously assumed.[62] West presumes that the whole Rhapsodic collection served as a sacred text for the mystery rites, and that the function of the various texts from which it was formed was to articulate the religious ideas of a community for which they were written. "What they were constructing was a sacred story of a religious

---

[59] West 1983 imaginatively reconstructs the Eudemian and Hieronyman theogonies (116–226), and he discusses the authorship issues (116–117; 176–178).

[60] In his critique of West's reconstruction, Brisson 1985b: 405 notes: "Pour reconstituer cette théogonie d'Eudème, dont on ne sait qu'une chose: son premier principe était la Nuit, M. L. West a donc besoin de prés de 60 pages, au cours desquelles prolifèrent les hypothèses les plus diverses." Casadio 1986: 310 raises a similar complaint.

[61] Dam. *De princ.* 124 (III.162.19–163.13 Westerink = 1.319.7–320.5 Ruelle) (*OF* 20i, 1131 B = OF 28 K) spends equal time on Homer and Hesiod, and his references to Eudemos show that this systematization of the cosmologies of the poets dates back to the fourth-century Peripatetics, if not earlier. [Justin] *Coh. Gr.* 14.2 (*OF* 49 B = OT 98 K) likewise attributes a canonical, systematic cosmogony to Homer, on the basis of the same line that Damascius cites, *Il.* 14.201 = 302.

[62] The assumption that the *Orphic Rhapsodies* were a full-length epic theogony actually works against the idea that they could also serve as the basis for ritual. Cornford 1950: 110 comments on the difference between the allusive or excerpted cosmogonies and the full epic treatments: "Epics do not reflect ritual action; nor were they recited as incantations to reinforce the efficacy of a rite every time it was performed."

sect, culminating in events and assurances of special interest and validity for the initiates of that sect."[63] However, none of the evidence West cites from Proclus to support the idea that the *Rhapsodies* were considered by the Neoplatonists as the sacred text of the mystery rites actually makes such a claim. Rather, Proclus repeatedly claims that certain ideas he finds in the works of Plato are in agreement with the ideas in the works of Orpheus or in the rituals of the mysteries, but Proclus never mentions the Orphic texts as actual parts of any ritual, nor does the agreement of ideas necessitate any such connection.[64]

A text can be related to a ritual in many different ways, and the Orphic poems that were associated with rituals no doubt spanned this gamut, ranging from texts that merely seemed to convey ideas similar to those a sophisticated interpreter like Proclus might find in a ritual to texts that actually played some role in the performance of a ritual. While there is no evidence to suppose that the late *Rhapsodies* themselves might have been used in a ritual context, other Orphic poems, including the earlier poems that were adapted into the later *Rhapsodies*, could certainly have been performed in a ritual context.

The *Rhapsodies*, then, contained theogonic material, perhaps in the form of hymns to Zeus or other mythic narratives that alluded to the originary powers of the cosmos. This varied mythic material may not have been consistent in every detail, even if a basic pattern was familiar enough for Damascius to refer to it as the "usual Orphic theology." The whole collection of twenty-four *Rhapsodies*, however, is unlikely to have been a single narrative, coherent and consistent from start to finish, that started with the beginnings of cosmogony and led up to the creation of humanity. Indeed, the analogy with the *Sibylline Oracles* suggests that different books may have been separate compositions, each with its own proem and contents that were shaped by the individual focus of the poem.[65] These contents included

---

[63] West 1983: 128. He contrasts this religious nature of early Orphic theogonies with what he identifies as the Cyclic theogony, a poem that made up part of the epic cycle and was attributed to Orpheus solely on the basis of it similarities to earlier Orphic material: "His poem stood under the name of Orpheus only because it was drawn from Orphic sources" (West 1983: 129). However, West never attempts to justify these assumptions, neither the idea that other Orphic theogonies must have been the doctrinally significant sacred stories for a sect nor the contradictory hypothesis that the Cyclic theogony somehow could be considered Orphic without serving such a function.

[64] West 1983: 173: "Occasional references in Proclus show that he understood the Rhapsodies as a whole to be a sacred text of the mystery rites." West (n. 102) cites *Theol. Plat.* 5.35 (5.127.8 Saffrey-Westerink) (*OF* 213iv B = OF 151 K); Procl. *In Ti.* 2.146.21 Diehl (*ad* 35a); Procl. *In Ti.* 3.297.8 Diehl (*ad* 42cd) (OF 229 K), but none of these passages actually support West's assertion.

[65] The reference to "the fourth Rhapsody to Mousaios" (*Tübingen Theosophy* 61 [*OF* 138i B = OF 61 K]) suggests that the fourth book, at least, began with an address to Mousaios, and it is plausible to imagine that many or most of the books began with such an address.

not only theogonic myth, but the whole range of subjects covered in poems attributed to Orpheus. Rather than trying to trace a stemma, as though Orphic poetry were preserved and transmitted through fixed manuscripts, we may imagine that, at least until it was collected in the *Rhapsodies*, different works of Orpheus circulated in widely varying versions, with new additions and transformations made freely by each generation of pseudepigraphers, who adapted the older material to suit their own religious and philosophical perspectives. Like the Sibylline collection, the *Rhapsodies* brought together older material with new compositions, shorter material with longer poems, well-known works with more obscure Orphica. While other Orphic works continued to circulate and new Orphica were composed, the *Rhapsodies* seem to have been the form in which most of the Imperial and Late Antique world knew the poems of Orpheus.

CHAPTER SIX

Orphic mythology
The content of Orphic poems

What then was Orphic, both for these eras and in earlier periods?[1] What was the range of themes and subjects that were associated with Orpheus? Until a papyrus with the *Orphic Rhapsodies* surfaces from the sands of Egypt, we can only look to the fragments quoted and the testimonies preserved of the *Rhapsodies* and other Orphic works. While the late lexica list titles of Orphic works, perhaps the best indicator of the whole range of mythic themes and narratives associated with Orpheus comes from the *Orphic Argonautica*. This late work begins with a proem that serves to authenticate this poem in the tradition of Orphic poetry, adopting the familiar Orphic style of an address to Orpheus' pupil Mousaios. Orpheus begins by listing all his previous themes before announcing that he will now sing of his own expedition on the Argo in the quest for the Golden Fleece.

> Now it is for you, master of the lyre, to sing that dear song which my heart incites me to recount, the things that never before have I uttered, when driven by the goad of Bacchos and lord Apollo I revealed the terrifying afflictions, the remedies for mortal men, the great rites for the mystai.
>
> First, then, the implacable necessity of ancient Chaos, and Chronos (Time), how he brought forth by his immeasurable bands Aither and resplendent Eros, of double nature, facing all around, the famed father of ever-lasting Night, whom indeed brief mortals call Phanes – for he was first made manifest. And the offspring of powerful Brimo, and the destructive deeds of the Earthborn, who dripped painfully as gore from Heaven, the seed of a generation of old, out of which arose the race of mortals, who exist forever throughout the boundless earth. And the nursing of Zeus, the cult of the mountain-running Mother, the things she devised on the Cybelean mountains for maiden Persephone concerning her father, the invincible son of Kronos, the famous rending of Kasmilos and of Heracles, the rites of Ida,

---

[1] An earlier version of this chapter has appeared as Edmonds 2011c.

the mighty Korybantes. The wandering of Demeter and the great grief of Persephone and how she became Thesmophoros. And then the glittering gifts of the Kabeiroi, and the ineffable oracles of Night concerning lord Bacchos, and most holy Lemnos and seagirt Samothrace, steep Cyprus and Adonian Aphrodite, the rites of Praxidike and the mountainous nights of Athela, and the laments of the Egyptians and the sacred libations for Osiris.

You have learned the much-practiced paths of divination from beasts and birds and what the arrangement of entrails is and what is presaged in their dream-roaming paths by souls of ephemeral mortals struck to the heart by sleep; the answers to signs and portents, the stars' courses, the purification rite, great blessing to men, placations of gods, and gifts poured out for the dead.

And I have told you all I saw and learned when at Tainaron I walked the dark road of Hades trusting my cithara, for love of my wife, and the sacred tale I brought forth from Egypt when I went to hallowed Memphis and the holy towns of Apis, that the great Nile garlands around. All this you have learned truly from my breast.[2]

Many of these allusions to the Orphic mythic tradition remain enigmatic, but several basic themes emerge. First is cosmology, accounts of the creation and nature of the universe. After cosmology comes a collection of myths involving figures associated with Demeter and Dionysos, as well as the bands of ecstatic dancers known as Kouretes and Korybantes. The various didactic themes, instructions for divination and other ritual practices, offer

---

[2] *OA* 7–46 (*OF* 1018v B = OT 224 K): Νῦν γάρ σοι, λυροεργὲ, φίλον μέλος ἀείδοντι | θυμὸς ἐποτρύνει λέξαι τά περ οὔποτε πρόσθεν | ἔφρασ᾽ ὅταν Βακχοῖο καὶ Ἀπόλλωνος ἄνακτος | κέντρῳ ἐλαυνόμενος, φρικώδεα κῆλ᾽ ἐπίφασκον, | θνητοῖς ἀνθρώποισιν ἄκη, μεγάλ᾽ ὄργια μύσταις· | ἀρχαίου μὲν πρῶτα χάους ἀμέγαρτον ἀνάγκην, | καὶ Χρόνον ὡς ἐλόχευσεν ἀπειρεσίοισιν ὑφ᾽ ὁλκοῖς | Αἰθέρα καὶ διφυῆ περιωπέα κυδρὸν Ἔρωτα, | Νυκτὸς ἀειγνήτης πατέρα κλυτόν· ὃν ῥα Φάνητα | ὁπλότεροι κλήσκουσι βροτοί· πρῶτος γὰρ ἐφάνθη· | Βριμοῦς τ᾽ εὐδυνάτοιο γονάς, ἠδ᾽ ἔργ᾽ ἀΐδηλα | Γιγάντων, οἳ λυγρὸν ἀπ᾽ Οὐρανοῦ ἐστάξαντο, | σπέρμα γονῆς τὸ πρόσθεν, ὅθεν γένος ἐξεγένοντο | θνητῶν, οἳ κατὰ γαῖαν ἀπείριτον αἰὲν ἔασι· | τιτθείαν τε Ζηνὸς, ὀρεσσιδρόμου τε λατρείαν | μητρὸς ἄ τ᾽ ἐν Κυβέλοις ὄρεσιν μητίσατο κούρην | Φερσεφόνην περὶ πατρὸς ἀμαιμακέτου Κρονίωνος· | Κασμίλου τε καὶ Ἡρακλέος περίφημον ἄμυξιν· | ὄργιά τ᾽ Ἰδαίων, Κορυβάντων τ᾽ ἄπλετον ἰσχύν· | Δήμητρός τε πλάνην, καὶ Φερσεφόνης μέγα πένθος, | θεσμοφόρος θ᾽ ὡς ἦν· ἠδ᾽ ἀγλαὰ δῶρα Καβείρων, | χρησμούς τ᾽ ἀρρήτους Νυκτὸς περὶ Βάκχου ἄνακτος, | Λῆμόν τε ζαθέην ἠδ᾽ εἰναλίην Σαμοθράκην, | αἰπεινήν τε Κύπρον, καὶ Ἀδωναίην Ἀφροδίτην | ὄργια Πραξιδίκης, καὶ ὀρεινῆς νύκτας Ἀθηλῆς· | θρήνους τ᾽ Αἰγυπτίων ὠς Ὀσίριδος ἱερὰ χύτλα. | Ἀμφὶ δὲ μαντείης ἐδάης πολυπείρονας οἴμους, | θηρῶν οἰωνῶν τε καὶ ἥ σπλάγχνων θέσις ἐστίν· | ἠδ᾽ ὅσα θεσπίζουσιν ὀνειροπόλοισιν ἀταρποῖς | ψυχαὶ ἐφημερίων ὕπνῳ βεβολημέναι ἦτορ, | σημείων τεράτων τε λύσεις, ἄστρων τε πορείας· | ἀγνοπόλον τε καθαρμὸν ἐπιχθονίοις μέγ᾽ ὄνειαρ, | ἱλασμούς τε θεῶν, φθιμένων τ᾽ ἐπινήχυτα δῶρα. | Ἀλλὰ δέ σοι κατέλεξ᾽ ἅ περ εἴσιδον ἠδ᾽ ἐνόησα, | Ταίναρον ἡνίκ᾽ ἔβην σκοτίην ὁδόν, Ἄϊδος εἴσω, | ἡμετέρῃ πίσυνος κιθάρῃ δι᾽ ἔρωτ᾽ ἀλόχοιο· | ἠδ᾽ ὅσον Αἰγυπτίων ἱερὸν λόγον ἐξελόχευσα, | Μέμφιν ἐς ἠγαθέην περάσας, ἱεράς τε πόληας, | Ἄπιδος ἅς περὶ Νεῖλος ἀγάρροος ἐστεφάνωται· | πάντα μάλ᾽ ἀτρεκέως ἀπ᾽ ἐμῶν στέρνων δεδάηκας. (*TLG* text adapted according to Vian 1987).

little in the way of mythic narrative but indicate some of the areas of special knowledge associated with Orpheus, and the list concludes with stories from Orpheus' own life, his journey to the Underworld in search of his wife, as well as his journey to Egypt, which lead up to the announcement of his new theme, his journey on the Argo.

All these themes appear in other myths from the Greek mythological tradition. The *bricolage* of the Greek mythic tradition means that the pieces used by the authors of the Orphic poems come from the same stock that every other mythmaker uses, even if not every subject found in the whole mythic tradition appears in Orphic poems. Although every subject found in Orphic poems also appears elsewhere in the mythic tradition, the way the pieces are combined and the way the construct is framed marks them as Orphic.[3]

There was, therefore, no such thing as Orphic mythology. That is to say, there was no set of stories that could be found exclusively in the poems attributed to Orpheus or associated only with the rituals he was thought to have founded, no separate Orphic myth of Dionysos or special Orphic cosmology setting out peculiarly Orphic doctrines.[4] All the myths found in the Orphic poems appear in other contexts as well; the name of Orpheus was used, in different ways at different times, to lend authority to poems and rites that drew from the same traditional stock of Greco-Roman mythological tradition that other poets used. The label "Orphic" attached to a story implied no special doctrines or deities, no specific religion or rituals, no particular myths or mystic ideas. There is nothing "essentially Orphic": no doctrine, mythic motif, or divinity that defines something as Orphic.

Nevertheless, an examination of the tales with which the name of Orpheus was associated provides an indication of the criteria used by the ancient Greeks to apply this label of "Orphic" to certain extra-ordinary myths. The *Orphic Argonautica* prologue provides a list of themes in its survey of previous Orphic literature: cosmogony, myths associated with Demeter and Dionysos and their attendants, and the life of Orpheus. It is worth examining the evidence for each of these themes in turn to get a sense of what myths the ancient Greeks and Romans, from the earliest archaic evidence up to late antiquity, might have associated with the poems

---

[3] Lévi-Strauss 1966: 16–36.
[4] Contrast the discussions in, e.g., Parker 1995 of "the Orphic cosmogony" and "the Orphic myth" of Dionysos, Parker 2005: 358 of "that alternative Dionysos who in Orphic myth was a key eschatological figure", or Sourvinou-Inwood 2005: 169–189 of "Orphic mythology" and the "Orphic Dionysos" that infiltrate the mainstream polis cults and myths.

of Orpheus. As my definition of "Orphic" indicates, a number of cues indicate whether a myth is likely to be labeled as Orphic. While the name of Orpheus is the single explicit proof that a myth was in fact labeled "Orphic" in antiquity, a claim within the myth to extra-ordinary purity, sanctity, or divine authority might also distinguish it as likely to be labeled "Orphic." The most valid cues that indicate a classification as "Orphic", especially in the early Christian and later material that comprises the bulk of the evidence, are emphases on the tale's extra-ordinary antiquity, perversity, or alien nature.

Cosmogony

The first mythological theme the Argonautic Orpheus recounts is cosmogonic, the actions of the first principles – Chaos, Chronos, Night, and Air – as well as the manifestation of the principle of generation, Eros. Several late sources summarize cosmogonic myths derived from the poems of Orpheus, and numerous quotations of various Orphic poems involve cosmological material. This mythological material is, for the most part, taken from the common stock, with only a few strange names and epithets not attested elsewhere, so the label "Orphic" (applied by the pseudepigraphic authors or by other witnesses) derives not from the content of the poems, but rather from the deviant ways in which the mythological content is framed and manipulated.[5]

This very characteristic of deviance from the expected norm, however, makes Orphic poetry a suitable medium for innovative thinkers trying to develop new cosmological ideas, and traces remain of thinkers who tried to work out cosmological problems such as how something can come from nothing or how the cosmos can be both a unity and a multiplicity. Of course, these issues are the standard problems that all the so-called Presocratic philosophers were grappling with, as well as all the thinkers that followed them in the Greek scientific and philosophical tradition. The extant evidence, however, shows that not only did some of these thinkers choose to articulate their ideas in the form of Orphic poems, but that many

---

[5] In some sense, Orphic poetry was always marginal – either its claims to antiquity and direct revelation were accepted, putting its authority higher than Homer and Hesiod, or it was rejected, making it a spurious and later invention, deviant from the familiar and accepted tradition. Cp. Herodotus' famous claim (2.53 [*OF* 880i B = OT 10 K]) that Homer and Hesiod first laid out the names, genealogies, and honors of all the gods for the Greeks, which also disparages the claims of other poets (such as Orpheus) to be older and more authoritative. By contrast, Pausanias 9.30.12 (*OF* 531ii, 682 B = OF 304 K) rates the real *Orphic Hymns* as more loved by the gods than the *Homeric Hymns*, even if not quite as beautiful.

of these ideas, even if expressed under the name of a particular philosopher such as Empedokles or Pherekydes, were later classified as Orphic,
simply because of their strangeness, their distance from the normal ideas
(ever-changing though they might be from generation to generation) of
the nature of the cosmos.[6] The mythic narratives of the Orphic cosmogonies seem characterized by extra-ordinary perversions in the successions of
generations, as well as by an unusual concentration of elements that seem
marked as alien, while the poems themselves are often marked by claims
to extra-ordinary wisdom, a revelation that is limited to a select few. A few
particular formulations, notably the cosmic egg and Zeus' swallowing of
the cosmos, stand out as notable ways in which traditional elements are
manipulated in Orphic texts, but the evidence, as always, is fragmentary
and difficult to interpret.

The Orphic egg

The first piece of evidence included by Kern in his 1922 collection of Orphic
fragments is, quite literally, a joke, and it illustrates perfectly the problems
with the evidence. In Aristophanes' comedy, the *Birds*, the chorus of Birds
sings of the creation of the world, recounting a myth that puts the birth
of the race of birds before the race of the gods – thus justifying the later
action of the comedy in which the birds take over the universe from the
gods.

> Hearken, you men, by nature living in darkness, like the generation of
> leaves, feeble creations of clay, strengthless, shadowy tribes, unfledged and
> ephemeral, wretched mortal men like the phantasms of dreams, pay heed
> with your minds to us, immortal and existing forever, ethereal and unag-
> ing, pondering the imperishable, so that you may hear from us everything
> correctly about the skies. Knowing rightly about the nature of birds and the
> origin of the gods, the rivers, Erebos, and Chaos, you would tell Prodikos
> to wail for the rest from me.
>
> At first there was only Chaos, Night, black Erebos, and wide Tartaros. Not
> Earth, nor air, nor heaven existed. First of all, Night with her black wings
> laid a wind egg in the boundless bosom of Erebos, from which, as the
> seasons came around, lovely Eros sprung, his back gleaming with golden

---

[6] Bernabé collects the testimonia for the identification of Empedokles as an Orphic (Diog. Laert. 8.53
[*OF* 1108i B = OT 181 K]; Syrian. *in. Metaph.* 11.35, 43.11 [*OF* 1108ii–iii B = OF 29, 66 K]), as
well as listing the fragments in which he detects ideas similar to those found in the Orphica (*OF*
447–453 B). West 1983: 7–15 looks at the various fifth- and sixth-century authors to whom Orphica
were attributed, probably in the fourth-century BCE treatise of Epigenes; cp. Linforth 1941: 114–119.

wings, like to the whirlwind-swift tempests. He, mating in wide Tartaros with night-winged Chaos, hatched forth our race, and it was the first to come out into the light. Previously, there was no race of immortals, until Eros mingled together all things, and from this commingling of things with other things were born Heaven, Ocean, Earth and the imperishable race of blessed gods. Thus we are very much older than the other blessed ones.[7]

What is Orphic about this passage? While previous scholars have classified it as Orphic on the basis of a particular mythic element – the egg – I would argue that the ancients might have classified it as Orphic, if they did so at all, because of its claim to special knowledge. Cosmogonies attributed in brief references to Orpheus in late sources do include an egg in the same intermediary position between first principles and the generations of the gods, whereas there is no egg in Hesiod. The fifth-century CE Neoplatonist Damascius, in his survey of cosmogonic principles, attributes to the *Orphic Rhapsodies* a cosmogony in which Chronos produces an egg amidst Aither and Chaos, while he mentions another Orphic cosmogony in which water and earthy matter produce a monstrous Herakles/Chronos, who produces an egg.[8] In the *Rhapsodies*, the egg produces the monstrous hermaphroditic form of Eros/Phanes, whereas in the other tale, the egg splits in two, producing Heaven and Earth, the gods who give birth to the succeeding generations. The egg is indeed a peculiar starting point for the cosmos, an origin that puts emphasis on the derivation of the multiplicity of the cosmos from a single principle.

Damascius, however, also attributes the egg to the cosmogony of Epimenides the Cretan, another mythical poet and religious specialist,

---

[7] Ar. *Av.* 685–703 (*OF* 64 B = OF 1 K) (trans. O'Neil): ἄγε δὴ φύσιν ἄνδρες ἀμαυρόβιοι, φύλλων γενεᾷ προσόμοιοι, | ὀλιγοδρανέες, πλάσματα πηλοῦ, σκιοειδέα φῦλ' ἀμενηνά, | ἀπτῆνες ἐφημέριοι ταλαοὶ βροτοὶ ἀνέρες εἰκελόνειροι, | προσέχετε τὸν νοῦν τοῖς ἀθανάτοις ἡμῖν τοῖς αἰὲν ἐοῦσιν, | τοῖς αἰθερίοις τοῖσιν ἀγήρως τοῖς ἄφθιτα μηδομένοισιν, | ἵν' ἀκούσαντες πάντα παρ' ἡμῶν ὀρθῶς περὶ τῶν μετεώρων. | φύσιν οἰωνῶν γένεσίν τε θεῶν ποταμῶν τ' Ἐρέβους τε Χάους τε | εἰδότες ὀρθῶς, Προδίκῳ παρ' ἐμοῦ κλάειν εἴπητε τὸ λοιπόν. | Χάος ἦν καὶ Νὺξ Ἔρεβός τε μέλαν πρῶτον καὶ Τάρταρος εὐρύς, | γῆ δ' οὐδ' ἀὴρ οὐδ' οὐρανὸς ἦν· Ἐρέβους δ' ἐν ἀπείροσι κόλποις | τίκτει πρώτιστον ὑπηνέμιον Νὺξ ἡ μελανόπτερος ᾠόν, | ἐξ οὗ περιτελλομέναις ὥραις ἔβλαστεν Ἔρως ὁ ποθεινός, | στίλβων νῶτον πτερύγοιν χρυσαῖν, εἰκὼς ἀνεμώκεσι δίναις. | οὗτος δὲ Χάει πτερόεντι μιγεὶς νυχίῳ κατὰ Τάρταρον εὐρὺν | ἐνεόττευσεν γένος ἡμέτερον, καὶ πρῶτον ἀνήγαγεν ἐς φῶς. | πρότερον δ' οὐκ ἦν γένος ἀθανάτων, πρὶν Ἔρως ξυνέμειξεν ἅπαντα· | ξυμμιγνυμένων δ' ἑτέρων ἑτέροις γένετ' οὐρανὸς ὠκεανός τε | καὶ γῆ πάντων τε θεῶν μακάρων γένος ἄφθιτον. ὧδε μέν ἐσμεν | πολὺ πρεσβύτατοι πάντων μακάρων.

[8] Dam. *De princ.* 123–124 (III.159.17–164.9 Westerink = 1.316–319 Ruelle) (*OF* 69, 75i, 76i, 77, 78, 79i, 80i, 86, 109x, 111vi, 1138, etc. B = OF 54, 60 K). Athenagoras 18.3 (*OF* 75ii, 879iii, 1020ii, 1141iii B = OF 57 K) attributes to Orpheus the second cosmogony, which Dam. *De princ.* 123 (III.160.17 Westerink) (*OF* 69, 75i, 1138 B = OF 54, OT 242 K) describes as "the one according to Hieronymos and Hellanikos, if they are not the same person." On this question, see West 1983: 176–178, and above, p. 19.

associated particularly with the purification of Athens from blood guilt around the time of Solon. Damascius cites the fourth-century BCE Peripatetic Eudemos as recording that Epimenides has Air and Night produce an egg, along with Tartaros. There was a revival of interest in Epimenides in Athens around the beginning of the Peloponnesian War, and Aristophanes and his audience may well have associated the cosmic egg with Epimenides in particular, rather than Orpheus.[9] To make Aristophanes the earliest witness to an Orphic cosmogony is thus problematic; Aristophanes is parodying something, but what is not clear.

Whatever Aristophanes' audience may have thought, later Greeks did associate the egg with Orpheus, whether the verses of Epimenides were later attributed to Orpheus or whether some later Orphic poet simply borrowed the imagery from Epimenides (or even from Aristophanes). Plutarch indeed connects the egg as the symbol of generation with Orphica, recounting that some of his friends joked that he was following Orphic or Pythagorean precepts when he abstained from eating eggs at a party. The joke leads to a discussion of which came first, the chicken or the egg, and one person quotes the characteristically Orphic opening line:

> "And in addition," he said laughing, "'I shall sing for those of understanding' the Orphic and sacred account which not only declares the egg older than the chicken, but also attributes to it the absolute primordiality over all things together without exception . . . Whence it is not inappropriate that in the rites about Dionysos the egg is consecrated as a symbol of that which begets everything and contains everything within itself."[10]

For Plutarch and his contemporaries, the egg is linked, not just with Orphic cosmogony, but also with Dionysiac rituals of the sort founded by Orpheus. The Orphic tagline he quotes, marking the revelation as special wisdom intended only for the privileged, recalls the way the chorus of birds frames their revelation as surpassing the knowledge of ordinary mortals,

---

[9] As Guthrie 1952: 93 points out; see his discussion (92–95) of the scholarship on the Orphic Egg. Bremmer 2002: 21 comments, "it may well be that he offers us a *bricolage* of comparable poems." West 1983: 50–51 points out that in 432/1 BCE the stain on the Alkmaionids from the Kylonian coup was brought back into prominence when the Spartans brought it up against Perikles. The purification of Delos in 426 may also have been modeled on the Epimenidean purifications. As noted above, ch. 2, nn. 50 and 51, Orpheus tends to replace Epimenides and other such poets in later evidence.

[10] Plut. *Quaest. conv.* 2.3.2 636de (*OF* 1ii, 101i B = OF 334 K): 'τὸ δ' ἐπὶ τούτοις' ἔφη γελάσας "ἀείσω ξυνετοῖσι' τὸν Ὀρφικὸν καὶ ἱερὸν λόγον, ὃς οὐκ ὄρνιθος μόνον τὸ ᾠὸν ἀποφαίνει πρεσβύτερον, ἀλλὰ καὶ συλλαβὼν ἅπασαν αὐτῷ τὴν ἁπάντων ὁμοῦ πρεσβυγένειαν ἀνατίθησιν. . . . ὅθεν οὐκ ἀπὸ τρόπου τοῖς περὶ τὸν Διόνυσον ὀργιασμοῖς ὡς μίμημα τοῦ τὰ πάντα γεννῶντος καὶ περιέχοντος ἐν ἑαυτῷ συγκαθωσίωται.' Cp. 2.3.1 635ef (*OF* 645, 647i, 648 B = OF 291 K).

even the sophisticated (and sophistic) Prodikos.[11] It is precisely this kind of claim to extra-ordinary wisdom that might cause the *Birds* chorus to have been classified as Orphic in some way by Aristophanes' audience and later audiences, whether or not the image of the egg was originally attributed to Epimenides.[12]

Likewise, the line from Euripides' *Melanippe* that describes "how the heaven and earth were once a single form," becomes classified as Orphic cosmogony when inscribed on a bowl along with other verses attributed to Orpheus.[13] Of course, Euripides' verse is not Orphic in the same way that the cosmogony from Apollonios Rhodios' *Argonautica* is. Apollonios, while not writing Orphic verses, nevertheless has Orpheus, as a character in his story, recite a cosmogonic myth. This Orphic cosmogony bears little resemblance to those found in the Derveni papyrus or the fragments of the *Rhapsodies*.

> He sang how the earth and the heaven and also the sea,
> once upon a time still joined together in a single form,
> after destructive strife were divided each from the other;
> and how the paths of the stars and the moon and the sun
> have their boundary fixed forever in the ether;
> and how the mountains arose, and how the resounding rivers
> with their nymphs and all creeping things were born.
> And he sang how first Ophion and Eurynome,
> daughter of Ocean, held the power in snowy Olympos,
> and how by might and arms the one gave way to Kronos,
> and the other to Rhea, and how they plunged into the waves of Ocean;
> but the other two meanwhile ruled over the blessed gods, the Titans,
> while Zeus, still a child and still an infant in his thoughts,
> dwelt in the Dictaean cave; and not yet to him

---

[11] This frame resembles other revelations from Orpheus or other figures claiming such extra-ordinary insight; cp. *OF* 337 B = OF 233 K; Pyth. *Carm. Aur.* 54ff, as well as Epimen. 3 B 1 DK, *Isaiah* 6:9, Parm. 28 B 6.3ff DK, Emp. 2 DK; Ov. *Met.* 15.153; *Hom. Hymn Dem.* 256–262; cp. Richardson 1974: 243–244 and Dunbar 1995: 429–432.

[12] Aristophanes may also be parodying various ideas that his audiences would have associated with thinkers, like Empedokles, who made similar claims to extra-ordinary wisdom. The role of Eros (700) in bringing all things together recalls the role of Empedokles' Φιλότης, while the whirlwinds (697) recall Empedokles' δίνη by which all the elements swirl together. See further Dunbar 1995 *ad loc.* So too, Night produces the wind egg (that is, an unfertilized egg) with the help of Air, perhaps an allusion to the role of Air in the cosmologies of thinkers such as Anaximenes and Diogenes of Apollonia, but also to the idea, attributed to "the so-called Orphic poems" by Aristotle, that the soul enters the body blown in on the winds (*De an.* A5 410b27 [*OF* 421i B = OF 27 K]).

[13] Eur. *Melanippe* fr. 484 K (= fr. 5 J.-V.L.) (*OF* 66i B): ὡς οὐρανός τε γαῖα τ᾽ ἦν μορφὴ μία; Macrob. *Sat.* 1.23.22. Bernabé collects all the inscriptions as *OF* 66iii B. For further discussion, see above ch. 3, figure 1.

had the earthborn Cyclopes given power with the bolt,
with thunder and lightning; for these things give renown to Zeus.[14]

The creation from a single form into a multiplicity is a familiar feature of the Presocratic cosmologies, but this cosmogony has no egg, unlike those of Aristophanes or the *Rhapsodies*. The important role played by Strife (Νεῖκος) recalls Empedokles specifically, while the characters of Ophion and Eurynome are found in the cosmogony of Pherekydes of Syros.[15] Again, we find innovative philosophical cosmology in a poet's verses transformed into the wisdom of Orpheus, this time not by the later audience of the poet but by the poet himself. Empedokles and Pherekydes are themselves connected with Orphica in later sources, as well as with the legendary wise man Pythagoras, but both are themselves extra-ordinary figures, credited not only with exceptional wisdom but even with miraculous powers stemming from that wisdom.[16] Like the Birds of Aristophanes, who claim to outdo the cleverness of Prodikos, or the speaker in Plutarch, who describes his knowledge of the egg as special wisdom for the privileged alone, figures like Empedokles and Pherekydes mark their own extra-ordinary claims to wisdom, and this kind of claim can be used, by audiences contemporary or later, to categorize them with the authors of Orphica who make similar claims.

Close the doors of your ears

The line Plutarch quotes to mark the special nature of the forthcoming revelation, "I shall sing for those of understanding. Close the doors of your ears, ye profane," appears to have been a favorite line to mark the

---

[14] Ap. Rhod. *Argon.* 3.496–511: "Ἤειδεν δ᾽ ὡς γαῖα καὶ οὐρανὸς ἠδὲ θάλασσα, | τὸ πρὶν ἔτ᾽ ἀλλήλοισι μιῇ συναρηρότα μορφῇ, | νείκεος ἐξ ὀλοοῖο διέκριθεν ἀμφὶς ἕκαστα· | ἠδ᾽ ὡς ἔμπεδον αἰὲν ἐν αἰθέρι τέκμαρ ἔχουσιν | ἄστρα, σεληναίης τε καὶ ἠελίοιο κέλευθοι· | οὐρεά θ᾽ ὡς ἀνέτειλε, καὶ ὡς ποταμοὶ κελάδοντες | αὐτῇσιν νύμφῃσι καὶ ἑρπετὰ πάντ᾽ ἐγένοντο. | ἤειδεν δ᾽ ὡς πρῶτον Ὀφίων Εὐρυνόμη τε | Ὠκεανὶς νιφόεντος ἔχον κράτος Οὐλύμποιο· | ὡς τε βίῃ καὶ χερσὶν ὁ μὲν Κρόνῳ εἴκαθε τιμῆς, | ἡ δὲ Ῥέῃ, ἔπεσον δ᾽ ἐνὶ κύμασιν Ὠκεανοῖο· | οἱ δὲ τέως μακάρεσσι θεοῖς Τιτῆσιν ἄνασσον, | ὄφρα Ζεὺς ἔτι κοῦρος, ἔτι φρεσὶ νήπια εἰδώς, | Δικταῖον ναίεσκεν ὑπὸ σπέος, οἱ δέ μιν οὔπω | γηγενέες Κύκλωπες ἐκαρτύναντο κεραυνῷ, | βροντῇ τε στεροπῇ τε· τὰ γὰρ Διὶ κῦδος ὀπάζει.
[15] The parallel with Empedokles was noted by the ancient scholia; for the connections with Pherekydes, see Schibli 1990: 95–97.
[16] For Pherekydes and Orphica, cp. *Suda* s.v. Φερεκύδης (φ 216, IV.713.23–24 Adler) (*OF* 1127 B = OT 228 K), Tert. *De anim.* 2.3 (*OF* 1087ii B = OT 147 K); Empedokles, see above, ch. 3 n. 29. Diogenes Laertius relates that Empedokles was called the pupil of Pythagoras, while Pherekydes was credited with being his teacher; both associations indicate the exceptional nature of their claims to wisdom and their classification with the Pythagoreans. Diogenes Laertius preserves a number of miracle stories about Pherekydes (1.116) and Empedokles (8.58–62). Empedokles' claim to be like a god, no longer mortal (31 B 112 DK = Diog. Laert. 8.62), is perhaps matched by the epigram in which Pherekydes claims to be the perfection of wisdom (Diog. Laert. 1.120 = *Anth. Pal.* 7.93).

extra-ordinary nature of Orphic poetry. Bernabé makes this passage, rather than Aristophanes, the first fragment in his 2004 collection of Orphic fragments, since it also shows up in the Orphic poem in the Derveni papyrus, possibly the oldest Orphic verses extant.[17] This poem, preserved in quotations in the fragmentary treatise, appears to be a hymn to Zeus that recounts how he became the supreme power in the cosmos.[18] The myth neatly resolves the theological problem of how a god born so late in the succession of generations can legitimately be hailed as the primary power by having Zeus incorporate all of the cosmos into himself and then bring it back into existence from him.[19] In the Derveni poem, it appears that Zeus swallows the phallus of Ouranos, which has been floating about in the ether ever since Ouranos was castrated by Kronos, "He swallowed the phallus of [. . .], who sprang from the ether first."[20] Later authors quote Orphic poems (probably from the Rhapsodic collection) that have Zeus swallowing the first-born (Protogonos) Phanes and then giving birth to the whole cosmos anew.

> And so, engulfing then the might of the Firstborn, Erikepaios, the body of all things he held in the hollow of his own belly; and he mingled with his own limbs the power and might of the god. Wherefore together with him all things were made again within Zeus, the gleaming height of the broad ether and the heaven, the fundament of the barren sea and the renowned earth, great Ocean and the uttermost Tartarean depths of the earth, and the rivers and the boundless sea and all other things, and all the immortal and blessed gods and goddesses, as many things that until then had come into

[17] The date of the Orphic poem is a vexed question. While the papyrus itself comes from a tomb dated to the late fourth or early third century BCE (see Themelis and Touratsoglou 1997), the text seems to be older. Ever since Burkert's assertion that the text must be pre-Platonic due to the lack of influence of Platonic ideas (Burkert 1968 and 1970), scholars have tended to agree that the papyrus text must date to around the beginning of the fourth century (see the summary in Kouremenos *et al.* 2006: 9–10). The poem on which the text comments, then, must be even older, but there is no way to date the verses in comparison with the verses of Orpheus quoted by Plato that are the only others from around the same period.

[18] Whereas West 1983: 69 sees it as an abridgement of a hypothetical earlier Orphic cosmogony he calls the Protogonos Theogony, Bernabé 2002c: 94–95 identifies its form as more closely resembling the *Homeric Hymns*.

[19] A version in the *Rhapsodies* portrays Zeus asking Night, "Mother, highest of the gods, immortal Night, how am I to establish my proud rule among immortals?" and "How may I have all things one and each one separate?" (Procl. *In Ti.* 1.206.26 Diehl [*OF* 237i B = OF 164 K]; Procl. *In Ti.* 1.313.31 Diehl [*OF* 237iv B = OF 165 K])

[20] col. 13.4: αἰδοῖον κατέπινεν, ὃς αἰθέρα ἔχθορε πρῶτος. The Derveni commentator interprets this phallus as the sun, which is responsible for all generation. By contrast, West 1983: 85 argues that Zeus swallowed the revered (αἰδοῖον) Protogonos, rather than his phallus (αἰδοῖον), and commentators have been divided whether the Derveni papyrus matches the later Rhapsodic version in this way or represents a different version. Cp. Brisson 2003. I have followed the cogent arguments of Betegh 2004, who reviews the controversies (111–122), emphasizing, among other things, the parallels with Hittite Kumarbi raised by earlier commentators.

being and all that were yet to come, it all was born in there, and in the belly of Zeus it all streamed together.[21]

In either case the idea is the same: Zeus incorporates within himself the generative principle, whether it is the hermaphroditic Phanes who generates the other gods by copulating with himself/herself or it is the generative member of the oldest god, Ouranos. Thus, the last-born Zeus becomes the first-born, the generating principle for the whole cosmos, the father of all.

Although Hesiod's cosmogony has its fair share of castrations and swallowings, the Orphic tale makes even more elaborate use of these motifs, provoking increased outrage as well as prompting more profound interpretations. Kronos' assault on Ouranos and swallowing of his children in Hesiod posed enough problems for Greek thinkers, but the idea of swallowing a severed phallus or even the entire cosmos goes even further. If indeed some version of the Hittite Kumarbi myth was known to Greek audiences as coming from the Near East, the Orphic tale would carry the added allure of alien nature.[22]

Whereas Hesiod has Zeus come to supreme power like an archaic tyrannos, by overthrowing the old aristocracy of the gods (the Titan children of Ouranos) and setting up a new order based on the principle of Justice (Δίκη), redistributing the honors and authority (τιμαί) to those who aided him in his coup, the Orphic story focuses on Zeus' omnipotence, his supreme transcendence of the cosmic order. "Zeus was the first, Zeus last, of the bright lightning's bolt, Zeus head, Zeus middle, from Zeus are all things made. Zeus the king, Zeus the beginning/ruler of all, of the bright lightning's bolt."[23] While an early version of these lines seems known to Plato, later Orphic poets embellish this theme in various ways, adding epithets particularly appropriate for Stoic or Neoplatonic or even Jewish

---

[21] Procl. *In Ti.* 1.324.29–325.3 Diehl, 1.313.9–16 (*OF* 241 B = OF 167 K): ὡς τότε Πρωτογόνοιο χανὼν μένος Ἡρικεπαίου | τῶν πάντων δέμας εἶχεν ἑῇ ἐνὶ γαστέρι κοίλῃ, | μῖξε δ' ἑοῖς μελέεσσι θεοῦ δύναμίν τε καὶ ἀλκήν, | τοὔνεκα σὺν τῷ πάντα Διὸς πάλιν ἐντὸς ἐτύχθη | αἰθέρος εὐρείης ἠδ' οὐρανοῦ ἀγλαὸν ὕψος, | πόντου τ' ἀτρυγέτου γαίης τ' ἐρικυδέος ἕδρη, | Ὠκεανός τε μέγας καὶ νείατα τάρταρα γαίης, | καὶ ποταμοὶ καὶ πόντος ἀπείριτος ἄλλα τε πάντα | πάντες τ' ἀθάνατοι μάκαρες θεοὶ ἠδὲ θέαιναι, | ὅσσα τ' ἔην γεγαῶτα καὶ ὕστερον ὁππόσ' ἔμελλεν, | ἐνγένετο, Ζηνὸς δ' ἐνὶ γαστέρι σύρρα πεφύκει. (trans. Guthrie). Cp. Athenagoras, *Leg.* 20.4 (*OF* 81, 80iii, 85 B = OF 58 K), Procl. *In Ti.* 3.101.9 Diehl (*OF* 240vi B = OF 82 K), Procl. *In Crat.* 62.3 Pasquali (*OF* 240i B = OF 129 K).

[22] The parallels of the Hittite Kumarbi with Hesiod were explored by Güterbock 1948, and Burkert 1987 discusses the similarities with the Derveni theogony. Cp. Betegh 2004: 119. The most complete study of the cross-cultural contacts and the parallels in the cosmogonies is López-Ruiz 2010, esp. 84–129.

[23] *OF* 14 B reconstructed from Derveni papyrus col. 17.6, 12; 18.12–13; 19.10. Bernabé postulates another line mentioning μοῖρα because of the discussion of μοῖρα in col. 18 ([Ζεὺς πνοιὴ πάντων, Ζεὺς πάντων ἔπλετο] μοῖρα).

theology.[24] Indeed, this theme of the transcendent Zeus, without the story of his swallowing Phanes or the phallus, appears in the so-called *Testament of Orpheus*, an Orphic poem that portrays itself as Orpheus' conversion to monotheism and his recantation of all his previous themes.[25]

The cosmogonic myths found in the Orphica, then, seem to play at *bricolage* with the same pieces of the mythic tradition found in Hesiod, but the Orphic combinations are characteristically weirder, even more full of monsters and perversions of the generational succession. The egg or the bizarre multi-headed, double-sexed Phanes serves to begin the process of generation, creating something out of nothing. Zeus' swallowing and re-producing the world likewise makes the cosmogonic process an endless loop, as the youngest god becomes the oldest, last becomes first. While the later cosmogonies put the figure of Chronos at the beginning of all, in place of Night, Chronos does not seem to be marked as a particularly Orphic feature (like the egg) in any of the evidence.[26] Moreover, although previous generations of scholars have hailed the Orphic cosmogonies as originating the idea of a Creator God, even the notion of Zeus swallowing and re-producing the world does not really fit in with the God of Genesis, or even the demiurgic creator of Plato's *Timaeus*.[27] Orphic poets may have used the medium of Orphic poetry to put forth new and extra-ordinary philosophical and theological ideas, but they did so using the

---

[24] Pl. *Leg.* 715e, with scholiast *ad loc.* (317 Greene) (*OF* 31iii–iv B = OF 21 K). Another version appears in Arist. [*Mund.*] 401a25 (*OF* 31iB = OF 21a K), while Porph. fr. 354 F Smith (*Peri agalm.*) = Euseb. *Praep. evang.* 3.8.2 (*OF* 243i B = OF 168 K) preserves a later Platonic one.

[25] Cp. the studies by Riedweg 1993, Holladay 1996, and Jourdan 2010. *The Testament of Orpheus* played an important role in the later reception of Orphica, since it put him among the figures of Classical antiquity that prefigured Christian truth.

[26] *Contra* West 1983: 263, who claims that Orphic mythology provided the main channel for the transmission of the Time-cosmogony. Brisson 1990: 2886 argues to the contrary that Chronos did not enter the cosmogony until the first century CE. Betegh 2004: 157–158 sums up the earlier controversies over Chronos (see especially his n. 117). None of these controversies, however, takes into account the absence of any evidence marking Chronos as pertaining peculiarly to Orphica, in the way that Plutarch's evidence marks the egg. Moreover, despite the arguments of Brisson 1997, Chronos appears as a divine figure as early as Pindar and is even conflated with Kronos in Pind. *Ol.* 10.50–55.

[27] *Contra* Guthrie 1952: 106: "The conception that seems to me to have the best right to be called an Orphic idea is that of a creator." Betegh 2004: 180–181 argues that the poem used the verb μήσατο (cp. col. 23.4) to describe Zeus' reproduction of the world as a conscious devising of the cosmos, rather than "simply spew[ing] up the previously swallowed entities." Nevertheless, the verb may have only described Zeus' plan to swallow and spew back up, since the poem contains no references to the kind of demiurgic planning and creating that appears in other kinds of accounts. The Neoplatonists, of course, attributed the whole elaborate scheme of Plato's *Timaeus* to the Orphica, including the creator's rational devising of the cosmos, but, even if such activity appeared explicitly in the *Orphic Rhapsodies* version, such a feature is an example of the Platonic shaping of the Orphica, not an independent development of the idea by hypothetical Orphics.

same traditional mythic figures and schemas found in other cosmogonies. Even the egg and Zeus' swallowing were not part of all Orphic cosmogonies, and, when Apollonios Rhodios portrays Orpheus reciting a cosmogony in his *Argonautica*, he includes neither of these features.[28]

Among the myths found in Orphic poems, then, cosmogony and cosmology took a prominent place, and thinkers who wished to propagate their own ideas found in Orphic poetry an effective vehicle for expression. The evidence for the specific content of any of these poems is problematic, however, since most of it comes from fragmentary quotations in very late sources, and it is thus difficult to know how much any poem cited actually contained.[29] Hymns to the gods, like the Orphic hymn to Zeus in the Derveni papyrus as well as the *Homeric Hymns*, provided the occasion for numerous and rich mythological narratives, while didactic poetry could elaborate physical and cosmological themes using the traditional elements of the mythic tradition. These cosmologies, each laying claim with their competing imagery and ideas to special wisdom, did not form a coherent or consistent whole, much less an identifiable Orphic doctrine about the nature and history of the cosmos. Rather, the Orphic cosmological myths were marked by the extra-ordinary manner in which they employed the traditional mythic material, the peculiar perversions of the successions of generations, whether through castration or swallowing or even the production of a generative god from an unfertilized wind egg.

Poems for the sacred rites

The cosmologies, however, are not the only or even best known myths with which Orpheus is associated. Orpheus is, first and foremost, a poet of the sacred rites, and he is credited with founding or providing the songs for many different rites honoring a selection of deities.[30] Orpheus founds rites for only a limited set of deities, however. The majority of the testimonies credit him with rituals for Demeter and Persephone, as well as for goddesses such as the Mother of the Gods or Hekate. He is also at times credited with

---

[28] See above, pp. 167–168.

[29] See above, p. 157 on Damascius' reference to Homer's cosmogony (*De princ.* 124 [III.162.19–163.13 Westerink = 1.319.7–320.5 Ruelle] [*OF* 20i, 1131 B = OF 28 K]), which, like that of [Justin] *Coh. Gr.* 2bc, derives a canonical, systematic cosmogony from Homer, on the basis of *Il.* 14.302.

[30] Bernabé collects the testimonies to Orpheus as the originator of mysteries and rites in general in *OF* 546–562 B. His collection is more comprehensive than the earlier collection of Kern, OT 90–104, 108–110 K.

founding the rites for deities like the Idaian Dactyls, who are associated with the Mother of the Gods, or for Bacchic figures like Dionysos.[31]

The list in the *Orphic Argonautica*, therefore, again provides an overview that tallies with the evidence surviving elsewhere; Orpheus founds rituals for Demeter or similar Great Mother figures and for Dionysos or similar Bacchic figures.[32] These two types of deities are the ones most often honored by special kinds of rituals, cults that are sometimes called mysteries.[33] Such cults, whether called *mysteria* or not, provide a special relation between the deity and the select number of worshipers who undertake the rituals honoring the god. The myths of Orpheus' poetry that are associated with such rites thus relate the tales of these divinities, honoring them for their vicissitudes and celebrating their power in overcoming them.[34] These myths need not provide the story of the origin of the cult; any myth describing the nature of the deity and narrating its triumphs could serve as a *hymnos physikos* in Menander Rhetor's sense, offering praise to the deity that

---

[31] Linforth 1941: 262–263 lists the rites Orpheus is said to have founded; Bernabé includes more testimonies, not all relevant, *OF* 510–535 B: Athenian mysteries for Persephone: Eur. *Rhes.* 938–949 (*OF* 511 B = OT 91 K); Eleusinian Mysteries: *Marm. Par.* (= *IG* xii.5 444) (*OF* 379, 513 B = OT 221 K); Clem. Al. *Protr.* 2.20.1–21.1 = Euseb. *Prep. evang.* 2.3.30–35 (*OF* 392iii, 391ii, 394i, 395i, 515i B = OF 52 K); Aristid. *Or.* 22.1 Keil (*OF* 516 B); Procl. *In R.* 2.312.16 Kroll (*OF* 517i B = OT 102 K), *Theol. Plat.* 6.11 (6.50.12 Saffrey-Westerink) (*OF* 517ii B = OT 102 K); Thdt. *Graec. Aff. Cur.* 1.21 (108.21 Canivet) (*OF* 511 B = OT 103 K); cp. also Ar. *Ran.* 1032 (*OF* 510, 626i B = OT 90 K), [Dem.] 25.11 (*OF* 512 B = OT 23 K); Diod. Sic. 4.25.1 (*OF* 514, 713ii, 916 B = OT 97 K); Phrygian Mother cults: Ap. Rhod. *Argon.* 1.1117–1151 (*OF* 526 B); – by way of Midas: Conon, *FGrH* 26 F 1.1 *ap.* Phot. *Bibl.* 186.130b 28 (*OF* 527i B = OT 160 K); Ov. *Met.* 11.92 (*OF* 499, 527ii B = OT 160 K), Just. *Epit.* 11.7.14 (*OF* 527iv B = OT 160 K), Clem. Al. *Protr.* 2.13.3 (*OF* 527iii B = OT 160 K); Idaean Dactyls: Ephorus, *FGrH* 70 F 104 *ap.* Diod. Sic. 5.64.4 (*OF* 519, 940i B = OT 42 K); Demeter Chthonia and Kore Soteira at Sparta: Paus. 3.14.5 (*OF* 533 B = OT 108 K), Paus. 3.13.2 (*OF* 534 B = OT 109 K); Megale at Phlya: Hippol. *Haer.* 5.20.4 (*OF* 532i B = OF 243 K), cp. Paus. 9.27.2 (*OF* 531i B = OF 305 K), 9.30.12 (*OF* 531ii, 682 B = OF 304 K), 1.22.7 (*OF* 1119 B) and 4.1.5 (which refers to a hymn to Demeter by Mousaios sung at Lycomidan rites at Phlya); Hekate in Aigina: Paus. 2.30.2 (*OF* 535i B = OT 110 K), cp. Origen, *C. Cels.* 6.22 (*OF* 535ii B), Lib. *Orat. pro Aristoph.*14.5 (2.89.13 Foerster). Praxidike is identified with Persephone in *OH* 29.5. Diodorus Siculus attributes some Dionysiac cults to Orpheus: cult of Dionysos, son of Semele, at Thebes: Diod. Sic. 1.23.2 (*OF* 48iii, 327iv, 497iv B = OT 95 K); Dionysus in Crete: Diod. Sic. 5.77.3 (*OF* 529 B); Eleusinian, Samothracian, Thracian, Cretan: Diod. Sic. 5.75.4 (*OF* 283i, 311xii, 530 B = OF 303 K).

[32] Cp. also the titles in the *Suda* listing s.v. Ὀρφεύς (o 654, III.565.5 Adler) (*OF* 605i, 835, 1102 B = OT 175, 223d K): Enthronements for the Mother of the Gods and Bacchica, Θρονισμοὺς Μητρῷους καὶ Βακχικά.

[33] The term *mysteria* seems to be associated in the Classical period primarily with the rites of Eleusinian Demeter and similar goddesses, as well as with the rituals of attendant deities, such as the Samothracian Great Gods or the Kabeiroi. In later periods it is also applied to rites for Isis and Osiris, Mithras, and even Dionysos. For an overview, see Graf nd s.v. Mysteries in *BNP*.

[34] Bianchi 1965 sets out the category of deities who suffer "vicissitudes," such as rape, dismemberment, or death, and importantly points out that the meaning of these vicissitudes to the worshipers could vary enormously in different contexts.

binds the god closer to the worshiper in the reciprocal networks of Greek religion.[35]

Myths of Demeter and Dionysos, of course, are not confined to Orphic poems, nor are the cults of these deities limited to rites founded by Orpheus. Certainly the cults of maternal goddesses like Demeter, Rhea, or the Mother of the Gods are found in many places with no connection to Orpheus, just as Bacchic cults abound throughout the Greek world, whether honoring Dionysos, Sabazios, or other similar figures. The Orphic versions must be understood within the context of the larger Greek mythological and religious tradition as extra-ordinary versions, marked in different ways and for different reasons by the attribution to Orpheus.

The aggrieved goddess

Perhaps the best-known mythic theme from the *Argonautica*'s list is "the wanderings of Demeter and the grief of Persephone." One Orphic poem even begins, "Sing, goddess, of the wrath of Demeter of the gleaming fruit," just as Homer's *Iliad* begins, "Sing, goddess, of the wrath of Achilles son of Peleus."[36] Many sources associate Orpheus with the myths and rituals connected with an aggrieved goddess, be it Demeter angry and mourning over the loss of her daughter or Persephone grieved over her abduction or even some other variation on the theme. Such aggrieved goddesses must be appeased, and these myths often conclude by telling how the goddess gains new honors among the gods as well as honors from mortals by the institution of propitiatory rites. Again, many such stories appear throughout the mythic tradition, but the Orphic versions bear some stamp of strangeness that marks them as extra-ordinary.

Of course, as with most Orphic poetry, only fragments remain to attest to the peculiarities, but a papyrus from the mid-first century BCE preserves portions of a hymn to Demeter attributed to Orpheus and marked as

---

[35] Burkert 1987: 78 concludes: "Thus in general and in detail, in correspondence and opposition, myth provided a framework for verbalizing more or less important aspects of the mysteries. This is 'speaking about god' *theologia*, yet it remains experimental, allusive, and incidental – far from a systematic theology."

[36] [Justin] *Coh. Gr.* 17.1 (*OF* 386 B = OF 48 K): μῆνιν ἄειδε, θεά, Δημήτερος ἀγλαοκάρπου. Cp. *Il.* 1.1. While the mythic pattern of the wrath of the aggrieved goddess is certainly more ancient even than Homer, appearing in earlier Near Eastern and Indo-European sources, there is no reason to believe the early Christian apologist who sees Homer as trying to outdo his earlier rival, Orpheus; the traditional formula was more likely adapted by an Orphic *bricoleur* at some later point precisely to contrive that effect of poetry older than Homer. Cp. Sowa 1984: 95–120, Nickel 2003 on this pattern.

Orphic by an address to Mousaios.[37] This papyrus has received little attention in recent years and has mostly been relegated to the role of supporting
evidence for the *Homeric Hymn to Demeter*. While this hymn may have
begun with "Sing, goddess, the wrath . . . ," it also includes a number of
hexameter verses that also appear in the *Homeric Hymn to Demeter*, and
the storylines share many similarities.

In this version, Persephone, daughter of Demeter and Zeus, is abducted
by Hades, the lord of the Underworld, while she is picking flowers among
a group of Oceanid nymphs and other maiden goddesses. The abduction
was arranged by Zeus and Hades without the knowledge of Demeter,
and Zeus even prevents Artemis and Athena from interfering.[38] Demeter
wanders the earth, searching for her child, waving torches and raving in her
wrath and sorrow.[39] Finally, she comes to Eleusis, where, disguised as an
old woman, she meets a mother and her daughters. In a scene missing from
the fragmentary papyrus but reported elsewhere, the mother, Baubo, cheers
the mourning Demeter by joking and exposing her genitals, and she gets
the goddess to break her fast by drinking the *kykeon*.[40] The goddess then
agrees to become the nurse of the infant son of the house. Demeter attempts
to make the child immortal by anointing him with ambrosia and putting
him in the fire, but she is interrupted by the mother and the child is burned
to death.[41] Demeter then reveals her divinity, castigating mortals for their
foolishness and asking if anyone knows who has abducted Persephone. We
may note a few differences in this narrative from the better-known *Homeric
Hymn to Demeter*.[42] In this Orphic version, the mourning Demeter is

---

[37] *P. Berol.* 13044 (*OF* 383, 387, 388, 389, 392, 393, 396, 397ii B = OF 49 K). Cp. Richardson 1974:
66–67, 77–86. The lines that also appear in the *Homeric Hymn to Demeter*: 21–26 ≈ *Hom. Hymn
Dem.* 418–423 (list of Oceanids – the papyrus is missing 419); 63–75 ≈ *Hom. Hymn Dem.* 8–18 (the
papyrus is missing 13–16), 32–36 (skips from πολυδέγμων of 18 to 31 – Narcissus and abduction);
92–94 ≈ *Hom. Hymn Dem.* 248–249 (mother's cry); 96–100 ≈ 256–262 (Demeter's rebuke, skipping
the oath); 102 ≈ *Hom. Hymn Dem.* 268, 54; 103–105 ≈ *Hom. Hymn Dem.* 55–56.

[38] Cp. Eur. *Hel.* 1314–1318; Claud. *De raptu* 2.204–246.

[39] Euripides (*Hel.* 1301–1369) depicts the wandering Demeter like the Phrygian or Cretan Mother of
the Gods, accompanied by rattling castanets and finally appeased by Bacchic ceremonies with drum
and flute, just like those associated with Kybele.

[40] Clem. Al. *Protr.* 2.20.1–21.1 = Euseb. *Prep. evang.* 2.3.30–35 (*OF* 392iii, 391ii, 394i, 395i, 515i B =
OF 52 K). Cp. the role of Iambe in *Hom. Hymn Dem.* 200–205, with the comments of Richardson
1974: 213–217. The papyrus mentions Baubo as the one who hands the baby over to Demeter, and
it is probable that this version thus resembles the one quoted by Clement that also features Baubo.
On Baubo, see Olender 1990.

[41] Although the child is saved in the *Homeric Hymn*, Apollod. *Bibl.* 1.5.1 also relates the death of the
child. Thus, although the fate of the child is obviously of crucial importance to each particular
telling, the general pattern of the myth could admit either alternative.

[42] It is worth noting that, although this hymn is relatively well known to contemporary scholars,
it may not have been as well known in antiquity. See Richardson 1974: 65–66 on the dramatic

cheered, not by Iambe jesting but by Baubo exposing her genitals, and the child whom Demeter nurses in the Orphic version perishes in the flames, rather than just wailing at being returned to his mortal mother.

Although the papyrus breaks off shortly after this point, the tale may be reconstructed from other references to tellings of the myth attributed to Orpheus. Some of the local inhabitants of Eleusis have witnessed the abduction of Persephone, and Demeter rewards Triptolemos, Eumolpos, and Eubouleus for their information by giving special agricultural wisdom, whether it is the gift of grain for the first time or some similar benefit.[43] The ending of the story also seems to have varied greatly; in some versions Demeter or Hekate (as her daughter or friend) goes down into Hades to seek Persephone, and in some variants Persephone herself chooses to remain in the Underworld.[44] Not enough remains of these texts for us to judge just how Orphic versions might differ from other tellings that were current, but the varying indications in the sources show that no single version was connected solely with Orpheus.[45]

The aggrieved goddess, who has lost both her daughter and her own honor through the violation, must be appeased, and the polemics of the early Christian apologists make clear that these tales were associated with rites that honored the goddesses, both mother and daughter. Unfortunately, these polemicists are little concerned about precision of detail, so it is impossible to sort out which versions of the myths are connected with which rituals and how.[46] Nevertheless, the tale of Demeter and Persephone

---

discovery of the single manuscript of the text in a Moscow stable in the eighteenth century, since this *Homeric Hymn* did not come down in the same manuscript tradition that preserved many of the other *Hymns*.

[43] Clement refers to them as γηγενεῖς, autochthons or primordial peoples born from the earth, and designates Triptolemos as a cowherd (βουκόλος), Eumolpos as a shepherd, and Eubouleus as a swineherd. The title of βουκόλος appears in a variety of Bacchic mysteries, and the swine of Eubouleus that fall into the chasm out of which Hades appears are associated with the piglets at the Thesmophoria. The gift of grain became a major theme in Athenian imperial propaganda, but the *Homeric Hymn* omits this episode, substituting a temporary famine, which Demeter ends when appeased.

[44] Demeter's descent: *OH* 41.5ff, cp. Ov. *Fast.* 4.611ff, *Met.* 5.533; Claud. *De raptu* 3.105–108. Hekate: Callim. fr. 446 Pfeiffer (*OF* 400ii B = OF 42 K); vase illustration Beazley, ARV² 1012. Persephone not returning: Verg. *G.* 1.39 and Servius *ad loc.*; Columella, *Rust.* 10.272ff; Luc. 6.698ff, 739ff.

[45] The vexed question of why the Orphic version of the Berlin papyrus seems more reflective of the local traditions of Attica than the Homeric Hymn is easily resolved when we understand that this story was given the label of Orpheus' name by a local mythic *bricoleur* seeking prestige for his version, rather than trying to postulate a creeping influence of Orphic sectaries in Attica, encroaching upon the dominance of the Eleusinian Mysteries. On such theories, see Graf 1974: 151–158, Richardson 1974: 84–86.

[46] Clem. Al. *Protr.* 2 provides a comprehensive overview of and attack upon the Greek mysteries, and his polemic served as a source and model for many later ones. See the studies in Jourdan 2010, 2011 and Herrero 2010.

was associated first and foremost with the Thesmophoria festival, which was celebrated all over the Greek world, as well as with the Eleusinian Mysteries, the local Athenian festival which was the most prestigious target of the polemics.[47] Demeter seems to be celebrated primarily as the mourning mother, lamenting and searching for her lost child, and this focus on her mourning causes this tale to be grouped, in the ancient sources, with other myths of a mourning goddess, like Isis seeking Osiris, Aphrodite mourning Adonis, and Kybele bewailing Attis. Even though, in these tales, the goddess is lamenting the loss of a lover rather than a daughter, the imagery of the goddess roaming the world seeking or bewailing her lost one is similar, and it is the laments that seem to have been the focus of the rituals.[48] Here, I would note, attending to ancient acts of classification proves methodologically significant, producing a grouping of mother mourning child with goddess mourning lover that is unexpected from a modern scholarly perspective. Although we have no more than mere references, Orpheus is credited with poems on all these myths, so this theme of the mourning goddess seems particularly associated with Orphic poetry.

Not only must the anguish of the mother be appeased, but the ravished maid herself must be compensated for her griefs. Persephone's new role as Queen of the Underworld brings her new honors, both among the gods and from mortals, that serve as recompense for her experience.[49] However, other variations of the myth present her trauma in a different way: the Kore is also raped by her father Zeus, often in the form of a chthonic snake, either before or after her marriage to Hades.[50] An *Orphic Hymn* celebrates

[47] Orpheus as founder of the Eleusinian Mysteries: *Marm. Par.* (= *IG* xii.5 444) (*OF* 379, 513 B = OT 221 K); Clem. Al. *Protr.* 2.20.1–21.1 = Euseb. *Prep. evang.* 2.3.30–35 (*OF* 392iii, 391ii, 394i, 395i, 515i B = OF 52 K); Aristid. *Or.* 22.1 Keil (*OF* 516 B); Procl. *In R.* 2.312.16 Kroll (*OF* 517i B = OT 102 K), *Theol. Plat.* 6.11 (6.50.12 Saffrey-Westerink) (*OF* 517ii B = OT 102 K); Thdt. *Graec. Aff. Cur.* 1.21 (108.21 Canivet) (*OF* 511 B = OT 103 K); cp. also Ar. *Ran.* 1032 (*OF* 510, 626i B = OT 90 K), Eur. *Rhes.* 938–949 (*OF* 511 B = OT 91 K), [Dem.] 25.11 (*OF* 512 B = OF 23 K); Diod. Sic. 4.25.1 (*OF* 514, 713ii, 916 B = OT 97 K). Theodoretos also attributes the Thesmophoria to Orpheus, but other sources, starting with Herodotus 2.49.1 (*OF* 54 B), sometimes credit Melampous with importing both Dionysiac and Demetriac rites from Egypt; cp. Clem. Al. *Protr.* 2.13.5 (*OF* 385 B), Diod. Sic. 1.97.4 (*OF* 56 B). On the Thesmophoria, see Chlup 2007; Versnel 1993: 228–288; Parker 2005: 270–283.

[48] As Roller 1999: 252 notes, with many examples of myths and rites associated with such goddesses, "The tone can be solemn or humorous, respectful or critical, but the mourning rite is always the central core of the narrative." I have explored this theme in greater detail in my "Dionysos in Egypt" (Edmonds 2013).

[49] Pind. fr. 133 S.-M. = Pl. *Meno* 81bc (*OF* 443 B) refers to the ποινή that Persephone accepts from mortals for her ancient grief (παλαιοῦ πένθεος), and Hades consoles her in the *Homeric Hymn* with the promise of the honors she will receive from every mortal (*Hom. Hymn Dem.* 362–369, cp. Claud. *De raptu* 2.277–306). See below, pp. 304–326.

[50] A detail preserved not only in early Christian polemic (Athenagoras, *Leg.* 20.3 [*OF* 84, 87i, 89i B = OF 58 K], cp. *OF* 276i, 281iii B = OF 153 K), but narrated with characteristic relish by Nonnos,

the otherwise unknown Melinoe, who is described in terms reminiscent of Hekate and the Erinyes, as a daughter of Persephone by Zeus, who came disguised as Plouto.[51] The identity of the victimized daughter sometimes varies as well. Mise, for whom rites similar to those celebrated for Kore were performed, is described in the *Orphic Hymn* as the daughter of Demeter at Eleusis, of Meter in Phrygia, of Cythera in Cyprus, and Isis in Egypt – that is, she is the daughter of the mourning mother in whatever aspect she might appear.[52]

In some versions, the aggrieved mother herself is the rape victim. The wrath of Demeter might come from her violation by Zeus, who is either her brother or, when she is identified with Meter or Rhea, actually her own son. Clement associates Zeus' rape of his mother with the wrath (μῆνις) of Demeter as well as with the rites of Kybele.

> Then there are the mysteries of Deo, and Zeus' sexual embraces of his mother Demeter, and the wrath of Deo (I know not what to call her now, mother or wife), on account of which, it is said, she is named Brimo; also the supplications of Zeus, and the draught of gall, the extractions of the hearts of sacrifices, and unspeakable deeds. Such rites the Phrygians are accustomed to perform for Attis and Kybele and the Korybantes. And the vulgar story relates how Zeus, having ripped off the testicles of a ram, brought them out and hurled them into the bosom of Deo, paying a false recompense for his violent embrace, as if he had cut off his own.[53]

Dion. 6.155–164. A similar myth is told of the Roman Bona Dea, raped by her father Faunus in the form of a snake, and Plut. *Vit. Caes.* 9.4 (*OF* 584 B) (cp. Macrob. *Sat.* 1.12.20–29) compares this tale to the Orphica. See Versnel 1993: 228–288, on the similarities of the Bona Dea festival with the Thesmophoria complex.

[51] *OH* 71 to Melinoe. On the difficulties with this text, see Morand 2001: 181–188, and Ricciardelli 2000: 494–499, who also discuss a lead tablet on which the name Melinoe appears associated with Persephone.

[52] *OH* 41 to Mise, which also describes her as a feminine aspect of Iacchos. Asklepiades of Tragilos, *FGrH* 12 F 4 (*OF* 391i B) makes Misa the daughter of Dysaules and Baubo at Eleusis, and Misme receives Demeter in her wanderings in Ant. Lib. *Met.* 24(*OF* 657ii B). The Kathodos festival of Mise is mentioned in a mime of Herod. (1.56), and an inscription from Aeolic Kyme identifies her with Kore (*IGSK* 5.38: Ἀνθὶς ἱέρεια Μίσῃ Κόρῃ τὸν βωμὸν ἀνέθηκε.). Hsch. s.v. Μίση (1442) preserves two more pieces of information about Mise, that she has something to do with Meter and oaths, and that she is connected with feminine insatiable desire, quoting a fragment of the comic poet Cratinus to the effect that women who are "misetai" use dildos: [Μισατὶς] Μίση· τῶν περὶ τὴν μητέρα τις, ἣν καὶ ὁμνύουσι. 1450. μισήτην· τὴν καταφερῆ λέγουσιν μισήτην· 'μίσηται δὲ γυναῖκες ὀλίσβοισι χρήσονται' (Cratin. fr. 354 ΚΑ/ 316K), οἱ δὲ ἁπλῶς μισητὸν τὸν ἀνίκανον, ἢ ἄπληστον τῇ τροφῇ.

[53] Clem. Al. *Protr.* 2.15.1 (*OF* 589i B): Δηοῦς δὲ μυστήρια καὶ Διὸς πρὸς μητέρα Δήμητρα ἀφροδίσιοι συμπλοκαὶ καὶ μῆνις (οὐκ οἶδ᾽ ὅ τι φῶ λοιπὸν μητρὸς ἢ γυναικός) τῆς Δηοῦς, ἧς δὴ χάριν Βριμὼ προσαγορευθῆναι λέγεται, ἱκετηρίαι Διὸς καὶ πόμα χολῆς καὶ καρδιουλκίαι καὶ ἀρρητουργίαι· ταὐτὰ οἱ Φρύγες τελίσκουσιν Ἄττιδι καὶ Κυβέλῃ καὶ Κορύβασιν. Τεθρυλήκασιν δὲ ὡς ἄρα ἀποσπάσας ὁ Ζεὺς τοῦ κριοῦ τοὺς διδύμους φέρων ἐν μέσοις ἔρριψε τοῖς κόλποις τῆς Δηοῦς, τιμωρίαν ψευδῆ τῆς βιαίας συμπλοκῆς ἐκτιννύων, ὡς ἑαυτὸν δῆθεν ἐκτεμών.

While Clement is undoubtedly mixing up different rites and emphasizing the most obscene elements in his polemic, the Derveni author also refers to the rape of Demeter[54] as well as Zeus' desire for his own mother, which he characteristically explains as a profound allegory.[55] While this earlier Orphic poem may not have narrated the rape itself or gone further to describe Zeus' other erotic pursuits, the Christian polemicists can pick out a succession of rape stories, perhaps from different episodes in the *Orphic Rhapsodies*, in which Zeus rapes first his mother and then the daughter he produces from this union. Athenagoras and Clement describe how Zeus first violated his mother in the form of a serpent, producing a child so monstrous that her mother would not nurse her.[56] This child, Persephone, he later raped, again in the form of a serpent, and this union produced Dionysos.[57] These incestuous rapes in every case produce offspring from the angered goddess, which may be the meaning of the reference in the *Argonautica* list to the offspring of Brimo, since Clement understands Brimo as a name signifying the goddess' anger.[58]

All this violence demands recompense, and the mystery rites seem to have been the special ceremonies by which the goddess' grief and anger were celebrated and appeased. The special honors paid to the goddess in such

---

[54] Col. 22.12–13 equates Demeter, Rhea, Ge, Meter, Hestia, and Deio and explains the name Deio from the fact that she was ravaged (ἐδηιώθη) in intercourse (μείξει). Kouremenos *et al.* 2006 understand this μεῖξις as parturition rather than copulation, but the parallel with Herodian they cite (3.2.420.9–10 Lentz) explains the ravaging by the plowing of the earth. The parallels with the rapes of Demeter mentioned in Pausanias suggest sexual violence that leaves Demeter with a wrath that must be propitiated. It is notable that at both Thelpusa and Phigaleia, Demeter bears a daughter from this rape who corresponds with Persephone (even though the rapist in the local stories is Poseidon as a horse rather than Zeus as a serpent), and that mystery rites with the familiar torches and mystic *cista* are instituted to propitiate her (Paus. 8.25.6, 8.42.2–3). Ov. *Met.* 6.114–119 has Arachne depict Jove's rape of Deo in the form of a snake and Neptune's of Ceres in the form of a horse.

[55] col. 26.8–13. The Derveni author explains that Orpheus meant that Zeus desired to have sex, not with his own mother (μητρὸς ἑαυτοῦ) but with the good mother (μητρὸς ἑᾶς – as if ἑᾶς were the equivalent of ἐάων), a piece of etymologizing that has won him perhaps more gratuitous condemnation from modern scholars than anything else in the treatise.

[56] Athenagoras *pro Christ.* 20.3 (*OF* 84, 87i, 89i B = OF 58 K). Athenagoras relates that, because Rhea/Demeter would not give this four-eyed, two-faced, horned infant the breast (θηλή) to suckle, she was called Athela the maiden (Kore), not to be confused with the maiden Athena. Cp. *OA* 31: ὀρεινῆς νύκτας Ἀθηλῆς.

[57] Clem. Al. *Protr.* 2.16.1–3; Clement associates the symbolon of the Sabazian mysteries, ὁ διὰ κόλπου θεός, with this rape in serpent form. This symbolon appears also in the Gurôb papyrus (*P. Gurôb* 1 [*OF* 578 B = OF 31 K] col. 1.24).

[58] *OA* 17: Βριμοῦς τ' εὐδυνάτοιο γονάς. Hippolytos, *Haer.* 5.8.41 claims that the Eleusinian Mysteries culminated with the pronouncement that Brimo has borne a son, Brimos, but he understands Brimo as "mighty" rather than "wrathful." Brimos might be identified with Iacchos/Dionysos, but, as the *Orphic Hymn to Mise* shows, even the gender of the offspring seems to have been fluid in these myths. Parker 2005: 358–359 reviews the possibilities for the son of Brimo in the Eleusinian evidence, settling tentatively on Ploutos, the personification of prosperity.

rites, through sacrifices and hymns and other ritual activities, provided a recompense to the goddess for the vicissitudes she had undergone, assuaging her anger through the positive attentions paid to her and transforming her grief into joy. The worshipers in such rites looked for the mollified goddess to provide favorable attentions to them in return, whether the blessings of health and wealth in life or a good lot in the afterlife in the realm of Persephone. Whether these were Eleusinian rites for Demeter and Persephone, Phrygian rites for Meter or Kybele, Phlyan rites for Megale, or the rites of another figure like Hekate, Praxidike or Athela, Orpheus was often (but not always) associated with them, as founder or simply as the singer whose hymns were part of the ritual or told the related myths.[59]

Threatened infant god

In addition to the cult of the mountain-roaming Mother, the Argonautic Orpheus mentions the nursing of Zeus as one of his previous themes, and the mythic pattern of a threatened infant god, be it Zeus or Dionysos or some other, appears in various ways in the evidence for the Orphic poems. When the infant god is born, since he is a potential heir to the kingship of heaven, he is hidden away with special nurses and with a special band of male guardians to protect him. He re-appears from hiding or destruction as an adult to assert his power against the forces of the earlier generation and claim his place among the gods.

Little survives of any Orphic tellings of the infancy of Zeus, but the myth found in other sources recounts how Rhea hid Zeus away from Kronos, who was swallowing all the children Rhea bore to prevent them from overthrowing him. He was nursed by nymphs or bees or a goat and protected by the Kouretes or Korybantes, who did their characteristic ecstatic armed dance around the cave in which the god was hidden, drowning out his infant cries with the clashing of their arms. Zeus grows up and defeats his father Kronos and the Titans in a mighty battle, having first tricked his father into vomiting back up the other children he has swallowed and then having obtained other divine allies.[60] Quotations or references to Orpheus in Neoplatonic authors confirm that some version of this tale appeared in the *Orphic Rhapsodies*, but it is difficult to tell what

---

[59] See note 31 above.

[60] Apollod. *Bibl.* 1.1.5–1.2.1 (*OF* 194ii, 200i, 203iv, 205, 208ii, 209iii, 213vi, 214ii, 215ii, 228i, 235i, 236i B), but different details appear in various sources. For an overview, see Gantz 1993: 41–45.

version or versions were recounted or how early any of these stories were recounted under the name of Orpheus.[61]

The infant Zeus has little trouble evading the threat of his father and becoming master of the universe, but other infant deities face more serious threats. Various sources attribute to Orpheus myths of the infancy of Dionysos, who goes through the same pattern of threat and return, although different versions have radically different elements in each part of the tale. Whereas Rhea always gives birth to Zeus, Dionysos has many births – from the ashes of Semele, from the thigh of Zeus, from Demeter, from Persephone, from the collected pieces of his own dismembered body. Some systematizing mythographers attempt to reconcile these births into a sequence, like that found in Nonnos, whereby Dionysos Zagreus, the child of Persephone and Zeus, is reborn after his dismemberment as the child of Semele. It is important to note, however, that this sequence does not hold in all of the evidence and that it creates other problems in narrative chronology, suggesting that the different tales coexisted in the tradition, however troubling the inconsistencies might be to tidy-minded scholars, both ancient and modern.[62] Nor was any version peculiarly Orphic, since various sources attest to Dionysos as the child of Semele, Persephone, and Demeter in different Orphic myths.[63]

---

[61] To defeat the previous generation, Zeus receives oracular advice from the primordial goddess Night and binds his father Kronos, having made him drunk with honey. The regurgitation of the other gods and the Titanomachy may follow, but Zeus also apparently learns from the defeated Kronos that he must swallow Phanes to become the supreme ruler of the cosmos. West 1983: 72 tries to reconstruct the story with reference to the fragments.

[62] Some of the versions have the dismemberment occur after the birth from Semele, including one of the earliest in date, Philodemos' reference to Euphorion, Phld. *Piet.* 44 (*P. Herc.* 247 III 1 p. 16 Gomperz) = Euphorion fr. 39 Van Groningen (= 53 De Cuenca) (*OF* 59i B = OF 36 K), which lists the three births of Dionysos as first from his mother, second from the thigh, and third after his dismemberment. Note that Diod. Sic. 3.62.6 (*OF* 59iii B = OF 301 K) also makes the birth after the dismemberment the third, not the second. Diodorus expresses his dismay at the conflicting traditions about Dionysos (3.62.2 [*OF* 59iii B = OF 301 K], 3.74.6). Bernabé 1998b tries to reduce all the versions to two variant storylines, both of which contributed elements to the *Orphic Rhapsodies*. The "primary version" has Dionysos born of Persephone, torn apart by the Titans, and then reborn from Semele, while the "secondary version," which he associates with Egypt and Osiris, has Dionysos born of Demeter/Rhea and reborn from the reassembled pieces collected by her after his dismemberment. Apart from the methodological problems of reducing mythic variants to simple stemmata, Bernabé's hypothesis founders on the fact that the sequence of mothers from Persephone to Semele does not hold in all the evidence.

[63] Despite the assumption, in much modern scholarship, that the son of Persephone is the "Orphic Dionysos," Diodorus Siculus 1.23.7 (*OF* 327iv, 497iv B = OT 95 K) shows that the Orphic rites were celebrated in honor of the son of Semele rather than the son of Persephone. However, he also attributes the version that Dionysos' mother was Demeter to the Orphica (3.62.8 [*OF* 58 B = OF 301 K]). Cp. Cicero's catalog of different Dionysoi in Cic. *Nat. D.* 3.58 (*OF* 497i B = OT 94 K) (note the other testimonia from later authors probably indebted to Cicero in *OF* 497 B). The fourth

After his birth, from whatever mother (or father), the infant god is entrusted to the care of women (whether to nymphs of some sort or to a nurse like Ino, Hipta, or even Rhea) and to the protection of male guardians (Satyrs, Kouretes, or Korybantes).[64] The forces of the older generation, however, try to destroy the child, whether a jealous Hera incites his adult protectors to violence or whether some band of attackers slips past the defenders.[65] The Christian polemic of Clement preserves the most detailed account of an Orphic version of this attack, in which a band of Titans sneak past the dancing Kouretes, distract the child with toys, tear him limb from limb, and then start to cook the pieces. Zeus blasts the Titans with lightning, and Apollo gathers the limbs and brings them to Delphi.

> The mysteries of Dionysos are perfectly inhuman. While he was still a child, the Kouretes danced around with clashing arms, and the Titans crept up by stealth and deceived him with childish toys. Then these Titans dismembered Dionysos while he was still an infant, as the poet of this mystery, the Thracian Orpheus, says: "Top, and spinner, and limb-moving toys, And beautiful golden apples from the clear-voiced Hesperides." And it is not useless to put forth to you the useless symbols of this rite for condemnation. These are knucklebone, ball, hoop, apples, spinner, looking-glass, tuft of wool. So, Athena, who abstracted the heart of Dionysos, was thus called Pallas, from the palpitating of the heart. The Titans, on the other hand, who tore him limb from limb, set a cauldron on a tripod and threw into it the limbs of Dionysos. First they boiled them down and, then fixing them on spits, "held them over Hephaistos (the fire)." But later Zeus appeared; since he

Dionysos is the child of Jove and Luna (probably arising from a confusion of Semele and Selene), and it is in his honor that Orphic rites are celebrated, not the son of Jove and Proserpine, who is first on the list. Bernabé 1998b: 34–36 presents the evidence for Semele as part of the Orphic tradition.

[64] Again, while the variant mothers, nurses, etc. are important for each particular telling, the concern here is for the general pattern, since not enough evidence survives to analyze the nuances of particular tellings. Hipta as the nurse of Dionysos Sabazios appears in *OH* 49 (*OF* 329 B = OF 199 K), as well as in the papyrus published in Obbink 2011, where she is identified with Demeter as the mother of the god (fr. 1, col. ii. 8–9). Nymphs and satyrs, the familiar companions of Dionysos, appear in *OH* 51.1 and *OH* 54.1, Ino Leukothea in *OH* 74.2. Apollod. *Bibl.* 3.4.3 puts them in sequence, with Dionysos going to the nymphs after the disasters in Ino's house, while Nonnos, *Dion.* 9.1–169 reverses the sequence, having Hermes bring Dionysos to Ino after the nymphs go mad and start chopping up babies. The god is nursed there by Mystis before being brought to Kybele. The Kouretes appear in Clem. Al. *Protr.* 2.17.2–18.2 (*OF* 306i, 588i, 312i, 315i, 318i, 322i B = OF 34 K), and Procl. *Theol. Plat.* 5.35 (5.127.21 Saffrey-Westerink) (*OF* 198ii, 278ii, 297i B = OF 151 K). Pausanias 3.24.3–5 preserves a peculiar local version in which Dionysos is put in a chest like Perseus and nursed by Ino when washed ashore. He notes that the spot is marked by statues of Korybantes (or Dioskouroi) with Athena.

[65] The similarity between the groups of adult women or men who are supposed to be protecting the child and those who attack the child is striking – the nymph nurses who become child-menacing maenads or the protective Kouretes who are replaced by attacking Titans. In some myths, the Kouretes themselves become the killers, as in Apollodoros' tale of Epaphos (*Bibl.* 2.1.3). Cp. Edmonds 2006: 353–358.

was a god, he speedily perceived the savor of the cooking flesh, which your gods agree to have assigned to them as their portion of honor. He assails the Titans with his thunderbolt and consigns the limbs of Dionysos to his son Apollo for burial. And Apollo, for he did not disobey Zeus, bearing the dismembered corpse to Parnassos, deposited it there.[66]

The toys by which the Titans distract the child become the tokens of a mystery rite that celebrates and propitiates the deity who has suffered this vicissitude, and a third-century BCE papyrus from Gurôb refers to these tokens, along with invocations of the Kouretes, Pallas, Brimo, Demeter, Rhea, and Dionysos.[67] The role of Apollo in gathering the pieces probably reflects the influence of Platonic allegorizing on the myth, since the Platonists understand the dismemberment as the cosmic process of movement from One to Many, and Apollo, read as a-pollon, Not-Many, is the principle which restores Unity.[68] Other Orphic versions feature Demeter/Rhea in the role of collector; under her care he is restored to life in some fashion.[69] This version is often connected with the myth of Isis and Osiris, another of the themes of Orpheus, even though the restored Osiris seems to remain in the Underworld, while the revived Dionysos goes on to establish his

---

[66] Clem. Al. *Protr.* 2.17.2–18.2 (*OF* 306i, 588i, 312i, 315i, 318i, 322i B = OF 34 K): Τὰ γὰρ Διονύσου μυστήρια τέλεον ἀπάνθρωπα· ὃν εἰσέτι παῖδα ὄντα ἐνόπλῳ κινήσει περιχορευόντων Κουρήτων, δόλῳ δὲ ὑποδύντων Τιτάνων, ἀπατήσαντες παιδαριώδεσιν ἀθύρμασιν, οὗτοι δὴ οἱ Τιτᾶνες διέσπασαν, ἔτι νηπίαχον ὄντα, ὡς ὁ τῆς Τελετῆς ποιητὴς Ὀρφεύς φησιν ὁ Θρᾴκιος· "κῶνος καὶ ῥόμβος καὶ παίγνια καμπεσίγυια, | μῆλά τε χρύσεα καλὰ παρ' Ἑσπερίδων λιγυφώνων." Καὶ τῆσδε ὑμῖν τῆς τελετῆς τὰ ἀχρεῖα σύμβολα οὐκ ἀχρεῖον εἰς κατάγνωσιν παραθέσθαι· ἀστράγαλος, σφαῖρα, στρόβιλος, μῆλα, ῥόμβος, ἔσοπτρον, πόκος. Ἀθηνᾶ μὲν οὖν τὴν καρδίαν τοῦ Διονύσου ὑφελομένη Παλλὰς ἐκ τοῦ πάλλειν τὴν καρδίαν προσηγορεύθη· οἱ δὲ Τιτᾶνες, οἱ καὶ διασπάσαντες αὐτόν, λέβητά τινα τρίποδι ἐπιθέντες καὶ τοῦ Διονύσου ἐμβαλόντες τὰ μέλη, καθήψουν πρότερον· ἔπειτα ὀβελίσκοις περιπείραντες "ὑπείρεχον Ἡφαίστοιο." Ζεὺς δὲ ὕστερον ἐπιφανείς (εἰ θεὸς ἦν, τάχα που τῆς κνίσης τῶν ὀπτωμένων κρεῶν μεταλαβών, ἧς δὴ τὸ "γέρας λαχεῖν" ὁμολογοῦσιν ὑμῶν οἱ θεοί) κεραυνῷ τοὺς Τιτᾶνας αἰκίζεται καὶ τὰ μέλη τοῦ Διονύσου Ἀπόλλωνι τῷ παιδὶ παρακατατίθεται καταθάψαι. Ὁ δέ, οὐ γὰρ ἠπείθησε Διί, εἰς τὸν Παρνασσὸν φέρων κατατίθεται διεσπασμένον τὸν νεκρόν.

[67] *P. Gurôb* 1 (*OF* 578B = OF 31 K). The text may contain instructions for a ritual, as well as poetic texts to be recited, but its fragmentary state makes it difficult to reconstruct. See Hordern 2000 for details of this text. Levaniouk 2007 provides a fascinating analysis of these toys as indices, in the Peircean sense, of the ritual experience, rather than direct elements of the ritual practice, an idea that is particularly useful when considering these rituals within an imagistic, rather than doctrinal, religious system. The papyrus published in Obbink 2011 provides an explanation of the role of the ῥύμβος as a device that Hipta used to make a noise to cover the cries of the infant god, like the noise of the Kouretes or Korybantes in other versions.

[68] Cp. Plut. *De E ap. Delph.* 388e. The Platonic interest in this myth as signifying the Many and the One accounts for the disproportionate number of references preserved in the Neoplatonists to the dismemberment story. For the role of Neoplatonic allegorization in transmitting and shaping the myth, see Edmonds 2009.

[69] Diod. Sic. 3.62.6 (*OF* 59iii B = OF 301 K) lists his rebirth after his members are collected by Demeter as the third birth of Dionysos and claims that this version agrees with the Orphica (3.62.8 [*OF* 58 B = OF 301 K]); cp. Corn. *ND* 30 (58.6 Lang) (*OF* 59iv B).

power as a god in the lands of the living.[70] In some versions, Dionysos is restored from his collected limbs or from the heart that Athena managed to take away from the Titans; in a few variants, this heart is ground into a potion that is fed to Semele, who gives birth to a new Dionysos.[71] In any case, a restored Dionysos emerges after the dismemberment to claim his honor as a god.[72]

The dismemberment is not the only version of the threat that the infant god needs to avoid. Other vicissitudes, such as being healed by Rhea/Kybele of madness inflicted by Hera or escaping from some threat by plunging into water and coming back out again after care from Thetis or the like, appear in other sources and may have appeared in Orphic versions as well. In every case, the young god is menaced by a member of the older generation, either a paternal kingly figure like Lykourgos or a maternal figure like Hera, and rescued by some sort of nurse, be it grandmother Rhea or nymphs associated with the sea or the rivers.

Many myths of Dionysos, in sources throughout the tradition, tell of his entry into some community, the resistance to him and its consequences, culminating in the acknowledgment of the god's power and divinity.[73] Such myths would naturally have been appropriate themes for poetry linked with rituals honoring Dionysos, and Orpheus would certainly have been

[70] Plut. *De Is. et Os.* 35 364e–365a (*OF* 47 B) unhesitatingly identifies Dionysos and Osiris, but Herodotus too seems to draw a connection (2.24.2; 2.59.2, 2.144.2; 2.156.5). Cp. Burkert 2004: 72–74. The myth of Epaphos, the son of Zeus by Io, may provide the link between Dionysos and Osiris. Io, who appears in Egypt as a cow, is often assimilated to Isis (cp. Acus. *FGrH* 2 F 26–27; Pherec. *FGrH* 3 F 67; Hdt. 1.1; 2.41; 3.27), and Diodorus lists Epaphos as the Egyptian Dionysos who is responsible for the Dionysiac rites there (3.74.1). Moreover, Apollod. *Bibl.* 2.1.3 recounts that Epaphos was killed by the Kouretes at the behest of Hera, while Hyginus preserves the tale that Hera tried to get the Titans to kill Epaphos (*Fab.* 150). For further discussion of Dionysos, Epaphos, and Osiris, see Edmonds 2013.

[71] Cp. Hyg. *Fab.* 167 (*OF* 327iii B); Procl. *H.* 7.11–15 (275 van den Berg) (*OF* 327ii B). This variant bears the marks of systematizers creatively trying to get all the different versions to line up. Firm. Mat. *Err. prof. rel.* 6.1–4 (88–89 Turcan) (*OF* 304iii, 309vii, 313iii, 314iv, 318v, 325, 332 B = OF 214 K) provides a euhemerized version in which a plaster model is made into which the heart is placed.

[72] The creation of mankind from the remains of the Titans does not follow the dismemberment of Dionysos, as many modern scholars continue to imagine. An anthropogony is a common sequel to the myth of the Titanomachy or Gigantomachy, but only the sixth-century CE Neoplatonist Olymp. *In Phd.* 1.3 (*OF* 174viii, 190ii, 227iv, 299vii, 304i, 313ii, 318iii, 320i B = OF 220 K) combines the myth of the dismemberment with the anthropogony, drawing on a tradition of Neoplatonic allegorizing that reads both the Titanomachy and the dismemberment as signifying the opposition of unity and multiplicity (cp. Procl. *In R.* 1.90.7–13 Kroll). I have discussed Olympiodorus' innovation, as well as its consequences in modern scholarship, in Edmonds 2009 and Edmonds 1999, *contra* Bernabé 2002a, 2003.

[73] Cp. Detienne 1986. Sourvinou-Inwood 2005: 149–240 discusses the mythico-ritual complex of Dionysos' arrivals. After the conquests of Alexander, the myths of the conquests of Dionysos shift from the scale of the individual polis to the whole *oikoumene*, but the pattern remains much the same.

an authoritative name for such poems. Little evidence, however, survives of such poetry, making it difficult to determine what features distinguished the Orphic versions from others. The dismemberment appears in both Orphic and non-Orphic versions, and some Orphic versions may have had other vicissitudes, such as madness or battles. Nonnos makes Dionysos' victories in a Gigantomachy a triumph parallel to Zeus' victories in the Titanomachy, and the Argonautic Orpheus mentions the destructive deeds of the earth-born Gigantes, born from the blood of Heaven, as one of his previous themes.[74] The systematizer Diodorus, on the other hand, complains that, although everyone knows that Dionysos took part in the Titanomachy, it is very difficult to get the chronology to work out right, and it is likely that conflicting stories were used by different mythic *bricoleurs*, both Orphic and non-Orphic, as they composed their tales for different audiences and occasions.[75]

The confusion between Gigantes and Titans is only part of a wider conflation of similar bands of primordial races; these earth-born men are at times associated with other primeval autochthons, not just the Kouretes or Korybantes who protect the infant god from their assaults, but also Telchines, Dactyls, Kabeiroi, and even Satyrs.[76] The fundamental ambivalence of these figures is clear from the versions in which the protective group is infiltrated or replaced by a group of assailants, as the Kouretes are by the Titans in Clement's version, as well as from the stories in which the

---

[74] Nonnos, *Dion.* 48.1–89. These destructive deeds are more likely to be the war against the gods, with its many battles and episodes, than the murder of the infant Dionysos, although the Gigantes are sometimes the perpetrators in that episode, particularly when the earth-born are interpreted as earth-working farmers tearing apart Dionysos the vine to produce wine. Cp. Diod. Sic. 3.62.6–7 (*OF* 59iii B = OF 301 K). The birth of the giants as the race of mortals born from the earth and blood of heaven is found even in Hes. *Theog.* 183–187 and becomes a common anthropogony in the mythic tradition. See Edmonds 2010 and Yates 2004, as well as Clay 2003: 96–99. One of the three references to a specific book of the *Orphic Rhapsodies* (book 8) also refers to the race of Gigantes, born from Earth and the blood of Heaven (*Etym. Magn.* s.v. Γίγας (231.21)· [*OF* 188 B = OF 63 K]). Cp. a quote from the fourth Rhapsody to Mousaios in the *Tübingen Theosophy* 61(*OF* 138i B = OF 61 K), as well as a reference to the twelfth revelation in Malalas' quotations (*Chron.* 4.8 [73.12 Dindorf] [*OF* 102i B = OF 62 K]).

[75] Diod. Sic. 3.62.8 (*OF* 58 B = OF 301 K).

[76] Not only do the Kouretes or Korybantes guard the infant Zeus and Dionysos, but, in some Orphic tales, they are protecting the young Kore before her abduction by Hades, Procl. *Theol. Plat.* 6.13 (6.65.17 Saffrey-Westerink) (*OF* 279i B = OF 191 K). Proclus frequently discourses at length on the protective function of the Kouretes and Korybantes as a cosmic principle in his Neoplatonic system, e.g., Procl. *In Crat.* 58.1 Pasquali (*ad* 396b) (*OF* 198i B = OF 151 K), *In Ti.* 1.317.11 Diehl (*ad* 28c) (*OF* 213ii B = OF 151 K), *Theol. Plat.* 5.3 (5.16.24 Saffrey-Westerink) (*OF* 213iv B = OF 151 K), 5.35 (5.127.21 Saffrey-Westerink) (*OF* 198ii, 278ii, 297i B = OF 151 K). Athena seems to be designated the leader of the Kouretes in some Orphic texts, e.g., Procl. *In Crat.* 185.20–22 Pasquali (*ad* 406d) (*OF* 267i B = OF 185 K); *Theol. Plat.* 5.35 (5.128.5 Saffrey-Westerink) (*OF* 267ii B = OF 151 K). Cp. the statue of Athena with Korybantes in Paus. 3.24.5.

Kouretes themselves are the killers.[77] The Kabeiroi, often identified with the Kouretes and Korybantes, appear in the Argonautic Orpheus' list not only in the references to their cult sites of Lemnos and Samothrace, but also in the tale of the rending of Kasmilos, one of the names given the Kabeiroi in Samothrace.[78] The myth remains obscure, but Kasmilos may here be the younger Kabeiros, often assimilated to Dionysos Sabazios, or perhaps the third Korybantic brother killed by the other two, whose remains became the object of cult.[79] All of these types, as Strabo tells us, are terrifying figures who dance ecstatically with weapons to the accompaniment of the flutes and cymbals in the train of the mother goddess.[80] Orpheus, as the poet most associated with such rituals, seems often to have been credited with poems that recount myths involving these figures.[81]

Alien and perverse tales

In addition to cosmological myths, then, myths associated with the festivals of Demeter and Dionysos and their attendants were the subject of Orphic poems. Many of these rites involved lamentation of the deities' vicissitudes (be it loss, rape, dismemberment, or some other trouble), as well as ecstatic celebration (wild dancing with characteristic flutes, cymbals, and drums), and these festivals served to win the favor of these deities for the mortals propitiating them.[82] Obviously, not all the songs performed at all these

---

[77] Cp. the killing of Epaphos by the Kouretes in Apollod. *Bibl.* 2.1.3, replacing the Titans in Hyg. *Fab.* 150(*OF* 327iii B), see note 70 above.

[78] ΣAp. Rhod. *Argon.* 1.917 (78 Wendel), who identifies Kasmilos as Hermes and the others as Demeter, Hades, and Persephone. Heracles, also mentioned in *OA* 24, is sometimes identified as one of the Idaean Dactyls. Cp. Strabo 10.3.22.

[79] Clem. Al. *Protr.* 2.19.1; cp. Firm. Mat. *Err. prof. rel.* 11. Clement assimilates the Kabeiroi to the Korybantes and claims that the rites have to do with the head of the murdered brother or with the phallus of Bacchos (here perhaps identified with the brother), which the brothers take to Etruria.

[80] Strabo 10.3.7 describes Kouretes, Korybantes, Dactyls, Telkhines, and Kabeiroi as all the same types; in 10.3.19 he adds Satyrs as similar Bacchic figures who protect the infant Dionysos, even though they are not armed dancers. Lucian, interestingly, groups Titans with Korybantes and Satyrs, *Salt.* 79.15 (*OF* 600i B = OT 209 K).

[81] Works on the Kouretes and Korybantes are also attributed to Epimenides (Diog. Laert. 1.113), a figure who, like Orpheus, was associated with mystery rites (cp. Strabo 10.4.14 and Plut. *Vit. Sol.* 12.7). In the Hellenistic period and later, the poems of Epimenides may have been credited to Orpheus, just as the work of many other lesser-known poets with similar themes seems to have been classified as Orphic. Such fusion of attributions may account for the Argonautic poems attributed to Epimenides. West 1983: 39–61 remains the best treatment of such figures, although the fragments of Mousaios, Linos, and Epimenides are collected in Bernabé's final volume of Orphic fragments.

[82] West's model of initiations into a group unduly restricts the scope of the Orphic poetry, and his derivation of such societies from shamanistic practices lacks historical credibility. "What the myth itself suggests is a ritual of initiation into a society – presumably a Bacchic society – which has taken on, at least at the mythic level, the special form of the shaman's initiation" (West 1983: 150). See

rituals throughout the Greek world were attributed to Orpheus, just as Orpheus was not credited with founding every one of these rites, but Orpheus was the most prestigious author of rite or poem for such festivals, and many must have been credited to him. Pausanias, it may be noted, dismisses most of this mass of poetry as not truly by Orpheus, with the single exception of the *Orphic Hymns* for the mysteries of Megale, the Great Goddess, celebrated by the Lycomidae at Phlya, which he describes as receiving great honor from the gods, although relatively short and inferior in beauty to the *Homeric Hymns*.[83] While the mythic narratives may not have been as compressed as those in the extant *Orphic Hymns*, the *Homeric Hymns* provide a better analogy for the form in which the myths of Orpheus appeared than the epic narratives of Hesiod.[84] Such hymns propitiate the divinity by a brief and allusive recounting of a myth that highlights in some way the honors of the deity, and this kind of poetry, whether in hymnic or other form, may have been performed in religious contexts along with sacrifices and other rituals.[85]

While the Hymns attributed to Homer celebrate, for example, Apollo at his Delian festival, a celebration that unites all the Ionian Greeks, the label Orphic is attached to more exotic myths, tales that mark their distance from the common stream. While Demeter and the Mother of the Gods may be as Greek as Dionysos, the myths associated with Orpheus seem

---

Bremmer 2002: 27–40 for a thorough deconstruction of the idea of Greek "shamans," so favored by earlier scholars as an explanation of Orpheus' reputation for wisdom deriving from his descent to the underworld. Private Bacchic associations certainly existed in the Hellenistic and Imperial periods, but even in those periods they must have represented only one context in which these myths were deployed. The spectrum ranged from itinerant specialists with individual clientele to civically sponsored ceremonies, and, while the details of a particular telling might help uncover the social and religious context in which it was performed, the general pattern of the myth cannot indicate a limitation to any particular point on the spectrum.

[83] Paus. 9.30.12 (*OF* 531ii, 682 B = OF 304 K), cp. Paus. 9.27.2 (*OF* 531i B = OF 305 K). Hippolytos provides the information that these mysteries are for a goddess Megale, clearly some form of Magna Mater (Hippol. *Haer.* 5.20.4 [*OF* 532i B = OF 243 K]). Pausanias denies that any other Orphica are authentic besides the hymns of the Lycomidae, and his habit of referring to Orphica he considers spurious as works of Onomakritos has caused much confusion among scholars, especially when they take such references as evidence of a sixth-century BCE date.

[84] All these poems drew on a common stock of hexametrical poetic language and formulae from the oral poetic tradition. In addition to the shared language between the *Homeric Hymn to Demeter* and the Orphic poem preserved on the Berlin Papyrus (see note 37), line 7 in the *Homeric Hymn to Heracles* also appears in the Orphic poem in the Derveni papyrus (col. 12.2 [*OF* 14 B]). The Derveni poem also uses lines that appear in the larger Homeric epics (*Od.* 8.335 ≈ DP col. 26.4; *Il.* 24.527–528 ≈ DP col. 26.6–7).

[85] The extant *Orphic Hymns* each begin with instructions for a sacrificial offering of some kind of incense, but it is difficult to reconstruct fully the ritual contexts in which they might have been performed. Such a task is obviously even more difficult for poems that are no longer extant. The connection between the *Homeric Hymns* and ritual is even less clear, although they too must have been performed in the context of some religious festival, i.e., a ritual setting.

to emphasize the alien nature of the gods, the Cretan Dionysos or Zeus or Phrygian Sabazios, the Phrygian Kybele or the Egyptian Demeter, the Kabeiroi of Samothrace, etc. Regardless of the actual origin of such cults, they were marked as alien elements present in Greek religion in the fifth century BCE and the Orphic label appears as early as the fourth century.[86] No doubt the number of Orphic poems on these subjects grew with the increasing popularity of such cults in the Hellenistic and later periods, since Orpheus' name signified not only expertise on these topics but also the authority of great antiquity for these newly developed rites. The mythic patterns repeated across generations – the infancy of Zeus and Dionysos or the rape of Rhea/Demeter/Persephone – permitted innovation within familiar storylines, and, although such repeating patterns cause difficulties for systematizers both ancient and modern, the twists of intergenerational relations create shocking tales – full of mystic significance for the initiates guided by allegorizers like the Derveni author or marks of pagan degeneracy for the Christian polemicists who preserve so much of the material.

Tales from the life of Orpheus

The last group of mythic themes for Orphic poetry comes from the life of Orpheus himself. Although the expedition of the Argo and Orpheus' descent into the Underworld in search of his wife appear in many forms in other tellings throughout the mythic tradition, there is little evidence for Orphic poems on these subjects, beyond the surviving *Orphic Argonautica*. While it is not impossible that earlier poems claiming to be by Orpheus had recounted the Argonautic legends, the myths of the heroes (Trojan, Theban, or otherwise) are not elsewhere attributed to Orpheus, and there is no surviving evidence for such a poem – even the Byzantine *Suda* does not include an *Argonautica* in its long list.[87]

---

[86] Euripides' *Cretans* refers to the initiates of Idaean Zeus and Zagreus Nyktipolos, as well as the rites of the Kouretes and the Mountain Mother, although there is no indication that these rites were labeled Orphic, even by Porphyry, who preserves the fragment: Eur. *Cret.* fr. 472 K (= fr. 2 J.-V.L.) *ap.* Porph. *Abst.* 4.19.21–23 (*OF* 567 B). Cp. Versnel's reading of Euripides' *Bacchae* in the context of such alien cults (Versnel 1990: 96–205). Plato and Isokrates seem to be aware of Orphica devoted to such myths, cp. Isoc. 11 (*Bus.*).39 (*OF* 26ii B = OF 17 K).

[87] *Suda* s.v. Ὀρφεύς (ο 654, III.564.27–565.11 Adler) (*OF* 91, 92, 411, 605i, 606, 608, 609, 611, 612, 685i, 692, 709, 725, 782, 800ii, 805, 809, 811, 835, 838, 839, 840, 1018iv, 1100ii, 1101iii, 1102, 1105, 1106iii, 1111, 1120, 1123, 1125iii B = OT 173, 174, 175, 178, 179, 184, 186, 196, 199, 223, 223d K). In the briefer ο 657, III.565.17–19 Adler (*OF* 727i, 1104i B = OT 177 K), Orpheus (of Croton) is credited just with an *Argonautica* and "some other stuff" (καὶ ἄλλα τινά). Note, however, that Diogenes Laertius does attribute Argonautic poems to Epimenides, so Argonautic material may have been in the Orphic repertoire. For the prehistory of the *Orphic Argonautica*, see Vian 1987.

The *Suda* does mention a *Katabasis*, the *Descent to the Underworld*, attributed to Herodikos of Perinthos, but this Orphic work does not seem to have had the impact on the mythic tradition that other versions of Orpheus' descent had.[88] Indeed, when ancient authors refer to myths of the Underworld, Orpheus himself does not make the list.[89] Despite the assumption in much modern scholarship that Orphic doctrines about the soul must have come from a *katabasis* poem narrated by Orpheus himself, no ancient source ever credits Orpheus with special knowledge about the soul and its fate on the basis of his own descent to the Underworld.[90] Even the Orphic fragments quoted, in Proclus and others, about the soul and its fate show no signs of coming from an autobiographical account, while the instructions for the Underworld journey in the gold lamellae resemble more an oracular response than an excerpt from a narrative *katabasis*.[91] The evidence from Diodorus suggests that descriptions of the Underworld and the fate of the soul might have been framed as revelations which Orpheus brought back from his trip to Egypt, but it is impossible to know what other tales might have mentioned such ideas.[92]

[88] The earliest reference to Orpheus' descent comes in Euripides' *Alcestis* 357–362 (*OF* 980 B = OT 59 K), but it is clearly a familiar story in the mythic tradition before then and is developed in many ways by various authors. Bernabé collects all the testimonies in *OF* 978–999 B, with his notes in Bernabé 2004: 445–457. Herodikos of Perinthos might be the same as Herodikos of Selymbria, the doctor mentioned in Pl. *Phdr.* 227d3–4 as recommending long walks for exercise, which would put him among the fifth-century Presocratic Orphic authors. This conjecture of authorship (which appears in Clement as Prodikos of Samos) appears to come from the fourth-century BCE scholar Epigenes (Clem. Al. *Strom.* 1.21.131.5 [*OF* 406, 800i, 1100i, 1101ii, 1128i B = OT 222, 173 K], cp. West 1983: 9–13, Linforth 1941: 114–119).

[89] Plut. *Quomodo adul.* 17b7 mentions Homer, Pindar, and Sophocles as authors who tell of the Underworld, while Pausanias (10.28.7) compares the Underworld vision in Polygnotos' painting at Delphi with the well-known *katabases* in Homer and the (lost) epics *Nostoi* and *Minyas*. By contrast, Orpheus is often listed as an expert in rites and purifications, as well as oracles and other special divinatory knowledge.

[90] *Contra* Parker 1995: 500: "Orphic poetry can almost be defined as eschatological poetry, and it was in such poems perhaps that 'persuasive' accounts of the afterlife – accounts designed, unlike that in *Odyssey* xi, to influence the hearer's behaviour in the here and now – were powerfully presented for the first time." Cp. West 1983: 12, who supposes that the references to the *Katabasis* must be to a poem "in autobiographical form." The lack of emphasis on ideas of the soul in Orphic literature renders even more problematic Bernabé's definition of Orphism in terms of doctrines of the soul (Cp. Bernabé 1998a: 172).

[91] Bernabé collects the fragments quoted from Orphica that pertain to the fate of the soul in *OF* 337–350 B. The gold tablets or lamellae can only be considered Orphic in that they claim a special status for the deceased on the basis of her purity or divine connections, since the name of Orpheus appears nowhere in any of the texts. See Edmonds 2004a. Riedweg 1998, 2002, and 2011, tries to reconstruct, in a fundamentally misguided attempt, an Orphic *katabasis* poem from which all the tablet texts derive. For the semiotic features that suggest a resemblance between some of the tablets and oracles, see Edmonds 2011c.

[92] Diod. Sic. 1.96.1–97.6 (*OF* 61, 62 B = OT 96 K). Cp. *OA* 43–45 (*OF* 40 B = OT 224 K) on the sacred tale brought back from Egypt.

Exotic myths

The myths of Orpheus are exotic tales within the Greek mythical tradition. They tell of familiar gods, like Zeus or Demeter or Persephone, doing strange things, or they tell of strange gods, like Sabazios or Kybele or Mise, doing familiar things. Orphic mythology – that is, the myths attributed to Orpheus – draws on the same stock of mythic elements and patterns as the rest of Greek mythology, but the label "Orphic" was not applied to ordinary and common myths of familiar gods or heroes doing familiar things. A poet might put the name of Orpheus on his own work – or a city might claim that Orpheus founded their local ritual – because that name would carry the authority of antiquity and direct divine inspiration, just as a poem or rite deemed exceptionally holy might be attributed to Orpheus by later observers ignorant of the true author. On the other hand, the label of Orpheus' name might be applied by ancient thinkers to classify texts or rites that were exceptionally strange – alien rites or tales of perverse and horrifying deeds by the gods. While in earlier periods, other names, such as Epimenides or Mousaios, might be used for such things, starting with the Hellenistic period the name of Orpheus becomes the dominant label, absorbing the others as later thinkers classify their works as "Orphic" or even attribute their poems to Orpheus.[93]

A survey of the mythic themes in Orphic poems shows that myths associated with the mysteries of Demeter and Dionysos, in their various aspects, names, and forms, are the most likely to be attributed to Orpheus, although cosmogonies also had their place. The mourning mother goddess, whether Demeter seeking Persephone or the mountain mother Kybele with her attending train of Korybantes, is celebrated in many myths attributed to Orpheus, as are the griefs of Persephone. The births of Dionysos or Zeus, as well as the threats the young god must overcome, form another theme, while tales associated with the attending Kouretes are also seen as characteristic of Orpheus. Orpheus also relates myths like that of the

---

[93] As Burkert 1972: 131 says of Pythagoras, "Whoever wanted to find a tangible personality in the chaotic mass of Ὀρφικά hit upon Pythagoras, and those who wanted to cast doubt on his originality used Orphism for this purpose." While this point is applicable to many authors to whom Orphica were attributed, Pythagoras himself is a special case, for two reasons. First, Pythagoras himself was reputed not to have written anything, so pseudepigrapha in his name were common. Second, the Neopythagorean movement in the first century BCE revitalized the authority of Pythagoras himself in a way that Epimenides, Mousaios, Linos or others never received. Iamblichus, at the end of this Neopythagorean movement, recounts that Pythagoras derived his most profound ideas from the most mystical works of Orpheus, even quoting a line of Pythagoras which claims he received the idea of number from the initiator Aglaophamos, who derived it from Orpheus (Iambl. *VP* 28.145–147 [*OF* 507i, 1144iv B = OT 249 K]).

cosmic egg or of Zeus' swallowing the cosmos, and his tales are populated by strange creatures, multiformed monstrosities who nevertheless behave less strangely than some of the more familiar gods. These themes, however, are not very valid cues for the Orphic label, since they often appear in other contexts as well. The features of alien origin or strange and perverse elements woven into the tale provide more valid cues to distinguish the things labeled Orphic; it is the exoticism, the stamp of strangeness that connects with the name of Orpheus.

These exotic myths, many ancient thinkers felt, must contain the most sublime truths, and Orpheus' myths are continuously the subject of exegesis, from the earliest commentaries found in the Derveni papyrus to the complex allegories of Neoplatonists like Proclus and Olympiodorus. These interpretations shape the myths, as the meanings are built into the story by each successive generation of poets who use the name of Orpheus. These *bricoleurs* weave new myths from the patterns and themes of the old, validating their innovations with the legendary antiquity and authority of the oldest and most inspired of poets. There was no fixed set of Orphic myths or doctrines, no Orphic mythology, just a bewildering array of rituals and myths to which different ancient authors and audiences, at different times and for different reasons, gave the magical name of Orpheus.

PART III

Orphic doctrines or the pure from the pure?

CHAPTER SEVEN

Orphic purity
Piety or superstition?

Introduction: Pure from the pure

Pure I come from the pure, Queen of those below the earth . . .

Ἔρχομαι ἐκ καθαρῶ<ν> καθαρά, χθονί<ων> βασίλεια[1]

The deceased on the gold tablet from Thurii proclaims to Persephone that she is pure and that she comes out of a line or group of others who are pure. Even the first line of this enigmatic gold tablet raises a host of questions – Who is she who was buried with this scrap of gold foil? What does it mean for her to be pure (καθαρά)? How did she become pure? The tablet texts tantalize us with their brevity, raising these questions we can never fully answer. Nevertheless, the emphasis on purity provides an important clue to reconstructing, if not the precise details of the identity of the deceased or the rituals she underwent in order to claim this pure status, then at least the general religious context in which such claims could be made.

Although these gold tablets have been linked by modern scholars to Orphism since their discovery in 1879, those links have been made largely on fallacious grounds, and it is rather the emphasis on purity and special privilege that mark these tablets as the sort of thing that might well have been categorized with the Orphic label by the ancients. In the ancient tradition, the rituals that provide purification and create special relationships with the gods were the specialty of Orpheus, and anyone who made the kind of claims made by the deceased on the Thurii tablets might thus have been associated with Orpheus by an outside observer, whether or not the poetic texts of the tablets or the rituals of purification implied by them were thought, by the deceased or whoever was responsible for providing

---

[1] Gold tablet A1 from Thurii (*OF* 488 B = OF 32c K) ln. 1, cp. the first lines in A2(*OF* 489 B = OF 32d K), A3 (*OF* 490 B = OF 32e K) and A5 (*OF* 491 B = OF 32g K). The adjective καθαρά indicates the feminine gender of the deceased; see Edmonds 2004a: 65–67. I have discussed the claim to purity on these tablets in Edmonds 2004a: 69–70.

her with the tablet, to be the work of Orpheus himself. Such a loose association with the works of Orpheus is, I suggest, characteristic of the use of
the label "Orphic" in the ancient sources, rather than some kind of Orphic
identity, membership in a group that proclaimed themselves Orphics, or
adherence to a recognized set of Orphic doctrines.[2]

By contrast, when previous scholars have set out their visions of
Orphism, they first and foremost imagine people, Orphics (*Orphici*), who
live an Orphic life, believing in Orphic doctrines and performing Orphic
rituals and observances.[3] As familiar as such a vision might be from modern religions such as Christianity, Judaism, or Islam, where one finds self-
identifying Christians (or Jews or Muslims– but the scholarship has mostly
used Christianity as the implicit model), living what they see as a Christian
life, believing in Christian doctrines, and regularly performing Christian
rituals and observances as a way of marking their Christian identity, it
presents a distorted picture of the evidence from antiquity associated with
the name of Orpheus. No ancient evidence attests to the existence of a
self-identifying group of Orphics, and, even though there is an abundance
of evidence for rituals or religious observances associated with Orpheus,
participation in such religious activities neither marked an Orphic identity nor indicated belief in particular doctrines. The label of Orphic was
at times applied to people, but only rarely in a direct manner, as a way
of indicating the group of unknown forgers of poems under the name
of Orpheus. More often, the Orphic label was used indirectly for people,
through an association of certain people with the poems or the rituals
attributed to Orpheus.

No consistent principles for such association appear in the evidence to
provide a monothetic definition of a proper Orphic ritual or to differentiate an Orphic person from a non-Orphic. However, there are certain cues
which correlate, to a greater or lesser degree, with the labeling of a ritual or
practice (or person engaged in that rite or practice) as Orphic, and one of
the cues most likely to indicate the label of Orphic is an emphasis on maintaining or obtaining purity, especially during the Classical and Hellenistic

---

[2] Cp. Burkert 1998: 393: "Die Realität, die hinter diesen Texten steht, läßt sich mit hinlänglicher
Sicherheit fassen. Nichts spricht für eine bakchische oder orphische 'Kirche' mit Klerus und Dogma.
Es handelt sich um wandernde Reinigungspriester, καθαρταί, τελεσταί, die ihren Klienten durch
Weiherituale, 'Lösung' aus allerlei Not und Ängsten bieten, einschließlich der Angst vor dem Tod
und vor Jenseitsstrafen."

[3] Bernabé 2004: 224: *Orphici agebant vitam religiosam, quem initiati in ritu privato adipiscebantur;
habebant libros tradentes et servantes doctrinam Orpheo adscriptos; credebant animam immortalem esse,
sed culpam vetustam quae hereditas a Titanibus devenit, sibi expiandam esse ritus certos celebrando,
praecepta instituta quaedam observando; credebant quoque animas suas in nova corpora transituras esse
antequam corpore liberatae aeternam vitam beatam ad inferos consequi possent.*

periods. Orpheus is known as the originator of many practices of purification, and the people associated with Orpheus and his practices are often depicted as obsessed with purity, usually with a negative valuation rather than a positive. The rituals founded by Orpheus often involve purification of the individual as an instrument to special and privileged relations with the divine, but, while such a goal might in some circumstances be the very definition of pious intent, the element of excess or the use of alien means tends to mark the Orphic. Nevertheless, the special rituals designed to perfect the individual's relation to a particular deity, often called *teletai* or mysteries, are unusual by their very nature; they are designed to provide a positive relation to a degree beyond that obtainable from the normal ritual interactions of mortals and gods in sacrifice and prayer. This extra-ordinary nature of such rituals is indicated by the fact that, in some sources, Orpheus is the inventor of all *teletai*, but some particular rituals of which Orpheus is said to be the particular founder have an even stronger correlation with the label "Orphic."

In this chapter, I examine the evidence for the rituals associated with Orpheus, both those that seem strictly purificatory and the more complex rites termed *teletai* or mysteries, as well as the people linked with such rituals. I shall first look at the people, both the ritual experts who perform the kind of rites that have been labeled with the name of Orpheus and their clientele. The majority of the evidence for such people tends to come in the Classical and Hellenistic periods, either from comic caricature or philosophic polemic, two different types of labeling someone else with the name of Orpheus for negative purposes. People who call themselves Orphic in a positive sense and live lives of exceptional purity, observing the practices of Orpheus and engaging in his rituals, exist only in the imaginary – mostly of modern scholars, although a few ancient positive imaginings appear as well. However, the label of Orpheus' name was also attached to various ritual practitioners, not so much to indicate that they performed only rituals attributed to Orpheus as to associate them either with the kind of special mysteries credited to Orpheus or simply with the level of excess in ritual practices that is correlated with Orpheus and his rituals. The name of Orpheus thus tends to mark either extra-ordinary rituals or extra-ordinary performance of ordinary rituals, especially ritual practices associated with purification. I survey such practices of purification, noting the ways and extents to which they are associated with Orpheus or Orphic rituals. I also examine the ways in which the Orphic label is attached to the complex rituals termed *teletai* or mysteries. Although Orpheus is sometimes credited with the invention of all such rites, specific sources attribute particular rites to Orpheus, usually to gain the authority or antiquity of this famous founder. Such specific attributions tend more often to be positive, whereas the general label of Orphic for purifications or *teletai* may be either positive or negative.

An absence of Orphics

Although modern scholars are accustomed to speak of Orphics, as they do of Pythagoreans or Christians, indicating a group of people who identify themselves as followers of a religious leader, the ancient sources never use such terms. The adjective "Orphic" is used to describe, first and foremost, the poetry ascribed to Orpheus, and, secondarily, the rites that Orpheus founded. The term is not applied to people until late; the first attestation is in a second-century CE commentary on Aratus' *Phainomena*, in which Achilles Tatius remarks that the Orphics compare the cosmos to an egg.[4] In this passage, as in others referring to Orphic people, the reference is to the authors of Orphic poetry. Another reference, in the mythographical work attributed to Apollodoros, seems itself to be a later interpolation, written into the margins of the main text, which perhaps dates to the first or second century CE. "Apollodoros" records a version found in some Orphic poems of a particular myth (Asklepios' resurrection of Hymenaios), and he refers vaguely to the pseudepigraphers who have passed their version down under the name of Orpheus.[5] The Neoplatonists, who find in Orphic poetry divine authority for their philosophical systems, refer in various ways to the Orphic poems, but not to Orphic people. Sometimes they cite Orpheus himself (ὥς φησιν Ὀρφεύς); sometimes the Orphic theology (ἡ Ὀρφικὴ θεολογία); sometimes the Orphic traditions (αἱ Ὀρφικαὶ παραδόσεις). Most of the uses of the term Orphic refer to the poems, although there are occasional instances where the term could refer to Ὀρφικοί as the authors of Orphic poems. Even the frequent citation, παρὰ τοῖς Ὀρφικοῖς, means "in the Orphic works," not, as Linforth took it, "in the works of the Orphics."[6]

---

[4] Ach. Tat. *Intr. Arat.* 4.42 (12.6 Di Maria) (*OF* 114iv B = OF 70 K); at 6.2 (17.11 Di Maria) (*OF* 114v B = OF 70 K), Achilles refers to ritual practitioners, οἱ τὰ Ὀρφικὰ μυστήρια τελοῦντες. In the much disputed passage in Hdt. 2.81 (*OF* 43, 45, 650 B = OT 216 K), Ὀρφικοῖσι is probably neuter, referring to rites or customs, rather than masculine, referring to people (or even λόγοι). See below, n. 44.

[5] The same reference accounts for several other references to Orphic people, in ΣEur. *Alc.* 1.18 and ΣPind. *Pyth.* 3.96. Of the 159 instances in the *TLG* of an adjective or adverb deriving from the ὀρφικ- stem, only a few actually refer to people instead of Orphic works.

[6] Procl. *In R.* 1.93.24 Kroll, *Theol. Plat.* 1.28 (1.121.6 Saffrey-Westerink) (*OF* 109vi B = OF 68 K), *Theol. Plat.* 4.22 (4.67.4 Saffrey-Westerink) (*OF* 174iv B), etc. Cp. Linforth 1941: 279. Linforth also

Figure 3 Line drawing of bone tablet from Olbia, figure 1 from West 1982: 18, reproduced courtesy of M. L. West.

Many modern scholars have become very excited over the possibility that the bone tablets from Olbia provide an exception, furnishing evidence of a self-identifying group of Orphics in the Classical period, but the argument hardly bears serious scrutiny. Given the weight that is often placed upon this flimsy piece of evidence, however, it is worth examining in detail. (See Figure 3.) First, although everything hangs on the reading of a single word scratched into the bone fragment, the text of the tablet in question is by no means clear. ΟΡΦΙΚ may be clearly read, but the scratches on the tablet following the kappa are hardly legible, and only a strong desire for a predetermined result can find an omicron and iota following. Given all the parallels for the use of the adjective, some neuter form referring to Orphic rituals is most probable.[7] Secondly, even if the word were actually Ὀρφικοί rather than Ὀρφικῶν or some other form, there is no reason the masculine form could not be referring to λόγοι, rather than people.[8] Thirdly, even

reads παρὰ τῶν Ὀρφικῶν in Iambl. *VP* 28.151 (*OF* 508ii, 1144viii B) as referring to Orphic people, in parallel with παρὰ τῶν Αἰγυπτίων ἱερέων, but the phrase is also parallel with παρὰ τῆς τελετῆς τῆς ἐν Ἐλευσῖνι γινομένης, suggesting that παρά is used indiscriminately here of people and things.

7 Cp. West 1982: 20; Burkert 1982: 12.
8 Cp. the uses of the adjective in Plut. *Quaest. conv.* 363e (with λόγον) and *De E ap. Delph.* 15.391d (*OF* 25ii B) (with λόγον implied). Procl. *In R.* 2.169.25 Kroll (*OF* 702iv B = OF 315 K) uses the masculine adjective with ὕμνος.

if the text read Ὀρφικοί in the sense of people, there is no evidence from context to determine what people are being so labeled or why. The single word, scratched along with a few other words on a bone tablet found in the colony of Olbia, hardly provides evidence for any particular form of religious community, much less for a long-standing group that identified themselves as Orphics. That the tablets might have been used in a ritual for Dionysos (although Zeus is just as probable, given the ΔΙΟ scratched on the tablet) by some religious expert is plausible, but we can draw no conclusion about such a practitioner's status within the community or about the clientele for whom he performed such a ritual, or even, indeed, what sort of ritual he might have performed. Only the desire to find self-labeling Orphics in the Classical period can motivate such a reading of this piece of evidence, a reading that rejects all the parallel evidence for the use of the term.[9]

The absence of ancient uses of the word "Orphics" to refer to the kind of followers of Orpheus whom Bernabé and others have imagined is reinforced by the periphrastic constructions ancient authors use when they are trying to refer to people associated with Orpheus and his works. Plato refers to οἱ ἀμφὶ Ὀρφέα to describe those who compose and interpret the poems of Orpheus, while Plutarch uses a different prepositional phrase, οἱ περὶ τὸν Ὀρφέα, for the composers of Orphic works.[10] Only in post-Christian writings do authors start to refer to disciples of Orpheus in explicit comparison to those of Christ, and, even in this period, the term "Orphics" is never used to designate a group of worshipers as "Christians" is, whether by themselves or by their enemies.[11]

Ritual experts and their clients

Apart from the poets who write poetry under the name of Orpheus, the people who are tagged with the label of Orpheus' name in the ancient sources fall into two categories: ritual practitioners and their clients. The rituals of Orpheus, like the poems of Orpheus, are not easily accessible to normal folk, so specialists provide the service of interpreting the poems and performing the rites for maximum efficacy. Greek religion, as scholars

[9] Olbian tablets (OF 463–465 B). Note that Bernabé assumes that ΔΙΟ = Διό(νυσος) on all three tablets and reads Ὀρφικοί on OF 463 B.

[10] Pl. Cra. 400c (quoted by Clem. Al. Strom. 3.3.16 and Stob. Flor. 1.41.9 [1.292.13 Wachsmuth]) (OF 430i B = OF 8 K); Plut. Comp. Cim. et Luc. 1.2 (OF 431ii B = OF 4 K).

[11] Discipuli Orphei in Myth. Vat. 3.12.5 (OF 333i B = OF 213 K); ἀκροατάς in [Justin] Coh. Gr. 15.1 (43 Marcovich) (OF 372, 377i B = OF 245 K). Ap. Ty. Ep. 16 (42.25 Penella) (OF 818 B = OT 85 K) refers periphrastically to τοὺς ἀπὸ Ὀρφέως to indicate those who follow the teachings of Orpheus.

have often noted, does not rely on a priestly class of ritual experts to maintain normal ritual performance. Instead, most rituals, even sacrifice or divination, can be performed by anyone, but some individuals are better qualified, through position, family lineage, or experience, to engage in the reciprocal relations with the gods that Greek religious acts entail. An officially appointed priest of Apollo, for example, is presumed to be more effective, when offering prayers and sacrifices, at obtaining a positive response, just as a practiced diviner will be able to offer a more informed interpretation of the omens provided by the entrails of a sacrificial victim. In the absence of a rigid hierarchy, however, there is always a potential competition, explicit or implicit, for the authority to perform a ritual act.[12] Certain individuals put themselves forward as experts in ritual practice, offering (or selling) their services to those in need of ritual performance who lack the confidence in their own ability to perform the rites successfully. Sometimes this expertise is validated by community sanction, as in the diviners or exegetes who are appointed by assembly decree, but there is always a marketplace for a wide range of such practitioners, offering services with varying levels of prestige and cost, vying with one another for clients.

Perhaps the most complete description of both experts and their clientele comes in the polemic of Plato, who has Adeimantos complain in the *Republic* that religious specialists undermine the value of justice by claiming that they have extra-ordinary powers to remove the penalties for wrongdoing. The passage is worth quoting again in full:

> But of all these arguments the most astounding are those they make about the gods and excellence, how indeed the gods also allot misfortune and a bad life to many good people, and the opposite fate to their opposites. Begging priests and diviners, going to the doors of the rich, persuade them that there is a power provided to them by the gods in sacrifices and incantations to make amends with pleasures and feasts if he or any of his ancestors has committed some injustice. And if he wants to harm some enemy, he will harm just and unjust alike with spells and curses for only a small expense, having persuaded, as they claim, the gods to obey them. And as witnesses for their claims, they bring in the poets. Some, on the topic of vice, granting

---

[12] Cp. Helen's intervention when she interprets the omen while Menelaus is hesitating (*Od.* 15.169–178). When the Delphic oracle provides the "wooden walls" message, Themistokles wins the competition in the assembly over its interpretation (Hdt. 7.143.1–3). See Chaniotis 2008 on the distinction between ritual practitioners whose authority is grounded in personal expertise and those who obtain office by election, lot, or purchase. Flower 2008a: 188–189 makes this same distinction between seer and priest, but the terminology is imprecise, and, as Chaniotis points out, even those appointed by lot can distinguish themselves through their personal performance of their roles.

ease, say that "vice may readily be seized in abundance; the way is easy and she dwells nearby. But the gods have placed sweat before excellence," and a long, steep, rough road. Then they call on Homer as a witness that the gods may be swayed by men; since that poet says: "Even the gods themselves may be moved by prayers; and men avert their wrath by praying to them and by sacrifices and soothing pleas, and by libations and the smell of burning fat, when someone has transgressed and done wrong." And they present a hubbub of books by Musaios and Orpheus, offspring of Selene and the Muses, as they say, according to which they perform their rituals. And they persuade not only individuals but whole cities that there are absolutions and purifications from unjust deeds through sacrifices and the pleasures of play, both for them while still living and after they have died. These *teletai*, as they call them, release us from evils in the hereafter, but terrible things await those who have not performed the rituals.[13]

The ritual experts here are described as ἀγύρται, begging-priests, and μάντεις, diviners. Such specialists use the books of Orpheus and Mousaios as the tools of their trade, along with the *katadesmoi*, the binding spells that Plato elsewhere associates with lead curse tablets and wax figurines. While they can at times dupe entire communities, their clientele are primarily the rich, that is, those who can afford the fees for their services. Plato has an aristocrat's disdain for those who earn their living, likening to a prostitute anyone who sells his services to please a client, a condemnation directed at the rival sophists who take fees for their lessons no less than these ritualists. The specialists employ a type of ritual, the *teletê*, which they promise provides benefits both during life and afterwards. Each element of this rich testimony deserves explication – the experts, their clients, and their practices, although the fact that Plato is undoubtedly engaged in harsh and ultimately unfair polemic must always be borne in mind.

---

[13] Pl. *Resp.* 364b2–365a3 (*OF* 573i B = OF 3 K): τούτων δὲ πάντων οἱ περὶ θεῶν τε λόγοι καὶ ἀρετῆς θαυμασιώτατοι λέγονται, ὡς ἄρα καὶ θεοὶ πολλοῖς μὲν ἀγαθοῖς δυστυχίας τε καὶ βίον κακὸν ἔνειμαν, τοῖς δ᾽ ἐναντίοις ἐναντίαν μοῖραν. ἀγύρται δὲ καὶ μάντεις ἐπὶ πλουσίων θύρας ἰόντες πείθουσιν ὡς ἔστι παρὰ σφίσι δύναμις ἐκ θεῶν ποριζομένη θυσίαις τε καὶ ἐπῳδαῖς, εἴτε τι ἀδίκημά του γέγονεν αὐτοῦ ἢ προγόνων, ἀκεῖσθαι μεθ᾽ ἡδονῶν τε καὶ ἑορτῶν, ἐάν τέ τινα ἐχθρὸν πημῆναι ἐθέλῃ, μετὰ σμικρῶν δαπανῶν ὁμοίως δίκαιον ἀδίκῳ βλάψει ἐπαγωγαῖς τισιν καὶ καταδέσμοις, τοὺς θεούς, ὥς φασιν, πείθοντές σφισιν ὑπηρετεῖν. τούτοις δὲ πᾶσιν τοῖς λόγοις μάρτυρας ποιητὰς ἐπάγονται οἱ μὲν κακίας πέρι, εὐπετείας διδόντες, ὡς "τὴν μὲν κακότητα καὶ ἰλαδὸν ἔστιν ἑλέσθαι | ῥηϊδίως· λείη μὲν ὁδός, μάλα δ᾽ ἐγγύθι ναίει· | τῆς δ᾽ ἀρετῆς ἱδρῶτα θεοὶ προπάροιθεν ἔθηκαν" καί τινα ὁδὸν μακράν τε καὶ τραχεῖαν καὶ ἀνάντη· οἱ δὲ τῆς τῶν θεῶν ὑπ᾽ ἀνθρώπων παραγωγῆς τὸν Ὅμηρον μαρτύρονται, ὅτι καὶ ἐκεῖνος εἶπεν "λιστοὶ δέ τε καὶ θεοὶ αὐτοί, | καὶ τοὺς μὲν θυσίαισι καὶ εὐχωλαῖς ἀγαναῖσιν | λοιβῇ τε κνίσῃ τε παρατρωπῶσ᾽ ἄνθρωποι | λισσόμενοι, ὅτε κέν τις ὑπερβήῃ καὶ ἁμάρτῃ." βίβλων δὲ ὅμαδον παρέχονται Μουσαίου καὶ Ὀρφέως, Σελήνης τε καὶ Μουσῶν ἐκγόνων, ὥς φασι, καθ᾽ ἃς θυηπολοῦσιν, πείθοντες οὐ μόνον ἰδιώτας ἀλλὰ καὶ πόλεις, ὡς ἄρα λύσεις τε καὶ καθαρμοὶ ἀδικημάτων διὰ θυσιῶν καὶ παιδιᾶς ἡδονῶν εἰσι μὲν ἔτι ζῶσιν, εἰσὶ δὲ καὶ τελευτήσασιν, ἃς δὴ τελετὰς καλοῦσιν, αἳ τῶν ἐκεῖ κακῶν ἀπολύουσιν ἡμᾶς, μὴ θύσαντας δὲ δεινὰ περιμένει.

From begging priests and diviners to magicians and orpheotelests

While *mantis* is a term that is often used positively to designate a professional diviner whose skill is officially recognized by the community, *agyrtês* has less positive connotations.[14] The name itself, deriving from ἀγείρω, to collect, emphasizes the fact that the *agyrtês* is dependent on collecting money from those who respect his expertise or holiness.[15] It is often employed as a term of abuse, to denigrate a religious specialist, like the mythical Teiresias or the historical *mantis* Lampon, who would in other circumstances be treated with great respect for their extra-ordinary abilities.[16] Strabo in fact uses the term of Orpheus himself. "There (at Dion) they say Orpheus the Kikon spent his time, a sorcerer, working at first as a begging-priest (ἀγυρτεύοντα) with his music and also with divination and the rituals pertaining to the initiations."[17] Strabo elsewhere makes the same collocation of Orphica with sorcery, divination, and ecstatic rituals, and, although not every use of the term *agyrtês* in the ancient sources is connected with Orpheus, the same idea of extra-ordinary ritual practice is implied, almost always in a negative fashion – charlatanry or ridiculous frenzies of religious activity.[18]

Apollonios of Tyana, who prides himself on being a philosopher and follower of Pythagoras, complains that extra-ordinarily holy people like himself are lumped by the ignorant with the magicians (μάγους) and those who derive their rituals from Orpheus (τοὺς ἀπὸ Ὀρφέως). If that is the case, he argues, then anyone who is just and divine ought to be called a

---

[14] Philokhoros, *FGrH* 328 F 76 *ap.* Clem. Al. *Strom.* 1.21.134.4 (*OF* 1015i B = OT 87, OF 332 K) lists Orpheus as the first *mantis* in his work on divination. On the *mantis*, see now Flower 2008a, Johnston 2008, and Trampedach 2008, as well as Bowden 2003 and Dillery 2005. Flower 2008b now provides the most complete study of the seer in ancient Greece.

[15] As Jiménez 2002: 189 concludes from her survey of the evidence for the uses of the word, "Según todos estos ejemplos, el término ἀγύρτης designa al individuo errante que vive de las limosnas que le proporcionan mayoritariamente determinadas prácticas mágicas y adivinatorias."

[16] Lysippus fr. 6 *PCG* 5 (620 KA): καὶ Λάμπονα δὲ τὸν μάντιν (. . .) Λύσιππος ἐν Βάκχαις τὸν αὐτὸν ἀγύρτην κωμῳδεῖ. For Teiresias, cp. Soph. *OT* 388–390.

[17] Strabo 7a.1.18 (fr. 10a Radt) (*OF* 554, 659, 816 B = OT 40, 84 K): ἐνταῦθα τὸν Ὀρφέα διατρῖψαί φησι τὸν Κίκονα, ἄνδρα γόητα, ἀπὸ μουσικῆς ἅμα καὶ μαντικῆς καὶ τῶν περὶ τὰς τελετὰς ὀργιασμῶν ἀγυρτεύοντα τὸ πρῶτον.

[18] Strabo 10.3.23 (*OF* 670 B = OT 216 K): "Sorcery and magic are closely related to religious frenzies, worship, and divination. And such also is devotion to the arts, in particular to the Dionysiac and Orphic arts." τῶν δ' ἐνθουσιασμῶν καὶ θρησκείας καὶ μαντικῆς τὸ ἀγυρτικὸν καὶ γοητεία ἐγγύς. τοιοῦτον δὲ καὶ τὸ φιλότεχνον μάλιστα τὸ περὶ τὰς Διονυσιακὰς τέχνας καὶ τὰς Ὀρφικάς. Jiménez 2002: 182–215 surveys a variety of terms for ritual specialists, which are associated in some texts with Orphica, but mostly refer to such practitioners with no mention of Orpheus. See esp. Hippoc. *Morb. sacr.* 1.10 (*OF* 657ii B); Porph. *Ep. Aneb.* 2.18d; Herakleitos, 22 B 14 DK (fr. 87 Marcovich) = Clem. Al. *Protr.* 2.22.3–4 (*OF* 587 B).

magician.[19] Later Pythagorean and Platonic philosophers, of course, liked to cite Orpheus as the founder of philosophy, as the extra-ordinary source of the divine revelations that underlie their systems.[20] But, from the perspective of the ordinary citizen, philosophers and magicians, Pythagorean holy men and mendicants with Orphic texts, doctors and natural scientists, were all more or less a collection of strange folk with pretensions to superiority because of their arcane knowledge. Indeed, the evidence from comedy suggests that they could easily be lumped together in ways that would make the philosophers (and probably even those who identified themselves as *magoi*) cringe. Aristophanes, in *Wealth*, refers to a certain Eudamos, whom the scholiast identifies as a philosopher (φιλόσοφος) who makes a living selling enchanted rings (τετελεσμένους δακτυλίους πωλῶν) for protection against snakebite or *daimones*.[21] Philosopher or *mantis* might be a respectable (and respectful) title, while *agyrtês* or *magos* are more often used to denigrate, but the ancient sources seem to have no qualms about mixing them together, however carefully the specialists in divination might want to differentiate themselves from the physicists or the moral philosophers from magicians.

The one term for a ritual specialist that is specifically associated with Orpheus, the Orpheotelest, is always a negative one. The name, which must mean something like "one who performs Orphic *teletai*," appears only in a few sources and only as a label given to someone contemptuously dismissed or critiqued. The only Orpheotelest identified by name is a certain Philip, whom Plutarch tells us was a wretched beggar, mocked by

---

[19] Ap. Ty. *Ep.* 16 (42.25 Penella) (*OF* 818 B = OT 85 K): "You think you should call 'magicians' the philosophers who follow Pythagoras, and likewise also those who follow Orpheus. For my own part I think that those who follow no matter whom, ought to be called 'magicians', if they turn out to be divine and just men." Μάγους οἴει δεῖν ὀνομάζειν τοὺς ἀπὸ Πυθαγόρου φιλοσόφους, ὧδέ που καὶ τοὺς ἀπὸ Ὀρφέως. ἐγὼ δὲ καὶ τοὺς ἀπὸ τοῦ δεῖνος οἶμαι δεῖν ὀνομάζεσθαι μάγους, εἰ μέλλουσιν εἶναι θεῖοί τε καὶ δίκαιοι. Bernabé reads Διὸς for δεῖνος, which somewhat alters the sense of the argument, but not the complaint about categorization.

[20] Iamblichus' famous Aglaophamos story (*VP* 28.145–147 [*OF* 507i B = OT 249 K]) presents the most vivid version. Cp. Plut. *De Pyth. or.* 18 402e (*OF* 1021i B); Julian. *Or.* 7.10 (*OF* 1021ii B = OT 14 K); Diog. Laer. 1.5 (*OF* 8iii, 887ii, 1021iv, 1046ii, 1073 B = OT 14, 125 K); Anon. *Prolegomena philosophiae Platonicae* 7 (11 Westerink-Trouillard-Segonds) (*OF* 1021v B). Early Christian polemics, e.g., Clem. Al. *Strom.* 1.15.66.1 (*OF* 1021iii B) and 5.4.24.1 (*OF* 669v B) or Epiph. *Haer.* 4.2.5 (182.11 Holl) (*OF* 50, 1133vii B), show that the philosopher's claims to divine inspiration from the poets could be turned against them.

[21] ΣAr. *Plut.* 883.5–8: ὁ δ' Εὔδαμος φαρμακοπώλης ἢ χρυσοπώλης, τετελεσμένους δακτυλίους πωλῶν. φιλόσοφος δὲ ἦν οὗτος ὁ Εὔδαμος φυσικοὺς δακτυλίους ποιῶν πρὸς δαίμονα καὶ ὄφεις καὶ τὰ τοιαῦτα. Cp. the list in Ar. *Nub.* 331–334 of "sophists, Thurian diviners, medical practitioners, long-haired-onyx-seal-wearing idlers, song-twisters for the cyclic dances, and quacks with their heads in the clouds," σοφιστάς, Θουριομάντεις, ἰατροτέχνας, σφραγιδονυχαργοκομήτας, κυκλίων τε χορῶν ἀσματοκάμπτας, ἄνδρας μετεωροφένακας.

the Spartan king Leotychides for making such promises of afterlife bliss resulting from his rituals while he lived such a miserable and poor life.[22] The same story is told in Diogenes Laertius with the philosopher Antisthenes in the role of wise and unsuperstitious man, but here the ritual expert who performs Orphic rites for people is termed a priest (ἱερεύς), a much more respectable term.[23] Philodemos assimilates the Orpheotelest to the despised *metragyrtês*, the mendicant priest of the Mother of the Gods, by claiming that the tympanon, the tambourine, of the Orpheotelest is of little worth, since the tympanon was the characteristic instrument of the metroac rites.[24] The performers of Orphic rituals are thus lumped with other types of ritual experts, even when the name of Orpheus is used to mock and denigrate their extra-ordinary nature. The label of "Orpheotelest" seems not to have been a common one, and it certainly was not one that the practitioners themselves would have used to advertise their expertise (anymore than a modern practitioner might label himself a "new age guru"). Such experts might have labeled themselves as *manteis* or *mystai* in the rites that Orpheus founded, but no evidence survives of such self-labeling. Even the Derveni author, a ritual expert who consults oracles on behalf of others and provides *teletai* with exegesis for those disappointed in their experiences at more well-established rituals, does not explicitly label himself in the surviving fragments of the Derveni papyrus.[25]

Clientele – others associated with Orpheus

Such ritual experts cater to the demands of their clientele, offering *teletai* which they explain according to the hubbub of books by Orpheus, along with other forms of religious services. Only particular types of clients are associated in the ancient evidence with the rites of Orpheus: the excessively gullible or superstitious person, who seeks hyperbolic measures of religious

---

[22] Plut. *Apopth. Lacon.* 224d (*OF* 653 B = OT 203 K). "To Philip the Orpheotelest, who was entirely broke, but was claiming that those who underwent the rites with him were happy after the end of this life, Leotychidas said, 'Why then, you fool, don't you die as soon as possible so that you may at the same time cease from bewailing your misfortune and poverty?'" Πρὸς δὲ Φίλιππον τὸν ὀρφεοτελεστὴν παντελῶς πτωχὸν ὄντα, λέγοντα δ' ὅτι οἱ παρ' αὐτῷ μυηθέντες μετὰ τὴν τοῦ βίου τελευτὴν εὐδαιμονοῦσι, "τί οὖν, ὦ ἀνόητε" εἶπεν, "οὐ τὴν ταχίστην ἀποθνήσκεις, ἵν' ἅμα παύσῃ κακοδαιμονίαν καὶ πενίαν κλαίων;"
[23] Diog. Laert. 6.1.4: "When he was being initiated in the Orphic mysteries, and the priest said that those who were initiated partook of many good things in Hades, 'Why, then,' said he, 'do not you die?'" Μυούμενός ποτε τὰ Ὀρφικά, τοῦ ἱερέως εἰπόντος ὅτι οἱ ταῦτα μυούμενοι πολλῶν ἐν ᾅδου ἀγαθῶν μετίσχουσι, "τί οὖν," ἔφη,"οὐκ ἀποθνήσκεις;" There is no reason to believe either story is historically accurate.
[24] Phld. *De poem.* (*P.Herc.* 1074) fr. 30 (181.1–10 Janko) (*OF* 655 B = OT 208 K).
[25] Cp. Edmonds 2008a for self- and other-labeling and the Derveni author.

purity or divine contact out of fear of divine anger, or the excessively pious and smug person, who likewise seeks hyperbolic measures of religious purity or divine contact out of desire to outdo his neighbors in his piety. Most of the descriptions of such people are thus labels put on them by others, generally with a negative implication – their religious devotion is extra-ordinary in an abnormal, unhealthy, or absurd way. Most of the evidence consists of brief passing references, like the allusion to "the doors of the rich" in Plato, but a few substantive descriptions in extended polemics give more detail of the kinds of features associated with such folk. Their polemic context naturally creates a distorted picture, but the caricatures of stereotypes found in Euripides, Theophrastos, and Plutarch actually provide a full range of the elements in the category, even if all the elements might never have been found in any one real, historical example.

In the one remaining instance of the term Orpheotelest not mentioned above, Theophrastos' ridiculously superstitious man (*deisidaimon*) goes to visit the Orpheotelest for the performance of a ritual (τελεσθησόμενος) every month, bringing along his children in the care of his wife (or the nursemaid).[26] The fact that he is the regular client of such a figure is one of the culminating indicators of his aberrant religiosity, his exaggerated fear of divine anger and the extra-ordinary steps he takes to avoid or appease it. Theophrastos' whole caricature is worth setting out, since it provides the best collection of associated elements in all the ancient evidence.

> Superstition would simply seem to be cowardice with respect to the divine. The Superstitious Man is the kind who washes his hands in three springs, sprinkles himself with water from a temple font, puts a laurel leaf in his mouth, and then is ready for the day's perambulations. If a weasel runs across his path he will not proceed on his journey until someone else has covered the ground or he has thrown three stones over the road. When he sees a snake in the house he invokes Sabazios if it is the red-brown one, and if it is the holy one he sets up a hero-shrine there and then. Whenever he passes the shiny stones at the crossroads he pours oil from his flask over them and falls to his knees and kisses them before leaving. If a mouse nibbles through a bag of barley, he goes to the exegete and asks what he should do; and if the answer is that he should give it to the tanner to sew up he disregards the advice and performs an apotropaic sacrifice. He is apt to purify his house frequently, claiming it is haunted by Hekate. If owls hoot while he is walking, he is disturbed and says "Athena is quite a power" before going on. He refuses to step on a tombstone or go near a dead body or a woman

---

[26] Theophr. *Char.* 16.11 (*OF* 654 B = OT 207 K): καὶ τελεσθησόμενος πρὸς τοὺς Ὀρφεοτελεστὰς κατὰ μῆνα πορεύεσθαι μετὰ τῆς γυναικός – ἐὰν δὲ μὴ σχολάζῃ ἡ γυνή, μετὰ τῆς τίτθης – καὶ τῶν παιδίων.

in childbirth, saying that he cannot afford to risk contamination. On the fourth and seventh of the month he orders his household to boil down some wine, then goes out and buys myrtle-wreaths, frankincense and cakes, and on his return spends the whole day garlanding the Hermaphrodites. When he has a dream he visits not only dream-analysts but also seers and bird-watchers to ask which god or goddess he should pray to. He makes a monthly visit to the Orphic ritualists to take the sacrament, accompanied by his wife (or if she is busy, the nurse) and his children. He would seem to be one of the people who scrupulously sprinkle themselves at the seashore. If ever he observes a man wreathed with garlic <eating?> the offerings at the crossroads, he goes away and washes from head to toe, then calls for priestesses and tells them to purify him with a squill or a puppy. If he sees a madman or epileptic, he shudders and spits into his chest.[27]

As Diggle notes, it is not the particular practices that mark the superstitious man as abnormal, but the excessive degree to which he does them all. "His actions and his attitudes, taken one by one, would probably not have seemed abnormal to the ordinary Athenian. What sets him apart is the obsessiveness and compulsiveness of his behaviour."[28] Nevertheless, certain types of behaviors are parodied in Theophrastos' portrait – the avoidance of the processes of generation and death, attention to oracles and omens, and participation in special kinds of rituals.

[27] Theophr. *Char.* 16(*OF* 654 B): Ἀμέλει ἡ δεισιδαιμονία δόξειεν <ἂν> εἶναι δειλία πρὸς τὸ δαιμόνιον, ὁ δὲ δεισιδαίμων τοιοῦτός τις, οἷος ἀπὸ <τριῶν> κρηνῶν ἀπονιψάμενος τὰς χεῖρας καὶ περιρρανάμενος ἀπὸ ἱεροῦ δάφνην εἰς τὸ στόμα λαβὼν οὕτω τὴν ἡμέραν περιπατεῖν. καὶ τὴν ὁδὸν ἐὰν ὑπερδράμῃ γαλῆ, μὴ πρότερον πορευθῆναι, ἕως <ἂν> διεξέλθῃ τις ἢ λίθους τρεῖς ὑπὲρ τῆς ὁδοῦ διαβάλῃ. καὶ ἐπὰν ἴδῃ ὄφιν ἐν τῇ οἰκίᾳ, ἐὰν παρείαν, Σαβάζιον καλεῖν, ἐὰν δὲ ἱερόν, ἐνταῦθα ἡρῷον εὐθὺς ἱδρύσασθαι. καὶ τῶν λιπαρῶν λίθων τῶν ἐν ταῖς τριόδοις παριὼν ἐκ τῆς ληκύθου ἔλαιον καταχεῖν καὶ ἐπὶ γόνατα πεσὼν καὶ προσκυνήσας ἀπαλλάττεσθαι. καὶ ἐὰν μῦς θύλακον ἀλφίτων διαφάγῃ, πρὸς τὸν ἐξηγητὴν ἐλθὼν ἐρωτᾶν, τί χρὴ ποιεῖν, καὶ ἐὰν ἀποκρίνηται αὐτῷ ἐκδοῦναι τῷ σκυτοδέψῃ ἐπιρράψαι, μὴ προσέχειν τούτοις, ἀλλ' ἀποτροπαίοις ἐκθύσασθαι. καὶ πυκνὰ δὲ τὴν οἰκίαν καθᾶραι δεινός, Ἑκάτης φάσκων ἐπαγωγὴν γεγονέναι. κἂν <κικκαβάζωσι> γλαῦκες βαδίζοντος αὐτοῦ ταράττεσθαι, εἴπας· Ἀθηνᾶ κρείττων, παρελθεῖν οὕτω. καὶ οὔτε ἐπιβῆναι μνήματι οὔτ' ἐπὶ νεκρὸν οὔτ' ἐπὶ λεχὼ ἐλθεῖν ἐθελῆσαι, ἀλλὰ τὸ μὴ μιαίνεσθαι συμφέρον αὑτῷ φῆσαι εἶναι. καὶ ταῖς τετράσι δὲ καὶ ἑβδόμαις προστάξας οἶνον ἕψειν τοῖς ἔνδον, ἐξελθὼν ἀγοράσαι μυρσίνας, λιβανωτόν, πόπανα καὶ εἰσελθὼν εἴσω στεφανοῦν τοὺς Ἑρμαφροδίτους ὅλην τὴν ἡμέραν. καὶ ὅταν ἐνύπνιον ἴδῃ, πορεύεσθαι πρὸς τοὺς ὀνειροκρίτας, πρὸς τοὺς μάντεις, πρὸς τοὺς ὀρνιθοσκόπους, ἐρωτήσων, τίνι θεῶν ἢ θεᾷ προσεύχεσθαι δεῖ. καὶ τελεσθησόμενος πρὸς τοὺς Ὀρφεοτελεστὰς κατὰ μῆνα πορεύεσθαι μετὰ τῆς γυναικός – ἐὰν δὲ μὴ σχολάζῃ ἡ γυνή, μετὰ τῆς τίτθης – καὶ τῶν παιδίων. καὶ τῶν περιρραινομένων ἐπὶ θαλάττης ἐπιμελῶς δόξειεν ἂν εἶναι. κἂν ποτε ἐπίδῃ σκορόδῳ ἐστεμμένον τῶν ἐπὶ ταῖς τριόδοις <ἐσθίοντα>, ἀπελθὼν κατὰ κεφαλῆς λούσασθαι καὶ ἱερείας καλέσας σκίλλῃ ἢ σκύλακι κελεῦσαι αὐτὸν περικαθᾶραι. <καὶ> μαινόμενον δὲ ἰδὼν ἢ ἐπίληπτον φρίξας εἰς κόλπον πτύσαι. (Text and translation from Diggle 2004, slightly modified).

[28] Diggle 2004: 350. Cp. Gordon 1999: 192: "Nothing he does is exactly wrong, let alone illicit, but the sheer scale of his enterprise, his credulity before religious professionals, the unmanliness of his fears, all make him ridiculous to a sound understanding."

The *deisidaimon* does all these things because of an excess of fear, but the other kind of caricature that appears is the prig, the one who engages in excessive religious activity with self-satisfaction and a superior attitude, disdaining the profane who do not make the same efforts. The most vivid portrait of such a person is Theseus' denunciation of his son, Hippolytos, in Euripides' play. Theseus produces a similar list of extreme religious practices by which Hippolytos distinguishes himself from normal people, but he charges that Hippolytos gives himself an air of superiority from his ways and, furthermore, that his piety is just a sham, a cloak under which he hides his true vices.

> Do you, then, walk with the gods, as an extraordinary man? Are you so chaste and undefiled by evil? I would not believe your boasting, vilely attributing to the gods such ignorance in thinking. All right then, vaunt and puff yourself up through your vegetarian diet of soulless foods, and taking Orpheus as your leader engage in Bacchic revels, honoring the smoke of many books. For you have been caught now. I sound the warning for all to flee such men as you. For they do their hunting with reverent words while they devise evils.[29]

Hippolytos does not, in the play, seem actually to do any of the things with which his father charges him, except claim to be the special companion of the gods, specifically Artemis, but, for Euripides' audience, that sort of holier-than-thou attitude could plausibly be coupled with such a list of practices, which resembles the list in Theophrastos – the avoidance of the processes of generation and death, attention to oracles and omens, and participation in special kinds of rituals. This list is neither coherent nor accurate, but provides evidence for the kinds of associations that Euripides' audience might make with someone who could be said to "take Orpheus as his leader." Just as with the client of the Orpheotelest, the evidence provides a picture of someone who is excessively concerned with purity and who engages in ritual practices to obtain or maintain that purity and the consequent special relations with the gods.

The works of Orpheus: *Teletai* and *katharmoi*

The role of Orpheus as supreme founder of mystery rites, of "initiations" and purifications, is the clearest point that emerges from a survey of all the

---

[29] Eur. *Hipp.* 948–957 (*OF* 627 B = OT 213 K): σὺ δὴ θεοῖσιν ὡς περισσὸς ὢν ἀνὴρ ξύνει; σὺ σώφρων καὶ κακῶν ἀκήρατος; οὐκ ἂν πιθοίμην τοῖσι σοῖς κόμποις ἐγὼ θεοῖσι προσθεὶς ἀμαθίαν φρονεῖν κακῶς. ἤδη νυν αὔχει καὶ δι' ἀψύχου βορᾶς σίτοις καπήλευ' Ὀρφέα τ' ἄνακτ' ἔχων βάκχευε πολλῶν γραμμάτων τιμῶν καπνούς· ἐπεί γ' ἐλήφθης. τοὺς δὲ τοιούτους ἐγὼ φεύγειν προφωνῶ πᾶσι· θηρεύουσι γὰρ σεμνοῖς λόγοισιν, αἰσχρὰ μηχανώμενοι.

evidence connected with Orpheus.[30] Not only do the earliest testimonies, such as Aristophanes and Plato, credit Orpheus with the invention of mystery rites in their lists of poetic culture heroes who brought the necessary elements of civilization to the Greeks (and mysteries are nearly always included in such lists), but later sources too remember Orpheus as the first founder of rites.[31] Pausanias, notwithstanding his general skepticism regarding the historical existence of Orpheus, puts him at the top of the list of poets, and marks his supremacy as the creator of *teletai* and purifications that cure disease and avert the anger of the gods.

> Orpheus, it seems to me, surpassed those before him in the beauty of his verse, and he came to a great height of power because he was believed to have discovered rites for the gods and purifications from unholy deeds, cures for diseases and ways of averting divine angers.[32]

In his capacity as poet, Orpheus creates the rituals, which naturally involve song and dance, music and words, as well as other actions.[33] Purifications and healing rituals are not a separate category from mysteries or the rites to avert divine wrath, since a disease that comes due to divine anger may be cured by purifying the afflicted one and by appeasing the god's anger with special mysteries.[34] The entire mode of intense religious activity, which is sometimes referred to as τὸ θρησκεύειν, is connected by some authors with the Thracian origins of Orpheus: to *thrêskeuein* is thus to act according to the Thracian poet. The wordplay appears first in Plutarch (although there is no reason to suppose it was original with him) and recurs throughout the scholiastic tradition as well as in various early Christian writers. The

---

[30] Cp. Linforth 1941: 261–276.

[31] Ar. *Ran.* 1032 (*OF* 510, 626i B = OT 90 K); Pl. *Prt.* 316de (*OF* 549i, 669iii, 806, 1013 B = OT 92 K).

[32] Paus. 9.30.4 (*OF* 546, 551, 1082i B): ὁ δὲ Ὀρφεὺς ἐμοὶ δοκεῖν ὑπερεβάλετο ἐπῶν κόσμῳ τοὺς πρὸ αὐτοῦ καὶ ἐπὶ μέγα ἦλθεν ἰσχύος οἷα πιστευόμενος εὑρηκέναι τελετὰς θεῶν καὶ ἔργων ἀνοσίων καθαρμοὺς νόσων τε ἰάματα καὶ τροπὰς μηνιμάτων θείων.

[33] Linforth 1941: 269 n.1 surveys the verbs used to describe Orpheus' founding of the rites, which range from verbs of discovering (εὑρεῖν) to showing (καταδεῖξαι) to establishing (καταστήσασθαι) and more. He also notes, however, that most often Orpheus is seen first as a poetic composer of poems connected with the mysteries. The disjunction between poetic composer and ritual founder would not, however, have been meaningful to the ancient sources in the way that it is from our modern perspective. Cp. Tatianus *Ad Gr.* 1.2 (*OF* 558, 1024iii B = OT 258 K), who links song and mystery: Ποίησιν μὲν γὰρ ἀσκεῖν καὶ ἄιδειν Ὀρφεὺς ὑμᾶς (the Greeks) ἐδίδαξεν, ὁ δὲ αὐτὸς καὶ μυεῖσθαι. Paus. 10.7.2 (*OF* 552 B) does draw a distinction between mystery poetry and the poetry of Panhellenic competitions, claiming that Mousaios, in imitation of Orpheus, refused to enter the contests.

[34] This overlap has puzzled many modern scholars, especially those who see healing as a non-religious activity within the context of the history of medicine. The understanding of Korybantic rites has been particularly confused by the attempt to see it as primarily a healing ritual aimed at curing madness. Cp. Linforth 1946.

Suda generalizes in its entry for θρησκεύει: "be reverent, serve the gods. For it is said that Orpheus the Thracian first devised the mysteries of the Greeks, and they called honoring the gods θρησκεύειν, since the invention was Thracian."[35] The Neoplatonists, who revered Orpheus even more highly than their predecessors, gave credit to Orpheus for all ancient Greek religion; Orpheus is the mystagogue for all theology among the Greeks, proclaims Proclus, securing the authority of Orpheus for his own systematic theology that he thinks underlies all of the Greek tradition.[36]

Orpheus' name can thus be associated with any mystery ritual, even one founded in historical times by someone else, since he is the ultimate creator of mystery rituals in general. This association can be used negatively in the sources, dismissing as Orphic foolishness any kind of special ritual or its participants – Theophrastos' client of the Orpheotelest remains a prime example. However, the name of Orpheus can also lend a special glamor to an otherwise undistinguished ritual, giving it the weight of antiquity as well as the authority of the greatest specialist. Many sources attach the name of Orpheus to many different rituals, and Linforth concluded his survey in despair, pointing out that there are no common features of all these rituals, either in deities or in practices, that could be used to define what is Orphic.[37] Nevertheless, by abandoning the search for monothetic definitions, we can detect patterns in the way the name of Orpheus was used as a label, both in the content of the rites and in the desired effect of the labeling.

In contrast to the sources, mostly from comedy or philosophic polemic, that link the name of Orpheus with absurd excesses in purificatory rites or extravagant mysteries, the sources that credit Orpheus with the foundation of particular mysteries are generally positive.[38] As for the nature of the rites, most of the testimonies fall into two rough groups – ceremonies

---

[35] *Suda* s.v. Θρησκεύει (θ 486, II.728.12–15 Adler) (*OF* 556vii B = OT 37 K): θεοσεβεῖ, ὑπηρετεῖ τοῖς θεοῖς. Λέγεται γὰρ ὡς Ὀρφεὺς Θρᾷξ πρῶτος τεχνολογῆσαι τὰ Ἑλλήνων μυστήρια. καὶ τὸ τιμᾶν θεὸν θρησκεύειν ἐκάλεσαν, ὡς Θρᾳκίας οὔσης τῆς εὑρέσεως. For all the plays on the Thracian/θρησκεύειν see *OF* 556i–ix B.

[36] Procl. *Theol. Plat.* 1.5 (1.25.26 Saffrey-Westerink) (*OF* 507iv B = OT 250 K). Cp. [Nonn.] *ad Gregor. Orat. in Iulian.* 4.69 (137 Nimmo Smith) (*OF* 556iv B).

[37] Linforth 1941: 266–267: "Obviously, all the things that are said about all the mysteries with which Orpheus' name is connected cannot be added together to produce a sum that would have any tolerable or credible unity. . . . For it must be carefully remarked that nothing is to be inferred from the comparative frequency with which the various myths and other features of the mysteries are alluded to except the comparative interest of the various writers in these matters."

[38] The exceptions are the early Christian polemics, which take lists of Orpheus' achievements and invert their valuation, critiquing him for setting up these blasphemous, idolatrous, and superstitious rituals. It is worth noting that the early Christian writers label as superstition all the things that the earlier Greek philosophers had, but add all the normal pagan rites as well. Martin 2004 and Gray

concerned with Demeter or the Mother of the Gods and her various attendants or those concerned with Dionysos or similar Bacchic figures. Such a breakdown is, of course, unsurprising, since the type of rituals known as *teletai* or mysteries are most often associated with Demeter and Dionysos.[39] Some, but not all, such mysteries are linked with Orpheus, and, even for those that are so linked, that association is not made in all the sources. Such inconsistency is best understood as the result of the fact that Orphic is not a precise term to any of these sources, with a fixed content defined by doctrines, practices, or even deities, but rather a label whose use was intended to have a particular effect – in this evidence, primarily an effect of increasing the authority, antiquity, and holiness of the rituals so described.

The mysteries of Orpheus: Special relations with the gods

Orpheus may be known as the archetypal founder of *teletai* or mysteries, but what these *teletai* or mysteries might be remains rather mysterious.[40] Hesykhios defines *teletai* as festivals, sacrifices, or mysteries (ἑορταί. θυσίαι. μυστήρια), but the exact nature of any of the rites referred to as *teletai* is difficult to discern from the surviving evidence. Some indeed were public festivals like the Panathenaia, celebrated by large groups of citizens, involving multiple sacrifices to a variety of deities along with many other ritual acts designed to honor and please the gods.[41] Others may have been celebrated by a smaller community, perhaps a private *thiasos* like the one led by the mother of Aiskhines (probably for Sabazios). Participation in such a ritual was more of a deliberate choice than participation in the public festivals, a choice motivated by the individual's feeling of a need for closer connection with the god than provided by the normal public festivals. Demosthenes' vicious mockery of this ritual remains the best description of a private *teletê* surviving in the evidence.

2003 both survey the way the category of superstition was developed in early Christianity from the earlier philosophical category.

[39] Cp. Burkert 1987: 2–11; Bowden 2010: 14.

[40] Graf nd s.v. Mysteries in *BNP* suggests that the general term μυστήρια derives from the Attic festival of that name later applied to other rituals that seemed similar, although the evidence is too sparse to fully establish this plausible hypothesis.

[41] Pind. *Pyth.* 9.97 refers to the Panathenaia as a *teletê*, for example, and also to the Olympic Games (*Ol.* 10.51). Euripides calls the Choes a *teletê* (*IT* 959). Ar. *Pax* 418–422 refers to a series of the great festivals of Athens – Panathenaia, Eleusinian Mysteries, Dipolia, and Adonia – as *teletai* that could be transferred to the honor of Hermes if he helps bring Peace back to the world. Schuddeboom 2009 revises and expands the earlier studies of Zijderveld and van der Burg on the uses of the words *teletê* and *orgia*.

When you become an adult, you read out the scrolls for your mother performing her rites (τῇ μητρὶ τελούσῃ), and generally assisting with other matters. At night you poured libations and robed those undergoing the ritual in fawn-skins, purifying them by smearing mud and bran mash around their bodies, and then you raised them up from their lustration and told them to say: "I have escaped evil; I have found the better." And you gave yourself airs that no one ever wailed that cry so strongly as you did. (I can well believe it! For you wouldn't think he gives tongue so loudly now, if you heard him doing his ritual wailing!) During the day you led your noble band of revelers through the streets, crowned with fennel and white poplar, stroking the sacred snakes or waving them over your head. And you danced around and bellowed "Euoi Saboi!" and "Hyes Attes! Attes Hyes!", and you were called Leader of the Dance and Guide and Ivy-bearer and Carrier of the Mystic Fan and such things by all the old women, taking your pay for these things in tipsy-cakes, and pastry twists, and fresh-baked buns. Truly, who would not call himself and his lot happy with such things?[42]

While Demosthenes is hardly an unbiased and trustworthy guide to the true activities and status of his archrival's mother, his picture of the rites must at least have seemed plausible and familiar to his audience in the jury. We may note the multiple steps in the ritual – libations, washings and costumings, a purification with mud and bran, the chanting of a mystic slogan, culminating with a public procession and a feast; this was a complex and lengthy process. Demosthenes unfortunately does not provide us with any account of who the clientele were for this ritual, but it seems unlikely that there was a stable community that celebrated together regularly.[43]

Teletai are not, as they are often translated, initiations, in the sense of a ritual that initiates an individual into a religious community.[44] While

---

[42] Dem. 18.259–260 (*OF* 577i B = OT 205 K): ἀνὴρ δὲ γενόμενος τῇ μητρὶ τελούσῃ τὰς βίβλους ἀνεγίγνωσκες καὶ τἄλλα συνεσκευωροῦ, τὴν μὲν νύκτα νεβρίζων καὶ κρατηρίζων καὶ καθαίρων τοὺς τελουμένους καὶ ἀπομάττων τῷ πηλῷ καὶ τοῖς πιτύροις, καὶ ἀνιστὰς ἀπὸ τοῦ καθαρμοῦ κελεύων λέγειν 'ἔφυγον κακόν, εὗρον ἄμεινον,' ἐπὶ τῷ μηδένα πώποτε τηλικοῦτ' ὀλολύξαι σεμνυνόμενος (καὶ ἔγωγε νομίζω· μὴ γὰρ οἴεσθ' αὐτὸν φθέγγεσθαι μὲν οὕτω μέγα, ὀλολύζειν δ' οὐχ ὑπέρλαμπρον), ἐν δὲ ταῖς ἡμέραις τοὺς καλοὺς θιάσους ἄγων διὰ τῶν ὁδῶν, τοὺς ἐστεφανωμένους τῷ μαράθῳ καὶ τῇ λεύκῃ, τοὺς ὄφεις τοὺς παρείας θλίβων καὶ ὑπὲρ τῆς κεφαλῆς αἰωρῶν, καὶ βοῶν 'εὐοῖ σαβοῖ,' καὶ ἐπορχούμενος 'ὑῆς ἄττης ἄττης ὑῆς,' ἔξαρχος καὶ προηγεμὼν καὶ κιττοφόρος καὶ λικνοφόρος καὶ τοιαῦθ' ὑπὸ τῶν γραδίων προσαγορευόμενος, μισθὸν λαμβάνων τούτων ἔνθρυπτα καὶ στρεπτοὺς καὶ νεήλατα, ἐφ' οἷς τίς οὐκ ἂν ὡς ἀληθῶς αὑτὸν εὐδαιμονίσειε καὶ τὴν αὑτοῦ τύχην;

[43] A succession of different clients seeking her services better suits Demosthenes' description of Aiskhines' mother as a prostitute earlier in the speech. Stable communities of religious deviants were more often attacked as political conspiracies, cp. the Bacchanalian affair in Rome or even the Pythagoreans.

[44] Cp. Dowden 1980: 412–417 on the terminology. Robertson 2003: 220 is right to point out that *mystai*, as participants in mystery rites, were not necessarily initiated into a group, but were often just select members of the community performing special rites on behalf of the whole. At times when the primary form of religious social organization for such rites was the polis group, *mystai* were

some religious communities, we may speculate, may have required that their members undergo such a ritual in order to be qualified to join, the purpose of the *teletê*, as with any other ritual, is first and foremost to please the god and to bind the worshiper into a closer relation with the deity. Insofar as *teletai* are special rituals, either private, elective rites or even mysteries (whether celebrated by the polis community or by a private group), participation in a *teletê* does create a change in status, marking the individual as somehow different than before performing the ritual. This difference may be analyzed on two planes – that of the interrelation of mortal worshiper and god (what we might call the vertical axis) and that of the worshiper and the other members of his or her community (what we might call the horizontal axis). On the vertical axis, the *teletê* brings the mortal closer to the god and strengthens the relationship between them – because of the special honors the mortal has provided, the god is bound by reciprocity to show special favor. On the horizontal axis, the worshiper marks his distance from the normal crowd by the special efforts made to please the god.

The purpose of the rites, seen on the vertical axis, is thus to win the god's favor, to appease any anger the divinity may feel, and to put oneself in the position to request special treatment from the god. The *mystês*, the one who has gone through a special *teletê*, especially one termed a *mysterion*, is proclaimed blessed, favored by the gods. Being blessed with the favor of the gods means peace and prosperity in life, success in one's ventures and all the components of a happy life.[45] This favored status continues after death, and various sources refer to *teletai* as the way to ensure a better lot in the afterlife.

> Blessed is he of men on earth who has beheld them, whereas he that is uninitiated in the rites, and he that has no part in them, never has a like portion once he has perished down in the shadows.[46]

members of the polis, whereas, in the Hellenistic period and following, when private religious groups became a more important form of social organization for the practice of religion, membership in that kind of group provided the occasions for the celebrations for the *mystai*. Robertson, however, imagines an evolution from primitive fertility magic to religious sects with soteriological concerns – a Frazerian paradigm that distorts the evidence and distracts from the very useful set of evidence he presents. For Robertson, as for so many earlier scholars with evolutionary models of religion, "the Orphics" are imagined to provide the crucial link between the primitives and the sophisticates.

[45] Lévêque 1982 explores the different connotations of the term ὄλβιος, which is used in different contexts to describe the blessed happiness of one favored by the gods. Despite the shifts in the semantic range of the term that Lévêque traces, the term always refers to one possessed of the things that, in the given circumstance, are deemed to make up a happy life, whether those things be material possessions, a stable family, power and respect in the community, or a guarantee of a happy life after death.

[46] *Hom. Hymn Dem.* 480–482: ὄλβιος ὃς τάδ' ὄπωπεν ἐπιχθονίων ἀνθρώπων· | ὃς δ' ἀτελὴς ἱερῶν, ὅς τ' ἄμμορος, οὔ ποθ' ὁμοίων | αἶσαν ἔχει φθίμενός περ ὑπὸ ζόφῳ εὐρώεντι. Cp. Pind. fr. 137 S.-M.

The traditional ways to obtain a favored afterlife, heroic deeds or divine parentage, are, of course, not feasible options for most people, but these *teletai* offer a way to create the special connection with the gods that only mythic heroes could otherwise obtain.[47]

Too much emphasis, however, has been put, in modern scholarship, on the role of *teletai* in providing a favored afterlife. Plato, as usual, is largely responsible for the distortion, since he harps on this aspect of the *teletai* in the *Republic*.[48] In this dialogue, of course, Plato is attacking the inadequacy of traditional rationales for leading the just life, and he finds the fear of punishment in the afterlife a particularly weak motivation. First, as the character of Kephalos shows, most normal people don't bother to worry much about the afterlife until they are approaching death, so that fear does little to cause people to behave justly.[49] Furthermore, if they do worry about divine anger at their unjust way of living, the *teletai* offered, not just by itinerant ritual practitioners but even by the most respected rites of the polis of Athens, the Eleusinian Mysteries, provide a means to appease the gods and thus escape the consequences of any injustice. Plato plays on the word *teletê*, deriving it from the word for the deceased, to highlight this connection between *teletai* and afterlife:

> There are absolutions and purifications from unjust deeds through sacrifices and the pleasures of play, both for them while still living (μὲν ἔτι ζῶσιν) and after they have died (δὲ καὶ τελευτήσασιν). These initiations (τελετάς), as they call them, release us from evils in the hereafter, but terrible things await those who have not performed the rituals.[50]

(*OF* 444i B) and Soph. fr. 837 R (= 753 N) (*OF* 444ii B); Isoc. 4.28. Ar. *Pax* 371 also notes the importance of initiation for the afterlife: "For I must be initiated before I die." δεῖ γὰρ μυηθῆναί με πρὶν τεθνηκέναι.

47 Cp. Edmonds 2004a: 198–207 on the ways the mythic tradition provides of obtaining a favorable afterlife, along with Plato's transpositions of them into philosophy as the ultimate solution.

48 Of course, Plato's emphasis on eschatology was compounded by modern historians of religion who imagined eschatology as one of the concerns of real religion and saw it as a mark of evolution toward Christianity.

49 Pl. *Resp.* 330d–331a (*OF* 433iii B). Only the neurotically superstitious worry all the time about punishment in the afterlife, like Plutarch's caricature of the superstitious man (*De superst.* 167a). Indeed, it is only through such an exaggerated fear of divine anger that afterlife punishment becomes a serious motivator for behavior in this life. Most people, like Kephalos, don't really think themselves deserving of afterlife punishment, even if they believe it might exist for the really unjust. (see further below, pp. 258–259).

50 Pl. *Resp.* 365a (*OF* 573i B = OF 3 K): λύσεις τε καὶ καθαρμοὶ ἀδικημάτων διὰ θυσιῶν καὶ παιδιᾶς ἡδονῶν εἰσι μὲν ἔτι ζῶσιν, εἰσὶ δὲ καὶ τελευτήσασιν, ἃς δὴ τελετὰς καλοῦσιν, αἳ τῶν ἐκεῖ κακῶν ἀπολύουσιν ἡμᾶς, μὴ θύσαντας δὲ δεινὰ περιμένει. There has been much dispute as to the exact sense of the participle τελευτήσασιν, since it has been taken to mean either 'for those who have already died' in contrast to those who are now living or 'for them when they have died' in contrast to the same people while they are living. Graf 2011a: 61–62 has argued for the former meaning, noting

Plato also links these rituals with benefits in the afterlife, mocking the vision of the symposium of the blessed as a kind of everlasting drunkenness.[51] In the course of the dialogue, Plato tries to build an argument for leading the just life on its own merits, without the added incentives provided by afterlife reward or punishment. Indeed, Socrates specifically removes such incentives from the argument, only allowing the traditional ideas back in at the very end, with his myth of Er.[52] Plato's emphasis on the afterlife aspect of *teletai* in the *Republic* must thus be seen as part of his philosophic project, his critique of inadequate traditional motivations for justice, rather than as a simple and straightforward testimony to the nature of *teletai* in Plato's world.

On the horizontal axis, the special relation between the worshiper and the deity that is enacted in the ritual is also performed for an audience of other mortals; it marks the change of status of the individual in the larger world of humans.[53] Any rite that excludes others inherently creates an in-group apart from the out-group, however subtle or dramatic the distinction might be. The Eleusinian Mysteries admitted men and women, children and slaves – potentially the whole community, but barbarians and murderers were still prohibited, and anyone who had elected not to undergo the Mysteries would be excluded, for example, from the courts while matters pertaining to the Mysteries were discussed.[54] The very *makarismoi*, the formulae

that the clientele for these rituals are not just individuals but whole cities, which cannot, as cities, look forward to benefits after death but which do have members who have already died. However, as he also notes, cities are also not really living in that same sense. I think the latter meaning is much preferable; the *teletai* provide benefits both during life and after death. The inclusion of both individuals and whole cities allows Plato to mix into a single critique both the private, elective rites catering to individuals and the public rituals, like the Eleusinian Mysteries, that are sponsored by the whole polis. Johnston 1999: 53 argues that rites for those who have already died are purification rituals to avert the danger from the polluted dead.

[51] Pl. *Resp.* 363c4–d2, cp. *Phd.* 69c (*OF* 434iii, 549ii, 576i, 669ii B) and Plotinus, *Enn.* 1.6.6 (*OF* 434iv B), where he provides a more positive picture of the benefits, dwelling with the gods in the pure and delightful realms on the true earth.

[52] The rewards and punishments in the afterlife, which are removed from consideration early in the discussion (366a–367e[*OF* 574, 910ii B = OF 3 K]), are restored at the end (614a) after justice has been proven to be inherently worthwhile. Afterlife compensations are "owed" to the argument; they are not merely a superfluous addition. See Morgan 2000: 206–207 for the imagery of debt and interest that runs through the dialogue.

[53] All analogies with Christian practices risk distortion, but, to provide a point of comparison, undergoing a *teletê* is a rite of passage more like a pilgrimage than a baptism. It is a process that can be repeated more than once without losing the intended effects, and, while it creates a certain distinction between those who have done such a pilgrimage and those who have not, it is not the necessary process to become a member of a specific group.

[54] The courts were famously cleared for the trial of Alkibiades (Andoc. 1.12). For the *prorrhesis* excluding murderers and barbarians, see, e.g., Isoc. *Paneg.* 157. Cp. the parody in Ar. *Ran.* 354–367. See Bowden 2010 for a recent synthetic account of the evidence for the rites connected with the Mysteries.

that describe the blessings obtained by those who performed the *teletê*, these utterances themselves set the initiated apart from the *atelestoi*. The selfsame utterance that describes the privileges of the privileged also enacts their separation from the unprivileged, and this distinction between the favored ones and the ordinary profane recurs in many settings, notably in the famous seal line that marked the beginning of poems attributed to Orpheus, "Close the doors of your ears, ye profane."[55]

Participation in such rites could be a cause of pride, a mark of piety and holiness, and some, like Apuleius, could point to the fact that they had undergone many such rites as a proof of their status as respectable worshipers of the gods.[56] On the other hand, excess in such exercises might be seen as ridiculous, like the superstitious client of the Orpheotelest who comes once a month to undergo the ritual.[57] The superior attitude affected by those with much experience of *teletai* would of course be easily resented, and Theseus' diatribe against his son harnesses such familiar resentment, as well as the suspicion that such affectations of superiority must be a mask for hidden vices.[58] Expertise in the performance of such rituals presents the same double-edged effect on relations within the society. Plato's Euthyphro complains that everyone laughs at him when he speaks in the Assembly on the basis of his superior understanding of such rites, and, while historical figures such as Lampon and Hierokles may be lampooned in Aristophanes, they are honored by the city in official inscriptions.[59] The Derveni author likewise takes his own ritual expertise very seriously, disparaging other practitioners who are unable to rival the understanding of the divinatory, sacrificial, and mystic rituals that he parades in his treatise.[60]

The name of Orpheus is only loosely associated with all such folk, insofar as the claim to special connections and purity obtained through rituals is apt to be tagged with the Orphic label. Orpheus is more closely connected with specific rituals, especially important mystery celebrations whose prestige is enhanced by association with the greatest founder of rites in the Greek mythic tradition. All mystery rites, all *teletai*, and even all practices of special purification may be credited to Orpheus, however, depending on the purposes of the author making the attribution. The name

[55] Bernabé collects the testimonies for this verse as *OF* 1 B, and Brisson 2010 discusses the opposition of initiate and profane in the context of the Derveni papyrus. Cp. also Jiménez 2002: 93–99 for the terms applied to the uninitiate.

[56] Apul. *Apol.* 55.   [57] Theophr. *Char.* 16.11a (*OF* 654 B = OT 207 K).

[58] Eur. *Hipp.* 948–957 (*OF* 627 B = OT 213 K).

[59] See above, ch. 4, *The epideixis of exegesis*, esp. n. 62.

[60] See Edmonds 2008a and above, pp. 129–135.

of Orpheus can be used to mock the excesses of the superstitious obsessed with purity or to praise the antiquity and sanctity of a local festival. I shall first survey practices of purification that are associated with Orpheus, and then turn in more detail to the more complex rituals termed *teletai* or mysteries.

Practices of purity

Camporeale draws a distinction between preventative (*preventiva*) and contingent (*contingente*) purification, between practices intended to avoid contamination and those intended to remove or expiate contamination that may have occurred.[61] In the evidence for people and practices associated with Orpheus, this distinction is useful for sorting out the practices used to maintain an excessive level of purity and those used to obtain or regain such a level of purity when the individual feels stained by something, either personal wrongdoing or that of some ancestor. The need for contingent purifications is often signaled by an omen or an oracle that informs the person suffering (or about to suffer) the anger of the gods that something must be done to appease them. Hence, the excessive concern for oracles and omens is part of the caricature of the superstitious man or the one who claims special privilege with the gods, since omens and oracles communicate the gods' will to mortals. But the excessively pious or superstitious person, the kind linked with Orpheus and his rituals of purification and initiation, is not content to wait for the gods' omens to warn of wrongdoing; such a person engages in practices that maintain an exaggerated level of purity in everyday life, often showcasing that exceptionally pure status to all those around.

One must be more pure than usual in order to properly approach a divinity, and various inscriptions in sanctuaries provide the best insight into the sorts of purifications that were thought necessary for someone to enter a sacred space. Different sacred spaces had different regulations, and the kinds of purity required vary widely in the evidence from different times and places, ranging from the prohibition of certain animals or items within the sanctuary to abstentions from certain foods or activities for a prescribed period of time before entering.[62] These sacred laws describe the

---

[61] Camporeale in the Premessa (pp. 1–2) to Paoletti 2004. This article in ThesCRA provides a good survey of the evidence for purification processes in the ancient Greek world.
[62] Lupu 2005: 14–21 surveys the purity requirements attested for sanctuaries, providing examples of the particular regulations in different sacred laws. Chaniotis 1997 traces the development of the idea of purification of the mind or soul, in addition to that of the body, in literary and epigraphical

preparations needed to move from the ordinary space of the profane world into the sacred space of the sanctuary, but the extra-ordinarily pure person makes such preparations all the time, either self-righteously, as though about to consort with gods at any moment, or fearfully, as though always afraid of offending the gods.

The primary way in which the offensively self-righteous Hippolytos in Euripides parades his purity, of course, is in his avoidance of the impurities of sex. His unusual complete avoidance of the works of Aphrodite pro-vokes the warnings of the chorus and motivates the plot, as the shunned goddess seeks revenge. This hyperbolic purity seems to be the main reason Theseus associates his son with Orpheus, but avoidance of sex is not asso-ciated with Orphica in other evidence. Indeed, celibacy, so familiar from debates over purity in the Christian tradition, makes only a few appearances in the Greek tradition. Sex was generally regarded as involving some minor pollution, and a deity might be offended by sexual intercourse within a sanctuary, but only a few cult regulations specify any regulation of sexual activity. Most of these merely specify that people should purify themselves before sacrificing or entering the temple if coming "from a woman" (or "from a man"), that is, directly after engaging in sexual intercourse.[63] A few festivals seem to have required abstinence from sexual activity as a preparation beforehand, but even for these it may have only been a few important participants leading the ceremony.[64] The idea of sexual absti-nence as an expiation or special propitiation for the gods was not unknown, since Orestes asks his sister whether her husband has avoided sex with her since their marriage from some sacred requirement (ἄγνευμ᾽ ἔχων τι θεῖον), but it was not a practice that was normally prolonged.[65] Hippolytos' life-long abstinence is seen as an exaggerated, even perverted, form of this kind of temporary purification, and it is the exaggeration that creates the association with the extra-ordinary purity associated with Orpheus.

Much of the impurity associated with sex probably stems, as Parker notes, from the bodily fluids mixed about outside their normal internal places, but the processes of generation and death also create impurity.[66]

---

evidence. Cp. Graf 2011b on the difference between purifications for sanctuaries and those connected with initiations into mystery cults. See also the typology of purificatory rituals in Petersen 2011, derived from Honko 1979.

[63] Cp. Parker 1983: 74–75 n. 4.

[64] Cp. Parker 1983: 85: "it was only seldom, to judge by the surviving evidence, that the layman was required to keep himself pure in preparation for a festival." Contra Burkert 1987: 108.

[65] Eur. El. 256, cp. the story about King Agis of Sparta who avoids his wife's bed after an earthquake in Plut. Vit. Alc. 23.9.

[66] Parker 1983: 76–77.

Theophrastos' client of the Orpheotelest goes out of his way to avoid any contamination coming from birth or death, "He refuses to step on a tombstone or go near a dead body or a woman in childbirth, saying that he cannot afford to risk contamination."[67] Greek religion had a variety of purificatory practices designed to cleanse those who were obliged to incur the pollution through their participation in the birth process or the rites of the funeral and mourning, but those excessively concerned with purity went out of their way to avoid any contact. Plutarch's superstitious man is notable for his anxiety about death and birth, and Plutarch notes that this anxiety is projected even onto the gods, who likewise avoid hanging corpses, women in childbirth, or houses where mourning is taking place.[68] On the positive side, the chorus of prophets of Zeus in Euripides' *Cretans* proudly proclaim their purity by claiming, "I flee from the birth of mortals and never go near their tombs."[69] Their isolation from these normal processes of human life is a mark of their superior connection with the gods, just as the superstitious caricatures in Theophrastos and Plutarch avoid the impurities of birth and death in order to maintain a level of purity that they think necessary to avert the gods' anger. Again, it is the extra-ordinary level of purity, rather than any specific practice that may provoke an ancient author to associate such folk with Orpheus.

Abstinence from the eating of meat, however, has a much higher cue validity for association with the name of Orpheus. That Hippolytos vaunts himself on his vegetarian diet and avoidance of ensouled food is perhaps the most absurd of all the charges Theseus makes against his son, given that Hippolytos' favorite activity is slaughtering beasts in the hunt. Nevertheless, the vegetarian diet is one of the clearest marks of the kind of hyperpure life associated with Orpheus. Many texts attribute to Orpheus a prohibition on the slaughter of animals; indeed, for Aristophanes, Orpheus' great achievements in the list of poetic culture heroes are the prohibition on slaughter and the institution of mystic rituals.[70] Sextus Empiricus, quoting from an Orphic poem, credits the cessation of primitive allelophagy to the

---

[67] Theophr. *Char.* 16.9: καὶ οὔτε ἐπιβῆναι μνήματι οὔτ' ἐπὶ νεκρὸν οὔτ' ἐπὶ λεχὼ ἐλθεῖν ἐθελῆσαι, ἀλλὰ τὸ μὴ μιαίνεσθαι συμφέρον αὑτῷ φῆσαι εἶναι.

[68] Plut. *De superst.* 170ab. Note that Artemis, at the end of Euripides' play (*Hipp.* 1437–1438), deserts Hippolytos for fear of being contaminated by his death: ἐμοὶ γὰρ οὐ θέμις φθιτοὺς ὁρᾶν | οὐδ' ὄμμα χραίνειν θανασίμοισιν ἐκπνοαῖς.

[69] Eur. *Cret.* fr. 472 K (= fr. 2 J.-V.L.) *ap.* Porph. *Abst.* 4.19.21–23 (*OF* 567 B). Note that these prophets are not associated with Orpheus in the ancient sources. Porphyry, who elsewhere knows Orphic material, does not draw the link when he quotes the passage, and nothing we know of the play would suggest any connection with Orpheus.

[70] Ar. *Ran.* 1032 (*OF* 510, 626i B = OT 90 K). Cp. Hor. *Ars P.* 391–392 (*OF* 626ii B = OT 111 K): *silvestris homines sacer interpresque deorum | caedibus et victu foedo deterruit Orpheus.*

Thesmophoric goddesses (probably Demeter and Persephone), which may allude to this combination of Orpheus' achievements, since Orpheus is associated with the Thesmophoria and the myth of Demeter linked to it in various sources.[71] Plutarch, an ardent defender of vegetarianism, likewise credits Orpheus as the originator of the meatless diet, while a fragment of the lost *Orpheus* by fourth-century BCE comic poet Antiphanes jokes about stuffing oneself with leaves.[72]

The abstention from all meat is also associated by Plutarch with Pythagoras and with Empedokles, and he provides a range of arguments in his treatises on vegetarian diet, some of which link the abstention to the idea of reincarnation.[73] Plutarch, like the later Porphyry and the earlier Empedokles, incorporates the argument for abstention from meat into a vision of humanity's decline from a state of primeval purity – before meat-eating was invented, through desperation or decadence, humans lived on cereals and honey, avoiding bloodshed and leading a pure and simple life. Such a life is referred to by Plato (although not by Empedokles, Plutarch, or Porphyry) as the Orphic life ('Ορφικός βίος):

> Athenian: Indeed, we may see that the practice of men sacrificing one another survives even now among many peoples; and we hear of the opposite practice among others, when they dared not even taste an ox, and the offerings to the gods were not living creatures, but rather meal cakes and grain steeped in honey, and other such pure sacrifices, and they abstained from meat as though it were unholy to eat it or to stain the altars of the gods with blood. Rather, those of us men who then existed lived so-called Orphic lives, partaking entirely of inanimate food and doing the opposite with things animate.[74]

---

[71] Sext. Emp. *Math.* 2.31–32 (90.10–22 Mau) (*OF* 641i, 642 B = OF 292 K). As noted above, ch. 3, n.12, the cessation of allelophagy is linked to the advent of civilization, humans becoming more than the beasts. Civilization brings justice, and with laws (*thesmoi*) comes agriculture, the other gift of the Thesmophoric goddesses. Orpheus himself is credited with the institution of the Thesmophoria by some late sources, cp. Thdt. *Graec. Aff. Cur.* 1.21 (108.21 Canivet) (*OF* 511 B = OT 103 K), although others credit a different ritual practitioner, Melampous, with bringing these rites from Egypt (Hdt. 2.49.1 [*OF* 54 B], Clem. Al. *Protr.* 2.13.5 [*OF* 385 B], Diod. Sic. 1.97.4 [*OF* 56 B]).

[72] Plut. *Conv. sept. sap.* 16 159c (*OF* 629 B = OT 215 K), cp. Jer. *Adv. Iovinian.* 2.14 (*PL* 23.304c) (*OF* 630 B). Antiph. *Orph.* fr. 178 KA = 180 Kock (*OF* 631 B): Βύστραν τιν' ἐκ φύλλων τινῶν. Them. *Or.* 30. 349b (*OF* 632 B = OT 112 K) plays with the idea, like Sextus linking it to the advent of agriculture. Porphyry *Abst.* 2.36 (*OF* 635 B) attributes the Pythagorean abstention from meat to ὁ θεολόγος, which often refers to Orpheus, although here it may simply mean Pythagoras himself. For the debate, see Bernabé *ad loc.*

[73] Plut. *De esu carn.* 1.996bc (*OF* 313i, 318ii B = OF 210 K); 2.997e–998d.

[74] Pl. *Leg.* 782c1 (*OF* 625i B = OT 212 K): ΑΘ. Τὸ δὲ μὴν θύειν ἀνθρώπους ἀλλήλους ἔτι καὶ νῦν παραμένον ὁρῶμεν πολλοῖς· καὶ τοὐναντίον ἀκούομεν ἐν ἄλλοις, ὅτε οὐδὲ βοὸς ἐτόλμων μὲν γεύεσθαι, θύματά τε οὐκ ἦν τοῖς θεοῖσι ζῷα, πέλανοι δὲ καὶ μέλιτι καρποὶ δεδευμένοι καὶ τοιαῦτα ἄλλα ἁγνὰ θύματα, σαρκῶν δ' ἀπείχοντο ὡς οὐχ ὅσιον ὂν ἐσθίειν οὐδὲ τοὺς τῶν θεῶν βωμοὺς

Such a life is not elsewhere credited to the inspiration of Orpheus, however, although the motifs of a simple and peaceful Golden Age existence that Plato here evokes appear widely in Greek mythology from Hesiod onward. Plato actually refers elsewhere to a Pythagorean life, which makes Pythagoras' followers stand out from the rest of mankind, although he does not specify the features of that life that distinguish it.[75] Later authors such as Porphyry and Iamblichus describe the Pythagorean life in great detail, but the Neopythagorean "revival" of the first century BCE is doubtless responsible for many of these details.[76] Of course, Iamblichus credits Pythagoras' ideas to the teachings of Orpheus, transmitted through the rituals of Aglaophamos, neatly providing Orphic authority for all of the Neopythagorean ideas he describes in his life of Pythagoras.[77]

Although Orpheus is at times credited with a ban on all meat, he is also sometimes said to have prohibited just the eating of certain parts, particularly the heart or the brain. Here, however, the credit is often shared with Pythagoras. Plutarch recounts how one of his friends mocked him for avoiding eggs at dinner, taunting him for holding to the teachings of the Orphica and Pythagorica. In this passage, Plutarch lists not only hearts and brains, but also eggs and beans as prohibited by such teachings.

> But when Sossius Senecio was hosting us, they suspected me of adhering to the Orphic or Pythagorean teachings and holding the egg taboo, as some hold the heart and brain, because I considered it the first principle of creation.[78]

αἵματι μιαίνειν, ἀλλὰ Ὀρφικοί τινες λεγόμενοι βίοι ἐγίγνοντο ἡμῶν τοῖς τότε, ἀψύχων μὲν ἐχόμενοι πάντων, ἐμψύχων δὲ τοὐναντίον.

[75] Pl. *Resp.* 600b: "And Pythagoras himself was exceedingly revered in this way, and his successors still even now, refer to a Pythagorean mode of life and seem somehow to be distinguished from others." Πυθαγόρας αὐτός τε διαφερόντως ἐπὶ τούτῳ ἠγαπήθη, καὶ οἱ ὕστεροι ἔτι καὶ νῦν Πυθαγόρειον τρόπον ἐπονομάζοντες τοῦ βίου διαφανεῖς πῃ δοκοῦσιν εἶναι ἐν τοῖς ἄλλοις.

[76] On the subject, see Riedweg 2005: 123–128 and the still indispensable Burkert 1972. Such Neopythagorean figures as Apollonios of Tyana distinguish themselves by, among other things, their scrupulous purity in the avoidance of meat. Cp. Philostr. *VA* 6.11 (*OF* 636 B). Note that the hermit Sarapion, who keeps only the book of Orphica with him, is said to live the life of Kronos (τὸν μυθευόμενον Κρόνιον βίον), rather than the βίος Ὀρφικός (*Suda* s.v. Σαραπίων [σ 116, IV.324.20 Adler] = Dam. *Isid.* fr. 41 [p. 37 Zintzen] [*OF* 677v B = OT 240 K]: μόνον σχεδὸν τὸν Ὀρφέα ἐκέκτητο καὶ ἀνεγίνωσκεν).

[77] Iambl. *VP* 28.145–147 (*OF* 507i, 1144iv B = OT 249, 250 K). The legend of Aglaophamos is a favorite for those, ancient and modern, who want to see an unbroken wisdom tradition from the oldest, most divine authority of Orpheus through Pythagoras and Plato, but Lobeck already argued decisively against its validity in his 1829 work of the same name. Cp. Burkert 1972: 128–129.

[78] Plut. *Quaest. conv.* 2.3.1 635e (*OF* 645, 647i B = OF 291 K): ὑπόνοιαν μέντοι παρέσχον, ἑστιῶντος ἡμᾶς Σοσσίου Σενεκίωνος, ἐνέχεσθαι δόγμασιν Ὀρφικοῖς ἢ Πυθαγορικοῖς καὶ τὸ ᾠόν, ὥσπερ ἔνιοι καρδίαν καὶ ἐγκέφαλον, ἀρχὴν ἡγούμενος γενέσεως ἀφοσιοῦσθαι· For the abstention from hearts

Plutarch then quotes the charmingly vivid line, "eating beans is like eating the heads of your parents" (ἴσόν τοι κυάμους ἔσθειν κεφαλάς τε τοκήων,), which is attributed in various sources to Pythagoras or simply the ancients, although only in the late collection of *Geoponica* to Orpheus. Likewise, the line, "wretches, utter wretches, keep your hands from beans!" (δειλοί, πάνδειλοι, κυάμων ἄπο χεῖρας ἔχεσθαι) is credited to Orpheus by the same source, but by earlier sources to Empedokles and to the Pythagoreans.[79] Orpheus is again connected with a prohibition on beans by Pausanias, who mysteriously remarks that anyone who has read the Orphica or seen the rites at Eleusis will understand his reference to a myth in which beans were *not* discovered by Demeter.[80] The prohibition on beans was explained in many different ways by different sources, but it is more often associated with Pythagoras than with Orpheus, and the Pythagorean aversion to beans becomes the theme of a number of stories illustrating the extreme purity of various Pythagoreans who give up their lives rather than touch beans in any manner.[81] The prohibitions on beans and all meat (ensouled food) are perhaps the elements in which the labels of Orphic and Pythagorean most overlap, but the sources do not consistently link any single set of prohibitions with either label – for example, beans with Pythagoreans and meat with followers of Orphic rules. The Pythagorean label becomes dominant in the later sources, after the influence of the Neopythagorean revival of the first few centuries, and the emphasis on purity becomes a much less valid cue for the Orphic label in the writings of the early Christians and their contemporaries.[82]

Some sources provide a whole list of foods that the pure and pious person must avoid, but remarkably similar lists appear credited to Pythagoras, Eleusinian regulations, or even just wise ancients.[83] Diogenes Laertius, relying on Alexander Polyhistor, provides a list of Pythagorean

---

and beans, see also Diog. Laert. 8.19 = Arist. fr. 194 Rose (*OF* 647ii B) and Suda s.v. Πυθαγόρας (π 3124, IV.265.12–13 Adler).

[79] Plut. *Quaest. conv.* 2.3.1 635e–636a (*OF* 648v B = OF 291 K). Cp. Gell. *NA* 4.11.9 = Emp. 31 B 141 DK (fr. 128 Wright): *in Empedocli carmine qui disciplinas Pythagorae secutus est, versus hic invenitur* 'δειλοί . . . ἔχεσθαι'. See the list of places in *OF* 648 B, as well as extensive bibliography on the debates over the 'true' origin of these sentiments, although Bernabé's listing of these fragments in *OF* 648 B is more than usually difficult to follow.

[80] Paus. 1.37.4 (*OF* 649i B = OT 219 K).

[81] E.g., for Pythagoras in Diog. Laert. 8.39, 8.45 (= *Anth. Pal.* 7.122); for Pythagoreans Myllias and Timycha in Iambl. *VP* 31.192–194 (= Neanthes, *FGrH* 84 F 31). Cp. Burkert 1972: 183–184.

[82] The exceptions that prove the rule are Jer. *Adv. Iovinian.* 2.14 (= *PL* 23.304c) (*OF* 630 B), who cites Orpheus among a long list of Greek philosophers who advocate vegetarianism, and Greg. Naz. *Or.* 27.10 (94 Gallay-Jourjon = *PG* 36.24c) (*OF* 648xiii = OF 291 K), who refers to 'Pythagorean silence and Orphic beans' as pagan practices to attack. For discussion, see Jourdan 2011: 232–233.

[83] Cp. Burkert 1972: 177 for a discussion of the various lists of foods.

abstentions that includes not only beans and eggs, but also all creatures that lay eggs, all meat, and two kinds of fish (τρίγλη and
μελάνουρος), as well as anything else prohibited by those who conduct the rites in the sacred places (τὰς τελετὰς ἐν τοῖς ἱεροῖς). Elsewhere Diogenes Laertius provides a slightly different list of Pythagorean
observances, mentioning hearts, rather than eggs, and adding a few
more fish (ἐρυθῖνος and μήτρα).[84] Porphyry attributes a similar list
to the Eleusinian Mysteries, including all domestic fowl (perhaps
as egg layers), fish, beans, and a collection of significant fruits –
apples and pomegranates (ῥοιᾶς τε καὶ μήλων).[85] Here again the overlap
between Pythagorean, Eleusinian, and Orphic appears in the sources, and
various scholars have sought in vain to discern which prohibitions might
actually historically have been enforced in any such rituals or lifestyles or to
sort through the varying and contradictory rationalizations given for these
abstentions. However, it is better to recognize that all these abstentions
were recognized as tokens of extra-ordinary purity and that such a level of
purity was associated at different times and to different degrees with all
three of these, as well as other ritual practices of purification.

This level of extra-ordinary purity appears also from a negative perspective, as a set of useless and superstitious practices that achieve nothing.
The Hippocratic author, in his polemic against his rivals, denounces the
purifiers who recommend such abstentions from fish, fowl, and fruit as
charlatans without any true understanding of how health is to be achieved,
conjurors, purificators, mountebanks, and charlatans (μάγοι τε καὶ καθάρ-
ται καὶ ἀγύρται καὶ ἀλαζόνες), who appear to be excessively religious
(σφόδρα θεοσεβέες).[86] The negative aspect of such abstentions comes out
in the evidence from comedy as well, where it forms part of the caricature
of the overly religious and superstitious person.

The scrupulous care for purity ascribed to the Orphic or Pythagorean
life does not even end with the person's death, for Herodotus, one of
the earliest sources to provide clear evidence of such practices, notes that
Egyptian practices forbid wearing woolen garments in temples or in burial,

[84] Alex. Polyh. *FGrH* 273 F 93 *ap.* Diog. Laert. 8.33 (*OF* 628i B = OT 214 K); cp. Diog. Laert. 8.19 =
Arist. fr. 194 Rose (*OF* 647ii B).

[85] Porph. *Abst.* 4.16.6. Cp. ΣLucian, *Dial. meret.* 7.4 (80,7 4.29 = 280.23 Rabe), who claims a similar
list of fruits, beans, meat and fish (including the τρίγλη, μελανούρος, and ἐρυθῖνος, as well as
κάραβος and γαλεός) is found in the mystic rite (ἐν τῷ μυστικῷ), probably from the Lucianic
context, the Haloa. A fragment from the comic poet Cratinus (fr. 236 KA = 221 Kock = Ath. 7.127
325e) suggests that those undergoing the purificatory preparations for consulting the Trophonius
oracle had to abstain from τρίγλη, μελάνουρος, and τρυγών. See Bonnechere 2003: 147–148.

[86] Hippoc. *Morb. sacr.* 1.22–40. Note that Porph. *Abst.* 4.16.1–4 too associates such purificatory
abstinences with the μάγοι, imagined here not as charlatans but the actual Persian priests.

customs that he claims agree with those called Orphic and Bacchic, but which are really Egyptian and Pythagorean.

> But nothing woolen is brought into temples or buried with them, for that is unholy. In this they agree with the things which are called Orphic and Bacchic, but are in fact Egyptian and Pythagorean. For it also is unholy for one partaking of these rites to be buried in woolen wrappings. There is a sacred legend told about these things.[87]

The purity from animal products in life is extended to the purity of the body in the burial process, so that purity may be taken to its final extreme. Other evidence attests to special burial practices for Pythagoreans, but there are no other mentions of Orpheus as the originator of funerary rites or even of special purifications for burial.[88] The archaic inscription from a burial ground in Cumae that proclaims "it is not right for any to lie here who has not been bacchic" certainly indicates the sort of exclusivity and superior attitude associated with Orphic purity, but it is the Bacchic nature of the rites, rather than any authority from Orpheus, that qualifies the one who has undergone them to receive burial.[89] In Herodotus, by contrast, even if he casts doubt on the authenticity of the attribution to Orpheus, the prohibition against wool is clearly marked as Orphic, although Herodotus also provides evidence for the blurring of categories, Orphic with Pythagorean, local Greek Bacchic customs with foreign Egyptian ones, that recurs elsewhere in the evidence.

Certain practices for maintaining an extra-ordinary level of purity are thus associated with Orpheus in the sources, although this association appears primarily in the earlier sources and disappears almost entirely in the early Christian and later sources. Neither any of the specific practices

---

[87] Hdt. 2.81 (*OF* 43, 45, 650 B = OT 216 K): Οὐ μέντοι ἔς γε τὰ ἱρὰ ἐσφέρεται εἰρίνεα οὐδὲ συγκαταθάπτεταί σφι· οὐ γὰρ ὅσιον. Ὁμολογέουσι δὲ ταῦτα τοῖσι Ὀρφικοῖσι καλεομένοισι καὶ Βακχικοῖσι, ἐοῦσι δὲ Αἰγυπτίοισι, καὶ <τοῖσι Πυθαγορείοισι· οὐδὲ γὰρ τούτων τῶν ὀργίων μετέχοντα ὅσιόν ἐστι ἐν εἰρινέοισι εἵμασι ταφθῆναι. Ἔστι δὲ περὶ αὐτῶν ἱρὸς λόγος λεγόμενος. Variant manuscript readings have provoked a long-standing dispute over which names Herodotus was actually using, since one family of manuscripts omits Bacchic and Egyptian, leaving only Orphic and Pythagorean: Ὁμολογέουσι δὲ ταῦτα τοῖσι Ὀρφικοῖσι καλεομένοισι καὶ Πυθαγορείοισι. Burkert's arguments (1972: 127–128) seem most convincing, especially the point that the longer version preserves all four as neuter (customs) rather than masculine (people), which corresponds to the absence of any other testimony to people called Orphikoi in the early evidence. For more bibliography, see Bernabé *ad loc.* Apul. *Apol.* 56 (31.21 Helm) (*OF* 651 B = OT 217 K) is clearly referring to this passage of Herodotus, although he abbreviates to Orpheus and Pythagoras, and he makes explicit the reasoning for avoiding wool as *corporis excrementum*.

[88] For references to secret Pythagorean funerary practices, see Plut. *De gen.* 585ef.

[89] *IGASMG* III 15 (*Iscrizioni greche arcaiche di Sicilia e Magna Grecia*, III: *Iscrizioni delle colonie euboiche*) (*OF* 652 B = OT 180 K): οὐ θέμις ἐντοῦθα κεῖσθαι ἰ μὲ τὸν βεβαχχευμένον.

(abstention from meat, beans, wool, etc.) nor the general exaggeration of normal levels of purity are at any point exclusively labeled as Orphic, and the label of "Pythagorean" becomes more common in the later evidence. Although the Orphic life appears in Plato as a term for an idealized Golden Age existence, no evidence exists for people actually living such a life, in contrast to the evidence, idealized or parodic as it may be, for people who carried out the Pythagorean lifestyle. Particular practices, carried out at specific times, may be associated with Orpheus or attributed to his invention, and those who engage in them may thus be linked with Orpheus, but the idea of Orphic communities living the pure and holy Orphic life is purely the fantasy of modern scholarship. Even the closest equivalent in the ancient evidence, the chorus of Cretan prophets of Zeus in Euripides, is firmly located in the mythical past as they address King Minos, however much they may provide a distorted reflection of certain aberrant individuals of Euripides' day, whose exaggerated practices of preventative purification mark them as extra-ordinary.[90]

Contingent purifications

Perhaps even more than with preventative purifications like abstention from meat, Orpheus is associated with contingent purifications, special rituals designed to remove the impurities incurred in the course of life or inherited from the past. The ritual experts denounced by Plato appeal to their clients by promising them relief from their own crimes or those of their ancestors.

> Begging priests and diviners, going to the doors of the rich, persuade them that there is a power provided to them by the gods in sacrifices and incantations to make amends with pleasures and feasts if he or any of his ancestors has committed some injustice.[91]

Plato mocks the rituals these *agyrtai* put forth as mere feasts and enjoyable games, an occasion to eat heartily on the excuse of appeasing the god and to dress up and do silly things on the pretence of honoring the offended deity.

---

[90] *Contra* Jiménez 2008: 785–799, who pulls together much of the evidence relating to practices of purification in the attempt to describe the features of the Orphic life as an actual practice. Parker 1995: 485 is far more cautious: "it seems to follow that certain initiates sought to lead 'Orphic lives' (the phrase is Plato's) by abstaining from meat; they 'took Orpheus as their master', therefore, for longer than the duration of the initiation alone."

[91] Pl. *Resp.* 364b (*OF* 573i B = OF 3 K): ἀγύρται δὲ καὶ μάντεις ἐπὶ πλουσίων θύρας ἰόντες πείθουσιν ὡς ἔστι παρὰ σφίσι δύναμις ἐκ θεῶν ποριζομένη θυσίαις τε καὶ ἐπῳδαῖς, εἴτε τι ἀδίκημά του γέγονεν αὐτοῦ ἢ προγόνων, ἀκεῖσθαι μεθ' ἡδονῶν τε καὶ ἑορτῶν.

Demosthenes makes similar critiques of the ritual performed by Aiskhines' mother, emphasizing the theatrical and sensual aspects of the ritual, the holiday spirit of the holy day's performance.[92]

Such purifications, however, were taken seriously in other circumstances, from the age-old rites of purification from blood crimes, attested from Homer onward, to the purifications of whole cities, like those famously performed by Epimenides in Athens after the Kylonian conspiracy. Aeschylus weaves the tragic story of the *Oresteia* around the theme of inherited guilt that needs purification lest it lead to further crimes that bring even more divine anger, and the myths of Oedipus and his descendants likewise feature the idea. The purpose of rituals of purification is to appease the anger of the gods at some wrongdoing and to bring the one being purified into such a state as to be able to resume positive relations with the gods. For this process to work, first the offense that triggers the divine anger must be identified, along with the one who committed the offense and the god who is offended. Next, the necessary actions to appease the god must be identified and undertaken. These may consist of direct purification of the individual or a more indirect approach, asking a deity, whether the offended one or some other, to remove the divine anger and its detrimental effects in the world of mortals. This appeasement usually consists of sacrifices and prayers to honor the god and persuade the divinity to relent (or to intervene and make another deity relent). Such a process of diagnosis and prescribed ritual cure appears repeatedly throughout the myths of the Greeks, from the plague in the *Iliad*, to the *Oresteia* of Aeschylus, to Sophocles' Oedipus and beyond.

What is characteristic of the association with Orpheus is thus not the process itself, but an excess in any part of that process. Ritual experts who flaunt the poems of Orpheus try to convince anyone who can pay that they need such purification, while some folk, like Theophrastos' *deisidaimon*, are so neurotic that they think they need such purification all the time. To seek extra-ordinary purification, rites meant to resolve a crisis, in ordinary situations, with no real crisis at hand, is behavior associated with Orpheus, with the people who perform rites attributed to Orpheus, or with those who seek the ritual expertise of such people.

Diagnosis through omens and oracles

One element of the extra-ordinary concern for purity that characterizes the type associated with the Orphica, especially in hostile sources, is an

---

[92] Dem. 18.259–260 (*OF* 577i B = OT 205 K).

exaggerated attention to omens and oracles, a continual suspicion that the gods are always trying to communicate their anger at lapses in purity or at other transgressions. Theophrastos' *deisidaimon* sees an omen in many of the chance events he encounters in his day: a weasel crossing his path, the sight of a snake, or the hoot of an owl. If a mouse gnaws through a sack of grain, he is convinced that it signifies some divine displeasure that must be appeased with sacrifices. Such a person takes his dreams seriously as communications from the gods, since he always fears that some misdeed of his may have prompted their anger. Anything even slightly out of the ordinary appears as a sign from the gods, instead of being taken as part of the diversity of experience, as a normal person would.

> This, however, is not the way of the superstitious man; but if even the smallest ill has befallen him, he sits down and builds around himself, in addition to his pain, great, harsh, and unbearable sufferings, and he also piles on himself fears and terrors and suspicions and disturbances, laying on with every sort of lamentation and groaning. For no man nor fortune nor circumstance nor even himself does he blame for everything, but the divine, and he says that from that source a daimonic stream of trouble has come carried down; and he thinks that it is not because he is unlucky, but because he is hateful to the gods, that any man is punished by the gods and that he pays the penalties appropriate to his own conduct.[93]

Plutarch indeed defines superstition (δεισιδαιμονία) as an excessive fear of the gods, and, from his Platonic philosophical perspective, tries to argue that the essential goodness of the gods means that they should never be feared as bringers of evil. As Martin points out, however, such a definition of superstition stems from philosophic debates and does not accurately reflect the ideas of the mainstream of Greek and Roman society. Superstition is invented as a category in the process of defining true piety as an Aristotelian mean between the atheist's ignorant denial of all gods and the superstitious man's ignorant fear of their malignity.[94] Nevertheless, Plutarch and others

---

[93] Plut. *De superst.* 168a: τοῦ δὲ δεισιδαίμονος οὐχ οὗτος ὁ τρόπος, ἀλλ᾽ εἰ καὶ μικρότατον αὐτῷ κακόν τι συμπεπτωκός ἐστιν, ἄλλα κάθηται πάθη χαλεπὰ καὶ μεγάλα καὶ δυσαπάλλακτα τῇ λύπῃ προσοικοδομῶν, καὶ προσεμφορῶν αὐτῷ δείματα καὶ φόβους καὶ ὑποψίας καὶ ταραχάς, παντὶ θρήνῳ καὶ παντὶ στεναγμῷ καθαπτόμενος· οὔτε γὰρ ἄνθρωπον οὔτε τύχην οὔτε καιρὸν οὔθ᾽ ἑαυτὸν ἀλλὰ πάντων τὸν θεὸν αἰτιᾶται, κἀκεῖθεν ἐπ᾽ αὐτὸν ἥκειν καὶ φέρεσθαι ῥεῦμα δαιμόνιον ἄτης φησί, καὶ ὡς οὐ δυστυχὴς ὢν ἀλλὰ θεομισής τις ἄνθρωπος ὑπὸ τῶν θεῶν κολάζεσθαι καὶ δίκην διδόναι καὶ πάντα πάσχειν προσηκόντως δι᾽ αὐτὸν οἴεται. (Loeb translation, with slight modifications). Cp. Clem. Al. *Strom.* 7.4.24: "They imagine that all occurrences are signs and causes of evils. If a mouse tunnels through a clay altar and, not having anything else, gnaws through an oil flask; if a rooster being reared crows in the evening, they take this as a sign of something." πάντα σημεῖα ἡγοῦνται εἶναι τὰ συμβαίνοντα καὶ κακῶν αἴτια· ἐὰν μῦς διορύξῃ βωμὸν ὄντα πήλινον κἂν μηδὲν ἄλλο ἔχων διατράγῃ θύλακον, ἀλεκτρυὼν τρεφόμενος ἐὰν ἀπὸ ἑσπέρας ᾄσῃ, τιθέμενοι τοῦτο σημεῖόν τινος.

[94] Martin 2004 traces this development, esp. 21–35 on the contribution of Theophrastos.

draw their examples of superstition from the stock of comic tropes and exaggerations that would be familiar to the mainstream audience, even if they explain them differently. Even someone who did not accept the Platonic postulate that the gods could never do evil, relying instead on the mythological tradition that showed them doing evil through jealousy and anger fairly often, even such a one would find ridiculous the exaggerated precautions and anxieties of the caricatures in Theophrastos or Plutarch. Indeed, the comic poets seem to have enjoyed mocking the excesses of the superstitious, who find meaning in a sneeze or a broken shoelace and who engage in all sorts of extravagant practices to appease the divinities they imagine to be offended.[95]

Another phenomenon often taken to be a sign of divine displeasure is illness, particularly unexplained illness or madness.[96] In the treatise on the so-called *Sacred Disease*, the inexplicable and dramatic disease of epilepsy, the Hippocratic author rails against his rival healers, who attribute all the symptoms to divine agency and attempt to redress the problem with expiatory rituals of purification.[97] Again, the line between normal, mainstream belief and superstition is not, as the philosophers or the Hippocratic doctors would have it, the idea that the gods could cause such things, but the excessive credulity that each and every instance of such a phenomenon must be a divine sign. When the massive plague afflicts the Achaeans at the beginning of the *Iliad*, no one is surprised to find that divine anger is responsible, but most folk would not see a sign of divine anger in every illness.

Madness, however, is sufficiently abnormal and disturbing to provoke a reaction even from the mainstream, although most people would not, like Theophrastos' *deisidaimon*, make an apotropaic spitting gesture at the mere sight of a madman.[98] Nevertheless, the extra-ordinary nature of the phenomenon creates a need for interpretation. Plato's Socrates indeed praises madness precisely because it provides an indication that purification and divine propitiation are needed.

> But indeed, for illnesses and the greatest troubles, which arise in certain families from ancient causes of divine anger, madness is generated within

---

[95] Men. fr. 106 KA = 109 Kock mocks the superstitious man who calls on the gods for luck when his shoelace breaks by having another character point out that it broke because he was too miserly to buy himself new ones, while Philemon, fr. 101 KA = 100 Kock scorns those who find meaning in a sneeze. Both of these examples are quoted in the critique of superstition by Clement of Alexandria (*Strom.* 7.4.24–25), who draws on the philosophic category of superstition in his polemic against pagan religion as a whole as superstition.

[96] See, in general, the treatment by Parker 1983: 207–234.

[97] Hippoc. *Morb. sacr.* 1.22–28.

[98] Theophr. *Char.* 16.14: "If he sees a madman or epileptic, he shudders and spits into his chest." μαινόμενον δὲ ἰδὼν ἢ ἐπίληπτον φρίξας εἰς κόλπον πτύσαι.

and provides oracular wisdom that tells from whom it is necessary to seek relief, having recourse to prayers and worship of the gods, from which, when it occurs, it obtains purifications and mystic rituals (*teletai*), and madness makes safe from harm the one having it for the present and for time to come. Madness discovers a release from present evils for the one possessed by it and raving rightly.[99]

Madness, like the spectacular plagues of the *Iliad* or Sophocles' *Oedipus*, requires interpretation; it is a sign from the gods that some offense has been committed, that some impurity stains the individual or the community and prevents positive relations with the divine. But experts are often needed to provide this interpretation, just as Kalkhas is summoned in the *Iliad* or Teiresias in Sophocles, since the cause of the divine anger may not be apparent.

Such hermeneutic experts are needed for any omen, although the magnitude of the omen usually determines the expertise required for its proper interpretation. No one would summon Teiresias to explain a chance sneeze – anyone nearby who cares will offer an interpretation. Such small-scale omens, like the weasel crossing the path or the owl's hoot, tend to indicate minor and immediate infractions, although they may be taken as the first warnings of divine anger about a larger matter. Such offenses may have occurred, not just in the recent past, but even much longer ago, and the business of the diviner is more often concerned with the past than the future, seeking out what event in the past has created the present sign rather than looking ahead to see what the consequences will be.[100] The transgressions of the past may be by the individual who receives the sign, be it the anomalous animal behavior or raving madness, but it may also indicate a crime committed by someone in the individual's community or by an ancestor of the individual. As Hesiod notes, often the whole community suffers from the injustice of a single person, and the cycles of crime and punishment over the generations provide tragedy with one of its greatest themes.[101]

---

[99] Pl. *Phdr.* 244de (*OF* 575 B = OF 3 K), Plotinus, *Enn.* 1.6.6 (*OF* 434iv): ἀλλὰ μὴν νόσων γε καὶ πόνων τῶν μεγίστων, ἃ δὴ παλαιῶν ἐκ μηνιμάτων ποθὲν ἔν τισι τῶν γενῶν ἡ μανία ἐγγενομένη καὶ προφητεύσασα, οἷς ἔδει ἀπαλλαγὴν ηὕρετο, καταφυγοῦσα πρὸς θεῶν εὐχάς τε καὶ λατρείας, ὅθεν δὴ καθαρμῶν τε καὶ τελετῶν τυχοῦσα ἐξάντη ἐποίησε τὸν [ἑαυτῆς] ἔχοντα πρός τε τὸν παρόντα καὶ τὸν ἔπειτα χρόνον, λύσιν τῷ ὀρθῶς μανέντι τε καὶ κατασχομένῳ τῶν παρόντων κακῶν εὑρομένη.

[100] Arist. *Rh.* 3.17.10 (1418a21–26) claims that the famous diviner Epimenides said that the diviner is concerned more for the past than the future.

[101] Hes. *Op.* 240. Aeschylus' *Oresteia* is, of course, the best example of the theme of inherited guilt, and the dramatic appearance of the Erinyes is an outstanding example of the depiction of divine anger.

The expert is needed, not just to diagnose, but also to prescribe the remedy for the problem. Although the means of purification are many and varied, there are two basic modes which may be distinguished in theory, although in practice they were seldom separated except in the most simple of procedures. Some rites of purification involve direct symbolic action, purging away or transferring the impurity, while others depend on soliciting divine action, making sacrifices or prayers to appropriate divinities who will remove the impurity or dissolve the divine anger. The first sort of actions fall into the class of performative acts, actions undertaken in a ritual manner that have a symbolic function, while the latter involve a supplication to the divine, but it would be a mistake to use the old magic/religion dichotomy to distinguish them. Although the performative acts of purgation do involve, to borrow the criteria Versnel has outlined, impersonal action rather than personal divine action, concrete and individual goals instead of intangible long-term goals, and an attitude of manipulation of the materials rather than a submissive attitude to divine will, the other associations modern scholars group with magic are not necessarily present – the anti-social aims or societal disapproval.[102] Likewise, although such rites are often seen by modern scholars as awkward survivals of primitive magical practices, no such denigration or even temporal separation from other kinds of practices appears in the ancient sources. Indeed, the performative acts of purification are often combined with the supplicative as a series of purifications or as various stages in complex rituals that have as their goal the purification of the individual (or community) and the establishment of more positive relations with the divinity.

In Aristophanes, when Bdelycleon tries to cure his father of his obsession with the courts, he treats him as a madman, afflicted by the gods, and subjects him to a series of cures, starting with generic purifications and culminating in the complex rituals of the Korybantes and incubation in the healing shrine of Asklepios.

> But he didn't obey, so he dragged him off for ritual purification. But he was still no better. After that he was doing the Korybantic rite, but the old man darted off still with the tambourine and, plunging right into the New Court, sat in as a juror. Since he got nothing from those rites, his son sailed off with him to Aegina and compelled him to lie one night in the

---

[102] For the criteria distinguishing magic from religion in modern scholarly discourse, see Versnel 1991. One of the factors that distinguishes Parker's excellent treatment of the subject from earlier studies is his avoidance of this evaluative dichotomy.

temple of Asklepios, but he popped up before daylight at the gate of the courts.[103]

None of these cures works, of course, this being comedy, but the range of possibilities open to an Athenian in the age of Perikles is instructive.

Prescriptions for purification

A brief survey of the means of purification available within Greek religion may prove useful to provide a context for practices that are labeled Orphic.[104] Certain common practices of purification are linked with Orpheus only insofar as those who practice them to an extreme are apt to be associated with the extreme purity of Orpheus. Within the category of performative purifications, purification by purgation may be distinguished from purification by transfer. Purgation involves symbolic removal of the impurity by contact with water, fire, air, or some other substance thought to wipe away the taint. Water, of course, is the simplest and most common element, easily available to anyone. Theophrastos' *deisidaimon*, who regularly visits the Orpheotelest for professional help in purification, also engages in frequent purifications of his own. He cleanses himself with water from three fountains on a daily basis, to rid himself of impurities he may have incurred unnoticed.[105] Such sprinkling with water was indeed a standard mode of purification, as the basins of lustral water, the *perirrhanteria*, placed outside temple sanctuaries attest. It was customary for someone entering the sacred space to sprinkle himself before entering, as a symbolic cleansing of the impurities of the profane world before entering the sacred space, but only the extreme purifiers would feel the need to so purify themselves before conducting their daily business.[106] Using

---

[103] Ar. *Vesp.* 118–124: ὁ δ' οὐκ ἐπείθετο. εἶτ' αὐτὸν ἀπέλου κἀκάθαιρ'· ὁ δ' οὐ μάλα. μετὰ τοῦτ' ἐκορυβάντιζ'· ὁ δ' αὐτῷ τυμπάνῳ ἄξας ἐδίκαζεν εἰς τὸ Καινὸν ἐμπεσών. ὅτε δῆτα ταύταις ταῖς τελεταῖς οὐκ ὠφέλει, διέπλευσεν εἰς Αἴγιναν· εἶτα ξυλλαβὼν νύκτωρ κατέκλινεν αὐτὸν εἰς Ἀσκληπιοῦ· ὁ δ' ἀνεφάνη κνεφαῖος ἐπὶ τῇ κιγκλίδι. Cp. the explanation of ἐκορυβάντιζεν by the scholiast *ad loc.*: τὰ τῶν Κορυβάντων ἐποίει αὐτῷ μυστήρια ἐπὶ καθαρμῷ τῆς μανίας.
[104] For further references, see Parker 1983: 232–234.
[105] Theophr. *Char.* 16.2: "The Superstitious Man is the kind who washes his hands in three springs, sprinkles himself with water from a temple font, puts a laurel leaf in his mouth, and then is ready for the day's perambulations." ὁ δὲ δεισιδαίμων τοιοῦτός τις, οἷος ἀπὸ τριῶν κρηνῶν ἀπονιψάμενος τὰς χεῖρας καὶ περιρρανάμενος ἀπὸ ἱεροῦ δάφνην εἰς τὸ στόμα λαβὼν οὕτω τὴν ἡμέραν περιπατεῖν. (Text and translation from Diggle 2004; see his explanation of the text, pp. 351–353.)
[106] As Diggle 2004: 353 notes, such purifications before sacred activity would be unremarkable; the point is that the *deisidaimon* does this without a special occasion. Cp. instances of preliminary purifications in Homer, *Il.* 1.449, 6.266–267, 9.171–174, 16.230, 24.302–305; *Od.* 2.261, 3.440–446,

water from three different sources is a comic exaggeration that appears also in a line from Menander that Clement of Alexandria cites to mock the superstitious and their fake cures for fake ills.

> If, O Phidias, you had any true problem, you should seek a true remedy for it. But now you have none, and I have found a fake cure for your fake problem. Consider how it will help you. Let women in a circle smear you around and sanctify you. Sprinkle water from three fountains, tossing in salt and lentils.[107]

Clement lists bits of wool, salt, torches, sulphur, and the squill plant as the sort of thing employed by sorcerers and charlatans who prey on the superstitious.[108] Theophrastos' *deisidaimon* uses squill, which, like hellebore, was probably chosen for its sharp smell, in a purification ritual.[109] Burning sulphur is used even in Homer for purification after Odysseus slaughters the suitors, and the combination of this sharp-smelling substance with fire creates an effect that symbolically washes away the bad things on an olfactory level, just as water does on a visual.[110] But the fire of torches, waved over the one being purified, could be used in the same way, as could the waving of a fan. Servius indeed claims that in all sacred rites there are three modes of purification – purging by fire and sulphur, washing by water, and ventilating by air. Servius links the airy method to the winnowing fan, also used as a basket, that was used agriculturally to separate the wheat from the chaff and ritually to separate the pure from the impure.[111] Iconographic evidence confirms the role of the winnowing fan,

---

4.750, 12.336; and Hes. *Op.* 724–725. For discussions, see Parker 1983: 19–20, as well as Ginouvès 1962: 311–313. Theophrastos' caricature also purifies himself with sea water whenever he gets the opportunity, καὶ τῶν περιρραινομένων ἐπὶ θαλάττης ἐπιμελῶς δόξειεν ἂν εἶναι (13), although Diggle condemns this line as an interpolation.

[107] Clem. Alex. *Strom.* 7.4.27 = Men. *Phasma* 50–56: εἰ μέν τι κακὸν ἀληθὲς εἶχες, Φειδία, | ζητεῖν ἀληθὲς φάρμακον τούτου σ᾽ ἔδει. | νῦν δ᾽ οὐκ ἔχεις· κενὸν εὑρὲ καὶ τὸ φάρμακον | πρὸς τὸ κενόν· οἰήθητι δὲ ὠφελεῖν τί σε. | περιμαξάτωσάν σε αἱ γυναῖκες ἐν κύκλῳ | καὶ περιθεωσάτωσαν· ἀπὸ κρουνῶν τριῶν | ὕδατι περίρραναι ἐμβαλὼν ἅλας, φακούς.

[108] Clem. Al. *Strom.* 7.4.26: "tufts of tawny wool, and lumps of salt, and torches, and squills, and sulphur, bewitched by sorcerers, in certain impure purifications." ἔρια πυρρὰ καὶ ἁλῶν χόνδρους καὶ δᾷδας σκίλλαν τε καὶ θεῖον δεδίασι, πρὸς τῶν γοήτων καταγοητευθέντες κατά τινας ἀκαθάρτους καθαρμούς.

[109] Theophr. *Char.* 16.13.   [110] *Od.* 22.481.

[111] Serv. *In Aen.* 6.471: "Wherefore in all sacred rites there are three such types of purifications. For either they purify by torch and sulphur, or they wash with water, or they ventilate with air, which is what it was in the rites of Liber." *unde etiam in sacris omnibus tres sunt istae purgationes: nam aut taeda purgant et sulphure, aut aqua abluunt, aut aere ventilant, quod erat in sacris Liberi.* Cp. Serv. *In Bucol.* 1.165: "That is the grain basket. Indeed it is said to be *mystic* and *of Iacchos* because the rites of Liber Pater pertain to the purification of the soul. And thus men are purified in his mysteries,

along with the torch, in mystery rituals that may be Dionysiac (as Servius suggests) or perhaps Eleusinian.[112]

None of these methods of purification provokes much criticism, even from the philosophers, nor are they associated with Orpheus or practitioners of Orphic rites, except when taken to extremes as by Theophrastos' *deisidaimon.* Some of the methods of transference, on the other hand, seem to draw more criticism and are lumped, from early on, with rituals that are seen as more extra-ordinary. The idea behind rituals of transference is no more complicated than that of purgation; instead of directly brushing away the impurity, using fire, air or water to remove the invisible taint, the impurity is transferred to another substance, a visible material that is then visibly removed. The same basic idea lies behind Theophrastos' *deisidaimon* throwing stones after a weasel has crossed his path, transferring the bad luck or other form of taint to the stones that are removed, or his waiting for another person to pass, so that the contamination passes to him.[113] The transfer of evils from the person to eggs in a ritual mentioned by Clement works in the same way: the person goes away pure, while the eggs retain the taint (and are perhaps then dedicated to Hekate).[114]

But the more dramatic forms of such purification involve smearing the one to be purified with blood or mud or some other impure material that is wiped off in the course of the ritual, leaving the subject clean and visibly purified. Herakleitos (deliberately) ignores the logic of the ritual that transfers the invisible impurity to the visible impurity and then removes both together, when he rails, "They purify themselves with other blood when they are polluted by blood, as if a man who had fallen into mud should

---

just as the grain is purified by the winnowing fans." *Id est cribrum areale.* **Mystica** *autem* **Iacchi** *ideo ait quod Liberi Patris sacra ad purgationem animae pertinebant: et sic homines eius Mysteriis purgabantur, sicut vannis frumenta purgantur.*

[112] For more on some of these images, including the so-called Torre Nova Sarcophagus (LIMC Ceres 146), the Lovatelli Urn (LIMC Ceres 145), and a fragment of terracotta also from the Lovatelli collection (LIMC Ceres 147), see Kinney 1994: 78–86, and Clinton 2003: 50–60, with further discussion in Edmonds 2006: 358–360.

[113] Theophr. *Char.* 16.3: "If a weasel runs across his path he will not proceed on his journey until someone else has covered the ground or he has thrown three stones over the road." καὶ τὴν ὁδὸν ἐὰν ὑπερδράμῃ γαλῆ, μὴ πρότερον πορευθῆναι, ἕως <ἂν> διεξέλθῃ τις ἢ λίθους τρεῖς ὑπὲρ τῆς ὁδοῦ διαβάλῃ.

[114] Clem. Al. *Strom.* 7.4.26.3: "Observe that the eggs, taken from those who have been purified, if they are warmed, produce living offspring. But this would not happen if they were taking on the evils of the man that had undergone purification." ὁρᾶν γοῦν ἔστι τὰ ᾠὰ τὰ ἀπὸ τῶν περικαθαρθέντων, εἰ θαλφθείη, ζωογονούμενα. οὐκ ἂν δὲ τοῦτο ἐγίνετο, εἰ ἀνελάμβανεν τὰ τοῦ περικαθαρθέντος κακά. Cp. Lucian, *De mort. Peregr.* 1.1, who refers to ᾠὸν ἐκ καθαρσίου left at the crossroads for Hekate as the sort of supper a poor cynic might pick up.

wash himself in mud."[115] Mud was indeed another possible substance for purification, as Demosthenes attests in his mockery of Aiskhines for assisting his mother in some mystery rite by purifying the initiates, wiping off (ἀπομάττων) the mud and the bran mash.[116] The same word for wiping off is used in connection with cheese cakes, which the lexicographer Hesykhios explains were used for purification, although the precise way they were used is left to our imagination.[117] In all these transfer purifications, the impure substance was then disposed of out of the way somewhere, leaving the purified one clean.[118]

These direct means of purification, by purgation or transfer, are often part of a more complex ceremony, like the Eleusinian preliminary purifications or the rites of Aiskhines' mother, which combine performative action with appeals for divine assistance through prayers and sacrifices.[119] When Theophrastos' *deisidaimon* goes to the priestesses for purification, purgation with squill (σκίλλη) is combined with the sacrifice of a puppy (σκύλαξ) to Hekate.[120] Plutarch seems to suggest that the sacrificed puppies then were used to smear those needing purification, a rite he calls περισκυλακισμόν ("puppifrication").[121] Of course, tangible offerings in the form of sacrifices or other dedications, combined with prayers or

---

[115] Herakleitos, 22 B 88 DK (fr. 41 Marcovich) = Plut. *Cons. Apol.* 106e (*OF* 454 B): καθαίρονται δ' ἄλλωι αἵματι μιαινόμενοι οἷον εἴ τις εἰς πηλὸν ἐμβὰς πηλῶι ἀπονίζοιτο. For more on purification with blood, which was not limited to purification from blood crimes, see Parker 1983: 371–373.

[116] Dem. 18.259 (*OF* 577i B = OT 205 K): καθαίρων τοὺς τελουμένους καὶ ἀπομάττων τῷ πηλῷ καὶ τοῖς πιτύροις. Harp. s.v. ἀπομάττων (36 Keaney) (*OF* 308ii, 577vii B = OT 206 K) claims that the mud coating is in imitation of the myth in which the Titans coated themselves with gypsum to dismember Dionysos. As Parker 1983: 231 comments on the Demosthenes passage, "the use of a bran mash for the same purpose is less easy to explain."

[117] Hsch. s.v. μαγίδες: μαγίδες· αἷς ἀπομάττουσι καὶ καθαίρουσι. καὶ μᾶζαι, ἃς καταφέρουσιν οἱ εἰς Τροφωνίου κατιόντες. μαγμόν· τὸ καθάρσιον· ἀπομάσσειν γὰρ λέγουσιν, ὅταν περικαθαίρωσι τοὺς ἐνοχλουμένους τινὶ πάθει. Note that the cakes are associated with those used in the ritual of the Trophonius oracle. Parker 1983: 231 n. 141 speculates that these cakes, like the eggs in Clement, may have been considered 'corpse food'.

[118] The best description of this disposal, which usually goes unmentioned in the ancient evidence, is in the Hippocratic polemic *Morb. sacr.* 1.100–102: "And some of the purifications they conceal in the earth, and some they throw into the sea, and some they carry to the mountains where no one can touch or tread upon them." Καὶ τὰ μὲν τῶν καθαρμῶν γῇ κρύπτουσι, τὰ δὲ ἐς θάλασσαν ἐμβάλλουσι, τὰ δὲ ἐς τὰ οὔρεα ἀποφέρουσιν, ὅπη μηδεὶς ἅψεται μηδὲ ἐπιβήσεται·

[119] See Clinton 2003 on the relation of preliminary purifications to the other stages of the Eleusinian Mysteries, although the terminological distinctions are perhaps not as clear and simple as Clinton argues. Cp. Dowden 1980.

[120] Theophr. *Char.* 16.13: "He calls for priestesses and tells them to purify him with a squill or a puppy." ἱερείας καλέσας σκίλλῃ ἢ σκύλακι κελεῦσαι αὑτὸν περικαθᾶραι. The wordplay between σκίλλη and σκύλαξ is probably deliberate and significant, but no evidence of contemporary exegesis survives.

[121] Plut. *Quaest. Rom.* 68 280c: "All the Greeks, so to speak, used to make use of a dog as the sacrificial victim for ceremonies of purification, and some do so even still. And for Hecatê they bring out puppies along with the other materials for purification, and they rub round about with puppies

hymns or other verbal means of offering honor to the deity, are the standard way to win the god's favor in Greek religion generally, so anyone seeking to appease divine anger or asking divine assistance would naturally employ such means. Some gods, however, specialize in turning away the consequences of impurity or divine anger, and gods such as Apollo, Zeus, and Athena bear epithets like Apotropaios, Soter, and Alexikakos, that indicate their aptitude for such purifications.[122] Damascius quotes some Orphic verses that praise Dionysos' power as the Releaser, Lysios.

> Dionysos is the cause of release, whence the god is also called the Releaser (Lyseus). And Orpheus says: "Men performing rituals will send hecatombs in every season throughout the year and celebrate festivals, seeking release from lawless ancestors. You, having power over them, whomever you wish you will release from harsh toil and the unending goad."[123]

The divine assistance may remedy any sort of impurity, from a minor infraction to a major impiety to an unpunished crime committed by someone in the community, either currently or among the ancestors long ago. Those sacrificing hecatombs at public festivals, or Plato's troubled folk, who visit the shrines of apotropaic deities when afflicted with an urge to commit sacrilege, are just the serious version of Theophrastos' ridiculous *deisidaimon*, who sacrifices to the apotropaic gods when a mouse nibbles through one of his bags.[124]

---

those who are in need of consecration, and they call this kind of purification *periskylakismos* ('puppification')." τῷ δὲ κυνὶ πάντες ὡς ἔπος εἰπεῖν Ἕλληνες ἐχρῶντο καὶ χρῶνταί γε μέχρι νῦν ἔνιοι σφαγίῳ πρὸς τοὺς καθαρμούς καὶ τῇ Ἑκάτῃ σκυλάκια μετὰ τῶν ἄλλων καθαρσίων ἐκφέρουσι καὶ περιμάττουσι σκυλακίοις τοὺς ἁγνισμοῦ δεομένους, περισκυλακισμὸν τὸ τοιοῦτο γένος τοῦ καθαρμοῦ καλοῦντες·

[122] Poll. *Onom.* 1.24 links the epithets of Apotropaios with Hikesios, Lysios, Katharsios, Phyxios, Soter, and others, signaling their shared functions. Epigraphic evidence attests to cults of Apollo Apotropaios in Attic Erchia, fourth century BCE (*LSAM* no. 18 A 33, G 33) and of Zeus Apotropaios in third-century BCE Erythrai (*LSAM* no. 25, 82). See further Farnell 1896: s.v. Zeus 130 (p. 166), s.v. 140–144 (pp. 172–174). Ἀπόλλον ἀποτρόπαιε appears as a protective invocation in Aristophanes (*Vesp.* 161, *Av.* 61, *Pl.* 359 and 854) and in later literature (Sopat. *Διαίρεσις ζητημάτων* 8.62.28; Nicephorus Basilaces, *Progymnasmata* 50.81; Aristaenetus, *Epist.* 2.1.8).

[123] Dam. *In Phd.* 1.11 (35 Westerink) (*OF* 350 B = OF 232 K): ια. Ὅτι ὁ Διόνυσος λύσεώς ἐστιν αἴτιος· διὸ καὶ Λυσεὺς ὁ θεός, καὶ ὁ Ὀρφεύς φησιν · | 'ἄνθρωποι δὲ τελήσσας ἑκατόμβας | πέμψουσιν πάσησιν ἐν ὥραις ἀμφιέτησιν | ὀργιά τ' ἐκτελέσουσι λύσιν προγόνων ἀθεμίστων | μαιόμενοι· σὺ δὲ τοῖσιν ἔχων κράτος, οὕς κε θέλησθα | λύσεις ἔκ τε πόνων χαλεπῶν καὶ ἀπείρονος οἴστρου'. Cp. Iambl. *Myst.* 3.10.14–16: τοῦ Σαβαζίου δ' εἰς Βακχείας καὶ ἀποκαθάρσεις ψυχῶν καὶ οἰκειότητα παρασκευάσται λύσεις παλαιῶν μηνιμάτων.

[124] Pl. *Leg.* 854ac (*OF* 37ii B); Theophr. *Char.* 16.6. Cp. references to the apotropaic deities to avert the omens of dreams in Aesch. *Pers.* 201–204, 216–219; Xen. *Symp.* 4.33; Hippoc. *Acut.* 4.89, at a sacrifice (Xen. *Hell.* 3.3.4), or for aid against diseases (Plut. *Conv. sept. sap.* 159f), or other unnatural occurrences (Plut. *de Am. Pro.* 497d). See further Parker nd s.v. Apotropaic Gods in *BNP*.

While a hecatomb could hardly be imagined as anything except a large public festival, the rites of the Korybantes, like the rites celebrated by Aiskhines' mother, seem not to have been publicly sponsored, but, at least at Athens, to have been carried out by private practitioners for their clientele.[125] From the descriptions in Classical sources, these rites seem to have involved prayers and sacrifices as well as the more direct means of purification. Such concerns for purity and closer relations with the divine appear also in the texts of the mysterious gold tablets, but we have very little idea of what sort of ritual practices might have produced these testimonies, labeled "Orphic" in modern scholarship since their first discovery. The fact that all the tablets with reliable information about their findspots have come from graves, in addition to the texts that provide information about the afterlife, suggests that they had some funerary function, but they might have also been involved in some kind of ritual before death.[126]

Three of the gold tablets from Thurii have the deceased's claim, "pure I come from the pure," which suggests some form of ritual purification, but the tablets provide no clear details about the process of purification that underlies such a claim. Some scholars have imagined a ritual based on the cryptic claims in A1 ("I flew out of the circle of wearying heavy grief; | I came on with swift feet to the desired crown; | I passed beneath the bosom of the Mistress, Queen of the Underworld") or even some sort of baptismal rite from the enigmatic "a kid I fell into milk" formula, but no plausible parallels exist for such imagined rites, and these lines are better understood as symbolic expressions of the initiate's experience than as literal representations of a mimetic rite.[127]

The two tablets from a grave in Pelinna instruct the deceased to "tell Persephone that Bacchios himself has freed you," which suggests the kind of release from divine anger that Dionysos Lysios specializes in, but again the tablet provides no details of how this process of release might have worked.[128] A tablet from Pherai justifies the request to join the *thiasos* of *mystai* in the afterlife by citing participation in the rites of Demeter Chthonia and the Mountain Mother.[129] The claim, on the tablets of the B type, to

---

[125] See Clinton 2003 for evidence of public sponsorship for Korybantic *thronosis* at Samothrace.

[126] A complete list of findspots, with some archaeological context, can be found in Edmonds 2011b: 41–48. Graf 1991 and 1993 raises the question of funerary context rather than pre-death initiation, while Riedweg 2011 suggests multiple ritual functions for the texts.

[127] Pure from the Pure: A1 (*OF* 488 B = OF 32c K) ln. 1, A2 (*OF* 489 B = OF 32d K) ln. 1, A3 (*OF* 490 B = OF 32e K) ln. 1, A5 (*OF* 491 B = OF 32g K) l.1. See Edmonds 2004a: 69–70. Ritual details: A1 (*OF* 488 B = OF 32c K) ll. 5–7, ln. 10. See Edmonds 2004a: 104–108.

[128] D1 (*OF* 485 B) and 2 (*OF* 486 B) ln. 2. See Edmonds 2004a: 60–61.

[129] D5 (*OF* 493a B) ln. 2): πέμπε με πρὸς μυστῶ<ν> θιάσους· ἔχω ὄργια [ἰδοῦσα] | Δημητρος Χθονίας, τε <τέ>λη καὶ Μητρὸς Ὀρεί[ας]. Regardless of the reconstruction of the end of the first

be the child of Earth and starry Heaven, like the claim in the Thurii tablets to be of Persephone's blessed race, suggests an alternate means of winning divine favor. Rather than using purification by ritual to achieve proximity to the divine, the deceased lays claim to a genealogical connection, like the heroes who trace their lineage to a divine parent or the autochthons who claim the parentage of Earth for their families. Such a boast of lineage enhances the deceased's appeal as a suppliant, begging for the favor of Persephone or asking the guardians for a drink of the water of Memory.[130] If the deceased buried with the gold tablet went through any ritual while still living, we might imagine a complex ritual that involved both such supplications and direct symbolic purifications. The evidence, however, does not allow us to uncover the exact nature of such a ritual, if indeed the tablets are the product of such a ritual, rather than simply being amulets sold to the relatives of the deceased by a ritual practitioner after her death.

The gold tablets provide no direct information about whether Orpheus was considered as the author of the hexameters in the tablet texts, but the extra-ordinary emphasis on purity, as well as the claims to superior connections with the gods, mark the gold tablets as the sort of materials that might well have been classified as Orphic by the ancient Greeks. The begging priests and diviners described in Plato, who make use of the books by Orpheus and Mousaios, advertise their rituals as being efficacious both before death and after, and no doubt some of the ritual experts who sought clientele ascribed the authority of Orpheus to their rituals. While such rituals of purification are credited to other mythic purifiers, such as Epimenides, Bakis, or Melampous, Orpheus remains the most prestigious and most widely cited founder of these rituals.

Orpheus as the founder of mysteries for the Mother

The discovery of the gold tablet from Pherai mentioning the rites of Demeter Chthonia and the Mountain Mother, which has caused so much difficulty for recent efforts to relegate all the gold tablets to the Bacchic mysteries, has, if anything, strengthened the case for attributing the tablets to an "Orphic" milieu – if such a context is properly understood.[131] Orpheus

---

line, the deceased's participation in ritual is the basis for the claim to preferential treatment in the afterlife.

[130] For the confrontation with Underworld guardians in the B tablets, see Edmonds 2004a: 61–63. For the claims to divine lineage, see Edmonds 2004a: 75–82, as well as Edmonds 2008b on the "child of Earth and starry Heaven" formula.

[131] Tablet D5 (*OF* 493a B). The place of Demeter and Meter in this tablet, like the name of Brimo in D3 (*OF* 493 B), reinforces the central importance of Persephone in the Thurii tablets (A1–3, A5

is perhaps most often associated with the rites of Demeter, as in the Orphic poems quoted by Sextus Empiricus and others that relate to the wanderings of Demeter in search of her daughter, Persephone, and her establishment of the Thesmophoria.[132] These rites were often identified with the rites of Isis, which Orpheus (or sometimes Melampous) was thought to have brought back to Greece from Egypt.[133] Theodoret identifies these Egyptian rites with both the Thesmophoria and the Eleusinian Mysteries, and other testimonies associate the founding of the Eleusinian Mysteries with Orpheus.[134] Several testimonies directly attribute the Eleusinian Mysteries to Orpheus, while others merely suggest the association by connecting the name of Orpheus to "the holiest of our mysteries."[135] Orpheus is also credited with founding the rites of Demeter Chthonia and Kore Soteira at Sparta, although it remains unclear how similar these rites might be to the Athenian Eleusinia or Thesmophoria.[136]

Orpheus is also connected with rituals for other goddesses related to Demeter and the story of Persephone's abduction, such as Hekate. Pausanias tells us that the Aiginetans claim that Orpheus founded the mysteries of Hekate on Aigina.[137] This attribution is clearly a local bid for the prestige of the panhellenically famous Orpheus, adding authority and antiquity to the rites of Hekate, which were the most important on the island. Orpheus'

from Rome [*OF* 488–491 B = OF 32c–e, g K]) and the two from Pelinna, D1 and D2 (*OF* 485–486 B). The two Pelinna tablets do have a significant role for Dionysos, as does D4 from Amphipolis (*OF* 496 B), but the mere reference to *mystai* and *Bacchoi* in B10 from Hipponion (*OF* 474 B), while sufficient to dispel Zuntz's arguments that the tablets had nothing to do with Dionysos, hardly suffices to make all the rest of the tablets Bacchic. The different tablets come from different religious contexts and appeal to special connections with different divinities to secure a favorable afterlife. See the attempts to explain away the problem in Graf and Johnston 2007: 121.

[132] See above ch. 6, *Poems for the Sacred Rites*.
[133] Diod. Sic. 1.96.3 (*OF* 48ii B = OT 96 K); for Melampous, cp. Clem. Al. *Protr.* 2.13.5 = Euseb. *Praep. evang.* 2.3.13 (*OF* 385 B).
[134] Thdt. *Graec. Aff. Cur.* 1.21 (108.21 Canivet) (*OF* 511 B = OT 103 K).
[135] Direct: *Marm. Par.* (*IG* xii.5 444) (*OF* 379, 513 B = OT 221 K); Clem. Al. *Protr.* 2.20.1–21.1 = Euseb. *Prep. evang.* 2.3.30–35 (*OF* 392iii, 391ii, 394i, 395i, 515i B = OF 52 K); Aristid. *Or.* 22.1 Keil (*OF* 516 B); Procl. *In R.* 2.312.16 Kroll (*OF* 517i B = OT 102 K), *Theol. Plat.* 6.11 (6.50.12 Saffrey-Westerink) (*OF* 517ii B = OT 102 K). Cp. [Dem.] 25.11 (*OF* 512 B = OT 23 K): ὁ τὰς ἁγιωτάτας ἡμῖν τελετὰς καταδείξας Ὀρφεύς. Cp. also Ar. *Ran.* 1032 (*OF* 510, 626i B = OT 90 K). Eur. *Rhes.* 938–949 (*OF* 511 B = OT 91 K) refers to Athenian mysteries for Persephone, while Diod. Sic. 4.25.1 (*OF* 514, 713ii, 916 B = OT 97 K) names Mousaios, son of Orpheus, as the founder of the Eleusinian Mysteries. Ov. *Met.* 11.92 (*OF* 499, 527ii B = OT 160 K) refers to Orpheus handing over rites to Eumolpos, which are presumably the Eleusinian ones.
[136] Paus. 3.14.5 (*OF* 533 B = OT 108 K), 3.13.2 (*OF* 534 B = OT 109 K). Note that Pausanias also refers to a statue (ξόανον) of Orpheus in the shrine of Demeter Eleusinia on Mount Taygetus, 3.30.5 (*OF* 1085 B), which further suggests a connection with Eleusinian rites.
[137] Paus. 2.30.2 (*OF* 535i B = OT 120 K); cp. Origen *C. Cels.* 6.22 (*OF* 535ii B), Lib. *Orat. pro Aristoph.*14.5 (2.89.13 Foerster) (*OF* 535iii B), for further attestations of the Hekate mysteries, although with no mention of Orpheus.

name is used often in such competitions for prestige, and the claims of various sources contradict one another freely. Hippolytos, in his polemic against the gnostics, who derive their ideas from pagan mysteries, claims that the Phlyan mysteries of Megale, the great mother Earth, were founded before those of Demeter at Eleusis, but that both derive their doctrines from the theology of Orpheus. There is little reason to accept Hippolytos' account of the highly sexualized nature of the rites, but that mystery rites at Phyla were associated with Orpheus and with Meter, Ge, or Demeter is confirmed by other testimonies.[138] The presence of other deities in the sanctuaries at Phlya need not complicate the fact that the mysteries themselves are centered around Megale, nor does the particular constellation of deities provide any real insight into the nature of the rites performed there.[139]

Orpheus is linked, not just with the Great Mother at Phlya, but also with the Phrygian Mother of the Gods. Plutarch identifies the rites of Bona Dea in Rome with those of the Phrygian Meter and claims that they greatly resemble the Orphica, again associating the rites of Orpheus with ecstatic celebrations for a maternal goddess.[140] Just as Orpheus passed down the Eleusinian rites to Cecropian Eumolpos, Ovid tells us, so too he passed down the Phrygian rites to Midas, and Midas appears as the intermediary for Orpheus' teachings in a number of sources.[141] Apollonios,

[138] Hippol. *Haer.* 5.20.4 (*OF* 532i B = OF 243 K). Cp. Paus. 9.27.2 (*OF* 531i B = OF 305 K), 9.30.12 (*OF* 531ii, 682 B = OF 304 K), where Pausanias claims to have seen the mysteries of the Lycomidae at Phlya himself and attests to hymns by Orpheus used in the ceremonies. Paus. 4.1.5–9 recounts a myth whereby a descendant of the eponymous Phlyos brought the rites of the Great Goddesses from Eleusis to Messene, thereby linking the rites at Phlya to both the Eleusinian and Andanian mysteries. Paus. 1.22.7 (*OF* 1119 B) also mentions a hymn to Demeter for the Lycomidan rites at Phlya, composed by Mousaios, that proclaims Phlyos a child of Earth (if not also of starry Heaven).

[139] Cp. Paus. 1.31.4: "Phlya and Myrrhinus have altars of Apollo Dionysodotus, Artemis Light-bearer, Dionysus Flower-god, the Ismenian nymphs and Earth, whom they name the Great goddess; a second temple contains altars of Demeter Anesidora, Zeus Ctesius, Tithrone Athena, the Maid First-born and the goddesses named the Semnae. The wooden image at Myrrhinus is of Colaenis." Φλυεῦσι δέ εἰσι καὶ Μυρρινουσίοις τοῖς μὲν Ἀπόλλωνος Διονυσοδότου καὶ Ἀρτέμιδος Σελασφόρου βωμοὶ Διονύσου τε Ἀνθίου καὶ νυμφῶν Ἰσμηνίδων καὶ Γῆς, ἣν Μεγάλην θεὸν ὀνομάζουσι· ναὸς δὲ ἕτερος ἔχει βωμοὺς Δήμητρος Ἀνησιδώρας Διὸς Κτησίου καὶ Τιθρωνῆς Ἀθηνᾶς καὶ Κόρης Πρωτογόνης καὶ Σεμνῶν ὀνομαζομένων θεῶν· τὸ δὲ ἐν Μυρρινοῦντι ξόανόν ἐστι Κολαινίδος. *Contra*, e.g., Casadio 1989: 1336, who suggests that the presence of Apollo with Dionysos is "una chiara allusione al mito del salvataggio di Dioniso da parte di Apollo dopo lo sparagmos titanico." See Bernabé 2004: 104 for further bibliography on the issue. Ultimately, we should remember the cautious analysis of Graf 2003.

[140] Linforth 1941: 244 shrewdly comments: "One suspects that when a Greek writer had occasion to speak of *foreign* orgiastic ritual and was reminded of *Greek* orgiastic ritual, he was naturally led to refer to the Greek ritual as Orphic." Here it is the ecstatic intensity of the rituals that prompts the classification, rather than the authority or antiquity claimed for them.

[141] Ov. *Met.* 11.92 (*OF* 499, 527ii B = OT 160 K): *Midan, cui Thracius Orpheus orgia tradiderat cum Cecropio Eumolpo.* Cp. Conon, *FGrH* 26 F 1.1 *ap.* Phot. *Bibl.* 186.130b 28 (*OF* 527i B = OT 160 K); Just. *Epit.* 11.7.14 (*OF* 527iv B = OT 160 K), Clem. Al. *Protr.* 2.13.3 (*OF* 527iii B = OT 160 K).

however, depicts Orpheus as inventing the rites for Phrygian Rhea for the Argonauts on their voyage. The Argonauts need to propitiate her and the Idaean Dactyls when the winds turn against them after they accidentally slaughter their hosts, the Doliones, and Orpheus sets up a ritual dance for youths in arms and armor, like that of the Kouretes or Korybantes.[142] Orpheus is also credited with devising the rituals of Korybantic enthronement for the Mother in a list of Orphic works preserved in the *Suda*.[143] Plato may hint at such a connection between Korybantic rites and Orpheus when he has Alkibiades quote the familiar Orphic opening tag ("close the doors of your ears") when talking of the Korybantic frenzy inspired by the words of Socrates.[144] The late *Orphic Argonautica* plainly lists the works of the Korybantes and Kouretes as some of the past themes of Orpheus' songs:

> the famous rending of Kasmilos and of Heracles, the rites of Ida, the mighty Korybantes. The wandering of Demeter and the great grief of Persephone and how she became Thesmophoros. And then the glittering gifts of the Kabeiroi, and the ineffable oracles of Night concerning lord Bacchos, and most holy Lemnos and seagirt Samothrace.[145]

---

[142] Ap. Rhod. *Argon.* 1.1117–1151 (*OF* 526 B). For the dances of the Kouretes and Korybantes, see Strabo 10.3.22 and the studies by Blakely 2000 and 2006, as well as Edmonds 2006.

[143] *Suda* s.v. Ὀρφεύς (ο 654, III.565.5 Adler) (*OF* 605i, 835, 1102 B = OT 175, 223d K), although the Orphic pseudepigrapha are credited to Nikias of Elea. West 1983: 9 traces this list back to Epigenes in the fourth century BCE. Note that the *Suda* also credits the historical poet Pindar with composing such *thronismoi*. See further Edmonds 2006: 351.

[144] Pl. *Symp.* 218b (*OF* xxviii B = OF 13 K). At 215ce, Alkibiades compares Socrates' words to the tunes of Marsyas: "The tunes alone can make people possessed, and disclose those who are in need of the gods and for the *teletai*. You differ from him only to this extent, that, with bare words and without instruments you do the same thing.... For, whenever I hear them, my heart pounds and my tears pour out – even more than among the Korybantes – from the effect of this man's words." μόνα κατέχεσθαι ποιεῖ καὶ δηλοῖ τοὺς τῶν θεῶν τε καὶ τελετῶν δεομένους διὰ τὸ θεῖα εἶναι. σὺ δ' ἐκείνου τοσοῦτον μόνον διαφέρεις, ὅτι ἄνευ ὀργάνων ψιλοῖς λόγοις ταὐτὸν τοῦτο ποιεῖς.... ὅταν γὰρ ἀκούω, πολύ μοι μᾶλλον ἢ τῶν κορυβαντιώντων ἥ τε καρδία πηδᾷ καὶ δάκρυα ἐκχεῖται ὑπὸ τῶν λόγων τῶν τούτου.

[145] *OA* 24–29 (*OF* 1018v B = OT 224 K): Κασμίλου τε καὶ Ἡρακλέος περίφημον ἄμυξιν· | ὀργιά τ' Ἰδαίων, Κορυβάντων τ' ἄπλετον ἰσχύν. | Δήμητρός τε πλάνην, καὶ Φερσεφόνης μέγα πένθος, | θεσμοφόρος θ' ὡς ἦν· ἠδ' ἀγλαὰ δῶρα Καβείρων, | χρησμούς τ' ἀρρήτους Νυκτὸς περὶ Βάκχου ἄνακτος, | Λῆμνόν τε ζαθέην ἠδ' εἰναλίην Σαμοθράκην. The Kabeiroi, often identified with the Kouretes and Korybantes, appear in the Argonautic Orpheus' list not only in the references to their cult sites of Lemnos and Samothrace, but also in the tale of the rending of Kasmilos, one of the names given the Kabeiroi in Samothrace. Cp. ΣAp. Rhod. *Argon.* 1.917 (78 Wendel), who identifies Kasmilos as Hermes and the others as Demeter, Hades, and Persephone. Herakles, also mentioned in *OA* 24, is sometimes identified as one of the Idaean Dactyls. Cp. Strabo 10.3.22. Clem. Al. 2.19.4 (*OF* 520 B) assimilates the Kabeiroi to the Korybantes and claims that the rites have to do with the head of the murdered brother or with the phallus of Bacchos (here perhaps identified with the brother), which the brothers take to Etruria. Cp. Firm. Mat. *Err. prof. rel.* 11.

Orpheus is also credited by Ephorus with instituting *teletai* learned from the Idaian Dactyls themselves, as Diodorus Siculus relates.[146] Diodorus elsewhere also associates Orpheus, not only with the Eleusinian Mysteries, but also with the Kabeiroi and the mysteries in Samothrace, just as the *Orphic Argonautica* includes these among Orpheus' prior themes.[147]

In all this evidence, the name of Orpheus is a mark of distinction conferred upon these rites, marking them as extra-ordinary in several ways. In some cases, like the foundation of the rites of the Phrygian Rhea in Apollonios or Hekate's mysteries in Aigina, the connection with Orpheus lends authority – the divine singer himself set forth the ritual. In others, like Plutarch's assimilation of the rites of Bona Dea, the Phrygian Meter, and the Orphica, the name of Orpheus marks the unusual intensity, the ecstatic character of the rites, providing a Greek label for things otherwise marked as foreign and strange.

Orpheus as the founder of Bacchic rites

The label of Bacchic often has similar connotations, indicating rituals that seem, in their intensity and wildness, somehow unHellenic, just as Dionysos always appears as a stranger, coming in from the outside. Earlier generations of scholars took this alien nature literally, imagining a historical invasion of Dionysiac cult, just as they attributed the ecstatic mysteries of Demeter or Meter to a late invasion from the barbaric and mystical Orient. Evidence such as the tablets from Pylos and Khania with the name of Dionysos in Linear B indicates that Dionysos is no newcomer, and the myths of the incursion of Dionysos or the Metroac mysteries are best understood as expressions of the stamp of strangeness that the Greeks always felt to mark these religious activities – the alien within.[148] The name of Orpheus was another way to mark this internal alien status, and many sources credit Orpheus with the creation of Dionysiac mysteries.

---

[146] Ephorus, *FGrH* 70 F 104 *ap.* Diod. Sic. 5.64.4 (*OF* 519, 940i B = OT 42 K).

[147] 4.43.1 (*OF* 522 B = OT 105 K) and 4.48.6 (*OF* 523 B) = Dion. Scyt. *FGrH* 32 F 14 (= fr. 18 Rusten). In 5.77.3 (*OF* 529 B), Diodorus attributes the Eleusinian and Samothracian mysteries to things Orpheus learned in Crete.

[148] Palaima 2004: 448–449. Tablet KH Gq5 from Khania records the offering of honey to Dionysos, while a tablet from Pylos (PY Ea 102) refers to a fire altar for Dionysos. Detienne 1986: 57 refers to "Dionysos, le dieu qui vient," arguing that "l'epiphanie du dieu et ses commencements parmi les hommes et les cités de la Grèce" are "l'essence de sa nature divine." Detienne draws on the earlier work of Otto to reject the historicizing understanding of the advent of Dionysos found in Rohde and others. Rohde 1925: 253–266, e.g., describes the invasion of Dionysiac cult, bringing the seeds of the belief of the immortality of the soul. The works of Henrichs have done the most to shift previous understandings of Dionysos.

Although various sources claim that Orpheus founded particular Demetriac rites in specific places, the sources that credit Orpheus with Dionysiac rites tend to be more general, giving him credit for the invention of all Dionysiac mysteries or for a particular type, rather than for, say, the rites of Dionysos Lysios in Megara. Often Orpheus is depicted as the agent who popularized and transmitted the rites of Dionysos to the Greeks, composing the hymns and the rituals, acting, as Clement puts it, as the poet of the mysteries.[149] Diodorus recounts how Orpheus learned the rites of Dionysos from earlier Thracian kings, who had received them directly from Dionysos, and, since Orpheus modified and passed them on to all, Dionysiac *teletai* are often called Orphic.

> . . . the rites which afterwards Orpheus, the son of Oiagros, learned from his father. Orpheus, who excelled all men by nature and by education, also made many changes in the rites, wherefore the rites which had been established by Dionysus were also called "Orphic."[150]

Diodorus' generalization, however, does not always hold, even within Diodorus' own work, since he also relates that the Egyptians claim that the rites for Dionysos, son of Semele, in Thebes are Orpheus' adaptation of the Egyptian rites for Osiris, whereas the Cretans claim that the rites of Dionysos, son of Zeus and Persephone, were taken by Orpheus from Crete.[151] Other sources similarly limit Orpheus' connection to the Dionysiac rites to a particular Dionysos out of a list of many. Diodorus connects the Orphic rites for Dionysos with the particular Dionysos born from Demeter, who comes second in his historicizing account of three figures with the name of Dionysos.[152] Cicero links the Orphic rites to the fourth Dionysos on his list, the one born of Jove and Luna, in contrast to the one born from Proserpina, the child of Cabirus to whom the Sabazian

---

[149] Clem. Al. *Protr.* 2.17.2 (*OF* 306i, 588i B = OF 34 K); cp. Euseb. *Praep. evang.* 2.3.23; Palaeph. Περί ἀπίστων 33 (50.7 Festa) (*OF* 500 B); Apollod. *Bibl.* 1.3.2 (*OF* 501, 901ii, 954ii, 987, 1035i B = OT 63 K); Joannes Lydus, *De mens.* 4.53 (109.13 Wünsch) (*OF* 504 B = OT 101 K); Lactant. *Div. inst.* 1.22.15 (234 Monat) (*OF* 505 B = OT 99 K); Aristid. *Or.* 41.2 Keil (*OF* 328i, 684 B = OF 307 K); Pomp. Melam 2.17 (*OF* 924 B = OT 33 K); Damagetus, *Anth. Pal.* 7.9 (*OF* 1071 B = OT 124 K); Thdt. *Graec. Aff. Cur.* 1.21 (108.21 Canivet) (*OF* 511 B = OT 103 K), 1.114 (132.25 Canivet) (*OF* 51iiii B = OT 100 K), 2.32 (147.9 Canivet) (*OF* 51ii B).

[150] Diod. Sic. 3.65.6 (*OF* 502, 893 B = OT 23 K): τελετάς, ἃς ὕστερον Ὀρφέα τὸν Οἰάγρου μαθόντα παρὰ τοῦ πατρός, καὶ φύσει καὶ παιδείᾳ τῶν ἀπάντων διενεγκόντα, πολλὰ μεταθεῖναι τῶν ἐν τοῖς ὀργίοις· διὸ καὶ τὰς ὑπὸ τοῦ Διονύσου γενομένας τελετὰς Ὀρφικὰς προσαγορευθῆναι. As Linforth 1941: 219 notes, "the story, as it is told, is a device to reconcile the view which prevailed among mythographers that Dionysus had founded the mysteries himself, with the fact that they were called Orphic and the legend that Orpheus was the great originator of mysteries."

[151] Diod. Sic. 1.23.2 (*OF* 48iii, 327iv, 497iv B = OT 95 K); 5.75.4 (*OF* 283i, 311xii, 530 B = OF 303 K).

[152] Diod. Sic. 3.64.1, cp. 3.62.8 (*OF* 58 B = OF 301 K).

mysteries are dedicated, or even the one born of Thyone for whom the trieteric festivals are celebrated.[153] Not all Bacchic mysteries, then, are Orphic,
but the label of "Orphic" may be applied to various Dionysiac mysteries
by different authors.

Some sources even draw a distinction between Orphica and Bacchica,
even while they lump them together as extra-ordinary ecstatic religious
rites. Strabo, in concluding his survey of the various ecstatic religious rites,
from the Kouretes and Korybantes to the Satyrs and Kabeiroi, puts the
Orphic rites in the same classification with the Dionysiac: "sorcery and
magic are closely related to religious frenzies, worship, and divination.
And such also is devotion to the arts, in particular to the Dionysiac and
Orphic arts."[154] When Plutarch describes the wild rituals that Alexander's
mother performed in barbaric Macedonia, he claims that, "all the women
there having been extremely addicted to the Orphica and the ritual festivities pertaining to Bacchos," they performed rituals like those of the
Thracians.[155] Plutarch here distinguishes the Orphic rites and the Bacchic
orgia as two different types of extra-ordinary rituals, which Olympias takes
to even more barbaric extremes. Not all Orphic mysteries, then, are Bacchic, either; the categories may overlap differently in the perspective of
different sources.[156]

Proclus speaks of those being consecrated (τελούμενοι) through Orpheus
to Dionysos and Kore,[157] and the sources do frequently locate Orphic rituals
in the service of these two deities and the ones associated with them, be it
Kore's mother and attendants or the Bacchic band of maenad nymphs and
satyrs. The idea, however, that there are two types of Orphica, Demetriac
and Bacchic, while not entirely misleading, is too simplistic. First, these

---

[153] Cic. *Nat. D.* 3.58 (*OF* 497i B = OT 94 K): *Dionysos multos habemus: primum Iove et Proserpina
    natum; secundum Nilo, qui Nysam dicitur interemisse; tertium Cabiro patre, eumque regem Asiae
    praefuisse dicunt, cui Sabazia sunt instituta; quartum Iove et Luna, cui sacra Orphica putantur
    confici; quintum Nyso natum et Thyone, a quo trieterides constitutae putantur.* Cp. Joannes Lydus,
    De mens. 4.51 (107.10 Wünsch) (*OF* 327i B, 497ii = OT 94 K), where the fourth Dionysos is listed
    as the son of Zeus and Semele. As Linforth 1941: 223–225 notes, it is likely that some confusion
    of Semele for Selene produced Luna as a mother for Dionysos in Cicero, but it remains unclear
    whether such confusion was deliberate wordplay or linguistic error.
[154] Strabo 10.3.23 (*OF* 670 B = OT 216 K): τῶν δ' ἐνθουσιασμῶν καὶ θρησκείας καὶ μαντικῆς τὸ
    ἀγυρτικὸν καὶ γοητεία ἐγγύς. τοιοῦτον δὲ καὶ τὸ φιλότεχνον μάλιστα τὸ περὶ τὰς Διονυσιακὰς
    τέχνας καὶ τὰς Ὀρφικάς.
[155] Plut. *Vit. Alex.* 2.7 (*OF* 579 B = OT 206 K): πᾶσαι μὲν αἱ τῇδε γυναῖκες ἔνοχοι τοῖς Ὀρφικοῖς
    οὖσαι καὶ τοῖς περὶ τὸν Διόνυσον ὀργιασμοῖς.
[156] Cp. the famous Venn diagram in Burkert 1977: 1–10, that portrays Orphic, Bacchic, and Eleusinian
    as overlapping circles. In general, such a diagram provides a good sense of the interrelation of these
    categories, although with the proviso that each source might define the boundaries differently.
[157] Procl. *In Ti.* 3.297.8 Diehl (*OF* 348i, 598 B = OF 229 K).

rituals themselves intertwine, as the presence of Bacchic Iacchos (son of Semele) in the Eleusinian Mysteries or of Rhea in various versions of the dissolution and reintegration of Dionysos (whether through madness or dismemberment) attests.[158] Second, the classification Orphic, as I have argued, is a polemic label, not a factual statement about the content of the thing so labeled. The label could be applied to mysteries honoring Demeter and Persephone, or their attendants, or to rites honoring Dionysos, in any one of his various forms, but it was not applied consistently to any of these, so we cannot designate any particular ritual as Orphic or deduce objective criteria by which to separate the Orphic rites from the non-Orphic.

Conclusion: The Orphic label for rites and people

The name of Orpheus, then, was a tag that was used to label both certain rituals and the people who were associated with them, either as ritual experts or as their clients, but the collection of rites and people found in the ancient evidence never adds up to a coherent set of people or practices that could be defined as Orphic. Neither the ritual experts nor their clients ever thought of themselves as "Orphics", nor did participation in any of the different rites or practices attributed to the founding genius of Orpheus ever constitute an "Orphic life" of the kind set by Plato in the mythic past of the Golden Age. The practices of purification and the more complex mystery rituals and other *teletai* attributed to Orpheus in the ancient evidence cannot be separated by any kind of defining criterion from the same kind of practices and rituals that were not so attributed. The choice to attribute a rite or practice to Orpheus depends rather on the specific purpose of the source making the attribution. To be sure, Orpheus was credited with only certain kinds of rituals; he was the inventor of mysteries or *teletai*, not sacrifice or ritual curses. The rituals with which the name of Orpheus is associated, however, are distinguished, not by their form and mechanics or by the deities to whom they are addressed, but rather by their distance from normal ritual practice. A practice of purification

---

[158] For Iacchos as a local form of Dionysos in Eleusinian and other contexts, cp. Soph. *Ant.* 1146–1154, Eur. *Bacch.* 725, and especially ΣAr. *Ran.* 479: ἐν τοῖς Ληναϊκοῖς ἀγῶσι τοῦ Διονύσου ὁ δᾳδοῦχος κατέχων λαμπάδα, λέγει, καλεῖτε θεόν. καὶ οἱ ὑπακούοντες βοῶσι, «Σεμελήϊ’ Ἴακχε πλουτοδότα». Graf 1974: 51 refutes Mylonas 1961: 238, cp. 318, for the identification. Clinton 1992: 66–67 remains cautious about a complete identification. For the connection of Rhea and Dionysos, cp. Ath. 5.201 (with Pl. *Leg.* 672bd), referring to the story that Dionysos was healed of madness by Rhea; a different version appears in Nonnos, *Dion.* 9.137–169. For Rhea as the agent in restoring the dismembered Dionysos, see, e.g., Corn. *ND* 30 (58.6 Lang) (*OF* 59iv B). For the presence of Rhea and the Kouretes and Korybantes in Bacchic cult, cp. Eur. *Bacch.* 120–132.

may be linked with Orpheus, not because Orpheus invented it or because it differs in form from any other normal type of purification practiced in the cities of Greece, but merely because the one who engages in it, like Euripides' Hippolytos, takes it to an extra-ordinary, abnormal extreme. A *teletê* may be labeled Orphic because Orpheus is the first inventor of all such rites that create a special relation with Demeter or with Dionysos, or the Orphic label may be applied to guarantee the prestige of this greatest of ritual founders for the local festival, to distinguish it from all others. The Orphic label may signify the scorn and contempt for the outlandish practices of disreputable charlatans or, albeit less frequently, it may mark the exceptionally pious man who has dedicated his time and resources to an extra-ordinary extent to preserve his purity and to honor the gods beyond the normal expectations.

Orphic rituals of purification purge the participants from the same taints of disease, madness, misfortune, or simple anxiety that all other purification rites within the Greek religion do, whether the impurities are caused by the individual or one of his ancestors. Every individual has different faults to redress, but only the exceptional individual is so concerned with the anger of the gods as to spend excessive amounts of energy trying endlessly to purify himself. In none of the evidence for purifications is there any indication that all mortals must atone for the same, single sin; indeed, the diversity of anxieties and the obsession with multiple purifications and rituals provide the comedians and other critics with much fodder in their attacks on the superstitious fools they associate with Orpheus and his rituals. Theophrastos' client of the Orpheotelest does not go monthly to purify himself from the murder of Dionysos Zagreus; he undertakes that experience to cleanse himself of all the incidental impurities that, despite all his neurotic precautions on a daily basis, he has nevertheless managed to acquire. Plutarch's caricature of the superstitious man may worry about ancestral crimes as much as his own, just like the rich clients mentioned by Plato, but none of them are concerned with a universal Titanic heritage staining all mankind. It is rather the differences in their fortunes and that of others that provokes them to seek special ritual treatment to avert the anger of the gods.

While there may well have been individuals like Hippolytos who, through their extra-ordinary attempts to maintain purity, became the object of scorn from their fellow citizens, there is no evidence that people living the Orphic life were a recognizable part of Greek society at any time in the nearly thousand-year span from which our evidence comes – in contrast to, say, the Pythagoreans or the Christians. While individual ritual practitioners no doubt paraded their piety with ostentatious displays of abstinence, figures such as the chorus of prophets of Zeus in Euripides' *Cretans* belong in the imaginary along with other features of Golden Age mythology. And, while such figures could be associated with Orpheus, their extra-ordinary practices of purity and long list of ritual credentials are not necessarily (and nowhere explicitly) linked to the sometime mythic founder of such practices.

Extra-ordinary purity is a cue with greater validity for evidence from the earlier periods, especially the Classical, than for the evidence of the early Christian writers and even the Neoplatonists. For these writers, Pythagoras is linked to practices of purity more often than Orpheus, even if Pythagoras is at times said to have derived his ideas from Orpheus. The emphasis on Orphic purity was revived in modern scholarship, when nineteenth-century scholars were seeking the roots of early Christian practices. The idea of Orphic puritanism played its part in the European scholarly debates over religion that were deeply influenced by the conflicts between Protestant and Catholic Christianity, and the Classical evidence linking Orpheus and purity was deployed in the reconstructions of Orphic religion.[159]

Even if the Orphic "church" imagined by Macchioro and his contemporaries is no longer taken seriously, the modern scholar's vision of Orphics living their Orphic life, celebrating Orphic rituals because of their Orphic beliefs, is still based on a model of religious organization unsuited to the practices of Greek religion as the ancient evidence presents it to us. This reconstruction is based upon the model of a doctrinal religion, like Christianity, rather than the imagistic model that better suits the social structures of ancient Greek religious practice. Whereas a doctrinal religion defines its religious communities through the regular practice of certain rituals that encode certain fundamental doctrines, anthropologists of religion such as Whitehouse have shown that another mode of religious practice, the imagistic religion, relies on individual experiences without communicable doctrines.[160] While scholars have imagined Orphism as doctrinal, the evidence better supports an imagistic system, in which rites attributed to

---

[159] Cp. Harrison 1922: 461 on a vase image of the death of Orpheus: "Orpheus was a reformer, a protestant; there is always about him a touch of the reformer's priggishness; it is impossible not to sympathize a little with the determined looking Maenad who is coming up behind to put a stop to all this sun-watching and lyre-playing." For the Protestant/Catholic debates, see above all Smith 1990.

[160] Cp. Whitehouse 2000: 14: in imagistic traditions, "virtually no attempt was made to communicate religious ideas as bodies of doctrine. Revelations were codified in iconic imagery, transmitted primarily through the choreography of collective ritual performances. Religious representations were structured as sets of revelatory images connected by loose (and somewhat fluid) thematic associations, rather than as cohering strings of logically connected dogma."

Orpheus are performed in extraordinary circumstances for extraordinary effects – expiation of past crimes that are bringing the anger of the gods now, fear of approaching death, etc. The superstitious man, the one who takes Orpheus as his lord, engages in these activities all the time, has continuous extraordinary experiences, lives life in full crisis mode. As such he is either an object of awe or of ridicule, depending on whether his extraordinary efforts are seen as worthwhile or not. The label of Orpheus' name marks the extra-ordinary, the absurdly superstitious or the extremely pious, the bizarre barbarian practice or the most ancient and holy of rites. Such practices, and the people who engage in them, are what receive the label of "Orphic" in the ancient evidence, and this evidence – properly considered – fills in the gap left by the absence of Orphics in our ongoing attempts to understand the nature and practices of ancient Greek religion.

CHAPTER EIGHT

Life in the afterlife
The initiates' privilege and the mythic tradition

Life in the afterlife

The survival of the dead is in some sense a culture universal, since it is undeniable; they survive in our memories of them, in the consequences of their acts, in their judgement of us which we carry with us internalized as an ethical standard. Most people have imagined this persistence as the presence of the dead in some kind of other world; since that world represents the dead for the living it will be an extension of this one.[1]

If the survival of the dead is indeed a culture universal, the question, in any given culture and at any given time, is how that survival is understood and articulated, how that other world is imagined. The survival of the dead through the memory of the living, however, is rarely the primary way such survival is conceptualized; an elaborately depicted world of the dead holds far more fascination. Different tellings within the Greek mythic tradition elaborate different aspects of the afterlife to suit their various purposes, but the category of Orphism is often defined in modern scholarship precisely by the presence of certain kinds of ideas about the afterlife, the nature and fate of the soul.

Orphic ideas of the soul and afterlife are most often defined by explicit contrast with the Homeric view of the afterlife, which is taken as the standard view for ancient Greek culture. As Parker puts it, "Orphic poetry can almost be defined as eschatological poetry, and it was in such poems perhaps that 'persuasive' accounts of the afterlife – accounts designed, unlike that in *Odyssey* xi, to influence the hearer's behaviour in the here and now – were powerfully presented for the first time."[2] In this section,

---

[1] Redfield 1991: 105. Recent scholars (such as Boyer 2001) have turned to cognitive psychology to reaffirm this idea, showing that people tend to attribute mental and emotional activities to deceased people even while affirming that their physical functions have ceased. I have articulated an earlier version of some of these ideas about the Homeric afterlife in Edmonds 2011d.

[2] Parker 1995: 500. Not only does such a claim ignore the mass of Orphic material on other subjects (which indeed Parker mentions elsewhere in his discussion), but it suggests that the Homeric *nekyia*

I argue that such an approach provides a misleading picture not only of Orphic ideas of afterlife, but even of the normative ideas in ancient Greek culture about the nature and fate of the soul, in life and afterwards. The ideas in Homeric poetry that are usually taken to be standard in fact represent a special perspective that stresses the power of poetry to provide immortality through memory, while the range of ideas that are actually marked in the ancient evidence as extraordinary or linked with Orpheus and his ilk is much smaller. The persistence of the soul and the lively afterlife are not the exclusive province of Orphism but rather the normal and most widely accepted ideas in the tradition. Only a limited range of ideas about the relation of the soul to the body seem consistently to be labeled, in some way or other, as Orphic in the evidence.

In their attempts to define Orphism by its doctrines, scholars over the past century and a half have put forth various lists of Orphic doctrines, but Bernabé has recently listed the central points of Orphic doctrine that have met with (more or less) general agreement: a belief in a soul–body dualism, an idea of an original sin (or *peché antécédent*) from which purification can be sought to attain salvation, and the idea of a cycle of reincarnations over which this process occurs.[3] I argue, to the contrary, that the dualism of the soul and body is an idea found throughout the tradition, whereas reincarnation is only found occasionally in texts labeled Orphic (even in its broadest sense) and cannot be read back into other texts. While a number of Orphic texts do emphasize the idea of purification, the idea of an Orphic doctrine of original sin is a modern fabrication, and the idea of obtaining a favorable afterlife (salvation) is not in itself an idea restricted to Orphism. The attempt to define Orphism by these doctrines includes in the category evidence that was never regarded as Orphic by the ancients themselves, as well as attributing all of these doctrines to evidence that displays only some or none of these ideas.

The supposed centrality of these doctrines to Orphism accounts in large part for the interest that Orphism has aroused over the last century and a half, since scholars regarded Orphism as the channel through

---

had no effect on the behavior of its audiences. Any traditional tale, particularly so influential a myth as the *Odyssey nekyia*, provides for its audience a model of the world and for behavior within it. See Edmonds 2004a: 4–13.

[3] Bernabé 1998a: 172: "El creyente órfico busca la salvación individual, dentro de un marco de referencia en que son puntos centrales: el dualismo alma-cuerpo, la existencia de un pecado antecedente, y el ciclo de trasmigraciones, hasta que el alma consigue unirse con la divinidad." Cp. Bernabé 1997: 39, Bernabé 2002d: 208–209. Guthrie 1952: 73 puts the same ideas in less guarded terms: "The Orphic doctrines included a belief in original sin, based on a legend about the origin of mankind, in the emphatic separation of soul from body, and in a life hereafter."

which the idea of the immortality of the soul, as well as the idea of sin and salvation, entered the Judaeo-Christian tradition. "It was the Orphic Mysteries," proclaims Smyth, "that gave birth to the most profound ideas of Greek religion – the divine origin of the soul, its eternal nature, and personal immortality."[4] Dieterich's influential *Nekyia* seeks to trace the Christian imagery of Hell back to Orphic sources, while Macchioro's *Orpheus to Paul* derives the theology of St. Paul from Orphic beliefs.[5] The contrast between the idea of mere persistence of souls beyond physical death and a true and authentic idea of immortality of the soul has been seen as the contrast between the dreary Homeric afterlife, where everyone shares the same bleak fate, and the other visions of a more lively afterlife, with different fates for different folks.[6] In his fundamental study of the issue, Rohde argues for the evolution of a real idea of the immortality of the soul coming from new ideas of the soul and of afterlife that arise out of the Dionysiac invasion and the Orphic reform. For Rohde, drawing upon the ideas of his friend Nietzsche, Dionysiac ecstasy provided the worshiper with a mystic identification with the deity, a feeling of immortal life, but it was only the rationalizing (Apolline) ideas of the Orphics that shaped this primitive feeling into a real doctrine.[7] Hence, by this argument, the Orphics are responsible for the entry into Greek religion of a real concept of the immortality of the soul, and the appearance of such ideas in other texts can be attributed to the influence of the Orphics.[8]

---

[4] Smyth 1912: 274. Cp. Moore 1912: 113–114: "Whatever extravagances Orphism fell to, it must be kept in mind that it had introduced into the European world certain doctrines pregnant with spiritual fruit. . . . It remained for Plato to bring the Orphic seed to fruit by giving an intellectual basis to the doctrine of the divine nature of the soul, which he thus raised out of the plane of mere emotional belief."

[5] Dieterich 1893; Macchioro 1930.

[6] Rohde 1925: 9 complains: "To speak of an 'immortal life' of these souls, as scholars both ancient and modern have done, is incorrect. They can hardly be said to *live* even, any more than the image does that is reflected in the mirror; and that they prolong to eternity their shadowy image-existence – where in Homer do we ever find this said?"

[7] Rohde 1925: 266: "Reflexion upon the nature of the world and of God, the changing and deceptive flow of appearance with the indestructible One Reality behind it; the conception of a divinity that is One, a single light that, divided into a thousand rays and reflected from everything that is, achieves its unity again in the soul of man: such thoughts as these, allied to the dim half-conscious impulse of an enthusiastic dance-worship, might allow the pure waters of the stream of mysticism to run clear at last, freed from the turbid and unsatisfying enthusiasm of popular religious practices."

[8] Cp. Lucas 1946: 67: "The modern reader, baffled and dismayed by the apparent crudity of much of conventional Greek religion, is inclined to look everywhere for signs of Orphism, because it gives more of what he has come to expect from religion, and he is loath to believe that the Greeks did not demand it too."

Even though the historical premises of Rohde's argument have long since been rejected, the relation of the Homeric ideas of afterlife to the Orphic is still relentlessly depicted in terms of a chronological development. Thus, for example, despite her caveats, Johnston's recent survey of Greek beliefs of death and afterlife takes the lifeless afterlife in Homer as primary in both time and importance. "In earliest times, the Greeks apparently believed that everyone got the same deal after death . . . The souls existed in a state that was not unpleasant but not particularly enjoyable."[9] Other views are presented as later developments, starting with the Archaic period – or rather with the elements in Homer (and Hesiod) that seem to clash with the ideas that are presumed to be "earliest."[10] Despite the notorious problems of dating the Homeric epics or even various elements within them, scholars have put forth a circular argument: the earliest material can be identified as the truly Homeric idea of afterlife, while the later material can be identified as such because it conflicts with the truly Homeric version, which is the earlier. The problem, I suggest, lies in the confusion of the world *in* the Homeric poems with the world *of* the Homeric poems, that is, the world of their audience. The ideology of death and afterlife expressed in the Homeric poems does not necessarily correspond to the ideas that were generally accepted by the audiences of the Homeric poems over the years in which the poems were being composed and performed.[11] Rather, the poems articulate their own ideology of death and afterlife that resonates with the ideas of heroic glory and the poetic celebration thereof within the poems. Scholars have mistaken the special ideology within the poems for the ideas of death and afterlife of the audience outside the poems.

---

[9] Johnston 2004: 486.
[10] Cp. Albinus 2000: 16: "The Archaic attitude towards death was confined to remembrance and adoration of the dead through hero-cult and epic song. Under the sway of Homeric discourse, the fate of mortals was regarded, with only a few exceptions, as a departure for the House of Hades, inhabited by the ghost-like images of former lives. However, a specific interest in the *hereafter*, representing a continuation of individual existence in its own right, developed from the Archaic to Classical times, much under the influence of Orphic discourse, and accompanied by extensive changes in social life." Sourvinou-Inwood 1995 links the shift in attitudes to death and afterlife to the rise of the city-state and sees the role of Orphic sectaries merely as developing the most extreme form of the ideas.
[11] *Pace* Rohde 1925: 26: "If the Homeric creed had not been so constructed in essentials that it corresponded to the beliefs of the time, or, at least, could be made to correspond, then it is impossible to account (even allowing for the poetic tradition of a school) for the uniformity that marks the work of the many poets that had a hand in the composition of the two poems. In this narrow sense it can be truly said that Homer's poems represent the popular belief of the time." Sourvinou-Inwood 1995 has a far more nuanced model, but she still assumes that the Homeric poems represent the earliest stage of a development of ideas.

The Homeric afterlife

The Homeric epics present a mixed picture of what happens to an individual after death, but scholars have focused on one element in that picture as the standard view of the afterlife, not just in Homer but in Greek religion more broadly. This supposedly standard view is that the souls of the dead lack all mind or force; once a hero leaves the light of the sun, only a grim, joyless and tedious existence awaits, with no particular suffering but no pleasure either. Such a view is supported by a few key passages in the epics. The shade of Patroklos refers to the other ghosts as ψυχαὶ εἴδωλα καμόν-των – souls, phantoms of the worn out, and Achilles encapsulates this view after his dream vision of Patroklos: "Ah me! So even in the house of Hades there is something, a soul and a phantom, but the wits are not there at all." Whatever it is (τις) that survives lacks φρένες, the force of mind or emotion that is an essential element of the living individual.[12] Achilles' lament at the condition of the soul of the deceased comes after he has attempted to embrace the shade of his dearly departed companion, and the same pathetic scene produces the same idea when Odysseus tries to embrace the shade of his mother in the Underworld. She tells him that she is not a trick or false image, but "this is the appointed way with mortals when one dies. For the sinews no longer hold the flesh and the bones together, but the strong might of blazing fire destroys these, as soon as the life leaves the white bones, and the spirit, like a dream, flits away, and hovers to and fro."[13] This idea is reinforced in the *Odyssey* when Circe describes Teiresias as the only shade in the Underworld who has retained his mind (νόον); all the rest are mere gibbering ghosts, unable to speak or think without the blood supplied by Odysseus' ritual.[14] This bleak vision of death and afterlife is fundamental to the Homeric idea of the hero's choice – only in life is there any meaningful existence, so the hero is the one who, like Achilles, chooses to do glorious deeds. Since death is inevitable, Sarpedon points out, the hero should not try to avoid it but go out into the front of

---

[12] *Il.* 23.103–104: ὢ πόποι ἦ ῥά τίς ἐστι καὶ εἰν Ἀΐδαο δόμοισι ψυχὴ καὶ εἴδωλον, ἀτὰρ φρένες οὐκ ἔνι πάμπαν. Cp. *Il.* 23.72. For differing approaches to the components of the Homeric self, see for example Claus 1981 or Clarke 1999: 42–47.

[13] *Od.* 11.218–222: ἀλλ' αὕτη δίκη ἐστὶ βροτῶν, ὅτε τίς κε θάνῃσιν. | οὐ γὰρ ἔτι σάρκας τε καὶ ὀστέα ἶνες ἔχουσιν, | ἀλλὰ τὰ μέν τε πυρὸς κρατερὸν μένος αἰθομένοιο | δαμνᾷ, ἐπεί κε πρῶτα λίπῃ λεύκ' ὀστέα θυμός, | ψυχὴ δ' ἠΰτ' ὄνειρος ἀποπταμένη πεπότηται. Rohde and others have taken this statement to imply that it is the process of cremation that removes the φρένες and θυμός from the soul that goes to Hades, but see below.

[14] *Od.* 10.493–495: "Teiresias whose mind (*phrenes*) is still firm. To him alone even in death has Persephone left his consciousness (*noos*), but the other shades just flit about." τοῦ τε φρένες ἔμπεδοί εἰσι· τῷ καὶ τεθνηῶτι νόον πόρε Περσεφόνεια, οἴῳ πεπνῦσθαι, τοὶ δὲ σκιαὶ ἀΐσσουσιν.

battle and win honor and glory.[15] Such glory (κλέος) is the only thing that really is imperishable (ἄφθιτον), the only meaningful form of immortality, since the persistence of the soul after death is so unappealing.[16] As powerful as this grim vision of the afterlife is in the Homeric epics, commentators since antiquity have noticed that this uniformly dreary life for the senseless, strengthless dead is not the only vision of afterlife presented in the Homeric poems.[17] Outside the few passages that emphasize the helplessness of the shades, the Homeric references to life after death provide a much more lively picture of the afterlife, a picture that corresponds with the evidence found outside the Homeric epics. The dead have feelings and emotions, memories of their lives in the sun, and the ability to know of and even interfere in the world of the living. They appreciate the attentions paid to them by the living, not simply the burial and funeral rituals, but the offerings made subsequently at the tomb. Moreover, the world of the dead itself is not so dreary, nor are all the shades merely flitting about, gibbering mindlessly. The pursuits of the dead mirror the world of the living, and the social hierarchies of the living world persist in some form after death. This afterlife is not uniform for all; those who have angered the gods continue their punishments in the afterlife, while those who have won their favor continue to enjoy its benefits. This differentiated afterlife is in direct conflict with the uniformly dreary one that underscores the importance of the heroic glory.

Sourvinou-Inwood has pointed out that the supposedly standard view of the dreary afterlife is actually confined to a very few emphatic passages surrounding the encounter of Achilles with the shade of Patroklos and Odysseus' journey to the Underworld, while the lively afterlife appears in a broader range of contexts. The scenes with Achilles and Patroklos or Odysseus and his mother are notable for their pathos, but, while these few passages clearly articulate the idea that the shades of the dead live mindless and meaningless existences,[18] the other references to the life after death are much less marked, suggesting that the audience needs less grounding to accept the ideas of lively afterlife introduced in them. It is the ideas of

---

[15] *Il.* 12.322–328.

[16] Thus, even Achilles, who chose to die young and glorious, would rather be alive again, although he does not repudiate his earlier choice and is delighted (γηθοσύνη) to hear that his son, Neoptolemos, is also securing himself immortality through his glorious deeds (*Od.* 11.486–540).

[17] Sourvinou-Inwood 1995: 84 n. 210: "The vividness of the Homeric image of the senseless ghosts is so strong and striking in its starkness that it has coloured modern scholars' visions of this Hades; without doubt it is partly responsible for the monolithic interpretations put on it."

[18] As Claus 1981: 98 notes of *Il.* 23.103–104, "What is impressive about these lines is not that they explain the particular nature of the shade but that they show a need to explain and define."

mindless shades and lifeless afterlife that need careful handling – put in the mouths of authoritative speakers like Achilles, Circe, and Odysseus as explanations of strange visions, these ideas are marked as special, in contrast to the expected and accepted ideas of a lively afterlife. As Sourvinou-Inwood notes, "Outside this context he [Homer] does not stick to the constraints of the belief in witless shades; for to him (and to his audience), by whom the belief in the lively shades was taken for granted, the articulation of behaviour or belief involving the shades as lively did not register as other than 'natural'."[19]

Even within the Homeric poems, many of the dead seem to have consciousness, feel emotions such as joy and anger, and have awareness of the world of the living. Gallons of ink have been spilled by scholars over the millennia trying to reconcile these inconsistencies in the Homeric text with the idea that Teiresias is the only shade with νόος before drinking the blood, but such solutions cannot resolve all the problems. One might imagine that Achilles can only feel sorrow at being in Hades and joy for his son's achievements because he has drunk the blood, but Ajax can recall their past quarrel and remain angry at Odysseus while sulking at a distance.[20] So too, Achilles worries in the *Iliad* lest Patroklos get angry at learning that he has given Hektor's corpse back to his father. Patroklos is now safely cremated and celebrated in funeral games and thus fully integrated into Hades; if the "rule" of the standard version is that the deceased loses all consciousness once cremated, Patroklos should have no way of knowing what Achilles has done nor any emotions to feel if he did learn.[21]

This conflict has been explained in many ways by scholars of many different approaches. The two basic modes, however, may be categorized as "survivals" and "interpolations," that is, the conflict is usually explained by the persistence of an older idea or the addition of a newer idea. Either

---

[19] Sourvinou-Inwood 1995: 79, referring to *Od.* 11, *Od.* 10.493–495, *Il.* 23.103–107. "But if, as I suggest, the filters of both poet and audience were shaped by a belief in a Hades which (whether or not it was explicitly hierarchically articulated) involved inhabitants with faculties, values, and behaviour-patterns at least minimally comparable to those they had in life, Achilles' superior status in Hades would have appeared 'only common sense', and so accepted unexamined" (80).

[20] Cp. Zaborowski 2005. The shade of Elpenor, to take another example, can plead with Odysseus for burial and threaten retribution, but these signs of intelligence and emotion have been taken as indication that the rules of the mindlessness of the dead do not apply to those still unburied.

[21] Rohde championed the view, based on *Od.* 11.221–222, that cremation is the point at which the soul loses the φρένες and θύμος, and that a shift from cremation to inhumation in the post-Homeric period brought new ideas of the survival of consciousness for the soul (or brought them back from previous periods of inhumation). Sourvinou-Inwood 1981: 33, however, relying on more recent archaeology that tracks the variation between practices at different times and in different regions, points out: "The choice between cremation and inhumation can be shown to be a matter of fashion, with no significance." Cp. Snodgrass 1971: 143–147.

older ideas of lively dead have survived into the Homeric era and remain fossilized in the text, or the older text of Homer has been altered by the intrusion of new conceptions of the afterlife which are alien to its original essence. Some scholars try a combination of both approaches, explaining the interpolations as revivals of an older substratum of belief, perhaps Mycenaean.[22] In any case, the Homeric attitude toward death and afterlife remains an anomaly, a hiatus between periods of different beliefs. As Rohde comments, "If we think how different it must have been before the time of Homer, and how different it certainly was after him, we can hardly help feeling surprise at finding at this early stage of Greek culture such extraordinary freedom from superstitious fears in that very domain where superstition is generally most deeply rooted."[23]

These inconsistencies cease to be problematic if we understand that the lively afterlife in Homer is in fact the rule rather than the exception, that the bleak and lifeless afterlife appears only to highlight the epic alternative of poetic immortality. In the imagination of the living, the souls of the dead retain their consciousness and memory, their abilities to think and emote, just as they retain the distinguishing marks of their former physical selves.[24] Many scholars have traced the idea of a conscious soul that lives a lively afterlife from the earliest extant writings onwards, in poetry and prose, from tragedy, comedy, and lyric to the writings of the historians and philosophers. As Claus concludes from his study of the word, "The development of the ψυχή as a psychological agent in popular usage after Homer does not seem to be owed to the introduction into Greece of new conceptions of the afterlife or to the development of some new sense of psychological sense-conception after Homer."[25] Rather, there is a continuity of usage between the Homeric references to the soul and its actions and other forms of Greek literature: the ψυχή is a life force that survives the death of the body and preserves certain elements of personality.

---

[22] Cp. Sourvinou-Inwood 1995: 77 n. 193, arguing specifically *contra* Rohde 1925: 38. Note the recurrence of geologic metaphors of fossils, substrata, intrusions, and the like, since geology provided the framework for the theories of evolution (both biological and cultural) that were developed in the nineteenth century.

[23] Rohde 1925: 24.

[24] An image of the deceased represented like the living person but with the wounds that caused his death appears in Homer (*Od.* 11.40–41), where Odysseus sees "many fighting men killed in battle, stabbed with brazen spears, still carrying their bloody armor on them," as well as on numerous vases, where the depiction of dead men with bandaged wounds was a recognized topos. Plato manipulates this idea in the *Gorgias*, where souls retain the scars of their wrongdoing (see Edmonds 2012). Dodds 1959: 379 *ad loc.* points out the tradition of scarred souls following Plato: Lucian, *Catapl.* 24–29; Philo, *Leg.* 1.103; Plut. *De sera* 22 564d; Epictetus, *Diss.* 2.18.11; Tac. *Ann.* 6.6; Them. *Or.* 20 234a.

[25] Claus 1981: 181.

The evidence of cult reinforces the conclusion that the audiences of Homer, in every age, would have generally imagined the dead to retain some form of consciousness and awareness of the world of the living. Although the changes in burial practice from the Iron Age to the Hellenistic world were numerous and complex, with significant variations in different regions, most of the practices that can be reconstructed – placing grave goods in the tomb, making regular offerings as well as special dedications and requests – attest to the idea that the dead retained some connection to and awareness of the world they had left. As Johnston concludes, "Greek funerary rites attest to the expectation that the deceased had some sentience in the afterlife and some of the same desires that he or she had while alive, and to the idea that the living could – and should – gratify those desires."[26] Indeed, so important was the performance of these rites that the right to inherit property could hinge on them, and Athenian law speeches show that this was an important consideration in the adoption of an heir.[27] Properly satisfied dead could bring benefits to the community, be it the family or the polis,[28] while the unsatisfied dead could become the source of trouble – disease, madness, drought, etc.[29] Nor is this idea purely a later development; not only do the Erinyes in Homer personify the anger of the dissatisfied dead, but Odysseus, while he is performing libations and sacrifices to the dead at the entrance to the Underworld, even makes an elaborate promise to perform further rituals upon his return to Ithaka for the satisfaction of the dead.[30] As Sourvinou-Inwood comments, "These ritual acts necessitate shades able to register, and rejoice at, rites addressed

[26] Johnston 1999: 43. See Humphreys 1980 for discussion of the Athenian evidence for family tombs; Whitely 1995 discusses the archaeological debates over the evidence.

[27] The idea comes up in several of the speeches of Isaios (Isae. 2.10, 37; 6.65; 8.38–39); cp. Arist. [*Ath. Pol.*] 55; Xen. *Mem.* 2.2.13. See further Johnston 1999: 39.

[28] The idea of the helpful dead appears, e.g., in Pl. *Leg.* 927b1–4; specific requests to the dead for aid occur in tragedy, e.g., Soph. *El.* 1066–1081; Eur. *HF* 490–495, *Hel.* 961–968, *El.* 678–681, *Or.* 1225–1245. In Ar. fr. 322 KA, dead heroes boast of their influence over the world of the living.

[29] Johnston discusses Herodotus' tale (5.92η) of Melissa, the wife of Periander of Corinth, who compelled him to strip the women of Corinth to provide the clothes that he had neglected to put in her grave. "Melissa's proof not only reveals Periander's personal proclivities but shows that she knows what has been happening in the upper world since she died, as does her knowledge of where Periander's lost object can be found. Finally, the story shows that dealing with the dead may become a civic concern even if their anger is caused by the act of a single citizen" (Johnston 1999: viii).

[30] *Od.* 11.29–33: "I swore many times to the strengthless heads of the dead that, when I returned to Ithaka, I would slaughter in my halls a barren cow, whichever one was the best, and heap up the pyre with treasures, and to Teiresias alone, apart from the rest, I would dedicate an all-black ram, the one which stood out from all in our flocks." πολλὰ δὲ γουνούμην νεκύων ἀμενηνὰ κάρηνα, | ἐλθὼν εἰς Ἰθάκην στεῖραν βοῦν, ἥ τις ἀρίστη, | ῥέξειν ἐν μεγάροισι πυρήν τ' ἐμπλησέμεν ἐσθλῶν, | Τειρεσίη δ' ἀπάνευθεν ὄϊν ἱερευσέμεν οἴῳ | παμμέλαν', ὃς μήλοισι μεταπρέπει ἡμετέροισι. Cp. *Od.* 10.521–526.

to them by Odysseus both in Hades and in Ithaca; they thus make sense in terms of, and so can be seen as refracting, a funerary ideology in which ritual acts were addressed to shades capable of registering, and rejoicing at, them."[31] Homer's audience, in whatever era, would have understood such rituals, not as pointless mummery vainly trying to attract the witless dead, but rather as a meaningful attempt to influence conscious entities who could make a substantive response.

In most of the evidence, then, the dead are not witless ghosts, faintly moaning as they flit mindlessly about, and the afterlife is indeed different for different people. Even in Homer, the world of the dead is much like that of the living, and individuals pursue their own activities as they did in life. Orion continues his hunting, while Minos continues giving judgment and resolving conflicts, suggesting that, in the world of the dead, the shades carry on with the characteristically Greek pursuit of lawsuits.[32] Minos' position among the dead, not to mention Achilles', suggests that the social hierarchies from the world of the living are reproduced in the land of the dead – the gods' favorites remain favored. Likewise, those who won favor from the gods by their deeds in life continue to reap the benefits, while those who incurred the wrath of the gods continue to suffer their displeasure. Much ingenuity has been needlessly exercised in the attempt to explain away the punishments of Tantalos, Tityos, and Sisyphos in the Homeric *nekyia* so that their suffering does not contradict the mindlessness of the dead, but those three simply represent notable figures who are suffering in the afterlife, just as Odysseus also meets other notables with different fates.[33] The Erinyes appear in oaths (*Il.* 3.276–280; 19.259–260) as figures who punish beneath the earth those who have transgressed oaths, but the Homeric poems do not elaborate, as other sources do, on the range of crimes and punishments, as well as punishers.

Differentiated afterlives

The fifth-century BCE painting of Odysseus in the Underworld by Polygnotos, which Pausanias saw at Delphi, provides a wider selection of punishers

---

[31] Sourvinou-Inwood 1995: 77. Rohde 1925: 38, by contrast, refers to these rituals as "what can only be called an oversight" that "hopelessly contradicted" the poet's previous ideas.

[32] Vase paintings depict the dead engaged in a variety of pleasant pursuits – games like *pessoi* or dice – and Pind. fr. 130 S.-M. (*OF* 440 B) has the dead engaging in horsemanship, gymnastics, and lyre-playing as well. Cp. Garland 1985: 68–72.

[33] *Pace* Sourvinou-Inwood 1986, there is no reason to imagine they didn't really die or that they are "cosmic" sinners or otherwise representative of special kinds of crimes.

and punished. In addition to the ones mentioned in the *Odyssey*, Polygnotos depicts a man who maltreated his father being abused in turn by the
father, while someone who committed sacrilege is left to the attentions of
a *pharmakeutria*, a witch or a poisoner.[34] Further torments are provided
by a horrible monster named Eurynomos – a demon unknown, Pausanias notes, to the *nekyiai* of the *Odyssey*, the *Minyas*, and the *Nostoi*. A
Demosthenic speech attests to other such paintings depicting the afterlife
torments of the impious,[35] and the idea of afterlife punishment is common
enough for Plato to depict the old man Kephalos as starting to think that
perhaps he might have something to worry about after death. Kephalos
refers to myths he has heard – not special doctrines but familiar traditional
tales – that assign punishment in the afterlife for injustices committed in
life. While he had not taken them seriously while younger, he says that
the approach of death causes people to examine their lives to see if they
will have any penalties to pay.[36] Those who discover crimes they have not
paid for get anxious, while those who can't think of any wrongs they have
done are buoyed up by hope.[37] Indeed, those who have won the favor of
the gods during their lives can expect that the gods will care specially for
them after death as well, as Hypereides claims in his funeral oration.[38]

While this basic idea of a differentiated afterlife seems both traditional
and widespread, the precise way in which the differentiations were made

---

[34] Paus. 10.27–31.

[35] [Dem.] 25.53: The speaker condemns his opponent: "But he is implacable, unsettled, unsociable;
he has no kindness, no friendliness, none of the feelings which an ordinary person knows; all those
things with which the painters depict the impious in Hades – Curses, Blasphemy, Envy, Faction,
Strife, with those will he be surrounded. This man, then, who is not likely to propitiate the gods in
Hades, but to be cast among the impious because of the depravity of his life . . . will you not punish
him?" ἀλλ' ἄσπειστος, ἀνίδρυτος, ἄμεικτος, οὐ χάριν, οὐ φιλίαν, οὐκ ἀλλ' οὐδὲν ὧν ἄνθρωπος
μέτριος γιγνώσκων· μεθ' ὧν δ' οἱ ζωγράφοι τοὺς ἀσεβεῖς ἐν Ἅιδου γράφουσιν, μετὰ τούτων, μετ'
ἀρᾶς καὶ βλασφημίας καὶ φθόνου καὶ στάσεως καὶ νείκους, περιέρχεται εἶθ' ὃν οὐδὲ τῶν ἐν Ἅιδου
θεῶν εἰκός ἐστιν τυχεῖν ἵλεων, ἀλλ' εἰς τοὺς ἀσεβεῖς ὠσθῆναι διὰ τὴν πονηρίαν τοῦ βίου . . . οὐ
τιμωρήσεσθε;

[36] Pl. *Resp.* 330d–331a (*OF* 433iii B). Kephalos is a good representative of the common tendency not
to believe that any such justice or retribution will concern one personally until faced with the
imminent prospect. Cp. Pl. *Grg.* 523a and 527a. The Derveni author too rebukes those who refuse
to believe in the terrors of Hades; col. V.6 (*OF* 473 B): Ἅιδου δεινὰ τί ἀπιστοῦσι;

[37] Of course, most people tend to assume that nothing they have done is really all that bad. As
Garland 1985: 17 notes, "There is little evidence for the claim that the majority of Greeks spent
their declining years consumed with guilty foreboding at the prospect of making a reckoning in
the hereafter. Fear, combined with a healthy fatalism, seems to be the worst that the average Greek
moribund had to cope with."

[38] Hyp. 6.43: "But if in Hades there is still some consciousness and care from some divinity, as
we believe, then it is likely that those who defended the honors of the gods, when they were
being destroyed, would meet with the greatest solicitude from the divinity." εἰ δ' ἔστιν αἴσθησις
ἐν Ἅιδου καὶ ἐπιμέλεια παρὰ τοῦ δαιμονίου, ὥσπερ ὑπολαμβάνομεν, εἰκός τοὺς ταῖς τιμαῖς τῶν
θεῶν καταλυομέναις βοηθήσαντας πλείστης κηδεμονίας ὑπὸ τοῦ δαιμονίου τυγχάνειν . . .

varies in the evidence. Kephalos describes the process that every person might go through of self-judgment, but other sources attest to the idea of judges who decide the fate of the deceased, be it the gods in a vague and unspecific sense or particular entities who carried out a detailed process of examination. In the *Laws*, Plato refers to the idea that the soul must give an account of its life to the gods as an ancestral belief (ὁ νόμος ὁ πάτριος), and the Platonic *Seventh Letter* urges belief in the ancient and holy accounts (τοῖς παλαιοῖς τε καὶ ἱεροῖς λόγοις) that tell of judges that provide punishment for wrongdoing committed in life.[39] Other sources specify the judges as Underworld divinities – Hades or a Zeus below the earth – or as particular semi-divine figures, Minos, Rhadamanthys, Aiakos, and even Triptolemos.[40] Plato's assignment of Minos as the judge of newly dead souls at *Gorgias* 524a (*OF* 460 B) is a clever bit of creative misprision of *Od.* 11.568–571, while the choice of Rhadamanthys may likewise adapt the reference in *Od.* 4.564.[41] Socrates includes Triptolemos among the judges at *Apology* 41a (*OF* 1076i B = OT 138 K), which may suggest that the idea was connected, for the Athenians, with the Eleusinian Mysteries.[42] Perhaps the earliest extant reference to the process of judgment comes in Pindar's *Second Olympian*, where an unspecified judge assigns recompense for the deeds of life, a blissful existence without toil for the good, unbearable toil for the bad.[43]

---

[39] Pl. *Leg.* 959b4: "It is well said that the bodies of the dead are just images of those who have died, but that of each of us which is truly real, the soul which we say is immortal, departs to the presence of other gods, there (just as our ancestral tradition says) to render its account. For the good this is a thing to inspire courage, but for the evil great dread." καὶ τελευτησάντων λέγεσθαι καλῶς εἴδωλα εἶναι τὰ τῶν νεκρῶν σώματα, τὸν δὲ ὄντα ἡμῶν ἕκαστον ὄντως, ἀθάνατον εἶναι ψυχὴν ἐπονομαζόμενον, παρὰ θεοὺς ἄλλους ἀπιέναι δώσοντα λόγον, καθάπερ ὁ νόμος ὁ πάτριος λέγει – τῷ μὲν γὰρ ἀγαθῷ θαρραλέον, τῷ δὲ κακῷ μάλα φοβερόν. Pl. *L.* 7.335a3–5: "But truly it is necessary always to believe the ancient and holy accounts which reveal to us that the soul is immortal and that it has judges and pays the greatest penalties, whenever someone is released from his body." πείθεσθαι δὲ ὄντως ἀεὶ χρὴ τοῖς παλαιοῖς τε καὶ ἱεροῖς λόγοις, οἳ δὴ μηνύουσιν ἡμῖν ἀθάνατον ψυχὴν εἶναι δικαστάς τε ἴσχειν καὶ τίνειν τὰς μεγίστας τιμωρίας, ὅταν τις ἀπαλλαχθῇ τοῦ σώματος. *Pace* Bernabé, not all references to ancient tradition in Plato (and elsewhere) refer to Orphic sources. At times, such references refer, not to esoteric formulations from extraordinary sources, but on the contrary to the best known and most widely accepted traditions.

[40] Aesch. *Eum.* 273–274: "Great Hades is the auditor for mortals there under the ground." μέγας γὰρ Ἅιδης ἐστὶν εὔθυνος βροτῶν ἔνερθε χθονός. Cp. *Supp.* 230–231: κἀκεῖ δικάζει τἀμπλακήμαθ', ὡς λόγος, Ζεὺς ἄλλος ἐν καμοῦσιν ὑστάτας δίκας. "As the story goes, another Zeus among the dead devises their final punishment."

[41] Aiakos is a more difficult question; see Dover 1993: 54–55, and my discussion in Edmonds 2004a: 148–149. For Plato's manipulations of the myths, see also Edmonds 2004a: 159–220.

[42] Cp. Graf 1974: 121–126.

[43] Pind. *Ol.* 2.56–67 (*OF* 445 B = OF 142 K): "But if one has it and knows what is to come, that the helpless souls of those who have died here immediately receive recompense. And all the wicked deeds in the realm of Zeus here someone beneath the earth judges, passing his sentence with hateful

Pindar brings in another element of the differentiated afterlife that appears in various places in the mythic tradition, the division of the deceased among various places for the afterlife. Pindar promises that those who have thrice lived a good life will go to the Isles of the Blessed, and these islands are the destination of the blessed dead in a number of sources, starting with Hesiod.[44] Homer refers rather to the Elysian Field as the destination where Menelaus will receive his reward, but this particular destination does not appear again in the texts until the self-consciously Homerizing Apollonios Rhodios. While in the *Odyssey*, the punished dead suffer in the same region as the rest of the shades Odysseus sees, in other texts Tartaros appears as the place of punishment. While Tartaros seems to become the standard name for the Underworld place of punishment, in Homer and Hesiod it is just a place of confinement for gods who defy Zeus, including the Titans from whom Zeus wrested control of the cosmos.[45] Plato creates vivid images of the otherworldly crossroads to dramatize the split between the good and the evil and their lots after death. Depending on Plato's purposes in the dialogue, the crossroads may lead to Tartaros and the Isles of the Blessed (*Gorgias*), up to the realm of the gods and down to the places of punishment (*Republic*), or simply in a bewildering variety of directions that compel the soul to follow the guidance of its appointed *daimon* (*Phaedo*). Such geographical distinctions appear elsewhere in the evidence, from the marginal gold tablets to the Athenian drinking song that puts Harmodios in the Isles of the Blessed.[46]

compulsion. But having the sun always in equal nights and equal days, the good receive a life most free of toil, not disturbing with the strength of their arms the earth, nor the water of the sea, for the sake of a paltry sustenance. But in the presence of those gods they honored, those who rejoiced in faithful oaths dwell forever without tears, while the others suffer toil that is unbearable to look at." εἰ δέ νιν ἔχων τις οἶδεν τὸ μέλλον, | ὅτι θανόντων μὲν ἐνθάδ' αὐτίκ' ἀπάλαμνοι φρένες | ποινὰς ἔτεισαν – τὰ δ' ἐν τᾷδε Διὸς ἀρχᾷ | ἀλιτρὰ κατὰ γᾶς δικάζει τις ἐχθρᾷ | λόγον φράσαις ἀνάγκᾳ· | ἴσαις δὲ νύκτεσσιν αἰεί, | ἴσαις δ' ἁμέραις ἄλιον ἔχοντες, ἀπονέστερον | ἐσλοὶ δέκονται βίοτον, οὐ χθόνα ταράσσοντες ἐν χερὸς ἀκμᾷ οὐδὲ πόντιον ὕδωρ | κεινὰν παρὰ δίαιταν, ἀλλὰ παρὰ μὲν τιμίοις | θεῶν οἵτινες ἔχαιρον εὐορκίαις ἄδακρυν νέμονται | αἰῶνα, τοὶ δ' ἀπροσόρατον ὀκχέοντι πόνον.

[44] Hes. *Op.* 168–173.

[45] *Il.* 8.10–16, 14.274–279, 8.478–491, 5.898. Cp. Hes. *Theog.* 713–745, *Hymn. Hom. Ap.* 335–336. The only reference before the *Gorgias* to a mortal being punished in Tartaros is a papyrus fragment from the Hesiodic *Catalogue of Women* (fr. 30 Merkelbach-West) that refers to Salmoneus being punished in Tartaros.

[46] The gold tablets (A2 [*OF* 489 B = OF 32d K] and A3 [*OF* 490 B = OF 32e K] ln. 4) from Thurii refer to the seats of the blessed (ἕδρας εὐαγέων), whereas the longer B tablets mention a split in the road between the first spring and the second. See Edmonds 2004a: 49–52, 84–85, for further analysis. Cp. the Harmodios skolion, *Carmina Convivialia* fr. 11 *PMG* : "Dear Harmodios, surely you have not perished. No, they say, you live in the blessed islands where Achilles the swift of foot, and Tydeus' son, Diomedes, are said to have gone." φίλταθ' Ἁρμόδι', οὔ τί πω τέθνηκας, νήσοις δ' ἐν μακάρων σέ φασιν εἶναι, ἵνα περ ποδώκης Ἀχιλεὺς Τυδεΐδην τέ †φασι τὸν ἐσθλὸν† Διομήδεα.

Some sources make less of a geographic distinction between the places of reward and punishment; the mode of separation seems to depend primarily on the medium and the author, rather than any doctrinal difference. Polygnotos' painting of the Underworld, for example, fits the punished dead in next to those whose lot in the afterlife is less painful, and Aristophanes puts his chorus of blessed dead close to the muck in which those who have transgressed must lie. Darkness and mud characterize an unhappy afterlife in a variety of sources, in contrast to light and air for the happy. Dodds attributes this idea of darkness and dirt to a natural confusion of Hades and the grave, just as the soul and the corpse are often confounded, but, while such associations may be valid in, e.g., Lucian, in general darkness and filth simply are thought of as unpleasant and bad – not the sort of conditions one would want to exist in.[47] While Hades is shadowy even in Homer, sources like Aristophanes take the notion to an extreme and emphasize the filth and muck, transforming the mud (βόρβορος or πηλός) that appears in other sources into everflowing excrement (σκῶρ ἀείνων).[48] In other sources, the punished are submerged, not in mud, but in the rivers of the Underworld, suffering the burning heat of Pyriphlegethon or the freezing cold of Kokytos or Styx or simply being submerged, smothered, and lost in the waters.[49]

The ideas of differentiated afterlife, and even the specific punishments therein, thus seem to be part of the widespread mythic tradition, used without any need to specify the source and for purposes as varied as those of Aristophanes, Plato, and the gold tablets. Nevertheless, these ideas are also, naturally enough, often associated specifically with the practitioners of *teletai* aimed at procuring a better lot in the afterlife. Plato refers to the idea of afterlife punishment for wrongs committed on earth as the sort of story citizens might hear from the kind of people who get seriously involved with

---

[47] Dodds 1951: 172 n. 102. Lucian has the recurring theme of the shades in the afterlife being nothing more than their corpses – skulls and bones, e.g., *Dial. Mort.* 5.

[48] Εἰς Ἀΐδεω δόμον εὐρώεντα (*Od.* 10.512, 23.322; cp. Hes. *Op.* 153). Ar. *Ran.* 145, cp. 273; βόρβορος in Aristid. *Or.* 22.10 Keil.

[49] The rivers are simply geography in *Od.* 11.513–515, but they appear as part of the apparatus of afterlife punishment in Pl. *Phd.* 112e–113c; Plotinus, *Enn.* 1.6.6 (*OF* 434iv B). Damascius' exegesis of the passage (*In Phd.* 2.145 [363 Westerink] [*OF* 341iv, 342 B = OF 125 K]) provides a special significance to each: "The power of delimitation is symbolized by the Okeanos, that of purification by the Acheron, that of chastisement by heat by the Pyriphlegethon, that of chastisement through cold by the Kokytos." τὴν διοριστικὴν κατὰ τὸν Ὠκεανόν, τὴν καθαρτικὴν κατὰ τὸν Ἀχέροντα, τὴν κολαστικὴν διὰ θερμότητος κατὰ τὸν Πυριφλεγέθοντα, τὴν κολαστικὴν διὰ ψυχρότητος κατὰ τὸν Κωκυτόν. Cp. Plutarch's citation of Pind. fr. 130 S.-M. (*OF* 440 B) at *De lat. viv.* 1130c, which compares being in the rivers to oblivion and living concealed with no light or recognition.

such things in the *teletai*.[50] Other sources, too, refer to such punishments and rewards as the sort of thing one hears of in the *teletai*.[51] The *teletai* represented one way to ensure a happy afterlife, so neglect of such rites could be seen as a ticket to an unhappy life after death. Polygnotos' painting shows the uninitiated trying to scoop water in broken pitchers, and such an endless, fruitless toil seems to have been a commonly imagined punishment for those who failed to do the service to the gods that participating in the ritual implied.[52]

By contrast, various sources describe the happy dead in pleasant conditions – sunlight, shade, cool breezes, etc. – surrounded by flowers and meadows, near cool, running water. A good afterlife is full of the things that make for a good life, which is to say the life of a nobleman or other privileged type. Although Pindar describes the fortunate dead as engaged in aristocratic pursuits like riding and hunting, the most popular aristocratic activity for the afterlife (as in life) seems to be the symposium.[53] Hundreds of funeral reliefs depict the deceased reclined on a symposiastic couch, often with cup in hand and sometimes even with a woman at the foot of the couch.[54] The afterlife is imagined as the best experiences of life – the festivals – and numerous inscriptions attest to the idea of choral

---

[50] Pl. *Leg.* 870de (*OF* 433ii B): "Concerning all these matters, let these preludes be announced, and, in addition to them, that story which many believe when they hear it from those who seriously concern themselves with such things in the mystic rites (*teletai*), that there is vengeance for such acts in Hades, and that those coming back again to this earth are bound to pay the penalty according to their nature, the penalty of suffering just what he himself inflicted, and to have that next life ended by such a fate at the hands of another." τούτων δὴ πάντων πέρι προοίμια μὲν εἰρημένα ταῦτ᾽ ἔστω, καὶ πρὸς τούτοις, ὃν καὶ πολλοὶ λόγον τῶν ἐν ταῖς τελεταῖς περὶ τὰ τοιαῦτα ἐσπουδακότων ἀκούοντες σφόδρα πείθονται, τὸ τῶν τοιούτων τίσιν ἐν Ἅιδου γίγνεσθαι, καὶ πάλιν ἀφικομένοις δεῦρο ἀναγκαῖον εἶναι τὴν κατὰ φύσιν δίκην ἐκτεῖσαι, τὴν τοῦ παθόντος ἅπερ αὐτὸς ἔδρασεν, ὑπ᾽ ἄλλου τοιαύτῃ μοίρᾳ τελευτῆσαι τὸν τότε βίον.

[51] Cp. Pl. *Phd.* 69c (*OF* 434iii, 549ii, 576i, 669ii B), Plotinus, *Enn.* 1.6.6 (*OF* 434iv B). The reference in *Gorgias* 493a (*OF* 434ii B) to a 'clever Sicilian', whether it is a specific reference to Empedokles or not, probably refers to a similar figure with ritual expertise.

[52] Paus. 10.31.9 (*OF* 434v B). The punishment of carrying water in broken pitchers probably lies behind the image in Pl. *Grg.* 493a (*OF* 434ii B), although Olymp. *In Grg.* 153.20 (*OF* 434vii B) sees it as specifically Pythagorean. It is included in lists of standard Underworld punishments like [*Ax.*] 371d (*OF* 434ix B), and so familiar an image is it that Philetairos, fr. 17 KA (*OF* 434viii B) can poke fun at it with the idea that the unmusical will suffer in Hades, carrying water in pierced vessels.

[53] Cp. Plut. *De sera* 565f = fr. 178 Sandbach (*OF* 594 B); Lucian, *Ver. hist.* 2.14–16, cp. 5. Both gold tablets from Pelinna, D1 (*OF* 485 B) ln. 6 and P2 (*OF* 486 B) ln. 6, promise wine to the deceased in her new life after death: οἶνον ἔχεις εὐδαίμονα τιμήν. The Platonic *Axiochus* adds to these physical pleasures the intellectual delights of philosophical conversations. [*Ax.*] 371d (*OF* 434ix B): "Here are discourses of philosophers, and performances of poets, cyclic dances, and concerts, well arranged drinking parties, and self-furnished feasts." διατριβαὶ δὲ φιλοσόφων καὶ θέατρα ποιητῶν καὶ κύκλιοι χοροὶ καὶ μουσικὰ ἀκούσματα, συμπόσιά τε εὐμελῆ καὶ εἰλαπίναι αὐτοχορήγητοι.

[54] For these Totenmahl reliefs, see Thönges-Stringaris 1965, who classifies them by the different components present (woman, horsehead, etc.). These reliefs date from the fifth to second centuries BCE and are found across the Greek world.

dancing in the afterlife.[55] Comedians, of course, have fun with the idea of an endless party in the afterlife, and Plato too mocks the idea that the best reward for living well is to be drunk for eternity.[56] Plato associates this idea of the symposium of the blessed with Mousaios, while Plutarch uses the same phrase of eternal drunkenness (μέθην αἰώνιον) to describe the ideas of those associated with Orpheus (τοὺς περὶ τὸν Ὀρφέα),[57] but there is no reason to suppose that all those who had Totenmahl reliefs on their graves had gone through special *teletai* or that all those who got the joke in a comic performance at a major Athenian festival thought of the symposium of the blessed as something only associated with Orpheus and his ilk. The rites associated with Orpheus and Mousaios may indeed have promised special access to the symposium of the blessed for those who thought their chances of admission were otherwise slim, but the idea of such a symposium itself was not limited to the Orphic sphere; it was an idea available in the mythic tradition for anyone who wanted to use it to think with about life and afterlife, as well as virtue, justice, and theodicy.

The symposium of the blessed, like the Isles of the Blessed, was the best afterlife that mortals could achieve, but, for some specially favored ones, death could mean the transition from mortality to a more divine state, although the boundaries between blessed dead, immortal hero, and even god are, at times, hard to discern.[58] Many of the heroes from the wars at Troy or Thebes that Hesiod puts on the Isles of the Blessed received cult in the festivals of city-states around Greece, and an even more select crew (e.g., Asklepios, Semele, Herakles) were elevated to divinity. While such a transcendence remained a theoretical possibility, it was generally reserved in practice for colonial *oikists* or others who transformed a whole

---

[55] As Hershbell notes in his commentary on the *Axiochus* (Hershbell 1981: 67), χωρὸς εὐσεβῶν appears in numerous funerary inscriptions, cp. *Epigr. Gr.* 151.5; 189.6; 218.16; 411.4; 506.8 in Kaibel 1878. It is worth noting that none of these inscriptions stress previous initiation as the means to joining the chorus.

[56] Ar. fr. 504 KA (*OF* 432i B), Pherekrates 113.30ff. KA (*OF* 432ii B). Aristophont. fr. 12 KA (*OF* 432iii B) also makes fun of the idea by depicting the Pythagorists having a Spartan-style syssitia with Pluto instead of a raucous symposium. Plato's critique in *Resp.* 363c (*OF* 431i B = OF 4 K) is part of his larger attack on the traditional ideas of the rewards for virtue.

[57] Plutarch's emphasis on the drunkenness, without the rest of the symposiastic trappings, indicates that he understands Plato's polemical purpose here, rather than, as Linforth 1941: 88 suggests, that "Plutarch and all postclassical authors lack the fine sense of order which adds infinitely to the delicacy of expression in classical Greek prose, and consequently give a blunted and mistaken report of what Plato said."

[58] *Contra* Rohde 1925: 253–254: "The first real principle of the religion of the Greek people is this – that in the divine ordering of the world, humanity and divinity are absolutely divided in place and nature, and so they must remain. A deep gulf is fixed between the worlds of mortality and divinity. The relations between man and God promoted by religion depend entirely on this distinction."

society that would then provide worship for their benefactor.[59] Empedokles seems to be one of the few who proclaimed his own divinity, but two gold tablets from Thurii suggest that some of the dead there also believed they had found the way to become a god.[60] Few ordinary mortals could hope to achieve immortality in this way, however; a perfect existence of festivals and symposia with the other blessed dead was the most they could hope for.

Poetic immortality and the Homeric afterlife

The testimony to a widespread and long-lasting tradition of a lively afterlife, both outside the Homeric poems and within them, suggests that the vision of the strengthless dead in the Homeric poems should not be seen as the standard or normal vision of the afterlife, but rather as a special concept devised within the poetic tradition of the Homeric poems and bearing a special relation to this kind of poetry that celebrates the glories of men (κλέα ἀνδρῶν).[61] The Homeric view of the afterlife as dreary and meaningless is not the byproduct of a Homeric period with a particularly vigorous and healthy attachment to life, in contrast to earlier and later periods that were overcome with primitive fears or decadent superstitions.[62] Such a period is

---

[59] As Nagy 1979: 116 notes, a hero is essentially epichoric, that is, his cult is a local phenomenon, carried out by a local community. The hero thus stands between the ordinary dead, to whom only the family pays cult (in the form of funerary and tomb rituals and only for a limited time), and the Panhellenic deity, to whom epichoric communities in a number of places pay cult in a variety of ways. The difference between mortals and gods is thus not so much an ontological category difference as a question of power, influence, or honor. See the sensible remarks of Parker 2011: 110, "Heroes are biographically dead mortals, functionally minor gods," as well as his appendix on hero cult (287–292).

[60] A1 (OF 488 B = OF 32c K) ln. 10: "Happy and most blessed one, a god you shall be instead of a mortal." ὄλβιε καὶ μακαριστέ, θεὸς δ' ἔσηι ἀντὶ βροτοῖο. Cp. A4 (OF 487 B = OF 32f K) ln. 4: θεὸς ἐγένου ἐξ ἀνθρώπου· See Edmonds 2004a: 73–75, for this fate after death as modeled upon the apotheosis of figures such as Semele and Herakles. Emp. 31 B 112 DK claims to go among the people of Akragas, honored as a god: "I go about among you as a god immortal, no longer mortal, honored among all, just as is seemly, crowned with fillets and flowery garlands." ἐγὼ δ' ὑμῖν θεὸς ἄμβροτος, οὐκέτι θνητός | πωλεῦμαι μετὰ πᾶσι τετιμένος, ὥσπερ ἔοικα, | ταινίαις τε περίστεπτος στέφεσίν τε θαλείοις.

[61] Although Johnston falls into the same trap as Rohde and others who see the Homeric poems directly reflecting the beliefs of Homeric audiences, she at least raises the possibility that ideas might be absent from Homer for thematic reasons: "It is my view that the *absence* from the poems of phenomena that are well attested in later sources must be understood to reflect the absence of those phenomena in the societies in which the poems developed, unless other cogent explanations for their absence can be found within the thematic concerns of the poet.... If the poems do not mention ideas about the dead that are amply attested in later sources, this is because the ideas were not available at the time that poems underwent their main development" (Johnston 1999: 7 n. 3).

[62] Cp. Rohde 1925: 242: "Nor were they very susceptible **during their best centuries** to the infectious malady of a 'sick conscience'. What had they to do with pictures of an underworld of purgatory

the fantasy of scholars whose particular idealization of the Greeks derived from reading the Homeric poems in isolation from the historical contexts in which they were formed and performed.[63] The clear and consistent message put forth by the ideas of afterlife identified as the standard Homeric view of afterlife is that poetic immortality in song is the only meaningful and desirable form of survival after death.

Such a message is not surprising in poems that are providing exactly that kind of immortality for the heroes they celebrate. Not only does Achilles make his famous choice of a brief life devoted to winning fame, but the other Iliadic heroes consistently choose their courses of action so that they may become a subject of song for men in time to come, on the principle that such poetic fame is the most valuable thing achievable.[64] The passages that present the bleak and lifeless view of the afterlife highlight the choices that central heroes of the epics make in opting for the immortality brought by epic song rather than any other alternative. While the *Iliad* centers on Achilles' choice of deaths, glorious death in battle instead of ignominious death at home, the *Odyssey* frames the issue as a choice of immortalities. Odysseus actually rejects the immortality offered by Kalypso because such a life, whatever its other attractions, would result in his own story, his poetic immortality, becoming lost.[65] More often, though, the possibility of any other kind of immortality is simply denied in the Homeric poems, even though the apotheosis of, e.g., Herakles and the Dioskouroi, was well known to the Homeric audience.[66] The Homeric poet again and

---

and torment in expiation of all imaginary types and degrees of sin, as in Dante's ghastly Hell?" (emphasis added).

[63] Cp. again Rohde 1925: 3–4: "Nothing may be said [in the Homeric poems] expressly of the joy and happiness of life, but that is because such things go without saying among a vigorous folk engrossed in a movement of progress, whose circumstances were never complicated and where all the conditions of happiness easily fell to the strong in activity and enjoyment. And, indeed, it is only for the strong, the prudent, and the powerful that this Homeric world is intended. Life and existence upon this earth obviously belongs to them." The resonances with the German Romantics on the one hand and with Rohde's friend, Nietzsche, on the other, are clear.

[64] The choice of Achilles, *Il.* 9.410–416. Cp. *Il.* 2.119; 3.287; 3.460; 6.358; 22.305; *Od.* 3.204; 8.580; 11.76; 21.255; 24.433. Helen, by contrast, laments that she and Paris will be the subject of such poetic memory: οἷσιν ἐπὶ Ζεὺς θῆκε κακὸν μόρον, ὡς καὶ ὀπίσσω | ἀνθρώποισι πελώμεθ' ἀοίδιμοι ἐσσομένοισι (*Il.* 6.356–358).

[65] Crane points out that Kalypso (the concealer) hides Odysseus in her cave on Ogygia, preventing him from receiving the honor and glory he would receive if he returned home and the story of his exploits was told, since no one ever comes to Ogygia. Unlike other heroes who disappear into caves, Odysseus would have no cult at his cave to maintain his honor. Crane 1988: 18: "Even if Amphiaraos, Rhesus, and Trophonius disappear, there remains some place where they can receive honor. Having vanished forever from the world of men, Odysseus has also lost the κλέος which he had won."

[66] As Crane 1988: 89 notes, the mixed immortal status of the Dioskouroi is a well-attested Indo-European tale that must have entered the tradition long before the Homeric poems were formulated:

again drives home the message that only the kind of poetic immortality he can provide is valuable; all other things that one might desire in life are secondary.[67]

There can be no doubt that such poetic immortality was indeed valued, and sought after, by the audiences of Homeric poetry from the archaic age onwards.[68] Survival in memory is indeed a real form of immortality, one sought after particularly by the aristocrats who competed for the honor of recognition by their society in games and in war, in the assemblies and in the symposia.[69] Pindar and his like provided a similar sort of immortality for the victors in the Panhellenic contests, while Simonides' poems on the victory at Plataia attest to the continuation of this competition for epic glory. Not only does Simonides' epigram on those who fell at Plataia proclaim that their glory in the world above will lead them back from Hades, but the whole epic on the battle (the "new Simonides") shows that the Homeric mode of celebrating κλέα ἀνδρῶν is still in demand in the fifth century.[70]

It is not surprising that the few references to the idea of poetic immortality as replacing any other form come precisely from the lyric poets who are emphasizing their own power and authority as poets to determine who will live forever. Sappho vaunts over another woman, taunting her bitingly (and, in the event, accurately) that she will be forgotten after death, flitting like a Homeric shade, while Sappho herself will be remembered because of

"In the *Iliad*, Achilles specifically states that even Heracles died (*Il.* 18.117), and there is no reference to immortality for Heracles, Achilles, or for any hero. This testimony, however, must be taken with caution. In the Teichoskopia, we hear that the Dioskouroi are dead, whereas the myth that they share death and immortality between them, being Indo-European in origins, antedates our *Iliad*. If the narrative pointedly ignores the immortality of the Dioskouroi, then references to the death of Heracles (or even of Achilles) do not prove that popular traditions situating Heracles on Olympus did not predate our *Iliad*."

[67] Rohde 1925: 43: "When a man dies his soul departs into a region of twilit dream-life; his body, the visible man perishes. Only his glorious name, in fact, lives on. His praises speak to after ages from the monument to his honour on his grave-mound – and in the song of the bard. A *poet* would naturally be inclined to think such things."

[68] Nagy 1979: 116 indeed suggests that part of the Panhellenic appeal of the Homeric poems was in their presentation of a kind of view of afterlife that transcended the local, epichoric funerary ideology, where different local traditions depicted the fate of the local heroes in different ways.

[69] Sourvinou-Inwood 1981: 32–33: "A good death which brings glory ensures a man's 'survival' in memory. Memory-survival is one of the ways in which men could leave their mark on life, continue to 'exist' – other than as ghostly shades in Hades . . . Memory-survival, survival of one's social persona in the collective memory of the community, or, through song, of many communities, depends on excellence and is not open to all; in terms of class it is limited to the aristocracy."

[70] Simon. 7.251: Ἄσβεστον κλέος οἵδε φίλῃ περὶ πατρίδι θέντες κυάνεον θανάτου ἀμφεβάλοντο νέφος· οὐδὲ τεθνᾶσι θανόντες, ἐπεί σφ' ἀρετὴ καθύπερθε κυδαίνουσ' ἀνάγει δώματος ἐξ Ἀίδεω. For the "new" Simonides poem on Plataia, cp. Boedeker and Sider 2001. The rhetoric of funeral orations continues the same ideals, and Herodotus' proem puts him in the same tradition.

her poetry. "After death you will be forgotten, and there will never be any longing for you, because you have no share of the roses of Pieria. Unseen in the house of Hades, flown from our midst, you will wander amidst the shadowy dead."[71] The Homeric poetic view of a lifeless afterlife remained in the tradition, available for access by any who wanted to make use of it, but it was never the dominant idea, either in literature or in cult.

Orpheus and eschatology

While the ideas of a lively afterlife are often labeled Orphic by modern scholars, it is important to note that neither Orpheus nor Orphica are associated in the ancient evidence either with the origination of such ideas or with a particular concern for them. Various sources attribute a Descent to Hades poem to Orpheus, but Orpheus is hardly the only poet to have described life in the afterlife. Indeed, when Plutarch, in his treatise on how to moderate the dangers of young people reading poetry, refers to authors who tell of the terrors of the Underworld, Orpheus does not make the list.[72] Homer is obviously the first to be mentioned, but, less obviously to a modern scholar, Pindar and Sophocles are the others listed. When Pausanias (10.28.7) suggests that Polygnotos innovated by including the demon Eurynomos, he lists other well-known Underworld journeys that have no such being. Again, he mentions Homer first, but he also includes the *Minyas* and the *Nostoi*, with no mention of Orpheus.

Plenty of evidence survives of epic *katabases*, not just Homer's Odysseus, but Heracles and Theseus and perhaps even other heroes. Despite the arguments that scholars such as Dieterich and Norden advanced, there is little reason to believe that the whole mythic tradition of *katabases* comes from some original Orphic model.[73] To be sure, Orpheus' *katabasis* might have a novel twist, in that the poet himself had undergone the journey, but, given that Orphica are by definition pseudepigraphic, the difference between a poet reciting Orpheus' narration of his journey and a poet reciting Homer's version of Odysseus' narration is less significant. Scholars have often assumed that Orpheus' *katabasis* would be autobiographical and thereby in some way more powerful or authentic, but it is noteworthy

---

[71] Sappho fr. 55 LP: κατθάνοισα δὲ κείσηι οὐδέ ποτα μναμοσύνα σέθεν | ἔσσετ' οὐδὲ †ποκ'†ὕστερον· οὐ γὰρ πεδέχηις βρόδων | τῶν ἐκ Πιερίας· ἀλλ' ἀφάνης κἀν Ἀίδα δόμωι | φοιτάσηις πεδ' ἀμαύρων νεκύων ἐκπεποταμένα. Plutarch's quotations (*Coniug. praec.* 145f–146a; *Quaest. conv.* 646ef) contextualize it as being directed against someone rich or ignorant (πρός τινα πλουσίαν or πρός τινα τῶν ἀμούσων καὶ ἀμαθῶν γυναικῶν).

[72] Plut. *Quomodo adul.* 17b7. [73] Cp. Dieterich 1893 and Norden 1927.

that, despite the variety of testimonia to Orpheus' *katabasis* poem and to his descent to find Eurydice, no ancient source ever draws the connection explicitly.[74] Modern scholars, by contrast, have emphasized the connection of Orpheus with eschatological poetry, seeking to trace to Orphic influence the appearances of the lively afterlife elsewhere in Greek literature and art. Such a misplaced emphasis would have surprised Pausanias, who links Polygnotos' fifth-century BCE painting of the Underworld with the epic *Minyas* and who merely mentions the presence of Orpheus in the Underworld within the painting without any further comment.[75]

Orpheus' own journey to the Underworld is not the only reason modern scholars associate him with eschatology in particular; his role as originator of rituals that provide a better afterlife has also led scholars to imagine him as the one responsible for the very idea of a differentiated afterlife. However, when Diodorus Siculus claims that Orpheus borrowed much of his mythic material on the Underworld from Egypt, he is not claiming that Orpheus brought the whole idea of a lively afterlife from Egypt, but rather that some of the specific imagery in his rites for Dionysos and Demeter was adapted from the rites of Osiris and Isis.[76] In this passage, following the age-old tradition of attributing wisdom to the orient, Diodorus lists Orpheus among many other wise men who brought their ideas from Egypt

---

[74] *Contra* Parker 1995: 500: "Orphic poetry can almost be defined as eschatological poetry, and it was in such poems perhaps that 'persuasive' accounts of the afterlife – accounts designed, unlike that in *Odyssey* xi, to influence the hearer's behaviour in the here and now – were powerfully presented for the first time." Cp. West 1983: 12, who supposes that the references to the *Katabasis* must be to a poem "in autobiographical form."

[75] Paus. 10.28.2.

[76] The names of the meadow of the blessed, the names of the rivers or of Charon the ferryman, the punishment of collecting water in a sieve, etc. Diod. Sic. 1.96.4–5 (*OF* 48ii, 61 B = OT 96 K): "For Orpheus brought [from Egypt] most of his mystic *teletai*, the ceremonies that concerned his wanderings, and his fabulous account of the things in Hades. For the *telete* of Osiris is the same as that of Dionysus and that of Isis most like that of Demeter, with only the names switched; and the punishments in Hades of the impious, the meadows of the pious, and all the popular products of the imagination, these were all introduced by Orpheus in imitation of the burial customs among the Egyptians." Ὀρφέα μὲν γὰρ τῶν μυστικῶν τελετῶν τὰ πλεῖστα καὶ τὰ περὶ τὴν ἑαυτοῦ πλάνην ὀργιαζόμενα καὶ τὴν τῶν ἐν ᾅδου μυθοποιίαν ἀπενέγκασθαι. τὴν μὲν γὰρ Ὀσίριδος τελετὴν τῇ Διονύσου τὴν αὐτὴν εἶναι, τὴν δὲ τῆς Ἴσιδος τῇ τῆς Δήμητρος ὁμοιοτάτην ὑπάρχειν, τῶν ὀνομάτων μόνων ἐνηλλαγμένων· τὰς δὲ τῶν ἀσεβῶν ἐν ᾅδου τιμωρίας καὶ τοὺς τῶν εὐσεβῶν λειμῶνας καὶ τὰς παρὰ τοῖς πολλοῖς εἰδωλοποιίας ἀναπεπλασμένας παρεισαγαγεῖν μιμησάμενον τὰ γινόμενα περὶ τὰς ταφὰς τὰς κατ' Αἴγυπτον. Cp. 1.92.2–3 (*OF* 48i B = OF 293 K) for Charon: "A ferryman is designated for this, whom the Egyptians call in their own language a *charon*. Wherefore they say that Orpheus, having visited Egypt once upon a time and seen this custom, fabricated a myth of the things in Hades, imitating some of these things and making up others on his own account." ἐφέστηκε δὲ ταύτῃ ὁ πορθμεύς, ὃν Αἰγύπτιοι κατὰ τὴν ἰδίαν διάλεκτον ὀνομάζουσι χάρωνα. διὸ καί φασιν Ὀρφέα τὸ παλαιὸν εἰς Αἴγυπτον παραβαλόντα καὶ θεασάμενον τοῦτο τὸ νόμιμον, μυθοποιῆσαι τὰ καθ' ᾅδου, τὰ μὲν μιμησάμενον, τὰ δ' αὐτὸν ἰδίᾳ πλασάμενον·

to Greece – not just the other ritual specialists Melampous and Mousaios, but also Homer, Daidalos, Lykourgos, Solon, Plato, Pythagoras, Eudoxos, Demokritos, and Oinopides. Diodorus does not portray Orpheus as the discoverer of the idea of the lively afterlife, but rather as the originator of various mystic rites that involve images of the afterlife, and the Egyptian images of the afterlife found on the temple walls (and perhaps the Books of the Dead) provide a vivid and graphic source for this particular type of wisdom. According to Diodorus, Orpheus elaborated the general idea of a lively and differentiated afterlife with specific images from Egypt that amazed his Greek audiences. Homer too made use of these images in his *Odyssey*, and Diodorus quotes lines he thinks derive directly from Egyptian sources.[77] Diodorus does not, as modern scholars have, explain these Egyptian influences on Orpheus and Homer as the introduction of a different concept of the afterlife to a Greek tradition that previously only imagined a pale and shadowy world of unanimated dead who share a common fate, because Diodorus does not, as modern scholars have, imagine that this bleak "Homeric" afterlife is the standard tradition from which the "Orphic" vision deviates.

Orphic ideas of the soul

While the lively afterlife of the soul is a popular notion that is not exclusively associated with Orphica or even the erudite speculations of the philosophers, certain ways of characterizing the soul's relation with the body do appear to be marked as unusual, extra-ordinary, or limited to a few esoteric thinkers – in a word, Orphic. The sources link some of these images directly with Orphica, while others are more loosely associated, but the context of the references makes it clear that these ways of thinking about the relation of body to soul differ from the ordinary ways, providing either extraordinarily wise insight or extraordinarily foolish mistakes. In this evidence, the body can be the tomb of the soul, its prison, or its guard post, while the soul appears as a living or even divine entity, passing time within the body and passing into and out of the body or even from body to body.

Most of the discussions of Orphic ideas of the relation of soul to body start with the passage in Plato's *Cratylus*, in which Socrates provides a number of etymologies for the word σῶμα, body, each of which depicts

---

[77] Diod. Sic. 1.96.6–7 (*OF* 61 B = OT 96 K). He explains Hermes in *Od.* 24.1–2, 11–14, as well as Ocean, the gates of the sun, and the Acheron river.

the relation in a different way. This starting point reveals the predominance of Plato in the evidence for such ideas, and, as so often happens, Plato's testimony is a dangerous guide to the ideas of his predecessors. However, with sufficient caution and awareness of Plato's tendency to "transpose" the ideas of others into his own agenda, we can uncover a range of ideas about the soul and its relation to the body, all of which are marked by their presentation in this sophistic etymological game.

> This, I think can be explained in many ways. If someone should make even a little change, a very little change. For some say it is the tomb (σῆμα) of the soul, as if the soul is buried in the present life; and then again, because by this means the soul signifies (σημαίνει) whatever it signifies, it is in this way also rightly called "sign" (σῆμα). But it seems most likely to me that those connected with Orpheus (οἱ ἀμφὶ Ὀρφέα) gave this name, as if the soul were paying the penalty for whatever it is paying; they think it has the body as an enclosure so that it is kept safe (σῴζηται), like a prison, and this is, as the name itself denotes, the safe (σῶμα) for the soul, until the penalty incurred is paid, and it is not even necessary to change a single letter.[78]

The passage includes several different images of the relation of the body to the soul: a tomb, a marker, a prison, a protective covering. Controversy has raged over the origins of each of these ideas and which of them come from the same source, because this is one of the very few early pieces of evidence in which an idea of the soul is explicitly attributed to people connected in some way to Orpheus (οἱ ἀμφὶ Ὀρφέα).[79] Plato's circumlocution shows that those who made use of the poems of Orpheus did not label themselves as and were not thought of as "Orphics," but it also shows that the defining feature of such people, for Plato's purposes here, was indeed their connection with Orphic texts.[80] The idea that Socrates attributes to them is specifically the idea that the soul is in the body for punishment, like a prison, but it is unclear how many of the etymologies in the passage may have come from an Orphic text. The adversative μέντοι does suggest that the τινες who give the σῶμα–σῆμα etymology may be different people from

---

[78] Pl. *Cra.* 400bc (*OF* 430i B = OF 8 K): Πολλαχῇ μοι δοκεῖ τοῦτό γε· ἂν μὲν καὶ σμικρόν τις παρακλίνῃ, καὶ πάνυ. καὶ γὰρ σῆμά τινές φασιν αὐτὸ εἶναι τῆς ψυχῆς, ὡς τεθαμμένης ἐν τῷ νῦν παρόντι· καὶ διότι αὖ τούτῳ σημαίνει ἃ ἂν σημαίνῃ ἡ ψυχή, καὶ ταύτῃ "σῆμα" ὀρθῶς καλεῖσθαι. δοκοῦσι μέντοι μοι μάλιστα θέσθαι οἱ ἀμφὶ Ὀρφέα τοῦτο τὸ ὄνομα, ὡς δίκην διδούσης τῆς ψυχῆς ὧν δὴ ἕνεκα δίδωσιν, τοῦτον δὲ περίβολον ἔχειν, ἵνα σῴζηται, δεσμωτηρίου εἰκόνα· εἶναι οὖν τῆς ψυχῆς τοῦτο, ὥσπερ αὐτὸ ὀνομάζεται, ἕως ἂν ἐκτείσῃ τὰ ὀφειλόμενα, [τὸ] "σῶμα," καὶ οὐδὲν δεῖν παράγειν οὐδ' ἓν γράμμα.

[79] Bernabé 1995 provides an excellent analysis of the debates, with important attention to the role of Platonic transposition.

[80] Linforth 1941: 148; cp. Bernabé 1995: 217–218.

οἱ ἀμφὶ Ὀρφέα, but it is entirely possible that, in a text such as the Derveni papyrus, the author (who is certainly someone who might be described as ἀμφὶ Ὀρφέα) might have provided the whole series of etymologies in the exegesis of a verse of Orpheus. The verse of Orpheus itself might or might not have anything to do with the imprisonment of the soul in the body; indeed, it is entirely plausible to imagine someone like the Derveni author providing an explanation of the body as a tomb, a sign, and a prison, in a verse that referred to some other kind of body entirely.[81]

Of course, the idea of the body as the tomb (σῆμα) of the soul has different ramifications than the idea of the body as the indicator (σῆμα) or even as the prison (δεσμωτήριον) or safeguard (ἵνα σώζηται), but, in the context of an exegetical exercise, those ramifications would not be pursued. The consequences of each interpretation are less important, in this context, than the fact that the exegete can devise them, that the exegete can demonstrate his acumen to his audience to bolster his own religious authority. Such a display is persuasive not because it expounds dogma in which the audience fervently believes but rather because it shows the exegete as a wise person whose expertise can be relied upon.[82] This process is, of course, precisely what Socrates is mocking with his display in the *Cratylus*, so efforts to uncover serious dogmas and their origins here are doubly problematic, since even if Plato is simply borrowing Socrates' etymologies from another text, there is little reason to suppose that the ramifications of any or all of them were seriously explored in such a (hypothetical) source.

Nonetheless, these images do appear in other evidence as well, so it is worth separating out each of the images to see how they are used, since all of these, regardless of their particular origin (even were that actually recoverable), can be categorized as Orphic, that is, the sort of thing that Socrates can somewhat carelessly associate with the people who have something to do with Orpheus. The very controversies in modern scholarship over which images can be associated with οἱ ἀμφὶ Ὀρφέα suggests that ancient audiences in general also would have been likely to lump all of them together as Orphic, even if some of the more erudite might have been able to trace particular doctrines to particular Pythagoreans or particular Orphic texts. Such a generalizing classification does not, however, mean that any one of these ideas implies the others; each is marginal in its own way, and the

---

[81] E.g., the line from the Orphic Hymn to Zeus quoted by Porphyry in Eusebios *Prep. Ev.* 3.8.2 (*OF* 243.22 B): σῶμα δέ οἱ περιφεγγές, ἀπείριτον, ἀστυφέλικτον.

[82] Cp. the rhetoric of the Derveni author in the discussion above regarding the contestive nature of the exegetical context and its importance for understanding the Derveni author's text.

differences may have been vitally important to those on the margins, even if the distinctions were ignored by a general audience.

Body and soul

In the *Gorgias*, Plato has Socrates claim that he has heard the idea of the soul buried in the body and the etymology σῶμα–σῆμα from some wise man, and he associates with some clever mythologizer from Sicily or Italy (τις μυθολογῶν κομψὸς ἀνήρ, ἴσως Σικελός τις ἢ Ἰταλικός) a further etymological play between the appetitive part of the soul as subject to persuasion (πιθανόν) and the jar (πίθος) that the souls try to fill in the Underworld.[83] Again, whether these wise guys are one and the same, real or imaginary, they serve in the context of the dialogue to support the idea that what Kallikles and others normally think of as life is really like death, and vice versa, a key notion in the arguments that Socrates makes to Kallikles that he has all his values reversed.[84] The idea is introduced by the notorious quote from Euripides, "Who knows if life is death and death life?" This is one of the bizarre ideas of Euripides that Aristophanes mocks repeatedly in the *Frogs*, finally skewering the poet with it when Dionysos quotes it at him as consolation for being left in the Underworld instead of being brought back to the world of the living.[85] Whatever its real origin, then, Aristophanes' testimony suggests that the idea that life is really death was recognizable to fifth-century Athenian audiences as a marginal and mockable idea, the speculation of someone with a claim to wisdom that could, in other contexts, be respected. Socrates' use of the idea in the *Gorgias* is characteristically complex and ironic, playfully introducing an

---

[83] Speculation has run rampant on the precise identity of this clever mythologizer. Olympiodorus, in his fifth-century commentary, assumed that this description referred to Empedokles, reputedly the teacher of Gorgias (*In Grg.* 157.15–17). Dodds 1959 ad loc. believes that a respectable Presocratic philosopher like Empedokles would never be called a *mythologos*, despite the fact that Plato uses terms like μυθολογεῖν to describe the discussions in his dialogues. Empedokles, moreover, wrote verses that appear, from the extant fragments, to have contained numerous mythological personages and scenes. Kingsley, on the other hand, believes that, while Plato might have called Empedokles a *mythologos*, he would never have referred to him as "some Italian or Sicilian," for he was too well known in Athens: "his audience in Athens will also have been familiar enough with it not to be taken in – let alone amused – by such a pointless equivocation" (Kingsley 1995: 114). If indeed it is necessary to hazard a specific identification of Plato's source for the fable, Empedokles remains a viable possibility for the clever Sicilian or Italian, despite these objections. Bernabé 2004: 365, on the other hand, suggests that Plato may have made the etymology up himself: *veri simillimum mihi videtur etymologias a Platone ipso inventas.*

[84] Pl. *Grg.* 492e. Cp. Kallikles' protests and Socrates' exhortations at the end of the dialogue.

[85] Ar. *Ran.* 1082 = Eur. *Phrixos* fr. 833 K (= fr. 17 J.-V.L.) and *Ran.* 1477 = Eur. *Polyidos* fr. 638 K (= fr. 12 J.-V. L.) (*OF* 457 B).

idea he acknowledges to be a bit strange (ὑπό τι ἄτοπα) but seriously urging Kallikles to consider it.[86] This double characterization of strange and mockable with strange and specially wise fits the category of Orphic, even though Plato does not here attribute the σῶμα–σῆμα idea to those connected with Orpheus.

Clement of Alexandria quotes the Pythagorean Philolaos, who attributes to ancient wisdom the idea that the soul is buried in the body: "The ancient theologians and seers testify that the soul is conjoined to the body to suffer certain punishments, and is, as it were, buried in this tomb."[87] Another Pythagorean, Euxitheos, appears in Athenaios as the source of the idea that the soul is yoked to the body for punishment.[88] A related image of torture, that combines the ideas of tomb and prison, is associated with the idea of the soul in the body for the payment of penalties. In his exhortation to live a philosophic life, Aristotle uses the image of a torture apparently practiced by certain Tyrrhenian pirates, who tied their living captives to dead bodies, to describe the soul placed in the body for punishment.[89] Like Philolaos, Aristotle attributes the idea that the soul is in the body for punishment (ἐπὶ τιμωρίᾳ) to extraordinary sources, both the *teletai* and the divinely inspired

---

[86] Pl. *Grg.* 493c3–4. Cp. the hedges that Socrates provides elsewhere, e.g., *Phd.* 114d.

[87] Clem. Al. *Strom.* 3.3.17.1 = Philolaos, 44 B 14 DK (*OF* 430iii B = OF 8 K): μαρτυρέονται δὲ καὶ οἱ παλαιοὶ θεολόγοι τε καὶ μάντιες, ὡς διά τινας τιμωρίας ἁ ψυχὰ τῷ σώματι συνέζευκται καὶ καθάπερ ἐν σήματι τούτῳ τέθαπται. Various doubts have been expressed about whether Philolaos or the Pythagoreans in general believed this idea, but Clement's quotation does not reveal whether Philolaos accepted this idea himself.

[88] Ath. 4.157c (*OF* 430vi B). Anaximander 12 B 1 DK, despite Nietzsche (*Philosophie im tragischen Zeitalter der Griechen* 6), probably refers not to the creation of the material cosmos by an injustice for which it must atone by destruction (in analogy to a certain understanding of the soul in the Orphica), but rather to the interplay of opposing elements. Cp. Kahn 1985: 193–196.

[89] Iambl. *Protr.* 43.21–44.9 (77.27 Des Places) = Arist. fr. 60 Rose (*OF* 430v B = OF 8 K): "So who could look at all this and think themselves successful and happy, if, right from the start, we are naturally put together as if for punishment, all of us, as they say in the initiation rites? For the ancients have an inspired saying that says that the soul 'pays penalties', and we live for the atonement of certain great failings. For the conjunction of the soul with the body looks very much like a thing of this sort; for as the Tyrrhenians are said to torture their captives often by chaining corpses right onto the living, face to face, fitting limb to limb, similarly the soul seems to be extended through and stuck onto all the sensitive members of the body." τίς ἂν οὖν εἰς ταῦτα βλέπων οἴοιτο εὐδαίμων εἶναι καὶ μακάριος, οἳ πρῶτον εὐθὺς φύσει συνέσταμεν, καθάπερ φασίν οἱ τὰς τελετὰς λέγοντες, ὥσπερ ἂν ἐπὶ τιμωρίᾳ πάντες; τοῦτο γὰρ θείως οἱ ἀρχαιότεροι λέγουσι τὸ φάναι διδόναι τὴν ψυχὴν τιμωρίαν καὶ ζῆν ἡμᾶς ἐπὶ κολάσει μεγάλων τινῶν ἁμαρτημάτων. πάνυ γὰρ ἡ σύζευξις τοιούτῳ τινὶ ἔοικε πρὸς τὸ σῶμα τῆς ψυχῆς. ὥσπερ γὰρ τοὺς ἐν τῇ Τυρρηνίᾳ φασὶ βασανίζειν πολλάκις τοὺς ἁλισκομένους προσδεσμευόντας κατ' ἀντικρὺ τοῖς ζῶσι νεκροὺς ἀντιπροσώπους ἕκαστον πρὸς ἕκαστον μέρος προσαρμόττοντας, οὕτως ἔοικεν ἡ ψυχὴ διατετάσθαι καὶ προσκεκολλῆσθαι πᾶσι τοῖς αἰσθητικοῖς τοῦ σώματος μέλεσιν. Hutchinson and Johnson 2005 convincingly argue that this section of Iamblichus' *Protrepticus* comes directly from Aristotle's own lost *Protrepticus*. The argument is supported by Augustine's use of the same image, which he derives from a Ciceronian quotation of Aristotle (August. *C. Iul. Pelag.* 4.15.78 [*OF* 430iv B = OF 8 K]).

ancients, but it is not clear whether the gruesome image of pirate torture actually stems from his sources or is his own rhetorical flourish.[90] In any case, Aristotle too links the idea that the soul is attached to the body for purposes of torment, in expiation for unspecified crimes, to the authority of ancient wisdom and to the practice of rituals. None of these sources specifies the crimes for which the soul is being punished; the reference is always indefinite – certain crimes, the things for which the soul pays the penalty, etc.[91] The soul is placed in the body to suffer the torments of life as a way of paying the penalty, like a prisoner in a torture chamber, and the life of the body is consequently imagined as the source of all these woes.

It is worth noting, however, the contexts in which this idea is introduced. Whereas the image of the tomb highlights the contrast of life and death, the image of the soul as prisoner in the body naturally brings up the question of how the soul can be freed. In his consolation to his wife for the loss of their young daughter, Plutarch compares the soul to a bird trapped in a cage, who is sooner free to spread her wings again when released early from the imprisonment of the body. Plutarch supports his positive approach to this premature death by reminding his wife of the mystic symbola of the Dionysiac rites (τὰ μυστικὰ σύμβολα τῶν περὶ Διόνυσον ὀργιασ-μῶν) that prevent them from believing the Epicurean idea that death brings only nothingness.[92] For Plutarch, this happy release from the body comes after an untimely death, but Aristotle is trying to turn his audience to the practice of philosophic living as the way to free the soul from bodily constraints during life.

By contrast, the reference in Athenaios to the Pythagorean Euxitheos is used in an argument against a different way of freeing the soul from the

---

[90] Since the ramifications of such an anti-somatic view are hardly in keeping with Aristotle's ideas for living a good life elsewhere in his works, it is tempting to suspect that it is a rhetorical flourish, a vivid image that is merely intended to stick in the memory – which it certainly did, turning up in Augustine even though Aristotle's work and the work of Cicero who quoted it have been lost.

[91] The indefinite nature of such references suggests that no single original sin is imagined for which all need to pay the penalty. Rather, it reflects the assumption that, somewhere in everyone's ancestry, there must have been something done that would anger the gods, since such is human – and divine – nature. Cp. Pl. *Phdr.* 244de (*OF* 575 B = OF 3 K) on such problems in particular families. Iambl. *Myst.* 4.4–5 reflects that the apparent injustice of the world, where good things happen to bad people and bad things to the good, makes sense if one understands that the gods may punish for misdeeds committed by souls in prior incarnations; cp. 3.10.14–16. In contrast to this assumption throughout the tradition, August. *C. Iul. Pelag.* 4.15.78 (*OF* 430iv B = OF 8 K) develops the idea that the crime in everyone's ancestry is in fact the same original sin of Adam and Eve. Cp. Jourdan 2011: 84 n. 301, 85 n. 304.

[92] Plut. *cons. Ux.* 611df. Contrast Epicurus, *Ep. Men.* 124. The reference to the consolatory benefits of knowing the symbola is the only reference to the process of initiation bringing some sort of special knowledge to the initiate, rather than improving relations with the deity. Cp. however, Cic. *Tusc.* 1.13 (29): *reminiscere, quoniam es initiatus, quae tradantur mysteriis.*

body – suicide. The prohibition of suicide is also the context for the famous
and problematic image of the φρουρά in Plato's *Phaedo*. Socrates responds
to the amazement of his interlocutors that he welcomes the approaching
hour of his death with the argument that, just as he refuses Crito's offer to
help him escape because of his respect for the laws, he believes that suicide,
as a premature and unauthorized escape from the body, is forbidden. "Now
the tale that is told in the secret rites (ἐν ἀπορρήτοις) about this matter,
that we men are in a kind of prison (φρουρά) and must not set ourselves
free or run away, seems to me to be weighty and not easy to understand."[93]
Socrates presents this image as an expression that comes from rites of the
kind which cannot be spoken openly (ἀπόρρητα), and his respect for the
cult prohibitions is reinforced by his evaluation of the image as impressive
and profound. The scholiast on the passage identifies the idea as coming
from Orpheus, but Socrates' characterization of his source as both special
and profound already marks the idea as Orphic in the broadest sense.

The term φρουρά itself has been the subject of much debate, since it
more often means some sort of garrison outpost than the sense of prison
that it seems to have in the above passage.[94] At issue is whether the soul's
relation to the body is negative, an imprisonment for crimes committed
previously, or whether it is more positive, a kind of protective custody or
dangerous garrison service overseen by the gods. The controversy over the
meaning raged even in the ancient Academy, and Damascius preserves a
list of the different interpretations. "Using these principles, we shall easily
prove that 'the custody' is not the Good, as some say, nor pleasure, as
Noumenios would have it, nor the Demiurge, as Paterios says, but rather,
as Xenokrates has it, that it is Titanic and culminates in Dionysos."[95] Some
of these interpretations are extremely puzzling, and it is hard to see what
φρουρά would mean in the *Phaedo* if it were identified with, e.g., the
Good.[96] Scholars have also struggled with what Damascius means in the
reading of Xenokrates that he favors, but understanding it, as Damascius
himself does, in terms of the Many deriving from the One makes sense
in the Platonic tradition, since the placement of souls in bodies can be

---

[93] Pl. *Phd.* 62b (*OF* 429i, 669iv B = OF 7 K): ὁ μὲν οὖν ἐν ἀπορρήτοις λεγόμενος περὶ αὐτῶν λόγος,
ὡς ἔν τινι φρουρᾷ ἐσμεν οἱ ἄνθρωποι καὶ οὐ δεῖ δὴ ἑαυτὸν ἐκ ταύτης λύειν οὐδ᾽ ἀποδιδράσκειν,
μέγας τέ τίς μοι φαίνεται καὶ οὐ ῥᾴδιος διιδεῖν· Cp. Σ*ad loc.* (10 Greene) (*OF* 429ii B = OF 7 K).

[94] Cp. the debates discussed in West 1983: 21 n. 53; Bernabé 2004: 357; Edmonds 2004a: 175–178. Cic.
Sen. 73 glosses it as *praesidium et statio.*

[95] Xenokrates fr. 219 Isnardi Parente = Dam. *In Phd.* 1.2 (29 Westerink) (*OF* 38i B).

[96] Westerink 1977 ad *loc.* examines the possibilities, explaining the interpretation of φρουρά as the
Good as a post-Plotinian concept of protective divine Providence, while identifying the φρουρά as
pleasure makes it the prison of bodily passions. Cp. also Boyancé 1963.

understood as part of the process by which the One is dispersed into multiplicity. The reading of the Titans' dismemberment of Dionysos in terms of the movement from the One to the Many also appears in other Platonic sources, although Xenokrates would be the earliest.[97] Xenokrates must have related the dismemberment story in terms of the One and the Many (or at least Damascius understood him to do so), since Damascius nearly always uses the peculiar term ἀποκορυφοῦται ('culminates in') to refer to the process of making (or returning to) a single, undivided one out of many.[98]

Regardless of the later interpretations, in the *Phaedo* Socrates clearly links the life of the philosopher as a practice for dying (μελέτη θανάτου) with this image of the soul in the body, whether as a prisoner like Socrates awaiting release or as an Athenian sent out for dangerous service at a garrison outpost. In both Athenaios and Plato, the argument against suicide hinges on the idea that the gods have placed the soul in the body for their own purposes and, however painful life might be, humans have no right to remove the soul from the body before the gods decide the time of service is over. In the Platonic *Axiochus*, by contrast, the image of the φρουρά is used, not as an argument against suicide, but rather as a consolation for an old man fearing death – unlike Socrates in the *Phaedo*, who was an old man so unafraid of death that he needed to explain to his friends why suicide was not a good shortcut. "For each of us is a soul, an immortal being shut up in a mortal fortress (ἐν θνητῷ φρουρίῳ); and Nature has put this hut together for evil . . . the aching soul yearns for the heavenly and kindred ether, and even thirsts for it, striving upwards for the feasting and dancing there."[99]

The φρουρά also appears in the consolatory discourse of Dio, where the idea is presented as a worst case scenario and attributed to a pessimist who had suffered much.[100] The brilliant youth on his deathbed, Kharidemos, who is the notional speaker of the discourse, tells his family not to mourn his untimely demise. Even if we take the gloomy view, he says, that souls are placed in bodies because the gods hate humans as the descendants

---

[97] See discussion below, pp. 381–388.

[98] Likewise the word κορυφή. Cp. Dam. *In Prm.* 213 = 94.26 Ruelle and 213 = 95.9 Ruelle; *De princ.* 2 (I.2.24 Westerink = 1.2.19 Ruelle), 2 (I.5.15 Westerink = 1.5.1 Ruelle), 4 (I.7.16 Westerink = 1.6.17 Ruelle) and many others.

[99] ἡμεῖς μὲν γάρ ἐσμεν ψυχή, ζῷον ἀθάνατον ἐν θνητῷ καθειργμένον φρουρίῳ· τὸ δὲ σκῆνος τουτὶ πρὸς κακοῦ περιήρμοσεν ἡ φύσις . . . ἡ ψυχὴ συναλγοῦσα τὸν οὐράνιον ποθεῖ καὶ σύμφυλον αἰθέρα, καὶ διψᾷ, τῆς ἐκεῖσε διαίτης καὶ χορείας ὀριγνωμένη.

[100] Dio Chrys. 30.10–25. The source is τις ἀνὴρ δυσάρεστος καὶ πολλὰ λελυπημένος κατὰ τὸν βίον (30.25). Bernabé excerpts pieces of this discourse as *OF* 429iii and 320vii–viii B, but does not include the whole argument in context.

of the Titans who rebelled against them in the Titanomachy, they should rejoice, since he will soon be freed of all the tortures of the sensible world.[101] Kharidemos produces an impressive list of all these torments, starting with the weather and going through earthquakes to disease and emotions, and argues that, while most people are not freed from them until after they have produced some offspring to take their place in the torture chamber, some are lucky enough to be released sooner. In his description of these torments, Dio clearly takes his cue from the *Phaedo*, where the experience of the sensible world is compared, implicitly and explicitly, to the torments of the Underworld, so it is difficult to determine whether Dio is merely playing his own variations on a theme by Plato or whether he is also drawing from other sources that he would suppose his second sophistic audience to be able to recognize.[102] Nevertheless, Kharidemos presents his account as extraordinary in nature, amazing and difficult to accept (τὸν δυσχερέστατον τῶν λόγων, ἔχοντα δέ τι θαυμαστὸν ἴσως), marking it as the kind of account that his family may not know of but that certain very educated (if perhaps not happy) men have worked out.

Whereas Dio presents his account as a sort of rhetorical counterexample (of the *a fortiori*, "even if my client did kill the man, you should acquit him of murder" variety), the pessimistic view of the body as a prison deliberately manufactured by hostile gods appears in some later texts of the sort often labeled "gnostic." In the Hermetic *Kore Kosmou*, souls which acted in disobedience to the cosmic order are imprisoned in bodies made from the residue of previous creation mixed with water, to which the planetary rulers contribute their influences, while in Zosimus the body is formed from the four elements as a prison for the spiritual man, Phos.[103] In the latter text, indeed, the body is the product of evil gods or *daimones*, hostile divine forces who are not imprisoning the soul to pay the penalty for unjust deeds, but rather to entrap and exploit the blameless divine soul for their own foul purposes.

A far more positive image comes from the other possible sense of φρουρά, the idea that the body is somehow a protective guard for the soul, a fortification in perhaps a hostile world, but something set up by gods who are not simply maliciously trying to torment mortals. In the *Phaedo*,

---

[101] On the connection of the punishment to the generation of humans from the Titans, see further below, pp. 360–374, 386–388; but it is worth noting that Dio clearly refers here to the Titanomachy, *pace* Bernabé.

[102] For the imagery in the *Phaedo*, cp. Edmonds 2004a: ch. 4.

[103] Κόρη κόσμου in Stob. 1.49.44 (Wachsmuth) = *Corp. Herm.* 23.26–30; Zos. *On the Letter Omega* 9–11.

the philosophic life is a kind of heroic venture, from which it would be shameful to desert like a soldier slipping away from the fortified frontier φρουρά to return to his comfortable home in Athens.[104] While the sense of φρουρά as prison is certainly dominant in the dialogue, given the prison setting, Plato manages to add in a more positive sense of the word, which may indeed be why he uses φρουρά, a word which, as Burkert has noted, cannot have come from a poetic text.[105] A similar type of transposition, as Bernabé calls it, may be at work in the *Cratylus*. Socrates refers to the body as a prison for the purpose of paying a penalty, but he extends the idea to make this δεσμωτηρίον into a protective περίβολος and derives the word σῶμα from σώζω, softening the harshness of the tomb imagery and putting a more positive spin on the incarceration. A comparison with the image in the *Phaedrus* of the soul emerging from the body as from an oyster shell reinforces this image of a tough, protective covering, rather than simply a restrictive prison.[106]

As Ferwerda notes, this idea that the soul needs to be protected by the body is developed at length in the *Timaeus'* account of the formation of the body. "For life's chains, as long as the soul remains bound to the body, are bound within the marrow, giving roots for the mortal race. . . . So, to preserve (διασώζων) all of the seed, he [the Demiurge] fenced it in with a stony enclosure (περίβολον)."[107] Later, in discussing how the soul departs from the body when it dies of old age, he uses the image of the soul slipping through the interlocking triangles that hold the soul in. "Eventually the interlocking triangles around the marrow can no longer hold on, and come apart under stress, and when this happens they let the bonds of the soul go. The soul then is released in a natural way, and finds it pleasant to take its flight."[108] The image of prison, recalled in the *Timaeus* by περίβολον and διασώζων that echo the *Cratylus*, makes way here for a woven fabric that holds the soul in the body until it wears out or is prematurely broken.

---

[104] Cp. the image of trimming one's hair in mourning for abandoning the argument in *Phd.* 89bc, as well as Socrates' refusal to leave Athens.

[105] Burkert 1972: 126 n. 33. While φρουρά may not come from dactylic hexameter, Plato may have borrowed the word from Aristophanes, as I suggest below, n. 164.

[106] Pl. *Phdr.* 250c. Bernabé 1995: 233–234 notes similar wordplay with σῶμα and σῆμα (in the form of ἀσήμαντοι) in the passage.

[107] Pl. *Ti.* 73b, 74a. Ferwerda 1985: 275 compares this account to the etymology from σώζω in the *Cratylus*: "At the end of our passage Plato has Socrates say that he likes the Orphic interpretation of σῶμα even better than the Pythagorean one, because not even a letter need to be changed. He is, methinks, also happy with it because it harmonizes perfectly with his own view which, later on, he propounded in his *Timaeus*." I would suggest rather that Plato modifies the Orphic interpretation to suit his own ideas.

[108] Pl. *Ti.* 81d.

The image in the *Timaeus* is closer to an image that appears in Aristotle, which he attributes to the verses of Orpheus, that an entity comes into being like the weaving of a net.[109] Other sources attest to the existence of an Orphic poem with the title of the *Net* (Δίκτυον), which is attributed in the *Suda* to a Pythagorean author, either Zopyros or Brontinos.[110] While the image is not entirely clear, West suggests that the soul is imagined as air occupying the interstices of the physical elements that make up the net.[111] In any case, the image of the body as a net that holds the soul together within the body, like the *Timaeus'* image, suggests a much more positive interaction of soul and body – the body protects and maintains the soul. However, the image of the body as a net woven together to hold the soul until it deteriorates emphasizes the temporary nature of the body's hold on the soul. Rather than a heavy tomb (or even an oyster shell), a net is a lighter and briefer thing, less burdensome in its binding and easier to unravel and remove. This idea of the body as temporary and easily removable is even more notable in a related image, the body as the garment of the soul. The *Suda* mentions a *Robe* (Πέπλος) in the same list of Pythagorean Orphica as the *Net*, and, like a net, a robe or tunic may be woven together to bind and cover the soul. In his allegorical explanation of the Cave of the Nymphs in Homer, Porphyry depicts the nymphs, weaving together on their looms of stone the sea-purple substance of bodies for the souls descending into birth. He compares the work of these nymphs to the weaving of Kore in a poem by Orpheus, noting also that the ancients described the heavens as a robe.[112]

---

[109] Arist. *Gen. an.* B1 734a16 (*OF* 404 B = OF 26 K): "How, then, does it make the other parts? For either all the parts, such as the heart, lung, liver, eye, and each of the others, come into being all together or they come into being in succession, as in the so-called verses of Orpheus, for there he says that an animal comes into being in the same way as the weaving of a net. That it is not all at once is apparent even by perception, for some of the parts are clearly visible as already existing while others are not yet." Τὰ οὖν ἄλλα πῶς; ἢ γάρ τοι ἅμα πάντα γίγνεται τὰ μόρια οἷον καρδία πνεύμων ἧπαρ ὀφθαλμὸς καὶ τῶν ἄλλων ἕκαστον, ἢ ἐφεξῆς ὥσπερ ἐν τοῖς καλουμένοις Ὀρφέως ἔπεσιν· ἐκεῖ γὰρ ὁμοίως φησὶ γίγνεσθαι τὸ ζῷον τῇ τοῦ δικτύου πλοκῇ. ὅτι μὲν οὖν οὐχ ἅμα καὶ τῇ αἰσθήσει ἐστὶ φανερόν· τὰ μὲν γὰρ φαίνεται ἐνόντα ἤδη τῶν μορίων τὰ δ' οὔ.

[110] *Suda* s.v. Ὀρφεύς (ο 654, III.565.7–8 Adler) (*OF* 403, 1018iv B = OT 223 K). Cp. *Suda* s.v. Ἵππος Νισαῖος (ι 578, II.664.25–29 Adler) (*OF* 405 B = OF 289 K), where Orpheus is said to have mentioned the Nisaian horses in his Δίκτυον; the *Suda* entry derives from Pausanias Atticus, Ἀττικῶν ὀνομάτων συναγωγή s.v. ι 8 (187.22 Erbse).

[111] West 1983: 10. He compares the idea to Philolaos' number cosmogony in which the world is built up element by element like the loops in a net. Lobeck 1829: 380–381 sarcastically dismisses Eschenbach's suggestion that it refers to a cosmogonic interpretation of Hephaistos' capture of Ares and Aphrodite, like that found in Procl. *In R.* 1.142–143 Kroll.

[112] Porph. *De antr. nymph.* 14 (56.10 Simonini) (*OF* 286i B = OF 192 K). Orpheus' poem describing the weaving of Kore, which is more likely to be the Πέπλος (cp. Lobeck 1829: 381), mentioned in the same *Suda* testimony as the *Net*, or perhaps another poem regarding the abduction of Kore.

The image of the body as a garment that covers the soul surfaces first in Empedokles, although it may possibly have appeared in an early Pythagorean Orphic Πέπλος that was later incorporated into the *Rhapsodies*. Plutarch quotes a couple of bits of Empedokles in a discussion of the straightforwardness of Empedokles' poetic style, which uses clear images to convey the nature of the things he is discussing. The body, in Plutarch's opinion, is thus clearly and simply labeled as the mortal-covering earth (ἀμφιβρότην χθόνα). In another treatise, Plutarch presents Empedokles' idea of reincarnation as part of his argument against the eating of meat, presenting the image of souls putting on new bodies, Nature is "clothing souls with an unfamiliar tunic of flesh."[113] Plutarch refuses to make his argument depend on Empedokles' peculiar idea of reincarnation, but he argues, among other things, that the mere possibility that the animal one eats might be a relative should be enough to deter one from eating flesh.[114]

Reincarnation

Modern scholars have often debated whether the idea of reincarnation should be classified as Orphic, Pythagorean, or in some other way, but the ancient evidence shows that, while the idea was certainly attributed to Orpheus in some evidence, as well as to the Pythagoreans, it is not characteristic of all evidence connected with Orpheus. Reincarnation is thus Orphic in the sense that it is the sort of marginal idea that could be attributed to Orpheus, not in the sense that all evidence for Orphic ideas of the soul must incorporate an idea of reincarnation. Plutarch's hesitation shows that, despite the place of reincarnation in various Platonic texts, the idea is still dubious and marginal for a wider audience, such as those

Bernabé suggests that the Pythagorean *Πέπλος* was later incorporated into the *Rhapsodies*, so he puts this passage of Porphyry among the Rhapsodic fragments. I would suggest that Porphyry's allegorical understanding of the weaving of Kore as signifying the oversight of Persephone over the process of genesis may result from the exegesis of a scene of Kore's weaving before her rape by Hades or Zeus in terms of an earlier (or later) *Peplos* poem that discussed the formation of material bodies (and perhaps the cosmos itself) in terms of the weaving of a garment, perhaps something like Pherekydes' image, fr. 2, of the robe that Zas gives to Chthonie as a wedding gift that makes her the physical manifestation of Earth. Cp. West 1983: 97.

[113] Emp. 31 B 126 DK (fr. 110 Wright) = Plut. *De esu carn.* 2.998c (*OF* 450 B): ἀλλάσσει δὲ ἡ φύσις ἅπαντα καὶ μετοικίζει "σαρκῶν ἀλλογνῶτι περιστέλλουσα χιτῶνι." Cp. the excerpt from Porphyry in Stob. *Flor.* 1.49.60.21–24 (1.446.7 Wachsmuth): μετακοσμήσεως εἱμαρμένη καὶ φύσις ὑπὸ Ἐμπεδοκλέους δαίμων ἀνηγόρευται 'σαρκῶν... χιτῶνι' καὶ μεταμπίσχουσα τὰς ψυχάς.

[114] Plut. *De esu carn.* 2.998d uses the analogy of a battle at night time, when one comes across a fallen body whose identity is concealed by the armor and hears from another that it might be a friend or relative instead of an enemy. It is better not to kill, even though the identification is unconfirmed, than to go ahead with the slaughter just because the identification is unconfirmed.

whom Plutarch hopes to convince with his arguments for vegetarianism. Porphyry's references to the bodily tunic in his treatise against meat-eating likewise do not present it in the context of reincarnation but rather in the context of purity. The body is one layer of clothing that we wear, and, just as someone entering a holy place should come with clean clothes and shoes, so too we should approach the gods with bodies pure from the taint of the slaughter of animals.[115] Proclus, in discussing Plato's myth of Er at the end of the *Republic* (which does culminate in reincarnations), uses the image, not to speak of the souls changing incarnations like garments, but rather of the process of punishment, in which the evil have the faults and vices that an ill-spent life has woven into them flayed off of them. The shadowy garment, the tunic of skin around the soul, is not here the bodily incarnation, but part of the soul that can be tainted with bodily faults.[116]

Even if the Platonists Plutarch, Porphyry, and Proclus probably did accept reincarnation, the image of the body as the garment of the soul, which it sheds at death, does not always entail a theory of reincarnation. When Castor is trying to justify Roman practice by Pythagorean ideas, his symbolic interpretation of the practice of covering the head while worshiping the gods as signifying that the body covers the soul does not entail reincarnation; the significance lies in the fact that the human soul is concealed within the body.[117] A late (second-century CE) Italian epitaph includes the image of the tunic of the body in lines that also refer to the soul as everliving and going to the gods and the blessed, and the injunctions to the relatives not to mourn contain no indication that the deceased expects to be back in another form at any point.[118] The same seems true of the images on Roman sarcophagi of genii taking a veil off the deceased; the process of unveiling is the removal of the body from the soul, but there is no reason to suppose that the deceased will shortly be donning a new garment.[119] That the image has passed into common parlance is clear from

---

[115] Porph. *Abst.* 2.46: "In the temples set off by men for gods, even footwear must be pure, and sandals spotless; in the sanctuary of the father, this cosmos, is it not fitting for us to keep holy our last external garment, the skin tunic, and live with it holy in the sanctuary of the father?" οὐ γὰρ δὴ ἐν μὲν ἱεροῖς ὑπ' ἀνθρώπων θεοῖς ἀφωρισμένοις καὶ τὰ ἐν ποσὶ καθαρὰ δεῖ εἶναι καὶ ἀκηλίδωτα πέδιλα, ἐν δὲ τῷ νεῷ τοῦ πατρός, τῷ κόσμῳ τούτῳ, τὸν ἔσχατον καὶ ἐκτὸς ἡμῶν χιτῶνα τὸν δερμάτινον οὐχ ἁγνὸν προσήκει διατηρεῖν καὶ μεθ' ἁγνοῦ διατρίβειν ἐν τῷ νεῷ τοῦ πατρός; Porphyry alludes to the image at 1.31 and perhaps also at 1.1.

[116] Procl. *In R.* 2.182.19 Kroll. Cp. Greg. Naz. *Carm. arcana* 7.36 Sykes = *Carm. dogmatica* 8.36 (*PG* 37.449.9), who does use the image of the body as a garment in the context of a succession of different incarnations.

[117] Castor, *FGrH* 250 F 15 = Plut. *Quaest. Rom.* 10 266e.   [118] *IG* xiv 2241 (*OF* 469 B).

[119] Zuntz 1971: 406 refers to these third-century CE images, with some other evidence, citing Macchioro, Zagreus, 532ff.; Sen. *Ep.* 92.13. Cp. *P. Bonon.* 4 (*OF* 717 B).

Epictetus, certainly no proponent of reincarnation, who refers to the body as the last little tunic, the final material possession by which another can constrain someone.[120]

The image of the body as the garment of the soul is thus fairly widespread, appearing not just in Empedokles and the whole Platonic tradition but in funerary inscriptions and even in Epictetus. Only in certain sources is this garment thought of as one of a succession of garments which the soul may put on as it passes through the cycle of reincarnations; more often, even in authors who talk about reincarnation in other passages, only a single wearing of the garment is envisaged. The image of the body as a protective covering also provides an explanation of the incarnation of the soul (and its exit), but nothing in the theory as it is explained, e.g., in the *Timaeus*, necessitates a cycle of reincarnations, endless or terminal. The same is true of the body as a prison and place of punishment for the soul. While Casadio is quite right to note that often one lifetime seemed insufficient for the workings of divine justice, such concerns did not always entail the idea of reincarnation.[121] Dio's pessimist rules out reincarnation by allowing for the possibility that a man may beget a son to take over his spot in the gods' prison camp and receive his share of the gods' torments.[122] Afterlife punishment might bring compensatory justice, adding to the miseries of this life the horrors of the Underworld; the solutions to the problems of theodicy can vary greatly, depending on the author and his agenda. The image of the body as the tomb of the soul primarily serves to flip the expectations of life and death – life is death and therefore death may be (an even better) life. The focus on the contrast between the two terms makes the σῶμα–σῆμα image less likely to be associated with a series of reincarnations than with the idea of the body as a prison.

Just as certain images of the soul's relation to the body are marked as extraordinary in some way, associated either with the wise and mysterious ancients or certain crazy crackpots, the notion of reincarnation is always

---

[120] Epictetus, *Diss.* 1.25.21: καὶ τὸ τελευταῖον χιτωνάριον, τοῦτ' ἔστι τὸ σωμάτιον, τούτου ἀνωτέρω οὐδενὶ οὐδὲν εἰς ἐμὲ ἔξεστιν.

[121] Casadio 1991: 126: "Se il corpo è per l'anima uno strumento di *timoria* e *kolasis*, una sola *ensomatosis* certamente non basta per garantire l'espiazione dei molti peccati di cui l'anima ha subito il giogo."

[122] Dio Chrys. *Or.* 30.17 (*OF* 429iii, 320vii B): "By so many tortures and of such a kind, then, do men remain surrounded in this outpost and dungeon, each for his appointed time; and most do not get out until they produce another person from their own selves and leave him as heir to the punishment in place of themselves, some leaving only one and others even more." τοιαῖσδε μὲν δὴ καὶ τοσαῖσδε βασάνοις ξυνεχομένους τοὺς ἀνθρώπους ἐν τῇδε τῇ φρουρᾷ καὶ τῷδε τῷ δεσμωτηρίῳ μένειν τὸν τεταγμένον ἕκαστον χρόνον, καὶ μὴ πρὶν ἀπιέναι τοὺς πολλοὺς πρὶν ἂν ἐξ αὐτοῦ ποιησάμενος ἄλλον ἀνθ' ἑαυτοῦ καταλίπῃ διάδοχον τῆς κολάσεως, οἱ μὲν ἕνα, οἱ δὲ καὶ πλείους.

marked as exceptional and is often attributed to figures like Orpheus or Pythagoras.[123] The cycle of reincarnations is thus Orphic in the sense defined in this study, in that it is applied to phenomena that bear the stamp of strangeness. Often the notion is attributed to a foreign source. Herodotus claims that the idea of reincarnation is Egyptian, but, since the Egyptians did not, in fact, have any such notion for the fate of the deceased, Herodotus is presumably attributing Egyptian origin to something he knows from a Greek source.[124] Since he elsewhere claims that practices thought to be Orphic and Bacchic are really Egyptian and Pythagorean, it seems plausible that he associates the idea of reincarnation with certain Orphica with which he was familiar. Diogenes Laertius, in his excursus on the sources of philosophy among the barbarians, says that Theopompos attributes the idea to the Persian *magoi*, another type of alien wisdom.[125]

The identification is not always as clearly foreign, however. Plato refers to some ancient story (παλαιός τις λόγος) with the idea, although the Neoplatonic commentators Damascius and Olympiodorus identify the story as Orphic and Pythagorean.[126] In the *Meno*, Plato refers to wise priests and poets who put forth the idea, quoting a poet who is surely Pindar for the idea that Persephone sends mortals back into life, rewarding the good with the lot of kings.[127] Empedokles and Pythagoras, as Plutarch tells us, both preached the doctrine of reincarnation as a basis for their arguments against the eating of flesh, but Plutarch is hesitant to add this peculiar idea to his own arguments for vegetarianism, fearing it will seem too incredible to his audience.[128] Plutarch refers to their arguments that eating animal food is running the risk of consuming one's own relatives;

---

[123] I use the Latinate word "reincarnation," rather than "metempsychosis," because of the objections of certain ancient Platonists, who argued that metempsychosis should imply a body having a series of souls, rather than a soul having a series of bodies, the term for which would be *metensomatosis* (cp. Procl. *In R.* 2.322.28 Kroll). While Pythagoras is usually credited with the origination of the idea of reincarnation, the *Suda* s.v. Φερεκύδης (φ 214, IV.713.11–18 Adler [*FGrH* 3 T 1]) makes Pherekydes the one who gave Pythagoras the idea.

[124] Hdt. 2.123.1 (*OF* 423 B). Cp. 2.81 (*OF* 43, 45, 650 B = OT 216 K).

[125] Diog. Laert. 1.9 = Theopomp. *FGrH* 115 F 64 (*OF* 427ii B = OF 28 K).

[126] Pl. *Phd.* 70c (*OF* 428i B = OF 6 K). Cp. Olymp. *In. Phd.* 10.6 (*OF* 428ii B = OF 6 K) and Dam. *In Phd.* 1.203 (*OF* 428iii B). The fragment of Diogenes of Oenoanda (fr. 40 Smith) (*OF* 427i B) is too heavily restored to help identify the source of the idea as Orphic, rather than Pythagorean, and even the nature of the idea at issue in the fragment depends heavily upon the speculations of the editors.

[127] Pl. *Meno* 81 (*OF* 424, 666 B), quoting Pind. fr. 133 S.-M. (*OF* 443 B).

[128] Plut. *De esu carn.* 1.996b: "I still hesitate, however, to frame an argument of the principle underlying my opinion, a principle that is great and mysterious and incredible, as Plato says, to merely clever men thinking mortal thoughts," τὴν δὲ μεγάλην καὶ μυστηριώδη καὶ ἄπιστον ἀνδράσι δεινοῖς, ἦ φησιν ὁ Πλάτων (*Phdr.* 245c), καὶ θνητὰ φρονοῦσιν ἀρχὴν τοῦ δόγματος ὀκνῶ μὲν ἔτι τῷ λόγῳ κινεῖν.

eating meat is no better than cannibalism.[129] Pythagoras was thought to remember a series of his own incarnations, starting with Euphorbos during the Trojan War, but the earliest testimony to his belief in reincarnation comes from the mockery of Xenophanes, who portrays him as recognizing an old friend's voice in the howling of a puppy.[130] Empedokles relates that he has gone through a series of incarnations, both animal and vegetable, in his exile from heaven.[131]

In post-Platonic evidence, the idea of reincarnation is often introduced in the context of a moral argument, where the next life becomes a recompense for the deeds of the previous one, either for good or for ill. The connection, however, between reincarnation and compensation is not strictly a necessary one, although such an ethicized idea of reincarnation can be useful to explain the apparent injustice of bad things happening to good people as well as serve as an exhortation to good behavior, even if divine justice does not seem immediately forthcoming.[132] In the myths of Plutarch, for instance, visions of judgment and recompense in the Underworld for the previous life are combined with an assignment of a new incarnation that serves as further recompense (for good or ill) of the prior life.[133] In the earlier evidence, however, the idea of reincarnation as recompense, familiar to modern scholars in the Indian system of karma, does not always seem to underlie the movement of the soul from one body to the next. Empedokles' list of incarnations – male, female, bird, plant, fish – baffles any attempt to find the reasons behind his change of lives.[134] Aristotle likewise complains that the Pythagoreans imagine transmigration of any soul to any body, regardless of the suitability of the soul for the body.[135]

---

[129] Plut. *De esu carn.* 2.997ef, cp. Emp. 31 B 136–137 DK (frr. 122 +124 Wright = Sext. Emp. *Math.* 9.129.2–3, 5–10).

[130] Xenophanes, 21 B 7 DK = Diog. Laert. 8.36.

[131] Emp. 31 B 117 DK (fr. 108 Wright) = Hippol. *Haer.* 1.3.2.3–4 = Diog. Laert. 8.77: "I have once upon a time already been a boy and a girl and a shrub and a bird and a mute fish that leaps from the sea." ἤδη γάρ ποτ' ἐγὼ γενόμην κοῦρός τε κόρη τε θάμνος τ' οἰωνός τε καὶ ἔξαλος ἔλλοπος ἰχθύς.

[132] Cp. Obeyesekere 2002 for a cross-cultural study on ethicization of the afterlife as a process of rationalizing and universalizing. By contrast, Long 1948: 27 denies that any non-ethicized idea of reincarnation could ever have been viable: "It is difficult to believe that any Greek would have taught metempsychosis as a purely mechanical and non-moral process, and if he did that other Greeks would have taken it up, especially men of education and culture."

[133] Cp. Plut. fr. 200.48–59 Sandbach and *De sera.* 565de, for Plutarchan adaptations of these Platonic ideas.

[134] Empedokles' vegetable incarnations do not seem to have created the same problem for eating vegetable food, which should caution us against taking this fragment too literally and out of the context of Empedokles' ideas about the elements reforming into different types of matter. Proclus of course does take it literally and worries about the issue (*In R.* 2.333 Kroll).

[135] Arist. *De an.* 407b20; cp. Xenophanes, 21 B 7 DK = Diog. Laert. 8.36.

Such notions of reincarnation seem grounded in the idea of the mutability of physical elements that transform into different combinations, and the new incarnation may be taken as random instead of dependent on past behavior.

The most elaborate descriptions of the process of reincarnation come in sources like Plato's myths, where a vision of the cycle of life and afterlife is ethicized and manipulated for philosophical purposes.[136] In each dialogue, Socrates attributes the ideas of the myth to some unspecified but special source, hedging, in characteristically Platonic fashion, the authority of the source. For example, in the *Phaedo*, Socrates insists on the fundamental truth of the ideas, even while he simultaneously marks their strangeness and opens them up to (philosophical) questioning. "No sensible man would insist that these things are exactly as I have described them, but I think that it is fitting for a man to risk the belief – for the risk is a noble one – that this, or something like this is true about our souls and their dwelling places, since soul evidently is immortal."[137] The complicated details of the process of reincarnation differ among the *Phaedo*, the *Phaedrus*, and the *Republic*, and these differences meticulously correspond to the details of the arguments in the respective dialogues.

Proclus tries to reconcile all the ideas about reincarnation in all the different myths of Plato, insisting that, in some way at least, all these things are exactly as Socrates describes them, and he quotes several verses of Orpheus in support of his grand unified theory. For Proclus, in his exegesis of the myth of Er at the end of the *Republic*, human souls are governed by rules of reincarnation dependent on a strict theodicy like that depicted in the *Republic*, suffering punishment in the afterlife and then continuing to suffer the consequences of their choices in their next incarnations. As in the *Republic*, afterlife reward or punishment does not substitute for, but complements, a cycle of reincarnations, and Proclus works to harmonize all the references to reincarnation and afterlife judgment in the *Gorgias*, the *Phaedo*, the *Phaedrus*, and the *Republic*. Not only may the soul going to its next incarnation receive a better or worse human life, depending on its behavior in the last incarnation, but, if it lived a

---

[136] See my treatment of the *Phaedo* myth in Edmonds 2004a: 159–220. The myths in the *Phaedrus* and *Republic* have even more elaborate systems of reincarnation, but Plato does not try to maintain a consistent system between the dialogues. Indeed, it is debatable whether the myth in the *Gorgias* even involves a process of reincarnation, since the focus is entirely upon judgment and recompense.

[137] Pl. *Phd.* 81e–82a: Τὸ μὲν οὖν ταῦτα διισχυρίσασθαι οὕτως ἔχειν ὡς ἐγὼ διελήλυθα, οὐ πρέπει νοῦν ἔχοντι ἀνδρί· ὅτι μέντοι ἢ ταῦτ' ἐστὶν ἢ τοιαῦτ' ἄττα περὶ τὰς ψυχὰς ἡμῶν καὶ τὰς οἰκήσεις, ἐπείπερ ἀθάνατόν γε ἡ ψυχὴ φαίνεται οὖσα, τοῦτο καὶ πρέπειν μοι δοκεῖ καὶ ἄξιον κινδυνεῦσαι οἰομένῳ οὕτως ἔχειν – καλὸς γὰρ ὁ κίνδυνος.

life without exercising its human reason, it might receive the life of an animal and suffer through another whole lifetime without being able to exercise that capacity of reason. Proclus argues that human souls, who inherently possess the capacity for reason, can transmigrate into animal bodies, but that animal souls, which do not inherently possess reason, cannot ever transmigrate into human bodies. The descriptions in Plato and other sources of humans passing into animal forms or vice versa must then, according to Proclus, refer to human souls passing into or out of animal bodies. Proclus cites Orpheus to support both the idea of human to human reincarnation, as well as transmigration between human and animal.[138] Orpheus also authenticates the idea that human souls, whether they have just been in animal or human bodies, receive a different fate at the end of a lifetime from animal souls. "When the souls of beasts or winged birds flit forth, and the sacred life leaves them, for them there is no one to lead the soul to the house of Hades, but rather it flutters vainly about itself until, mingled with the breath of the wind, another body snatches it in. But when a human being leaves the light of the sun, Kyllenian Hermes leads the immortal souls to the enormous depths of the earth."[139] Humans thus undergo the process of afterlife judgment and recompense that befits their rational natures, as well as the provident care that the Platonic divine takes for them, while the souls of animals are turned loose to the breezes until they find new incarnations.

[138] Procl. *In R.* 2.338.10–339.9 Kroll (*OF* 338 B = OF 224 K): "Next, that there is also passage of human souls into other animals, this also Orpheus clearly teaches, when he declares: 'On account of this a soul returning according to certain cycles of time goes into different animals from humans at different times. One time it becomes a horse, then a [. . .]; another time a sheep, then a bird dreadful to behold; another time a canine body and growling voice, and the race of cold serpents creeps upon the divine earth.'" Ἔπειθ' ὅτι καὶ εἰς τὰ ἄλλα ζῷα μετάβασίς ἐστι τῶν ψυχῶν τῶν ἀνθρωπίνων, καὶ τοῦτο διαρρήδην Ὀρφεὺς ἀναδιδάσκει, ὁπηνίκα ἂν διορίζηται· "οὕνεκ' ἀμειβομένη ψυχὴ κατὰ κύκλα χρόνοιο | ἀνθρώπων ζώοισι μετέρχεται ἄλλοθεν ἄλλοις· | ἄλλοτε μέν θ' ἵππος, τότε γίνεται . . . | ἄλλοτε δὲ πρόβατον, τότε δ' ὄρνεον αἰνὸν ἰδέσθαι, | ἄλλοτε δ' αὖ κύνεόν τε δέμας φωνή τε βαρεῖα, | καὶ ψυχρῶν ὀφίων ἕρπει γένος ἐν χθονὶ δίῃ." Proclus links the passage of various souls into various bodies, some human and others not, to the generation of all living things from the Titans, the favorite Neoplatonic myth to explain the generation of many from the originary unity: "For does not Orpheus transmit such ideas clearly, when after the mythical punishment of the Titans and the genesis of all mortal living things from them he says first that souls pass from one life to another according to certain revolutions and various souls enter into various bodies, often those of humans." ἢ οὐχὶ καὶ Ὀρφεὺς τὰ τοιαῦτα σαφῶς παραδίδωσιν, ὅταν μετὰ τὴν τῶν Τιτάνων μυθικὴν δίκην καὶ τὴν ἐξ ἐκείνων γένεσιν τῶν θνητῶν τούτων ζῴων λέγῃ πρῶτον μέν, ὅτι τοὺς βίους ἀμείβουσιν αἱ ψυχαὶ κατὰ δή τινας περιόδους καὶ εἰσδύονται ἄλλαι εἰς ἄλλα σώματα πολλάκις ἀνθρώπων.

[139] Procl. *In R.* 2.339.20–26 Kroll (*OF* 339 B = OF 223 K): αἱ μὲν δὴ θηρῶν τε καὶ οἰωνῶν πτεροέντων | ψυχαὶ ὅτ' ἀΐξωσι, λίπῃ δέ μιν ἱερὸς αἰών, | τῶν οὔ τις ψυχὴν παράγει δόμον εἰς Ἀίδαο, | ἀλλ' αὐτοῦ πεπότηται ἐτώσιον, εἰς ὅ κεν αὐτὴν | ἄλλο ἀφαρπάζῃ μίγδην ἀνέμοιο πνοῇσιν· | ὁππότε δ' ἄνθρωπος προλίπῃ φάος ἠελίοιο, | ψυχὰς ἀθανάτας κατάγει Κυλλήνιος Ἑρμῆς | γαίης ἐς κευθμῶνα πελώριον.

Blowing in the wind

This idea of wandering souls, blowing in the wind, resembles an idea that Aristotle attributes to the Pythagoreans, that the soul simply goes into whatever body it happens to meet, regardless of the suitability of the soul for the body.[140] Although Aristotle does not explicitly connect the two, he also mentions the idea, which appears in the so-called verses of Orpheus (ὁ ἐν τοῖς Ὀρφικοῖς ἔπεσι καλουμένοις λόγος), that bodies breathe in the soul as it is carried about by the winds. The blowing of the winds could produce the random incarnations implied by the Pythagorean theory, and the image of the soul borne upon the winds until breathed in may well be an image from an early Orphic poem, perhaps one composed by a Pythagorean, that is picked up and incorporated into the later *Rhapsodies* that Proclus quotes. The role of Hermes in guiding humans to the Underworld need not present insuperable contradictions, since his function as psychopomp is so familiar in the mythic tradition and the human souls could be turned over to the winds for rebirth, rather than, e.g., descend in shooting stars as they do at the end of the myth of Er.[141]

The image is also interesting for the concept of the nature of the soul that is implicit in it. Aristotle's commentators add little that could not be derived from this notice, but Iamblichus attributes the idea to a specific work, the *Physika*.[142] This title, as Gagné points out, is likely a later name for a poem that was perceived to set out ideas relating to the composition of the physical cosmos, but he suggests that we can identify a particular work, extant in the fourth century, to which Aristotle is alluding. Gagné speculates that this Orphic text may have portrayed the Tritopatores, the personifications of the ancestral spirits who watch over the health and fertility of the family or community, as winds that bring the souls into bodies.[143] Iamblichus suggests that the individual souls are parceled out from the One soul in these individual acts of breathing, but it is unclear whether this speculation on the relation of the many and the one comes from the early Orphic text, in the context of Presocratic speculations on the topic, or is yet another Neoplatonic interjection of Neoplatonic cosmology

---

[140] Arist. *De an.* 407b21.   [141] Pl. *Resp.* 621b.

[142] Arist. *De an.* A5 410b27 (*OF* 421i B = OF 27 K). Neither Aristotle nor his commentators explicitly refer this process of incarnation to a theory of reincarnations. Iambl. *De an. ap.* Stob. *Flor.* 1.49.32 (1.366.17 Wachsmuth) (*OF* 421vi B = OF 27 K). Gaisford emended the MSS reading of φυσικοῖς to match Aristotle's Ὀρφικοῖς, but Iamblichus provides more information than is contained in Aristotle's passage, and Gagné suggests that Iamblichus may have known the Orphic text as the *Physika*.

[143] Gagné 2007.

into older texts.[144] In any case, the idea that the soul might enter the body by the breath of the winds can be securely linked with the name of Orpheus by the time of Aristotle, even if none of the sources explicitly connect this idea with reincarnation, rather than simply with incarnation.

The idea that the soul is breathed in also appears attributed to Orpheus by Vettius Valens, who quotes several verses that link the soul with air: "for humans, the soul derives its roots from the ether" and "it is by drawing in the air that we acquire a divine soul."[145] Valens, however, does not link the idea with reincarnation, but rather uses Orpheus' authority to bolster his claims about the immortality and divine nature of the soul.[146] The association of the soul with an airy element (be it αἰθήρ or ἀήρ) is, however, a widespread idea that can hardly be limited to an Orphic sphere. The idea of an airy soul is a natural extension of the image of the soul as the last breath of the dying person, and Bernabé cites a wide variety of parallels to the idea that the soul is airy and the body earthy, ranging from funerary inscriptions to drama to philosophical speculations.[147] Clement even accuses Orpheus of plagiarizing Herakleitos with his verses on the soul's airy nature and the danger of water to the soul.[148] Valens' Orphic text may not be the same one as Aristotle's (or Clement's), but, whereas Aristotle mentions a peculiar idea of the soul breathed in on the winds that seems to be associated only with Orpheus, Valens (and Clement) refer to an idea of the airy nature of the soul that, while it may also be associated with Orpheus, appears in a variety of other sources.

---

[144] Cp. Finamore and Dillon 2002: 144–145.

[145] Vett. Val. 9.1.42–44 (OF 436, 422 B = OF 228ab K): ψυχὴ δ' ἀνθρώποισιν ἀπ' αἰθέρος ἐρρίζω-ται... ἀέρα δ' ἕλκοντες ψυχὴν θείαν δρεπόμεσθα. The notion of drawing in a divine soul by breathing is reminiscent of imagery from the Chaldaean Oracles (and also the Mithras Liturgy); cp. Edmonds 2000.

[146] Vett. Val. 9.1.44–45 (OF 426, 425 B = OF 228cd K): ψυχὴ δ' ἀθάνατος καὶ ἀγήρως ἐκ Διός ἐστιν... ψυχὴ δ' ἀθάνατος πάντων, τὰ δὲ σώματα θνητά. It is a pity, but characteristic of the harm done by previous scholarship, that Komorowska 2004: 324 concludes that Valens could have had no real knowledge of the Orphica but must have found the text from some other source, simply because these lines quoted from Orpheus fail to match the supposed doctrines of "the necessity to recover the Dionysiac element" and other corollaries of the Zagreus myth.

[147] Bernabé 2004: 368 ad OF 436 B: multi (non tantum Orphici) credebantur animam aetheri affinem esse. Diog. Ap. 64 B 4 DK; Eur. Supp. 532, Hel. 1014–1016. For the idea of the psyche as the dying breath, which can be found as early as Homer, see Rohde 1925: 30–31, with Claus 1981: 1–8, and Bremmer 1983: 21–24.

[148] Clem. Al. Strom. 6.2.17.1 (OF 437 B = OF 226 K); cp. Herakleitos, 22 B 36 DK (fr. 66 Marcovich). As Bernabé 2002d: 223 points out, it is likely that the Orphic text known to Clement bears the influence of Stoic ideas that draw upon Herakleitos, and he compares Ar. Did. Epit. Phys. 39.471.11 Diels (SVF 2.821) = Chrysippos fr. 821 von Arnim (SVF 2.225.18) = Posidonius fr. 351 Theiler, as well as Herm. Irris. 14 = Cleanthes fr. 496 (SVF 1.11.6) and Diog. Laert. 7.143 = Chrysippos fr. 633 von Arnim (SVF 2.191.34).

While the idea of the soul blowing in the wind can be reconciled with reincarnation, it neither necessarily entails it nor is entailed by it – the sources attest to ideas of reincarnation without an air-borne soul as well as an airy soul that comes to incarnation only once. Moreover, different thinkers imagined the cycle of reincarnations in different ways, and not every element of one theory of reincarnation appears in all the others.[149] In some versions, the cycle of reincarnations may be endless; in others the whole point is that some means of escape exists. The fundamental principle that death is followed by new life, just as life is followed by death, does not differ much from the basic idea of afterlife. "Now you have died, now you have been born, on this very day, thrice blessed one," proclaim the tablets from Pelinna, but these tablets, like the bone plaques from Olbia with the slogan "life-death-life" merely indicate a sort of life after death, not a full theory of reincarnation.[150] By contrast, most of the references to Pythagorean ideas of reincarnation imply an endless cycle, and even the Platonic adaptations only hint at the possibility of escape.[151] Some of the Neoplatonists seem to have imagined a permanent escape from rebirths; Augustine mentions that Porphyry imagined an escape, although Servius denies any such possibility.[152] Proclus cites as a prayer said by those going through the rites an Orphic verse that refers to an escape from the wheel and a respite from evils.[153]

However, not every reference to a wheel can be taken as an allusion to the cycles of reincarnation, since the image of a wheel could also signify, as it does in Aristotle, the affairs of human life.[154] The gold tablet from

---

[149] Cp. Edmonds 2004a: 95–98 on some of the different types of reincarnation and the debates surrounding the idea in the gold tablets.

[150] Pelinna tablets, D1 (*OF* 485 B) ln. 1, D2 (*OF* 486 B) ln. 1: νῦν ἔθανες καὶ νῦν ἐγένου, τρισόλβιε, ἄματι τῶιδε; Olbian bone tablet *OF* 463 B.

[151] Cp. Plutarch's story (*De gen.* 585ef) of the Pythagorean Lysis, whose friends are concerned, not that he be given Pythagorean burial so that he could escape the cycle of rebirths, but so that his soul could pass on to its next rebirth. In Plato's *Republic*, every soul must choose its next birth; the best that one can hope for is to make a good philosophic choice (*Resp.* 614de, 617d–620d [*OF* 1037ii, 1077i B = OT 139 K]). In the *Phaedrus*, it is theoretically possible for a well-governed soul to avoid falling into birth every single time it passes through the struggle to see at the Plain of Truth (248c), but there is no real escape. In the *Phaedo*, by contrast, the fully purified would seem to pass up to the region of the gods with no reason ever to descend again. The Neoplatonic commentators, however, spotted the inconsistency of this idea with the Cyclic argument earlier in the dialogue. Cp. Dam. *In Phd.* 1.547, 2.147, and Olymp. *In Phd.* 10.14. See further Edmonds 2004a: 97–99, 215–218.

[152] August. *De civ. D.* 10.30, 13.19, 22.27; Serv. *Ad Aen.* 6.745.

[153] Procl. *In Ti.* 3.297.3 Diehl (*ad* 42cd) (≈ *OF* 348i, 598 B = OF 229 K): οἱ παρ᾽ Ὀρφεῖ τῷ Διονύσῳ καὶ τῇ Κόρῃ τελούμενοι τυχεῖν εὔχονται, "κύκλου τ᾽ ἂν λήξαι καὶ ἀναπνεῦσαι κακότητος". A variation of the passage appears also at Simpl. *in Cael.* 377.12 Heiberg (*OF* 348ii B = OF 230 K) (who refers to Zeus, instead of Dionysos and Persephone).

[154] Arist. *Ph.* 4.14 223b24; [*Pr.*] 17.3 916a28. Cp. Hdt. 1.107.2.

Thurii, which imagines apotheosis for the deceased after her escape from the circle of grief, may not have envisaged a whole preceding series of incarnations, and the first-century funerary inscription that congratulates Hekataios for his early escape from the cycle of woes is merely consoling him for his premature death in middle-age, not hailing his departure from the cycle of reincarnations.[155] So too, Clement's quotation from Orpheus that describes how all things cycle around is drawing rather on the tradition of comparing human lives to the cycle of leaves that grow and fall.[156] Herakleitos' paradoxical equation of life and death likewise is quoted by Plutarch in the context of the brevity of human life and the ongoing process of nature, not to console Apollonios with the hope of reincarnation.[157] Too many of the so-called Presocratic thinkers were fascinated by the idea of a cyclical nature of things to take every such reference as implying a doctrine of reincarnation; the cycle was used in many even more interesting ways.

Likewise, not every reference to vegetarianism implies a doctrine of reincarnation or vice versa. Some theorists denied the transmigration of souls from animals to humans or the other way around,[158] and Plutarch and Porphyry, among others, found many other reasons to avoid the eating of meat. The earliest references to vegetarianism associated with Orpheus stress purity with no hint of the idea of reincarnation.[159] Like the idea of the cycle, abstention from meat could be used in many different ways, and we must not let the assumption of a doctrine of reincarnation distract us from other interesting possibilities.

---

[155] Aι (*OF* 488 B = OF 32c K) ln. 6: κύκλο<υ> δ' ἐξέπταν βαρυπενθέος ἀργαλέοιο (*OF* 488 B). *SEG* 41 no. 624 (*OF* 467 B) is a funeral stele from Panticapaeum that is dated somewhere in the first century BCE or CE. Nock 1940 [1986] sensibly and convincingly argues that the sentiments are not Orphism but "popular philosophy."

[156] Clem. Al. *Strom.* 5.8.45.4 (*OF* 438 B = OF 227 K). Clement is discussing symbolic language and explicitly provides the exegesis of the symbol: "The branches either stand as the symbol of the first food, or they are that the multitude may know that fruits spring and grow universally, remaining a very long time; but that the duration of life allotted to themselves is brief." οἱ θαλλοὶ ἤτοι τῆς πρώτης τροφῆς σύμβολον ὑπάρχουσιν, ἢ ὅπως ἐπιστῶν-ται οἱ πολλοὶ τοὺς μὲν καρποὺς δι' ὅλου θάλλειν καὶ αὔξεσθαι διαμένοντας ἐπὶ πλεῖστον, σφᾶς δὲ αὐτοὺς ὀλίγον εἰληχέναι τὸν τῆς ζωῆς χρόνον. Cp. the famous image in *Il.* 6.145. Plutarch cites this and a large number of similar sentiments in his *Consolation to Apollonius*, 103b–104e.

[157] Herakleitos, 22 B 88 DK (fr. 41 Marcovich) = Plut. *Cons. Apol.* 106e (*OF* 454 B).

[158] Aug. *De civ. D.* 10.30 points out that, while Plotinus, *Enn.* 3.4.2 agreed with Plato about the transmigration of animals and humans, Porphyry disagreed. Cp. Euseb. *Præp. evang.* 13.16.

[159] Cp. Pl. *Leg.* 782cd (*OF* 625i B = OT 212 K) on the Ὀρφικὸς βίος, Eur. *Hipp.* 952 (*OF* 627 B = OT 213 K): ἄψυχος βορά. On purity, see further above, chapter 7.

Conclusions

What then constitutes the Orphic idea of the soul's relation to the body, both during life and after (and perhaps before as well)? A few ideas stand out in the sources as marked with that stamp of strangeness that is our best guide to the category of Orphic, but we cannot reconstruct from them an Orphic doctrine of the soul, since these ideas are not all compatible with one another and different parts of them appear separately and combined in different ways in the evidence.[160] Reincarnation appears as Orphic in all of its attestations, whether that label is applied to Pythagorean teachings or Empedokles or Platonic myths, but the converse is not true, since there are many ideas about the soul that preclude or ignore the idea of reincarnation that nonetheless are clearly marked as Orphic. The various images from the *Cratylus* passage may all be labeled Orphic, since the attention to the soul's relation to the body during life, be it as tomb or prison or safe house, appears in limited contexts and is always marked as a special revelation, an extraordinary idea that will transform the hearer's outlook on life and death. These images are presented in protreptic or consolatory speeches, turning the audience's value system on its head, either to convince them to fear death no longer or to fear continuing to live as they do. One danger of such contexts, however, for the modern scholar seeking to understand the different types of doctrines of the soul and afterlife from antiquity is that the images may be piled up with little regard for either discrimination or consistency. The stirring sermon in the Hermetic corpus that calls upon its hearers to awake from their moral sleep and renew their lives reviles the body with a string of epithets familiar from a variety of sources: "But first you must rip off from yourself the tunic you wear, the woven garment of ignorance, the prop of evil, the bond of corruption, the shadowy enclosure, the living death, the sentient corpse, the portable tomb, the robber in your house, who hates you through the things he loves and who envies

---

[160] It is worth noting that the transformation of the soul into a divine being, the ὁμοίωσις θεῷ which plays such an important role in Platonic theology, is not linked with the name of Orpheus in the ancient sources, neither in Plato (cp. *Tht.* 176b) nor in the Neoplatonists (where it becomes the standard definition of philosophy). Although two gold tablets refer to becoming a god (above n. 60), this kind of immortalization (ἀπαθανατίζειν) does not appear associated with Orpheus, despite the reference to Thracian Zalmoxis (*Chrm.* 156d); even in Neoplatonic thought such processes are linked with theurgy and the Chaldaean Oracles, rather than the ancient name of Orpheus. The apotheosis of mortals appears from the earliest literary evidence, e.g., Ino (*Od.* 5.333) or Ganymede (*Il.* 20.232), and Odysseus suggests that, because of his great gratitude, he will worship Nausicaa as a goddess (*Od.* 6.280).

you through the things he hates."[161] We cannot trace each image back to different sources and extrapolate the significance and ramifications of each.

On the other hand, we must also be careful not to lump all roughly similar ideas together, as Clement does in his attack on the Marcionites for their rejection of the body. Clement cites a huge variety of sources, from Homer to Philolaos, from Herakleitos to Herodotus, and from Plato to the Sibyl, anything that supports the notion that the Marcionites plagiarized, from Classical antiquity in general and Plato in particular, the idea that birth is an evil. For Clement, Herodotus' story of Kleobis and Biton or Sophocles' rejoicing that he had grown too old to be a slave to sexual desires have the same point as Philolaos' image of the body as a prison for punishment or Pindar's *makarismos* for the initiate in the Eleusinian Mysteries. Clement's indiscriminate collection has no room for the kind of information most useful to the modern scholar in determining the nature of these different citations, the context of each text and the way in which the ideas about the soul and the body are presented. While we can know the context of the excerpts from Herodotus or Plato, the excerpts from Pindar or Herakleitos or Philolaos create much more of a problem for the scholar trying to figure out the attitude toward the relation of the soul and body that is expressed in the text. Plato's φρουρά can be compared with the arguments in the whole of the *Phaedo*, and we can see that the idea is marked as extraordinary both by the source to which Socrates attributes it and by the interlocutors' reactions. For Pindar we have no such information, only Clement's assertion that the lines pertain to the Eleusinian Mysteries. Nevertheless, careful comparisons can help us sort the evidence to reconstruct the outlines of the categories of ordinary and extraordinary ideas about the soul and its experiences.

The Orphics were not characterized in the ancient sources by their ideas of a lively afterlife and their concern with the hereafter, but rather by their peculiar ideas about the relation of the body to the soul in the here and now. An ordinary man like Plato's Kephalos might worry a bit about suffering in the afterlife (especially as the afterlife approached), but he wouldn't think too much about his body as a prison or burden in this life, nor would he be inclined to think of his current life as a kind of death. Such ideas were the province of the strange and marginal figures, the intellectuals who

---

[161] *Corp. Herm.* 7.2.9–13: πρῶτον δὲ δεῖ σε περιρρήξασθαι ὃν φορεῖς χιτῶνα, τὸ τῆς ἀγνωσίας ὕφασμα, τὸ τῆς κακίας στήριγμα, τὸν τῆς φθορᾶς δεσμόν, τὸν σκοτεινὸν περίβολον, τὸν ζῶντα θάνατον, τὸν αἰσθητὸν νεκρόν, τὸν περιφόρητον τάφον, τὸν ἔνοικον λῃστήν, τὸν δι' ὧν φιλεῖ μισοῦντα καὶ δι' ὧν μισεῖ φθονοῦντα. Cp. Clarke 1999: 14, who cites Monty Python's dead parrot sketch as an example of conflated and contradictory ideas of death.

wondered if life was really death and who lived in this life as if already dead.

Aristophanes pokes fun at such figures in his portrayal of Socrates' students in the *Clouds*; they are pale as corpses and take no care for the necessities of ordinary life.[162] When the old man Strepsiades tries to join them, he laments that he is becoming half-dead (ἡμιθνὴς) like Socrates' follower, Khairophon, and, when Socrates curses his stupidity, he replies that he has already perished.[163] While sitting around trying to think deep, philosophical thoughts, he complains that he has not only lost material things (money and shoes), but he has also become pale and lacking his vital force (ψυχή). He compares his situation to a frontier guardsman reduced to singing guardpost songs (φρουρᾶς ᾄδων) as he wastes away at his lonely post.[164] The imagery of being dead in life arises repeatedly throughout the play, although it is notable that these thinkers are never portrayed as speculating about the afterlife, even among all the other peculiar things they ponder. Life as one of these marginal intellectuals is much like death in this Aristophanic comedy, and Aristophanes' audience no doubt found the humor in this mockery of familiar strange figures.

Plato too attests to such mainstream ideas of speculative thinkers. When Socrates provides his famous definition of philosophy as the practice of death (μελέτη θανάτου), Simmias laughs, pointing out that most people would agree that philosophers are practically dead already (and that, if not, someone should kill them).

> You sure made me laugh, although I don't feel much like laughing just now. For I think the many, if they heard what you just said about the philosophers, would think it entirely right, and those people where we come from would agree totally, that in truth philosophers *are* already dead, nor would they omit to say that they think the philosophers deserve to suffer this.[165]

We may understand such a joke, like the ones in Aristophanes, as the flip side of the body–soul doctrines that appear, not just in the *Phaedo*, but also, for example, in the *Cratylus*. The distinction between those who postulate

---

[162] Pale skin, e.g., *Nub.* 103, 1171.
[163] *Nub.* 504: ἡμιθνὴς; *Nub.* 726: ἀλλ' ὦ 'γάθ' ἀπόλωλ' ἀρτίως.
[164] Ar. *Nub.* 718–721: ὅτε μου φροῦδα τὰ χρήματα, φροῦδη χροιά, φροῦδη ψυχή, φροῦδη δ' ἐμβάς· καὶ πρὸς τούτοις ἔτι τοῖσι κακοῖς φρουρᾶς ᾄδων ὀλίγου φροῦδος γεγένημαι. That he uses the word φρουρά is no doubt a wordplay on φροῦδα ("lost"), but Plato may well have had this passage in mind when choosing the word for the *Phaedo*.
[165] Pl. *Phd.* 64b: οὐ πάνυ γέ με νυνδὴ γελασείοντα ἐποίησας γελάσαι. οἶμαι γὰρ ἂν τοὺς πολλοὺς αὐτὸ τοῦτο ἀκούσαντας δοκεῖν εὖ πάνυ εἰρῆσθαι εἰς τοὺς φιλοσοφοῦντας – καὶ συμφάναι ἂν τοὺς μὲν παρ' ἡμῖν ἀνθρώπους καὶ πάνυ – ὅτι τῷ ὄντι οἱ φιλοσοφοῦντες θανατῶσι, καὶ σφᾶς γε οὐ λελήθασιν ὅτι ἄξιοί εἰσιν τοῦτο πάσχειν.

a cycle of reincarnations that provides the basis for an ascetic, vegetarian lifestyle and those who see the body as a net woven to support the soul in its sojourn in the material realm may be very clear to the proponents of each idea and even discernible to the modern scholar who carefully examines the evidence for each view. Such a marginal distinction, however, is likely to have been entirely ignored by Aristophanes' audience or any other ancient mainstream group.[166] From the perspective of the center, all such ideas reverse the value of life and death, turning normative values on their head, and these ideas will be classified together as extra-ordinary, perhaps even explicitly Orphic.

These ideas of the relation of soul to body and life to death may be termed "Orphic" in the broadest sense, as ideas that would have been perceived either as laughable conceits of pretentious intellectuals by Aristophanes' audience or as extraordinary insights into the human condition by more sympathetic observers – be they self-designated philosophers like the followers of Plato or even someone like Strepsiades in the *Clouds* before he figures out the scam. The idea that the soul had an airy nature would only be perceived as out of the ordinary if developed further in certain ways, whereas the idea that the soul persisted in an active fashion after death would not have been perceived as extra-ordinary at all.

The lively afterlife, including the differentiations of reward and punishment based on behavior within life, is thus not an extraordinary idea for the ancient Greeks of any period for which we have evidence to check. The Homeric idea of immortality coming only from the memory of the dead preserved in the minds of the living through poetic song remains, no doubt, a viable alternative model throughout all the periods in which Homeric poetry was a significant presence in education, but even the Homeric poems present, along with the idea of poetic immortality, reinforcement of the normal ideas of the persistence of souls and a lively afterlife. This normal idea, the ordinary idea of afterlife, is at times challenged by marginal philosophical ideas that cast the relation of life and afterlife in a different way, suggesting that life was really death and the afterlife after death was the real life. These ideas, however, have less to say about the nature of the afterlife than about the relation of the soul to body during life – the soul

---

[166] Dover 1968: lii perfectly captures the problem of perspective, especially as it afflicts modern scholars, who are naturally inclined to side with the intellectuals: "In order to understand *Nu.* we must make an imaginative effort to adopt an entirely different position, the position of someone to whom all philosophical and scientific speculation, all disinterested intellectual curiosity, is boring and silly. To such a person distinctions which are of fundamental importance to the intellectual appear insignificant, incomprehensible, and often imperceptible."

is entombed in the body, alive in death, or perhaps it is just trapped there, imprisoned to undergo punishment or caught in the net until it can win release. Such extra-ordinary ideas about life thus provoke extra-ordinary solutions for action within life, ranging from ascetic lifestyles to rituals of purification, and such solutions also appear in the evidence associated with the label of Orphic.

CHAPTER NINE

Original sin or ancestral crimes
Zagreus and the concern with purification

The web of Penelope

And she devised yet another trick. Setting up a great loom within the halls, she wove a delicate and great-sized web ... And thus by day she was weaving at the great loom, but by night she was unraveling it, since she had placed torches nearby her.[1]

Alberto Bernabé has compared the scholarship on Orphism in the past century to the web of Penelope, a succession of cunning weavings of the threads followed by unravelings, in which any apparent progress in formulating a coherent picture of Orphism by one wave of scholars is undone by the next group of critics.[2] So the proto-Protestant Orphic church imagined by Kern and Macchioro was unraveled by skeptics like Wilamowitz, while the more balanced Orphic religious movement depicted by Guthrie was challenged by the rigorous critique of Linforth. Bernabé now objects to the attempts made recently to tear apart his own careful reconstruction of Orphic religion, articulated in a series of articles over the past decade and culminating in his new edition of the Orphic fragments.

Orphism, as Bernabé and other scholars such as Parker, Graf, and Johnston define it, is a religious movement that can be identified, not by social structures like an Orphic church, but rather by a set of doctrines about the origin and fate of the soul.[3] The doctrines of the soul's immortality and

---

[1] Hom. *Od.* 2.93–95, 104–105: ἡ δὲ δόλον τόνδ' ἄλλον ἐνὶ φρεσὶ μερμήριξε· | στησαμένη μέγαν ἱστὸν ἐνὶ μεγάροισιν ὕφαινε, | λεπτὸν καὶ περίμετρον·... ἔνθα καὶ ἠματίη μὲν ὑφαίνεσκεν μέγαν ἱστόν, | νύκτας δ' ἀλλύεσκεν, ἐπὴν δαΐδας παραθεῖτο.

[2] Bernabé 2002a: 402: "Le titre que j'ai donné à cette analyse du mythe orphique de Dionysos et des Titans, 'La toile de Pénélope', vise à être une espèce de métaphore des phases de reconstitution et de déconstruction que les spécialistes ont fait subir à ce mythe, tout au long de son histoire." An earlier version of this chapter has been published online as *Recycling Laertes' Shroud: More on Orphism and Original Sin*. Center for Hellenic Studies online (http://chs.harvard.edu/chs/redmonds).

[3] Bernabé 1997: 38 sees this nucleus of doctrines as the reference point by which the ancients labeled something Orphic: "Debemos denunciar la falacia de un argumento reiteradamente expresado: que

296

its transmigration from body to body are founded, in this hypothesis, on a particular narrative of the origin of human beings within the cosmos.[4] Scholars weave together four strands into this central mythic narrative: the dismemberment of Dionysos Zagreus by the Titans, the punishment of the Titans by Zeus, the generation of human beings from the ashes of the lightning-blasted Titans, and the burden of guilt that human beings inherited from their Titanic ancestors because of this original sin. I argue to the contrary that this "Zagreus myth" (as I will refer to this construct of the four elements) is a modern fabrication and that the coherent picture of Orphism scholars have so cleverly woven must be unraveled, so that all of the strands of evidence may be recycled, put back into their proper contexts within ancient Greek religion.[5]

The four strands of the myth never appear all bound together in any of the extant evidence, but scholars defend the reconstruction of this Zagreus myth as the only possible way to explain the appearance in the evidence of all four strands in various contexts and combinations. In response to recent critiques, Bernabé tries to weave the pieces together into one coherent tale to sustain the idea of an Orphic religion that persisted over the centuries, defined by its essential nucleus of doctrines despite the shifting cultural milieux in the Mediterranean between the sixth century BCE and the sixth CE.[6] Bernabé presents as clear a case as may be made about the most crucial pieces of evidence for each of these strands belonging to a single fabric, but his arguments nevertheless fail to prove even that such a Zagreus myth ever existed before its formulation in modern scholarship. While it

no existe un orfismo como moviemento religioso, sino sólo libros atribuidos a Orfeo. Basta con preguntarse cuál es el motivo de que alguien atribuya un libro a Orfeo para descubrir que hay un punto referencial, un núcleo de pensamiento en el que cada escritor se integra o no. El orfismo es un ideología, y atribuirse una obra órfica es el resultado de haber optado previamente por una forma de pensar en materia de religión." Parker 1995 is more tentative in his reconstruction, but nevertheless identifies something as Orphism that he discusses in terms of specific doctrines, even if he leaves the unity of Orphism in doubt. Graf and Johnston 2007, despite their appeals to *bricolage* as the fundamental mechanism of the mythic and religious tradition, nevertheless make the eschatological doctrines derived from the Orphic myth of Dionysos' murder the essence of their interpretation of the gold tablets and the religious context from which they come.

4 Bernabé 1998a: 172: "El creyente órfico busca la salvación individual, dentro de un marco de referencia en que son puntos centrales: el dualismo alma-cuerpo, la existencia de un pecado antecedente, y el ciclo de trasmigraciones, hasta que el alma consigue unirse con la divinidad." Cp. Bernabé 1997: 39, Bernabé 2002d: 208–209, Bernabé 2008b: 1645–1647.

5 See Edmonds 1999 for the modern fabrication of the Zagreus myth. Bernabé 2002a and 2003 attempt to directly refute the textual arguments in that article, but leave largely unaddressed the arguments about the place of the creation of the Zagreus myth and Orphism in the scholarship on the history of religions.

6 Bernabé 2002a: 423: "Il doit donc correspondre à un mouvement religieux d'une longue durée lui aussi, d'une longue présence. Quel autre candidat à une aussi longue durée pourrions nous trouver, sinon l'orphisme?"

is ultimately impossible to prove that such a myth never did exist, that all four elements were not ever at any point woven together, I shall show that none of the evidence combines all four elements, that some of the evidence that Bernabé and others have claimed combines several strands does not in fact weave together the elements in such a way, and that some of the evidence that attests to the presence of one element in fact precludes the presence of some of the other elements. Moreover, despite the claim that the evidence can be explained in no other way, I shall show that each of these threads can easily be explained within the wider context of Greek religion and mythology. The result is not a single, tightly woven myth like the one Bernabé and others have fabricated, but rather an assortment of shreds and patches that nevertheless provides a better understanding of the nature and variations of ancient Greek religion.

It is impossible to disprove that some author unknown, at some point in the twelve centuries between Pindar and Olympiodorus, might have combined all four of the strands of the Zagreus myth or even that such a story was designed to provide a rationale for a special religious program involving purifications. Likewise, it is impossible to prove conclusively that such a combination was actually never made, that no one until the nineteenth century ever combined the elements into a single story. Too many texts are missing from antiquity to make a simple argument from silence persuasive. The hypothesis that a telling of the Zagreus myth existed must therefore be evaluated on other grounds.

One important difference between the two unprovable hypotheses is falsifiability.[7] My contention that the Zagreus myth never existed could be falsified by the discovery of a text that recounted the myth including all four elements. My hypothesis that such a story did not provide a doctrinal basis for a coherent Orphic religion could be falsified by a new text like the Derveni papyrus that provides exegesis of cultic practice on the basis of the myth. By contrast, the hypothesis that the Zagreus myth existed as a secret tradition that was never clearly and explicitly recorded is completely unfalsifiable. No potential discovery of myth or ritual, exegesis or argument, could possibly shake the assertion that such a myth existed in an underground tradition, since the absence of clear evidence is in fact one of the proofs that the tradition was secret. To make the comparison somewhat melodramatically, the hypothesis of the Zagreus myth shares this

---

[7] The criterion of falsifiability provides a way of choosing between two potentially valid theories, both of which can provide meaningful ways of explaining the evidence. Popper 1963: 35 comments on the fact that unfalsifiable theories frequently seem strong because almost any evidence can be fitted into the theory, but that "this apparent strength was in fact their weakness."

characteristic of unfalsifiability with UFO and other conspiracy theories.[8] No amount of evidence can prove that the black helicopters or aliens or the Illuminati or whatever it happens to be do not exist. The lack of evidence merely reinforces the conviction that the secret was important enough to be kept secret. Logically, such theories are weaker than those whose truth can be tested by the appearance of new evidence.

Accepting the Zagreus myth involves accepting a number of premises that are rarely made explicit in the arguments for its plausibility. First is the idea of a secret doctrinal tradition, a secret that is recognizable by allusion to those in the know but which it is not licit to make explicit. Such a premise is used to explain all the indirect references to the myth and the absence of any direct exposition of either the story or the doctrines it supports. According to this hypothesis, modern scholars have cracked this secret code, unlike the still mysterious references to the rituals of the Eleusinian Mysteries. The Zagreus myth explains all the secret references made not only by the pious initiates like Pausanias and Diodorus Siculus, who respect the mysteries, but also by the philosophers like Plato and Plutarch, who only make use of the ideas without fully accepting the myth. And, of course, even Christian polemicists like Clement and Firmicus dare not do more than allude vaguely to the crucial doctrines and ideas, even in the midst of their revelation of the actions of the rituals. Hence, all their evidence can be seen to point to this myth, even though none of the evidence actually expresses it openly.

A related premise is that this secret doctrine, the need for humanity to seek purification from the original sin of the Titanic ancestors' murder of Dionysos, remained unchanged throughout the span of more than a millennium from which the evidence comes. The myth of the murder of Zagreus always had this meaning to the Orphic faithful, who preserved the essential tenet of their faith despite the absence of any social structure or organization to help them transmit their doctrines over the generations. One consequence of this premise is that scholars can ignore the explicit meaning assigned to any part of the myth in the evidence, as well as the context in which the myth is related. The true context, according to this premise, is the secret Orphic tradition, not the particular text in which the element or idea just happens to be found.

In addition to these premises, accepting the Zagreus myth requires that one accept that not only did the true meaning remain unchanged over

---

[8] Guthrie 1952: 253 even speaks of a "conspiracy of silence" that hides the evidence for the Orphic mysteries in the earlier periods.

the centuries, but none of the reinterpretations that were done, by various unbelieving philosophers and allegorists, had any real impact on the form and shape of the story. Therefore, all the evidence that mentions the dismemberment, the Titans' punishment, the anthropogony, or the guilt borne by the human race can be used to reconstruct the same story. Any variants can be explained away like the variants in a manuscript tradition, as errors that do not reflect the true and original text.

The first premise of the secret doctrine is susceptible to the logical critique of unfalsifiability, but the others, I would argue, go counter to the fluid and dynamic nature of the Greek mythic tradition. Greek myths were never, even after the efforts of the late systematizing mythographers, a set of fixed texts whose archetype could be recovered from a collation of the manuscripts. Rather, they remained a dynamic tradition that was constantly in contest, with new versions narrated in different ways all vying for authority with each other. While the internal coherence of the Zagreus myth hypothesis lends it plausibility, the premises on which the whole structure rests cannot be accepted.

To make his argument for the existence of the Zagreus myth and its centrality to Orphic doctrine from the sixth century BCE to the sixth century CE, Bernabé provides a set of thirty-seven testimonies (selected from the more than one thousand Orphic fragments in his new edition).[9] He arranges these texts into six basic categories: the early testimony of Pindar to inherited guilt, the references in Plato to inherited guilt and the punishment of the Titans, the allusions to the dismemberment in Plutarch's *De Esu Carnium*, the evidence for rituals connected with the dismemberment, references to the generation of the human race from the blood of the Titans, and Neoplatonic texts (from Proclus and Damascius to Olympiodorus' crucial passage).[10] The reconstruction of the Zagreus myth and of Orphism in general does indeed rest on such few and such slender threads.[11] I shall treat each of these categories in turn, showing that the evidence does not support the hypothesis of a Zagreus myth combining the strands of dismemberment, punishment of Titans, anthropogony, and inherited guilt. On the contrary, the evidence associated with the dismemberment

[9] Bernabé 2002a: 426–433.
[10] Bernabé 2002a covers all these categories, whereas Bernabé 2003 focuses in more textual detail upon Olympiodorus, Plutarch, Plato, and the blood of the giants in the *Orphic Argonautica*.
[11] Cp. Festugière in his review of Guthrie's reconstruction of Orphic doctrines: "Toutes les reconstructions de l'orphisme ont pour fondement un très petit nombre de témoignages sûrs et un plus grand nombre de textes dont l'exégèse me paraît arbitraire" (Festugière 1936: 310). One of the significant differences between the current debate and the older Linforth–Guthrie controversy is precisely that the current argument is grounded in the particular pieces of evidence and their interpretation.

of Dionysos attests to a variety of myths and rituals which had different meanings in their assorted contexts. Although Persephone and Dionysos are indeed both associated in some evidence with relief from divine anger, this function is not directly associated with the dismemberment myth but belongs to other aspects of their cults. Nor is the Dionysos who is dismembered always the child of Persephone; at times he is born from Semele or even Demeter. So, too, the Titans were punished in myth both after their dismemberment of Dionysos and after their rebellion against the gods, but, except in the sixth-century CE innovation of Olympiodorus, the generation of human beings only follows the Titanomachy.

At stake in the recycling of this evidence is not merely the validity of the Zagreus myth, but a variety of other issues in ancient Greek religion, as each text replaced in context enhances the understanding both of the particular facet and of the broader dynamics of the tradition. For example, my treatment of the anthropogonic myths that relate mankind's origin from a previous race will show that the Orphic evidence is indeed part of a broader tradition of such tales, even if the scattered and mostly local evidence for such myths is too often overshadowed by the Hesiodic tales. My rereading of Pindar fr. 133 raises important questions about the relation of Persephone cult (especially perhaps in Magna Graecia) to the myth of her abduction, touching on that perennial problem in the study of Greek religion – the relation of myth to ritual. If the cult honors paid to her are in some sense a recompense for her abduction, we can gain a better understanding of Persephone's role as *kourotrophos* and patron of marriage, as well as a better sense of the ideas of women and marriage that structure the societies that related the myths and celebrated the cults. So, too, the evidence for rituals involving the dismemberment of Dionysos provides insight into the whole range of ways in which the god was significant for the Greeks in different times and different places.

More importantly, understanding that the dismemberment myth did not have a single meaning helps us to see the underlying dynamic of the Greek religious tradition, the ceaseless change and contestation within the relatively stable and coherent tradition. The workings of this fluid and dynamic tradition are also explored in my treatment of Plato's references in the *Laws*, as well as the allegorical readings of Plutarch and the Neoplatonists Proclus, Damascius, and Olympiodorus. Plato is continually struggling with the balance between innovation and tradition as he formulates rules for a new society in the *Laws*, and the passages I treat are only a small part of his manipulation of traditional religious ideas in the service of his philosophic ideals. Moreover, Plato's use of myths does not differ so greatly from the later thinkers who follow in the Platonic philosophic tradition. By treating the interpretations of Plutarch and Olympiodorus as a real part of the Greek mythic and religious tradition, rather than an excrescence that needs to be wiped away for the "original" meaning to shine through, my analysis presents a broader view of the ways the Greeks dealt with their myths. Plutarch provides the viewpoint of an educated religious thinker of the early Imperial period, while Olympiodorus and the other Neoplatonists show the ways in which the religious tradition continued to be significant, even as Greek paganism faced the challenges of Christianity. Recycling this material, removing it from its artificial frame and replacing it in its original contexts, helps us better to understand the ancient evidence and religious traditions from which it comes.

The apparent coherence of the Zagreus myth can only be achieved by taking the pieces of evidence out of their proper contexts; when viewed in the context of the texts from which they come, the pieces provide instead a series of tantalizing glimpses of the wider fabric of Greek religion and mythology. The collections of Orphic fragments by Kern and Bernabé both presume the existence of the Zagreus myth and arrange the evidence to provide the clearest picture of their reconstruction of the myth, trimming out the surrounding texts in which the fragments are found.[12] As Catherine Osborne has noted, however, any collection of fragments creates interpretive problems, because the texts are stripped of the contexts from which they come. "Thus it is the collection of 'fragments' in groups by modern editors, working on the basis of their own preconceptions, which provides the context in which they are currently read."[13] In the context of a collection of fragments, the Zagreus myth seems a plausible hypothesis, but its coherence disappears when the strands are seen, not in the limited context of "Orphism," defined in a particular way, but in the broader context of Greek religion as a whole.

---

[12] One of the few ways in which Bernabé's excellent edition of the Orphic fragments does not represent an advance over his predecessor Kern is in his deliberate choice to cut back the context of the fragments even further. Bernabé 2000: 74: "Non mi interesso di quei frammenti contenuti nei commentari neoplatonici che non offrono nessuna informazione per la ricostruzione del poema orfico. Il Kern è stato troppo generoso, a mio avviso, nella inclusione di questi commenti."

[13] Osborne 1987: 8. Osborne recognizes the problem of biased sources and peculiar interpretations that leads scholars to discard the contexts, but, as she argues, "Reading an embedded instead of a fragmented text we read it as a functioning and meaningful system, governed by the preoccupation of an interpreter whose interests we can assess, rather than a set of disjointed parts, detached from the context in which they might mean something. Each interpretation will start from a biased approach, but once this factor is recognised we are in a better position to proceed" (Osborne 1987: 10).

Although Bernabé protests that Orphism is the only known religious movement that could explain the persistence of the mythic elements, the entire Greek mythic tradition itself provides the proper context for interpreting the presence, persistence, and permutations of these elements.[14] The *bricolage* performed by countless narrators of myth over the millennia combines and recombines the various elements in the mythic tradition in a stunning variety of ways for a plethora of purposes.[15] The story of Dionysos' dismemberment, like any other myth, meant different things to different people and even different things to the same people in different contexts. The mere presence of the tale elements over a long stretch of time does not mean that its religious or philosophical meaning remained the same; on the contrary, without explicit evidence that a myth somehow meant the same thing to people in significantly different times and places, we must assume that it was reinterpreted to suit the ideas of its current users. No such explicit evidence exists, and the evidence to the contrary, which does indeed exist, is suppressed when the texts are examined without their contexts.

Some of the evidence is labeled in the ancient sources as Orphic, that is, associated with a poem or a ritual composed by Orpheus, but much of the evidence Bernabé and his predecessors cite is brought into consideration only because it attests to one of the four mythic strands of the Zagreus myth. Whereas Linforth simply refused to consider such evidence, I suggest that it is more useful to try, however tentatively, to recycle the material, to attempt to place it back into its context within the larger fabric of Greek religion. To be sure, we are left with an incomplete picture, disconnected shreds of the vast and complex tapestry of ancient Greek religion, but such shreds more accurately represent the puzzle we have before us than a neatly woven web that binds together disparate elements for the sake of having a simple solution.[16]

---

[14] Bernabé 2003: 39: "Une telle persistance s'explique seulement si tous les passages renvoient à un schéma commun, qui a gardé sa cohésion en tout temps. Il doit donc correspondre à un mouvement religieux lui aussi d'une longue durée, d'une longue présence. Quel autre candidat à une aussi longue durée pourrions nous trouver, sinon l'orphisme?"

[15] For the concept of *bricolage*, see Lévi-Strauss 1966: 16–36. Cp. the attempt to explore some of the ramifications of the idea for myths of the journey to the underworld often labeled "Orphic" in Edmonds 2004a. Graf and Johnston 2007, esp. 70–71, make use of the concept to discuss the religious context of the gold tablets, but their discussion is vitiated by the attempt to pin down a single act of bricolage that created the Zagreus myth, rather than seeing the pieces as the product of many acts of *bricolage* over the entire span of time from which the evidence comes.

[16] Bernabé uses the puzzle image of Henrichs in Burkert 1977: 21 to argue that all these pieces should be seen as part of the same Orphic puzzle. "Bref, nous possédons les pièces d'un puzzle.

Recompense for the ancient grief

Pure I come from the pure, Queen of those below the earth,
And Eukles and Eubouleus and the other gods and daimons;
For I also claim that I am of your blessed race.
Recompense I have repaid on account of deeds not just;
Either Fate mastered me or the lightning bolt thrown by the thunderer.
Now I have come, a suppliant, to holy Phersephoneia,
That she, gracious, may send me to the seats of the blessed.[17]

In one of the gold tablets from Timpone Piccolo in Thurii, the speaker seeks the favor of Persephone, Queen of the Underworld, asking for an afterlife in the company of the blessed. In support of her plea, she claims not only that she comes of the lineage of the gods, but that she is ritually pure, and that she has made recompense for unjust deeds. These enigmatic qualifications, which she clearly expects Persephone to understand, have fascinated scholars ever since the discovery of this tablet in 1879, and the answers that have been provided to this enigma have been fundamental to the reconstruction of the religious context of the gold tablets and the wider phenomenon of Orphism.

The discovery of the Thurii tablets provided the impetus for the formulation of Orphism as a religion centrally concerned with sin and salvation, and, even if Orphism is no longer seen as foreshadowing the importance of these doctrines in Early Christianity, the idea persists that humanity is stained with the crime of the Titans who murdered the infant Dionysos Zagreus, child of Persephone. The conjunction of Persephone and a ποινή paid for unjust deeds has accordingly been understood as a claim that the deceased has learned the secret of humanity's origin from the Titanic murderers of Dionysos and has paid to Dionysos' mother the blood-price owed by all humans for the ancestral crime.

The interpretation of this gold tablet from Thurii rests crucially upon the mistaken interpretation of another enigmatic text, a fragment of Pindar

---

Elles s'assemblent, ne serait-ce que manière incomplète. Certains philologues cherchent à montrer qu'elles n'appartiennent pas à un puzzle, mais que ce sont des réalités indépendantes. Seul un partis pris préalable peut conduire à nier ce qui est évident: il s'agit ici d'une attitude qui se manifeste particulièrement en relation avec l'orphisme, tout comme s'il existait une volonté déterminée d'en donner l'idée de quelque chose d'insignifiant, d'inconsistant, de tardif ou, qui pis est, d'inventé" (Bernabé 2002a: 420). I would simply suggest that one must consider the "puzzle" to be reconstructed with this evidence as "Greek religion" rather than "Orphism."

[17] Gold tablet A2 from Thurii (*OF* 489 B = OF 32d K), cp. A3 (*OF* 490 B = OF 32e K): ἔρχομαι ἐκ καθαρῶν καθαρά, χθονίων βασίλεια, | Εὐκλῆς καὶ Εὐβουλεύς καὶ θεοὶ δαίμονες ἄλλοι | καὶ γὰρ ἐγὼν ὑμῶν γένος ὄλβιον εὔχομαι εἶναι. | ποινὰν δ' ἀνταπέτεισ' ἔργων ἕνεκ' οὔτι δικαίων· | εἴτε με μοῖρ' ἐδάμασσ' εἴτε ἀστεροπῆτι κεραυνῶ | νῦν δ' ἱκέτης ἥκω παρ' ἁγνὴν Φερσεφόνειαν | ὥς με πρόφρων πέμψῃι ἕδρας ἐς εὐαγέων.

preserved in a Platonic dialogue, in which Persephone is said to accept the recompense (ποινή) for her ancient grief (πένθος). I argue that, in both these texts, the ποινή Persephone accepts is not a blood-price, but rather ritual honors in recompense for her traumatic abduction to the Underworld by Hades. Persephone's πένθος is not grief over a murdered son but rather her anguish over this turbulent passage from Kore to Queen of the Underworld. I will first examine the meanings of these terms in Pindar, and then explore parallel stories in which the grief of a maiden's disrupted passage is appeased or her anger averted by ritual honors paid to her, not by the guilty party as weregild, but by mortals seeking to win her favor, to make her gracious (πρόφρων) toward them just as the deceased hopes in the Thurii tablet.

By resituating these pieces of evidence in their proper religious context, I hope to contribute to a better understanding of the religious phenomena labeled Orphic in antiquity, showing how familiar patterns of myth and ritual are manipulated and taken to extra-ordinary extremes. The Orphic is not one who believes that all humanity must atone for the original sin of the Titans' murder of Dionysos, but rather one who believes that she can win special favor, in the afterlife as well as in this life, by special attentions paid to Persephone and other chthonic powers. These special attentions might include rites of appeasement, special placatory honors, or rites of purification and release. These latter rites are likely to have had a Dionysiac aspect, since Dionysos is the god who presides over purification and release. The presence of Dionysos in the evidence, therefore, stems from his complementary role in this traditional pattern of myth and ritual, rather than from the particular mythic strand that made Persephone the mother of Dionysos, of which there is no trace in this evidence.

The enigmatic reference, contained in a fragment of Pindar quoted in Plato's *Meno*, to the recompense Persephone receives for the ancient grief has been taken as the earliest evidence for the Orphic doctrine of humanity's guilt inherited from the Titans.

Those from whom Persephone receives the recompense for the ancient grief,
their souls in the ninth year she sends back to the sun above,
and from them arise glorious kings and men swift with strength and very great
in wisdom;
and in time to come they are called sacred heroes among men.[18]

---

[18] Plato, *Meno* 81bc = Pind. fr. 133 (*OF* 443 B): οἷσι γὰρ ἂν Φερσεφόνα ποινὰν παλαιοῦ πένθεος | δέξεται, εἰς τὸν ὕπερθεν ἅλιον κείνων ἐνάτῳ ἔτει | ἀνδιδοῖ ψυχὰς πάλιν, ἐκ τᾶν βασιλῆες ἀγαυοὶ | καὶ σθένει κραιπνοὶ σοφίᾳ τε μέγιστοι | ἄνδρες αὔξοντ'· ἐς δὲ τὸν λοιπὸν χρόνον ἥρωες | ἁγνοὶ πρὸς ἀνθρώπων καλέονται.

This passage was not considered Orphic by Kern, but Bernabé has included it in his recent edition on the strength of the arguments made by H. J. Rose. Even Linforth, although he expresses reservations, accepts this passage as evidence that an idea of humans paying the penalty for the Titans' murder of Dionysos was known in the sixth century BCE.[19] Such a payment would seem to imply all four of the elements of the so-called Zagreus myth: the dismemberment of Dionysos Zagreus, the punishment of the Titans, the anthropogony from their remains, and the burden of inherited guilt to be expiated by the payment. The problem is that Rose's interpretation is dependent on the particular detail of Olympiodorus' telling that seems most likely to be his own innovation – the composition of human beings not just from the Titans but also from the fragments of Dionysos which they consumed before being blasted with lightning.[20] However, the alternatives to Rose's interpretation previously suggested by Rohde and Linforth are too weak to supplant Rose's analysis, so I shall argue for an alternative explanation dismissed by Rose, Persephone's grief over her abduction by Hades, and show the flaws in Rose's argument for dismissing this explanation. Without this crucial early testimony, the hypothesis that the Zagreus myth existed from the sixth century BCE is untenable, and the Thurii tablet demands an alternative explanation.

Rose makes his argument on the basis of the meanings of two crucial words: ποινή and πένθος. The ποινή, he argues, must have its basic Homeric sense of weregild, the payment of blood-money that a murderer or his kin make to the kin of the murdered man. The word πένθος he likewise claims must have the sense of grief over the death of a loved one, especially a close kinsman. Rose is refuting the interpretation by earlier scholars such as Rohde that reads πένθος as guilt (*Schuld*) in the sense of something that causes grief and takes it as the guilt of humans for their misdeeds during

---

[19] Linforth 1941: 350 does note, however, "It is a curious thing that nowhere else, early or late, is it said or even expressly implied that guilt descended to men in consequence of the outrage committed upon Dionysos. Even Olympiodorus does not say so." West 1983: 110 n. 82, on the other hand, sees other possible explanations of the fragment, comparing the perjury in Empedokles 31 B 115 DK (fr. 107 Wright) (*OF* 449 B).

[20] Edmonds 1999: 48–49. Cp. Rose 1936: 88: "For if men are not the descendants of the Titans (again it is of little moment whether they were actually called by this name so early), what share have they in the guilt which grieves Persephone and causes her to accept an atonement at their hands? Again, if their ancestors did not devour the divine infant, what claim have they, their satisfaction once made, to such especial grace as she shows them? Mere Titan-men might well be content if they escape Tartaros, with such an inheritance of guilt; these pardoned sinners are raised to the highest rank on earth and afterwards heroized." In Rose's response to Linforth, he can do no more than reiterate the fact that he can think of no other way to interpret the passage (Rose 1943).

previous lives.[21] Rose is correct to claim that πένθος is unlikely to have the sense of "cause of guilt," but, as we shall see, he unduly limits the feeling of grief to mourning for slain kin.

Rose's argument follows fairly straightforwardly upon these two premises of the meanings of the words. If Persephone feels grief at the loss of a close relative, who could that relative be but her son, Dionysos? The fact that Dionysos is not recorded as the son of Persephone before the Hellenistic period must therefore be an accident of preservation. The ποινή that Persephone accepts must therefore be the weregild for her son's death. Since the murderers of Dionysos in the later evidence are named as the Titans, the human beings who pay this blood-price must somehow be descendants of the Titan-murderers, who carry the debt inherited from their ancient progenitors. Therefore, the fact that no other text – from any period, including Olympiodorus – that mentions the death of Dionysos refers to an inherited guilt borne by human beings descended from his murderers must also be an accident of preservation.

A closer examination of the two key words in this text, however, reveals the flaws in Rose's argument. In the first place, although it may most often mean blood-price in Homer, ποινή never has the sense of weregild in Pindar. The only use of the word which comes close is undoubtedly the one in the forefront of Rose's mind, the reference in *Ol.* 2.58 to the ποινή that the dead pay in the afterlife for the kind of life they have lived on earth.[22] However, even this usage has a much wider scope than weregild paid to a kinsman, especially since Pindar goes on to talk of the recompense that those who have lived good lives receive, a blissful life in paradise.[23] The other uses of ποινή in Pindar show that the term nearly always has a positive connotation, not a penalty paid to the victim of wrongdoing, but a reward given to someone who has gone through exceptional experiences or shown exceptional effort. Indeed, most often the term ποινή or ἄποινα refers to Pindar's own victory song, which Pindar with characteristic modesty

---

[21] Rohde 1925: 442 (ch. xii, n. 34) suggests that "the underworld gods themselves (as guardians of the Souls) are immediately injured by the deed and stricken by grief and must receive satisfaction on their own account." He can cite no evidence, however, to support the claim that mortal injustice would be felt as a personal grief by the underworld gods.

[22] Pind. *Ol.* 2.56–67 (*OF* 445 B = OF 142 K): εἰ δέ νιν ἔχων τις οἶδεν τὸ μέλλον, | ὅτι θανόντων μὲν ἐνθάδ' αὐτίκ' ἀπάλαμνοι φρένες | ποινὰς ἔτεισαν – τὰ δ' ἐν τᾷδε Διὸς ἀρχᾷ | ἀλιτρὰ κατὰ γᾶς δικάζει τις ἐχθρᾷ | λόγον φράσαις ἀνάγκᾳ· | ἴσαις δὲ νύκτεσσιν αἰεί, | ἴσαις δ' ἁμέραις ἅλιον ἔχοντες, | ἀπονέστερον | ἐσλοὶ δέκονται βίοτον, οὐ χθόνα ταράσσοντες ἐν χερὸς ἀκμᾷ | οὐδὲ πόντιον ὕδωρ | κεινὰν παρὰ δίαιταν, ἀλλὰ παρὰ μὲν τιμίοις | θεῶν οἵτινες ἔχαιρον εὐορκίαις ἄδακρυν νέμονται | αἰῶνα, τοὶ δ' ἀπροσόρατον ὀκχέοντι πόνον.

[23] As Rohde 1925: 443 (ch. xii, n. 35) points out, the ἀπάλαμνοι φρένες are not just the souls of the unjust, but the helpless souls of all facing judgment for their lives.

proclaims as the best reward for any achievement.[24] Even in Pindar, of course, a victory ode is not the only possible recompense for effort, however, and ποινή is used with an extended sense of an offering that is due to someone's honor. In *Pyth.* 9.58, the land that the nymph Cyrene receives as a bridal gift after her rape by Apollo is οὔτε παγκάρπων φυτῶν νάποινον, "not without a fitting return of all kinds of crops." When Battos seeks some help for his stammer, he is granted the kingship of Cyrene as a ποινή, whereas Herakles is granted a blissful paradise of peace as a ποινή for all the great deeds he has undertaken and specifically for his aid to the gods in their fight against the giants.[25]

It is worth noting that in none of these cases is the ποινή paid by someone who is any way responsible for the efforts that the person receiving it had to undertake or the sufferings she has undergone. Pindar certainly did not cause the athletes to strive for their prizes; he is merely on hand to provide the fitting tribute to them. Apollo is the one who rapes Cyrene, but Libya personified undertakes to provide a bridal gift in compensation. The giants, rather than the gods, are responsible for the exertions Herakles must make in the Gigantomachy, but the gods provide the ποινή. Such a recompense is the τιμή due to the recipient, the honor that properly accrues, rather than the payment of a debtor.

Rose's analysis of the word πένθος in Pindar also unduly restricts its meaning, limiting it to the grief felt at the loss of an intimate. In two cases, Polydeukes' grief over his twin Kastor's death and the dirge sung by the Gorgons after Medusa's slaying, the word does indeed have this sense.[26] However, in other cases, the nature of the grief is clearly different. Pindar grieves at Strepsiades' death in battle in *Isthm.* 7.37, but the grief is the sorrow felt at the loss of a splendid stranger who achieved much and might yet have achieved more, not the anguish of losing a relative or even a personal friend. The mighty griefs that Pindar is trying to put behind him in *Isthm.* 8.1–7 are again unlikely, from the context, to be personal griefs, and, even if Rose is correct in connecting them with the troubles of

---

[24] Pind. Pyth. 1.58–59: Μοῖσα, καὶ πὰρ Δεινομένει κελαδῆσαι πίθεό μοι ποινὰν τεθρίππων· Cp. with ἄποινα: *Ol.* 7.16, *Pyth.* 2.14, *Nem.* 7.16, *Isthm.* 3.7, *Isthm.* 8.4.

[25] Battos – *Pyth.* 4.59–63: ὦ μάκαρ υἱὲ Πολυμνάστου, σὲ δ᾽ ἐν τούτῳ λόγῳ | χρησμὸς ὤρθωσεν μελίσσας Δελφίδος αὐτομάτῳ κελάδῳ· | ἅ σε χαίρειν ἐστρὶς αὐδάσαισα πεπρωμένον | βασιλέ᾽ ἄμφανεν Κυράνᾳ, | δυσθρόου φωνᾶς ἀνακρινόμενον ποινὰ τίς ἔσται πρὸς θεῶν. Herakles – *Nem.* 1.67–72. καὶ γὰρ ὅταν θεοὶ ἐν πεδίῳ Φλέγρας Γιγάντεσσιν μάχαν | ἀντιάζωσιν, βελέων ὑπὸ ῥιπαῖσι κείνου φαιδίμαν γαίᾳ πεφύρσεσθαι κόμαν | ἔνεπεν· αὐτὸν μὰν ἐν εἰρήνᾳ τὸν ἅπαντα χρόνον ἐν σχερῷ | ἡσυχίαν καμάτων μεγάλων ποινὰν λαχόντ᾽ ἐξαίρετον | ὀλβίοις ἐν δώμασι, δεξάμενον θαλερὰν Ἥβαν ἄκοιτιν καὶ γάμον | δαίσαντα πὰρ Δὶ Κρονίδᾳ, σεμνὸν αἰνήσειν νόμον.

[26] *Nem.*10.77 and *Pyth.* 12.10.

Thebes in the Persian War, these troubles are of widespread concern, not so much the deaths of particular individuals as the turmoil and disruption of life that follow in the wake of war.[27] Rose stretches even further when he tries to argue that the πένθος of the daughters of Kadmos in *Olympian* 2 must likewise be limited to grief over the loss of kin. He claims, "Every one of their misfortunes or griefs involved a death, whether of Semele, Aktaion, Pentheus, or the children of Ino."[28] While Agave and Autonoë would indeed be mothers grieving over the loss of their children Pentheus and Aktaion, it is very odd to claim that Semele's grief must be mourning the loss of herself as a close relative! On the contrary, Semele's griefs are the vicissitudes she went through before her death: the attentions of Zeus, the malice of Hera, and her incineration by Zeus' embrace. As a result she descends into the Underworld before being retrieved by her son, Dionysos, and raised to glorious divine honors. Likewise, Ino is specifically mentioned as having received immortality after plunging into the sea. Her griefs may include the death of her children, but the vicissitudes of caring for the infant Dionysos, the madness of her husband, and the trauma of being chased off a cliff should not be ignored. In both these cases, simple grief over the death of a child cannot be the referent of πένθος here. Pindar's point is that the daughters of Kadmos suffered many things during their lives but were recompensed by the gods with immortality, for which they receive honors from mortals. Agave and Autonoë, whose primary grief *does* have to do with the death of their sons, are not mentioned here, precisely because they don't get this sort of recompense. The πένθος of the daughters of Kadmos thus has a fairly broad scope, including all the hardships suffered by this family, from the molestation of Semele by an eager Zeus to the mad Bacchic frenzies many of them underwent to the tragic deaths of family members at the hands of their own family.

[27] Rose himself shows how he is stretching his point; he suggests that these misfortunes must have "either actually involved the deaths of those near to Pindar and his friends or at least such sorrow as men might feel for a like disaster" (Rose 1936: 83). Euxantios, in Plutarch's quotation (*De exil. 9* 602f) of *Pae.* 4.50–53 (fr. 52d Snell-Maehler = D4 Rutherford), οὐ πενθέων δ' ἔλαχον, οὐ στασίων (53), "has no share of griefs or quarrels," which seems a general statement of a life free from troubles, not, as Rose 1936: 83 argues, a specific claim that "he has had neither a quarrel or fight with any one else nor mourn the loss in such frays of his own friends."

[28] Rose 1936: 83. Pind. *Ol.* 2.22–30: ἕπεται δὲ λόγος εὐθρόνοις | Κάδμοιο κούραις, ἔπαθον αἷ μεγάλα· πένθος δὲ πίτνει βαρύ | κρεσσόνων πρὸς ἀγαθῶν. | ζώει μὲν ἐν Ὀλυμπίοις ἀποθανοῖσα βρόμῳ | κεραυνοῦ τανυέθειρα Σεμέλα, φιλεῖ δέ νιν Παλλὰς αἰεὶ | καὶ Ζεὺς πατήρ, μάλα φιλεῖ δὲ παῖς ὁ κισσοφόρος· | λέγοντι δ' ἐν καὶ θαλάσσᾳ | μετὰ κόραισι Νηρῆος ἁλίαις βίοτον ἄφθιτον | Ἰνοῖ τετάχθαι τὸν ὅλον ἀμφὶ χρόνον.

If πένθος is not necessarily grief over the death of a relative and ποινή in Pindar means not blood-price but reward, Rose's identification of Persephone's ancient grief must be reconsidered. As Rose himself notes, the most obvious cause of grief for Persephone is her rape by Hades, the central element in almost every mythic story that mentions her name. Rose, however, dismisses this possibility in favor of Persephone's grief over the murder of her son Dionysos Zagreus. Rose cites no texts that mention such grieving, however, and I have found only one that could provide any evidence for Persephone's grief over the murder of her son. In Nonnos' sixth-century CE conglomeration of tales about Dionysos, Hera appeals to Persephone to send an Erinys to drive Dionysos, son of Semele, into a frenzy, arguing that this Dionysos might receive the honors that her murdered son Zagreus should have had.[29] Even in this text, Persephone is not depicted as grieving, and any grief she might feel is less important than the stereotypical jealous rage of a neglected woman. In contrast to this single, very late, and very idiosyncratic text, the grief of Persephone over her rape by Hades appears in texts as early as the *Homeric Hymn to Demeter* and continues throughout the mythological tradition. The *Orphic Argonautica* even refers to the great grief of Persephone when separated from her mother as a theme of previous Orphic poetry.[30]

Rose claims that the less-well known tale of Persephone's grief over her son's murder must be the referent of the ancient grief because humans are the ones paying the ποινή, and humans would have no reason to pay a ποινή for Persephone's rape. He argues, "Two events stand out in her myths as likely causes of sorrow. One is of course her rape by Hades. But even if we allow that this would naturally be called a πένθος, no man had anything whatsoever to do with it from first to last."[31] Here the distinction between the Homeric sense of ποινή as blood-price paid by a relative of the slayer and the Pindaric use of ποινή as a fitting recompense that might be provided by someone unconnected is most significant for the argument. For while no human may have been involved in *causing* her grief, humans are explicitly involved, even in the *Homeric Hymn to Demeter*, with *assuaging* her grief. In his attempts to reassure his bride and convince her of the advantages of staying as his wife, not only does Hades

---

[29] Nonnos, *Dion.* 31.32–70. Note that Rose provided the introduction and mythological footnotes to the Loeb edition of Nonnos published in 1940 (Rouse 1940), so Nonnos' obscure version would have been in in the forefront of his mind a few years before.

[30] *OA* 26: Δήμετρός τε πλάνην καὶ Φερσεφόνης μέγα πένθος. Cp. Ov. *Met.* 5.506: *illa quidem tristis neque adhuc interrita vultu.*

[31] Rose 1936: 85.

urge his worthiness as a spouse, but he also promises that she will gain great honors (τιμαί), for all will have to make sacrifices, perform rituals, and make gifts to her.[32] Rudhardt has pointed out the importance of the distribution of the gods' τιμαί in ancient Greek religious thought, and the myth of Persephone's abduction marriage served to establish her position among the gods and articulate the honors due to her.[33] Hades himself pays no ποινή for his rape, but the honors that every human being who hopes for a favorable reception in the Underworld after death pays to Persephone serve as the compensation for the experience she has been through.

Such a link between Persephone's abduction and her cultic honors seems not to be confined to the evidence of myth. While ritual evidence is always harder to interpret, the cults of Persephone, particularly in Magna Graecia, seem to have put the honors and festivals of Persephone in the context of her abduction. For example, many of the *pinakes* found in the cult area of Persephone near Epizephyrian Locri depict the abduction of Persephone by Hades, while others show her enthroned next to her spouse in the Underworld, receiving homage from various visitors. The so-called "Young Abductor" *pinakes*, which have a youthful bridegroom instead of the bearded Hades in the role of abductor, seem to indicate that Persephone's abduction was taken as a model of the transition of marriage for a young woman – a terrifying change, perhaps, but one that provides a new status and position in society.[34] Such a cultic model would certainly have been familiar to Pindar and his audience in Magna Graecia, and the mention of Persephone's ancient grief and the compensation provided by human activity would be easily recognizable as a reference to her abduction and the τιμαί due to her as compensation.

---

[32] *Hom. Hymn to Dem.* 362–369: μηδέ τι δυσθύμαινε λίην περιώσιον ἄλλων. | οὔ τοι ἐν ἀθανάτοισιν ἀεικὴς ἔσσομ᾽ ἀκοίτης | αὐτοκασίγνητος πατρὸς Διός· ἔνθα δ᾽ ἐοῦσα | δεσπόσσεις πάντων ὁπόσα ζώει τε καὶ ἕρπει, | τιμὰς δὲ σχήσησθα μετ᾽ ἀθανάτοισι μεγίστας, | τῶν δ᾽ ἀδικησάντων τίσις ἔσσεται ἤματα πάντα | οἵ κεν μὴ θυσίαισι τεὸν μένος ἱλάσκωνται | εὐαγέως ἕρδοντες ἐναίσιμα δῶρα τελοῦντες. Cp. the description of the foundation of the mysteries, 473–479.

[33] Rudhardt 1994, esp. 208–211. See also Clay 1989 on the *Homeric Hymn to Demeter* and Foley 1994: 55, 104–112, where she contextualizes the issue within the institution of marriage. Rudhardt's analysis of the distribution of τιμαί in the *Hymn* focuses particularly on Persephone's returns in her mediation of the worlds of the living and the dead, but the articulation of Persephone's τιμή may have been different in other regions of the Greek world, e.g., Pindar's audiences in Magna Graecia, than at Eleusis. A greater focus on her role as Queen of the Underworld would be appropriate if, as it seems in some versions, Persephone did not return to her mother.

[34] Redfield 2003: 369: "These representations thus use the myth of Persephone to catch both the terror of marriage – the dislocation of transfer from father to husband – and its triumph, the transformation of the bride into the matron, sovereign of her domestic dominion." For a discussion of Persephone and the *pinakes* in their Locrian context, see Redfield 2003: ch. 11 (346–386). Useful earlier studies include Sourvinou-Inwood 1991: 147–188.

Plato's audience for the *Meno*, in which Socrates quotes the lines, would also have had no trouble understanding the reference to Persephone's abduction and cult. The cult of Kore at Eleusis may have emphasized different aspects of the myth, but, as the *Homeric Hymn to Demeter* shows, the Eleusinian Mysteries were considered part of the honors that were due Persephone in recompense for her rape. While we can't be sure what ideas of afterlife were associated with the cults of Persephone in Magna Graecia, we can at least be sure that the cult at Eleusis did include the promise of benefits after life on earth ended, not only during life.[35]

Pindar fr. 133, then, does not support the idea that the Zagreus myth lies behind the mention of Persephone and ποινή in the Thurii tablet, nor that the idea of inherited guilt through a Titanic heritage was known in the Archaic period of Pindar or even in Plato's Athens. Rose's interpretation depends upon taking the words ποινή and πένθος in a restricted sense that does not fit with Pindar's other uses of the words.[36] The ancient grief of Persephone, which must be assuaged by the honors paid to her in ritual, arises from the traumatic experience of her passage from the land of the living to the realm of the dead, from the stage of unmarried maiden Kore to the married matron Persephone, Queen of the Dead.

Indeed, many kinds of evidence show that both Plato and Pindar could expect their audiences to be familiar with the story pattern of Persephone's abduction and to link it with paying cult honors to her in hopes of favorable treatment from her, whether such favor came in the form of a blissful afterlife in the Isles of the Blessed or a better reincarnation.[37] The place of πένθος, ποινή, and Persephone in Pindar and the Thurii tablets must be

---

[35] The *Homeric Hymn to Demeter*, 480–482 and 486–489, proclaims blessed the one who takes part in the Mysteries, promising a better lot after death than the uninitiate's as well as prosperity during life. Cp. Sophocles fr. 837 R (753 N) (*OF* 444ii B) and Isoc. *Paneg.* 4.28. Clem. Al. *Strom.* 3.3.17, in the context of the Eleusinian Mysteries, quotes Pind. fr. 137 S.-M. (*OF* 444i B), which makes a similar claim.

[36] Nevertheless, it could be argued that, while improbable, Rose's interpretation is not impossible, so it is worth examining the consequences of accepting such an interpretation. To take the fragment as evidence for the existence of the Zagreus myth in the Archaic period would imply that not only did Pindar know of the story of Persephone's son being dismembered and eaten by the Titans and of humans created from the ashes, but he expected his audience in a public performance not only to understand the reference but also to accept the story as an explanation. Plato too would have to presume not only that his audience was familiar with the story but also that the contradictions between the Zagreus myth's explanation of the human condition and the one Socrates is putting forth in the dialogue would not have bothered his readers.

[37] Both Pindar and Plato show that both reincarnation and a stay in paradise were options for the afterlife known to them, and that such options need not be mutually exclusive. For Pindar, e.g., *Ol.* 2.70–77 and fr. 130 (*OF* 440 B); Plato combines different types of options in his various myths of the afterlife; see Edmonds 2004a: 198–219.

understood in this broader context, for, as Sarah Johnston has shown, this pattern of disrupted maiden's transition appears in a number of places in the Greek religious tradition, associated with a variety of different ritual complexes in which the maiden whose transition to adult womanhood is disrupted by death is honored and appeased by a festival. The ritual celebration serves to avert the wrath of the spirit, with its attendant famine, plague, or other disasters, and to bring to the community the positive aspects of chthonic powers, fertility and fecundity for the land and its people.[38] Stories such as those of Erigone, Carya, and Iphinoë show how this pattern of providing recompense for the maiden's grief could be adapted in different ways, and we can better understand the religious background of the Pindar fragment, and thereby the Thurii gold tablets, if we see them in the context of this kind of pattern.

Erigone's story is told in various ways in the sources, but she is generally associated with the Athenian Anthesteria and specifically with the Aiora, the ritual swinging that takes place at one point during the larger festival. The young girls of Athens must swing in the trees during this rite to placate the spirit of Erigone Aletis, the wandering one, who hangs herself from a tree after the death of her father.[39] Either Erigone is the daughter of Klytaimnestra and Aigisthos, who wanders into Attica in vengeful pursuit

[38] As Jennifer Larson points out to me, this pattern is familiar in traditional myth not simply for maidens in transition to adulthood, but for heroes and heroines in general, where cult often is established to propitiate the wrath of some hero or heroine. The offense can be imagined in a wide variety of forms, just as the propitiatory cult may vary greatly from instance to instance (cp. Larson 1995: 131–133). Nevertheless, the underlying pattern is familiar.

[39] *Etym. Magn.* s.v. Ἀλῆτις (62.9): "Aletis: Some say that she is Erigone, the daughter of Ikarios, since she wandered everywhere seeking her father. Others say she is the daughter of Aigisthos and Klytaimnestra. Still others say she is the daughter of Maleotos the Tyrrhenian; others that she is Medea, since, having wandered after the murder of her children, she escaped to Aigeus. Others say that she is Persephone, wherefore those grinding the wheat offer some cakes to her." Ἀλῆτις· Τινὲς τὴν Ἠριγόνην τὴν Ἰκαρίου θυγατέρα, ὅτι πανταχοῦ ζητοῦσα τὸν πατέρα ἠλᾶτο· οἱ δὲ Αἰγίσθου καὶ Κλυταιμνήστρας φασίν· οἱ δὲ, τὴν τοῦ Μαλεώτου τοῦ Τυρρηνίου θυγατέρα· οἱ δὲ, τὴν Μήδειαν, ὅτι μετὰ τὸν φόνον τῶν παίδων πρὸς Αἰγέα κατέφυγεν ἀλητεύσασα· οἱ δὲ, τὴν Περσεφόνην· διότι τοὺς πυροὺς ἀλοῦντες πέμματα τινὰ προσέφερον αὐτῇ. Serv. *In Bucol.* 2.389: "But after a certain time, a sickness afflicted the Athenians to such an extent that their maidens were driven by some kind of frenzy." *sed post aliquantum tempus Atheniensibus morbus immisus est talis, ut eorum virgines quodam furore compellerentur.* *Etym. Magn.* s.v. Αἰώρα (42.4): "Aiora: A festival for the Athenians, which they call a feast offered to departed souls. For they say that Erigone, daughter of Aigisthos and Klytaimnestra, came with her grandfather Tyndareus to Athens to prosecute Orestes. When he was acquitted, she hung herself and became a cause of pollution for the Athenians. In accordance with an oracle, the festival is performed for her." Αἰώρα· Ἑορτὴ Ἀθηναῖς, ἣν καλοῦσιν εὔδειπνον. Λέγεται γὰρ Ἠριγόνην τὴν Αἰγίσθου καὶ Κλυταιμνήστρας θυγατέρα σὺν Τυνδαρέῳ [τῷ πάππῳ] ἐλθεῖν Ἀθήναζε, κατηγορήσουσαν Ὀρέστου· ἀπολυθέντος δὲ, ἀναρτήσασαν ἑαυτήν, προστρόπαιον τοῖς Ἀθηναίοις γενέσθαι· κατὰ χρησμὸν δὲ ἐπ' αὐτῇ συντελεῖσθαι τὴν ἑορτήν.

of Orestes and kills herself after he is acquitted,[40] or she is the daughter of the local farmer Ikarios, to whom Dionysos first introduces wine and viticulture. When Ikarios gives wine to his neighbors, they kill him in a drunken fury and hide his body when they wake up with the first hangover. When she cannot find her father, Erigone wanders around seeking him, finally hanging herself when she discovers his corpse.[41] As Johnston has pointed out, whether Erigone is described as the daughter of Ikarios or of Aigisthos, in both cases the death of her father means that she has no one to arrange her marriage and facilitate her transition to adult womanhood.[42] Nonnos' version (47.185–186) even has the bloody ghost of her father appear to her and specifically lament that she will never know marriage.

This death of a maiden in the disrupted transition to adulthood naturally stains the community with the miasma of her untimely death, and the maidens of Athens are afflicted with a violent impulse to end their own lives in the same fashion until an oracle ordains the festival of the Aiora as a way of averting the anger of Erigone.[43] The festival includes the girls' swinging that is so cheerfully depicted in vase paintings, as well as the Ἀλῆτις song, no doubt a choral song and dance honoring the maiden, performed by the maidens who wish to avoid the grief she suffered by providing a recompense in ritual.[44]

In Laconia, the Caryatis chorus is performed by maidens in honor of the unfortunate Carya, who, seduced by Dionysos, never completed her transition to adulthood but was transformed into a tree. Lactantius (ad Statius Thebaid 4.25) tells how the local maidens went mad and hung themselves from the branches of this carya tree. The temple of Diana Caryatis was founded on that spot, and presumably the Caryatis festival

---

[40] Erigone, daughter of Klytaimnestra and Aigisthos: Marm. Par. (= IG xii.5 444) 40 (OF 379, 513 B = OT 221 K); Apollod. Ep. 6.25; Etym. Magn. s.v. Αἰώρα (42.4) and s.v. Ἀλῆτις (62.9); Hyg. Fab.122 ; Paus. 2.18.6.

[41] Erigone, daughter of Ikarios: Apollod. Bibl. 3.14.7; Ael. NA 7.28; Nonnos, Dion. 47.148–255; Hsch. s.v Αἰώρα; Etym. Magn. s.v. Ἀλῆτις (62.9); Hyg. Poet. astr. 2.4; Serv. In Bucol. 2.389.

[42] Johnston 1999: 220: "Underneath the accretions of each version lies the simple tale of a maiden whose life was cut off before she could marry. The fact that in both versions her tragedy is precipitated by the death of her father – the man who would have arranged her marriage – and in one version by the subsequent death of her brother as well – the man who would have arranged her marriage in her father's absence – makes this point even clearer: she is alone, without anyone to guarantee her proper passage from maiden to wife."

[43] Serv. In Bucol. 2.389; Etym. Magn. s.v. Αἰώρα (42.4): ἀναρτήσασαν ἑαυτήν, προστρόπαιον τοῖς Ἀθηναίοις γενέσθαι· κατὰ χρησμὸν δὲ ἐπ' αὐτῇ συντελεῖσθαι τὴν ἑορτήν.

[44] Swinging – Ath. 14.618e; Hsch. s.v Αἰώρα; Etym. Magn. s.v. Αἰώρα (42); Hyg. Poet. astr. 2.4; Serv. In Bucol. 2.389; Myth. Vat. 1.19, 2.61. Ἀλῆτις song – Ath. 14.618e; Poll. Onom. 4.55; Hesych. s.v. Ἀλῆτις; cp. Callim. fr. 178 Pfeiffer on Athenian women lamenting Erigone. Cp. Johnston 1999: 219–224; Burkert 1985: 241–242.

celebrated there arose at that time. As Johnston suggests, the rite serves to appease the maiden, who was stranded in a liminal zone, betwixt and between being a maiden and a woman, living and dead.[45] The grief of Carya is appeased by the ritual honors so that the maidens of Laconia do not suffer the same grief of disrupted transition to adult life.

The threat of the maiden's anger if unappeased appears explicitly in the cases of Erigone and Carya, but the same pattern appears, albeit without the explicit threat, in the case of the Proetid Iphinoë. Hesykhios defines the Agriania festival as one celebrated for one of the daughters of Proitos, but also as a festival of the dead.[46] Like the Anthesteria in Athens, the Agriania involved the appeasement of the spirits of the dead to ensure the fertility of the community in the coming year. Just as the appeasement of Erigone by ritual choruses of maidens seems to have been part of the Anthesteria to make sure that the maidens of Athens would be able to complete their transitions to mature womanhood, marriage and childbearing, so at the Agriania Iphinoë may have been honored. Whereas the other daughters of Proitos who went wild and wandered like cows in the hills were tamed and married off to Melampous and his brother, Iphinoë perished in the process, attaining death instead of marriage.[47] Pausanias tells us that maidens in Megara on the brink of marriage made libations and offerings of their hair to Iphinoë, here the daughter of the local hero Alkathoos, since she died before marriage, like the Hyperborean maidens at Delos.[48] The Agriania may have involved other kinds of rituals, since Pausanias and Apollodoros tell us that Melampous cured the girls with certain rites, purifications, and choruses that involved the youths as well as the maidens.[49] To judge by the parallel of the Anthesteria, the festival must have been concerned with the renewal of the fertility of the community through the appeasing and honoring of the powers of the dead, both collectively and as individuals like Iphinoë concerned with particular aspects.

---

45 Johnston 1999: 226–228.
46 Hsch. s.v. Ἀγράνια: "Agrania: a festival in Argos for one of the daughters of Proitos." Ἀγράνια· ἑορτὴ ἐν Ἄργει, ἐπὶ μιᾷ τῶν Προίτου θυγατέρων. "Agriania: a festival of the dead among the Argives and contests in Thebes." Ἀγριάνια· νεκύσια παρά Ἀργείοις καὶ ἀγῶνες ἐν Θήβαις.
47 Cp., e.g., Apollod. *Bibl.* 2.2.2.
48 Paus. 1.43.4: ἐντεῦθεν πρὸς τὸ Ἀλκάθου βαδίζουσιν ἡρῷον, ᾧ Μεγαρεῖς ἐς γραμμάτων φυλακὴν ἐχρῶντο ἐπ' ἐμοῦ, μνῆμα ἔλεγον τὸ μὲν Πυργοῦς εἶναι γυναικὸς Ἀλκάθου πρὶν ἢ τὴν Μεγαρέως αὐτὸν λαβεῖν Εὐαίχμην, τὸ δὲ Ἰφινόης Ἀλκάθου θυγατρός· ἀποθανεῖν δὲ αὐτήν φασιν ἔτι παρθένον. καθέστηκε δὲ ταῖς κόραις χοὰς πρὸς τὸ τῆς Ἰφινόης μνῆμα προσφέρειν πρὸ γάμου καὶ ἀπάρχεσθαι τῶν τριχῶν, καθὰ καὶ τῇ Ἑκαέργῃ καὶ Ὤπιδι αἱ θυγατέρες ποτὲ ἀπεκείροντο αἱ Δηλίων.
49 Apollod. *Bibl.* 2.2.2; cp. Paus. 8.18.7. Given Melampous' connection with Dionysiac rites, the *katharmoi* he used were presumably Dionysiac, especially since Apollodoros tells us that the maidens went mad because they had refused the *teletai* of Dionysos.

The associations of Melampous with Dionysiac rites, as well as the mention of ecstatic dancing and purificatory καθαρμοί, recall the presence of Dionysos in the other tales. In each case, Dionysos appears as a disruptive force who disturbs the maiden's expected path of transition from girl to wife. The Proetids' maiden madness is caused and/or cured by his power, and he seduces Carya and, in some versions, Erigone as well. While neither of these maidens ends up, like Ariadne, as the official bride of the god, it is worth noting the variants of Ariadne's story that conclude with her disrupted transition to marriage ending with suicide by hanging, like Erigone.[50] Johnston has indeed pointed out that, in this pattern of girl's transition, the positive and negative endings are two sides of the same coin.[51] Instead of having a normal transition into the adult roles of wife and mother by which they gain a new status in the human community, these mythic maidens suffer extraordinary experiences and never obtain a normal adult life. Some maidens end up dead, exerting power as vengeful spirits that threaten other maidens, whereas others end up divinized in some way, as cult statues, priestesses, or even brides of a god.

By her marriage to Hades, of course, Persephone does both, attaining full status as the divine wife of an important god but also going to the realm of death. So too, like Erigone, Persephone is known as Aletis, the wanderer, just as the Proetids also do not make an orderly transition from being girls to being wives but wander wildly in the hills.[52] Persephone's ancient grief therefore belongs in this wider context of maiden stories which are resolved by ritual honors to appease the Kore and avert her potential wrath, to win her favor for the community and bring the benefits of fertility, especially for maidens who are going through their own transitions. The particular ritual response may vary from Attica to Magna Graecia, from Eleusis to Locri or to Thurii, but the basic, underlying pattern remains the same.

Again, it is worth noting that the recompense to assuage the maiden's grief is never offered by those who are directly responsible for her suffering. Not only do Hades and Dionysos never offer recompense, but even the slayers of Ikarios do not offer ritual atonement for their blood guilt and their responsibility for Erigone's orphaned and thus marriageless condition.[53] Rather, the recompense is offered by those who want to gain something

---

[50] Ariadne is the bride of Dionysos in Hes. *Theog.* 947–949, but Plut. *Vit. Thes.* 20 tells of her death by suicide or in childbirth.

[51] Johnston 1999: 225, cp. 227 n. 83.   [52] *Etym. Magn.* s.v. Ἀλῆτις (62.9). Cp. Johnston 1999: 222.

[53] This transferred compensation is true not only for the mortal heroines, but for goddesses as well. Cp. Pausanias' story of Demeter's anger at being raped by Poseidon (Paus. 8.25.4–7). Here too humans pay cult honors to the goddess to appease the anger provoked by the actions of a god.

from the spirit; the ritual honors are paid by the girls who want the favor of the spirit upon them as they go through their own transition.[54]

Other texts in which the word ποινή appears in a ritual context do seem to support the idea that the term had the sense of a recompense paid, not by those guilty of an offense, but by others wishing to do honor to and to win the favor of a power in need of appeasement. Maidens who died before marriage or childbirth were not the only restless spirits whose anger might need to be averted or appeased, and the Derveni papyrus provides an example of recompense paid, not to Persephone, but to the spirits of the dead.

> prayers and sacrifices appease the souls, and the enchanting song of the *magoi* is able to remove the *daimones* when they impede. Impeding *daimones* are revenging souls. This is why the *magoi* perform the sacrifice, as if they were paying a penalty. On the offerings they pour water and milk, from which they make the libations, too. They sacrifice innumerable and many-knobbed cakes, because the souls, too, are innumerable.[55]

The *magoi*, whoever they may be precisely, perform rituals to appease the souls of the dead, the *daimones* who might somehow impede the aims of those for whom the rituals are being performed. It is unlikely that the *magoi* themselves (or even clients for whom they might be performing rituals) are personally responsible for the deaths of these unhappy souls.[56] Although the text is fragmentary and the context unclear, these revenging souls are generic, innumerable, not the specific victims of a particular crime for which an individual is taking responsibility and making atonement. The

---

54 The story of Koroibos and the Poinê that snatched children from their mothers seems to concern a similar situation, albeit with different complications and variations (Paus. 1.43.7–8, Conon *FGrH* 26 F 1.19). Apollo sends the personified spirit of Poinê to inflict upon the women of Argos the same grief, the loss of a child, that befell Psamathe, daughter of the king who had to expose her child by Apollo (the child, Linos, was eaten by dogs, while Psamathe herself was killed by her father). Although Koroibos destroys the child-snatching monster, the vengeance returns in the form of a plague. Only when Koroibos establishes a cult is sufficient recompense made to substitute for the ποινή inflicted by the god, be it the personified Poinê or the plague. While Pausanias does not describe the cult or who performs it after Koroibos founds it, the most obvious beneficiaries are the women of Argos, who no longer are losing their children to demon or plague. Larson 1995: 134 notes that, while male spirits often wreak their own revenge, females like Psamathe most often have a substitute avenger, be it Poinê or Erinys or even Apollo himself who is the agent for vengeance.

55 col. 6.1–11 (*OF* 471, 656i B): [εὐ]χαὶ καὶ θυσ[ί]αι μ[ειλ]ίσσουσι τὰ[ς ψυχάς,] ἐπ[ωιδὴ δ]ὲ μάγων δύν[α]ται δαίμονας ἐμ[ποδὼν] γι[νομένο]υς μεθιστάναι. δαίμονες ἐμπο[δὼν ὄντες εἰσὶ] ψ[υχαὶ τιμω]ροί τὴν θυσ[ία]ν τούτου ἕνεκε[μ] π[οιοῦσ]ι[ν] οἱ μά[γο]ι, ὡσπερεὶ ποινὴν ἀποδιδόντες. τοῖ<ς> δὲ ἱεροῖ[ς] ἐπισπένδουσιν ὕ[δω]ρ καὶ γάλα, ἐξ ὦνπερ καὶ τὰς χοὰς ποιοῦσι. ἀνάριθμα [κα]ὶ πολυόμφαλα τὰ πόπανα θύουσιν, ὅτι καὶ αἱ ψυχα[ὶ ἀν]άριθμοί εἰσι.

56 *Contra* Johnston 1999: 138: "Here, in Column VI, however, the penalty is to be paid to the *daimones empodôn* (i.e., the souls of the dead), not to Persephone, and it is hard not to infer that it is intended to atone for the deaths of the *daimones empodôn* themselves."

ποιναί take the form of ritual actions, sacrifices and libations accompanied with some form of sung prayers, since it is ultimately this enchanting song of the *magoi* that appeases and removes the impeding *daimones*.

The specific benefits of appeasing these spirits, other than to prevent them from impeding, are unclear, but parallels with other texts suggest some of the ends a practitioner might have in mind in presenting honors to the restless dead. A *defixio* from Olbia promises that the practitioner will honor the spirit and present a gift, if the spirit takes action against his legal opponents.[57] The combination of honor and sacrifices made to the spirit of an unknown dead person show that this kind of recompense need not be made by someone who is in any way responsible for the spirit's condition. On the contrary, the ritual sets up a reciprocal relation between a spirit who wants honor from one of the living and a mortal who wants a favor from one of the spirits in the Underworld.

Such favors need not be the direct and practical interventions characteristic of *defixiones*, binding and strangling the opponents in a lawsuit or tripping up the horses in a chariot race or the like. Just as the payment of ποιναί to the innumerable souls in the Derveni papyrus is performed by *magoi* to appease them, so too the ποιναί mentioned in the Gurôb papyrus are likely to be intended to win the favor of Brimo, whose aid is invoked in the next line. The restoration of the lines is uncertain, but the reference to some sort of recompense immediately precedes the request that Brimo, probably here Persephone, preserve the one making the prayer.[58]

Such preservation, to judge by the parallels in the Orphic Hymns and other prayers, is most likely to mean safety and good fortune in this world, but preservation from the perils of the afterlife is another possibility.[59] The *Homeric Hymn*, after all, promises that those who have paid honor to Persephone Kore at Eleusis will obtain a happy lot in the afterlife, while the gold tablet found at Pherai, which claims the initiate need no longer pay a ποινή, promises that the deceased will go to the sacred meadow, perhaps

---

[57] "And if you put a spell on them and capture them, I shall indeed honor you and shall prepare for you the best of offerings." ἤ]ν δέ μοι αὐτούς | κατάσχης καὶ κ[ατα]λάβης, ἐ<γ>ὼ δέ σε | τειμήσω καί σο[ι] ἄριστον δ[ῶ]ρ-|ρον παρασκε[υῶ]. (Text and translation from Jordan 1997a: 217.)

[58] *P. Gurôb* 1 (*OF* 578 B = OF 31 K) col. 1.4–5: "accept as my gift, the penalties . . . ; preserve me, great Brimo." δῶρον δέξ]ατ' ἐμὸν ποινὰς πατε[| σῶισόν με Βριμὼ με[γάλη. Text according to Hordern 2000, with the restoration of the line-end omitted. The first line is reconstructed as λύσιν πα[τερῶν ἀθεμίστων] according to West 1983, by comparison with Dam. In Phd. 1.11 (35 Westerink) (*OF* 350 B = OF 232 K): ὀργιά τ' ἐκτελέσουσι λύσιν προγόνων ἀθεμίστων μαιόμενοι. Note, however, the difference between offering a recompense to Brimo and obtaining release from the actions of ancestors. Brimo may be identified here with Persephone alone or there may be a more sweeping identification with Persephone, Demeter, and Rhea all together.

[59] Morand 2001: 218–219, cp. 342, appendix 7.3a.

a place for the blessed dead, like the seats of the blessed in the Thurii tablets.[60] Pindar fr. 133 sets the rewards for appeasing Persephone not just in the afterlife but in the next life. Whereas the Eleusinian Mysteries of the *Homeric Hymn* bring first prosperity in life and then a good lot after death, the rites to which Pindar refers bring first a good lot after death, in a new life, and then an even better lot after death comes again. The Queen of the Dead sends back to the world of the living those who have paid the recompense for her ancient grief, and their new life is one of such honor and power that, after they die once more, they receive honor as blessed heroes. The particular benefit sought may vary in each instance of this pattern, but the basic idea of the honor to the Underworld power providing benefits both before and after death remains the same.

The by-now familiar passage of Plato picks up on this same duality of purpose for such rituals, to provide benefits for the recipients while living as well as after they have died. In the *Republic*, Adeimantos complains to Socrates that the entire Greek religious tradition makes people prefer injustice.

> And they present a hubbub of books by Musaios and Orpheus, offspring of Selene and the Muses, as they say, according to which they perform their rituals. And they persuade not only individuals but whole cities that there are absolutions and purifications from unjust deeds through sacrifices and the pleasures of play, both for them while still living and after they have died. These *teletai*, as they call them, release us from evils in the hereafter, but terrible things await those who have not performed the rituals.[61]

These purifications from unjust deeds bring benefits for those still living and those who have died, that is both before and after death. Plato engages in wordplay, claiming that the reason some of these rites are called τελεταί is that they are for the τελευτήσασιν, the dead, since they release us (ἡμᾶς)

---

[60] Pherai tablet D3 (*OF* 493 B): "Passwords: Male child of the thyrsos, Male child of the thyrsos; Brimo, Brimo; Enter the sacred meadow. For the initiate is without penalty." Σύμβολα· ἀνδρικεπαιδόθυρ-σου – ἀνδρικεπαιδόθυρσου. Βριμώ – Βριμώ. Εἴσιθι ἱερὸν λειμῶνα· ἄποινος γὰρ ὁ μύστης. In the Pherai tablet, which also invokes Brimo, the initiate claims to be ἄποινος, which can only mean here that the ποινή has already been paid. However, I could find no other parallel to ἄποινος being used in this sense. Its other attestations seem to involve a different etymology, referring to wineless offerings.

[61] Pl. *Resp.* 2.364a–365b (*OF* 573i, 693, 910i B = OF 3 K): βίβλων δὲ ὅμαδον παρέχονται Μουσαίου καὶ Ὀρφέως, Σελήνης τε καὶ Μουσῶν ἐκγόνων, ὥς φασι, καθ᾽ ἅς θυηπολοῦσιν, πείθοντες οὐ μόνον ἰδιώτας ἀλλὰ καὶ πόλεις, ὡς ἄρα λύσεις τε καὶ καθαρμοὶ ἀδικημάτων διὰ θυσιῶν καὶ παιδιᾶς ἡδονῶν εἰσι μὲν ἔτι ζῶσιν, εἰσὶ δὲ καὶ τελευτήσασιν, ἃς δὴ τελετὰς καλοῦσιν, αἳ τῶν ἐκεῖ κακῶν ἀπολύουσιν ἡμᾶς, μὴ θύσαντας δὲ δεινὰ περιμένει.

from the sufferings in the afterlife (there – ἐκεῖ).[62] While this definition of τελεταί should never be taken as a transparent, simple description that proves that all such rituals had to do with the afterlife, Plato's wordplay confirms the double purpose of the rituals that appears in the other evidence.

This passage, however, raises other issues that are helpful for understanding the evidence. Adeimantos sneers at the beggar priests and prophets who go to the doors of the rich, and he claims that they convince not only individuals, but whole cities to perform their rituals. That both communities and individuals can perform the same sort of rites helps us understand the similarities between the communal festivals like the Anthesterian Aiora and the Eleusinian Mysteries and the individual rituals that appear in the Derveni papyrus and the gold tablets. The communal rituals had much more prestige, and their authority was accepted by the widespread community, while the individual practitioners had to vie to establish their authority with their clients, so for Plato to waive the question of legitimacy and authority and to lump all of them together is highly tendentious. No doubt the conflicting stories about such figures as Epimenides and his purification of Athens from the murder of the followers of Kylon help Plato blur the differences between the rites of mendicant beggar priests and rituals long sanctioned by the traditions of the community.[63] Nevertheless, in order to make his point about the superiority of philosophy to all these other practices, he manipulates the parallels of form and purpose between the communal and the individual rites. They all involve libations and sacrifices, singing and dancing, pleasures and play, and they all are designed to purify the participants and to win the assistance of the gods.

Plato's description of the purpose of these rituals raises yet a third distinction that is helpful for understanding the evidence, that between the rites of aversion and those of appeasement. Like the distinction drawn above between preventative and contingent purification, this is, in some sense, merely a temporal distinction, deflecting the anger of the divine power either before it occurs or afterwards. Rites of appeasement are made when the divine anger has already manifested itself, in plague or famine or a frenzy that impels maidens to suicide. Rites of aversion, on the other hand, are designed to prevent these bad effects from occurring by keeping the divine power happy and satisfied rather than angry. In some cases, this

---

[62] Although some have read this passage as implying that the *teletai* were performed by the living on behalf of the dead, the fact that Adeimantos refers to these rituals being performed for "us" indicates that he is referring to rituals that he and his interlocutors participate in for the sake of a better afterlife, rather than ones they might perform for the benefit of the dearly departed.

[63] Diog. Laert. 1.110, Plut. *Vit. Sol.* 12.4–5.

assumes a situation of what Redfield calls "normal danger," where there is a divine power that is always potentially angry and dangerous who can be kept from inflicting harm by a regular set of religious practices.[64] The Anthesterian Aiora, the Agriania, the Caryatis, and such festivals all fall into this category of rites of aversion that are said to have grown into regular practice from a ritual of appeasement in a particular crisis. The category includes not only public and communal rites, but the whole spectrum of public to private, communal to individual. Some such rites might come at particular moments, such as the *proteleia* sacrifices to Iphinoë or the Delian maidens, made to avert problems as a maiden embarks on the transition to marriage. The rites described in the Derveni papyrus that involve placating the impeding *daimones* likewise are designed to solve the potential problem before it occurs, to win the favor of the powerful spirits rather than risk their hostility. The Olbia *defixio*, like the *katadesmoi* mentioned in Plato, also serves to win the favor of the spirit and divert his anger onto the enemies of the individual performing the ritual.[65]

A ποινή like that offered to the impeding *daimones* in the Derveni papyrus or to Persephone in the Pindar fragment serves to appease the potentially hostile power, offering recompense to one who has suffered and providing honors that recognize the extraordinary experiences. Once the community or the individual is already in the grip of the divine anger, however, λύσις is needed to free the victim from the effects of that anger; καθαρμός is required to remove the miasma that infects the community or the individual. The λύσεις τε καί καθαρμοί Plato mentions are therefore, under the distinction I have been drawing, rites of appeasement. They work after the anger has already come, rather than serving to avert it beforehand.

---

[64] Redfield 1990: 123. Cp. Borgeaud 1999: 287: "One might think of rituals in general as being treatments of an original mistake." Borgeaud here raises the intriguing question of whether *guilt* was imagined to result from these mistakes, rather than simply an obligation to rectify and commemorate the mistake.

[65] A *Lex Sacra* found at Selinous provides an example of ritual prescriptions for both aversion and appeasement rituals, further confirming Plato's depiction in the *Republic*. One part of the lead tablet gives instructions for rituals to be performed at regular intervals by family groups in honor of the Tritopatores (the ancestral spirits), as well as Zeus Meilichios (benevolent chthonic Zeus) and the Eumenides (the benevolent aspect of these *daimones*). On the other side of the tablet, however, are instructions for an individual who wishes to purify himself and appease the anger of an *elasteros*. Since such an individual is instructed to do the same things as a murderer afflicted by an *elasteros*, the *elasteros* must be some sort of avenging Fury who enacts the anger of the dead or other power, be it a murder victim or some other spirit in need of appeasement. Whatever the occasion for the publication of the *Lex Sacra* may have been, it is significant that prescriptions were put in place both for regular rites to keep potentially hostile chthonic powers like the Eumenides benevolent and to appease already hostile spirits for an individual who had incurred their wrath. Cp. Jameson *et al.* 1993: 54.

Whereas the ποινή is offered directly to the potentially hostile power, these λύσεις τε καί καθαρμοί often seem to require the intervention of another divinity to break the grip of the divine anger once it has set in, whether that anger manifests itself as plague or famine or madness, the pursuit of the Furies or the appearance of a monster that wreaks havoc on the community.

There were a number of deities whose epithets attest to their power in this regard, and Plato makes reference to the shrines of the apotropaic deities whose aid should be sought by someone who is impelled to criminal activity by the Furies brought on by some ancient source of anger.[66] But while Zeus or Athena might serve this function, the primary deity associated with purification and release is of course Dionysos Lyseus. Damascius preserves lines from an Orphic poem that praises Dionysos for his power to release mortals from the pains they suffer because of the deeds of their ancestors.

> Dionysos is the cause of release, whence the god is also called the Releaser (Lyseus). And Orpheus says: "Men performing rituals will send hecatombs in every season throughout the year and celebrate festivals, seeking release from lawless ancestors. You, having power over them, whomever you wish you will release from harsh toil and the unending goad."[67]

Iamblichus claims that Sabazios handles the same sort of divine angers persisting from ancient times with Bacchic rites of purification and release.[68] The *locus classicus* for such rites is of course Plato's *Phaedrus*, where the madness of Dionysos provides release for those troubled by ancient crimes.[69]

---

[66] Pl. *Leg.* 854ac (*OF* 37ii B). Zeus Apotropaios and Athena Apotropaia are attested at Erythrai (Farnell 1896 s.v. Zeus 130 [p. 166]), but the function of purification or expiation for previous crimes is associated with several deities under several epithets. Poll. 1.24 links the epithet of Apotropaios with Hikesios, Lysios, Katharsios, Phyxios, Soter, and others. See Farnell 1896 s.v. Zeus 140–144 (pp. 172–174) for testimonies for such epithets for Zeus. Cp. Apollo Alexikakos mentioned by Pausanias (1.3.4). See further above, p. 235.

[67] Dam. *In Phd.* 1.11 (35 Westerink)) (*OF* 350 B = OF 232 K): Ὅτι ὁ Διόνυσος λύσεώς ἐστιν αἴτιος· διὸ καὶ Λυσεὺς ὁ θεός, καὶ ὁ Ὀρφεύς φησιν · | 'ἄνθρωποι δὲ τελήεσσας ἑκατόμβας | πέμψουσιν πάσῃσιν ἐν ὥραις ἀμφιέτῃσιν | ὀργιά τ᾽ ἐκτελέσουσι λύσιν προγόνων ἀθεμίστων | μαιόμενοι· σὺ δὲ τοῖσιν ἔχων κράτος, οὕς κε θέλησθα | λύσεις ἔκ τε πόνων χαλεπῶν καὶ ἀπείρονος οἴστρου'. This commentary was formerly attributed to Olympiodorus and is labeled as Olympiodorus B ιά in Kern (OF 232, not OF 237 as in Bernabé 2003: 37). Westerink 1977: 15–17, however, argues against Norvin for the attribution to Damascius, and his attribution has been generally accepted.

[68] Iambl. *Myst.* 3.10.14–16: τοῦ Σαβαζίου δ᾽ εἰς Βακχείας καὶ ἀποκαθάρσεις ψυχῶν καὶ οἰκειότητα παρασκευάσται λύσεις παλαιῶν μηνιμάτων.

[69] Pl. *Phdr.* 244de (*OF* 575 B = OF 3 K): "But indeed, for illnesses and the greatest troubles, which arise in certain families from ancient causes of divine anger, madness is generated within and provides oracular wisdom that tells from whom it is necessary to seek relief, having recourse to prayers and worship of the gods, from which, when it occurs, it obtains purifications and mystic rituals (*teletai*), and madness makes safe from harm the one having it for the present and for time to come. Madness discovers a release from present evils for the one possessed by it and raving rightly." ἀλλὰ μὴν νόσων γε καὶ πόνων τῶν μεγίστων, ἃ δὴ παλαιῶν ἐκ μηνιμάτων ποθὲν ἔν τισι

Dionysos thus plays a complementary role in the process of relieving the victim of divine angers; he is not himself the one who needs to be appeased, but his disruptive madness can provide the way for the victim to make the necessary atonements. Bacchic ecstasy can purge away the miasma, the stain of divine disfavor that clings to a whole community or family line for generations, and allow a positive relationship to be established with the once hostile power.

In this light, we can reconsider the presence of Dionysos in so many of the death and the maiden myths, in which the maiden's passage to adulthood is disrupted. Although it is often suggested that, for example, the presence of the Dionysiac Melampous is a later contamination of the Proetid story, a Dionysiac element may be an integral part of the whole process of the disruption and restitution of order that takes place in these stories. Rather than a contamination of an earlier pattern, stemming from an imagined later invasion of Dionysiac religion into Greece, the presence of Dionysos is one readily available possibility in the pattern, one of the traditional elements available to the *bricoleur*. In dealing with the social disruption caused by maidens' transitions, Dionysos was always one way of expressing the overturning of the social order, especially of portraying it as an invasion from outside. Other ways of portraying the disruption certainly existed, and such different *bricolages* are often found in the stories that make use of the pattern, but the presence of Dionysos is a piece that fits well into the pattern whenever needed. The disruptive and purificatory ecstasy of Bacchic frenzy complements the appeasement of the hostile spirit, who, after the Dionysiac disruption of the social order, becomes willing to accept recompense for her sufferings and cease to vent her anger upon the community.

The gold tablets from Pelinna provide the perfect illustration of this kind of complementarity.[70] "Tell Persephone that Bacchios himself has released you," the deceased is instructed, showing that the purifications of Dionysos are the prerequisite for winning favor with the Queen of the Underworld.

τῶν γενῶν ἡ μανία ἐγγενομένη καὶ προφητεύσασα, οἷς ἔδει ἀπαλλαγὴν ηὕρετο, καταφυγοῦσα πρὸς θεῶν εὐχάς τε καὶ λατρείας, ὅθεν δὴ καθαρμῶν τε καὶ τελετῶν τυχοῦσα ἐξάντη ἐποίησε τὸν [ἑαυτῆς] ἔχοντα πρός τε τὸν παρόντα καὶ τὸν ἔπειτα χρόνον, λύσιν τῷ ὀρθῶς μανέντι τε καὶ κατασχομένῳ τῶν παρόντων κακῶν εὑρομένη. This madness is labelled Dionysiac at 265b.

70 Gold tablet from Pelinna, D1 (*OF* 485 B): νῦν ἔθανες καὶ νῦν ἐγένου, τρισόλβιε, ἄματι τῶιδε. | εἰπεῖν Φερσεφόναι σ᾽ ὅτι Βάκχιος αὐτὸς ἔλυσε᾽ | ταῦρος εἰς γάλα ἔθορες᾽ | αἶψα εἰς γάλα ἔθορες᾽ | κριὸς εἰς γάλα ἔπεσες. | οἶνον ἔχεις εὐδαίμονα τιμήν. | κἀπιμένει σ᾽ ὑπὸ γῆν τέλεα ἄσσαπερ ὄλβιοι ἄλλοι. "Now you have died and now you have been born, | thrice blessed one, on this day. | Say to Persephone that Bacchios himself freed you. | A bull you rushed to milk. | Quickly, you rushed to milk. | A ram you fell into milk. | You have wine as your fortunate honor. | And rites await you beneath the earth, just as the other blessed ones."

Dionysos' power need not be explained by imagining that Persephone was thought of as Dionysos' mother in this text; the relation between Lyseus and the aggrieved maiden (Kore) could be imagined in many ways in different tales, as lovers like Erigone or Ariadne, as siblings (Roman Liber and Libera), or as mother and son, as with Semele whom Dionysos releases from Hades and brings to Olympos as a goddess. Each choice has its significance in the different myths (and the varying versions thereof), but the basic pattern of complementarity provides the background on which the variations are made.

The distinction between aversion rituals that involve preventative purification and rituals of appeasement that provide recompense is, of course, not always clear-cut; the complementary rituals can overlap and blend in particular situations. Theophrastos shows how these two types of ritual can overlap in his caricature of the superstitious man, who takes even small occurrences as omens of an offended deity and sees the need to purify himself after all sorts of things.

> The Superstitious Man is the kind who washes his hands in three springs, sprinkles himself with water from a temple font, puts a laurel leaf in his mouth, and then is ready for the day's perambulations. If a weasel runs across his path he will not proceed on his journey until someone else has covered the ground or he has thrown three stones over the road.... If a mouse nibbles through a bag of barley, he goes to the exegete and asks what he should do; and if the answer is that he should give it to the tanner to sew up he disregards the advice and performs an apotropaic sacrifice. He is apt to purify his house frequently, claiming it is haunted by Hekate.... He refuses to step on a tombstone or go near a dead body or a woman in childbirth, saying that he cannot afford to risk contamination.... When he has a dream he visits not only dream-analysts but also seers and bird-watchers to ask which god or goddess he should pray to. He makes a monthly visit to the Orphic ritualists to take the sacrament, accompanied by his wife (or if she is busy, the nurse) and his children.[71]

---

[71] Theophr. *Char.* 16.2–3, 6–7, 9, 11–12 (*OF* 654 B = OT 207 K): ὁ δὲ δεισιδαίμων τοιοῦτός τις, οἷος ἀπὸ τριῶν κρηνῶν ἀπονιψάμενος τὰς χεῖρας καὶ περιρρανάμενος ἀπὸ ἱεροῦ δάφνην εἰς τὸ στόμα λαβὼν οὕτω τὴν ἡμέραν περιπατεῖν. καὶ τὴν ὁδὸν ἐὰν ὑπερδράμῃ γαλῆ, μὴ πρότερον πορευθῆναι, ἕως διεξέλθῃ τις ἢ λίθους τρεῖς ὑπὲρ τῆς ὁδοῦ διαβάλῃ.... καὶ ἐὰν μῦς θύλακον ἀλφίτων διαφάγῃ, πρὸς τὸν ἐξηγητὴν ἐλθὼν ἐρωτᾶν, τί χρὴ ποιεῖν, καὶ ἐὰν ἀποκρίνηται αὐτῷ ἐκδοῦναι τῷ σκυτοδέψῃ ἐπιρράψαι, μὴ προσέχειν τούτοις, ἀλλ᾽ ἀποτροπαίοις ἐκθύσασθαι. καὶ πυκνὰ δὲ τὴν οἰκίαν καθᾶραι δεινός, Ἑκάτης φάσκων ἐπαγωγὴν γεγονέναι.... καὶ οὔτε ἐπιβῆναι μνήματι οὔτ᾽ ἐπὶ νεκρὸν οὔτ᾽ ἐπὶ λεχὼ ἐλθεῖν ἐθελῆσαι, ἀλλὰ τὸ μὴ μιαίνεσθαι συμφέρον αὑτῷ φῆσαι εἶναι.... καὶ ὅταν ἐνύπνιον ἴδῃ, πορεύεσθαι πρὸς τοὺς ὀνειροκρίτας, πρὸς τοὺς μάντεις, πρὸς τοὺς ὀρνιθοσκόπους, ἐρωτήσων, τίνι θεῶν – ἢ θεᾷ – προσεύχεσθαι δεῖ. καὶ τελεσθησόμενος πρὸς τοὺς Ὀρφεοτελεστὰς κατὰ μῆνα πορεύεσθαι μετὰ τῆς γυναικός – ἐὰν δὲ μὴ σχολάζῃ ἡ γυνή, μετὰ τῆς τίτθης – καὶ τῶν παιδίων. Text and translation from

Theophrastos' *deisidaimon* provides a negative picture of a person obsessed with these rituals, endless aversion rituals to ward off any possible harm as well as endless purification rituals, just in case some impurity was incurred. The superstitious man not only seeks to avoid any impurity or offense himself, but he takes precautions against suffering the consequences of any taint that might come from others he is associated with.

While the caricature represents the view of a disapproving observer, this same concern with purification and appeasement appears as a more positive self-presentation in the gold tablet from Thurii. Not only does the deceased come pure and from the pure, but she has established a special relation with Persephone and has offered the ποινή in recompense for the unjust deeds. The key to the deceased winning a favorable afterlife lies precisely in these two concerns, and her attention to purity and to establishing her relations with Persephone are what distinguish her from all the other dead who appear before the Queen of the Dead.[72] Rather than being tokens of initiation into a secret society that shares the secret of sin and salvation, these tablets reflect, in a positive portrayal, the same hyperbolic concern with purity and a special favor from the gods won by special sacrifices that Theophrastos mocks.

As I have argued elsewhere, this ambivalence in the evidence, this mix of positive and negative evaluations of the same extra-ordinary concerns with purity and special relations with the gods is characteristic of the evidence for the ancient idea of Orphism.[73] Theophrastos depicts his *deisidaimon* as making regular visits to the Orpheotelest, just as Euripides depicts his Theseus linking his son's obsessive and hypocritical concerns about purity with Orpheus and his books, while Plato represents the Orphic life as one of primordial purity and closeness to the gods, without any violence or blood sacrifice.[74] It is this extra-ordinary level of concern with purity and appeasement of the powers of the Underworld that characterizes the evidence labeled Orphic in the ancient sources, not any central nucleus of dogmas about the origins of human sin and suffering.

The ancient grief of Persephone and the ποινή she accepts for it in Pindar fr. 133 thus do provide a way of understanding the religious context of the gold tablets from Thurii that mention Persephone and ποινή, even if not the same way that Rose proposed. Persephone's πένθος is not her anguish at

---

Diggle 2004. Diggle renders τελεσθησόμενος tendentiously as "take the sacrament," following Guthrie to avoid the translation "being initiated," which implies, in English, a once and for all procedure.

[72] See Edmonds 2004a: 69–82.   [73] See Edmonds 2008a.

[74] Eur. *Hipp.* 948–957 (*OF* 627 B = OT 213 K), Pl. *Leg.* 782c1 (*OF* 625i B = OT 212 K).

the murder of her son, but the suffering she experienced from her traumatic rape by Hades, the disruption of her maiden's passage to womanhood that ended in the realm of the dead. Similar unhappy experiences, trials and tribulations, also beset figures such as Semele and Ino, Kyrene and Ariadne, Erigone and Iphinoë, but they too all end up with a recompense in the form of honors paid to them by others. This ποινή is never paid by the one who caused the disruption – the guilty party, as we might see it, in the story. Rather, this recompense, in the form of rituals, sacrifices, and choruses, is performed by mortals who wish to win the favor of the afflicted one and to avert her anger from themselves onto others. The gold tablets make use of this familiar pattern, not for a regular, civic ritual, but for an extra-ordinary and personal one, marking the deceased as an exceptional person who deserves extra-ordinary favor from the Queen of the Dead. Understanding the religious context, both the familiar patterns of myth and ritual and the way they are manipulated in the tablets, provides a better understanding of the tablets, a vision no longer obscured by the mirage of an Orphic myth of Zagreus and its dogma of original sin.

That old Titanic nature

Another of the best known and most persistently cited pieces of evidence for the supposed "Orphic" doctrine of original sin embodied in the Zagreus myth is the reference to the "Titanic nature" in Plato *Laws* 701bc (*OF* 37i B = OF 9 K) (Τιτανικὴν φύσιν). Taken out of the context of the Platonic argument, this reference has been read as an irrefutable indication that the whole myth of humans' creation from the Titans who murdered Dionysos was known to Plato. However, by examining the reference, not as a fragment of Orphic doctrine, but as part of Plato's illustration of his speaker's point, I show that it is clearly a reference, not to the secret tale of the murder of Zagreus, but rather to the well-known story of the Titans' rebellion against the gods. The referent of Plato's allusion was recognized by Cicero, but Bernabé has recently revived arguments for reading this passage in the context of Olympiodorus' dual nature of mankind. Bernabé attempts to defend his rereading of *Laws* 701bc by pairing it with another passage from the *Laws*, 854ac (*OF* 37ii B) and claiming that the two passages can only be seen as referring to the same Orphic idea. Both of these texts must be replaced in their proper contexts, and the strands of myth they employ must be seen in their proper place in the Greek mythic tradition. The first belongs to the myths of the rebellion against the gods by the Titans and Giants, which resulted in pitched battles before the gods restored order to the cosmos by defeating their foes. The second evokes the familiar idea of the Erinyes driving to madness and new crimes someone whose inheritance includes crimes that have not yet been expiated.

Plato alludes to the Titanic nature in the Athenian Stranger's discussion of the problems of a city that, like democratic Athens, allows too much license to its citizens. He describes a slippery slope, starting with those who disregard the rules of musical composition (playing off the double sense of νόμος as musical tune and law) and ending with a complete breakdown of societal order, in which no rules are respected at all.

> Next on this path to liberty would be the wish not to submit to the rulers; and, following this, to flee the service and authority of father and mother and the elders; and, near the end, to seek not to obey the laws, and, at the end itself, to pay no mind to oaths and promises and the entirety of the gods, displaying and imitating the fabled ancient Titanic nature, they return to the same things, experiencing a savage time, never to cease from evils.[75]

Bernabé claims that Plato must here be referring to the Orphic doctrine of the Titanic heritage of mankind, the predisposition to evil inherited from the Titan ancestors who murdered Dionysos. He argues that the way Plato refers to this Titanic nature as an ancient story is in keeping with the way Plato refers to Orphic material throughout his works, and that the idea must therefore come from an Orphic text. Moreover, he claims that, in order to display a Titanic nature (Τιτανικὴν φύσιν ἐπιδεικνύσι), humans must have it innately, which requires the anthropogony found in Olympiodorus.[76] According to his interpretation of this sixth-century Neoplatonist's version of the myth, humans have a double nature, Dionysiac and Titanic, since they are created from the ashes of the Titans who ate the dismembered Dionysos.[77] The lawless ones in the Platonic passage have abandoned their Dionysiac side and given themselves wholly over to the dark side, their Titanic heritage.[78]

---

[75] Pl. *Leg.* 701bc (*OF* 37i B = OF 9 K): ἐφεξῆς δὴ ταύτῃ τῇ ἐλευθερίᾳ ἡ τοῦ μὴ ἐθέλειν τοῖς ἄρχουσι δουλεύειν γίγνοιτ' ἄν, καὶ ἑπομένη ταύτῃ φεύγειν πατρὸς καὶ μητρὸς καὶ πρεσβυτέρων δουλείαν καὶ νομοθέτησιν, καὶ ἐγγὺς τοῦ τέλους οὖσιν νόμων ζητεῖν μὴ ὑπηκόοις εἶναι, πρὸς αὐτῷ δὲ ἤδη τῷ τέλει ὅρκων καὶ πίστεων καὶ τὸ παράπαν θεῶν μὴ φροντίζειν, τὴν λεγομένην παλαιὰν Τιτανικὴν φύσιν ἐπιδεικνῦσι καὶ μιμουμένοις, ἐπὶ τὰ αὐτὰ πάλιν ἐκεῖνα ἀφικομένους, χαλεπὸν αἰῶνα διάγοντας μὴ λῆξαί ποτε κακῶν.

[76] Bernabé 2003: 36: "Il s'agit donc de quelque chose d'inné, car on ne peut montrer d'autre φύσις que celle qu'on a."

[77] Olymp. *In Phd.* 1.3 (*OF* 174viii, 190ii, 227iv, 299vii, 304i, 313ii, 318iii, 320i B = OF 220 K). I treat this passage in detail below, pp. 374–391.

[78] Bernabé 2002a: 419: "Les hommes qui se soumettent à la loi sont ceux qui font accroître leur côté dionysiaque, tandis que les êtres qui se dégradent se rapprochent de plus en plus d'une nature

For these reasons, Bernabé rejects the argument of Linforth that Plato describes these lawless ones as behaving like the Titans rather than displaying their inherent Titanic heritage, but even he admits that the text itself poses problems for his interpretation.[79] For the lawless do not just display, but they display and imitate the fabled ancient Titanic nature (τὴν λεγομένην παλαιὰν Τιτανικὴν φύσιν ἐπιδεικνῦσι καὶ μιμουμένοις), and, as Linforth argued, the word "imitate" implies that the lawless do not already have the Titanic nature inherently but rather are imitating the legendary Titans.[80]

To resolve the apparent dilemma of imitating what one already has or displaying what one does not, one need only think of actors or other performers who, in their displays in the theater, imitate the natures of various personas from myth.[81] Plato indeed speaks elsewhere of the corrupting effect that such imitations and displays might have on the souls of those who engage in them; imitation of evil leads to further wickedness, as in the slippery slope of his argument in the *Laws*.[82] To display the nature of the legendary Titans while imitating their behavior does not imply an innate character, an inherited stain, or even a predisposition to sin caused by the original crime of Titanic ancestors. On the contrary, Plato, as he so often does, is illustrating his point by allusion to a traditional myth, enriching his argument with all the associations that the tale evokes in his audience without needing to recount the tale in full.

But what tale would Plato's audience have recognized in this allusion? Bernabé insists that it must be an Orphic myth, since the formula τὴν λεγομένην παλαιάν resembles the way Plato refers to other Orphica.[83] Plato does indeed use such tags to refer to Orphic texts, but he also uses such phrases to refer to mythic tales that are not, by any stretch of the imagination, Orphic. For example, in the *Statesman*, the interlocutors discuss τὰ παλαὶ λεχθέντα, ancient tales, with specific reference to three stories, the quarrel of Atreus and Thyestes, the reign of Kronos, and the birth of warriors from the earth.[84] Tales told long ago, τὰ παλαὶ λεχθέντα, is a natural way of referring, not just to tales attributed to Orpheus, but to any

---

titanique à l'état pur, rendant ainsi manifeste une nature titanique présente chez eux depuis toujours, mais avec une intensité qui fait qu'ils ressemblent aux Titans eux-mêmes, origine de cette nature."

[79] Bernabé 2002a: 419: "C'est le mot mimoumenois qui pourrait poser problème ici."

[80] Linforth 1941: 343. Cp. Alderink 1981: 70–71.

[81] Cp. the dancers mentioned by Lucian, *Salt.* 79.15 (*OF* 600i B = OT 209 K), who dance out the parts of Titans, satyrs, and Korybantes.

[82] E.g., Pl. *Resp.* 395b–396d.

[83] Bernabé 2003: 37, where he cites his study of Platonic usage in Bernabé 1998c.

[84] *Plt.* 268e7: τὰ παλαὶ λεχθέντα; the phrase is also found at 269b4 and 274c5.

and all tales familiar from the Greek mythic tradition. Such designations do signal that Plato is alluding to a traditional myth he expects his audience to be familiar with, but we cannot limit such a reference to myths that are imagined to be exclusively or even primarily Orphic in origin.

In fact, we can be quite certain what ancient audiences would have understood by Plato's reference, because we have the testimony of Cicero, who refers to this passage in his own *Laws*. "In truth, our Plato makes them of the kind of the Titans, those who rebel against the magistrates, in the same way as the Titans did against the gods."[85] Cicero sees the parallel set up in the Platonic passage between the lawless ones who think themselves beyond any rules or governors and the ancient Titans who thought themselves beyond the control of the gods. And, just as the revolt of the Titans in the Titanomachy led to miserable defeat and punishment, so too the lawless will end up in the same sort of condition as the Titans, experiencing a harsh and savage time as a result of their anarchic behavior and never escaping from the evils they have brought upon themselves.[86] Cicero was assuredly familiar with more Orphic material than survives to us today, so an allusion to an Orphic myth of the Titans' murder of Dionysos and mankind's heritage would not have escaped him, had it been at all recognizable.[87]

Bernabé, however, claims that Plato is deliberately making an obscure reference. "Mon impression est en effet qu'ici Platon a délibérément choisi d'être peu clair, parce qu'il ne partage que partiellement les croyances qu'il recueille."[88] That is, Plato must be making an obscure reference to the Zagreus story instead of a clear reference to the Titanomachy because he was not really a believer in the secret Orphic doctrine, but nevertheless wanted to use the idea of an inherited stain from the Titans to make his point. However, the allusion to the Titanomachy illustrates Plato's point better than an allusion to the Zagreus story could, and it is difficult

---

[85] Cic. *Leg.* 3.2.5: *noster vero Plato Titanum e genere statuit eos, qui, ut illi caelestibus, sic hi adversentur magistratibus.*

[86] Bernabé 2003: 37 calls attention to the parallel between the phrase μὴ λῆξαί ποτε κακῶν and the Orphic line cited in Proclus and Simplicius, whose original form was probably something like κύκλου τε λῆξαι καὶ ἀναπνεῦσαι κακότητος (Procl. *In Ti.* 3.297.3 Diehl [*ad* 42cd] [≈ *OF* 348i, 598 B = OF 229 K], cp. Simpl. *in Cael.* 377.12 Heiberg [*OF* 348ii B = OF 230 K]; reconstruction of the verse by Rohde 1925: 357 n. 48). The wording is not so close or exceptional, however, nor the idea of ceasing to experience trouble so unusual as to suggest any sort of direct borrowing, much less that it is "une expression que nous reconnaissons pour être caractéristique de l'orphisme." Bernabé also refers to the κύκλος mentioned in tablet A1 from Thurii as evidence of the Orphic origin of Plato's phrase, but there is no κύκλος in Plato.

[87] Cicero refers both to an Orphic poem and to Orphic rites that are familiar to his contemporaries, *Nat. D.* 1.107 (*OF* 889i, 1101iv B = OT 13 K) and 3.58 (*OF* 497i B = OT 94 K).

[88] Bernabé 2003: 35.

to see why Plato would deliberately make a muddled argument in this situation.[89]

Bernabé tries to bolster his interpretation of *Laws* 701bc (*OF* 37i B = OF 9 K) by citing another passage from the *Laws*, which he claims also alludes to the Zagreus myth. At *Laws* 854ac (*OF* 37ii B), the Athenian Stranger describes the mythic preamble that should precede the law against temple robbery, in accordance with the previously agreed principle that each of the laws of this new state the interlocutors are planning should be preceded by a preamble that expresses in the terms of traditional myths the ideas embodied in the law.

> And, in accordance with the plan we already agreed upon, it is necessary to prefix to all these laws preludes as brief as possible. And thus, one might say the following to reason with and encourage a man whom an evil desire calls by day and wakes up at night, driving him to despoil something from the temples: "You extraordinary man, neither human nor divine is the evil that now moves you, prompting you to go toward sacrilege, but it is some accursed impulse circling round, innate from ancient and unexpiated wrongs to men, against which you must take care with all your strength. What sort of care that is, learn now. When any such thoughts befall you, go to the expiatory sacrifices, go as suppliant to the temples of the apotropaic deities, go to the company of the men who are said to be good; and thus learn, partly from others, partly by self-instruction, that every man must honor the beautiful and just; but flee the company of evil men without looking back. And if when you do these things thus acting your illness abates somewhat, that is well and good; but if not, then deliver yourself from life, reckoning death the better thing."[90]

This preamble describes how the impulse to commit such a crime stems from ancient and unexpiated injustices and, in keeping with a pattern found throughout the *Laws* of blending traditional religion with philosophical innovation, states that the best way to resist the impulse is to couple traditional ritual purifications with philosophic training through

---

[89] Cp. the arguments of Linforth 1941: 343–345 on the relevance of the Titanomachy allusion to the context of the *Laws*.

[90] Plato, *Leg.* 854ac (*OF* 37ii B): προοίμια δὲ τούτοισι, κατὰ τὸν ἔμπροσθεν λόγον ὁμολογηθέντα, προρρητέον ἅπασιν ὡς βραχύτατα. λέγοι δή τις ἂν ἐκείνῳ διαλεγόμενος ἅμα καὶ παραμυθούμενος, ὃν ἐπιθυμία κακὴ παρακαλοῦσα μεθ' ἡμέραν τε καὶ ἐπεγείρουσα νύκτωρ ἐπί τι τῶν ἱερῶν ἄγει συλήσοντα, τάδε· ὦ θαυμάσιε, οὐκ ἀνθρώπινόν σε κακὸν οὐδὲ θεῖον κινεῖ τὸ νῦν ἐπὶ τὴν ἱεροσυλίαν προτρέπον ἰέναι, οἶστρος δέ σέ τις ἐμφυόμενος ἐκ παλαιῶν καὶ ἀκαθάρτων τοῖς ἀνθρώποις ἀδικημάτων, περιφερόμενος ἀλιτηριώδης, ὃν εὐλαβεῖσθαι χρεὼν παντὶ σθένει· τίς δ' ἐστὶν εὐλάβεια, μάθε. ὅταν σοι προσπίπτῃ τι τῶν τοιούτων δογμάτων, ἴθι ἐπὶ τὰς ἀποδιοπομπήσεις, ἴθι ἐπὶ θεῶν ἀποτροπαίων ἱερὰ ἱκέτης, ἴθι ἐπὶ τὰς τῶν λεγομένων ἀνδρῶν ὑμῖν ἀγαθῶν συνουσίας, καὶ τὰ μὲν ἄκουε, τὰ δὲ πειρῶ λέγειν αὐτός, ὡς δεῖ τὰ καλὰ καὶ τὰ δίκαια πάντα ἄνδρα τιμᾶν· τὰς δὲ τῶν κακῶν συνουσίας φεῦγε ἀμεταστρεπτί. καὶ ἐὰν μέν σοι δρῶντι ταῦτα λωφᾷ τι τὸ νόσημα· εἰ δὲ μή, καλλίω θάνατον σκεψάμενος ἀπαλλάττου τοῦ βίου.

the observation of good men. As with the previous passage, Bernabé claims that Plato's way of introducing the allusion, λέγοι δή τις ἄν, signals that the myth must be Orphic, an uncommon idea rather than a well-known one. "Il ne s'agit donc pas de quelque chose d'universellement accepté, mais de la doctrine de quelques-uns."[91] The context of the passage, however, makes it clear that the indefinite speaker is a hypothetical lawgiver speaking to a hypothetical and potential criminal. Moreover, the mythic preamble, far from being an esoteric doctrine, is deliberately designed to be a familiar and recognizable myth, an idea that will be persuasive from its mere familiarity.[92]

In this case, the familiar mythic idea is the Erinyes or other agents of the gods who drive men to terrible acts because of unexpiated crimes in the past. In his 1829 commentary on the passage, Lobeck already noted this as a well-known idea in Greek religious thought.[93] While the generation-by-generation sequence of crimes in the house of Atreus is perhaps the best-known example, the idea that the punishment could skip generations was not unknown, either. Pausanias relates that the wrath (μήνιμα) of the Furies of Laios and Oedipus fell not on Tisamenos, son of Tersander, son of Polyneikes, who became king of Thebes after the Trojan War, but on his son, Autesion. Autesion was removed from the city at the advice of an oracle, presumably after some disaster struck.[94] In Athens, not every Alkmaionid was thought to be driven by the Furies taking vengeance for the slaughter of the followers of Kylon, but the consequences of that stain were surely brought into political discourse at various moments in history when an Alkmaionid leader (Perikles and Alkibiades spring to mind) was attempting to pursue a policy deemed ruinous by his political opponents.[95]

---

[91] Bernabé 2003: 37.

[92] Cp. Brisson 1999: 120–121, 132–133 on the use of the preambles in the *Laws*, along with Appendix 4 (156–157), which lists fourteen laws and the myths connected with their preambles. Brisson's catalog is based on the use of forms of the word μύθος in the text, and so it does not include *Leg.* 854b or other preambles not labeled with the term, but the pattern is clear.

[93] Lobeck 1829: 635 n. *t.* He compares Hdt. 4. 149; Aesch. *Cho.* 283; Xen. Eph. *Ephes.* 1.5. Parker 1983: 191–206 has a longer list of references to inherited guilt, e.g., Solon fr. 1.25–35; Hes. *Op.* 282–285; *Il.* 4.160–162, 3.300ff, 6.200–205; *Od.* 20.66–78, 11.436; Aeschylus: *Sept.* 653–655, 699–701, 720–791; *Ag.* 1090–1097, 1186–1897, 1309, 1338–1342, 1460, 1468–1488, 1497–1512, 1565–1576, 1600–1602; Sophocles: *El.* 504–515; *Ant.* 583–603; *OC* 367–370, 964–965, 1299; Euripides: *El.* 699–746, 1306 ff.; *IT* 186–202, 987–988; *Or.* 811–818, 985–1012, 1546–1548; *Phoen.* 379–382, 867–888, 1556–1559, 1592–1594, 1611. Note that crimes of blood are not the only occasion for inherited guilt; cp., e.g., Lykourgos 1.79.

[94] Paus. 9.5.15–16. Oracles often prescribe ritual purifications, but we rarely have the specific information on what past crime caused what particular crisis. Nock 1958: 852 nn. 24–25 lists a number of oracles with ritual prescriptions.

[95] Cp. Hdt. 5.70–72; Thuc. 1.126–127.

Bernabé claims that the description of the impulse to criminality, the οἶστρος, as neither divine nor human means that it must be Titanic, but the Erinyes would equally fall into this sort of middle category as inhuman servants of the gods. Platonists, starting from the definition in the *Symposium* (203a), refer to such an intermediary as daimonic, partaking in neither the limitations of humanity nor the perfection of the gods.[96] Plato is unwilling to admit that the perfect gods could ever be directly responsible for wrongdoing, and the category of the daimonic becomes a convenient way to explain the traditional tales in which humans seem provoked by the gods to commit crimes. The impulse to a crime as dreadful as sacrilege or temple robbery, on the other hand, seems unlikely to come from the mere ignorance and greed of fallible humans, especially in a state as well-ordered as the one the interlocutors are putting together; some outside force must be driving these people to defy the gods and thus bring about their ruin.[97] The Furies are just one of the mythological entities that could personify these agents of the gods, and it is worth noting that the indefinite οἶστρος expresses well the vacillation in the tradition between a personification, like the Erinyes, and a more abstract miasma or stain that arises from the same sort of crime and has the same effect on the community.[98]

While Bernabé is surely correct to see the same idea of an οἶστρος at work in this passage and the Orphic verses preserved in Damascius, which also discuss release through rites from an οἶστρος that stems from unexpiated ancestral crimes, in neither passage is there any indication that these ancestors are Titans.[99] Once again, the idea of such expiation performed by later generations for crimes, known or unknown, specified

---

[96] Bernabé refers to the parallel with Plut. *De esu carn.* 1.996b (*OF* 318ii B = OF 210 K) (on which more below) as proof that both Plato and Plutarch are talking about a Titanic element, but Plutarch makes clear that he is using the Platonic category of the *daimon* to explain the myth of the Titans allegorically. When Plutarch refers to the irrational and violent element in man as not divine but daimonic, he is following his own Middle Platonic psychology/demonology. Humans have three parts – a divine reason, a daimonic soul, and a material body. The story of the Titans provides a model for the behavior of souls that are irrational and violent, who get chained to a body as the result of their crimes.

[97] The Athenian Stranger comments at *Leg.* 853be on how such a perversion as sacrilege is unlikely to arise in their state, but notes that they must prepare for all kinds of problems in the less than perfect world in which we live. Dodds 1951: 177 n. 133 sees the temptation to sacrilege in particular as indicating a special origin of the crime, but the context of the discussion in the *Laws* makes it clear that temple robbery is just an example of a crime that is not only injustice to humans but a crazy attempt to get away with injustice against the gods. Cp. Saunders 1990: 71–73 on this passage in the context of Plato's ideas of law and punishment.

[98] Cp. Parker 1983: 107–109, on the slippage between personified agents and abstract miasma from blood guilt.

[99] Dam. *In Phd.* 1.11 (35 Westerink) (*OF* 350 B = OF 232 K). See above, n. 67.

or unspecified, committed by members of the family who lived earlier, is a widespread and familiar theme, nor is Dionysos Lyseus the only god to whom such rituals might be performed, as the reference in Plato's *Laws* to the shrines of the apotropaic deities confirms.[100]

Bernabé attempts to limit the scope of the reference, however, by citing Dodds' note that the crimes for which one is paying are usually thought to be crimes committed by oneself in a previous incarnation; hence, humans are paying for the crimes of the Titans, with whom they are identified. Even Dodds, however, although he proposes the reading Bernabé adopts of this Platonic passage, does no more than claim that the idea of reincarnation creates a more philosophically satisfying solution to the problem of theodicy than other ideas of inherited guilt or post-mortem punishment.[101] Every reference to inherited guilt does not imply a theory of reincarnation, and there is no evidence in either the Platonic passage or the Orphic reference in Damascius that such a theory of paying for the crimes of a previous incarnation is involved. Indeed, the reference in the Orphic verses to the forebears (προγόνοι) seems to suggest a focus on the genetic rather than metempsychotic connection between the criminals and punished. Moreover, even the evidence that does make a genetic link between the Titans and humanity (on which more below) never suggests that all human beings are actually reincarnations of the small band of Titans (in some versions, seven in number) who murdered Dionysos.

Despite, then, the claim that these two passages from the *Laws* can only be understood in terms of a single mythic paradigm that stems from the Orphic myth of Zagreus, they are in fact easily explicable in terms of myths well-known in the Greek mythological tradition, the tales of the Titanomachy and the Furies that were recognizable in a variety of forms from a variety of sources to Plato's audience.[102] In each passage, the well-known referent makes better sense in the context of Plato's argument than would the imagined reference to an esoteric Orphic doctrine. The threads of the punishment of the Titans and the problems of inherited guilt that scholars have tried to weave into the Zagreus myth belong instead to other aspects of the ancient Greek religious and mythological tradition. Rather than hunting for Orphic influences and excerpting fragments out of context to recreate a lost esoteric doctrine, we must consider Plato's references in the context of the arguments he is presenting

---

[100] See above, n. 66.
[101] Dodds 1951: 150. Dodds' explanation of *Laws* 854 (*OF* 37ii B) is at p. 177 n. 133.
[102] Bernabé 2003: 37: "Elles ne peuvent s'expliquer que si elles renvoient à un seul paradigme, coïncidant avec les croyances orphiques."

to his audience. By such a method, we can gain a better appreciation of the ways in which Plato manipulates the mythic tradition of his society, reworking familiar and traditional tales and elements to suit his philosophic purposes.[103]

Misreading the eating

Plutarch's allusion to the Titans' dismemberment and cannibalism of Dionysos in his essay *On the Eating of Flesh* is another key thread used in the fabrication of the supposed Orphic doctrine of original sin, another strand that must be replaced into its proper context within Greek religious thought. Clarifying and developing the arguments of previous scholars, Bernabé reads this passage as clear proof that Plutarch knew a myth in which the Titans, after their murder and dismemberment of Dionysos, were punished by incarnation in human form, a version of the anthropogony. This interpretation, however, depends on the decontextualization of Plutarch's reference and the misreading of the allegorical interpretation that Plutarch is making of the myth. Plutarch is not using the myth to explain why humans first entered the cycle of reincarnations, to reveal the esoteric origin of humankind; rather, he cites the myth to bolster the credibility of the argument he has been making about the perils of eating flesh. The myth proves, for Plutarch, that his vegetarian ideal is not a bizarre, new-fangled idea, but something hallowed by tradition, an idea that was even encoded in allegorical fashion into ancient myth. However, by mixing up the vehicle of the allegory Plutarch presents with its tenor, scholars have misread the passage as evidence that the myth of the Titans' dismemberment of Dionysos concluded with their reincarnation into human forms.[104] It is impossible to disprove that some other, hypothetical, no longer extant text might have related the tale in such a way, but Plutarch's text cannot be used as evidence for the existence of such a missing myth.

Plutarch's two discourses on the eating of flesh survive only in incomplete form, excerpts perhaps from lectures that were included in the collections made of Plutarch's writings in late antiquity. In the first discourse, Plutarch

---

[103] Cp. Edmonds 2004a for an examination of Plato's manipulations of myth in the context of his arguments in the *Phaedo*.

[104] Dawson 1992 analyzes ancient allegory, making use of terminology developed for the study of figurative language: "It has become customary to distinguish between a metaphor's tenor, the idea expressed or the subject of the comparison, and its vehicle, the image by which that idea or subject is conveyed" (Dawson 1992: 5).

sketches a scenario for the development of meat-eating among humans, starting from the first savage killings in desperate hunger to the decadent and cruel butcheries of luxury-loving moderns, who slaughter animals merely to gratify their bloodlust and titillate their palates. Plutarch carries out his argument along several lines. First, the eating of meat is bad for the body. Humans were not fashioned to be carnivores, and excess meat causes digestive difficulties (*De esu carn.* 1.995ad [*OF* 318ii B = OF 210 K]). Secondly, the eating of meat makes the body a burden on the soul, clouding its natural brilliance: "In just the same way, then, when the body is turbulent and surfeited and burdened with improper food, the lustre and light of the soul inevitably come through it blurred and confused, aberrant and inconstant, since the soul lacks the brilliance and intensity to penetrate to the minute and obscure issues of natural life."[105] Thirdly, the training of the soul to treat all animals with respect will naturally make the person more virtuous toward human beings as well (1.996ab). Plutarch then moves to the principle underlying his arguments (ἀρχὴ τοῦ δόγματος), mentioning his hesitation in the face of the peculiarity of the idea of reincarnation, but citing Plato and then Empedokles to give his ideas credibility. The first fragment ends with the passage under discussion:

> It would perhaps not be wrong to begin and quote lines of Empedokles as a preface (. . .) For here he says allegorically that souls, paying the penalty for murders and the eating of flesh and cannibalism, are imprisoned in mortal bodies. However, it seems that this account is even older, for the legendary suffering of dismemberment told about Dionysos and the outrages of the Titans on him, and their punishment and their being blasted with lightning after having tasted of the blood, this is all a myth, in its hidden inner meaning, about reincarnation. For that in us which is irrational and disorderly and violent and not divine but demonic, the ancients used the name "Titans", and this pertains to one being punished and paying the penalty.[106]

---

[105] Plut. *De esu carn.* 1.995f-996a: οὕτω δὴ καὶ διὰ σώματος θολεροῦ καὶ διακόρου καὶ βαρυνομένου τροφαῖς ἀσυμφύλοις πᾶσ᾽ ἀνάγκη τὸ γάνωμα τῆς ψυχῆς καὶ τὸ φέγγος ἀμβλύτητα καὶ σύγχυσιν ἔχειν καὶ πλανᾶσθαι καὶ φέρεσθαι, πρὸς τὰ λεπτὰ καὶ δυσθεώρητα τέλη τῶν πραγμάτων αὐγὴν καὶ τόνον οὐκ ἐχούσης.

[106] Plut. *De esu carn.* 1.996bc (*OF* 313i, 318ii B = OF 210 K): οὐ χεῖρον δ᾽ ἴσως καὶ προανακρούσασθαι καὶ προαναφωνῆσαι τὰ τοῦ Ἐμπεδοκλέους· (. . .) ἀλληγορεῖ γὰρ ἐνταῦθα τὰς ψυχάς, ὅτι φόνων καὶ βρώσεως σαρκῶν καὶ ἀλληλοφαγίας δίκην τίνουσαι σώμασι θνητοῖς ἐνδέδενται. καίτοι δοκεῖ παλαιότερος οὗτος ὁ λόγος εἶναι· τὰ γὰρ δὴ περὶ τὸν Διόνυσον μεμυθευμένα πάθη τοῦ διαμελισμοῦ καὶ τὰ Τιτάνων ἐπ᾽ αὐτὸν τολμήματα, κολάσεις τε τούτων καὶ κεραυνώσεις γευσαμένων τοῦ φόνου, ἠνιγμένος ἐστὶ μῦθος εἰς τὴν παλιγγενεσίαν· τὸ γὰρ ἐν ἡμῖν ἄλογον καὶ ἄτακτον καὶ βίαιον οὐ θεῖον ἀλλὰ δαιμονικὸν οἱ παλαιοὶ Τιτᾶνας ὠνόμασαν, καὶ τοῦτ᾽ ἔστι κολαζομένου καὶ δίκην διδόντος.

Because the treatise breaks off here, it is difficult to follow Plutarch's argument clearly, especially since the manuscripts do not, in fact, preserve the quotation from Empedokles that Plutarch promises. Nevertheless, Plutarch has laid out his ideas clearly enough that the underlying principle is evident: the eating of meat impairs the soul, depriving it of divine light, which leads to further crimes of blood, murder and warfare, all of which further pervert the soul.[107] Plutarch introduces Empedokles to show the ultimate consequence of the soul's unhealthy relation to the body, reincarnation. Plato, in the *Phaedo* (81e), also makes reincarnation the result of a soul's failing to separate itself from its desire for the body and its pleasures, and Plutarch is elaborating the Platonic argument with specific reference to the lust for blood and the pleasures of eating flesh.

Plutarch describes Empedokles as allegorizing, concealing his meaning within a story that, on its surface, has a different sense. The story, the vehicle of Empedokles' allegory, is clearly the tale of the *daimon* who for a crime of bloodshed or oath-breaking is exiled from heaven and imprisoned in an alien body.[108] The allegorical meaning, the tenor, of this story of Empedokles is that the souls of those who eat meat will undergo reincarnation; the souls correspond to the *daimon* in the myth, the eating of meat to the crime of bloodshed, and the rebirth in human or animal bodies to the imprisonment of the daimon in mortal form. Empedokles' point in his allegorical tale is therefore the same as that which Plutarch has been making in his argument, even if he uses a different form of expression.

Plutarch then goes further to support his arguments, claiming that not only does Empedokles agree with him, but this message is enshrined in ancient myth as well. The λόγος (here meaning the reasoned account as opposed to the traditional narrative, μῦθος) that souls of those who succumb to the lust to eat meat may suffer reincarnation is actually the meaning, Plutarch claims, of the myth of the Titans' dismemberment of Dionysos. The correspondences between vehicle and tenor are again clear: the Titans represent the undisciplined element that impels a person to indulge in pleasures of the flesh and to commit crimes of violence; Dionysos is a living creature who is the victim of a bloody crime; the Titans' murder, dismemberment, and cannibalism corresponds to the slaughter, butchery, and eating of an animal; the punishment of the Titans who are blasted

---

[107] Many of the same ideas appear, moreover, in Plutarch's other writings which touch on the question, particularly *Terrestriane an aquatilia* and *Bruta animalia*. Note that the latter treatise takes Circe's transformation of Odysseus' men as the occasion for the dialogue.

[108] Commentators agree that the missing quotation from Empedokles must have been 31 B 115 DK (fr. 107 Wright) (*OF* 449 B) or another passage with the same images.

with lightning represents the effects of meat-eating on the individual, who is not only made physically uncomfortable by his excesses, but who is also chained to the body both in this life and in subsequent reincarnations.[109] The correspondences show, for Plutarch, that his argument is supported by the authority of the mythic tradition, since the meaning was enigmatically expressed in the ancient myth.

These correspondences in the allegory, however, should not be taken as identifying the parts of the tenor and vehicle, which is how the passage has often been read. Just as Dionysos is not actually an animal who is butchered to provide food, so too the Titans are not actually the undisciplined element in human beings, nor is the punishment of the Titans by lightning bolt (and perhaps Tartarosis) actually the same as reincarnation. Bernabé argues that Plutarch does not see the myth as an allegory, but rather that Plutarch claims to be making his own allegorical interpretation, an interpretation limited to his etymologizing of the name Titan in the myth.[110] The text, however, clearly shows that it is the myth, not Plutarch, that is the source of the allegorical meaning (ἠνιγμένος ἐστὶ μῦθος), since Plutarch never claims to be making a new symbolic interpretation of his own, but rather to be explicating the meaning that is already there.

Indeed, it would be strange if Plutarch had claimed otherwise, since the practice of ancient allegory always claimed that the meaning was inherent in the myth, whether it was put there by a sublimely wise poet (like Homer or Orpheus) or whether it was put there by the sublimely wise ancients who first composed the tale that was later corrupted and obscured by later poets (like Homer or Orpheus).[111] Plutarch's own practice of allegory shows that he consistently attributes the meaning to the mythmaker (whether a specific poet or unnamed ancients) and that he always maintains the distinction between the narrative of the myth (the vehicle) and its enigmatic meaning (tenor). While Plutarch uses words like ἠνιγμένος and αἰνίττονται in a

---

[109] The allegory is particularly neat if the Titans, in the story with which Plutarch expects his audience to be familiar, were imprisoned in Tartaros after or as a result of being struck with lightning. While different stories that involve the Titans specify different punishments, in several variants lightning and Tartarosis are part of the same retaliation by Zeus. Cp. Arn. *Adv. nat.* 5.19 (273.14 Marchesi) (*OF* 318vii B = OF 34 K); Nonnos, *Dion.* 6.205–210. Prometheus suffers a similar combination of lightning and plunge to Tartaros at the end of the *Prometheus Bound* (1048–1093). Cp. the Iapetid Menoitios, in *Theog.* 514–515.

[110] "Le Chéronéen ne nous dit que le mythe est symbolique, mais que c'est lui qui en fait une interprétation symbolique. Dans le mythe, par contre, la séquence complète des événements serait explicite." Bernabé 2002a: 409 = Bernabé 2003: 30.

[111] Dawson 1992 uses Herakleitos and Cornutus as representatives of these two types of allegorizing, showing that allegory was not used solely to defend the status of poets like Homer from the charge of telling immoral tales but also to bolster the authority of revisionary thinkers by showing that their ideas were in line with culturally accepted texts.

variety of circumstances to refer to puzzles that must be explained, from oracles to riddles to metaphors, the most complex kind of αἴνιγμα is a traditional mythic narrative that requires interpretation to bring out the hidden meaning concealed beneath the explicit text.[112] A few examples should be sufficient to illustrate the point.

In his treatise on Isis and Osiris (366c), Plutarch relates the tale that the goddess Nepthys was barren after her marriage with Typhon but produced a child after her adultery with Osiris. Now, since a goddess cannot really be infertile, claims Plutarch, there must be a hidden symbolic meaning, in this case that the earth, which is made barren by scorching heat, needs moisture to produce fertility. The correspondences between vehicle and tenor are clear: Nepthys is the earth, Typhon is heat, and Osiris is moisture. The distinction between myth and meaning is likewise clear: if they (unspecified and indefinite tellers of the myth) say (λέγουσιν) this thing, then they mean allegorically (αἰνίττονται) the other thing.[113]

The tale of Aphrodite's birth from the sea, mentioned in Plutarch's *Quaest. conv.* 5.10.4 685e, likewise conceals a hidden physical meaning; it is a fabricated story, a μῦθον πεπλασμένον, which enigmatically signifies the generative properties of brine, εἰς τὸ τῶν ἁλῶν γόνιμον αἰνιττομένους. The well-known narrative is merely alluded to: Aphrodite, goddess of love and sex, is born from the sea.[114] The meaning is that salt has generative properties, an idea which the speaker has been arguing on other grounds, such as the aphrodisiac effects of salt on dogs and rats' ability to conceive without copulation just by licking salt. The goddess Aphrodite corresponds to the power of generation (τὸ γόνιμον), while the sea stands for the salt that comes from its briny waters.

Plutarch's allegorical interpretations, however, do not always attribute a physical meaning to the myth; often Plutarch claims that the myths contain ideas about the soul and the cosmos, especially ideas in line with his own interpretation of Platonic cosmology. For example, in *Quaest. conv.* 745e, the Sirens in Homer are reinterpreted by one of the interlocutors, Ammonius, within the context of the Sirens in Plato's Myth of Er at the end of the *Republic* (617c). The Sirens in Homer (*Od.* 12.39–54, 158–208) are terrifying creatures, who lure men to their deaths with their song,

---

[112] Cp. the analysis of Bernabé 1999 of the variety of ways in which Plutarch uses such terms.

[113] In this case, Plutarch rules out the possibility that the myth itself could be true (since it is wrong to claim that a goddess could be infertile), but in most cases he leaves the literal truth of the myth out of the question, seeing no reason to challenge the traditional tale.

[114] The brief summary omits further complicating details found in sources like Hes. *Theog.* 178–200, such as the tale that Kronos castrates Ouranos and flings his severed members into the sea, from which Aphrodite arises.

and Odysseus' men can only get past them by stopping up their ears with wax. Ammonius claims that Homer conveyed a truth symbolically, ὀρθῶς ἠνίξατο, by this myth, namely that the harmony of the spheres creates a longing for the divine in the soul that is not made deaf by fleshly obstructions and passions. Here, the Sirens and their song represent the music of the celestial spheres, as they do in the myth of Er. The men lured to their death in Homer's tale correspond to the souls drawn back toward the heavenly realm by the recollection of the celestial harmonies, whereas Odysseus' crew, who survive because they are prevented from hearing the Sirens' song, represent the average person who is too bound up with flesh and desire to feel the attraction of the divine.

Odysseus' men figure in another of Plutarch's allegories, where they again stand in for the unphilosophic masses, in this case as they go through the cycle of reincarnations. In a fragment preserved in Stob. *Flor.* 1.49.60,[115] Plutarch argues that Homer has a theory of the soul which corresponds to the teachings of Pythagoras and Plato.

> The things said in Homer about Circe contain an admirable theory about the soul. It goes thus: "They had the heads of swine, the voice, the hair, and the form; but still the mind was steadfast as it was before." The story is an allegory of the things said by Plato and Pythagoras about the soul, how although imperishable of nature and eternal, it is not without suffering nor unchangeable, but in its so-called perishing and destruction it has a change and rearrangement to other forms of bodies, seeking according to pleasure the form suitable and familiar to it through the similarity and habituation to the mode of life.[116]

As Homer tells it, when Odysseus and his men stopped on the island of Aiaia, Circe transformed Odysseus' men into beasts by means of a magic potion. The true meaning behind the cover of poetic invention is the immortality of the soul and its passage through reincarnations that reflect its choices in life. Once again, it is the myth that is the αἴνιγμα, the container of allegorical meaning, and, once again, the hidden meaning

---

[115] fr. 200. The title in Stobaeus implies that the passage is, like the excerpt before it, by Porphyry, but for stylistic and other reasons, it is generally accepted as by Plutarch.

[116] Plut. fr. 200.1–13 Sandbach = Stob. *Flor.* 1.49.60.1–13 (1.445 Wachsmuth): Τὰ δὲ παρ' Ὁμήρῳ περὶ τῆς Κίρκης λεγόμενα θαυμαστὴν ἔχει τὴν περὶ ψυχὴν θεωρίαν. λέγεται γὰρ οὕτως· [*Od.* 10.239–240] "οἱ δὲ συῶν μὲν ἔχον κεφαλὰς φωνήν τε τρίχας τε | καὶ δέμας· αὐτὰρ νοῦς ἦν ἔμπεδος ὡς τὸ πάρος περ." ἔστι τοίνυν ὁ μῦθος αἴνιγμα τῶν περὶ ψυχῆς ὑπό τε Πυθαγόρου λεγομένων καὶ Πλάτωνος, ὡς ἄφθαρτος οὖσα τὴν φύσιν καὶ ἀίδιος, οὔ τι μὴν ἀπαθὴς οὐδ' ἀμετάβλητος, ἐν ταῖς λεγομέναις φθοραῖς καὶ τελευταῖς μεταβολὴν ἴσχει καὶ μετακόσμησιν εἰς ἕτερα σωμάτων εἴδη, καθ' ἡδονὴν διώκουσα τὸ πρόσφορον καὶ οἰκεῖον ὁμοιότητι καὶ συνηθείᾳ βίου διαίτης. Cp. Plato's arguments in *Phd.* 81e.

of the myth corresponds with a philosophic argument.[117] Odysseus' men represent the individual soul; their minds remain the same even when their bodily form has changed. Plutarch unpacks each element of the transformation by Circe on Aiaia as an allegory for the death of the body through the cycle of rebirths in the place where souls pass from one body to another. Death is a transformation; Circe stands for the circle of rebirths, a fact proved by the etymology of her name; just as her island of Aiaia is the place where lost souls wander lamenting "Ai, ai" until they fall back into new bodies.[118] The potion of Circe (κυκεῶνα) is the stirring together (κυκώσης) of eternal and mortal that produces incarnation. In this process of reincarnation, the soul gravitates to a body most apt to the dominant part of its nature. Those dominated by the appetitive element become donkeys and swine, while those in whom the competitive element has become dominant through their indulgence in strife and savagery end up as wolves or lions.[119] Only those who have restrained their passions and appetites, philosophically putting their reason in charge of their conduct, will go into human bodies or perhaps, if they have kept sufficiently pure, will avoid the process altogether.

All the etymologies serve to confirm the hidden meaning of Homer's tale, but Plutarch also draws support from a citation of Empedokles, who

---

[117] fr. 200.47–48 Sandbach and *De sera*. 565de: "And this is no longer myth nor poetry but truth and a physical account." καὶ οὐκέτι ταῦτα μῦθος οὐδὲ ποίησις ἀλλ' ἀλήθεια καὶ φυσικὸς λόγος.

[118] fr. 200.25–31 Sandbach: "Homer has called the revolution in a circle and rotation of rebirth by the name of Circe, child of the Sun, the Sun which eternally joins every death to birth and birth again to death, linking them together. The island of Aiaia is that fate and country receiving the man when he is dying, the place to which the souls wander when they first arrive, when they are wailing and feeling like strangers." Ὅμηρος δὲ τὴν ἐν κύκλῳ περίοδον καὶ περιφορὰν παλιγγενεσίας Κίρκην προσηγόρευκεν, Ἡλίου παῖδα τοῦ πᾶσαν φθορὰν γενέσει καὶ γένεσιν αὖ πάλιν φθορᾷ συνάπτοντος ἀεὶ καὶ συνείροντος. Αἰαίη δὲ νῆσος ἡ δεχομένη τὸν ἀποθνῄσκοντα μοῖρα καὶ χώρα τοῦ περιέχοντος, εἰς ἣν ἐμπεσοῦσαι πρῶτον αἱ ψυχαὶ πλανῶνται καὶ ξενοπαθοῦσι καὶ ὀλοφύρονται. Cp. *De vita et poesi Homeri* 126.

[119] fr. 200.48–59 Sandbach: "Those whom the appetitive element leaps forth to control and to dominate in the transformation and birth, Homer says that the change brings to them turbid and impure lives, through their love of pleasure and gluttony, and the bodies of donkeys and swine. Whenever a soul comes to second birth having a spirited element that has become thoroughly savage through bitter rivalries and murderous cruelties arising from some quarrel or ill will, then, full of fresh bitterness and melancholy, it hurls itself into the body of a wolf or lion, just as though latching onto and fitting around itself the body with its ruling passion as an instrument of retaliation." ὧν μὲν γὰρ ἐν τῇ μεταβολῇ καὶ γενέσει τὸ ἐπιθυμητικὸν ἐξανθοῦν ἐπικρατεῖ καὶ δυναστεύει, τούτοις εἰς ὀνώδη καὶ ὑώδη σώματα καὶ βίους θολερούς καὶ ἀκαθάρτους ὑπὸ φιληδονίας καὶ γαστριμαργίας φησὶ γίνεσθαι τὴν μεταβολήν. ὅταν δὲ φιλονεικίαις σκληραῖς καὶ φονικαῖς ὠμότησιν ἔκ τινος διαφορᾶς ἢ δυσμενείας ἐξηγριωμένον ἔχουσα παντάπασιν ἡ ψυχὴ τὸ θυμοειδὲς εἰς δευτέραν γένεσιν ἀφίκηται, πλήρης οὖσα προσφάτου πικρίας καὶ βαρυφροσύνης ἔρριψεν ἑαυτὴν εἰς λύκου φύσιν ἢ λέοντος, ὥσπερ ὄργανον ἀμυντικὸν τὸ σῶμα τῷ κρατοῦντι προσιεμένη πάθει καὶ περιαρμόσασα. Cp. *De sera*. 565de for another adaptation of these Platonic ideas.

also relates a story about reincarnation. Even though he uses different names than Homer does, they both are talking about the operation of Fate (Εἱμαρμένη) and Nature (Φύσις) that puts souls in new bodies. Instead of Circe and her potion, Empedokles refers to the *daimon* wrapping around an alien garment of flesh (σαρκῶν ἀλλογνῶτι περιστέλλουσα χιτῶνι), but the different vehicles have the same tenor; their mythic expressions have the same meaning.[120]

Plutarch's allegorical reading of this Homeric passage bears numerous resemblances to his reading of the myth of the Titans in *De esu carn.* 1.996bc (*OF* 313i, 318ii B = OF 210 K). In both, he makes use of etymologies to confirm the validity of the allegory. In both, he supports his claim with an additional reference to Empedokles. In both, he claims that the ancient myth has the same meaning as a philosophic argument regarding reincarnation, an argument going back to Plato's *Phaedo* that the soul needs to be guided by reason and separate itself from the passions of the body in order to avoid a bad (or possibly even any) reincarnation. Following the Platonic model of the soul, he speaks of the rational element that should be in charge, as well as the appetitive or passionate elements that attempt to take control. Such an uncurbed element (τὸ ἀκόλαστον), pursuing pleasure or a spirited desire for violence and bloodshed, can lead the individual into disaster, causing the soul to be caught up with the body. In life, this condition hampers the natural facilities of the soul, its ability to perceive the divine light, to reason. After the life of the body ends, such a soul is immediately attracted back into a bestial form that reflects the guiding element. In his arguments against eating flesh, Plutarch describes at length the appetites for the pleasures of gluttony or the impulses to violence and bloodshed that can lead a person astray if not kept in check and restrained by a philosophic mind and practice.

This is the irrational and disorderly and violent element in us that Plutarch claims the ancients named the Titans in the myth. Plutarch never claims that this element is actually a Titan, much less that the Titans are reincarnated in all human beings because of their primordial crime. To do so would be to mix the tenor and vehicle of his allegory and make nonsense of his argument. The punishment of the Titans represents allegorically the

---

[120] Plut. fr. 200.21–25 Sandbach and *De sera.* 565de: αὐτῆς γὰρ τῆς μετακοσμήσεως εἱμαρμένη καὶ φύσις ὑπὸ Ἐμπεδοκλέους δαίμων ἀνηγόρευται "σαρκῶν ἀλλογνῶτι περιστέλλουσα χιτῶνι" καὶ μεταμπίσχουσα τὰς ψυχάς. Plutarch quotes the same fragment of Empedokles (31 B 126 DK = fr. 110 Wright [*OF* 450 B]) in the second portion of *De esu carn.* 2.998c, arguing that the prospect of reincarnation will deter the unruly element (τὸ ἀκόλαστον) from pursuing its lusts for flesh.

punishment of the soul that falls back into a body because of its bloodlust and gluttony, just as Circe's transformation of Odysseus' men into swine represents the reincarnation of souls from human to animal bodies. Circe's transformation of Odysseus' men into animals does not also cause them to be reincarnated as animals; it merely represents it allegorically. So too, the Titans' murder of Dionysos and punishment by lightning does not also cause them to be reincarnated; Plutarch's myth is explicitly an allegory, not an aetiological myth.

Bernabé, by contrast, claims that the myth of the Titans here serves as the primordial crime, the *péché antécédent*, that is the cause of the fallen condition of humans in this world, a crime that is repeated every time a human yields to his Titanic element. Bianchi's idea of *péché antécédent* is useful for understanding certain kinds of myths that are told as the *aition* for a particular phenomenon, especially ritual practice.[121] Once upon a time, a god was angered at a certain occurrence, and so forever after humans have performed a certain rite that both reminds everyone of the problem and solves it by appeasing the god. Hesiod's tale of the quarrel between Zeus and Prometheus that resulted in the separation of men and gods is the canonical example of such a *péché antécédent*, an event that happened long ago but which produced the conditions that exist today. The ritual of sacrifice serves at the same time as a reminder of the separation and a way of healing the breach.

Hesiod's tale, however, is framed within his text as an explanation of why the lives of men are so hard; it is explicitly aetiological. By contrast, Plutarch frames his tale of the Titans as an allegory, using the same vocabulary that he uses to introduce other allegorical tales (ἠνιγμένος ἐστὶ μῦθος εἰς τὴν παλιγγενεσίαν). If the tale of Circe's transformation of Odysseus' men were taken as an *aition* instead of an allegory, the transformation would have to serve as the precedent and cause of the whole cycle of reincarnations – because Odysseus' men drank the potion and were transformed into swine, so now all mortals undergo reincarnation. Only the fragmentary state of *De esu carnium* makes the analogous interpretation of the myth of the Titans seem less obviously absurd.

It is not in the least surprising that Plutarch should see the myth of the Titans' murder of Dionysos as, in essence, an allegory of the fate of the soul, since the tale was preserved and transmitted by a number of different authors specifically because it was a useful vehicle for various

---

[121] Bianchi 1966 distinguishes between *péché antécédent*, found in the myths of many cultures, and the Christian idea of original sin, but his category has been used by later scholars to reintroduce a notion of original sin into non-Christian contexts, such as ancient Orphism.

ideas about the nature of the soul and the cosmos. Although the idea that the myth of Dionysos' dismemberment was about the grape vine remained popular,[122] the physical understanding of the myth was often replaced or supplemented by a metaphysical understanding that took the dismemberment of Dionysos as an allegory of division of the One into Many, that is, the process of differentiation that created the physical world and the individual.[123] Plutarch himself describes how the story of Dionysos' dismemberment is an allegory of this *diakosmesis*.

> The wiser ones, concealing it from the many, call the transformation into fire Apollo from its singleness, or Phoebus from its purity and lack of defilement. Regarding his change and the rearrangement of matter (*diakosmesis*) into winds, water, earth, stars, and the generation of plants and animals, they speak allegorically of this experience and transformation as "rending" and "dismemberment". And they name him Dionysos, Zagreus, Nyktelios, Isodaites, and they recount allegories and myths fitting the stories of destructions and disappearances and then the returns to life and rebirths.[124]

In the Platonic tradition, the physical division of the universe is often less significant than the process by which the world soul or originary soul is divided and dispersed throughout the cosmos. Plutarch, like his successors Plotinus, Proclus, and Damascius, sometimes reads the myth as being about the macrocosm – the division and reintegration of the world soul – and sometimes as about the microcosm – the fate of the individual soul in its incarnations and attempts to free itself and return to the divine. In his treatise on Isis and Osiris, for example, Plutarch describes Osiris, whom he identifies with Dionysos, as the world soul, the Intelligible Principle, which is divided out through the cosmos.[125] Proclus, in his commentary on

---

[122] Dionysos is seen as the vine, born of rain (Zeus) and earth (Demeter); the grapes are trampled apart by the peasants (*gegeneis*); the wine is prepared by boiling and comes out stronger after the processes. Cp. Diod. Sic. 3.62.6–7 (*OF* 59iii B = OF 301 K); Corn. *ND* 30 (58.6 Lang) (*OF* 59iv B). The idea of Dionysos as the personification of wine appears also in fragments of the *Rhapsodies* (collected in OF 216 K = *OF* 331, 321, 303 B). This evidence should not be dismissed as a mere Stoic accretion; it was clearly part of the story as it was told in the *Rhapsodies* (*contra* West 1983: 142, 245–246).

[123] For the Stoic doctrines of ἐκπυρώσεις and διακοσμήσεις, cp. Chrysippos fr. 527 von Arnim (*SVF* 2.168.11) = Stob. *Ecl.*1.184.8–185.24; Macrob. *Sat.* 1.17.7(*SVF* 2.1095).

[124] Plut. *De E ap. Delph.* 9.388e (*OF* 613ii B): κρυπτόμενοι δὲ τοὺς πολλοὺς οἱ σοφώτεροι τὴν μὲν εἰς πῦρ μεταβολὴν Ἀπόλλωνά τε τῇ μονώσει Φοῖβόν τε τῷ καθαρῷ καὶ ἀμιάντῳ καλοῦσι. τῆς δ' εἰς πνεύματα καὶ ὕδωρ καὶ γῆν καὶ ἄστρα καὶ φυτῶν ζῴων τε γενέσεις τροπῆς αὐτοῦ καὶ διακοσμήσεως τὸ μὲν πάθημα καὶ τὴν μεταβολὴν διασπασμόν τινα καὶ διαμελισμὸν αἰνίττονται· Διόνυσον δὲ καὶ Ζαγρέα καὶ Νυκτέλιον καὶ Ἰσοδαίτην αὐτὸν ὀνομάζουσι, καὶ φθοράς τινας καὶ ἀφανισμοὺς εἶτα δ' ἀναβιώσεις καὶ παλιγγενεσίας, οἰκεῖα ταῖς εἰρημέναις μεταβολαῖς αἰνίγματα καὶ μυθεύματα περαίνουσι.

[125] Plut. *De Is. et Os.* 54 373a: The Intelligible is Osiris, the Platonic receptacle is Isis, and the product of their interaction is Horus.

the *Cratylus*, refers to the division of the whole into many individual parts on every level – mind, soul, and perceptible matter. He even brings in the physical process of wine-making to the levels of meaning he finds in the myth of the Titans' dismemberment of Dionysos.[126] In his commentary on the *Phaedo*, on the other hand, Damascius brings out the personal and individual level of meaning, the life of the individual seeking divine perfection in a fragmented world. Like Plutarch, Damascius connects the Titans with the irrational element, a middle term between rational mind and mindless matter which corresponds to Plutarch's daimonic soul element.

> The Titanic mode of life is the irrational mode, by which rational life is torn asunder: It is better to acknowledge its existence everywhere, since in any case at its source there are Gods, the Titans; then also on the plane of rational life, this apparent self-determination, which seems to aim at belonging to itself alone and neither to the superior nor to the inferior, is wrought in us by the Titans; through it we tear asunder the Dionysus in ourselves, breaking up the natural continuity of our being and our partnership, so to speak, with the superior and inferior. While in this condition, we are Titans; but when we recover that lost unity, we become Dionysoi and we attain what can truly be called completeness.[127]

When we behave badly and follow the impulses of that spirited element, we act as Titans, pulling apart the Dionysos, the superior rationality, within us, but when we behave well, we become perfected Dionysoi, under the guidance of our rational and divine element. The present general temporal clauses indicate that the idea applies not to condition precedent, but to the general situation; the tale of Dionysos and the Titans is an allegory of the general human condition, not a tale of the preceding cause of it.

Plutarch's understanding of the myth of the Titans' dismemberment of Dionysos must therefore be seen within the context, not only of his own practice of allegorical interpretation, but also within the tradition of such allegorical interpretations of this very myth. Each of these allegorical readings is designed for the particular argument being made in the context in which the myth is cited, and the details of the myth that are recounted

---

126 Procl. *In Crat.* 109.9 Pasquali (*ad* 406c) (*OF* 331ii B = OF 216 K). Note that he refers to the θεολόγοι who put the meanings into the myth.

127 Dam. *In Phd.* 1.9 (trans. Westerink, modified): ὅτι ἡ Τιτανικὴ ζωὴ ἄλογός ἐστιν, ὑφ' ἧς ἡ λογικὴ σπαράττεται. Κάλλιον δὲ πανταχοῦ ποιεῖν αὐτήν, ἀπὸ θεῶν γε ἀρχομένην τῶν Τιτάνων· καὶ τοίνυν τῆς λογικῆς τὸ δοκοῦν αὐτεξούσιον καὶ οἶον ἑαυτοῦ βουλόμενον εἶναι μόνου, οὔτε δὲ τῶν κρειττόνων οὔτε τῶν χειρόνων, τοῦτο ἡμῖν οἱ Τιτᾶνες ἐμποιοῦσιν, καθ' ὃ καὶ τὸν ἐν ἡμῖν Διόνυσον διασπῶμεν, παραθραύοντες ἡμῶν τὸ ὁμοφυὲς εἶδος καὶ οἶον κοινωνικὸν πρὸς τὰ κρείττω καὶ ἥττω. οὕτω δὲ ἔχοντες Τιτάνές ἐσμεν· ὅταν δὲ εἰς ἐκεῖνο συμβῶμεν, Διόνυσοι γινόμεθα τετελειωμένοι ἀτεχνῶς.

are tailored to fit the argument.[128] When compared with Plutarch's other allegorizations, Plutarch's reading of the myth in *De Esu Carnium* clearly follows the same pattern, using not only the same kind of language and relation of the myth to the philosophical argument, but even coming up with the same point as some of his other allegorical interpretations. Despite the fragmentary condition of the text of Plutarch's treatise on the eating of flesh, we can reconstruct the shape of his argument from Plutarch's writings on related topics, and we can see how the allegorical understanding of the myth supports the argument he is making in this discourse, with its particular emphasis on flesh-eating rather than passions in general. However, by mixing up the tenor and the vehicle of Plutarch's allegorization, modern scholars have created a new pastiche of a myth, in which the Titans' actions in the myth of the dismemberment are followed by a sequel of the Titans' reincarnation into human form. This confusion distorts not only the reading of the Plutarch passage, but also, by postulating a myth known to Plutarch that combines dismemberment and anthropogony, causes scholars to misread the later allusions to and interpretations of the dismemberment myth. Rather than seeing all these references as evidence for an Orphic doctrine of original sin, a Titanic nature within humankind that comes from the reincarnation of the Titans into human form, we can use each of these references to gain a better understanding of the philosophical arguments of Plutarch and his successors, as well as the ways in which they manipulated the common mythic tradition. The complex designs of these thinkers should not be reduced to mere threads in a funerary shroud, fragments of a single story of the prefiguration of the Christian doctrine of original sin.

The playthings of Dionysos

In addition to the references to mythic narratives of the dismemberment of Dionysos, we must consider the texts that indicate some sort of ritual practice associated with the story.[129] Bernabé asserts that the various

---

[128] Cp. the emphasis on seven Titans and seven pieces of Dionysos in arguments that relate the story to the seven divisions of fate in the *Timaeus*. Cp. Procl. *In Ti.* 2.146.9 Diehl (*OF* 311i B = OF 210 K). Likewise, the preservation of Dionysos' heart by Athena is mentioned when the preservation of essential unity through forethought (*pronoia* = Athena Pronaia/Pronoia) despite material division is one of the points of the argument (cp. Procl. *In Ti.* 2.145.18 Diehl [*ad* 35a] [*OF* 314i B = OF 210 K]).

[129] Bernabé 2002a: 413 incorrectly sees this as a fundamental category neglected in Edmonds 1999: "Mais il nous reste encore à developper un argument à notre avis fondamental: le rapport qui existe entre le mythe de Dionysos et des Titans et les teletai, un lien sur lequel Edmonds n'a point

testimonies to rituals, some attributed to Orpheus, connected with the dismemberment of Dionysos are evidence for the doctrine of guilt inherited by humans from their Titanic ancestors for the murder of Dionysos. While I agree that the existence of certain rituals is undeniable, I argue that assuming that the motif of dismemberment can only imply the full story of anthropogony and original sin oversimplifies the step from ritual to doctrine. That there were rituals connected with the *sparagmos* of Dionysos cannot be doubted; that some of these rituals mentioned the Titans in connection with the destruction is certain; that any of these rituals had anything to do with anthropogony or purification from original sin is not only unprovable (as well as unfalsifiable) but unsupported by the evidence.

The evidence for ancient Greek ritual of any kind is desperately slim and deeply problematic, especially for efforts to recover not simply what was done but what the rituals meant in the religion of the people performing them. The references in texts that speak of ritual are even less transparent than the literary texts, and any deductions about the import of the ritual must be carefully culled from the evidence, always taking the context into due consideration. Rather than attesting to a single doctrine of original sin that was central to a marginal sect, the evidence for rituals associated with the *sparagmos* of Dionysos can provide valuable information on the practices of ancient Greek religion, not only for the worship of Dionysos, but also for the rites associated with divinities such as the Kouretes and Korybantes.

Just as the myth of the dismemberment did not have a single meaning but was reinterpreted in various ways by the various narrators and their audiences, so too the rituals associated with the story must have had a variety of significances. One of the few references extant for the context in which a ritual connected with the *sparagmos* might be performed is a scholiast to Clement, who explains the Lenaia festival as having to do with the dismemberment of Dionysos.

> *Lenaizontas* – a rustic song sung at the wine trough, which even itself has to do with the dismemberment of Dionysos. He has put very well and gracefully the bit about "binding up with ivy", at the same time showing the fact that the Lenaian festivals are dedicated to Dionysos and also how as drunken mischief these things have been clapped together by tipsy and drunken people.[130]

insisté, car il a toujours envisagé le mythe sous son aspect exclusivement littéraire, sans être occupé de son emploi rituel ou religieux."

[130] ΣClem. Al. *Protr.* 1.2.2 (p. 297.4–8 Stählin): ληναΐζοντας· ἀγροικικὴ ᾠδὴ ἐπὶ τῷ ληνῷ ᾀδομένη, ἣ καὶ αὐτὴ περιεῖχεν τὸν Διονύσου σπαραγμόν. πάνυ δὲ εὐφυῶς καὶ χάριτος ἐμπλέως τὸ "κιττῷ

Just as some authors interpret the myth of the dismemberment as signifying the process of making wine from grapes, so too in some festivals the
dismemberment was celebrated as part of the process of wine-making –
the harvesting of the grapes and their trampling out into wine.[131] The
scholiast is not alone in connecting the dismemberment of Dionysos with
the making of wine, and there is no reason to dismiss this interpretation
as a late and inauthentic allegorization that has nothing to do with what
the people celebrating the ceremony believed. The timing of the Lenaia
does not coincide with the time of the grape harvest, but the word ληνός
means the trough or vat in which the grapes are pressed for wine, while the
Lenai seem to have been the women celebrating the Dionysiac rituals as
Bacchic maenads.[132] We know little of the components of the Lenaia apart
from the dramatic competitions, but the equation of Dionysos with his
wine is a commonplace, so it is entirely plausible that the Lenaia festival
included a ritual that involved some commemoration of the dismemberment of Dionysos as part of its festivities, whether in some sort of dramatic
enactment or simply in song.

While the Lenaia was a public festival, the dismemberment of Dionysos
may also have played a role in festivals less open to the view of all. Clement
of Alexandria associates the dismemberment with the taboo on eating
pomegranates for women at the Thesmophoria.[133] This sort of ritual, not

---

ἀναδήσαντες" τέθεικεν, ὁμοῦ μὲν τὸ ὅτι Διονύσῳ τὰ Λήναια ἀνάκειται ἐνδειξάμενος, ὁμοῦ δὲ καὶ
ὡς παροινίᾳ ταῦτα καὶ παροινοῦσιν ἀνθρώποις καὶ μεθύουσιν συγκεκρότηται.

[131] Diod. Sic. 3.62.6–7 (*OF* 59iii B = OF 301 K); Corn. *ND* 30 (58.6 Lang) (*OF* 59iv B). This
interpretation appears to have been woven into the myth itself at least by the time of the *Rhapsodies*.
Cp. Proclus' quotations that equate Dionysos with wine (Procl. *In Crat.* 108.13 Pasquali [*OF* 331i,
321, 303 B = OF 214, 216b–c K]; *In Crat.* 109.9 Pasquali [*ad* 406c] [*OF* 331ii B = OF 216a K]).

[132] Diod. Sic. 3.63.4 explains the god's epithet Lenaios from the pressing of the grapes in the wine-
vats. Hesykhios equates λῆναι with βάκχαι, as does a ΣHerakleitos, 22 B 15 DK: ληναΐζουσιν·
βακχεύουσιν. λῆναι γὰρ αἱ βάκχαι. Burkert 1985: 290 compares the Lenai to the Thyiades who
roam the mountains around Delphi in a winter celebration or the women of Thebes celebrating the
Agrionia. Cp. Plut. *Quaest. conv.* 717a; *contra* Pickard-Cambridge 1968: 29–30, deriving the name
of the Lenaian festivals from the Lenai and from the ληνός are not mutually exclusive options.
Cp. Mayerson 2000 on the uses of ληνός that extend beyond the literal meaning of the stomping
trough; Spineto 2010: 18 on the Lenaia as festival of the ληνός that evokes the dismemberment
through the association with other parts of the viticultural process: "I Lenaia, però, per poter
accogliere in sé la celebrazione della torchiatura, dovevano avere un nesso di ordine simbolico
con essa o, almeno, risultare adatti, sempre per ragioni simboliche, a riferirsi ad essa. Questo
nesso è garantito, appunto, dalle attività agricole che si svolgevano nel periodo di tempo della
loro celebrazione. La potatura a secco evoca una violenza inferta alia rite ed evoca lo sparagmos, e
quindi lo smembramento di Dionysos."

[133] Clem. Al. *Protr.* 2.19.3: "Just as the women, in celebrating the Thesmophoria, abstain from eating
the seeds of the pomegranate, believing that pomegranates sprang from the drops of the blood
of Dionysus that had fallen to the ground." ὥσπερ ἀμέλει καὶ αἱ θεσμοφοριάζουσαι τῆς ῥοιᾶς
τοὺς κόκκους παραφυλάττουσιν ἐσθίειν· τοὺς γὰρ ἀποπεπτωκότας χαμαὶ ἐκ τῶν τοῦ Διονύσου
αἵματος σταγόνων βεβλαστηκέναι νομίζουσι τὰς ῥοιάς.

a private mystery but yet not something that should be spoken of publicly, may well be the kind alluded to by Herodotus. When discussing the rites of Osiris in Egypt, Herodotus famously refuses to provide details, claiming that it is not licit for him to speak of them, οὔ μοι ὅσιόν ἐστι λέγειν. Since the rites of Osiris in Egypt do not, from the available evidence, seem to have been unspeakable, many have hypothesized that Herodotus is identifying them with Greek rituals that do have such a taboo.[134] Osiris was often identified with Dionysos, and the stories of their dismemberments were easy for mythic narrators to conflate.[135] We need not follow the conjectures of scholars ancient and modern who have postulated that the Greek rituals actually came from Egypt (or vice versa!) to understand Herodotus' evidence as indicating that he knew of rituals having to do with the dismemberment (and probably rebirth) of Dionysos that he felt merited a degree of ritual silence.[136] However, although many of the rituals for Osiris may have concerned the fertility brought by the Nile, they were assuredly not limited to that aspect, so it is impossible to be certain what the significance was of the rituals Herodotus had in mind. Even though Herodotus believed that the Thesmophoria also derived from Egypt, the Thesmophoria is only one possibility for a ritual somehow involving the dismemberment of Dionysos that it is forbidden to speak about; there must have been many others, most of which we know nothing about.[137]

While Herodotus' Osiris rituals do seem to have been associated with Orphic rituals, Bernabé includes in his arguments a number of testimonies which seem to have little or no connection to an Orphic ritual

---

[134] Hdt. 2.61. However, Lloyd *ad* Hdt. 2.61 (p. 279) argues that this expression is simply Herodotus' way of rendering the Egyptian term Sšt3w, which refers to rituals excluded from the sight of all but the priests.

[135] Plut. *De Is. et Os.* 35 364e–365a (*OF* 47 B) is perhaps the most complete account of the identification of cults, but Bernabé collects the testimonies to Bacchic and Orphic rituals believed to stem from Egypt as *OF* 40–63 B. Cp. Edmonds 2013 for the conflation of Dionysos with Osiris and Apis and Epaphos as grounded in the similarities of ritual experience.

[136] Lobeck 1829: 671, Wilamowitz-Moellendorff 1931–32, II: 193, and Festugière 1935: 379 argued that the myth of Dionysos' dismemberment must have come from Egyptian Osiris cult, probably in the Hellenistic period, but Casadio 1996: 216 points out that the process might have gone the other way, since there is no evidence for the dismemberment of Osiris until the Ptolemaic era.

[137] Cp. Hdt. 2.171, where Herodotus mentions a rite of an unnamed god. He refuses to speak about this rite and then adds that he also refuses to speak of the rite for Demeter that the Greeks call the Thesmophoria. He traces the origins of this rite in Greece to the Danaids escaping from Egypt. Cp. Thdt. *Graec. Aff. Cur.* 1.21 (108.21 Canivet) (*OF* 51i B = OT 103 K), who claims that Orpheus transformed the Egyptian rites of Isis and Osiris into the Greek rites of Deo and Dionysos, mentioning the Eleusinia and the Thesmophoria as well as the Dionysia. Cp. 2.32, where the Thesmophoria and Dionysia are paired as the rites learned from the Egyptians. Cp. Herodotus' claim that Melampous brought Bacchic rituals from Egypt, 2.49.1 (*OF* 54 B).

associated with the dismemberment of Dionysos.[138] The story in Herodotus about the Olbian Skyles participating in Dionysiac cult assuredly attests to the intercultural relations between the Greeks and the inhabitants of the area, but there is no reason to connect it with the Olbian bone tablets, as if there were only one Dionysiac cult in the entire region over the entirety of the history of Greek colonization in Olbia.[139] Moreover, even if one of the Olbian bone tablets did refer to Orphik[oi instead of Orphik[a and Dio[nysos instead of Dio[s (of which I am not convinced), it would not follow that at Olbia there was a sect of Orphics who practiced Dionysiac rituals having to do with reincarnation.[140] The bone tablets do suggest the presence at some point in time at Olbia of a ritual specialist (whether established priest or itinerant charlatan) who made use of Orphic materials with a rather Heraclitean theology, but the evidence provides no indication of what rituals he might have practiced or for whom. The bone tablets have no Titans, no dismemberment, no lightning, and no anthropogony – nothing to narrow the field of reference of their cryptic and paradoxical inscriptions to the myth of Dionysos' dismemberment.

A second-century CE *lex sacra* from Smyrna does mention the Titans in a Dionysiac context, but its dietary prohibitions against beans and eggs hardly fit either with the myth of dismemberment or the Titanic anthropogony.[141] The inscription undoubtedly provides regulations for a private mystery association, but taboos on particular foods are not limited to a single context or rationale.[142] Eggs were forbidden to those participating in the Haloa, while Eleusinian initiates had to avoid beans as well as fish, fowl, and pomegranates.[143] Pausanias claims that anyone who has seen an initiation at Eleusis or read the so-called Orphic writings will understand his claim that beans were the one product of the earth that

---

[138] Herodotus claims that the Orphic and Bacchic rituals are really Egyptian and Pythagorean (2.81.2 [*OF* 45, 650 B = OT 216 K]).

[139] Hdt. 4.79 (*OF* 563 B). The bone tablets are listed as *OF* 463–465 B. For the value of this evidence, see above, pp. 199–200.

[140] Bernabé 2002a: 414 claims that this evidence "nous indiquent que le culte de Dionysos était pratiqué dans cette ville par des individus qui s'autodénommaient orphiques et qui croyaient en une séparation du corps et de l'âme et en une cycle vie-mort-vie, dans lequel ils impliquaient le dieu lui-même."

[141] *SEG* 14 752 (*OF* 582 B). See Nock 1958.

[142] Cp. Burkert's collection of food taboos in different rites, Burkert 1972: 177. The prohibition of certain fish in a variety of contexts is particularly striking. Parker 1983: 357–365 (appendix 4) reviews the evidence for food taboos and their rationales, suggesting (362) that an extension of the taboo on cannibalism may explain a number of the particular prohibitions.

[143] ΣLucian *Dial. Metr.* 7.4 (80,7 4.29 = 280.23 Rabe); Porph. *Abst.* 4.16.

Demeter did not provide.[144] Plutarch explains the food taboos of eggs and beans, as well as hearts and brains, as the avoidance of consuming the first principle of creation (γενέσεως).[145] The precise role of the Titans remains inexplicable even on the hypothesis of the Zagreus myth, since the inscription is too fragmentary to reconstruct, but the combination of dismemberment, Titanic anthropogony, and inherited guilt is hardly the only possible explanation for the mention of Titans.[146] Most plausibly, the Titans could here simply represent the mythic exemplars of cannibals, those who violate the basic rules of what (or who) can be eaten.[147]

A *defixio* from Lilybaeum also mentions the Titans, locating them in Tartaros along with Persephone, but there is no indication that they are invoked for any reason other than that they are Underworld powers, like the spirits of the dead and their queen, Persephone, who are also invoked.[148] The Titans indeed appear as deities in Tartaros from their earliest mentions in Greek literature, as Pausanias points out: "Homer first introduced the Titans into poetry, making them gods down in Tartaros, as it is called; the lines are in the oath of Hera. Onomakritos, borrowing the name from Homer, composed the rites of Dionysos and made the Titans the authors of the sufferings of Dionysos."[149]

---

[144] Paus. 1.37.4 (*OF* 649i B = OT 219 K); cp. 8.15.4 (*OF* 649ii B = OT 219 K), where Pausanias mentions a *hieros logos* associated with the rites of Eleusinian Demeter at Pheneus that explains why the Pheneatians consider the bean to be not *katharos*.

[145] Plut. *Quaest. conv.* 2.3.1 635e–636a (*OF* 645, 647i, 648v B = OF 291 K) jokes about his abstention from eggs causing his friends to speculate that he was picking up Orphic or Pythagorean superstitions and to quote at him the dramatic verses comparing the eating of beans to gnawing one's parents' heads. As Burkert 1972: 190 points out, the Pythagoreans seem to have extended the food taboos from preliminary purificatory practices to a lifelong practice.

[146] *Contra* Nilsson 1957: 138: "Something is to be expounded to the mystae about the Titans. This cannot be anything but their crime against the child Dionysos." Nock 1958: 848 supplements ἐχθροτάτην ῥίζαν κυάμων ἐκ σπέ[ρματος] | Τειτάνων and suggests "it almost seems as though the taboo on beans . . . is given a novel rationale — that beans spring from the seed of the race of the Titans." Such speculation based on a supplement is as close as one can come to a connection with the Titanic anthropogony.

[147] Cp. Parker 1983: 362, for the possibility of the cannibalism taboo underlying many ritual food prohibitions. Cp. also Detienne's interpretation of the dismemberment story as a protest against the normal sacrificial procedures of polis religion. Special food taboos seem connected with this sort of protest, but the particular doctrines about the soul and its incarnations may vary.

[148] Bernabé does not list this as an Orphic fragment, but refers to it on pp. 50–51 of his collection of fragments (Bernabé 2004); cp. Jordan 1997b: 395, who suggests that the Titans are thought of as avenging spirits like the Erinyes.

[149] Paus. 8.37.5 (*OF*39, 1113 B = OT 194 K): Τιτᾶνας δὲ πρῶτος ἐς ποίησιν ἐσήγαγεν Ὅμηρος, θεοὺς εἶναι σφᾶς ὑπὸ τῷ καλουμένῳ Ταρτάρῳ· καὶ ἔστιν ἐν Ἥρας ὅρκῳ τὰ ἔπη. παρὰ δὲ Ὁμήρου Ὀνομάκριτος παραλαβὼν τῶν Τιτάνων τὸ ὄνομα Διονύσῳ τε συνέθηκεν ὄργια, καὶ εἶναι τοὺς Τιτᾶνας τῷ Διονύσῳ τῶν παθημάτων ἐποίησεν αὐτουργούς.

Pausanias' claim that Onomakritos was the first to put the Titans into the story of the dismemberment raises an interesting question not often treated in the scholarship, which usually centers on the issue of Pausanias' naming of Onomakritos.[150] Regardless of who or when this innovator was, Pausanias' evidence implies that previous versions of the dismemberment had other figures involved. The Titans, then, are not an integral part of the dismemberment story, merely one element which the mythic *bricoleurs* may choose to include if it suits their purposes. References to the dismemberment of Dionysos, therefore, which do not mention the Titans cannot be presumed to include the Titans, since other villains – perhaps the Giants or the Telchines or even the Kouretes – may have substituted in these other versions.[151] The identity of the villains in the tale would undoubtedly provide a key to understanding the meaning of the story and the ritual to which it was connected. The γηγενεῖς, for example, are often mentioned in references that take the significance of the story to relate to Dionysos as the vine, since the earth-born and the earth-workers (γεωργοί – farmers) are easily linked.[152]

Once the innovation is recognized, we may speculate about the innovator and his reasons for innovation. Bernabé protests that, even if Pausanias means by the name Onomakritos Ps. Orpheus, there is no reason to put the date of this pseudepigrapher any later than the real Onomakritos.[153] However, since a telling of the dismemberment that involves the Titans

---

[150] Linforth 1941: 353, to my mind, has demonstrated conclusively that Onomakritos is Pausanias' way of referring to Orphic pseudepigrapha: "No one else throughout antiquity quotes from works of Onomacritus or makes any allusion to them. It is an extremely probable inference from these considerations that when Pausanias says Onomacritus he means Ps.-Orpheus, that all his quotations from Onomacritus are really quotations from Orphic poems, and that there were actually no poems by Onomacritus and never had been. His words cannot be taken as a statement of fact, but only as an echo of speculations concerning the authorship of Orphic poetry." Cp. Pausanias' attribution of poems to Onomakritos: 1.22.7 (*OF* 1119 B); 8.31.3 (*OF* 351, 1114ii B = OT 193 K); 9.35.5 (*OF* 254ii, 1114iii B). In each case, it seems likely that he is referring to a poem attributed to Orpheus that he believes is not actually by Orpheus. The topics of those poems also match themes attributed elsewhere to Orphic texts: the genealogy of the Graces (9.35.5 [*OF* 254ii, 1114iii B]) is given in *Orphic Hymn* 60, while there is a reference to Herakles and the Dactyls (8.31.3 [*OF* 351, 1114ii B = OT 193 K]) in the list of Orphic themes in the *Orphic Argonautica* (24–25), and Diod. Sic. 5.64.4 (*OF* 519, 940i B = OT 42 K) credits Orpheus with the introduction of the rites of the Idaian Dactyls.

[151] Cp. the curious myth in Apollod. *Bibl.* 2.1.3, in which the Kouretes do away with another child of Zeus, Epaphos, at the urging of jealous Hera.

[152] Cp. Corn. *ND* 30 (58.6 Lang) (*OF* 59iv B) for the etymological pun, as well as Diod. Sic. 3.62.6–7 (*OF* 59iii B = OF 301 K).

[153] Bernabé 2002a: 414: "Il est bien clair qu'on garde le souvenir qu'à une date ancienne (pourquoi nier la date traditionelle du VIe siècle avant J.-C.?) furent fondés certains rites dionysiaques faisant référence aux souffrances de Dionysos infligées par les Titans." Bernabé also makes an unwarranted leap here from the Orphic poem to rituals making use of the same innovation.

does not appear in the extant evidence until the versions of Diodorus Siculus and Clement of Alexandria, there is also no reason to date the Orphic poem much earlier than the second century BCE. In the absence of any other evidence for an Orphic poem that includes the Titans in the dismemberment story, we can only conclude from Pausanias' evidence that some poet in the centuries before Diodorus substituted the Titans for an older set of villains in the story for some purpose that remains unclear.

The earliest poetic references to the dismemberment do not actually resolve the problem, since, although Kallimachos and Euphorion tell of the dismemberment in the third century, the mention of the Titans comes only in the later sources that refer to them. Philodemos lists the three births of Dionysos, first from his mother, then from Zeus' thigh, and finally after his limbs were reassembled by Rhea when he had been dismembered by the Titans. Philodemos claims that Euphorion agrees with this account in his *Mopsiopiai*, and the scholiast on Lycophron cites both Euphorion and Kallimachos for the tale that the limbs of Dionysos were put in Apollo's Delphic tripod after the Titans dismembered him.[154] While the myth of Dionysos' dismemberment is thus finally attested by the third century, we cannot be certain of the details of these tellings. Euphorion or Kallimachos may have cast the Titans as villains or their role may only have become canonical later, causing the later sources to interpret the Gigantes, Korybantes, or other villains as the Titans.

Evidence from the fourth century for rituals that may involve imitation of the dismemberment of Dionysos unfortunately lacks any clear reference either to the Titans or to an Orphic source. Demosthenes describes initiands being covered with mud in a scandalous rite performed by Aiskhines' mother in her private cult practice. Harpocration tells us in his commentary that the Titans coated themselves with gypsum when they slaughtered the infant Dionysos and that those who are mimetically enacting the myth for those about to be initiated do likewise.[155] Even assuming that

---

[154] Phld. *Piet.* 44 (*P. Herc.* 247 III 1ss p. 16 Gomperz) = Euphorion fr. 39 Van Groningen (= 53 De Cuenca) (*OF* 59i B = OF 36 K): <πρώτην τούτ>ων τὴν ἐκ μ<ητρός>, ἑτέραν δὲ τ<ὴν ἐκ> τοῦ μηροῦ, <τρί>την δὲ τὴ<ν ὅτε διασπασθεὶς ὑπὸ τῶν Τιτάνων Ῥέ<ας τὰ> μέλη συνθεί<σης> ἀνεβίω[ι]. κἀν <τῆϊ Μοψοπίαι δ' Εὐ<φορί>ω<ν ὁ>μολογεῖ <τού>τοις, <οἱ> δ' Ὀρ<φικοὶ> καὶ παντά<πασιν> ἐνδιατρε<ίβουσιν>. ΣLycoph. 208 (Tzetzes) = Euphorion fr. 14 Van Groningen (= 13 De Cuenca) = Callim. fr. 643 Pfeiffer (*OF* 36 B = OF 210 K): ἐτιμᾶτο δὲ καὶ Διόνυσος ἐν Δελφοῖς σὺν Ἀπόλλωνι οὑτωσί· οἱ Τιτᾶνες τὰ Διονύσου μέλη σπαράξαντες Ἀπόλλωνι ἀδελφῷ ὄντι αὐτοῦ παρέθοντο ἐμβαλόντες λέβητι, ὁ δὲ παρὰ τῷ τρίποδι ἀπέθετο, ὥς φησι Καλλίμαχος καὶ Εὐφορίων λέγων ἂν πυρὶ Βάκχαν δίαν ὑπερ φιάλην ἐβάλοντο.

[155] Harp. s.v. ἀπομάττων (36 Keaney) (*OF* 308ii, 577vii B = OT 206 K): Ἀπομάττων· Δημοσθένης ἐν τῷ ὑπὲρ Κτησιφῶντος. οἱ μὲν ἁπλοϊκώτερον ἀκούουσιν ἀντὶ τοῦ ἀποψῶν καὶ ἀπολυμαινόμενος, ἄλλοι δὲ περιεργότερον, οἷον περιπλάττων τὸν πηλὸν καὶ τὰ πίτυρα τοῖς τελουμένοις, ὡς λέγομεν

Harpocration is indeed talking about the same practice as Demosthenes, the white gypsum with which the slayers of the god disguise themselves appears as a terrifying disguise in a number of other contexts, so we cannot be certain whether the name Titan was attached to the initiators in the ritual of Aiskhines' mother or merely added by the lexicographer to accord with later practice.[156] The fact that one word for this gypsum powder was τίτανος, however, suggests that it would be easy at any point to call the white-faced murderers Titans, sanctioning the mythological innovation with the etymological wordplay.[157] The ritual mentioned by Demosthenes is generally considered to be for Sabazios, but it is plausible to suggest that the books from which the ritual came (read out by the young Aiskhines) might have been considered Orphica.[158] However, even if we accept all these hypotheses, that Aiskhines' mother performed rituals from Orphic books that involved the Titans as murderers of Dionysos, we still have no evidence to indicate what the ritual was for. As is usually the case with the evidence for ancient Greek ritual practice, we get a few tantalizing details of what was done but almost nothing about why or what the practitioners thought they got out of the ritual.

Diodorus Siculus does provide evidence for the existence of an Orphic poem that narrated the dismemberment as well as rituals that somehow corresponded.[159] In his testimonies, Diodorus actually gives several different variations of the story in different places. Not only does Diodorus recount the other stories of Dionysos' birth and life, including a number of euhemerizing interpretations, but he also provides two different

ἀπομάττεσθαι τὸν ἀνδριάντα πηλῷ· ἤλειφον γὰρ τῷ πηλῷ καὶ τῷ πιτύρῳ τοὺς μυουμένους, ἐκμιμούμενοι τὰ μυθολογούμενα παρ᾽ ἐνίοις, ὡς ἄρα οἱ Τιτᾶνες τὸν Διόνυσον ἐλυμήναντο γύψῳ καταπλασάμενοι ἐπὶ τῷ μὴ γνώριμοι γενέσθαι. τοῦτο μὲν οὖν τὸ ἔθος ἐκλιπεῖν, πηλῷ δὲ ὕστερον καταπλάττεσθαι νομίμου χάριν. Cp. Eust. *Il.* 2.735 (I.519.6 van der Valk) (*OF* 320xii B) on *titanos* as the dust of gypsum: οἱ δὲ παλαιοί φασι τίτανος κόνις γύψος.

156 Euphorion fr. 92 Van Groningen (= 26 De Cuenca) (*OF* 35 B) refers to whitened faces in a Dionysiac context. Cp. Nonnos, *Dion.* 17.228, 27.204, 29.274, 34.144, 48.732. The motif is not purely found in Dionysiac contexts, as the Phokians' gypsum powder disguise shows in Hdt. 8.27 and Paus. 10.1.11. Cp. Polyaenus, 6.18.1.

157 *Contra* West 1983: 155, who does not believe that "the similarity of τίτανος and Τιτάν played any part in the formation of the story."

158 Cp. West 1983: 26–27. The attribution of the rites to the Phrygian Sabazios and Mother of the Gods is based on the claim of Strabo 10.3.18 (*OF* 577v B) (cp. Lobeck 1829: 647), rather than anything in the text itself, and several recent scholars have raised doubts; cp. Parker 1996: 159.

159 Diod. Sic. 5.75.4 (*OF* 283i, 311xii, 530 B = OF 303 K) and 3.62.2–8 (*OF* 58, 59iii, 327v, 399iii B = OF 301 K). ΣLucian *Deor. Conc.* 52.9 (212.25 Rabe) (*OF* 283iii B), which Bernabé 2002a: 414 cites in support of a dismemberment by the Titans, does not mention either the Titans or the dismemberment, merely providing evidence for rituals in honor of Dionysos, son of Persephone. Again, the existence of such rituals is not in question; it is their significance, about which the testimony provides no information, that is in question.

sets of parents for the dismembered Dionysos and two different sets of dismemberers.[160] He tells of a child of Zeus and Demeter, who was dismembered by the γηγενεῖς, but also of a Cretan-born Dionysos, son of Zeus and Persephone, who was dismembered by the Titans. In both cases, he comments that the story is in accord with Orphic poems and rituals, and he explicitly refers back from the latter passage to the earlier one, in which he gives an explanation of the dismemberment in terms of the vine. Bernabé is certainly right to suppose that Diodorus is drawing here, not on a single Orphic poem but on a variety of Orphica.[161] A variety of myths and rituals that made use of the dismemberment story may have been attributed to Orpheus – some of which included the Titans; some of which did not. Nothing in Diodorus, however, suggests that the murderers of Dionysos were the ancestors of mankind or that the point of the ritual was purification from this particular crime.[162]

Hypothetically, Diodorus may be discussing the same myths and rituals attributed to Orpheus to which Pausanias alludes, and these rituals might even be the same as Clement denounces in what is perhaps the most detailed account of a ritual that makes use of the myth of the dismemberment. Clement even cites verses from Orpheus describing the Titans' distraction of the infant god with toys, which serve as the *symbola* for initiates who have undergone the ritual.

[160] Cp. Cicero's catalog of different Dionysoi in *Nat. D.* 3.58 (*OF* 497i B = OT 94 K) (note the other testimonia from later authors probably indebted to Cicero in *OF* 497 B). The fourth Dionysos is the child of Jove and Luna (probably arising from a confusion of Semele and Selene), and it is in his honor that Orphic rites are celebrated, not the son of Jove and Proserpine, who is first on the list. Cp. Diod. Sic. 1.23.2 (*OF* 48iii, 327iv, 497iv B = OT 95 K) for another testimony that the Orphic rites were celebrated in honor of the son of Semele rather than the son of Persephone.

[161] Bernabé 2002b: 70, 89. Bernabé, however, tries to reduce all these versions to two variant storylines, both of which contributed elements to the *Orphic Rhapsodies*. The "primary version" has Dionysos born of Persephone, torn apart by the Titans, and then reborn from Semele, while the "secondary version," which he associates with Egypt and Osiris, has Dionysos born of Demeter/Rhea and reborn from the reassembled pieces collected by her after his dismemberment. See Bernabé 1998b for the most complete exposition of the hypothesis. Apart from the methodological problems of reducing mythic variants to simple stemmata, Bernabé's hypothesis founders on the fact that the sequence of mothers from Persephone to Semele does not hold in all the evidence. Nonnos may have a coherent story in which Zagreus, son of Persephone, is dismembered and reborn as Dionysos, son of Semele, but some of the versions have the dismemberment occur after the birth from Semele, including one of the earliest in date, Philodemos' reference to Euphorion, Phld. *Piet.* 44 (*P. Herc.* 247 III 1 p. 16 Gomperz) = Euphorion fr. 39 Van Groningen (= 53 De Cuenca) (*OF* 59i B = OF 36 K), which lists the three births of Dionysos as first from his mother, second from the thigh, and third after his dismemberment. In his list, Diod. Sic. 3.62.6 (*OF* 59iii B = OF 301 K) also makes the birth after the dismemberment the third, not the second.

[162] τελεταί in general may have had purification as one of their elements (as Jiménez 2001 argues), but we must be careful to draw the distinction between preliminary purification rituals intended to prepare the celebrants for a sacred festival and purifications intended to remove the miasma of past crimes as the central focus of the τελετή as in Pl. *Phdr.* 244de (*OF* 575 B = OF 3 K).

The mysteries of Dionysos are perfectly inhuman. While he was still a child, the Kouretes danced around with clashing arms, and the Titans crept up by stealth and deceived him with childish toys. Then these Titans dismembered Dionysos while he was still an infant, as the poet of this mystery, the Thracian Orpheus, says:

"Top, and spinner, and limb-moving toys,
And beautiful golden apples from the clear-voiced Hesperides."

And it is not useless to put forth to you the useless symbols of this rite for condemnation. These are knucklebone, ball, hoop, apples, spinner, looking-glass, tuft of wool.

So, Athena, who abstracted the heart of Dionysus, was thus called Pallas, from the palpitating of the heart. The Titans, on the other hand, who tore him limb from limb, set a cauldron on a tripod and threw into it the limbs of Dionysus. First they boiled them down and, then fixing them on spits, "held them over Hephaistos (the fire)." But later Zeus appeared; since he was a god, he speedily perceived the savor of the cooking flesh, which your gods agree to have assigned to them as their portion of honor. He assails the Titans with his thunderbolt and consigns the limbs of Dionysos to his son Apollo for burial. And Apollo, for he did not disobey Zeus, bearing the dismembered corpse to Parnassus, deposited it there.[163]

This description is part of Clement's diatribe against the religious rituals of the Greeks, which he claims are all celebrations of murders and perversions. Cannibalism of an infant is even better for Clement's purposes than Zeus' incestuous rapes of Demeter and Persephone, and he makes sure to make a dig at the Greek gods' gluttonous appetites for sacrificial meats. Clement's references to mystery rites and to the symbols of the initiates do indicate that he connected the Orphic poem about the dismemberment to certain Dionysiac rituals, but, while Clement provides details that appear less clearly elsewhere (such as the toys of Dionysos or the peculiar cooking

---

[163] Clem. Alex. *Protr.* 2.17.2–18.2 (*OF* 306i, 588i, 312i, 315i, 318i, 322i B = OF 34 K): Τὰ γὰρ Διονύσου μυστήρια τέλεον ἀπάνθρωπα· ὃν εἰσέτι παῖδα ὄντα ἐνόπλῳ κινήσει περιχορευόντων Κουρήτων, δόλῳ δὲ ὑποδύντων Τιτάνων, ἀπατήσαντες παιδαριώδεσιν ἀθύρμασιν, οὗτοι δὴ οἱ Τιτᾶνες διέσπασαν, ἔτι νηπίαχον ὄντα, ὡς ὁ τῆς Τελετῆς ποιητὴς Ὀρφεύς φησιν ὁ Θρᾴκιος· "κῶνος καὶ ῥόμβος καὶ παίγνια καμπεσίγυια, | μῆλά τε χρύσεα καλὰ παρ' Ἑσπερίδων λιγυφώνων." Καὶ τῆσδε ὑμῖν τῆς τελετῆς τὰ ἀχρεῖα σύμβολα οὐκ ἀχρεῖον εἰς κατάγνωσιν παραθέσθαι· ἀστράγαλος, σφαῖρα, στρόβιλος, μῆλα, ῥόμβος, ἔσοπτρον, πόκος. Ἀθηνᾶ μὲν οὖν τὴν καρδίαν τοῦ Διονύσου ὑφελομένη Παλλὰς ἐκ τοῦ πάλλειν τὴν καρδίαν προσηγορεύθη· οἱ δὲ Τιτᾶνες, οἱ καὶ διασπάσαντες αὐτόν, λέβητά τινα τρίποδι ἐπιθέντες καὶ τοῦ Διονύσου ἐμβαλόντες τὰ μέλη, καθήψουν πρότερον· ἔπειτα ὀβελίσκοις περιπείραντες "ὑπείρεχον Ἡφαίστοιο." Ζεὺς δὲ ὕστερον ἐπιφανείς (εἰ θεὸς ἦν, τάχα που τῆς κνίσης τῶν ὀπτωμένων κρεῶν μεταλαβών, ἧς δὴ τὸ "γέρας λαχεῖν" ὁμολογοῦσιν ὑμῶν οἱ θεοί) κεραυνῷ τοὺς Τιτᾶνας αἰκίζεται καὶ τὰ μέλη τοῦ Διονύσου Ἀπόλλωνι τῷ παιδὶ παρακατατίθεται καταθάψαι. Ὁ δέ, οὐ γὰρ ἠπείθησε Διί, εἰς τὸν Παρνασσὸν φέρων κατατίθεται διεσπασμένον τὸν νεκρόν.

procedures), he has no interest in relaying an exegesis of the ritual, in explaining what the participants thought they were doing and why.[164] Although Clement does confirm the existence of some associated ritual, he in fact provides almost no information about the ritual itself. As he does for the Eleusinian Mysteries, he quotes Orpheus to get the scandalous details of the myth, but he does not even provide the few details about what happens in the ritual that he does for the Mysteries at Eleusis.[165]

Firmicus Maternus does provide more details, real or imagined, about rites associated with the dismemberment of Dionysos as part of his own polemic against pagan rituals. Like Clement, he too denigrates the Dionysiac mysteries as perverse celebrations of murders, but he offers a full, euhemerized version of the myth, making Dionysus the son of a king of Crete murdered by jealous courtiers. The ritual, he claims, was instituted to placate the anger of the king over the murder of his son, who could not even receive a burial because he had been dismembered and eaten.

> To mitigate the savagery of the tyrant's fury, the Cretans established the day of the death as a religious festival, and put together an annual rite with a trieteric consecration, performing in order all that the dying child both did and suffered. They tore a live bull with their teeth, evoking the cruel feast in their annual commemorations, and by howling dissonant cries through the depths of the woods they imitated the madness of a raving spirit, so that it would be believed that the crime was done not by treachery but though madness. Before them was carried the chest in which the sister secretly stole away the heart, and with the song of flutes and the clashing of cymbals they mimicked the rattles by which the boy was deceived. Thus in the honoring of a tyrant by a subservient mob a god has been made out of one who was not able to find burial.[166]

---

[164] It is hard to believe that he would have missed the opportunity to heap scorn on the worship of dead, criminal ancestors if the myth as he knew it had included an anthropogony from the Titans, but an argument from silence can never prove conclusively that Clement did not simply omit an anthropogony that was in his source. Of course, Clement's evidence can hardly be used to prove that such an anthropogony was in his source, either, since his description of the dismemberment ends with the burial of Dionysos at Delphi.

[165] Jourdan 2006: 278 (cp. Jourdan 2005) points out that, in Clement's version, the Titans may not have actually consumed the parts of Dionysos they cooked, since Zeus can order Apollo to bury the remains. A story in which the Titans did not consume Dionysos could not, of course, end with the anthropogony as found in Olympidorus, since there would be no Dionysiac divine element in the composition of humans. Such a consideration makes it all the more unlikely that any of the versions which include Apollo or Demeter/Rhea gathering the pieces for burial could ever have included an anthropogony.

[166] Firm. Mat. Err. prof. rel. 6.5 (89 Turcan) (OF 572 B): *Cretenses ut furentis tyranni saevitiam mitigarent, festos funeris dies statuunt, et annuum sacrum trieterica consecratione conponunt, omnia per ordinem facientes quae puer moriens aut fecit aut passus est. vivum laniant dentibus taurum, crudeles epulas annuis commemorationibus excitantes, et per secreta silvarum clamoribus dissonis*

Firmicus associates the dismemberment story with the trieteric festivals of Dionysos and describes the *sparagmos* of a bull as part of a commemoration of the dismembered infant.[167] He also includes the *cista mystica*, which makes an appearance in various mystery rites from the Eleusinia to Isis, and the manic cries, flutes, and cymbals which are characteristic of Dionysiac and Metroac festivities. Firmicus, like Clement, denies that there is any point to the rituals except to honor dead royalty as gods; his polemic refuses the existence of any theological underpinning to pagan ritual.

In the absence of any evidence from the texts themselves, Bernabé deduces the meaning of all these rituals from the evidence of the Gurôb papyrus (*OF* 578 B = OF 31 K). This fragmentary papyrus from the third century BCE seems to contain some sort of ritual instructions for a Dionysiac ritual, and there are a number of remarkable parallels with Clement's description of the mysteries of Dionysos, the most striking of which is the presence of the toys of Dionysos, the knucklebones, tops, and mirror that Dionysos' murderers used to distract him before the murder (*P. Gurôb* 1 [*OF* 578 B = OF 31 K] col. 1.29–30). Whatever ritual was associated with this text, therefore, certainly evoked the dismemberment of Dionysos in some form, but the text of the papyrus is too fragmentary to show what this ritual might have been or even if the dismemberment was central to the ceremony or merely an element of Dionysiac myth recalled in passing. The presence of the Kouretes earlier in the text (col. 1.7–8) suggests that the whole scenario of the dismemberment was evoked, and Brimo, Demeter, and Rhea can also be fit into the narrative as it is found in other sources.

This text, unlike the other evidence, is not merely alluding to or describing a ritual, but seems actually to include instructions for things to be spoken and done in a ritual. However, despite Bernabé's claim that the meaning is evident, even this text does not provide sufficient information to determine the purpose of the ritual, much less its theological underpinnings. Bernabé claims not only that the fact that the dismemberment is enacted implies that the point of the ritual is the salvation of human beings

---

eiulantes fingunt animi furentis insaniam, ut illud facinus non per fraudem factum, sed per insaniam crederetur. praefertur cista in qua cor soror latenter absconderat, tibiarum cantu et cymbalorum tinnitu crepundia, quibus puer deceptus fuerat mentiuntur. sic in honorem tyranni a serviente plebe deus factus est qui habere non potuit sepulturam.

[167] As an expression of skepticism about the reality of such a ritual, one cannot do better than the (probably apocryphal but nevertheless wonderful) story that the logician Bertrand Russell offered to buy a bull for Jane Harrison on the condition that she and her female students tear it apart with their teeth.

from their Titanic original sin, but that the text explicitly asks Brimo for salvation from the crimes of these lawless ancestors.[168]

There is indeed a plea to Brimo in the text (col. 1.5: σῶισόν με Βριμὼ με[γάλη), but the "explicit" mention of lawless ancestors is only explicit in a restoration to the text. Bernabé, following West, has restored col. 1.4 as δῶρον δέξ]ατ᾽ ἐμὸν ποινὰς πατ[έρων ἀθεμίστων, from the papyrus reading... ετεμον ποινας πατ...[169] West's restoration is plausible, if one accepts the premise that a ritual involving the dismemberment of Dionysos must have to do with salvation from humanity's Titanic heritage, but it cannot be used as an argument for that same premise without circularity.

Even if we accept the circular argument and use the words from the Orphic fragment quoted by Damascius, it is not clear, either in Damascius or in the Gurôb papyrus, whether these fathers for whose crimes a recompense is offered are Titanic ancestors or merely human ones.[170] The text might, with West's restoration, include both the elements of the dismemberment story and the idea of inherited guilt, but, even so, the Titans are never explicitly mentioned and there is no trace of any anthropogonic element. The Gurôb papyrus certainly does provide evidence for a Dionysiac ritual in the third century BCE that makes reference to the dismemberment, as well as for the syncretism of different types of Dionysiac cults current in Egypt in the period.[171] However, the plea to Brimo for salvation and even the reference to some sort of recompense (ποινὰς) do not provide evidence for the meaning of the ritual, since such pleas and debts are a standard part of the relations between deities and worshipers in Greek religion, particularly in private cults.

---

[168] Bernabé 2002a: 416: "L'implication des êtres humains dans ce drame sacré est évidente, non seulement parce qu'il est représenté dans la telete, mais encore parce que le texte dit explicitement que ce dont il s'agit, c'est d'expier le crime des ancêtres et de demander à Brimô le salut."

[169] Bernabé notes the earlier conjectures of Smyly and Tierney in his apparatus to *OF* 578 B in Bernabé 2004, but Hordern 2000 also accepts the restoration. Cp. West 1983: 171.

[170] Dam. *In Phd.* 1.11 (35 Westerink) (*OF* 350 B = OF 232 K): "Ὅτι ὁ Διόνυσος λύσεώς ἐστιν αἴτιος· διὸ καὶ Λυσεὺς ὁ θεός, καὶ ὁ Ὀρφεύς φησιν "ἄνθρωποι δὲ τελήεσσας ἑκατόμβας | πέμψουσιν πάσησιν ἐν ὥραις ἀμφιέτησιν | ὄργιά τ᾽ ἐκτελέσουσι λύσιν προγόνων ἀθεμίστων | μαιόμενοι· σὺ δὲ τοῖσιν ἔχων κράτος, οὕς κε θέλησθα | λύσεις ἔκ τε πόνων χαλεπῶν καὶ ἀπείρονος οἴστρου." Note that Iambl. *Myst.* 3.10.14–16 attributes to Sabazios the power to free people through Bacchic ritual from the burdens of ancient divine angers: τοῦ Σαβαζίου δ᾽ εἰς βακχείας καὶ ἀποκαθάρσεις ψυχῶν καὶ οἰκειότητα παρασκεύασται λύσεις παλαιῶν μηνιμάτων. The plural angers of the gods once again indicates that a single Titanic crime is not imagined, but rather the variety of crimes that could accumulate over generations.

[171] The papyrus may indeed be an example of the *hieroi logoi* mandated by the edict of Ptolemy Philopator, although note Hordern's comments on the informal, even sloppy nature of the writing: "That the papyrus contains such a hieros logos is certainly likely, but that we may have here to do with a text belonging to a lower social and literary level is suggested by the somewhat messy script, occasional errors and perhaps by the irregular line-lengths" (Hordern 2000: 132).

Of course, the gold tablets from Pelinna do provide evidence for Dionysos as the one who, in conjunction with Persephone, frees human beings from the burden of previously committed crimes. "Tell Persephone that Bacchios himself set you free."[172] Other tablets from Thurii and Pherai attest that the bearer could approach Persephone with the claim to have paid any necessary penalties.[173] The gold tablets, however, have no mention of the Titans or the dismemberment, and the dismemberment story is hardly the only context in which Dionysos can function as the liberator.[174] Again, the evidence fails to bring together the pieces – the dismemberment of Dionysos, the punishment of the Titans, the generation of the human race, the inheritance of guilt. One or two of these pieces show up in each of these texts, but that in itself is no proof that all four elements are secretly part of each of the texts, and that the other elements must be supplied in order to interpret the texts.

The evidence examined here, therefore, while it attests to the existence of rituals attributed to Orpheus or connected with Orphic poems that somehow involve the story of the dismemberment of Dionysos, does not ever provide insight into the meaning of the rituals in the religious contexts in which they were performed. The evidence does show that a version of the dismemberment that involved the Titans existed before the second century BCE, but it also attests to a variety of stories and rituals that have to do with the dismemberment of Dionysos, which seem to have been performed for a variety of reasons. Just as the myth of the dismemberment was understood in many ways, as a tale about the natural processes of the vine, or about the formation of differentiated life in the cosmos, or even about the development of the moral and ethical individual, so too the rituals that made use of this traditional element of the dismemberment of Dionysos were understood in a variety of ways, as festivals celebrating the production of wine or as rites marking the renewal of the cosmos or even as mysteries that brought the celebrants into a new personal relation with the gods. While some rites might have served to purify the participants from divine anger stemming from a previous crime, none of the evidence that mentions the dismemberment actually provides any indication of such a function. Although such a function remains possible for some of the rites

---

[172] Tablet D1 (*OF* 485 B) ln. 2: εἰπεῖν Φερσεφόναι σ' ὅτι Β<άκ>χιος αὐτός ἔλυσε.

[173] Tablet from Pherai D3 (*OF* 493 B) ln. 2: πο<ινὰν δ' ἀνταπέ[ι]τε[σε]ι<σ>' ἔργων ἕνεκα οὔτι δικα<ί>ων. = Tablets A2 (*OF* 489 B = OF 32d K) and A3 (*OF* 490 B = OF 32e K) ln. 4; cp. ἄποινος γὰρ ὁ μύστης.

[174] The claim to be of the race of the gods (or in the B tablets to be the child of Earth and starry Heaven) is not a claim to be a Titan; cp. Edmonds 2004a: 75–79. For Dionysos Lyseus, cp. Edmonds 2004a: 60–61, 73.

mentioned, other evidence seems to indicate the connection of the ritual with Dionysos' aspect as a god of wine and growing things, as Dionysos Lenaios rather than Dionysos Lyseus. To restrict the evidence to a single ritual function, a single interpretation of a single myth, is to unduly limit the use of material that could be used to illuminate a variety of aspects of Dionysiac religion over the centuries of time and the wide variety of places from which it comes. A broader investigation of this material in the context, not just of Orphic texts that mention the Titans, but of the evidence for rituals involving the Kouretes and Korybantes or even the Kabeiroi and Telchines, might yield connections hitherto unsuspected and help clarify the mysteries that still surround these mystery rites.

The blood of the earthborn

Another passage used as a strand in the fabrication of an Orphic myth of original sin derived from a Titanic heritage is Orpheus' list of previous themes at the beginning of the *Orphic Argonautica*. To authenticate the pseudepigraphic *Argonautica* as a poem of Orpheus himself, the text starts with Orpheus referring to what must have been well-known previous works of his, including accounts of the creation from the primal gods like Night and Phanes, the grief (πένθος) of Persephone at her rape and the wandering search of her mother Demeter, the tale of Aphrodite and Adonis, accounts of Korybantes and Kabeiroi, and even the laments for Egyptian Osiris. In the midst of this collection is the passage in question, a reference to the Earthborn giants and the creation of mortals.

> And the offspring of powerful Brimo, and the destructive deeds
> of the Earthborn, who dripped painfully as gore from Heaven,
> the seed of a generation of old, out of which arose
> the race of mortals, who exist forever throughout the boundless earth.[175]

Bernabé takes this passage as a reference to the creation of the human race from the Titans after their dismemberment of Dionysos and concludes that the *Orphic Argonautica* must be reproducing the sequence of stories in the *Orphic Rhapsodies*, which therefore must have included the combination of a Titanic anthropogony with the dismemberment of Dionysos. The Earthborn in this passage must be Titans, he claims, because the

---

[175] *OA* 17–20 (*OF* 320v B): Βριμοῦς τ᾽ εὐδυνάτοιο γονάς, ἠδ᾽ ἔργ᾽ ἀΐδηλα | Γιγάντων, οἳ λυγρὸν ἀπ᾽ Οὐρανοῦ ἐστάξαντο, | σπέρμα γονῆς τὸ πρόσθεν, ὅθεν γένος ἐξεγένοντο | θνητῶν, οἳ κατὰ γαῖαν ἀπείριτον αἰὲν ἔασι· This text follows Vian 1987. Dottin 1930, whose text appears in the *TLG*, reads Γηγενέων for Γιγάντων, and both forms appear in the manuscripts.

birth of the Giants cannot come between the birth of Dionysos (child of Brimo/Persephone) and the creation of human beings.[176] Moreover, if there is a succession of races, one race cannot be born directly from another; each race must be created separately, as in the Hesiodic myth.[177]

When read in the context of the wider Greek tradition of anthropogonic myths, however, both the generation of the Giants from the blood of Ouranos and the succession of the current human race from an earlier generation of earthborn giants appear as perfectly familiar elements in the mythic tradition that do not need to be explained by reference to a secret Orphic anthropogony. While the Hesiodic myth of the metal ages (gold, silver, bronze, and iron) remains an influential model for the generation of humans throughout the Greek mythic tradition, even in Hesiod there are traces of another model that was perhaps even more widespread, the generation of the current race of humans from a previous generation of people born directly from the earth. More importantly, the sequence of the dismemberment of Dionysos, the punishment of the Titans, the creation of mankind, and the payment of the penalty for the murder does not actually appear, either in the passage from the *Orphic Argonautica* or in any of the other evidence Bernabé cites to support his claims. On the contrary, in this evidence, the creation of the human race follows upon the battle of the Earthborn against the gods. These threads, which Bernabé uses to try to weave together an Orphic myth of Titanic original sin, belong instead to the mythic traditions about autochthony and the first generations of humans.

The evidence for anthropogonic myth that survives from the *Orphic Rhapsodies* shows that both the artifice model of the myth of the metal races and the fertility model of the earthborn appeared in Orphic poems, but the sequence of the narrative culminating in the creation of the current human race is not as clear as Bernabé claims.[178] Proclus, in his commentary on

---

[176] However, Vian 1987: 8 notes that the events in 17–31 do not follow one another in chronological sequence, so Bernabé's objection to the ordering with 17–20 seems to depend on the assumption of a chronological arrangement that does not in fact exist in the poem.

[177] Bernabé 2003: 32: "Il ne semble pas logique que, dans les mythes sur les âges, il soit dit qu'une race provienne de la précédente. Même si on y parlait de la race de ceux qui sont nés des Géants, ceux-ci ne seraient pas pour cela les ancêtres de la race suivante. Dans le mythe hésiodique il est parfaitement clair que chaque race commence et se termine sans avoir nullement donné naissance à celle qui vient après."

[178] Loraux 2000: 2 distinguishes between the model of artifice and the model of fertility for the generation of mankind (and woman). The presence of both models, however, does not necessitate that there was a single consistent version in the *Rhapsodies* that blended the two together. While it might be possible to harmonize the various accounts, it remains likely that different accounts were told in different parts of the collection of Orphic texts known as the *Rhapsodies*. Cp. West

Plato's *Republic*, provides evidence that the Hesiodic myth of the metals that Plato plays with in his dialogue (546e) was also associated with the creation of men in an Orphic poem.[179] The gold race from Hesiod is associated with Phanes, while the silver race is ruled over by Kronos. The third race, whom Proclus connects with the craftsmen (*demiourgoi*) in the city of the *Republic*, is created by Zeus from the limbs of the Titans.[180] Each race is connected with a type of person: the gold are intellective and divine, the silver self-reflective (since Kronos' "crooked cunning" curves back on itself), and the Titanic concerned with inferior and irrational beings. Although Proclus only summarizes the Orphic reference, these races, like those in Hesiod, seem to live in separate ages of the world, created and ruled over by different gods, rather than succeeding one another. However, the last race in Proclus' list, the race generated from the Titans, seems to follow the pattern, not of the Hesiodic metal races fabricated by a creator god, but of the Earthborn races, springing up out of the earth from the remains of the previous generation. Orphic references to the generation of humans from the remains of the Titans or the Giants must therefore be understood in the context of this pattern of anthropogonic myth, a strand in the mythic tradition that survives mostly in antiquarian allusions and passing references to local tales.

As Loraux points out in her study of Greek anthropogonic traditions, the mythic tradition has a large number of different stories about the first humans, mostly local stories which attribute the origin of mankind to their own area. "It is not that each city yearns to narrate the birth of the first man in its own way, but that any national tradition is less interested in giving a version of the beginnings of humanity than in postulating the nobility of the stock from which it originated."[181] There are two basic ways in

---

1983: 98, 107, who imagines an adaptation of Hesiod's metal race in the earliest Orphic theogony that is later adapted to the Titanic tale by the compiler of the *Rhapsodies*.

[179] Procl. *In R.* 2.74.26 Kroll (*OF* 159, 216i, 320ii B = OF 140 K): ὁ μὲν θεολόγος Ὀρφεὺς τρία γένη παραδέδωκεν ἀνθρώπων· πρώτιστον τὸ χρυσοῦν, ὅπερ ὑποστῆσαι τὸν Φάνητά φησιν· δεύτερον τὸ ἀργυροῦν, οὗ φησιν ἄρξαι τὸν μέγιστον Κρόνον· τρίτον τὸ Τιτανικόν, ὃ φησιν ἐκ τῶν Τιτανικῶν μελῶν τὸν Δία συστήσασθαι. Cp. Procl. *In Hes. Op.* 127–129 (5.15 Pertusi) (*OF* 216ii B = OF 141 K).

[180] It is interesting to note that Proclus merely connects the Titans with demiourgic activity, rather than with vice and passion, especially since Proclus does explicitly connect the races of heroes and of iron in the Hesiod version with the irrational passionate and appetitive parts of the soul that lead humans to vice. If, as Bernabé and others have suggested, the Titanic nature from the Zagreus anthropogony is associated with such irrational passions and vices, it is quite strange that Proclus would not mention such a Titanic nature in this context. If, however, the Titans were associated with demiourgic activity in the differentiation of the cosmic elements rather than with inherited vice (as in Plut. *De E ap. Delph.* 9.388e [*OF* 613ii B] above, see further on Damascius below), Proclus' arguments about the Orphic and Hesiodic versions make sense.

[181] Loraux 2000: 9.

which these local traditions claim prestige for their origins: either their first ancestors are descended from gods or from the earth itself. In the former case, the first generation of mortals comes from the union of some god with a local minor divinity, such as a nymph. More often, however, the first generation of mortals springs directly from the earth. The Athenian myths of autochthony are perhaps the best known, the generation of Erichthonius (or Erechtheus) from the Earth after Hephaistos' attempted rape of Athena, as well as tales of the autochthons Cecrops, Amphictyon, and Cranaus.[182] Nevertheless, Erichthonius was hardly the only first man in the Greek mythic tradition. Hippolytos preserves a prose version of what might have been verses of Pindar that catalog the first humans of many different myths.

> "It is difficult," he says, "to discover whether for the Boeotians Alalkomeneus rose up over Lake Kephisos as the first of men; or whether the first were the Idaian Kouretes, a divine race; or the Phrygian Korybantes, whom first the sun looked upon as they sprung up, growing as trees do; or whether Arcadia brought forth Pelasgos, more ancient than the moon; or Eleusis produced Dysaules, dweller in Raria; or Lemnos of fair children begot Kabiros in unspeakable rites; or Pallene produced the Phlegraean Alkyoneus, oldest of the Giants. But the Libyans affirm that Iarbas, firstborn, on emerging from arid plains, commenced eating the sweet acorn of Jupiter."[183]

A full explication of this text is beyond the scope of this study, but it is worth noting that some of the candidates for the original humans are individuals (often descended from a god and a nymph), while others are a γένος, a whole group like the Kouretes and Korybantes. At times the first man is representative of a group that appears in other evidence, such as Kabiros for the Kabeiroi. These primordial people all seem to arise from the earth, their native soil; they are all γηγενεῖς, Earthborn, even if only some of them receive the label Gigantes.[184]

---

[182] Cp. the studies of Peradotto 1977 and Parker 1986. Luginbühl 1992 and Loraux 2000 examine not only the Athenian authochthony stories, but also the evidence for other areas.

[183] Hippol. *Haer.* 5.4.4 ≈ fr. 67b *Lyrica Adespota PMG*: χαλεπὸν δέ, φησίν, ἐξευρεῖν εἴτε Βοιωτοῖς Ἀλαλκομενεὺς ὑπὲρ λίμνης Κηφισίδος ἀνέσχε πρῶτος ἀνθρώπων· εἴτε Κουρῆτες ἦσαν Ἰδαῖοι, θεῖον γένος, ἢ Φρύγιο(ι) Κορύβαντες, οὓς πρώτους ἥλιος ἐπεῖδε δενδροφυεῖς ἀναβλαστάνοντας· εἴτε προσεληναῖον Ἀρκαδία Πελασγόν, ἢ Ῥαρίας οἰκήτορα Δυσαύλην Ἐλευσίν, ἢ Λῆμνος καλλίπαιδα Κάβιρον ἀρρήτῳ ἐτέκνωσεν ὀργιασμῷ· εἴτε Πελλήνη Φλεγραῖον Ἀλκυονέα, πρεσβύτατον Γιγάντων. Λίβυες δὲ Ἰάρβαντά φασι πρωτόγονον αὐχμηρῶν ἀναδύντα πεδίων γλυκείας ἀπάρξασθαι Διὸς βαλάνου.

[184] Dysaules, for example, is listed as one of the γηγενεῖς, the primordial inhabitants of Eleusis, who help Demeter in her search for Persephone (Clem. Al. *Protr.* 2.20.1–21.1 = Euseb. *Prep. evang.* 2.3.30–35 [*OF* 392iii, 391ii, 394i, 395i, 515i B = OF 52 K]); cp. Arn. *Adv. nat.* 5.25–27 (280.8 Marchesi) (*OF* 391iii B = OF 52 K). Cp. Luginbühl 1992: 136–143.

Strabo, trying to provide an overview of the stories about the Kouretes, sums up his rather bewildering review of varying stories and allusions by noting that many people identify the Kouretes with other similar groups. "So great is the complexity in these accounts that, while some represent the Korybantes and Kabeiroi and Idaian Dactyls and Telchines as the same as the Kouretes, others make them kin with one another and distinguish certain small differences from one another."[185] The Kouretes are linked to other groups of primitive, semi-mortals as well; Strabo quotes a fragment of Hesiod that makes the Kouretes kin to the Satyrs, and he describes the Kouretes as Satyrs in the service of Zeus.[186]

One group of primordial peoples often conflated, not only with the Gigantes, but with the Kouretes, Korybantes, Dactyls, and even the Satyrs, are the Titans. As Vian has shown, the myths of the Gigantomachy and the Titanomachy were intertwined at an early stage.[187] Perhaps the most surprising identification in the collection of primordial peoples is the connection made between the Satyrs and the Titans as bands of primitive, hubristic, ithyphallic males.[188] Lucian describes the Bacchic dances of Ionia as Satyric in nature, in which audiences spend the whole day watching Satyrs and Titans and Korybantes, as if they were all variations upon similar themes.[189] Even some of the names of individual Titans known from the genealogies of Hesiod show up as the names of Kabeiroi or Dactyls

---

[185] Strabo 10.3.7: τοσαύτη δ᾽ ἐστὶν ἐν τοῖς λόγοις τούτοις ποικιλία, τῶν μὲν τοὺς αὐτοὺς τοῖς Κουρῆσι τοὺς Κορύβαντας καὶ Καβείρους καὶ Ἰδαίους Δακτύλους καὶ Τελχῖνας ἀποφαινόντων, τῶν δὲ συγγενεῖς ἀλλήλων καὶ μικράς τινας αὐτῶν πρὸς ἀλλήλους διαφορὰς διαστελλομένων. Cp. Blakely 2006: 13–21 for a survey of the evidence regarding the Korybantes, Kouretes, Kabeiroi, Idaian Dactyls, and Telchines.

[186] Hes. fr. 10a.17–19 Merklbach-West = Strabo 10.3.19: ἐξ ὧν οὔρειαι Νύμφαι θεαὶ ἐξεγένοντο, καὶ γένος οὐτιδανῶν Σατύρων καὶ ἀμηχανοεργῶν, Κουρῆτές τε θεοὶ φιλοπαίγμονες ὀρχηστῆρες. Kouretes as satyrs in the service of Zeus: Strabo 10.3.11 (*OF* 570 B): ὥσθ᾽ οἱ Κουρῆτες ἤτοι διὰ τὸ νέοι καὶ κόροι ὄντες ὑπουργεῖν ἢ διὰ τὸ κουροτροφεῖν τὸν Δία (λέγεται γὰρ ἀμφοτέρως) ταύτης ἠξιώθησαν τῆς προσηγορίας, οἱονεὶ Σάτυροί τινες ὄντες περὶ τὸν Δία.

[187] Vian 1952: 169ff. Although Vian argues that the Gigantomachy and Titanomachy were originally separate stories, he shows that authors interchanged them from at least the Classical period onward. As with so many scholars interested in the origin of the stories, he deplores the imprecision of the ancient authors of myths who mix them up, rather than celebrating their creative ingenuity. In discussing the presence of elements of both Gigantomachy and Titanomachy in Aristophanes' *Birds*, he laments: "Malheureusement, Aristophane ne s'embarrasse pas de précisions mythologiques" (Vian 1952: 184).

[188] Cp. *Suda* s.v. Τιτανίδα γῆν (τ 677, iv.562.22–23 Adler): ἐνομίζοντο δὲ τῶν Πριαπωδῶν θεῶν εἶναι. Lucian, *Salt.* 21.4 suggests that Priapus may have been one of the Titans.

[189] Lucian, *Salt.* 79.15 (*OF* 600i B = OT 209 K): ἡ μέν γε Βακχικὴ ὄρχησις ἐν Ἰωνίᾳ μάλιστα καὶ ἐν Πόντῳ σπουδαζομένη, καίτοι σατυρικὴ οὖσα, οὕτω κεχείρωται τοὺς ἀνθρώπους τοὺς ἐκεῖ ὥστε κατὰ τὸν τεταγμένον ἕκαστοι καιρόν, ἁπάντων ἐπιλαθόμενοι τῶν ἄλλων, κάθηνται δι᾽ ἡμέρας τιτᾶνας καὶ κορύβαντας καὶ σατύρους καὶ βουκόλους ὁρῶντες.

or Kouretes.[190] Like these other primordial peoples, the Titans are often described as the first inhabitants of particular locales, the folk most closely linked to the soil from which they spring.[191] Attica was known as the Titanland, Τιτανίδα γῆν, from its primordial inhabitant, just as Titane near Sikyon is named for Titan, the first one to dwell there.[192] The Eretrians even claimed descent from a Titan, Eretrieus, son of Phaethon, who provided the people with his name.[193]

Whereas in the myth of the metal races each race is created separately to correspond with a separate age of the world, the myths of the earthborn provide a group of primordial peoples whose function is to bridge that awkward gap between the originary gods and normal, contemporary human peoples.[194] One consequence is that these folk are always being

---

[190] Cp. Phot. *Lexicon* s.v. Κάβειροι (κ 3 Theodoridis): δαίμονες ἐκ Λήμνου διὰ τὸ τόλμημα τῶν γυναικῶν μετενεχθέντες· εἰσὶ δὲ ἤτοι ῞Ηφαιστοι ἢ Τιτᾶνες. The Θεοὶ μεγάλοι at Imbros are identified as Kasmilos (the name of one of the Kabeiroi according to ΣAp. Rhod. 1.917 [78 Wendel] and Strabo 10.3.21), Koios, Kreios, Hyperion, Iapetos, and Kronos (*IG* xii.8 #74). Eurymedon is known as one of the Kabeiroi (Nonnos, *Dion.* 14.17–22, etc.), but he is also called the king of the giants (*Od.* 8.58–60) and the father (with Hera) of Prometheus, according to the Σ^T *Il.* 14.296 (the story appears to go back to Euphorion fr. 99 Van Groningen). Eustathios, commenting on the same passage, refers to Eurymedon as a Titan (III.646.20–23 van der Valk).

[191] Cp. Eust. *Il. ad* 2.735 (I.519.6 van der Valk) (*OF* 320xii B) on τίτανος as the dust of gypsum: οἱ δὲ παλαιοί φασι τίτανος κόνις γύψος. Detienne 1979: 80–81 argues further for an origin that marks the Titans as formed from a combination of earth and fire, τίτανος as quicklime, the ash formed by firing limestone: "So the Titans of the Orphic myth are not to be confused with the adversaries of Zeus in Hesiod's Theogony. In the tale of Dionysos's murder, the powers that take part are at once gods and men: gods, because like them they precede the human race, but also men because the affinities of these personages with a certain earthly substance, quicklime, qualify them to play the role of ancestors to a race as deeply rooted in the soil as the 'eaters of bread'" (Detienne 1979: 81).

[192] Attica: *Suda* s.v. Τιτανίδα γῆν (τ 677, IV.562.18–21 Adler): οἱ μὲν τὴν πᾶσαν, οἱ δὲ τὴν Ἀττικήν. ἀπὸ Τιτηνίου, ἑνὸς τῶν Τιτάνων ἀρχαιοτέρου, οἰκήσαντος περὶ Μαραθῶνα, ὃς μόνος οὐκ ἐστράτευσεν ἐπὶ τοὺς θεούς, ὡς Φιλόχορος ἐν Τετραπόλει, ῎Ιστρος δ' ἐν α' Ἀττικῶν. Sikyon: Paus. 2.11.5. Nic. *FGrH* 271–2 F 4–5 seems to have described Titans originating in his homeland of Aetolia. Cp. Detienne 1979: 80–81.

[193] Eust. *Il.* 2.537 (I.429.12–17 van der Valk) : Ἐρέτρια ἐκαλεῖτο μὲν καὶ Μελανηὶς ἀπὸ Μελανέως, πατρὸς Εὐρύτου· ἔσχε δὲ τὴν κλῆσιν ἀπὸ Ἐρετριέως, υἱοῦ Φαέθοντος, ἑνὸς τῶν Τιτάνων. ταύτης ὁ πολίτης Ἐρετριεύς, οὗ γενικὴ Ἐρετριέως καὶ συναιρέσει Ἐρετριῶς, ὡς Στειριεύς Στειριέως Στειριῶς, χοεύς χοέως χοῶς, εἶδος μέτρου, οὗ καὶ αὐτοῦ ἡ αἰτιατικὴ τὸν χοᾶ, ὡς Πειραιεύς Πειραιέως Πειραιῶς Πειραιᾶ.

[194] Cp. Loraux 2000: 3: "Humankind exists because there were 'first men', yet the greatest difficulty is not to assign them birth, but to give them posterity . . . Doubtless, the process did not proceed without delays and 'misfires', since in order to characterize the beginnings of humanity, myths multiply the repetition, the reduplication, the discontinuity. Sometimes men are born from primordial beings who are themselves derived from the earth, and who, in a sort of dress rehearsal, ensure the transition between the origin and the times of men." Most 1997b points out that, strictly speaking, even in Hesiod only three separate metal races are created, and the remaining ones are not explicitly created but arise somehow from the previous.

superseded by the human race, whether they are obliterated and replaced or whether some remain as relics of the older order, preserving secrets that belong to that time. Sometimes the previous generation provides helpful services for their descendants; they are culture heroes who discover fire (like Prometheus or Phoroneus) or technology (like the Dactyls or Telchines).[195] At other times, they rebel against the inevitable replacement and are blasted, leaving only their works or their blood behind.[196] The connection between γένη is sometimes genetic, as in the myths associated with the great flood, when the descendants of the Titans, Deucalion and Pyrrha, themselves have offspring who mingle with the new race of humans they produce from the bones of the earth.[197] In other cases, however, the human race arises only out of the destruction of the previous race.

Such a story is the tale of the myth of the Gigantomachy alluded to in the *Orphic Argonautica*. The Gigantes are one of the primordial races generated from the Earth, but, unlike some of the other primordial peoples, they are known in myth almost exclusively for their hubristic and violent attempts to overthrow the power of the gods. After some individual assaults, the Gigantes band together to make war on the gods. The gods, aided by Herakles, defeat the Gigantes, and from their remains, in some tales, the human race is born.[198] Bernabé, however, identifies the Giants in the *Orphic Argonautica* passage as Titans, their destructive deeds as the dismemberment of Dionysos, and the generation of humans from them as an allusion to Zeus' generation of mortals from the smoking remains of the Titans glutted with the flesh of the infant god.

To reach these conclusions, Bernabé wants first to alter Vian's reading of the lines describing the Gigantes.[199] Rather than having the Giants dripped as blood (ἐστάξαντο) painfully (λυγρόν) from Ouranos and being

---

[195] Phoroneus: Paus. 2.19.5, 2.15.5; Idaian Dactyls: Strabo 10.3.22; Hes. fr. 282 Merklbach-West, *Phoronis* (fr. 2 *PEG*); Telchines: Strabo 10.3.7, 19, 14.2.9, Diod. Sic. 5.55.1–3. Cp. Blakely 2006: 218–219 on the way the Telchines are represented either as envious and destructive because of being replaced or as culture heroes involved with artisanal and magical activities. Cp. Sourvinou-Inwood 2003 on the role of Pelasgians in such stories.

[196] For Pohlenz 1916: 585, the current humans' supersession of the Titans represents the historical conquest of a culture whose gods were the Titans by the Greeks. But there is no need to reduce a useful mythic symbol to a concrete historical reality. Kronos and the Titans always represent the order of the past, whether that past is imagined as harsh and savage or a pleasant Golden Age of peace. Cp. Versnel 1993: 90–132.

[197] Ov. *Met.* 1.393–394; cp. Apollod. *Bibl.* 1.7.2, where the flood is to destroy the race of Bronze (equated with the Giants). A similar combination of originary family and autochthons appears in the marriages between the race of Spartoi and the Cadmids at Thebes. Cp. Loraux 2000: 14. Pind. *Ol.* 9.43–56 emphasizes the descent from the Titan Iapetos.

[198] For a good summary of the mythic and artistic evidence, see Gantz 1993: 445–454. Cp. Vian 1952.

[199] *OA* 17–20 Βριμοῦς τ᾽ εὐδυνάτοιο γονὰς, ἠδ᾽ ἔργ᾽ ἀΐδηλα | Γιγάντων, οἳ λυγρὸν ἀπ᾽ Οὐρανοῦ ἐστάξαντο, | σπέρμα γονῆς τὸ πρόσθεν, ὅθεν γένος ἐξεγένοντο | θνητῶν, οἳ κατὰ γαῖαν ἀπείριτον

the seed (σπέρμα) from which a race of mortals came later, Bernabé wants to remove the comma and make λυγρόν go with σπέρμα, making the Earthborn the baneful seed from which mortals sprang, dripping as the blood spilled from them.[200] The result is to compress the allusion into one story, the generation of humans from the Titans who murdered Dionysos, instead of two, the generation of the Giants from the blood of Ouranos and the generation of humans from the Giants slain in the Gigantomachy.

Bernabé argues that ἐστάξαντο, as a middle, should take as its subject the bleeder, not the substance bled out, so the Gegeneis must be doing the bleeding. However, even in the active, the substance (usually blood) dripped out can be the subject of the verb, so the middle (rarely attested elsewhere) works perfectly to indicate that the subjects of the action are the very drops that are being bled out of Heaven/Ouranos.[201] Moreover, the origin of the Giants from the blood of Ouranos is a well-known myth, with variations from Hesiod to the *Orphic Rhapsodies*. Hesiod recounts how, when Kronos castrated Ouranos, drops of the blood fell onto the Earth/Gaia, who produced the race of Giants, the Furies, and the Meliae.[202] While the Furies and Giants are known from other sources, the nymphs called Meliae remain somewhat mysterious. These children of Earth and starry Heaven seem to be identified with the parents of the race of bronze when Hesiod recounts the myth of the metal races in the *Works and Days*, leading the scholiasts to suggest that the bronze race should be identified with the Giants born from the blood of Heaven.[203] Traces remain of tales of other races generated from the blood spilled in Ouranos' castration;

αἰὲν ἔασι. Dottin 1930, whose text appears in the *TLG*, reads Γηγενέων for Γιγάντων, and both forms appear in the manuscripts.

[200] Bernabé 2003: 33 is quite right to point out that the reference to this passage in Edmonds 1999: 56 n. 65 gives the impression that humans are generated from the seed of the Earthborn fallen from the sky, rather than the blood.

[201] The LSJ notes that the verb can be used in the active with the accusative or dative of the substance dripped, but also with the subject (blood, water, etc.) falling in drips itself, citing Hdt.6.74; Soph. *Phil.*783; Aesch. *Ag.* 179 (lyr.); Eur. *Rhes.* 566; Eur. *Andr.* 533 (lyr.); Soph. fr. 534 R (= 491 N) (anap.); Hippoc. *Epid.* 1.14. The LSJ makes no mention of a middle sense, and no other use of the aorist middle turns up in a search of the *TLG*.

[202] Hes. *Theog.* 183–187. Apollod. *Bibl.* 1.1.4 (*OF* 185, 186ii, 187i, 192i B) recounts the same story, but focuses only on the Furies.

[203] Hes. *Op.* 145 ἐκ μελιᾶν. Scholia on the passage identify these with the nymphs sprung from the blood of Ouranos and the bronze race themselves with the Giants: ΕΚ ΜΕΛΙΑΝ. Τρίτον φησὶ γενέσθαι γένος παρὰ τῆς Εἱμαρμένης, τὸ Γιγαντικὸν ἐκεῖνο, τὸ μάχιμον. Οἱ περὶ Πρόκλον τὸ ΕΚ ΜΕΛΙΑΝ, Δωρικῶς περισπῶσιν, ἐκ τῶν μελιῶν λέγοντες γενέσθαι τοὺς γίγαντας. Sometimes, however, they become the progenitors of the human race. Cp. Hsch. s.v. μελίας καρπός (693): τὸ τῶν ἀνθρώπων γένος. See also Σ^T *Il.* 22.127: ἢ ἐπεὶ μελιηγενεῖς λέγονται οἱ πρώην ἄνδρες καὶ "λαοὶ" ἀπὸ τῶν λίθων Δευκαλίωνος. Clay 2003: 96–99 sees this anthropogony from the blood of Ouranos as the *Theogony*'s version of the origin of the human race, in contrast to the myth of the metal races in the *Works and Days*. See now Yates 2004, for more on this anthropogony.

both Akousilaos and Alkaios claim that the Phaiakians (another primordial people, kin to the savage Cyclopes as well as the Giants in Homer) were actually born from the blood of Ouranos.[204] The *Etymologicum Magnum* preserves two lines of Orpheus, from the eighth book of the *Hieros Logos*, which explain the name of the Giants as the Earthborn, since they come from the blood of Heaven spilled on the earth.[205] In all these accounts, the castration of Ouranos leads to another set of offspring of Earth and Heaven, a race who are not Titans, but in the same generation.[206]

The lines from the *Rhapsodies* on the subject of the Gigantes, coupled with the mention of the destructive works of the Gigantes in the catalog of the *Orphic Argonautica*, suggest that a tale of the Giants and their works may have been recounted in an Orphic poem. Hesiod passes over recounting the deeds of the Giants, but his reference clearly depends on the tale being well known.[207] What might have happened to the Giants and their descendants in Orpheus' story we don't know, but Gigantomachies were popular in art, and they were obviously popular enough in myth for Xenophanes to inveigh against the Gigantomachy as the prime example of the sort of old-fashioned story that was narrated at symposia instead of enlightening philosophical discourse.[208] The battle of the Giants against the gods is certainly the most obvious referent for the allusion to their "destructive deeds" (ἔργ᾽ ἀΐδηλα), a term that suits the various combats and destructions that took place in the Gigantomachy much better than the single murder of an infant god.

Another reason to read the Giants' destructive deeds as a reference to the Gigantomachy instead of the dismemberment of Dionysos is that the creation of human beings is the sequel to the destruction of the Giants in several of the references to the Gigantomachy, just as it is in the passage of the *Orphic Argonautica*. Although the tale of humans generated from the

---

[204] Σ^L Ap. Rhod. *Argon.* 4.982–992a (309.13–17 Wendel): Ἀκουσίλαος ἐν τῆ γ᾽ (2 fr 4 J.) φησίν, ὅτι ἐκ τῆς ἐκτομῆς τοῦ Οὐρανοῦ ῥανίδας ἐνεχθῆναι συνέπεσεν, τουτέστι σταγόνας, κατὰ τῆς γῆς, ἐξ ὧν γεννηθῆναι τοὺς Φαίακας· οἱ δὲ τοὺς Γίγαντας. καὶ Ἀλκαῖος (fr 206 Lobel = 116 B. III 185) δὲ λέγει τοὺς Φαίακας ἔχειν τὸ γένος ἐκ τῶν σταγόνων τοῦ Οὐρανοῦ. *Od.* 7.58–60, 205–206.

[205] *Etym. Magn.* s.v. Γίγας (231.21)· (*OF* 188 B = OF 63 K): Παρὰ τὸ γῶ, τὸ χωρῶ, γίνεται γάς· καὶ κατὰ ἀναδιπλασιασμὸν, γίγας· ἢ παρὰ τὸ ἐκ τῆς γῆς ἰέναι· οἷον, Οὓς καλέουσι γίγαντας ἐπώνυμον ἐν μακάρεσσιν, οὕνεκα γῆς ἐγένοντο, καὶ αἵματος οὐρανίοιο.Οὕτως Ὀρφεὺς ἐν τῷ ὀγδόῳ τοῦ Ἱεροῦ Λόγου. The passage is one of the few citations of the *Rhapsodies* (the *Hieros Logos* in 24 Rhapsodies) by book or rhapsody.

[206] The claim in the gold tablets to be the child of Earth and starry Heaven may align the speaker, not with the Titans, but with some other primordial race of humanity, sprung directly from the Earth. Cp. Edmonds 2004a: 75–79, with further discussion in Edmonds 2010.

[207] Hes. *Theog.* 50. Like the passage from the *Orphic Argonautica*, this proem serves to distinguish the poet's current theme from other well-known stories.

[208] Xenophanes, 21 B 1.21 DK. See the exhaustive treatment of artistic and literary sources in Vian 1952.

blood of the enemies of the gods defeated in battle seems to go back even to Mesopotamian sources, Ovid's version is undoubtedly the best known, in which humans are born from the blood of the Giants seeping down into the Earth after their battle against the gods, the culmination of all their crimes and violations of justice.[209] In other versions, the same tale is told of the Titans and the Titanomachy; a race of violent, primordial people rises up against the authority of the gods and a bloody battle ensues. As one scholiast makes explicit through the etymology, mortal human beings (βροτοί) are born from the gore (βρότος) of the defeated Titans.[210] The scholiast is commenting on a passage of Oppian, who presents the birth of humans from the blood of the Titans as one alternative for the origin of humans, the other being their creation by Prometheus.[211] Dio attributes the tale of human descent from the blood of the Titans to a morose man who must have suffered much in life, since he blames the miseries of human existence in this foul world on the hatred of the gods for the descendants of their enemies, the Titans who fought a war against them.[212]

> All mankind, we are all from the blood of the Titans. Thus, because they were the enemies of the gods and fought against them, we are not beloved

---

[209] Ov. *Met.* 1.157–162. Note that, although Ovid identifies the Giants with the Hesiodic Iron race, he nevertheless has the next race succeed directly from the one previous. For the Mesopotamian tales, cp. *Atrahasis* 1.212–217 and *Enûma elis* VI.1.

[210] ΣOpp. *Halieutica* 5.1–10: "Some say that it was from the blood of the Titans warring against the Heavenly gods, particularly Zeus, and being beaten; whence, they say, man is called mortal (*brotos*) from the gore (*brotos*) or bloody defilement of the Titans." τινὲς δέ φασιν ἐκ τοῦ αἵματος τῶν Τιτάνων πολεμούντων μετὰ τῶν οὐρανίων θεῶν, μάλιστα δὲ τοῦ Διός, καὶ ἡττηθέντων, ὅθεν καί, φασί, βροτὸς ὁ ἄνθρωπος λέγεται ὡς ἀπὸ βρότου ἢ τοῦ αἱματηροῦ μολυσμοῦ τῶν Τιτάνων. A scholiast to Pind. *Ol.* 3.28c quotes an unknown poet Pherenikos, who claims that the Hyperboreans sprang up from the blood of the Titans.

[211] Opp. *Halieutica* 5.1–10 (*OF* 320xiv B): "But truly, someone created men to be a race like the blessed gods, but he gave lesser strength to them, whether the child of Iapetus, cunning Prometheus, made the race in the likeness of the blessed ones, mingling earth with water, and anointed his heart with the balm of the gods, or indeed we are born from the gore that divinely gushed from the Titans." ἀλλά τις ἀτρεκέως ἱκέλην μακάρεσσι γενέθλην ἀνθρώπους ἀνέφυσε, χερείονα δ' ὤπασεν ἀλκήν, εἴτ' οὖν Ἰαπετοῖο γένος, πολυμῆτα Προμηθεύς, ἀντωπὸν μακάρεσσι κάμεν γένος, ὕδατι γαῖαν ξύνωσις, κραδίην δὲ θεῶν ἔχρισεν ἀλοιφῇ, εἴτ' ἄρα καὶ λύθροιο θεορρύτου ἐκγενόμεθα Τιτήνων. It is worth noting that the story of Prometheus' creation of mankind is paralleled not only in Plato's *Protagoras* (320–321), but, as Procl. *In R.* 2.53.2–12 Kroll (*OF* 352i B = OF 143 K) tells us, Orpheus represented the descent of the soul into matter (i.e., the formation of human beings) by the myth of Prometheus' theft of fire.

[212] See pp. 276–277 above. Note that later in the oration (30.26 [*OF* 320viii B]), Dio proposes a better story (ἕτερος δὲ βελτίων ἐστὶ τοῦδε λόγος), that mankind descends not from the Titans or Giants but from the gods, who love us as their kin: ἔλεγε δὲ ὑμνῶν τόν τε Δία καὶ τοὺς ἄλλους θεοὺς ὡς ἀγαθοί τε εἶεν καὶ φιλοῖεν ἡμᾶς, ἅτε δὴ ξυγγενεῖς ὄντας αὐτῶν. ἀπὸ γὰρ τῶν θεῶν ἔφη τὸ τῶν ἀνθρώπων εἶναι γένος, οὐκ ἀπὸ Τιτάνων οὐδ' ἀπὸ Γιγάντων. Dio's use of Titans or Giants here reinforces the idea that the war against the gods, whether by Titans or Giants, was the context of the previous story. Cp. Dio Chrys. *Or.* 33.2 for another dismissive reference to the story of descent from the Titans.

by the gods either, but we are punished by them and we are born into retribution, being in custody in this life for a certain time as long as we each live ... This harsh and foul-aired prison, which we call the cosmos, has been prepared by the gods.[213]

Bernabé claims that this Dio passage must also be a reference to the dismemberment story, but waging war against the gods (τοῖς θεοῖς καὶ πολεμησάντων) cannot refer to the murder of Dionysos Zagreus; the verb πολεμέω makes the context of the Titanomachy clear.[214] Dio's references to mankind being in a prison (ἐν φρουρᾷ) do indeed recall the references in Plato's *Phaedo* and *Cratylus* to doctrines about the soul associated with Orpheus, but this fact merely reinforces the argument that such doctrines have no particular connection to the myth of dismemberment, but might be associated with any story of the creation of humanity. That human souls are ἐν φρουρᾷ and paying the penalty through their lives in bodies is the result of the Titanomachy in Dio's story; this is a rather pessimistic message to draw from the traditional story of the human race created from the blood of the defeated opponent of the gods, but, then again, Dio specifically frames it as the tale of a long-suffering pessimist.[215] Oppian, by contrast, has a much more positive interpretation of the same tale, befitting the context in which he relates it. Although somewhat inferior in their strength, humans are like the gods, and thus there is nothing they cannot accomplish.[216]

---

[213] Dio Chrys. *Or.* 30.10–11 (*OF* 429iii, 320vii B): ὅτι τοῦ τῶν Τιτάνων αἵματός ἐσμεν ἡμεῖς ἅπαντες οἱ ἄνθρωποι. ὡς οὖν ἐκείνων ἐχθρῶν ὄντων τοῖς θεοῖς καὶ πολεμησάντων οὐδὲ ἡμεῖς φίλοι ἐσμέν, ἀλλὰ κολαζόμεθά τε ὑπ' αὐτῶν καὶ ἐπὶ τιμωρίᾳ γεγόναμεν, ἐν φρουρᾷ δὴ ὄντες ἐν τῷ βίῳ τοσοῦτον χρόνον ὅσον ἕκαστοι ζῶμεν ... εἶναι δὲ τὸν μὲν τόπον τοῦτον, ὃν κόσμον ὀνομάζομεν, δεσμωτήριον ὑπὸ τῶν θεῶν κατεσκευασμένον χαλεπόν τε καὶ δυσάερον.

[214] Bernabé 2002a: 411: "Mais ce que Dion nous dit, c'est que nous sommes du sang des Titans, sans préciser quand celui-ci a été versé. Et ce n'est qu'après, lorsqu'il indique la raison pour laquelle les hommes sont punis, qu'il explique que les Titans ont lutté contre les dieux." On the contrary, Dio explains when the blood was shed, not somewhere later in his speech but in the sentence immediately following – the blood was shed when the Titans made war against the gods, that is, the Titanomachy.

[215] Bernabé 2002a: 411–412 protests that, if one denies a reference to the Orphic myth of dismemberment, one needs to find another myth that combines the element of the generation of humans from the Titans with a concern for inherited guilt. "D'où aurait-il bien pu sortir, ce mythe?" Since the idea of inherited guilt and the idea of generation of humans from a previous race of semi-divine opponents of the gods both appear in a variety of evidence in the mythic tradition, their combination in the text of Dio should not be terribly surprising. Dio (or his source) simply performed the *bricolage* characteristic of the mythic tradition, bringing together familiar elements to make a particular point. A particular combination of traditional mythic elements does not imply a long tradition of such a combination, however far back each element may be attested.

[216] Opp. *Halieutica* 5.1–5 (*OF* 320xiv B): ἔνθεν ἔπειτ' ἀΐων τεκμαίρεο, κοίρανε γαίης, ὡς οὐδὲν μερόπεσσιν ἀμήχανον, οὐκ ἐνὶ γαίῃ μητρὶ καμεῖν, οὐ κόλπον ἀν' εὐρώεντα θαλάσσης· ἀλλὰ

A reference in a letter of the Emperor Julian, cited as another testimony to the Zagreus anthropogony, comes from a context almost as positive as Oppian, although it may not even refer to the same type of Gigantomachy anthropogony. Julian is urging philanthropic treatment of men of all nations, good and bad alike. Among his arguments from reason and cult, he claims that all are deserving of good treatment because all men are kin and descendants of the gods, according to the sacred legend that the race of men arose from sacred drops of blood that fell when Zeus was setting the cosmos in order.[217] This allusion could be to the same tale as in Oppian, of humans' divine descent from the Titans after Zeus set the world in order after defeating them in the Titanomachy, but the reference remains uncertain, especially since Julian attributes the tale to the ancient theurgists (παραδέδοται διὰ τῶν ἀρχαίων ἡμῖν θεουργῶν). Theurgy in Julian always refers to the Chaldaean Oracles or those who make use of the texts for special interactions with the gods.[218] However, even if the reference is not to some unknown myth from the cosmology of the Chaldaean Oracles, the creation of mankind from blood neither follows the dismemberment nor fastens on mankind a burden of inherited guilt.

The last piece of evidence adduced is a Sibylline oracle inscribed at Perinthos from perhaps the second century BCE, which mentions blood, fire, and ash mingling when Bacchos cries Evoe.[219] Bernabé sees this combination of substances as a reference to the moment of creation of mankind, when the Titans are blasted by Zeus' lightning.[220] Of course, a sacrificial

---

τις ἀτρεκέως ἰκέλην μακάρεσσι γενέθλην ἀνθρώπους ἀνέφυσε, χερείονα δ' ὤπασεν ἀλκήν. Oppian's message is similar to the tales that link contemporary humans to divine ancestors and recalls traditional definitions of the difference between men and gods. Cp. Pind. *Nem.* 6.1–5.

[217] Julian. *Ep.* 89b107–118: εἴς τε τὸ διάφορον ἀποβλέψαντα τῶν ἠθῶν καὶ τῶν νόμων, οὐ μὴν ἀλλὰ καί, ὅπερ ἐστὶ μεῖζον καὶ τιμιώτερον καὶ κυριώτερον, εἰς τὴν τῶν θεῶν φήμην, ἢ παραδέδοται διὰ τῶν ἀρχαίων ἡμῖν θεουργῶν, ὡς, ὅτε Ζεὺς ἐκόσμει τὰ πάντα, σταγόνων αἵματος ἱεροῦ πεσουσῶν ἐξ οὐρανοῦ τὸ τῶν ἀνθρώπων βλαστήσειε γένος· καὶ οὕτως οὖν συγγενεῖς γινόμεθα πάντες, εἰ μὲν ἐξ ἑνὸς καὶ μιᾶς, ἐκ δυοῖν ἀνθρώποιν ὄντες οἱ πολλοὶ καὶ πολλαί, καθάπερ οἱ θεοί φασι καὶ χρὴ πιστεύειν ἐπιμαρτυρούντων τῶν ἔργων, ἐκ τῶν θεῶν πάντες γεγονότες.

[218] *Pace* Bernabé 2003: 34, citing Bidez *ad loc* for support: "Il semble évident que l'expression τῶν ἀρχαίων θεουργῶν dans le texte a désigne des Orphiques." However, of the seven uses of words derived from θεουργία in the corpus of Julian, three (*Or.* 7.14.8 219b1; *Or.* 5.20.17 180b; *Gal.* 203.11 224d) refer to magical practice in general, while the remainder (*Or.* 5.12.32 173a1; *Or.* 5.18.34 178d; *Gal.* 230.7 354b) refer specifically to the arts of the Chaldaeans. *Or.* 5.18.34 178d even quotes one of the Chaldaean Oracles (*CO* 129).

[219] εὐτυχεῖτε. χρησμὸς Σιβύλλης. | ἐπὰν δ' ὁ Βάκχος εὐάσας πλη<γή>σ<ε>τα<ϊ | τότε αἷμα καὶ πῦρ καὶ κόνις μιγήσεται. | Σπέλλιος Εὐήθις ἀρχιβουκόλος. (Adaptation of Dieterich 1891: 8, of the text of Kaibel 1879: 211 = *Epigr. Gr.* 1036a [*OF* 320xi B = OT 210 K].)

[220] Bernabé 2003: 34, following Dieterich 1911: 72 (= Dieterich 1891: 7): "L'oracle faisait référence à la création de l'homme dans le mythe orphique, au moment où le feu de la foudre de Zeus et le sang des Titans se mêlent à la terre."

celebration accompanied by Bacchic cries is the most likely context, since blood, fire, and ash would mingle in any sacrifice, but the context provides no way to prove that the Sibylline Oracle is authorizing a sacrificial rite for the Bacchic group that set up the inscription instead of making an enigmatic allusion to a secret anthropogonic myth that was somehow important to this group. However, Bernabé himself points out that it is unclear whose blood it would be in an anthropogonic context. The dual nature of mankind doctrine would seem to demand that it be the blood of Dionysos that provides the divine element that mingles with the ash of the Titanic element, but Bernabé admits that the mythic parallels would suggest that it must be the Titans' blood.[221] Such confusion suggests that the verses make more sense as reference to a sacrificial ritual performed by the Bacchic group that set up the inscription.[222]

However, even if the Perinthos inscription did refer to the anthropogonic moment, it would hardly support the claim that all these pieces of evidence show a clear sequence of events that must have been recounted in the *Orphic Rhapsodies*.[223] In fact, not a single one of these texts contains all of the elements that are claimed to be inseparable parts of the myth: the dismemberment of Dionysos, the punishment of the Titans by lightning, the creation of humans from the blood fallen from them, and the burden of expiation for the Titans' crime. On the contrary, this collection of texts that refer to an anthropogony from the blood of the Titans never connects that anthropogony with the dismemberment story, but rather with the tale of the Titanomachy. When the anthropogony is connected to a burdensome Titanic heritage, therefore, as in Dio, it is the crime of rebelling against the gods for which mankind reaps the consequences.

Bernabé, however, objects that, whatever the text itself might seem to say, these references cannot be to the Titanomachy because, he asserts, the Titanomachy always ends with the Titans imprisoned in Tartaros, whereas

---

[221] Bernabé 2003: 34 n. 15.

[222] Some might object that the sacrificial interpretation does not explain the word restored as πλη<γή>σ<ε>τα<ι in the inscription. Dieterich and Bernabé take this term to refer to the Titans' dismemberment of Dionysos, but beating is not normally part of the murder, which is described either in terms of a savage tearing apart or a perverted sacrificial carving up. I would venture to suggest that πλησ<ε>τα<ϊ might be a better restoration of ΠΛΗΣΤΑ, so that Dionysos gives his Bacchic shout, not as a death rattle but more characteristically as a cry of triumph and satisfaction. Indeed, I find that editors before Dieterich, such as Kaibel 1879, read the passive πλησ<θήσ>ετα<ι, but the middle requires less of a supplement. I would, of course, be hesitant to rest the weight of any argument on an uncertain textual restoration.

[223] Bernabé 2002a: 413: "Nous voyons donc comment un groupe de textes coïncident dans la référence à un mythe où l'on parlait du démembrement de Dionysos par les Titans, du foudroiement de ceux-ci, de la création des hommes à partir des cendres et du sang des Titans tombés par terre et de l'expiation du crime. Nous pouvons attribuer cette séquence aux Rhapsodies orphiques."

the dismemberment story ends in the death of the Titans by lightning.[224] While it would no doubt make the most sense to a scholar trying to arrange all the fragmentary tales neatly into a single coherent whole to have a Titanomachy ending with Tartarosis followed by a dismemberment ending in lightning, the evidence is unfortunately not so neat. The fifth-century CE Neoplatonist Damascius notes that there are three punishments related for the Titans in the tradition: lightning, shackling, and descent into lower regions, i.e., Tartarosis.[225] Different tales seem to have included different punishments according to the context of the tale; we cannot deduce the preceding crime from the punishment. Damascius associates the creation of humans not with the first punishment, lightning, but with the last, the imprisonment in Tartaros. By contrast, in at least one Orphic version, the binding of the Titans followed the dismemberment story, since the punishment of Atlas holding up the sky is cited as a consequence of the crime.[226] Such a story is absolutely incompatible with the idea that the generation of human beings from the ashes of the Titans was inseparable from the dismemberment story.[227] On the contrary, if any pattern is prevalent, it is the generation of human beings following upon the Titanomachy, parallel to the creation of humans after the Gigantomachy in other stories.

The passage from the *Orphic Argonautica*, then, does not provide evidence for a narrative from the *Orphic Rhapsodies* that included a sequence of Dionysos' dismemberment, Titans' punishment by lightning, and creation of human beings from the ashes of the Titans. Rather, as the parallels show, the myths alluded to in the passage are the generation of the race of Giants from the blood of Ouranos and the creation of human beings from the remains of the Giants after the Gigantomachy. Even if the events in the catalog of previous themes were all in a strict chronological sequence (which they most clearly are not), there is no problem with the sequence of

---

[224] Bernabé 2002a: 411: "La Titanomachie a comme suite, aussi bien dans Hésiode que dans les notices sure les Rhapsodies, l'emprisonnement des Titans dans le Tartare. Par contre le foudroiement serait le seul résultat des actions titaniques contre Dionysos."

[225] Dam. *In Phd.* 1.7 (33 Westerink) (*OF* 178iv, 235ii, 318iv B): ὅτι τριτταὶ παραδέδονται τῶν Τιτάνων κολάσεις· κεραυνώσεις, δεσμοί, ἄλλων ἀλλαχοῦ πρόοδοι πρὸς τὸ κοιλότερον. On this passage, see further below.

[226] Procl. *In Ti.* 1.173.1 Diehl (*OF* 319i B = OF 215K): καὶ γὰρ οἱ θεολόγοι μετὰ τὸν τοῦ Διονύσου διασπασμόν, ὃς δηλοῖ τὴν ἐκ τῆς ἀμερίστου δημιουργίας μεριστὴν πρόοδον εἰς τὸ πᾶν ὑπὸ τοῦ Διός, τοὺς μὲν ἄλλους Τιτᾶνας ἄλλας λήξεις διακεκληρῶσθαί φασι, τὸν δὲ Ἄτλαντα ἐν τοῖς πρὸς ἑσπέραν τόποις ἱδρῦσθαι ἀνέχοντα τὸν οὐρανόν· Ἄτλας δ' οὐρανὸν εὐρὺν ἔχει κρατερῆς ὑπ' ἀνάγκης, πείρασιν ἐν γαίης. Simpl. *in Cael.* 375.12 Heiberg (*OF* 319ii B = OF 215 K) also links the punishment of Atlas and the other Titans with the dismemberment of Dionysos.

[227] As claimed by, e.g., Detienne 1979: 80.

events in the passage, since the creation of human beings often occurs as the sequel to the Gigantomachy, and there is no reason that the Gigantomachy could not occur after the birth of Brimo's child. In any case, the existence of a race of Earthborn people between the births of the gods and the generation of the human race is a common feature of anthropogonic myths in the Greek tradition, even if these Earthborn are sometimes named Giants, sometimes Titans, and sometimes even Kouretes or Dactyls. Likewise, it is in no way exceptional for the previous race to be the seed from which the current race comes, since the complete separation of the races only comes in some versions of the Hesiodic metal races myth.

The idea of the generation of the human race from the Titans therefore does not imply familiarity with the version found in the sixth-century CE Olympiodorus. On the contrary, all the earlier versions of the Titanic anthropogony connect the generation of mortals with the Titanomachy rather than the dismemberment myth. Such a myth, as Dio shows, can indeed be used to saddle the human race with the burden of divine anger resulting from the deeds of the Titans, but the situation is hardly different from the vengeance taken upon human beings in Hesiod as the result of the deeds of Prometheus. Each of these mythic elements – the inherited anger of the gods, the creation of the human race from the blood of the previous race, the punishment of the Titans – appears in the broader mythic tradition, combined in different ways with different emphases by different authors performing mythic *bricolage*. To insist that they all can be reduced to a single text that has one particular meaning is to miss the richness of the Greek mythic tradition, its multiformity and polyvalence. If we unbind them from the artificial frame of the Zagreus myth, these strands of evidence can help us get a better understanding of the myths of anthropogony, their common patterns and their points of variation. Such an understanding is all the more important because so many of the variants are local traditions, preserved only by passing references in later authors and overshadowed by the better-known stories of Hesiod's Panhellenic epic.

Olympiodorus' innovation

Olympiodorus' recounting (*In Phd.* 1.3–6) of the Titan's dismemberment of Dionysos and the subsequent creation of humankind has served for over a century as the linchpin of the reconstructions of the supposed Orphic doctrine of original sin. From Comparetti's first statement of the idea in his 1879 discussion of the gold tablets from Thurii, Olympiodorus' brief testimony has been the only piece of evidence to pull together the threads of the

Zagreus myth, linking the dismemberment of Dionysos with the creation of human beings.[228] Scholars have repeatedly argued that Olympiodorus preserves the only complete version of the story, which exists elsewhere only in incomplete fragments or allusions.[229] These fragments, it is argued, must be restored by supplying the missing threads from Olympiodorus' story, which, despite the late sixth-century CE date and peculiar biases of the author as a pagan Neoplatonist scholar (and possibly alchemist) in a Christian era, nevertheless preserves essentially unchanged the central Orphic myth that dates from the sixth century BCE.

I show first that, while Olympiodorus does indeed link the dismemberment and the anthropogony, he does not include any element of inherited guilt, either in his narration of the myth or in his interpretation. Moreover, his telling of the myth, making the anthropogony the sequel to the dismemberment of Dionysos, is an innovation made for the purposes of his own argument. Rather than preserving in fossilized form a sacred myth more than a millennium old, Olympiodorus concocts an innovative tale of his own, manipulating a variety of sources that describe the dismemberment of Dionysos, as well as other sources that recount the punishment of the Titans for their rebellion in the Titanomachy and the subsequent creation of new races from them. Olympiodorus' sources include not only poetic treatments of the subjects but also allegorical readings of the myths, especially those by his predecessors Proclus and Damascius. Olympiodorus' narration of the dismemberment of Dionysos is not the key witness to a lost, secret tradition that prefigures the Christian doctrine of original sin, but rather a colorful example of a late antique Neoplatonic philosopher's manipulation of the Greek mythic tradition.

In the Greek mythic tradition, the interpretation of the myth cannot be kept separate from the way the narrative is recounted, since the author retelling a traditional tale always adapts the details of the story to fit the ideas he is trying to convey and the audience to which he is recounting the tale.[230] In this process of *bricolage*, the author strives to

---

[228] Comparetti in Cavallari 1879. For further discussion of Olympiodorus, see Edmonds 2009, from which the following is adapted.

[229] Not only Bernabé 2002a and 2003, but also, e.g., Bremmer 2004: 53, who claims that the story "started to appear in veiled form in our texts from the middle of the fifth century onwards... We unfortunately find this myth in its most detailed form only in the sixth-century philosopher Olympiodorus."

[230] *Contra* Bernabé 2002a: 423, who insists that, at least for the Zagreus myth, the various authors of the tale could only alter their interpretations, not any of the structural components: "Comme il arrive avec la plupart des mythes en général, les différents auteurs qui rapportent ce mythe puisent chacun à son gré dans différents éléments du paradigme, mais ils n'ajoutent jamais des éléments

render his version authoritative for his audience by engaging with previous versions of the tale, especially the best-known or most authoritative renditions. Olympiodorus adopts many of the same gambits used by earlier tellers of myth in the Greek tradition (including Plato), concealing his own innovations by starting with references to previous versions and then diverging from the earlier accounts. Olympiodorus crafts his myth to argue for a conclusion surprising for a Neoplatonist, that suicide is forbidden because the body contains divine elements. Olympiodorus' mythic innovations allow him to provide a new and startling explanation of a crux in the *Phaedo* that Damascius and Proclus had tried to explain earlier. By drawing on these previous interpretations to provide a better and more authoritative version of the myth, Olympiodorus is engaging in the same kind of agonistic myth-telling that is characteristic of the Greek mythic tradition from the earliest evidence. Olympiodorus is not pedantically preserving an ancient Orphic myth, he is rather making use of the authority of Orpheus among the Neoplatonists to support his own philosophical ideas, concocting a curious new version of the traditional tale of the dismemberment of Dionysos to explain Socrates' puzzling prohibition of suicide.

As with the reference in Plut. *De esu carn.* 1.996bc (*OF* 313i, 318ii B = OF 210 K) to the dismemberment myth, Olympiodorus' recounting and interpretation of the story must be understood in the context of the argument he is making as well as in the context of his Neoplatonic interpretive tradition. The text comes from Olympiodorus' commentary on the *Phaedo* of Plato, in his explanation of Socrates' puzzling prohibition of suicide. In addition to his own argument against suicide (1.2), Olympiodorus claims that the text itself contains two proofs, a mythical and Orphic argument and a philosophic and dialectic one.

> And the mythical argument is as such: four reigns are told of in the Orphic tradition. The first is that of Ouranos, to which Kronos succeeds after cutting off the genitals of his father. After Kronos, Zeus becomes king, having hurled his father down into Tartaros. Then Dionysos succeeds Zeus. Through the scheme of Hera, they say, his retainers, the Titans, tear him to pieces and eat his flesh. Zeus, angered by the deed, blasts them with his thunderbolts, and from the sublimate of the vapors that rise from them comes the matter from which men are created. Therefore we must not kill ourselves, not because, as the text appears to say, we are in the body as a kind of shackle, for that is obvious, and Socrates would not call this a mystery; but we must not kill ourselves because our bodies are Dionysiac; we are,

incompatibles avec le schéma retracé à l'intérieur de la structure narrative (ils peuvent le faire, par contre, dans l'interprétation, ce qui est tout autre chose)."

in fact, a part of him, if indeed we come about from the sublimate of the Titans who ate his flesh.[231]

Once again, as in Plutarch, a myth is used to provide traditional authority for a philosophical argument, and the meaning of the myth, properly interpreted, is the same as the conclusion of the dialectic. Olympiodorus insists that the allegorical meaning (ἡ τοῦ μύθου ἀλληγορία) must be uncovered in order to understand Socrates' reference to the esoteric tradition, dismissing as too obvious the possibility that the φρουρά is simply the shackle of the body. While Olympiodorus draws heavily on the commentaries of Damascius and Proclus,[232] he nevertheless must make a contribution of his own to the scholarship, finding new levels of meaning in the traditional story. Of course, to find the meaning he wants, he carefully selects and manipulates the details he provides of the traditional myth.

Olympiodorus concludes the narration of the myth at the end of the quoted passage, and it is important to note that the myth he relates does not contain the narrative element of a burden of inherited guilt passed on to mankind. In Olympiodorus' story, mankind receives its material from the Titans who cannibalized Dionysos; human bodies thus include an element of the god. The story begins with the kingship in heaven passing through four cosmic reigns: Ouranos, Kronos, Zeus, and Dionysos. Ouranos is castrated by Kronos; Kronos is sent to Tartaros by Zeus; Zeus hands over the throne to Dionysos. Hera is angry and incites the Titans to murder and cannibalism. Zeus blasts the Titans with lightning and humans are created from the particles that precipitate out of the smoke (ἐκ τῆς αἰθάλης τῶν ἀτμῶν) that rises from the blasted Titans. The idea that human beings inherited a burden of guilt, be it *péché antécédent* or original sin, from these Titans is not part of the story as Olympiodorus tells it, but has been read into his story by commentators since Comparetti.[233]

---

[231] Olymp. *In Phd.* 1.3 (*OF* 174viii, 190ii, 227iv, 299vii, 304i, 313ii, 318iii, 320i B = OF 220 K): Καὶ ἔστι τὸ μυθικὸν ἐπιχείρημα τοιοῦτον· παρὰ τῷ Ὀρφεῖ τέσσαρες βασιλεῖαι παραδίδονται. πρώτη μὲν ἡ τοῦ Οὐρανοῦ, ἣν ὁ Κρόνος διεδέξατο ἐκτεμὼν τὰ αἰδοῖα τοῦ πατρός· μετὰ δὲ τὸν Κρόνον ὁ Ζεὺς ἐβασίλευσεν καταταρταρώσας τὸν πατέρα· εἶτα τὸν Δία διεδέξατο ὁ Διόνυσος, ὅν φασι κατ' ἐπιβουλὴν τῆς Ἥρας τοὺς περὶ αὐτὸν Τιτᾶνας σπαράττειν καὶ τῶν σαρκῶν αὐτοῦ ἀπογεύεσθαι. καὶ τούτους ὀργισθεὶς ὁ Ζεὺς ἐκεραύνωσε, καὶ ἐκ τῆς αἰθάλης τῶν ἀτμῶν τῶν ἀναδοθέντων ἐξ αὐτῶν ὕλης γενομένης γενέσθαι τοὺς ἀνθρώπους. οὐ δεῖ οὖν ἐξάγειν ἡμᾶς ἑαυτούς, οὐχ ὅτι, ὡς δοκεῖ λέγειν ἡ λέξις, διότι ἔν τινι δεσμῷ ἐσμεν τῷ σώματι (τοῦτο γὰρ δῆλόν ἐστι, καὶ οὐκ ἂν τοῦτο ἀπόρρητον ἔλεγεν), ἀλλ' ὅτι οὐ δεῖ ἐξάγειν ἡμᾶς ἑαυτοὺς ὡς τοῦ σώματος ἡμῶν Διονυσιακοῦ ὄντος· μέρος γὰρ αὐτοῦ ἐσμεν, εἴ γε ἐκ τῆς αἰθάλης τῶν Τιτάνων συγκείμεθα γευσαμένων τῶν σαρκῶν τούτου.

[232] See Westerink 1976 on Olympiodorus' dependence on Damascius, as well as Damascius' connection with Proclus' lost commentary.

[233] As Linforth 1941: 350, notes, "It is a curious thing that nowhere else, early or late, is it said or even expressly implied that guilt descended to men in consequence of the outrage committed

Nor does original sin enter into Olympiodorus' interpretation of the myth's meaning. Each narrative element of the myth's vehicle corresponds with an element of meaning in its tenor. The four reigns in the succession of the kingship of heaven correspond to the degrees of virtue a soul can practice. The myth may divide them up in a temporal sequence, but the contemplative, purificatory, civic, and ethical virtues coexist, and the myth's temporal sequence represents the hierarchy of their value.[234] The dismemberment of Dionysos signifies that the ethical and physical virtues are not necessarily consistent with one another. The Titans represent division and particularity, and their chewing of Dionysos is the ultimate degree of breaking down the unity into little particles. Hera provides the motivation for this process of division because "she is the patron deity of motion and procession; hence it is she who, in the *Iliad*, is continually stirring up Zeus and stimulating him to providential care of secondary existents."[235] The lightning of Zeus signifies the reversion of the divided pieces back to the whole, since fire has an upwards motion. Dionysos is the patron of genesis, of the movement into life as well as back out of it, and so this divine process should not be undone by human will in suicide. The god oversees the processes of coming into and out of life, and humans have no right to take control away from the god. Thus, the mythic argument produces the same conclusion as the dialectic: "if it is the gods who are our guardians and whose possessions we are, we should not put an end to our own lives, but leave it to them."[236]

Although it is possible to invent an argument against suicide on the basis of human beings suffering the punishment of the Titans' crime and doomed to suffer even worse punishment by evading life in the prison of the body, Olympiodorus does not make such an argument. Neither the myth as he tells it nor the interpretation he provides of the details includes an idea

upon Dionysos. Even Olympiodorus does not say so." Bernabé extrapolates this episode from the conclusion drawn by Dio's pessimist, that the gods would automatically bear humans a grudge because of their relation to the Titans. To be sure, such a combination of elements by *bricolage* would have been possible for Olympiodorus or some other author, but none of the extant texts actually have it and to assert that it must have been in a missing, secret text is an unfalsifiable hypothesis.

[234] Olymp. *In Phd.* I.4.8–11: οὕτως καὶ παρὰ τῷ Ὀρφεῖ αἱ τέσσαρες βασιλεῖαι αὗται οὐ ποτὲ μέν εἰσι, ποτὲ δὲ οὔ, ἀλλ᾿ ἀεὶ μέν εἰσι, αἰνίττονται δὲ τοὺς διαφόρους βαθμοὺς τῶν ἀρετῶν καθ᾿ ἃς ἡ ἡμετέρα ψυχὴ ἐνεργεῖ σύμβολα ἔχουσα πασῶν τῶν ἀρετῶν, τῶν τε θεωρητικῶν καὶ καθαρτικῶν καὶ πολιτικῶν καὶ ἠθικῶν. Cp. *OF* 10iv B (*Addenda et corrigenda*, vol. 3, p. 444).

[235] Olymp. *In Phd.* I.5.18–20: κατ᾿ ἐπιβουλὴν δὲ τῆς Ἥρας, διότι κινήσεως ἔφορος ἡ θεὸς καὶ προόδου· διὸ καὶ συνεχῶς ἐν τῇ Ἰλιάδι ἐξανίστησιν αὕτη καὶ διεγείρει τὸν Δία εἰς πρόνοιαν τῶν δευτέρων.

[236] Olymp. *In Phd.* I.7: Καὶ τοῦτο μὲν τὸ μυθικὸν ἐπιχείρημα. τὸ δὲ διαλεκτικὸν καὶ φιλόσοφον τοιοῦτόν ἐστιν, ὅτι εἰ θεοὶ ἡμῶν εἰσιν ἐπιμεληταὶ καὶ κτήματα ἐκείνων ἐσμέν, οὐ δεῖ ἐξάγειν ἑαυτούς, ἀλλ᾿ ἐπιτρέπειν ἐκείνοις.

of human beings inheriting the guilt of the Titans' murder of Dionysos. While some scholars admit that Olympiodorus himself never brings up the idea, they nevertheless see him as providing evidence for another text that does include original sin as its central theme, Olympiodorus' source in the *Orphic Rhapsodies*.[237] By a circular argument, the element of original sin not found in Olympiodorus is supplied from an earlier text, even though that earlier text is reconstructed from Olympiodorus.

Bernabé argues that Olympiodorus faithfully reproduces a passage from the *Orphic Rhapsodies*, since some of the details he includes in the narrative correspond with details known from other sources to be in the Orphic poems.[238] The succession of rulers in heaven appears in a number of Orphic works, and the dismemberment story was also certainly treated in at least one Orphic poem. Such correspondences do not, of course, necessarily mean that Olympiodorus did not innovate in his telling of the story, since *bricolage*, the creative manipulation of traditional elements is, after all, the standard operation of the transmission of myth in the Greek mythic tradition. Bernabé assumes that Olympiodorus simply summarized a section of the *Orphic Rhapsodies* without presuming to alter the sacred text in any way – except of course to leave out the essential point at the end in which the guilt of the Titans descends upon mankind. Such an omission is taken as unproblematic, since it is the only logical conclusion to be drawn from the story. On this interpretation, Olympiodorus replaces this natural conclusion with his Neoplatonic allegorizing, which can be disregarded by modern scholars as inauthentic and thus without any influence on the narrative of the myth itself.

I argue, to the contrary, that we cannot neglect the interrelation of Olympiodorus' interpretation and his telling of the story, since the meaning he sees in the story directly affects the elements he chooses to include. The assumption that Olympiodorus' source is a single text which he summarizes without alteration is likewise unfounded; Olympiodorus refers to a whole mythic tradition associated with Orpheus rather than a single text, and some of his most important sources are the commentaries of his

---

[237] Cp. West 1983: 166: "Although Olympiodorus' interpretation of the Orphic myth is to be rejected, there is no denying that the poet may have drawn some conclusion from it about man's nature; . . . any such conclusion is likely to have concerned the burdens of our inheritance." The hypothetical nature of the element of inherited guilt in the narrative is revealed by the verb – "may have drawn."

[238] Bernabé 2003: 28: "Le résumé de ce qui était narré dans le poème orphique semble être assez fidèle. En effet, en ce qui concerne les autres détails du paragraphe, que l'on peut relever aussi dans d'autres sources, Olympiodore concorde avec d'autres citations, directes même, rapportées aux Rhapsodies. Il n'y a donc pas de raison valable de douter que la dernière affirmation soit aussi fidèle à la source que les autres."

Academic predecessors, Proclus and Damascius, rather than the particular texts attributed to Orpheus. Olympiodorus indeed shows himself willing to adapt the Orphic materials to his philosophic points, especially when those points have a precedent in the commentaries of his predecessors.

Olympiodorus begins his narration with a reference to the Orphic tradition (παρὰ τῷ Ὀρφεῖ . . . παραδίδονται), not with a quotation from an Orphic text. The imprecision of his reference is reinforced by his use of φασι, "they say," to continue his narrative. The indeterminate third person plural indicates that Olympiodorus is not citing or even summarizing a single text, but rather referring to the way the story is traditionally told. Olympiodorus situates his own retelling of the story within the mythic tradition, providing his account with the authority of that tradition.[239] However, his reference to four reigns in the succession of the kingship of heaven actually contradicts other accounts, surviving in Proclus and elsewhere, of six reigns.[240] As Westerink notes, Olympiodorus is drawing on the commentaries of Damascius and Proclus, but his identification of each of the reigns with a class of virtues shapes his telling.[241] Olympiodorus is clearly making use of Damascius' discussion of the virtues in his *Phaedo* commentary (1.138–151), although Damascius includes more classes of virtues, separating the ethical from the physical virtues and putting the paradigmatic and hieratic virtues above the contemplative. Westerink suggests that Olympiodorus may be following Ammonius in eliminating the paradigmatic and hieratic virtues as a way of devaluing theurgic practice in relation to philosophic contemplation, since these virtues could have been identified with the Orphic reigns of Phanes and Night if Olympiodorus had been concerned to stay as close as possible to the text of Orpheus.[242]

---

[239] Cp. Aristotle's advice (*Rh.* 2.21.11) for the orator to use mythic exempla to support his point, "For because they are common, they seem to be correct, since everyone agrees upon them." διὰ γὰρ τὸ εἶναι κοιναί, ὡς ὁμολογούντων πάντων, ὀρθῶς ἔχειν δοκοῦσιν.

[240] Cp. ch. 5 n. 40. Plato provides the earliest reference to the six reigns in *Phlb.* 66c8–9. As I argue above, Bernabé collects all nine quotations of this line in *OF* 25 B, but, when one examines the context of each fragment, it is clear that none of them refer directly to a sequence of divine generations. Plato is referring to elements of the good, describing pure and harmless pleasures as the fifth element; *OF* 25ii B = Plut. *De E* 391d refers to the same in a treatise on the number five. Damascius quotes the line several times but never in reference to generations of gods. In *OF* 25iv B = *in Phileb.* 251, he is just citing the Philebus passage. The other references (*OF* 25v B = *De princ.* 53, *OF* 25vi B = *in Parm.* 199, *OF* 25vii B = *in Parm.* 253, *OF* 25viii B = *in Parm.* 278; *OF* 25ix B = *in Parm.* 381) are all just making a list of six arguments. Proclus (*In R.* 2.100.23 = *OF* 25iii B) lists the hierarchy of entities in the myth of Er: Ananke and Fates, Sirens, celestial gods, guardian *daimones*, judges, and punishing *daimones*, but even this list of divine beings is not a theogonic sequence of generations.

[241] Westerink 1976: 40–41.

[242] Westerink 1976: 41. He cites Ammon. *in Int.* 135.19–32 and Phlp. *in Cat.* 141.25–142.3 for testimonies to Ammonius' scale of virtues.

However, only four reigns are needed to make Olympiodorus' point, so he has no compunction about jettisoning the first two of Proclus' six from his narration.

Olympiodorus takes fewer liberties with the next section of his narrative, although he still makes significant choices of what traditional elements to exclude from his retelling of the dismemberment. He mentions only the Titans, Dionysos, and Hera, leaving out Apollo, the Kouretes, and Athena. These other deities often play a role in the dismemberment narrative, for example in Clement's version, but Olympiodorus has no place for them in his interpretation, so he omits them.[243] Each of the elements he chooses to include not only has precedent in the traditional mythic narratives but also meaning within the preceding interpretive tradition.

The most obvious are the figures of the Titans and Dionysos, which have a long history of interpretation in terms of the Many and the One. The Titans represent the forces of division that make many particulars out of the original one.[244] Damascius suggests, in his commentary on this same section of the *Phaedo*, that the connection with the Titans and Dionysos goes back to Xenokrates in the early Academy, since Xenokrates explained the φρουρά mentioned in the *Phaedo* as being Titanic and culminating in Dionysos.[245] The sojourn in the body, whether it be understood simply as imprisonment, or more positively as garrison duty in the dangerous

---

[243] In contrast to, e.g., Procl. *In Ti.* 2.145.18 Diehl (*ad* 35a) (*OF* 314i B = OF 210 K), who includes Athena in the story as the one who preserves the heart of the dismembered Dionysos, signifying the divine providence (πρόνοια) that oversees the restoration of unity in the process of division. Athena's Delphic epithet of Pronaia was frequently allegorized to make Athena, goddess of wisdom, the representative of divine providence, Pronoia. Athena appears as Minerva in Firmicus Maternus' euhemerizing version (*De err. prof. relig.* 6.3 [*OF* 314iv B = OF 214 K]).

[244] The idea that the Titans are the ancestors of all living things because of the creation of the multiplicity of the material world from their remains appears in a number of texts, e.g., Procl. *In R.* 2.338.10–339.9 Kroll (*OF* 338 B = OF 224 K): "For does not Orpheus transmit such ideas clearly, when after the mythical punishment of the Titans and the genesis of all mortal living things from them he says first that souls pass from one life to another according to certain revolutions and various souls enter into various bodies, often those of humans." ἢ οὐχὶ καὶ Ὀρφεὺς τὰ τοιαῦτα σαφῶς παραδίδωσιν, ὅταν μετὰ τὴν τῶν Τιτάνων μυθικὴν δίκην καὶ τὴν ἐξ ἐκείνων γένεσιν τῶν θνητῶν τούτων ζῴων λέγῃ πρῶτον μέν, ὅτι τοὺς βίους ἀμείβουσιν αἱ ψυχαὶ κατὰ δή τινας περιόδους καὶ εἰσδύονται ἄλλαι εἰς ἄλλα σώματα πολλάκις ἀνθρώπων. Cp. *OH* 37.4–5: "origin and fount of all much-suffering mortal creatures, | those in the sea and winged in the air and who dwell on the earth" ἀρχαὶ καὶ πηγαὶ πάντων θνητῶν πολυμόχθων, | εἰναλίων πτηνῶν τε καὶ οἳ χθόνα ναιετάουσιν. See discussion of this idea in Plutarch and Damascius above in *Misreading the Eating*.

[245] Xenokrates fr. 219 Isnardi Parente = Dam. *In Phd.* 1.2 (29 Westerink) (*OF* 38i B): "We are in some kind of custody" ἔν τινι φρουρᾷ ἐσμεν (*Phd.* 62b): "Using these principles, we shall easily prove that 'the custody' is not the Good, as some say, nor pleasure, as Noumenios would have it, nor the Demiurge, as Paterios says, but rather, as Xenokrates has it, that it is Titanic and culminates in Dionysos." Ὅτι τούτοις χρώμενοι τοῖς κανόσι ῥᾳδίως διελέγξομεν, ὡς οὔτε τἀγαθόν ἐστιν ἡ φρουρά, ὥς τινες, οὔτε ἡ ἡδονή, ὡς Νουμήνιος, οὔτε ὁ δημιουργός, ὡς Πατέριος, ἀλλ', ὡς

frontier of the material world, or even as protective custody by provident and benevolent gods, is in any case a period in which the individual is separated from the whole, the unity of divine perfection.[246] Olympiodorus thus follows the precedent of Proclus and Damascius when he etymologizes the name of the Titans from the indefinite pronoun τι to emphasize their connection with the particular. "And he is torn apart by the Titans, of whom the something (τι) denotes the particular, for the universal form is broken up in genesis."[247] Likewise, Olympiodorus' designation of Dionysos as the overseer of the world of genesis is in keeping with the place of Dionysos in Proclus and Damascius as the monad of a demiurgic manifold.

It is worth noting the absence of Apollo from the narrative at this point, since Apollo is often mentioned in connection with Dionysos as the one responsible for gathering his scattered limbs, reintegrating his divided self.[248] While the connection between Dionysos and Apollo in Delphic ritual may have some part in the transmission of Apollo's role in the story, Apollo is generally included when the narrator of the story wants to emphasize the reintegration process and left out when only the process of division is important for the point.[249]

Hera, on the other hand, is not always mentioned in the retelling of the dismemberment of Dionysos, but Olympiodorus includes her because

Ξενοκράτης, Τιτανική ἐστιν καὶ εἰς Διόνυσον ἀποκορυφοῦται. This passage, like the allusion in Dio Chrys. 30.10–11 (OF 429iii, 320vii B), shows that other ways of interpreting the φρουρά were current, aside from the dismemberment story. Xenokrates must have related the dismemberment story in terms of the One and the Many, since Damascius nearly always uses ἀποκορυφοῦται (and κορυφή) to refer to the process of making (or returning to) a single, undivided one out of many (cp. Dam. In Prm. 213 = 94.26 Ruelle and 213 = 95.9 Ruelle; De princ. 2 [1.2.24 Westerink = 1.2.19 Ruelle], 2 [1.5.15 Westerink = 1.5.1 Ruelle], 4 [1.7.16 Westerink = 1.6.17 Ruelle] and many others).

[246] Cp. Boyancé 1963, as well as Westerink 1977: 28. Iambl. De an. ap. Stob. Flor. 1.49.32 (1.366.17 Wachsmuth) (OF 421vi B = OF 27 K) provides an overview of various reasons for the soul's descent into the body, which span the range from harsh imprisonment in the body for past crimes to altruistic concern for other souls.

[247] In Phd. 1.5.11–13: καὶ ὑπὸ τῶν Τιτάνων σπαράττεται, τοῦ "τί" μερικὸν δηλοῦντος, σπαράττεται δὲ τὸ καθόλου εἶδος ἐν τῇ γενέσει. Westerink 1976: 44 compares Procl. In Crat. 62.3 Pasquali (OF 240i B = OF 129 K), In R. 1.90.9–13 Kroll, and Dam. De princ. 57 (11.52.20–23 Westerink = 1.120.1–5 Ruelle) .

[248] Cp. Dam. In Phd. 1.129 (81 Westerink) (OF 309ii, 322ii B = OF 209 K): ὅτι τὰ ὅμοια μυθεύεται καὶ ἐν τῷ παραδείγματι. ὁ γὰρ Διόνυσος, ὅτε τὸ εἴδωλον ἐνέθηκε τῷ ἐσόπτρῳ, τούτῳ ἐφέσπετο καὶ οὕτως εἰς τὸ πᾶν ἐμερίσθη. ὁ δὲ Ἀπόλλων συναγείρει τε αὐτὸν καὶ ἀνάγει καθαρτικὸς ὢν θεὸς καὶ τοῦ Διονύσου σωτὴρ ὡς ἀληθῶς, καὶ διὰ τοῦτο Διονυσοδότης ἀνυμνεῖται.

[249] See West 1983: 150–152, for a discussion of the possible role of Delphic cult. Olympiodorus himself mentions Apollo when it suits his purpose later in the commentary, when he refers to the well-known Orphic myth that concludes with Apollo making Dionysos back into a unity. Olymp. In Phd. 7.10.5–7 (OF 291i, 311vii, 322iii B = OF 211 K): πῶς δὲ ἄρα οὐ τὰ Ὀρφικὰ ἐκεῖνα παρῳδεῖ νῦν ὁ Πλάτων, ὅτι ὁ Διόνυσος σπαράττεται μὲν ὑπὸ τῶν Τιτάνων, ἑνοῦται δὲ ὑπὸ τοῦ Ἀπόλλωνος;

of her meaning within the Neoplatonic interpretive tradition. Despite his explicit claim, Hera is not "in the *Iliad*, continually stirring up Zeus and stimulating him to providential care of secondary existents."[250] On the contrary, she is continually trying to prevent Zeus from intervening in the war and from exercising some sort of providential care over the particular secondary existents, the Trojans, whom she wants destroyed. However, as Westerink points out, Olympiodorus' claim refers not to the well-known text of the *Iliad*, but rather to Proclus' allegorical interpretation of one scene, Hera's seduction of Zeus on Mt. Ida.[251] In his allegorical interpretation of the infamously scandalous story of lust among the gods, Proclus reads the scene as the creative union of the One and the Secondary Principle, in which the Secondary Principle gets the One to begin the process that creates all things. Olympiodorus, therefore, like Proclus and other Neoplatonic interpreters, and indeed like other myth retellers and interpreters in the Greek mythic tradition, shows no compunction about altering the details or meaning even of a text as well-known as the *Iliad* in the service of his argument. For these transmitters of the mythic tradition, the essence of the myth lies in its meaning, its tenor, rather than the details of any textual vehicle, however prestigious.

Olympiodorus' focus on the meaning rather than the narrative of the traditional tale helps explain his innovations in the final parts of the myth, since his selection of details stems from the point he is trying to make with his mythic argument. Olympiodorus recounts that Zeus blasted the Titans with lightning and then created the human race from the remains. The lightning of Zeus is, after all, his standard weapon of punishment, and several versions of the dismemberment story do in fact include the blasting of the Titans by lightning.[252]

However, as Damascius notes, there are three punishments recounted in the tradition for the Titans for their various crimes: lightning, shackles, and Tartarosis.[253] Different tellings of the myths of the Titans' crimes (be it the revolt against the gods in the Titanomachy or the dismemberment of Dionysos or even Prometheus' theft of fire) made use of different punishments or combinations of punishments. Although some scholars have assumed that the blasting of the Titans after their cannibalism must have

---

[250] *In Phd.* 1.5.18–20: κατ' ἐπιβουλὴν δὲ τῆς "Ηρας, διότι κινήσεως ἔφορος ἡ θεὸς καὶ προόδου· διὸ καὶ συνεχῶς ἐν τῇ Ἰλιάδι ἐξανίστησιν αὕτη καὶ διεγείρει τὸν Δία εἰς πρόνοιαν τῶν δευτέρων.

[251] Westerink 1976: 45–46. Procl. *In R.* 1.132.13–136.14 Kroll.

[252] E.g., Plut. *De esu carn.* 1.996c (*OF* 313i B = OF 210 K); Clem. Al. *Protr.* 2.18; Arn. *Adv. nat.* 5.19 (273.14 Marchesi) (*OF* 318vii B = OF 34 K).

[253] Dam. *In Phd.* 1.7 (33 Westerink) (*OF* 178iv, 235ii, 318iv B); see above n. 225 and further below.

been the final event in the career of the Titans, this presumption, though specious, is not borne out by the evidence. As I have shown, the Titans survived the episode in some versions, being cast down into Tartaros and then later released. In one reference to the dismemberment story "as told by the theologians" (i.e., the Orphic versions), Proclus refers to the various lots of punishment that the other Titans received when Atlas was stationed to hold up the heavens on his back.[254] Arnobius' version of the Titans' punishment for the dismemberment includes not only lightning but also Tartarosis: "Jupiter, drawn in by the sweetness of the smells, rushed unbidden to the feast, and, discovering what had been done, overwhelmed the feasters with his terrible thunder and hurled them down to the lowest places of Tartarus."[255] In Nonnos, Zeus imprisons the Titans in Tartaros and then blasts the Earth with lightning, creating an ekpyrosis followed by a deluge.[256]

The same punishments of lightning, binding, and Tartarosis appear in versions of the Titanomachy, from Hesiod to the Neoplatonic citations of the Orphica. Scholars have tried to sort out the varying references into a consistent storyline, assigning the Tartarosis to the Titanomachy and the lightning to the dismemberment and putting the Titanomachy before the dismemberment, but such solutions presume not only that the Neoplatonists citing the Orphic accounts were summarizing the Rhapsodic version without altering any details but also that the *Orphic Rhapsodies* themselves presented a single consistent version. But, West's elegant reconstruction notwithstanding, we have no evidence that the *Rhapsodies* presented a single, coherent and internally consistent version rather than a collection of different Orphic works that may have alluded to or narrated the episode in a variety of ways.[257]

Olympiodorus chooses lightning as the punishment for the Titans in his story, rather than following the version Proclus cites, and he adds

---

[254] See n. 226 above.

[255] Arn. Adv. nat. 5.19 (273.9 Marchesi) (OF 312iii B = OF 34 K): *Iuppiter suavitate odoris inlectus, invocatus advolarit ad prandium compertaque re gravi grassatores obruerit fulmine atque in imas Tartari praecipitaverit sedes.*

[256] Nonnos, *Dion.* 6.205–210. In 48.1–89, Nonnos also has the Gigantomachy, which he casts as an explicit attempt to redo the death of Zagreus (48.25–29). Note that Dionysos in this episode uses a torch to incinerate the Giants as a parallel for his father's lightning.

[257] Even Damascius' claim (*De princ.* 123 [III.159.17 Westerink = I.316–317 Ruelle] [*OF* 90, 96, 109viii, 114viii, 677i B = OT 223d, OF 60 K]) that the *Rhapsodies* present the familiar Orphic theology (ἡ συνήθης Ὀρφικὴ θεολογία) does not presume a single consistent version or exclude references elsewhere in the *Rhapsodies* to versions that differ in details. West 1983 assumes consistency in the *Rhapsodies* at various points in his argument, but never argues for this hypothesis. See above, ch. 5, *The nature of the Rhapsodic collection.*

an anthropogony to the story of the dismemberment. The generation of human beings from the remains of the gods' enemies after their battle against the gods (whether Titanomachy or Gigantomachy) is, as we have seen, a familiar theme in the mythic tradition.[258] However, no other extant source explicitly connects the dismemberment crime of the Titans with the anthropogony, so Olympiodorus must either be following some version no longer extant or he must be innovating, combining mythic elements in a way that they have not been combined in the extant references. Given the gaps in our sources, the missing text hypothesis is always possible, but there are good reasons why Olympiodorus might innovate by combining the elements of dismemberment and anthropogony, blending the stories of the Titans' two great crimes and their aftermaths.

First of all, Olympiodorus can mix the two stories because they both, in the Neoplatonic interpretive tradition, have the same meaning. The Titans stand always for the forces of division, separating the elements of the cosmos and promoting the process of genesis. Whether they are waging open battle or committing secret murder, they are in these myths opposing the gods, who represent the divine perfection of unity. Proclus provides precisely this interpretation of the myths in a passage in his commentary on the *Republic* in which he links the two myths.

> Whence, I think, they say both that the Titans struggle against Dionysos and that the Giants struggle against Zeus. For to the gods, as craftsmen as it were of the cosmos, pertains the unification and the undivided creation and the wholeness before the division, but the latter propel into multiplicity the creative powers and they manage in a divided fashion the things in the universe and they are moreover the fathers of material things.[259]

For Proclus and those in his interpretive tradition, the Gigantomachy/Titanomachy myth really signifies this process of division and creation that is bounded by the unifying power of the gods, just as the story of the dismemberment of Dionysos is really another way of expressing the same idea.[260] Whereas Proclus equates two distinct stories, the Gigantomachy and the dismemberment, Damascius simply lumps

---

[258] Above, *The blood of the earthborn*.

[259] Procl. *In R.* 1.90.7–13 Kroll: ὅθεν οἶμαι καὶ τοὺς Τιτᾶνας τῷ Διονύσῳ καὶ Διὶ τοὺς Γίγαντας ἀνταγωνίζεσθαί φασιν· τοῖς μὲν γὰρ ὡς πρὸ τοῦ κόσμου δημιουργοῖς ἥ τε ἕνωσις προσήκει καὶ ἡ ἀμέριστος ποίησις καὶ ἡ πρὸ τῶν μερῶν ὁλότης, οἳ δὲ εἰς πλῆθος προάγουσιν τὰς δημιουργικὰς δυνάμεις καὶ μεμερισμένως διοικοῦσιν τὰ ἐν τῷ παντὶ καὶ προσεχεῖς εἰσιν πατέρες τῶν ἐνύλων πραγμάτων.

[260] Cp. Alex. Lyc. *Tractatus de placitis Manichaeorum* 5.10–14 (5.74 Brinkmann) (*OF* 311xi B): τὴν θείαν δύναμιν μερίζεσθαι εἰς τὴν ὕλην· ἐκ δὲ τῶν ποιητῶν τῆς Γιγαντομαχίας, ὅτι μηδὲ αὐτοὶ ἤγνοσαν τὴν τῆς ὕλης κατὰ τοῦ θεοῦ ἄνταρσιν.

together all the stories of the Titans related in the mythic tradition. He notes that three punishments are traditionally recounted for the Titans, lightning, shackles, and descents into lower regions, although he only associates the anthropogony with the last, the descent into lower regions, i.e., Tartarosis.

> Three punishments of the Titans are handed down in the tradition – lightning, shackles, descents into various lower regions. This last one is thus in the nature of a retribution, exacerbating their divisive nature and making use of their shattered remains for the constitution of individual entities, particularly humans. The middle one is coercive, holding back their divisive powers. The first is purificatory, bringing them to unity through participation. It is necessary, however, to regard all three as imposed upon each, even if the myth divides them up.[261]

Again, like Olympiodorus, Damascius is not quoting from a particular Orphic text, he is providing an overview of the mythic tradition and arguing that all the stories about the punishment of the Titans have the same meaning. Elsewhere in his argument, Damascius does make direct quotations of Orphic poems, specifically at the beginning and the end (I.4 and I.11). These two quotations, however, are designed to illustrate specific points while at the same time lending the authority of Orpheus to the whole of the argument, a common tactic in the Greek mythic tradition. Plato's quotation of Homer in his descriptions of the Underworld in his myths in the *Gorgias* and *Phaedo* provide particularly apt parallels for Damascius here. In each case, Plato brings in a single line of Homer to suggest that his description of the Underworld is as familiar (and thus authoritative) as Homer's, while nevertheless making radical innovations. Moreover, the descriptions of Minos giving judgments among the dead in the *Gorgias* (523e) or of Tartaros as a deep pit in the *Phaedo* (112ad) do not actually have the same meaning in Plato's myths as they did in Homer – Plato makes Minos the judge of newly arriving souls instead of the arbiter of disputes among the dead and his vision of Tartaros as a swirling, breathing whirlpool is far from the empty pit of Homer.[262] Damascius likewise makes use of an idea from an authoritative poet without either

---

[261] Dam. *In Phd.* 1.7 (33 Westerink) (*OF* 178iv, 235ii, 318iv B): ὅτι τριτταὶ παραδέδονται τῶν Τιτάνων κολάσεις· κεραυνώσεις, δεσμοί, ἄλλων ἀλλαχοῦ πρόοδοι πρὸς τὸ κοιλότερον. αὕτη μὲν οὖν οἷον τιμωρίας ἐπέχει τάξιν, ἐπιτρίβουσα αὐτῶν τὸ διαιρετικὸν καὶ ἀποχρωμένη τῷ κερματισμῷ αὐτῶν εἰς σύστασιν τῶν ἀτόμων ἄλλων τε καὶ ἀνθρώπων· ἡ δὲ μέση κολαστική, τὰς διαιρετικὰς ἐπέχουσα δυνάμεις· ἡ δὲ πρώτη καθαρτική, ὀλίζουσα αὐτοὺς κατὰ μέθεξιν. δεῖ δὲ περὶ ἕκαστον τὰς τρεῖς θεωρεῖν, εἰ καὶ ὁ μῦθος μερίζει·

[262] For Plato's use of Homer (and other sources), cp. Edmonds 2004a: 171–220.

keeping to the limits of the original text or necessarily preserving the poet's meaning.

Thus, although Bernabé cites this section of Damascius as evidence for an Orphic myth that contained the dismemberment, the anthropogony, and the idea of punishment for Titanic guilt, we can neither construct a narrative sequence in which these punishments occurred nor identify a particular narrative as the source of all these mythic elements. The myth may divide up these punishments into different stories, as retributions at different times or for different crimes, but they are all complementary, providing the same meaning for the myth.

There can be no doubt, however, that Damascius associates, not lightning, but the descent into Tartaros with the creation of human beings. In the above passage, Damascius lists the three punishments – lightning, shackles, and Tartarosis – and then discusses them in reverse order – Tartarosis, shackles, and lightning. Descent into the lower regions is equivalent to creation from fragments, shackles to coercive restraint, and lightning to purification. He expands his discussion of the punishments in the next few paragraphs, following this reversed order – Tartarosis in 1.8–9, shackles in 1.10, and purification in 1.11.[263] In the context of this procedure, he explains the creation of human beings from the fragments of the Titans as the ultimate in the process of division (εἰς ἔσχατον μερισμόν), since these entities are the lowest of the creative powers, the bottom link in the chain that connects the created materials with the divine creator. The details of the myth, that humans are created from the most divided particles of the dead bodies of the Titans, merely serve to emphasize the extreme of the process of division which the myth indicates, transferring the divided nature of human life to the extremely divided condition of the Titans.[264] To live a Titanic life, therefore, is to behave in such a manner that exacerbates the divided condition of life.

---

[263] Bernabé's abbreviation of Damascius (Bernabé 2002a: 406–408, T2) is particularly misleading in this case, since he retains only the elements (dismemberment, punishment of the Titans, and anthropogony) that he sees as the crucial sequence, without regard for their context or relation to one another. Cp. Bernabé 2003: 28.

[264] Dam. *In Phd.* 1.8 (33 Westerink) (*OF* 320iv B): Πῶς ἐκ Τιτανικῶν θρυμμάτων οἱ ἄνθρωποι γίνονται; Ἢ ἐκ μὲν τῶν θρυμμάτων, ὡς ἀπεστενωμένοι τὴν ζωὴν εἰς ἔσχατον μερισμόν· ἐκ δὲ τῶν Τιτανικῶν, ὡς ἐσχάτων δημιουργῶν καὶ τοῖς δημιουργήμασι προσεχεστάτων. ὁ μὲν γὰρ Ζεὺς "πατὴρ ἀνδρῶν καὶ θεῶν", οἱ δὲ ἀνθρώπων μόνων ἀλλ' οὐχὶ καὶ θεῶν, καὶ οὐκέτι πατέρες ἀλλὰ αὐτοί, οὐδὲ αὐτοὶ ἁπλῶς ἀλλὰ τεθνεῶτες, καὶ οὐδὲ τοῦτο μόνον ἀλλὰ καὶ συντεθρυμμένοι· ὁ γὰρ τοιοῦτος τρόπος τῆς ὑποστάσεως εἰς τοὺς αἰτίους ἀναπέμπεται. *Contra* Bernabé, the identification of the Titans as not the fathers of human beings, but they themselves (οὐκέτι πατέρες ἀλλὰ αὐτοί) should not be taken to imply the reincarnation of Titans into human forms, as the next phrase shows. It is the material of the dead bodies that provides the identification, not the reincarnation of the soul.

As Damascius asserts, "the Titanic mode of life is the irrational mode, by which rational life is torn asunder."[265] For Damascius, therefore, the meaning of the myth is that leading the irrational life breaks up the natural continuity of our being (τὸ ὁμοφυὲς εἶδος) and the partnership with the superior and inferior (οἶον κοινωνικὸν πρὸς τὰ κρείττω καὶ ἥττω), i.e., the links that bind the unity together. Acting like Titans is irrational and divisive to the self; acting in a unifying manner is to be like Dionysos. Damascius continues the allegory when he claims that "while in this condition [i.e., irrational and divided], we are Titans; but when we recover that lost unity, we become Dionysoi, having become thoroughly perfected." Nowhere in this exegesis is there a doctrine of a Titanic element and a Dionysiac element mixed into human nature by the creation of humankind from the Titans' remains. Rather, Damascius applies the general principle of division, which, as he points out, is everywhere (πανταχοῦ), to human life and behavior.

Olympiodorus takes the process of blending the stories Proclus identifies as having the same meaning one step further than Damascius; instead of just talking about all of the tales of the Titans' punishment as one idea, Olympiodorus actually recounts a version that blends the crime of the dismemberment with the anthropogony that sometimes follows on the crime of the revolt against the gods and then provides the exegesis of his myth. Olympiodorus, like Damascius, provides both an individual, ethical meaning for the myth and a theological, cosmological meaning, but Olympiodorus needs to provide a different angle on the problem than his predecessors, so he comes up with interpretations that are rather strange even among Neoplatonic allegorical exegeses.

The idea that bodies are simply a φρουρά for souls, a shackle or prison for individuals separated from the divine unity, is too obvious for Olympiodorus; the true meaning must be something more difficult to understand in order for Socrates to refer to it as an inexpressible mystery, ἀπόρρητον. Olympiodorus constructs an argument that makes suicide forbidden, not because of the nature of the soul and its punishment, but because of the nature of the body itself. If the Titans from whom the human body is created consumed Dionysos, then the human body itself must partake of

---

[265] Dam. *In Phd.* 1.9 (33 Westerink) : Ὅτι ἡ Τιτανικὴ ζωὴ ἄλογός ἐστιν, ὑφ᾽ ἧς ἡ λογικὴ σπαράττεται. Κάλλιον δὲ πανταχοῦ ποιεῖν αὐτήν, ἀπὸ θεῶν γε ἀρχομένην τῶν Τιτάνων· καὶ τοίνυν τῆς λογικῆς τὸ δοκοῦν αὐτεξούσιον καὶ οἶον ἑαυτοῦ βουλόμενον εἶναι μόνου, οὔτε δὲ τῶν κρειττόνων οὔτε τῶν χειρόνων, τοῦτο ἡμῖν οἱ Τιτᾶνες ἐμποιοῦσιν, καθ᾽ ὃ καὶ τὸν ἐν ἡμῖν Διόνυσον διασπῶμεν, παραθραύοντες ἡμῶν τὸ ὁμοφυὲς εἶδος καὶ οἶον κοινωνικὸν πρὸς τὰ κρείττω καὶ ἥττω. οὕτω δὲ ἔχοντες Τιτᾶνές ἐσμεν· ὅταν δὲ εἰς ἐκεῖνο συμβῶμεν, Διόνυσοι γινόμεθα τετελειωμένοι ἀτεχνῶς.

the divine. As Linforth comments, "It is an audacious conjecture, because nothing could be more extraordinary than that a Platonist or Neoplatonist should locate the divine element which is in man anywhere but in the soul."[266]

Olympiodorus' audacity may simply be due to his desire to provide something new in a long tradition of Platonic commentary on the φρουρά, but he may also have more complicated reasons for his argument about the composition of humans. As Brisson has argued, Olympiodorus may be making an alchemical allegory in his recounting of the myth, in addition to the ethical and cosmological allegories.[267] The descriptions of the fire of Zeus' lightning blasting the Titans and of the particles produced out of the smoke that become the material for the creation of mankind, Brisson suggests, lend themselves to interpretation in alchemical terms. If fire (lightning) is applied to lime (ἄσβεστος), then a sublimate (αἰθάλη) appears as solid particles falling from the smoke (ἀτμός). This sublimate (αἰθάλη) may be identified with the ever-fresh (ἀειθαλής) spirit (πνεῦμα) that animates a human being. Lime is identified etymologically with the Titans and symbolically with Dionysos, so the application of fire to the combination (the Titans stuffed with morsels of Dionysos) alchemically produces the human being. Bernabé points out that αἰθάλη usually has the simple meaning of soot or ash, rather than the technical meaning of the solid particles that fall as a sublimate from the fumes released by the process of burning.[268] Soot, however, is merely the most common, general form of such a sublimate, and the fact that the word has a general meaning in no way precludes it from being used in a technical sense. Indeed, for an interpreter like Olympiodorus, taking a common word in a technical and esoteric sense is precisely the way to discern the hidden, allegorical meaning.[269]

Of course, without further evidence, it is impossible to prove that Olympiodorus is making such an alchemical allegory, but it is equally impossible to disprove, and the hypothesis serves to explain the peculiar innovation that Olympiodorus makes in arguing for the divinity of the body. So too, even if αἰθάλη is a common word, it seems unnecessarily circuitous to refer to the soot from the smoke, ἐκ τῆς αἰθάλης τῶν ἀτμῶν, rather than

---

[266] Linforth 1941: 330.   [267] Brisson 1992: 493–494.   [268] Bernabé 2003: 27–28.
[269] The debate over whether Olympiodorus the sixth-century CE commentator on the *Phaedo* was the same as the sixth-century CE alchemical author does not really help resolve the issue, except insofar as the fact that it was plausible to attribute the alchemical works to the philosopher suggests that our commentator might have had familiarity with the terminology, whether or not he wrote the extant treatises.

simply refer to the ashes of the corpses. The alchemical hypothesis also serves to explain why Olympiodorus is the only evidence for an anthropogony from the ashes of the enemies of the gods instead of the blood. Bernabé himself admits that Olympiodorus' evidence produces uncertainty whether the *Orphic Rhapsodies* narrated the generation of humans from the blood or the ashes of the Titans, an unresolvable dilemma if it is presumed that Olympiodorus could not be innovating this detail for purposes of his own.[270]

Even if the alchemical allegory were to be rejected as too bizarre even for Olympiodorus, the version of the dismemberment story that Olympiodorus relates nevertheless seems to be the product of careful and deliberate manipulation of the mythic tradition, rather than the mindless preservation of a single text. Olympiodorus repeatedly demonstrates his willingness to alter the details and meanings of previous tellings in order to construct his arguments, and his combination of the dismemberment of Dionysos and the creation of human beings from the remains of the Titans is without precedent in the evidence. Olympiodorus' peculiar recounting of the myth of the dismemberment cannot be taken as evidence for a canonical Orphic tale of the generation of human beings from the ashes of the Titans. Not only is Olympiodorus' tale clearly not a precise reproduction of a single, standard Orphic text, but even if it were, the myth still does not include the dual Titanic and Dionysiac elements of human nature or any burden of guilt passed to humans, a stain of that original sin they all share. The innovative conclusion of Olympiodorus' tale, the anthropogony from the soot of the Titans, should not be read back into other tellings of the dismemberment story, since Olympiodorus chose to connect the dismemberment and the anthropogony for specific reasons, to make particular points within his argument. Such an innovation was made possible by the interpretations of the dismemberment, the Titanomachy, and the punishment of the Titans within the context of the Neoplatonic interpretive tradition, developing from Proclus to Damascius to Olympiodorus.

Olympiodorus' mythic argument against suicide is a fascinating filament within the wild and often gaudy tapestry of Neoplatonic myths. Careful analysis of the way Olympiodorus makes use of previous tellings of the myth of dismemberment as well as of the allegorical readings of the dismemberment and other myths provides insight into the relation of

---

[270] Bernabé 2004: 264: *incertum utrum in Rhapsodiis homines a Titanum cineribus (ut enarravit Olympiodor.) an ab eorum sanguine (ut Dion, Iulian, Ti. Perinth.) orti sint; probabiliter ab ambobus.* Cp. the attempts of Linforth 1941: 328–331 and West 1983: 164–166 to resolve the dilemma.

late antique thinkers to the Greek mythic tradition, suggesting that even a sixth-century pagan living in an increasingly Christian world could engage in the same kind of serious play with the mythic tradition as Plato had a millennium earlier, brewing up a curious concoction of his own from the familiar materials to suit his arguments.

CHAPTER TEN

Conclusions
Redefining ancient Orphism

Blunting Occam's Razor: Some methodological considerations

"There is always an easy solution to every human problem – neat, plausible and wrong."

(H. L. Mencken, "The Divine Afflatus", *New York Evening Mail*, 16 November 1917)

Why should scholars of Greek religion unravel the web so carefully woven by previous scholars that binds together all the messy threads of evidence that pertains to Orpheus? Surely a category of Orphism defined by a nucleus of doctrines provides a neat solution to the difficulties of evidence ranging over a thousand years of Greek culture, and defining Orphism by its doctrines seems to modern scholars the most plausible way of understanding a religion or "religious current." Everything that is reminiscent of such doctrines can be classified as "Orphic" or influenced by "Orphic ideas," which permits the collection of a large body of evidence and its arrangement in terms of such ideas. By contrast, a category of "Orphic" that relies on vague cues whose validity varies over time seems to provide an amorphous object of study that is at times indistinguishable from the background of Greek religion. Defining Orphism by its doctrines and relating those doctrines to a single aetiological myth seems to provide a much simpler solution with fewer variables; surely Occam's razor requires that scholars prefer the hypothesis that involves less complication? Why should we pick apart this web of Penelope that has been so carefully woven in the last hundred years of scholarship to provide a neat and plausible solution? Why should we instead accept a messy and complicated answer that leaves many pieces of evidence incompletely explained?

The first response to such a question is that the hypothesis of an Orphism defined by a nucleus of doctrines does not, in fact, accurately explain the data but requires divorcing the evidence from its contexts, both the immediate textual contexts and the larger context of Greek religion. More-over, the idea that a single myth could retain a soteriological meaning throughout all its uses and re-uses runs counter to the dynamic nature of Greek religion, which continually reshapes the traditional mythic and ritual elements to create new significance. The Greek religious tradition lacks the kinds of social structures and institutions needed to maintain the continuity of religious doctrines over the centuries from which the evidence comes, and only the fragmentary state of the evidence makes imagining a continuous current of religious doctrine and practice possible for those scholars who assume doctrines must provide the basic structure of any coherent religious tradition. Defining Orphism by its doctrines and deriving those doctrines from the Zagreus myth, as recent scholars have sought to do, distorts the interpretation both of the individual pieces of evidence and the larger background of Greek religion.

The understanding of individual texts suffers from such an interpreta-tion. The hypothesis of a Zagreus myth seems to provide a simple expla-nation of a complex collection of evidence, weaving all the pieces into a single whole – a myth that includes the dismemberment of Dionysos, the punishment of the Titans, the generation of humanity from their ashes, and the need for purification from the original sin of the Titans' murder. The myth, moreover, provides a doctrine of the nature and fate of the soul that can be used as the nucleus of a definition of Orphism in ancient Greece, providing a simple essence of a complex religious phenomenon. As I have shown in the last chapter, however, the claim that the anthropogony was an inevitable sequel to the dismemberment story is false. Not only is Olympiodorus the only text in which the anthropogony follows the dis-memberment, but, in many of the most substantive pieces of evidence, the two cannot be linked. To read the anthropogony into Plutarch's allegory in the *De Esu Carnium* is to distort the text, and Proclus also has the dismem-berment followed not by the generation of humanity out of the remains of the Titans, but by the shackling of the various Titans in a number of different places. Likewise, to assume that references to punishment of the Titans or to the creation of human beings must include the story of the dismemberment is to distort the evidence, to damage our understanding of the passages in question, from the Titanic nature of Plato's *Laws* to Dio's Titanic origin for humanity or the allusion to the blood of the earthborn in the *Orphic Argonautica*. The apparently simple explanation of the Zagreus myth only works with these texts if some of their complexities are ignored or if they are stripped of their context and woven into the fabric of the Zagreus myth as bare "Orphic fragments."

Even for the strands of evidence that do not present inherent contradictions to an interpretation in terms of the Zagreus myth, the assumption that they are all part of this single story unduly limits the scope of interpretation and misrepresents the nature of Greek myth. Not every reference to Titans as the ancestors of mankind or to Persephone and Dionysos relieving the burden of ancient crimes or to the dismemberment of Dionysos alludes to this single story. The Greek mythic tradition was far richer and more varied, and the evidence instead attests to many different variants. We miss perceiving the evidence for local anthropogonic traditions, or for purificatory rituals, or for a number of different rituals and philosophical or theological ideas associated with the dismemberment – from agricultural festivals to private initiations to Neoplatonic cosmologies. The simple explanation provided by the Zagreus myth blinds us to the complexity and richness of the religious context that produced all of this evidence, causing us to halt our investigations before we have explored all of the ramifications. The investigations in previous chapters have been a start at exploring some of these ramifications, the ritual and mythic traditions whose traces remain only in fragments and allusions but which played a larger role in Greek religion as a whole than the scarcity of the surviving evidence might suggest.

Not only does the simple explanation obscure the depth and variety of the sources from which the evidence comes, but it contradicts the dynamic and fluid way in which the Greek mythic tradition changed over the centuries. None of the evidence that has been put forth for the existence of the Zagreus myth, from the sixth century BCE to the sixth century CE, actually provides all of the pieces of the supposed myth. The sequence of dismemberment of Dionysos, punishment of the Titans, anthropogony from their remains, and mankind's burden of guilt simply does not appear in any of the evidence. All of the individual strands, of course, do appear independently and sometimes even in combination with one of the other elements. The Greek mythic tradition operates by *bricolage*, the piecing together of various scraps from the tradition rag-bag to create new variants of old, familiar tales as well as new tales from old pieces. The presence of one traditional element therefore never necessitates the presence of any other; the beginning, middle, or end of a story can be altered to suit the *bricoleur's* purpose as easily as the characters can be shifted around – one hero substituting for another or one monster for another. Any particular combination of traditional elements is therefore inextricably linked to the context in which the story is told, to the purpose for which the narrator relates the tale.[1]

---

[1] Cp. Edmonds 2004a, esp. 4–13.

The assumption that the story of the dismemberment of Dionysos provided the basis for Orphic doctrines for over a thousand years thus requires the tacit assumption that this myth is somehow an exception to the way Greek myth works in general. Not only is this assumption problematic in itself, but it would also require the even more problematic assumption of some form of social mechanism to transmit these doctrines in essentially unchanged form over this whole time period. As many scholars have repeatedly noted, however, such mechanisms as canonical scriptures and professional priests, so familiar from doctrinal religions like Judaism and Christianity, are noticeably absent from Greek religion.

There are several reasons why the hypothesis of the Zagreus myth and the attendant idea of a coherent Orphic religion might have been appealing to the scholars at the end of the nineteenth and beginning of the twentieth centuries who first put it forth.[2] Orphism, as reconstructed on the basis of the Zagreus myth, not only provides a simple, elegant, and coherent explanation of the evidence, but the model that it assumes of a doctrinally-based religion, focused on salvation from sin and relying on the authority of sacred texts, is familiar to modern scholars of religion who come from a Judaeo-Christian background. The very coherence of the model that the Zagreus myth assumes, therefore, comes not from the ancient evidence but from the familiarity of the religious model. However, such a model, forged in the debates between Protestantism and Roman Catholicism and shaped by the ideas of the Enlightenment as well as the Reformation, cannot be applied to ancient religion without anachronism.[3] Such a model is scarcely applicable to early Christianity, much less to ancient pagan Greek religion. We must turn to another model to make sense of the evidence.

Orphica within Greek religion

In this study, I have attempted to set out a model for understanding this evidence that makes better sense of the phenomena within the understanding of Greek religion as it has been developed in the last few decades by scholars such as Burkert and Parker. Greek religion is a religion without a professional class of priests, without a canonical set of sacred texts, and without a specific set of doctrines that make up an orthodoxy. Whitehouse's model of an imagistic religion, one that is transmitted not by repetition of doctrines but by the performance of intense rituals, can help modern scholars understand these absences from Greek religion that make it so different from the familiar doctrinal structure of the Judaeo-Christian

---

[2] Edmonds 1999, esp. pp. 57–66.   [3] Cp. Smith 1990.

tradition. Orphism, however, must not be understood as the exception to the rule, the doctrinal current within Greek religion or the forerunner of the doctrinal tradition of Christianity that followed. Rather, Orphism, to use a modern "-ism" term to designate a modern scholarly concept, can be understood as the category that includes those things that the ancient Greeks associated with the name of Orpheus, the Orphica – whether text or ritual. This category includes a variety of extra-ordinary religious phenomena labeled with the name of Orpheus or classified together with such things in the ancient evidence, and I have tried in this study to survey this evidence, putting it in the context of Greek religion as a whole.

The complexity of Greek religion as the background context justifies the complexity of the model to explain the category of Orphica within it. I have identified a set of cues that are associated with the things labeled Orphic in the ancient evidence – extra-ordinary purity or sanctity, extra-ordinary antiquity, or extra-ordinary strangeness or perversity. These cues have varying validity in different times and circumstances, and the category of Orphic itself shifts as the cues shift in importance. In the earliest surviving evidence, the most important cues appear to be extra-ordinary purity, like that of Euripides' Hippolytos, or the special claim to sanctity and divine favor that marks the *teletai* advertised by the itinerant ritual practitioners with their hubbub of books. Even in this early evidence, however, the stamp of strangeness, even perversity, appears in the descriptions of Orphic rites and tales, and the debates over the antiquity of Orpheus and his works have begun. The extreme antiquity of Orpheus becomes more important in the Hellenistic period and especially in the struggles between the early Christian apologists and their Neoplatonist opponents. The alien nature of the Orphica, and indeed, of Orpheus himself, likewise plays a role in the debates over the Hellenic tradition, and Orpheus becomes at times the pupil of Moses/Mousaios and at times an ignorant, illiterate Thracian, swindling the even more ignorant primitive barbarians among whom he lives. The Orphica become either the supreme example of alien wisdom or are dismissed as shocking barbarisms. The shocking quality of the perverse tales of Orpheus makes them the focus of allegorical interpretation from the earliest witnesses, as the apparent obscenity is interpreted as profound holiness, arcanely expressed. The Christian interpreters reject and condemn this allegorization, while the Neoplatonists bring it to new and complex heights, but they both emphasize the obscurity and apparent perversity of the Orphica as a representative of the Hellenic religious tradition. No single set of criteria characterizes every testimony to the ancient category of Orphism, but they all share this loose collection of cues that create a family resemblance among the pieces of evidence, even as that category shifts over time. Orphism always stands in relation to ideas of normal Greek religion, helping to define normality by its very distance from those ideas of normality (which themselves shift from person to person and period to period).

Understanding what sorts of rituals are labeled with the name of Orpheus (and which are not) helps to illuminate the nature of Greek religious practices of purification and even the rites associated with gods such as Demeter and Dionysos. Not all the rites that refer to the dismemberment of Dionysos or the search of Demeter for her lost daughter were considered Orphic by those who took part in them. Most were regular parts of the religion of the polis, while some others were indeed marked as extraordinary and liable to be associated with Orpheus. The idea of people living an Orphic life was merely a myth of a golden-age existence, and only a few practices of purification were so out of the ordinary as to be considered Orphic. Rites of preventative and contingent purification were part of many normal festivals, and mantic consultation to determine the past cause of divine anger was standard procedure for both individuals and entire cities. Finding such relief from the anger of the gods, as well as seeking favor with the gods through sacrifices and other rituals, was considered normal religious activity to secure a happy and blessed life, and the favor of the gods could improve not just this life but the afterlife as well. The idea of a differentiated afterlife, whether a continuation of the familiar life in the sun or a compensation for its injustices, was not the secret doctrine of Orphic believers, but rather a common assumption underlying most funerary practices and literary representations, the sort of idea that could be included without comment in a public funeral oration. A few ideas of life after death, such as a cycle of reincarnations, were indeed marked as extra-ordinary, the sort of crazy new age idea that those who took Orpheus' poems too seriously might come up with, but a variety of contradictory ideas about life after death coexisted within the mainstream of Greek religion, including the Homeric ideal of survival through poetic glory, which had a perennial appeal both to the aristocrats who could achieve lasting fame and to the poets who could provide it for them.

Throughout the millennia from which our evidence comes, poets continued to compose poems under the name of Orpheus, borrowing the glamor and authority of his name to ensure that their own creations were passed down. Little survives of these compositions beyond the selections made by the Neoplatonist philosophers and the early Christian apologists, who culled the materials that had survived to their day for the elements most apt to their own purposes. Nevertheless, the lists of titles preserved by ancient scholars show that, in addition to the hymns to the gods for which Orpheus was always best known, the magic name of Orpheus was attached to a variety of other poems, from didactic poems revealing the secrets of divination or the properties of stones to accounts of the cosmos that, like the hexameters of Empedokles or Parmenides (or Lucretius), explained the nature of things in the world. These poems were always a hubbub of books rather than an organized canon of sacred scriptures; only by the time of the Neoplatonic systematizers like Syrianus were these Orphic poems organized and systematized. The mythic elements involved with all these poems were the same as those from which other poets, who did not use the name of Orpheus, drew. Orphicists, like other poets, were *bricoleurs*, who patched together familiar bits from the mythic tradition to create their own new works, even if the Orphica were characterized by more strange and perverse twists of narrative than the works of Homer and Hesiod or even of Aeschylus and Euripides.

This study provides only a preliminary investigation of some of the most interesting pieces of evidence in the category of things that the ancient Greeks labeled "Orphic." Much more remains to be done, for example, to understand the physical, ritual, and even socio-political ideas of the Derveni author and the Orphicist who composed the poem he interprets. The gold lamellae still raise baffling questions of interpretation even as the number and variety of tablets found increases. The collection of *Orphic Hymns* that was so crucial to the Renaissance imagination of ancient Orphic wisdom is just beginning to receive the sort of critical scholarly re-examination that has been absent for so long, and even the *Orphic Argonautica* and *Lithika* are starting to receive some attention. A model for the category of Orphica that abandons earlier flawed assumptions about Greek religion and myth can help provide new insights into these fascinating texts as the evidence is examined anew.

While such a way of understanding the ancient category of Orphism, of the things labeled Orphic, does transform the understanding of the evidence, both for the things labeled Orphic and for other elements of Greek religion, it merely involves a change of perspective, rather than a wholesale rejection of the valuable work done by scholars of Greek religion in the past century. Indeed, in many cases, it simply involves continuing the shift begun by recent scholars who have transformed the study of Greek religion with new models from the disciplines of anthropology and history of religions. Among the avenues which have already proved fruitful are Levi-Strauss's concept of *bricolage*, employed so usefully by scholars such as

Graf and Johnston, and Whitehouse's model of an imagistic religion, which scholars such as Casadio and Martin have begun to apply to Greco-Roman religions. These ideas provide new insights into Greek religion which can be carried further. The new model that has perhaps been most developed is Burkert's model of itinerant religious specialists competing for religious authority among a varying clientele, which has been fruitful in replacing older ideas of priests and believers or of orientalizing cults creeping in with the decay of traditional Greek religion.[4] To return to the metaphor of Penelope's weaving, much of the work done by previous scholars can be worked into the fabric of the new understanding of Orphism and the new understanding of the wider field of Greek religion. While some of the conclusions drawn must be reworked to fit into this model and many of the individual threads must be placed in different contexts, much of the clever and careful work still provides useful pieces in the great tapestry of Greek religion that scholars continue to try to reconstruct and restore. Redefining ancient Orphism does not merely tear apart the labors of previous scholars, it provides a way to recontextualize and replace the evidence to better understand the nature of the category of things Orphic and its place within Greek religion.

---

[4] Burkert 1982 provides the first real articulation of this model, but others have begun to pick up on it in recent years, notably Redfield 1991, Calame 2002, and, to a certain extent, Parker 1995. Parker incorporates these ideas into his study of mainstream Greek religion in Parker 2011, and such a model is also at work in the recent studies of Herrero 2010 and Jourdan 2010, 2011.

Bibliography

Ábel, E. 1885. *Orphica. Accedunt Procli hymni, Hymni magici, Hymnus in Isim: aliaque eiusmodi carmina.* Bibliotheca scriptorum Graecorum et Romanorum Teubneriana. Leipzig and Prague: G. Freytag.

Albinus, L. 2000. *The House of Hades: Studies in Ancient Greek Eschatology.* Studies in Religion, 2. Aarhus: Aarhus University Press.

Alderink, L. J. 1981. *Creation and Salvation in Ancient Orphism.* American Classical Studies, 8. Chico, CA: Scholars Press.

———. 1993. "Foreword to the Mythos edition." In Guthrie, W. K. C. ed. *Orpheus and Greek Religion: A Study of the Orphic Movement.* Mythos. Princeton: Princeton University Press. xiii–xxxiv.

Anonymous. 1982. "Der orphische Papyrus von Derveni." *Zeitschrift für Papyrologie und Epigraphik* 47: 1–12 (after 300).

Athanassiadi, P. 2010. *Vers la pensée unique la montée de l'intolérance dans l'Antiquité tardive.* Histoire, 102. Paris: Les Belles Lettres.

Bastianini, G. 2005. "Euripide e Orfeo in un papiro fiorentino (PSI 15, 1476)." In Bastianini, G. and Casanova, A. eds. *Euripide e i papiri: atti del convegno internazionale di studi: Firenze, 10–11 giugno 2004.* Florence: Istituto Papirologico G. Vitelli. 227–242.

Baxter, T. M. S. 1992. *The Cratylus: Plato's Critique of Naming.* Philosophia Antiqua, 58. Leiden, New York and Cologne: E. J. Brill.

Beatrice, P. F. 2001. *Anonymi Monophysitae Theosophia: An Attempt at Reconstruction.* Supplements to *Vigiliae Christianae*, 56. Leiden and Boston: Brill.

Bernabé, A. 1995. "Una etimología platónica: ΣΩMA-ΣHMA." *Philologus* 139(2): 204–237.

———. 1996. "Plutarco e l'orfismo." In Gallo, I. ed. *Plutarco e la religione: Atti del VI Convegno plutarcheo (Ravello, 29–31 maggio 1995).* Naples: M. D'Auria. 63–105.

———. 1997. "Orfeotelestas, intérpretes, charlatanes: transmisores de la palabra órfica." In Bosch, M. d. C. and Fornés, M. A. eds. *Homenatge a Miguel Dolç: Actes del XII Simposi de la Secció Catalana i I de la Secció Balear de la SEEC, Palma, 1 al 4 de febrer de 1996.* Palma de Mallorca: Sociedad Española de Estudios Clásicos. 37–41.

———. 1998a. "La palabra de Orfeo: Religión y magia." In Vega, A., Rodríguez Tous, J. A. and Bouso, R. eds. *Estética y religión: El discurso del cuerpo y los sentidos.* Er, Revista de Filosofía, documentos. Barcelona: Literatura y Ciencia. 157–172.

1998b. "Naciementos y muertes de Dioniso en los mitos órficos." In Sánchez Fernández, C. and Cabrera Bonet, P. eds. *En los límites de Dioniso: Actas del simposio celebrado en el Museo Arqueológico Nacional, Madrid, 20 de junio de 1997.* Murcia: Caja de Ahorros. 29–39.

1998c. "Platone e l'orfismo." In Sfameni Gasparro, G. ed. *Destino e salvezza: tra culti pagani e gnosi cristiana. Itinerari storico-religiosi sulle orme di Ugo Bianchi.* Cosenza: Lionello Giordano Editore. 37–97.

1999. "Αἴνιγμα y αἰνίττομαι: exégesis alegórica en Platón y Plutarco." In Pérez Jiménez, A., García López, J. and Aguilar, R. M. eds. *Plutarco, Platón y Aristóteles: Actas del V Congreso Internacional de la I.P.S. (Madrid-Cuenca, 4–7 de mayo de 1999).* Madrid: Ediciones Clásicas. 189–200.

2000. "Nuovi frammenti orfici e una nuova edizione degli Ὀρφικά." In Tortorelli Ghidini, M., Storchi Marino, A. and Visconti, A. eds. *Tra Orfeo a Pitagora: Origini e incontri di culture nell'antichità. Atti dei Seminari Napoletani 1996–1998.* Naples: Bibliopolis. 43–80.

2002a. "La toile de Pénélope: A-t-il existé un mythe orphique sur Dionysos et les Titans?" *Revue de l'histoire des religions* 219(4): 401–433.

2002b. "Referencias a textos órficos en Diodoro." In Torraca, L. ed. *Scritti in onore di Italo Gallo.* Pubblicazioni dell'Università degli studi di Salerno. Sezione atti, convegni, miscellanee, 59. Naples: Edizioni scientifiche italiane. 67–96.

2002c. "La théogonie orphique du papyrus de Derveni." *Kernos* 15: 91–129.

2002d. "Orphisme et Présocratiques: Bilan et prespectives d'un dialogue complexe." In Laks, A. and Louguet, C. eds. *Qu'est-ce que la Philosophie Présocratique? / What is Presocratic Philosophy?* Cahiers de philologie, 20. Lille: Presses universitaires du Septentrion. 205–247.

2003. "Autour du mythe orphique sur Dionysos et les Titans: Quelques notes critiques." In Accorinti, D. and Chuvin, P. eds. *Des Géants à Dionysos: Mélanges de mythologie et de poésie grecques offerts à Francis Vian.* Hellenica, 10. Alessandria: Edizioni dell'Orso. 25–39.

2004. *Poetae epici Graeci: Testimonia et fragmenta. Pars II. Orphicorum et Orphicis similium testimonia et fragmenta. Fasciculus I.* Bibliotheca scriptorum Graecorum et Romanorum Teubneriana. Munich and Leipzig: K. G. Saur.

2005. *Poetae epici Graeci: Testimonia et fragmenta. Pars II. Orphicorum et Orphicis similium testimonia et fragmenta. Fasciculus 2.* Bibliotheca scriptorum Graecorum et Romanorum Teubneriana. Munich and Leipzig: K. G. Saur.

2007a. *Poetae epici Graeci: Testimonia et fragmenta. Pars II. Orphicorum et Orphicis similium testimonia et fragmenta. Fasciculus 3.* Bibliotheca scriptorum Graecorum et Romanorum Teubneriana. Berlin and New York: Walter de Gruyter.

2007b. "The Derveni Theogony: Many Questions and Some Answers." *Harvard Studies in Classical Philology* 103: 99–133.

2008a. "La teogonía órfica citada en las *Pseudoclementina*." *Adamantius* 14: 79–99.

2008b. "A modo de epílogo." In Bernabé, A. and Casadesús, F. eds. *Orfeo y la tradición órfica: Un reencuentro*. Akal universitaria, 280–281. Madrid: Akal. 1625–1648.

2013. "Dionysos in the Mycenean World." In Bernabé, A., Herrero de Jáuregui, M., Jiménez San Cristóbal, A. I., and Martín Hernández, R. eds. *Redefining Dionysos*. Berlin and Boston: Walter De Gruyter. 23–37.

Bernabé, A. and Casadesús, F. eds. 2008. *Orfeo y la tradición órfica: Un reencuentro*. Akal universitaria, 280–281. Madrid: Akal.

Bernabé, A. and Jiménez, A. I. 2001. *Instrucciones para el mas allá: Las láminillas órficas de oro*. Religiones antiquitatis, Series maior. Madrid: Ediciones Clásicas.

2008. *Instructions for the Netherworld: The Orphic Gold Tablets*. Religions in the Graeco-Roman World, 162. Leiden and Boston: Brill.

Betegh, G. 2002. "On Eudemus Fr. 150 (Wehrli)." In Bodnár, I. and Fortenbaugh, W. W. eds. *Eudemus of Rhodes*. Rutgers University Studies in Classical Humanities, 11. New Brunswick, NJ: Transaction Publishers. 337–357.

2004. *The Derveni Papyrus: Cosmology, Theology, and Interpretation*. Cambridge and New York: Cambridge University Press.

2007. "The Derveni Papyrus and Early Stoicism." *Rhizai* 4(1): 133–152.

Bianchi, U. 1965. "Initiation, mystères, gnose (Pour l'histoire de la mystique dans le paganisme gréco-oriental)." In Bleeker, C. J. ed. *Initiation: Contributions to the Theme of the Study-Conference of the International Association for the History of Religions Held at Strasburg, September 17th to 22nd 1964*. Studies in the History of Religions. Supplements to *Numen*, 10. Leiden: E.J. Brill. 154–171.

1966. "Péché originel et péché «antécédent»." *Revue de l'histoire des religions* 170(2): 117–126.

Blakely, S. 2000. "Madness in the Body Politic: Kouretes, Korybantes, and the Politics of Shamanism." In Hubert, J. ed. *Madness, Disability, and Social Exclusion: The Archaeology and Anthropology of "difference"*. One World Archaeology, 40. London and New York: Routledge. 119–127.

2006. *Myth, Ritual, and Metallurgy in Ancient Greece and Recent Africa*. Cambridge and New York: Cambridge University Press.

Boedeker, D. and Sider, D. eds. 2001. *The New Simonides: Contexts of Praise and Desire*. Oxford and New York: Oxford University Press.

Bonnechere, P. 2003. *Trophonios de Lébadée: Cultes et mythes d'une cité béotienne au miroir de la mentalité antique*. Religions in the Graeco-Roman World, 150. Leiden and Boston: Brill.

Borgeaud, P. 1999. "Melampous and Epimenides: Two Greek Paradigms of the Treatment of Mistake." In Assmann, J. and Stroumsa, G. G. eds. *Transformations of the Inner Self in Ancient Religions*. Studies in the History of Religions, 83. Leiden and Boston: E. J. Brill. 287–300.

Bos, A. P. 1991. "Supplementary Notes on the 'De mundo'." *Hermes* 119(3): 312–332.

Bowden, H. 2003. "Oracles for Sale." In Derow, P. and Parker, R. eds. *Herodotus and His World: Essays from a Conference in Memory of George Forrest*. Oxford: Oxford University Press. 256–274.

2010. *Mystery Cults of the Ancient World*. Princeton and Oxford: Princeton University Press.

Boyancé, P. 1963. "Note sur la phroura platonicienne." *Revue de philologie* 37: 7–11.

Boyer, P. 2001. *Religion Explained: The Evolutionary Origins of Religious Thought*. New York: Basic Books.

Bremmer, J. N. 1983. *The Early Greek Concept of the Soul*. Princeton: Princeton University Press.

1994. *Greek Religion*. Greece & Rome: New surveys in the classics, 24. Oxford and New York: Oxford University Press.

2002. *The Rise and Fall of the Afterlife: The 1995 Read-Tuckwell Lectures at the University of Bristol*. London and New York: Routledge.

2004. "Remember the Titans!" In Auffarth, C. and Stuckenbruck, L. T. eds. *The Fall of the Angels*. Themes in Biblical Narrative, 6. Leiden and Boston: E. J. Brill. 35–61.

2010. "*Manteis*, Magic, Mysteries and Mythography: Messy Margins of *Polis* Religion." *Kernos* 23: 13–35.

Brisson, L. 1985a. "La figure de Chronos dans la théogonie orphique et ses antécédents iraniens." In Tiffeneau, D. ed. *Mythes et représentations du temps*. Phénoménologie et herméneutique. Paris: Éditions du Centre national de la recherche scientifique. 37–55. (Reprinted in Brisson 1995.)

1985b. "Les théogonies orphiques et le papyrus de Derveni." *Revue de l'histoire des religions* 202(4): 389–420.

1987. "Proclus et l'Orphisme." In Pépin, J. and Saffrey, H. D. eds. *Proclus, lecteur et interprète des anciens: Actes du colloque international du CNRS, Paris, 2–4 octobre 1985*. Colloques internationaux du Centre national de la recherche scientifique. Paris: Éditions du Centre national de la recherche scientifique. 43–103. (Reprinted in Brisson 1995.)

1990. "Orphée et l'orphisme à l'époque impériale: Témoignages et interprétations philosophiques, de Plutarque à Jamblique." *Aufstieg und Niedergang der Römischen Welt* II(36.4): 2867–2931.

1992. "Le Corps 'dionysiaque'. L'anthropogonie décrite dans le *Commentaire sur le Phédon de Platon* (1, par. 3–6) attribué à Olympiodore est-elle orphique?" In Goulet-Cazé, M.-O., Madec, G. and O'Brien, D. eds. Σοφίης μαιήτορες «Chercheurs de Sagesse»: Hommage à Jean Pépin. Collection des études augustiniennes. Série Antiquité, 131. Paris: Institut d'études augustiniennes. 481–499.

1995. *Orphée et l'orphisme dans l'Antiquité gréco-romaine*. Collected Studies Series, 476. Aldershot: Variorum.

1997. "Chronos in Column XII of the Derveni Papyrus." In Laks, A. and Most, G. W. eds. *Studies on the Derveni Papyrus*. Oxford and New York: Oxford University Press. 149–166.

1999. *Plato the Myth Maker*. Translated, edited, and with an introduction by Gerard Naddaf. Chicago and London: University of Chicago Press.

2002. "La figure du Kronos orphique chez Proclus." *Revue de l'histoire des religions* 219(4): 435–458.

2003. "Sky, Sex and Sun: The Meanings of αιδοιος/αιδοιον in the Derveni Papyrus." *Zeitschrift für Papyrologie und Epigraphik* 144: 19–29.

2004. *How Philosophers Saved Myths: Allegorical Interpretation and Classical Mythology*. Chicago: University of Chicago Press.

2006. "The Derveni Papyrus [rev. of Betegh 2004]." *The Classical Review* 56(1): 7–11.

2008. "El lugar, la función y la significación del orfismo en el neoplatonismo." In Bernabé, A. and Casadesús, F. eds. *Orfeo y la tradición órfica: Un reencuentro*. Akal universitaria. Serie religiones y mitos, **280–281**. Madrid: Akal. 1491–1516.

2009. "Syrianus et l'orphisme." In Longo, A. ed. *Syrianus et la métaphysique de l'Antiquité tardive: actes du colloque international, Université de Genève, 29 septembre–1er octobre 2006*. Elenchos, 51. Naples: Bibliopolis. 463–497.

2010. "L'opposition profanes/initiés dans le papyrus de Derveni." In Rebillard, É. and Sotinel, C. eds. *Les frontières du profane dans l'antiquité tardive*. Collection de l'École française de Rome, 428. Rome: École française de Rome. 21–35.

2011. "Okéanos dans la colonne XXIII du Papyrus de Derveni." In Herrero de Jáuregui, M. *et al.* eds. *Tracing Orpheus: studies of orphic fragments in honour of Alberto Bernabé*. Berlin: De Gruyter. 385–392.

Buitenwerf, R. 2003. *Book III of the Sibylline Oracles and Its Social Setting*. Studia in Veteris Testamenti Pseudepigrapha, 17. Leiden and Boston: Brill.

Burkert, W. 1968. "Orpheus und die Vorsokratiker: Bemerkungen zum Deveni-Papyrus und zur pythagoreischen Zahlenlehre." *Antike und Abenland* 14: 93–114.

1970. "La genèse des choses et des mots: Le papyrus de Derveni entre Anaxagore et Cratyle." *Les études philosophiques* 4: 443–455.

1972. *Lore and Science in Ancient Pythagoreanism*. Trans. Minar, E. L., Jr. Cambridge, MA: Harvard University Press.

1977. *Orphism and Bacchic Mysteries: New Evidence and Old Problems of Interpretation*. Protocol of the colloquy of the Center for Hermeneutical Studies in Hellenistic and Modern Culture, 28. Berkeley, CA: Center for Hermeneutical Studies in Hellenistic and Modern Culture.

1982. "Craft Versus Sect: The Problem of Orphics and Pythagoreans." In Meyer, B. and Sanders, E. P. eds. *Jewish and Christian Self-Definition*. Volume 3: *Self-Definition in the Greco-Roman World*. Philadelphia: Fortress Press. 1–22.

1985. *Greek Religion: Archaic and Classical*. Trans. Raffan, J. Oxford: Blackwell.

1987. *Ancient Mystery Cults*. Carl Newell Jackson Lectures. Cambridge, MA and London: Harvard University Press.

1992. *The Orientalizing Revolution: Near Eastern Influence on Greek Culture in the Early Archaic Age*. Revealing Antiquity, 5. Cambridge, MA: Harvard University Press.

1998. "Die neuen orphischen Texte: Fragmente, Varianten, 'Sitz im Leben'." In Burkert, W. ed. *Fragmentsammlungen philosophischer Texte der Antike / Le raccolte dei frammenti di filosofi antichi. Atti del seminario internazionale, Ascona, Centro Stefano Franscini 22–27 settembre 1996*. Aporemata, 3. Göttingen: Vandenhoeck & Ruprecht. 387–400.

2004. *Babylon, Memphis, Persepolis: Eastern Contexts of Greek Culture*. Cambridge, MA: Harvard University Press.

Calame, C. 1995 "Invocations et commentaires 'orphiques': Transpositions funéraires de discours religieux." *Discours religieux dans l'antiquité* 150: 11–30.

2002. "Qu'est-ce qui est orphique dans les Orphica? Une mise au point introductive." *Revue de l'histoire des religions* 219(4): 385–400.

2006. "Itinéraires rituels et initiatiques vers l'au-delà: Temps, espace et pragmatique dans les lamelles d'or." In *Pratiques poétiques de la mémoire: Représentations de l'espace-temps en grèce ancienne*. Paris: Éditions la Découverte. 229–288.

Casadesús, F. 2010. "Similitudes entre el Papiro de Derveni y los primeros filósofos estoicos." In Bernabé, A., Casadesús, F. and Santamaría, M. A. eds. *Orfeo y el orfismo: Nuevas perspectivas*. Alicante: Biblioteca Virtual Miguel de Cervantes. 192–239.

2011. "The Castration of Uranus and its Physical Consequences in the Derveni Papyrus (cols. XIII and XIV) and the First Stoic Philosophers." In Herrero, M. ed. *Tracing Orpheus: Studies of Orphic Fragments in Honour of Alberto Bernabé*. Sozomena, 10. Berlin and Boston: De Gruyter. 377–383.

Casadio, G. 1986. "Adversaria Orphica et Orientalia." *Studi e materiali di storia delle religioni* 52 (n.s. 10): 291–322.

1987. "Adversaria Orphica: A proposito de in libro recente sull' orfismo." *Orpheus* 8: 381–395.

1989. "Antropologia gnostica e antropologia orfica nella notizia di Ippolito sui Sethiani." In Vattioni, F. ed. *Sangue e antropologia nella teologia*. Centro Studi Sanguis Christi, 6. Rome: Edizioni Pia Unione Preziosissimo Sangue. 1295–1350.

1991. "La metempsicosi tra Orfeo e Pitagora." In Bougeaud, P. ed. *Orphisme et Orphée: En l'honneur de Jean Rudhardt*. Recherches et rencontres, 3. Geneva: Librairie Droz. 119–155.

1996. "Osiride in Grecia e Dioniso in Egitto." In D'Auria, M. ed. *Plutarco e la religione: atti del VI Convegno plutarcheo (Ravello, 29–31 maggio 1995)*. Naples: M. D'Auria. 201–227.

Cavallari, F. S. 1879. "Sibari." *Notizie degli scavi di antichità* Anno 1879: 156–159.

Chaniotis, A. 1997. "Reinheit des Körpers – Reinheit des Sinnes in den griechischen Kultgesetzen." In Assmann, J. and Sundermeier, T. eds. *Schuld, Gewissen und Person*. Studien zum Verstehen fremder Religionen, 9. Gütersloh: Mohn. 142–179.

Chaniotis, A. 2008. "Priests as Ritual Experts in the Greek World." In Dignas, B. and Trampedach, K. eds. *Practitioners of the Divine: Greek Priests and Religious Officials from Homer to Heliodorus.* Hellenic Studies, 30. Washington, DC: Center for Hellenic Studies. 17–34.

Chlup, R. 2007. "The Semantics of Fertility: Levels of Meaning in the Thesmophoria." *Kernos* 20: 69–95.

Clarke, M. 1999. *Flesh and Spirit in the Songs of Homer: A Study of Words and Myths.* Oxford Classical Monographs. Oxford and New York: Oxford University Press.

Claus, D. B. 1981. *Toward the Soul: An Inquiry into the Meaning of ψυχή before Plato.* Yale Classical Monographs, 2. New Haven, CT: Yale University Press.

Clay, J. S. 1989. *The Politics of Olympus: Form and Meaning in the Major Homeric Hymns.* Princeton: Princeton University Press.

2003. *Hesiod's Cosmos.* Cambridge and New York: Cambridge University Press.

Clinton, K. 1992. *Myth and Cult: The Iconography of the Eleusinian Mysteries. The Martin P. Nilsson Lectures on Greek Religion, Delivered 19–21 November 1990 at the Swedish Institute at Athens.* Acta Instituti Atheniensis Regni Sueciae Series in 8o, 11. Stockholm: Svenska institutet i Athen.

2003. "Stages of Initiation in the Eleusinian and Samothracian Mysteries." In Cosmopoulos, M. B. ed. *Greek Mysteries: The Archaeology of Ancient Greek Secret Cults.* London and New York: Routledge. 50–78.

Cohn-Haft, L. 1956. *The Public Physicians of Ancient Greece.* Smith College Studies in History, 42. Northampton, MA: Department of History of Smith College.

Collins, J. J. 1983–85. "The Development of the Sibylline Tradition." In Charlesworth, J. H. ed. *The Old Testament Pseudepigrapha.* Garden City, NY: Doubleday. 421–459.

Comparetti, D. 1882. "The Petelia Gold Tablet." *Journal of Hellenic Studies* 3: 111–118.

1910. *Laminette orfiche.* Florence: Galletti e Cocci.

Cornford, F. M. 1950. *The Unwritten Philosophy and Other Essays.* Cambridge: Cambridge University Press.

Crane, G. 1988. *Calypso: Backgrounds and Conventions of the Odyssey.* Athenäums Monografien Altertumswissenschaft, 191. Frankfurt am Main: Athenäum.

Creuzer, F. 1810–12. *Symbolik und Mythologie der alten Völker, besonders der Griechen.* Leipzig and Darmstadt: Karl Wilhelm Leske.

Dawson, D. 1992. *Allegorical Readers and Cultural Revision in Ancient Alexandria.* Berkeley, Los Angeles and Oxford: University of California Press.

Delbrueck, R. and Vollgraff, W. 1934. "An Orphic Bowl." *Journal of Hellenic Studies* 54(2): 129–139.

Detienne, M. 1975. "Les chemins de la déviance: Orphisme, dionysisme et pythagorisme." In *Orfismo in Magna Grecia: Atti del quattordicesimo Convegno di Studi sulla Magna Grecia.* Naples: Arte Tipografica. 49–79.

1979. *Dionysos Slain.* Trans. Muellner, M. and Muellner, L. Baltimore, MD: Johns Hopkins University Press.

1986. "Dionysos dans ses parousies, un dieu épidémique." In *L'association dionysiaque dans les sociétés anciennes: Actes de la table ronde org. par l'École Française de Rome (Rome, 24–25 mai 1984).* Collection de École Française de Rome, 89. Rome: École Francaise de Rome. 53–83.

1996. *The Masters of Truth in Archaic Greece.* Trans. J. Lloyd. New York: Zone Books.

2003. *The Writing of Orpheus: Greek Myth in Cultural Context.* Trans. Lloyd, J. Baltimore, MD: Johns Hopkins University Press.

Dieterich, A. 1891. *De hymnis Orphicis capitula quinque: Ad veniam legendi in Universitate Philippina Marpurgensi a philosophorum ordine impetrandam.* Marburg: Impensis Elwerti Bibliopolae Academici.

1893. *Nekyia: Beiträge zur Erklärung der neuentdeckten Petrusapokalypse.* Leipzig: B. G. Teubner.

1911. *Kleine Schriften: Mit einem Bildnis und zwei Tafeln.* Leipzig and Berlin: B. G. Teubner.

Diggle, J. 2004. *Theophrastus: Characters.* Cambridge Classical Texts and Commentaries, 41. Cambridge and New York: Cambridge University Press.

Dignas, B. and Trampedach, K. eds. 2008. *Practitioners of the Divine: Greek Priests and Religious Officials from Homer to Heliodorus.* Hellenic Studies, 30. Washington, DC: Center for Hellenic Studies.

Dillery, J. 2005. "Chresmologues and Manteis: Independent Diviners and the Problem of Authority." In Johnston, S. I. and Struck, P. T. eds. *Mantikê: Studies in Ancient Divination.* Religions in the Graeco-Roman World. Leiden and Boston: E. J. Brill. 167–231.

Dodds, E. R. 1951. *The Greeks and the Irrational.* Sather Classical Lectures, 25. Berkeley: University of California Press.

1959. *Plato, Gorgias: A Revised Text with Introduction and Commentary.* Oxford: Clarendon Press.

Dottin, G. ed. 1930. *Les Argonautiques d'Orphée.* Nouvelle collection de textes et documents. Paris: Les belles lettres.

Dover, K. J. 1968. *Aristophanes: Clouds.* Oxford and New York: Oxford University Press.

1993. *Aristophanes, Frogs: Edited with Introduction and Commentary.* Oxford and New York: Oxford University Press.

Dowden, K. 1980. "Grades in the Eleusinian Mysteries." *Revue de l'histoire des religions* 197(4): 409–427.

Dunbar, N. 1995. *Aristophanes, Birds. Edited with introduction and commentary.* Oxford and New York: Oxford University Press.

Edmonds, R. G., III. 1999. "Tearing Apart the Zagreus Myth: A Few Disparaging Remarks on Orphism and Original Sin." *Classical Antiquity* 18(1): 35–73.

2000. "Did the Mithraists Inhale? A Technique for Theurgic Ascent in the Mithras Liturgy, the Chaldaean Oracles, and some Mithraic Frescoes." *Ancient World* 32(1): 10–24.

2004a. *Myths of the Underworld Journey: Plato, Aristophanes, and the "Orphic" Gold Tablets*. Cambridge and New York: Cambridge University Press.

2004b. [Untitled] Review of Bernabé 2004a. *Bryn Mawr Classical Review* 2004.12.29. http://bmcr.brynmawr.edu/2004/2004-12-29.html.

2004c. [Untitled] Review of Detienne 2003. *Bryn Mawr Classical Review* 2004.07.54. http://bmcr.brynmawr.edu/2004/2004-07-54.html.

2006. "To Sit in Solemn Silence? *Thronosis* in Ritual, Myth, and Iconography." *American Journal of Philology* 127(3): 347–366.

2008a. "Extra-Ordinary People: Mystai and Magoi, Magicians and Orphics in the Derveni Papyrus." *Classical Philology* 103(1): 16–39.

2008b. "Recycling Laertes' Shroud: More on Orphism and Original Sin." *Center for Hellenic Studies online*. http://chs.harvard.edu/chs/redmonds.

2009. "A Curious Concoction: Tradition and Innovation in Olympiodorus' 'Orphic' Creation of Mankind." *American Journal of Philology* 130(4): 511–532.

2010. "The Children of Earth and Starry Heaven: The Meaning and Function of the Formula in the 'Orphic' Gold Tablets." In Bernabé, A., Casadesús, F. and Santamaría, M. A. eds. *Orfeo y el orfismo: Nuevas perspectivas*. Alicante: Biblioteca Virtual Miguel de Cervantes. 98–121.

ed. 2011a. *The "Orphic" Gold Tablets and Greek Religion: Further Along the Path*. Cambridge and New York: Cambridge University Press.

2011b. "The 'Orphic' Gold Tablets: Texts and translations, with critical apparatus and tables." In Edmonds, R. G., III ed. *The "Orphic" Gold Tablets and Greek Religion: Further Along the Path*. Cambridge and New York: Cambridge University Press. 15–50.

2011c. "Sacred Scripture or Oracles for the Dead? The Semiotic Situation of the 'Orphic' Gold Tablets." In Edmonds, R. G., III ed. *The "Orphic" Gold Tablets and Greek Religion: Further Along the Path*. Cambridge and New York: Cambridge University Press. 257–270.

2011d. "Afterlife." In Finkelberg, M. ed. *The Homer Encyclopedia*. Chichester and Malden, MA: Wiley-Blackwell. 11–14.

2012. "Whip Scars on the Naked Soul: Myth and Elenchos in Plato's *Gorgias*." In Collobert, C., Destrée, P. and Gonzalez, F. J. eds. *Plato and Myth: Studies on the Use and Status of Platonic Myths*. Mnemosyne Supplements, 337. Leiden and Boston: Brill. 165–186.

2013. "Dionysos in Egypt? Epaphian Dionysos in the *Orphic Hymns*." In Bernabé, A., Herrero de Jáuregui, M., Jiménez San Cristóbal, A. I., and Martín Hernández, R. eds. *Redefining Dionysos*. Berlin and Boston: Walter De Gruyter. 415–432.

Forthcoming. "Misleading and Unclear to the Many: Allegory in the Derveni Papyrus and the Orphic Theogony of Hieronymus." In Santamaria, M. A.

ed. *50 Years of the Discovery of the Derveni Papyrus (1962–2012)*. Oxford: Oxford University Press.

Eliade, M. 1965. *The Myth of the Eternal Return. Or, Cosmos and History*. Bollingen Series, 46. Trans. Trask, W. R. Princeton: Princeton University Press.

1987. *The Sacred and the Profane: The Nature of Religion*. Trans. Trask, W. R. San Diego: Harcourt Brace Jovanovich.

Farnell, L. R. 1896. *The Cults of the Greek States*. Volume 1. Oxford: Clarendon Press.

Ferwerda, R. 1985. "The Meaning of the Word σῶμα in Plato's Cratylus 400C." *Hermes* 113(3): 266–279.

Festugière, A. J. 1935. "Les mystères de Dionysos." *Revue Biblique* 44: 192–211; 366–396.

1936. "Comptes rendus bibliographiques: Guthrie (W.K.C.) Orpheus and Greek Religion." *Revue des études grecques* 49: 306–310.

Finamore, J. F. and Dillon, J. M. 2002. *Iamblichus, De Anima: Text, Translation, and Commentary*. Philosophia Antiqua, 92. Leiden and Boston: Brill.

Flower, M. A. 2008a. "The Iamidae: A Mantic Family and its Public Image." In Dignas, B. and Trampedach, K. eds. *Practitioners of the Divine: Greek Priests and Religious Officials from Homer to Heliodorus*. Hellenic studies, 30. Washington, DC: Center for Hellenic Studies. 187–206.

2008b. *The Seer in Ancient Greece*. Berkeley, Los Angeles, and London: University of California Press.

Foley, H. P. 1994. *The Homeric Hymn to Demeter: Translation, Commentary, and Interpretive Essays*. Princeton: Princeton University Press.

Ford, A. 2005. "The Function of Criticism ca. 432 BC: Texts and Interpretations in Plato's Protagoras." Princeton/Stanford Working Papers in Classics no. 120501. http://papers.ssrn.com/sol3/papers.cfm?abstract_id=1426838##.

Foti, G. and Pugliese Carratelli, G. 1974. "Un sepolcro di Hipponion e un nuovo testo orfico." *La parola del passato* 29: 91–126.

Friedman, J. B. 1970. *Orpheus in the Middle Ages*. Cambridge, MA: Harvard University Press.

Furley, D. J. 1955. "[Aristotle]: On the Cosmos." In Forster, E. S. and Furley, D. J. eds. *Aristotle: On Sophistical Refutations; On Coming-to-be and Passing Away; On the Cosmos*. Loeb Classical Library. Cambridge, MA: Harvard University Press. 333–409.

Furley, W. D. and Bremer, J. M. 2001. *Greek Hymns: Selected Cult Songs from the Archaic to the Hellenistic Period*. Studien und Texte zu Antike und Christentum, 9–10. Tübingen: Mohr Siebeck.

Gagarin, M. 2002. *Antiphon the Athenian: Oratory, Law, and Justice in the Age of the Sophists*. Austin: University of Texas Press.

Gagné, R. 2007. "Winds and Ancestors: The Physika of Orpheus." *Harvard Studies in Classical Philology* 103: 1–23.

2008. "The Sins of the Fathers: C.A. Lobeck and K.O. Müller." *Kernos* 21: 109–124.

Gantz, T. 1993. *Early Greek Myth: A Guide to Literary and Artistic Sources.* Baltimore, MD: Johns Hopkins University Press.

Garland, R. 1985. *The Greek Way of Death.* Ithaca, NY: Cornell University Press.

Gesner, J. M. 1764. *Orpheōs Hapanta: Orphei Argonautica Hymni Libellus De Lapidibus Et Fragmenta.* Leipzig: Fritsch.

Ginouvès, R. 1962. *Balaneutikè; recherches sur le bain dans l'antiquité grecque.* Bibliothèque des Écoles françaises d'Athènes et de Rome, 200. Paris: De Boccard.

Gordon, R. 1999. "Imagining Greek and Roman Magic." In Ankarloo, B. and Clark, S. eds. *Witchcraft and Magic in Europe.* Volume 2: *Ancient Greece and Rome.* Philadelphia: University of Pennsylvania Press. 159–275.

Graf, F. 1974. *Eleusis und die orphische Dichtung Athens in vorhellenistischer Zeit.* Religionsgeschichtliche Versuche und Vorarbeiten, 33. Berlin and New York: De Gruyter.

1991. "Texts orphiques et rituel bacchique: A propos des lamelles de Pelinna." In Bougeaud, P. ed. *Orphisme et Orphée: En l'honneur de Jean Rudhardt.* Recherches et rencontres, 3. Geneva: Librairie Droz. 87–102.

1993. "Dionysian and Orphic Eschatology: New Texts and Old Questions." In Carpenter, T. H. and Faraone, C. A. eds. *Masks of Dionysus.* Myth and Poetics. Ithaca, NY: Cornell University Press. 239–258.

2003. "Lesser Mysteries–Not Less Mysterious." In Cosmopoulos, M. B. ed. *Greek Mysteries: The Archaeology of Ancient Greek Secret Cults.* London and New York: Routledge. 241–262.

2009. "Serious Singing: The Orphic Hymns as Religious Texts." *Kernos* 22: 169–182.

2011a. "Text and Ritual: The Corpus Eschatologicum of the Orphics." In Edmonds, R. G., III ed. *The "Orphic" Gold Tablets and Greek Religion: Further Along the Path.* Cambridge and New York: Cambridge University Press. 53–67.

2011b. "Baptism and Graeco-Roman Mystery Cults." In Hellholm, D., Vegge, T., Norderval, Ø., and Hellholm, C. eds. *Ablution, Initiation, and Baptism: Late Antiquity, Early Judaism, and Early Christianity.* Beihefte zur Zeitschrift für die neutestamentliche Wissenschaft und die Kunde der älteren Kirche, 176. Berlin and New York: De Gruyter. 101–118.

nd. "Mysteries." *Brill's New Pauly.* Brill Online, 2012. Reference. Bryn Mawr College. 15 October 2012. http://referenceworks.brillonline.com/entries/brill-s-new-pauly/mysteries-e814910.

Graf, F. and Johnston, S. I. 2007. *Ritual Texts for the Afterlife: Orpheus and the Bacchic Gold Tablets.* London and New York: Routledge.

Gray, P. 2003. *Godly Fear: The Epistle to the Hebrews and Greco-Roman Critiques of Superstition.* Atlanta: Society of Biblical Literature.

Griffith, M. 1990. "Contest and Contradiction in Early Greek Poetry." In Griffith, M. and Mastronarde, D. J. eds. *Cabinet of the Muses: Essays on Classical and Comparative Literature in Honor of Thomas G. Rosenmeyer.* Atlanta, GA: Scholars Press. 185–207.

Gruen, E. S. 1998. *Heritage and Hellenism: The Reinvention of Jewish Tradition.* Hellenistic Culture and Society, 30. Berkeley, CA: University of California Press.

Güterbock, H. G. 1948. "The Hittite Version of the Hurrian Kumarbi Myths: Oriental Forerunners of Hesiod." *American Journal of Archaeology* 52(1): 123–134.

Guthrie, W. K. C. 1952. *Orpheus and Greek Religion: A Study of the Orphic Movement.* Methuen's Handbooks of Archaeology. London: Methuen.

Halleux, R. and Schamp, J. 1985. *Les lapidaires grecs.* Collection des universités de France. Paris: Les Belles Lettres.

Hardie, A. 2000. "Pindar's 'Theban' Cosmogony (The First Hymn)." *Bulletin of the Institute of Classical Studies* 44: 19–40.

Harrison, J. E. 1903. *Prolegomena to the Study of Greek religion.* Cambridge: Cambridge University Press.

1922. *Prolegomena to the Study of Greek Religion.* 3rd edn. Cambridge: Cambridge University Press.

Havelock, E. A. 1963. *Preface to Plato.* A History of the Greek Mind, 1. Cambridge, MA and London: Belknap Press of Harvard University Press.

Henrichs, A. 1984a. "The Eumenides and Wineless Libations in the Derveni Papyrus." In *Atti del XVII Congresso Internazionale di Papirologia.* Naples: Centro internazionale per lo studio dei papiri ercolanesi. 255–268.

1984b. "The Sophists and Hellenistic Religion: Prodicus as the Spiritual Father of the Isis Aretalogies." *Harvard Studies in Classical Philology* 88: 139–158.

2003. "Writing Religion: Inscribed Texts, Ritual Authority, and the Religious Discourse of the Polis." In Yunis, H. ed. *Written Texts and the Rise of Literate Culture in Ancient Greece.* Cambridge and New York: Cambridge University Press. 38–58.

Hermann, G. 1805. *Orphica.* Leipzig: Caspari Fritsch.

Herrero, M. 2007a. *Tradición órfica y cristianismo antiguo.* Colección Estructuras y procesos, Serie Religión. Madrid: Editorial Trotta.

2007b. "Las fuentes de Clem. Alex., *Protr.* ii 12–22: un tratado sobre los misterios y una teogonía órfica." *Emerita* 75(1): 19–50.

2007c. "¿A quién dirige Gregorio de Nazianzo su crítica de la reencarnación (De anima 22–52)?" *Adamantius* 13: 231–246.

2010. *Orphism and Christianity in Late Antiquity.* Sozomena, 7. Berlin and New York: Walter de Gruyter.

Hershbell, J. P. 1981. *Pseudo-Plato, Axiochus.* Society of Biblical Literature. Texts and Translations, 21. Graeco-Roman Religion Series, 6. Chico, CA: Scholars Press.

Holladay, C. R. 1996. *Fragments from Hellenistic Jewish Authors.* Volume 4: *Orphica.* Society of Biblical Literature, Texts and translations 40. Pseudepigrapha series 14. Chico, CA: Scholars Press.

Honko, L. 1979. "Theories Concerning the Ritual Process: An Orientation." In Honko, L. ed. *Science of Religion: Studies in Methodology. Proceedings of the Study Conference of the International Association for the History of Religions,*

412   Bibliography

Held in Turku, Finland, August 27–31, 1973. Religion and Reason, 13. The
     Hague, Paris and New York: Mouton. 369–390.
Hordern, J. 2000. "Notes on the Orphic Papyrus from Gurôb (P. Gurôb 1; Pack2
     2464)." *Zeitschrift für Papyrologie und Epigraphik* 129: 131–140.
Humphreys, S. C. 1980. "Family Tombs and Tomb Cult in Ancient Athens:
     Tradition or Traditionalism?" *Journal of Hellenic Studies* 100: 96–126.
Huss, B. 2010. "Orpheus." In Moog-Grünewald, M. ed. *The Reception of Myth
     and Mythology.* Brill's New Pauly Supplements 4. Leiden and Boston: Brill.
     478–494.
Hutchinson, D. S. and Johnson, M. R. 2005. "Authenticating Aristotle's *Protrep-
     ticus.*" *Oxford Studies in Ancient Philosophy* 29: 193–294.
Isler-Kerényi, C. 2007. "Modern Mythologies: 'Dionysos' versus 'Apollo'."
     In *Dionysos in Archaic Greece: An Understanding through Images.* Reli-
     gions in the Graeco-Roman World, 160. Leiden and Boston: E. J. Brill.
     235–254.
Jaeger, W. 1945. *Paideia: The Ideals of Greek Culture.* Trans. Highet, G. New York:
     Oxford University Press.
Jameson, M. H., Jordan, D. R. and Kotansky, R. D. 1993. *A Lex Sacra from
     Selinous.* Durham, NC: Duke University Press.
Janko, R. 1997. "The Physicist as Hierophant: Aristophanes, Socrates and the
     Authorship of the Derveni Papyrus." *Zeitschrift für Papyrologie und Epigraphik*
     118: 61–94.
     2001. "The Derveni Papyrus (Diagoras of Melos, *Apopyrgizontes Logoi?*): A New
     Translation." *Classical Philology* 96(1): 1–32.
     2002. "The Derveni Papyrus: An Interim Text." *Zeitschrift für Papyrologie und
     Epigraphik* 141: 1–62.
     2002–03. "God, Science and Socrates." *Bulletin of the Institute of Classical Studies*
     46: 1–18.
     2005. [Untitled] Review of Betegh 2004. *Bryn Mawr Classical Review* 2005.01.27.
     http://bmcr.brynmawr.edu/2005/2005-01-27.html.
     2008. "Reconstructing (Again) the Opening of the Derveni Papyrus." *Zeitschrift
     für Papyrologie und Epigraphik* 166: 37–51.
Jiménez, A. I. 2001. "Consideraciones sobre las teletai Órficas." In Castro, J. F. G.
     and Vidal, J. L. eds. *Actas del X Congreso Espanol de Estudios Clásicos (21–25 de
     septiembre de 1999), III.* Madrid: Sociedad Espanola de Estudios Clasicos.
     2002. *Rituales órficos.* Thesis/dissertation, Universidad Complutense de Madrid.
     2008. "Los orfeotelestas y la vida órfica." In Bernabé, A. and Casadesús, F. eds.
     Orfeo y la tradición órfica: Un reencuentro. Akal universitaria. Serie religiones
     y mitos, 280–281. Madrid: Akal. 771–799.
Johnston, S. I. 1999. *Restless Dead: Encounters Between the Living and the Dead
     in Ancient Greece.* Berkeley and Los Angeles: University of California
     Press.
     2004. "Death, the afterlife, and other last things: Greece." In Johnston, S. I.
     ed. *Religions of the Ancient World: A Guide.* Cambridge, MA: Belknap Press.
     486–488.

2008. *Ancient Greek Divination*. Blackwell Ancient Religions. Malden, MA and Oxford: Wiley-Blackwell.

Jordan, D. R. 1997a. "An Address to a Ghost at Olbia." *Mnemosyne* 50(2): 212–219.

1997b. "Two Curse Tablets from Lilybaeum." *Greek, Roman and Byzantine Studies* 38(4): 387–396.

Jouan, F. and Van Looy, H. eds. 2000. *Euripide*. Volume 7: *Fragments, Part 2: Bellérophon-Protésilas*. Collection des universités de France. Série grecque, 406. Paris: Les Belles lettres.

Jouanna, J. 1975. *Hippocrates: La nature de l'homme. éd., trad. et comm.* Corpus medicorum Graecorum, I, 1,3. Berlin: Akademie-Verlag.

1999. *Hippocrates*. Trans. DeBevoise, M. B. Baltimore, MD: Johns Hopkins University Press.

Jourdan, F. 2003. *Le papyrus de Derveni*. Paris: Les Belles Lettres.

2005. "Manger Dionysos: l'interpretation du mythe du demembrement par Plutarque a-t-elle ete lue par les neo-Platoniciens?" *Pallas* 67: 153–174.

2006. "Dionysos dans le Protreptique de Clément d'Alexandrie: Initiations dionysiaques et mystères chrétiens." *Revue de l'histoire des religions* 223(3): 265–282.

2010. *Orphée et les chrétiens: La réception du mythe d'Orphée dans la littérature chrétienne grecque des cinq premiers siècles. Volume 1: Orphée, du repoussoir au préfigurateur du Christ: "réécriture d'un mythe à des fins protreptiques chez Clément d'Alexandrie"*. Anagôgê, 4. Paris: Les Belles lettres.

2011. *Orphée et les chrétiens: La réception du mythe d'Orphée dans la littérature chrétienne grecque des cinq premiers siècles. Volume 2: Pourquoi Orphée?* Anagôgê, 5. Paris: Les Belles lettres.

Kahn, C. H. 1985. *Anaximander and the Origins of Greek Cosmology*. Philadelphia, PA: Centrum Philadelphia.

1997. "Was Euthyphro the Author of the Derveni Papyrus?" In Laks, A. and Most, G. W. eds. *Studies on the Derveni Papyrus*. Oxford and New York: Oxford University Press. 9–22.

Kaibel, G. 1878. *Epigrammata Graeca ex lapidibus conlecta*. Berlin: G. Reimer.

1879. "Supplementum Epigrammatum Graecorum ex lapidibus conlectorum." *Rheinisches Museum für Philologie, Geschichte und griechische Philosophie* 34: 181–213.

Kern, O. 1888. *De Orphei, Epimenidis, Pherecydis theogoniis quaestiones criticae*. Berlin: Libraria Nicolai (R. Stricker).

1922. *Orphicorum Fragmenta*. Berlin: Weidmann.

King, C. 2003. "The Organization of Roman Religious Beliefs." *Classical Antiquity* 22(2): 275–312.

King, K. L. 2003. *What is Gnosticism?* Cambridge, MA: Belknap Press of Harvard University Press.

Kingsley, P. 1995. *Ancient Philosophy, Mystery, and Magic: Empedocles and Pythagorean Tradition*. Oxford: Clarendon Press.

Kinney, D. 1994. "The Iconography of the Ivory Diptych Nicomachorum-Symmachorum." *Jahrbuch für Antike und Christentum* 37: 64–96.

Komorowska, J. 2004. *Vettius Valens of Antioch: An Intellectual Monography.* Kraków : Księgarnia Akademicka.

Kouremenos, T., Parássoglou, G. M. and Tsantsanoglou, K. 2006. *The Derveni Papyrus.* Studi e testi per il Corpus dei papiri filosofici greci e latini, 13. Florence: L.S. Olschki.

Kowalzig, B. 2007. *Singing for the Gods: Performances of Myth and Ritual in Archaic and Classical Greece.* Oxford Classical Monographs. Oxford and New York: Oxford University Press.

Laks, A. 1997. "Between Religion and Philosophy: The Function of Allegory in the Derveni Papyrus." *Phronesis* 42(2): 121–142.

Lambert, W. G. and Millard, A. R. 1969. *Atra-ḫasīs: the Babylonian story of the Flood.* Oxford: Clarendon Press.

Larson, J. 1995. *Greek Heroine Cults.* Wisconsin Studies in Classics. Madison: University of Wisconsin Press.

Ledbetter, G. M. 2003. *Poetics Before Plato: Interpretation and Authority in Early Greek Theories of Poetry.* Princeton: Princeton University Press.

Levaniouk, O. 2007. "The Toys of Dionysos." *Harvard Studies in Classical Philology* 103: 165–202.

Lévêque, P. 1982. "Olbios et la félicité des initiés." In Hadermann-Misguich, L., Raepsaet, G. and Cambier, G. eds. *Rayonnement grec: Hommages à Charles Delvoye.* Université libre de Bruxelles, Faculté de philosophie et lettres, 83. Brussels: Editions de l'Université de Bruxelles. 113–126.

Lévi-Strauss, C. 1966. *The Savage Mind.* Chicago: The University of Chicago Press.

Lincoln, B. 1993. "Socrates' Persecutors, Philosophy's Rivals, and the Politics of Discursive Forms." *Arethusa* 26(3): 233–246.

Linforth, I. M. 1941. *The Arts of Orpheus.* Berkeley and Los Angeles: University of California Press.

——— 1946. "Telestic Madness in Plato, *Phaedrus* 244 DE." *University of California Publications in Classical Philology* 13(6): 163–172.

Lobeck, C. A. 1829. *Aglaophamus, sive, De theologiae mysticae Graecorum causis libri tres.* Königsberg: Fratrum Borntraeger.

Loisy, A. 1919. *Les mystères païens et le mystère chrétien.* Paris: Émile Nourry.

Long, A. A. 1992. "Stoic Readings of Homer." In Lambarton, R. and Keaney, J. J. eds. *Homer's Ancient Readers: The Hermeneutics of Greek Epic's Earliest Exegetes.* Magie Classical Publications. Princeton: Princeton University Press. 41–66.

Long, H. S. 1948. *A Study of the Doctrine of Metempsychosis: From Pythagoras to Plato.* Princeton: Princeton University Press.

López-Ruiz, C. 2010. *When the Gods Were Born: Greek Cosmogonies and the Near East.* Cambridge, MA and London: Harvard University Press.

Loraux, N. 2000. *Born of the Earth: Myth and Politics in Athens.* Trans. Stewart, S. Ithaca, NY and London: Cornell University Press.

Lucas, D. W. 1946. "Hippolytus." *Classical Quarterly* 40(3/4): 65–69.

Luginbühl, M. 1992. *Menschenschöpfungsmythen: Ein Vergleich zwischen Griechenland und dem Alten Orient*. Klassische Sprachen und Literaturen, 58. Bern: Peter Lang.

Lupu, E. 2005. *Greek Sacred Law: A Collection of New Documents (NGSL)*. Religions in the Graeco-Roman World, 152. Leiden and Boston: Brill.

Maass, E. 1898. *Commentariorum in Aratum reliquae*. Berlin: Weidmann.

Macchioro, V. 1922. *Eraclito: Nuovi studi sull'orfismo*. Biblioteca di cultura moderna. Bari: G. Laterza & figli.

——— 1930. *From Orpheus to Paul: A History of Orphism*. Studies in religion and culture: Schermerhorn Lectures, 1. New York: H. Holt and Company.

Macías Otero, S. 2010. "Euripides, fr. 912 Kannicht (*OF* 458)." In Bernabé, A., Casadesús, F. and Santamaría, M. A. eds. *Orfeo y el orfismo: Nuevas perspectivas*. Alicante: Biblioteca Virtual Miguel de Cervantes. 405–420.

Mansfeld, J. 1983. "Cratylus 402a-c: Plato or Hippias?" In Rossetti, L. ed. *Atti del Symposium Heracliteum 1981*. Volume 1: *Studi*. Rome: Edizioni dell'Ateneo. 43–55. (Reprinted in Mansfeld 1990.)

——— 1990. *Studies in the Historiography of Greek Philosophy*. Assen: Van Gorcum.

Marcel, R. 1958. *Marsile Ficin, 1433–1499*. Les Classiques de l'humanisme. Études, 6. Paris: Les Belles Lettres.

Martin, D. B. 2004. *Inventing Superstition: From the Hippocratics to the Christians*. Cambridge, MA and London: Harvard University Press.

Martin, L. H. and Pachis, P. eds. 2009. *Imagistic Traditions in the Graeco-Roman World: A Cognitive Modeling of History of Religious Research*. Acts of the Panel Held During the XIX C Congress of the International Association of History of Religions (IAHR), Tokyo, Japan, March 2005. Thessaloniki: Equinox.

Matelli, E. 2010. "Peripato e orfismo a Rodi." In Bernabé, A., Casadesús, F. and Santamaría, M. A. eds. *Orfeo y el orfismo: Nuevas perspectivas*. Alicante: Biblioteca Virtual Miguel de Cervantes. 421–454.

Mayerson, P. 2000. "The Meaning and Function of ληνός and Related Features in the Production of Wine." *Zeitschrift für Papyrologie und Epigraphik* 131: 161–165.

Moore, C. H. 1912. "Greek and Roman Ascetic Tendencies." In Smyth, H. W. ed. *Harvard Essays on Classical Subjects*. Boston and New York: Houghton Mifflin Co. 97–140.

Morand, A.-F. 2001. *Études sur les Hymnes orphiques*. Religions in the Graeco-Roman World, 143. Leiden, Boston and Cologne: Brill.

Morford, M. P. O. and Lenardon, R. J. 1999. *Classical Mythology*. 6th edn. Oxford and New York: Oxford University Press.

Morgan, K. A. 2000. *Myth and Philosophy from the Presocratics to Plato*. Cambridge and New York: Cambridge University Press.

Most, G. W. 1994. "Simonides' Ode to Scopas in Contexts." In Jong, I. J. F. d. and Sullivan, J. P. eds. *Modern Critical Theory and Classical Literature*. Mnemosyne. Supplementum, 130. Leiden and New York: E.J. Brill. 127–152.

1997a. "The Fire Next Time. Cosmology, Allegoresis, and Salvation in the Derveni Papyrus." *Journal of Hellenic Studies* 117: 117–135.

1997b. "Hesiod's Myth of the Five (or Three or Four) Races." *Proceedings of the Cambridge Philological Society* 43: 104–127.

Mylonas, G. E. 1961. *Eleusis and the Eleusinian Mysteries*. Princeton: Princeton University Press.

Nagy, G. 1979. *The Best of the Achaeans: Concepts of the Hero in Archaic Greek Poetry*. Baltimore, MD: Johns Hopkins University Press.

Nickel, R. 2003. "The Wrath of Demeter: Story Pattern in the *Hymn to Demeter*." *Quaderni Urbinati di Cultura Classica* 73(1): 59–82.

Nightingale, A. W. 1995. *Genres in Dialogue: Plato and the Construct of Philosophy*. Cambridge and New York: Cambridge University Press.

Nilsson, M. 1957. *The Dionysiac Mysteries of the Hellenistic and Roman Age*. Skrifter utgivna av Svenska institutet i Athen, 8.5. Lund: C. W. K. Gleerup.

Nock, A. D. 1940. "Orphism or Popular Philosophy?" *Harvard Theological Review* 33(4): 301–315. (Reprinted in Nock 1986: 503–515.)

1958. "A Cult Ordinance in verse." *Harvard Studies in Classical Philology* 63: 415–421. (Reprinted in Nock 1986: 847–852.)

1986. *Essays on Religion and the Ancient World. Selected and Edited, with an Introd., Bibliography of Nock's Writings, and Indexes, by Zeph Stewart*. Oxford and New York: Oxford University Press.

Norden, E. 1927. *P. Vergilius Maro Aeneis Buch VI*. Leipzig and Berlin: Teubner.

Obbink, D. 1994. "A Quotation of the Derveni Papyrus in Philodemus' *On Piety*." *Cronache Ercolanesi* 24: 111–135.

1997. "Cosmology as Initiation vs. the Critique of Orphic Mysteries." In Laks, A. and Most, G. W. eds. *Studies on the Derveni Papyrus*. Oxford and New York: Oxford University Press. 39–54.

2011. "Dionysos in and out of the Papyri." In Schlesier, R. ed. *A Different God? Dionysos and Ancient Polytheism*. Berlin and Boston: De Gruyter. 281–296.

Obeyesekere, G. 2002. *Imagining Karma: Ethical Transformation in Amerindian, Buddhist, and Greek Rebirth*. Comparative Studies in Religion and Society, 14. Berkeley and Los Angeles: University of California Press.

Olender, M. 1990. "Aspects of Baubo: Ancient Texts and Contexts." In Halperin, D. M., Winkler, J. J. and Zeitlin, F. I. eds. *Before Sexuality: The Construction of Erotic Experience in the Ancient Greek World*. Princeton: Princeton University Press. 83–107.

Oliver, J. H. 1950. *The Athenian Expounders of the Sacred and Ancestral Law*. Baltimore, MD: Johns Hopkins University Press.

Orlin, E. M. 1997. *Temples, Religion, and Politics in the Roman Republic*. Mnemosyne Supplements. History and Archaeology of Classical Antiquity, 164. Leiden, New York and Cologne: E. J. Brill.

Osborne, C. 1987. *Rethinking Early Greek Philosophy: Hippolytus of Rome and the Presocratics*. Ithaca, NY: Cornell University Press.

Otto, W. F. 1965. *Dionysus, Myth and Cult*. Trans. Palmer, R. B. Bloomington: Indiana University Press.

Palaima, T. G. 2004. "Appendix One: Linear B Sources." In Trzaskoma, S., Smith, R. S. and Brunet, S. eds. *Anthology of Classical Myth: Primary Sources in Translation*. Indianapolis: Hackett Publishing Co. 439–454.

Paoletti, O. 2004. "Purificazione." In *Thesaurus Cultus et Rituum Antiquorum (ThesCRA) II. Purification – Initiation – Heroization – Apotheosis – Banquet – Dance – Music – Cult Images*. Los Angeles: J. Paul Getty Museum. 3–35.

Parker, R. 1983. *Miasma: Pollution and Purity in Early Greek Religion*. Oxford: Clarendon Press.

1986. "Myths of Early Athens." In Bremmer, J. N. ed. *Interpretations of Greek Mythology*. Totowa, NJ: Barnes & Noble Books. 187–214.

1995. "Early Orphism." In Powell, A. ed. *The Greek World*. London and New York: Routledge. 483–510.

1996. *Athenian Religion: A History*. Oxford and New York: Oxford University Press.

2005. *Polytheism and Society at Athens*. Oxford and New York: Oxford University Press.

2011. *On Greek Religion*. Cornell Studies in Classical Philology, 60. Ithaca, NY: Cornell University Press.

nd. "Apotropaic Gods." *Brill's New Pauly*. Brill Online, 2012. Reference. Bryn Mawr College. 16 October 2012. http://referenceworks.brillonline.com/entries/brill-s-new-pauly/apotropaic-gods-e1289o.

Parker, R. and Stamatopoulou, M. 2004. "A New Funerary Gold Leaf from Pherai." *Archaeologike Ephemeris* 143: 1–32.

Pendrick, G. J. 2002. *Antiphon: The Fragments*. Cambridge Classical Texts and Commentaries, 39. Cambridge and New York: Cambridge University Press.

Peradotto, J. 1977. "Oedipus and Erichthonius: Some Observations on Paradigmatic and Syntagmatic Order." *Arethusa* 10(1): 85–101.

Petersen, A. K. 2011. "Rituals of Purification, Rituals of Initiation: Phenomenological, Taxonomical and Culturally Evolutionary Reflections." In Hellholm, D., Vegge, T., Norderval, Ø., and Hellholm, C. eds. *Ablution, Initiation, and Baptism: Late Antiquity, Early Judaism, and Early Christianity*. Beihefte zur Zeitschrift für die neutestamentliche Wissenschaft und die Kunde der älteren Kirche, 176. Berlin and New York: De Gruyter. 3–40.

Pickard-Cambridge, A. W. 1968. *The Dramatic Festivals of Athens*. Oxford and New York: Oxford University Press.

Pohlenz, M. 1916. "Kronos und die Titanen." *Neue Jahrbücher für das Klassiche Altertum* 38: 549–594.

Popper, K. R. 1963. *Conjectures and Refutations: The Growth of Scientific Knowledge*. London: Routledge & Kegan Paul.

Privitera, G. A. 1965. *Laso di Ermione nella cultura ateniese e nella tradizione storiografica*. Filologia e critica, 1. Rome: Edizioni dell'Ateneo.

Pugliese Carratelli, G. 1993. *Le lamine d'oro "orfiche"*. Milan: Libri Scheiwiller.

2001. *Le lamine d'oro orfiche: Istruzioni per il viaggio oltremondano degli iniziati greci*. Biblioteca Adelphi, 419. Milan: Adelphi.

Pulleyn, S. 1997. *Prayer in Greek Religion.* Oxford Classical Monographs. Oxford and New York: Oxford University Press.

Rangos, S. 2007. "Latent Meaning and Manifest Content in the Derveni Papyrus." *Rhizai* 4(1): 35–75.

Reale, G. and Bos, A. P. 1995. *Il trattato Sul cosmo per Alessandro attribuito ad Aristotele.* Temi metafisici e problemi del pensiero antico, 42. Milan: Vita e pensiero.

Redfield, J. 1990. "From Sex to Politics: The Rites of Artemis Triklaria and Dionysus Aisymnetes at Patras." In Halperin, D. M., Winkler, J. J., and Zeitlin, F. I. eds. *Before Sexuality: The Construction of Erotic Experience in the Ancient Greek World.* Princeton: Princeton University Press. 115–134.

1991. "The Politics of Immortality." In Borgeaud, P. ed. *Orphisme et Orphée: En l'honneur de Jean Rudhardt.* Recherches et rencontres, 3. Geneva: Librairie Droz. 103–117.

2003. *The Locrian Maidens: Love and Death in Greek Italy.* Princeton: Princeton University Press.

Reinach, S. 1909. *Orpheus: A General History of Religions.* Trans. Simmonds, F. New York: G. P. Putnam's Sons.

Ricciardelli, G. 2000. *Inni orfici.* Scrittori greci e latini. Milan: A. Mondadori.

Richardson, N. J. 1974. *The Homeric Hymn to Demeter.* Oxford: Clarendon Press.

Riedweg, C. 1993. *Jüdisch-hellenistische Imitation eines orphischen Hieros Logos: Beobachtungen zu OF 245 und 247 (sog. Testament des Orpheus).* Classica Monacensia, 7. Tübingen: G. Narr Verlag.

1994. *PS.-Justin (Markell von Ankyra?), Ad Graecos de vera religione (bisher "Cohortatio ad Graecos").* Schweizerische Beiträge zur Altertumswissenschaft, 25. Basle and Berlin: F. Reinhardt.

1998. "Initiation – Tod – Unterwelt: Beobachtungen zur Kommunikationssituation und narrativen Technik der orphisch-bakchischen Goldblättchen." In Graf, F. ed. *Ansichten griechischer Rituale: Geburtstags-Symposium für Walter Burkert.* Stuttgart and Leipzig: Teubner. 359–398.

2002. "Poésie orphique et rituel initiatique: Éléments d'un 'Discours sacré' dans les lamelles d'or." *Revue de l'histoire des religions* 219(4): 459–481.

2005. *Pythagoras: His Life, Teaching, and Influence.* Trans. Rendall, S. Ithaca, NY: Cornell University Press.

2011. "Initiation – Death – Underworld: Narrative and Ritual in the Gold Leaves." In Edmonds, R. G., III ed. *The "Orphic" Gold Tablets and Greek Religion: Further Along the Path.* Cambridge and New York: Cambridge University Press. 219–256.

Robertson, N. 2003. "Orphic Mysteries and Dionysiac Ritual." In Cosmopoulos, M. B. ed. *Greek Mysteries: The Archaeology of Ancient Greek Secret Cults.* London and New York: Routledge. 218–240.

Roessli, J.-M. 2008. "La cosmo-théologie orphique du roman pseudo-clémentin: Note sur ses sources et son utilisation dans les 'Homélies' et les 'Reconnaissances'." *Les Études Classiques* 76(1): 83–94.

Rohde, E. 1895. *Die Religion der Griechen: Rede zum Geburtsfeste des höchstseligen Grossherzogs Karl Friedrich und zur akademischen Preisvertheilung, am 22. November 1894.* Heidelberg: Universitäts-Buchdruckerei von J. Horning.

———. 1925. *Psyche: The Cult of Souls and Belief in Immortality among the Greeks.* Trans. Hillis, W. B. London: Kegan Paul, Trench, Trubner & Co.

Roller, L. E. 1999. *In Search of God the Mother: The Cult of Anatolian Cybele.* Berkeley and Los Angeles: University of California Press.

Rosch, E. and Mervis, C. B. 1975. "Family Resemblances: Studies in the Internal Structure of Categories." *Cognitive Psychology* 7: 573–605.

Rose, H. J. 1936. "The Ancient Grief: A Study of Pindar, Fr. 133 (Bergk)." In Bailey, C. ed. *Greek Poetry and Life: Essays Presented to Gilbert Murray on His Seventieth Birthday, January 2, 1936.* Oxford: Clarendon Press. 79–96.

———. 1943. "The Grief of Persephone." *The Harvard Theological Review* 36(3): 247–250.

Roth, P. 1984. "Teiresias as Mantis and Intellectual in Euripides' *Bacchae*." *Transactions of the American Philological Association* 114: 59–69.

Rouse, W. H. D. 1940. *Nonnos: Dionysiaca, Volumes i–iii.* Loeb Classical Library, 344, 354, 356. Cambridge, MA: Harvard University Press.

Rudhardt, J. 1994. "Concerning the *Homeric Hymn to Demeter*." In Foley, H. P. ed. *The Homeric Hymn to Demeter: Translation, Commentary, and Interpretive Essays.* Princeton: Princeton University Press. 198–211.

Rusten, J. S. 1985. "Interim Notes on the Papyrus from Derveni." *Harvard Studies in Classical Philology* 89: 121–140.

Santamaria, M. A. 2012. "Orfeo y el orfismo. Actualización bibliográfica (2004–2012)." *'Ilu. Revista de Ciencias de las Religiones* 17: 211–252.

Saunders, T. 1990. "Plato and the Athenian Law of Theft." In Cartledge, P. A., Millett, P. C. and Todd, S. C. eds. *Nomos: Essays in Athenian Law, Politics and Society.* Cambridge: Cambridge University Press. 63–82.

Schibli, H. S. 1990. *Pherekydes of Syros.* Oxford and New York: Oxford University Press.

Schuddeboom, F. 2009. *Greek Religious Terminology: Telete & Orgia. A Revised and Expanded English Edition of the Studies by Zijderveld and Van der Burg.* Religions in the Graeco-Roman World, 169. Leiden and Boston: Brill.

Scodel, R. 2011. "Euripides, the Derveni Papyrus, and the Smoke of Many Writings." In Lardinois, A. P. M. H., Blok, J. H., and Poel, M. G. M. v. d. eds. *Sacred Words: Orality, Literacy, and Religion.* Volume 8 of *Orality and Literacy in the Ancient World.* Mnemosyne Supplements, 332. Leiden and Boston: Brill. 79–100.

Smith, J. Z. 1978. *Map is not Territory: Studies in the History of Religions.* Studies in Judaism in Late Antiquity, 23. Leiden: E.J. Brill.

———. 1982. *Imagining Religion: From Babylon to Jonestown.* Chicago Studies in the History of Judaism. Chicago: University of Chicago Press.

———. 1987. *To Take Place.* Chicago: University of Chicago Press.

———. 1990. *Drudgery Divine: On the Comparison of Early Christianities and the Religions of Late Antiquity.* Chicago: University of Chicago Press.

Smyth, H. W. 1912. "Greek Conceptions of Immortality from Homer to Plato."
In Smyth, H. W. ed. *Harvard Essays on Classical Subjects*. Boston and New
York: Houghton Mifflin Co. 239–283.

Snell, B. 1966. "Die Nachrichten über die Lehren des Thales und die Anfänge der
griechischen Philosophie- und Literaturgeschichte." In *Gesammelte Schriften*.
Göttingen: Vandenhoeck & Ruprecht. 119–128.

Snodgrass, A. M. 1971. *The Dark Age of Greece: An Archaeological Survey of
the Eleventh to the Eighth Centuries* BC. Edinburgh: Edinburgh University
Press.

Sourvinou-Inwood, C. 1981. "To Die and Enter the House of Hades: Homer,
Before and After." In Whaley, J. ed. *Mirrors of Mortality: Studies in the Social
History of Death*. New York: St. Martin's Press. 15–39.

1986. "Crime and Punishment: Tityos, Tantalos, and Sisyphos in *Odyssey* 11."
Bulletin of the Institute of Classical Studies 33: 37–58.

1991. *"Reading Greek Culture": Texts and Images, Rituals and Myths*. Oxford:
Clarendon Press.

1995. *"Reading" Greek Death: To the End of the Classical Period*. Oxford and
New York: Oxford University Press.

2003. "Herodotos (and Others) on Pelasgians: Some Perceptions of Ethnicity."
In Derow, P. and Parker, R. eds. *Herodotus and His World: Essays from a
Conference in Memory of George Forrest*. Oxford and New York: Oxford
University Press. 103–144.

2005. *Hylas, the Nymphs, Dionysos and Others: Myth, Ritual, Ethnicity. Martin
P. Nilsson Lecture on Greek Religion, delivered 1997 at the Swedish Institute at
Athens*. Skrifter utgivna av Svenska institutet i Athen, 19. Stockholm: Paul
Aaström.

Sowa, C. A. 1984. *Traditional Themes and the Homeric Hymns*. Chicago: Bolchazy-
Carducci.

Spineto, N. 2010. "Spontaneità naturale e intervento umano: Aspetti religiosi della
viticoltura in Grecia." In Montero, S. and Cardete, M. C. eds. *Naturaleza y
religión en el mundo clásico: usos y abusos del medio natural*. Thema Mundi, 3.
Madrid: Signifer Libros. 9–18.

Stewart, A. 1998. "Nuggets: Mining the Texts Again." *American Journal of Archaeology* 102(2): 271–282.

Struck, P. 2003. "The Ordeal of the Divine Sign: Divination and Manliness in
Archaic and Classical Greece." In Rosen, R. M. and Sluiter, I. eds. *Andreia:
Studies in Manliness and Courage in Classical Antiquity*. Mnemosyne Supple-
mentum, 238. Leiden and Boston: Brill. 167–186.

2004. *Birth of the Symbol: Ancient Readers at the Limits of their Texts*. Princeton:
Princeton University Press.

Sutcliffe, S. 2003. *Children of the New Age: A History of Spiritual Practices*. London
and New York: Routledge.

Taylor, T. 1792. *The Hymns of Orpheus, Translated from the original Greek: With a
Preliminary Dissertation on the Life and Theology of Orpheus*. London: Printed
for the Author.

1824. *The Mystical Hymns of Orpheus. Translated from the Greek, and demonstrated to be the Invocations which were used in the Eleusinian Mysteries.* Chiswick: C. Whittingham.

Themelis, P. G. and Touratsoglou, G. 1997. *Οι Τάφοι του Δερβενίου. Δημοσιέυματα του Αρχαιολογικόυ Δελτίου*, 59. Athens: Ταμειο Αρχαιολογικων Πορων και Απαλλοτριωσεων.

Thomas, R. 2003. "Prose Performance Texts: Epideixis and Written Publication in the Late Fifth and Early Fourth Centuries." In Yunis, H. ed. *Written Texts and the Rise of Literate Culture in Ancient Greece.* Cambridge and New York: Cambridge University Press. 162–188.

Thönges-Stringaris, R. 1965. "Das griechische Totenmahl." *Mittheilungen des Deutschen Archaeologischen Instituts. Athenische Abtheilung* 80: 1–99.

Tiedemann, D. 1780. *Griechenlands erste Philosophen oder Leben und Systeme des Orpheus, Pherecydes, Thales und Pythagoras.* Leipzig: Weidmanns Erben und Reich.

Torjussen, S. S. 2008. *Metamorphoses of Myth: A Study of the "Orphic" Gold Tablets and the Derveni Papyrus.* PhD Thesis, University of Tromsø.

Tortorelli Ghidini, M. 2006. *Figli della terra e del cielo stellato: Testi orfici con traduzione e commento.* Speculum. Naples: M. D'Auria.

Trampedach, K. 2008. "Authority Disputed: The Seer in Homeric Epic." In Dignas, B. and Trampedach, K. eds. *Practitioners of the Divine: Greek Priests and Religious Officials from Homer to Heliodorus.* Hellenic Studies, 30. Washington, DC: Center for Hellenic Studies. 207–230.

Tsantsanoglou, K. 1997. "The First Columns of the Derveni Papyrus and their Religious Significance." In Laks, A. and Most, G. W. eds. *Studies on the Derveni Papyrus.* Oxford and New York: Oxford University Press. 93–128.

Versnel, H. S. 1990. *Ter Unus: Isis, Dionysos, Hermes: Three Studies in Henotheism.* Volume 1 of *Inconsistencies in Greek Religion.* Leiden: E. J. Brill.

———. 1991. "Some Reflections on the Relationship Magic–Religion." *Numen* 38(2): 177–197.

———. 1993. *Transition and Reversal in Myth and Ritual.* Volume 2 of *Inconsistencies in Greek Religion.* Leiden: E. J. Brill.

Vian, F. 1952. *La Guerre des Géants: le mythe avant l'époque hellénistique.* Paris: Librairie C. Klincksieck.

———. 1987. *Les argonautiques orphiques.* Paris: Les Belles Lettres.

Vicari, P. 1982. "Sparagmos: Orpheus among the Christians." In Warden, J. ed. *Orpheus, the Metamorphoses of a Myth.* Toronto and Buffalo: University of Toronto Press. 63–83.

Walker, D. P. 1953. "Orpheus the Theologian and Renaissance Platonists." *Journal of the Warburg and Courtauld Institutes* 16(1): 100–120.

Warden, J. 1982. "Orpheus and Ficino." In Warden, J. ed. *Orpheus, the Metamorphoses of a Myth.* Toronto and Buffalo: University of Toronto Press. 85–110.

Watmough, J. R. 1934. *Orphism.* Cambridge: Cambridge University Press.

West, M. L. 1982. "The Orphics of Olbia." *Zeitschrift für Papyrologie und Epigraphik* 45: 17–29.

1983. *The Orphic Poems*. Oxford and New York: Oxford University Press.

2007. *Indo-European Poetry and Myth*. Oxford and New York: Oxford University Press.

Westerink, L. G. 1976. *The Greek Commentaries on Plato's Phaedo: Damascius*. Amsterdam, Oxford, New York: North-Holland Publishing Co.

1977. *The Greek Commentaries on Plato's Phaedo: Olympiodorus*. Amsterdam, Oxford, New York: North-Holland Publishing Co.

Whitehouse, H. 2000. *Arguments and Icons: Divergent Modes of Religiosity*. Oxford and New York: Oxford University Press.

Whitely, J. 1995. "Tomb Cult and Hero Cult: The Uses of the Past in Archaic Greece." In Spencer, N. ed. *Time, Tradition, and Society in Greek Archaeology: Bridging the "Great Divide"*. Theoretical Archaeology Group (TAG). London and New York: Routledge. 43–63.

Wilamowitz-Moellendorff, U. v. 1931–32. *Der Glaube der Hellenen*. Berlin: Weidmannsche Buchhandlung.

Williams, M. A. 1996. *Rethinking "Gnosticism": An Argument for Dismantling a Dubious Category*. Princeton: Princeton University Press.

Wittgenstein, L. 1958. *Philosophical Investigations: The English Text of the Third Edition*. Trans. Anscombe, G. E. M. New York: Prentice Hall.

Woodbury, L. 1986. "The Judgment of Dionysus: Books, Taste and Teaching in the Frogs." In Cropp, M., Fantham, E. and Scully, S. E. eds. *Greek Tragedy and Its Legacy: Essays Presented to D.J. Conacher*. Calgary: University of Calgary Press. 241–258.

Yates, V. 2004. "The Titanic Origin of Humans: The Melian Nymphs and Zagreus." *Greek, Roman, and Byzantine Studies* 44(2): 183–198.

Zaborowski, R. 2005. "Meandres de la psychologie homerique: Le cas d'Ajax." *Organon* 34: 5–20.

Zuntz, G. 1971. *Persephone: Three Essays on Religion and Thought in Magna Graecia*. Oxford: Clarendon Press.

Index

423

Index locorum

CPSIA information can be obtained
at www.ICGtesting.com
Printed in the USA
LVHW082352081222
734884LV00015B/1201

9 781108 730075